AUSTRALIAN POETRY SINCE 1788

GEOFFREY LEHMANN has published seven collections of his poetry and a *Selected Poems* and *Collected Poems*. He has edited two anthologies of Australian comic verse, and co-edited (with Robert Gray) two previous anthologies of Australian poetry. He has also published a novel, two children's books and *Australian Primitive Painters*, a book of art criticism. Lehmann was the first Australian poet to be published by the London publishing house Faber & Faber. He has been a member of the Literature Board of the Australia Council. He continues to write as a literary reviewer for The *Australian* newspaper and his poems are widely published, most recently in *The New Yorker*. He has been a lawyer, specialising in corporate tax, was a partner of the international accounting firm PricewaterhouseCoopers, co-author of the five editions of Lehmann & Coleman's *Taxation Law in Australia*, and chairman of the Australian Tax Research Foundation.

ROBERT GRAY has published eight books of poetry, has written a prize-winning memoir, *The Land I Came Through Last* (2008), has edited the poetry of John Shaw Neilson and the journals of the painter John Olsen, and has won numerous awards for his poetry, including the National Poetry Prize of the Adelaide Arts Festival, the NSW Premier's Award, the Victorian Premier's Award, the *Age* Book of the Year for poetry, and the Patrick White Award. His work was a set text for the final high-school examinations in New South Wales and Victoria for many years. There have been book-length translations of his poetry published in China, Germany and the Netherlands, and a selected edition and several other volumes of his work have appeared in the UK. He has been a writer-in-residence in Japan, Germany, China, and Italy, and made reading tours of Germany, the UK and Ireland. At present, he is a regular reviewer of poetry for various newspapers.

Visit of Hope to Sydney Cove, near Botany Bay

WHERE Sydney Cove her lucid bosom swells,
And with wide arms the indignant storm repels;
High on a rock amid the troubled air
Hope stood sublime, and waved her golden hair;
Calmed with her rosy smile the tossing deep,
And with sweet accents charmed the winds to sleep;
To each wild plain she stretched her snowy hand,
High-waving wood, and sea-encircled strand.
"Hear me," she cried, "ye rising realms! record
Time's opening scenes, and Truth's prophetic word.
There shall broad streets their stately walls extend,
The circus widen, and the crescent bend;
There, rayed from cities o'er the cultured land,
Shall bright canals, and solid roads expand.
There the proud arch, colossus-like, bestride
Yon glittering streams, and bound the chasing tide;
Embellished villas crown the landscape-scene,
Farms wave with gold, and orchards blush between.
There shall tall spires, and dome-capped towers ascend,
And piers and quays their massy structures blend;
While with each breeze approaching vessels glide,
And northern treasures dance on every tide!"
Then ceased the nymph – tumultuous echoes roar,
And Joy's loud voice was heard from shore to shore –
Her graceful steps descending pressed the plain,
And Peace, and Art, and Labour, joined her train.

– Erasmus Darwin, 1789

AUSTRALIAN POETRY SINCE 1788

Edited by
GEOFFREY LEHMANN & ROBERT GRAY

UNSW PRESS

A UNSW Press book

Published by
University of New South Wales Press Ltd
University of New South Wales
Sydney NSW 2052
AUSTRALIA
www.unswpress.com.au

First published 2011

10 9 8 7 6 5 4 3 2 1

National Library of Australia
Cataloguing-in-Publication entry
Title: Australian poetry since 1788/
edited by Geoffrey Lehmann and Robert Gray.
ISBN: 978 174223 263 8 (hbk.)
Subjects: Australian poetry
Other Authors/Contributors:
Lehmann, Geoffrey, 1940
Gray, Robert, 1945
Dewey Number: A821.008

Design Di Quick
Printer Everbest
Endpapers Café curtain, 'Emu Track' screen-printed cotton made by Annan Fabrics, c1950s (Gift of Mrs Dorothy Nicholas, Collection: Powerhouse Museum, Sydney. Photo: Sotha Bourn)

This book is printed on paper using fibre supplied from plantation or sustainably managed forests.

UNSW Press Literary Fund
wishes to acknowledge the generous support of Bret Walker SC; Peter Farrell and the Farrell Family Foundation; and Australian Unity.

Australian Government

Australia Council for the Arts

This project has been assisted by the Australian Government through the Australian Council for the Arts, its arts funding and advisory body.

CONTENTS

INTRODUCTION

A PLEASURE-SEEKING AUDIENCE is the only audience for poetry worth having, Philip Larkin has said. This was the guiding principle in making our anthology. We wanted a book that could be lived with over a lifetime, a physical object to be picked up with pleasure and still able to surprise many years after it was purchased.

We sat down to work on the anthology with a cleared desk and a determination to experience everything published in Australian poetry; or to read it again, since most of it was already known to us: we have each been involved with this subject for at least 50 years.

The character of Australian poetry is the result of unique influences. There is, above all, the landscape: so immense, so relatively empty, so various, so strange to Europeans, with only the apparently light touch upon it of the Aboriginal people. The newcomers wanted to write their presence on this continent, and hence Australian poetry has been much concerned with nature. The uniqueness of the country has meant that poets here have concentrated in their work not so much on formal innovation, until recently, but on the peculiar content of the land itself, which has provided originality enough. Consequently, for a long time Australian poetry took the quatrain form of the ballad as almost synonymous with poetry: the form has been as ubiquitous in Australian poetry as the heroic couplet in eighteenth-century English verse. Contributing to such a preference was the prevalence of the Scots and Irish among the early European arrivals, with their love of their folk traditions and of recitation. There followed the immense popularity in the 19th century of the native-born balladeers, such as Gordon, Paterson, and Lawson, whose work everyone knew something of by heart.

Wanting to be objective in our choices – since all is lost if one doesn't endeavour to inhabit at least the edges of objectivity – we have found that we mainly judged poetry by a readily comparative measure, by its use of the techniques of poetry. Poetry is, to a large extent, defined by poetry and judged by poetry. Of course, content is what is most moving in a poem; but the language first has to be effective. A good poem is appreciated at least as much as poetry as it is as message. Content is often subjectively weighted for the reader. We make mistakes most readily, in choosing poems, when we allow ourselves to choose on the basis of subject, so we have been wary of humanist homily, of uplift, and of the politically right-minded.

What we looked for, instead, were the marks of poetry: imagery, rhythm, musical texture, aphoristic phrasing, mastery of form, and an original tone of voice (something that the poet can seldom hear accurately for him or her self, and can do least about). Conversely, we were not dissuaded by work whose content we disagreed with (except for the sentimental and its obverse, the sadistic). Liberal humanists ourselves, we have been affected by the work of communist and Catholic. We were attracted to all the manifestations of poetry, from concrete poems to prose poems, from the cerebral to the naïve, from the humorous to the confessional, and from formal to free verse – anything that persuaded us it was well done.

The extended critical biographies that introduce the more established poets' selections seemed necessary, because, by providing the context in which the work was made, they deepen appreciation. Biographical and historical criticism seems to us inevitable, so long as it is sensibly restrained. Keats's poem "To Autumn" gains in emotional effectiveness if one knows that he was dying of TB at the time it was written. To take extreme examples in this book, it is necessary to know that Francis Webb was confined in hospitals for long periods and was schizophrenic when his doctor trusted him to hold his five-day old baby. Or that Philip Hodgins, at the time he wrote his poems, was terminally ill with leukemia.

There is, of course, the danger of biographical and sociological commentary leading to poetry being used merely to illustrate theories or fashionable causes. This philistinism has been fully realised, particularly in the way poetry is taught in schools. The poem is an aesthetic and expressive object, and extra-literary information is simply a means to its appreciation.

Many of the poems here will only survive in anthologies (or else by drifting unselected in cyber space), since their authors have not written enough outstanding work to warrant republication of their books. Yet, it should be said that the single poem, or handful of poems, by these writers we have often found to be among our best inclusions. Countering a common complaint about anthologies, we have included a number of longer pieces. The space they required does not necessarily mean we consider them more significant than shorter poems.

The editors of this book were not involved in the selection of their own poetry. Each editor chose the poems of the other.

Many have helped us with this anthology. In particular we thank for their support and patience Kathy Bail, Heather Cam, Heather Champion, Phillipa McGuinness and Di Quick of UNSW Press.

TWO ABORIGINAL SONGS (Anonymous)

Over the last thirty years, anthologies of Australian poetry typically begin with Aboriginal poems, to acknowledge what Les Murray has called "the senior culture". We were surprised to discover this practice began with A. B. Paterson's *Old Bush Songs* (1905).

We preface our anthology with the two Aboriginal songs with which he opened his collection. He provided this comment: "These songs were supplied by Mr S. M. Mowle, a very old colonist, with much experience of the blacks fifty years ago. He writes – 'I could never find out what the words meant, and I don't think the blacks themselves knew.' Other authorities, however, say that the blacks' songs were very elaborate, and that they composed corroborees which reached a high dramatic level."

The Aboriginal presence is much stronger in Australian poetry than the Amerindian presence in North American poetry in English. One reason may be that Europeans settling in Australia were forced to see Australia to some extent through Aboriginal eyes, because of the radically different nature of the Australian landscape, its fauna and flora. Australia appeared a strange place to European eyes and the early settlers were happy to borrow Aboriginal words to name places and animals.

It is interesting that in the two Aboriginal songs below, the same word may appear several times, sometimes with the ending of the word varied. The repetitions suggest that perhaps there is some form of parallelism, as in the Hebrew psalms. This is the case with other Aboriginal songs that appear in translation later in this volume. No words are common to both songs. Are they in different languages? These poems, in their mysterious presence, signify the immemorial Aboriginal voice of the country.

Two Aboriginal Songs

I

Korindabriã, korindabriã, bogaronã, bogaronã. Iwariniang iwaringdo,
iwariniang, iwaringdo, iwariniang, iwaringdo, iwariniang, iwaringdo,
iwaringime. Iwaringiang. iwaringdõõ, ilanenienow, coombagongniengowe,
ilanenienow. coombagongiengowé, ilanenienowe combagoniengowé,
ilanenienimme.

II

Buddha-buddharo nianga, boomelanã, bulleranga, crobinea, narnmalã,
yibbilwaadjo nianga, boomelanã, a, boomelana, buddha-buddharo, nianga,
boomelana, buddharo nianga, boomelana, bullerangã, crobineã, narnmala,
yibbilwaadjo, nianga, croilanume, a, croilangã, yibbilwaadjo, nianga,
croilanga, yibbilwaadjo, nianga croilangã. coondheranea. tabiabina,
boorganmala, yibbilwaadjo, nianga, croilanoome.

VAN DIEMEN'S LAND (Anonymous)

"Van Diemen's Land" is justly the most famous convict ballad. It exists in many different versions. Rather than choose a particular one, we decided to combine the best of four variations. Two of the versions we considered had England as the home country of the three poachers, and used English names and references, and the other two had the poachers coming from Ireland. In general, our composite is based on the version in Russel Ward's *The Penguin Book of Australian Ballads* (1964) as being the liveliest and most idiomatic. In the ballad, all three men were sentenced under a law specifying transportation to Van Diemen's Land for fourteen years, if such a group was found together in a wood, and one had a gun or bludgeon (*Old Bush Songs*, edited Warren Fahey and Graham Seal (2005) at page 55). There was much public sympathy for poachers; this was widely regarded as a crime from the gentry's viewpoint only. In fact, few convicts were transported for poaching.

Van Diemen's Land

Come, all you gallant poachers, that ramble free from care,
That walk out of a moonlight night, with your dog, your gun, and snare;
Where the lusty hare and pheasant you have at your command,
Not thinking that your last career is on Van Diemen's Land.

Poor Thomas Brown from Nenagh Town, Jack Murphy, and poor Joe,
We was three daring poachers, as the gentry well does know;
One night we was trepanned, my boys, by keepers hid in sand,
And for fourteen years transported was unto Van Diemen's Land.

The first day that we landed upon that fatal shore,
The planters they came flocking round, full twenty score or more;
They ranked us up like horses, and sold us out of hand,
And they yok'd us up to to ploughs, brave boys, to plough Van Diemen's Land.

There was a girl from Dublin Town, Rosanna was her name,
For fourteen years transported was, for playing of the game.
Our planter bought her freedom, and he married her out of hand;
She gave to us good usage upon Van Diemen's Land.

The huts that we must live in are built of sods and clay,
With rotten straw for bedding and we dare not to say nay.
Our cots we fence with fire, we slumber when we can,
To drive away the dogs and tigers upon Van Diemen's Land.

Oh! oft when I am slumbering, I have a pleasant dream:
A-lying in old Ireland beside some purling stream,
With my true love upon my side, and a jug of ale in hand,
But I wake a brokenhearted man all in Van Diemen's Land.

God bless our wives and families, likewise that happy shore,
That isle of sweet contentment which we shall see no more.
As for our wretched females, see them we seldom can,
There's twenty to one woman upon Van Diemen's Land.

So all you jolly poacher lads, this warning take from me:
I'd have you quit night-walking and to shun bad company,
Throw by your dogs and snares, to you I do speak plain,
For if you knew our hardships you would never poach again.

BOTANY BAY (Anonymous)

"Botany Bay" was a stage song in the 1880s, long after transportation of convicts had ceased, but is likely to have an earlier origin. The version we use is from Russel Ward's *The Penguin Book of Australian Ballads*, which seems preferable to that in Stewart and Keesing's edition of *Old Bush Songs*. Ward notes that "rum-culls" means "old mates in crime". The Old Bailey is the Central Criminal Court in London.

Botany Bay

Farewell to old England for ever,
  Farewell to our rum-culls as well;
Farewell to the well-loved Old Bailey
  Where I used for to cut such a swell.

Chorus
Singing too-ra-lie, too-ra-lie, addity,
Singing too-ra-lie, too-ra-lie, aye,
Singing too-ra-lie, too-ra-lie, addity,
We're sailing for Botany Bay.

'Taint leaving Old England we cares about,
  'Taint 'cause we mis-spells what we knows;
But because all we light-fingered gentry
  Hops around with a log on our toes.

There's the captain as is our commandier,
  There's the bosun and all the ship's crew,
There's the first and the second class passengers
  Knows what we poor convicts goes through.

For fourteen long years I'm transported,
  For fourteen long years and a day,
Just for meeting a cove in the alley,
  And stealing his ticker away.

Oh, had I the wings of a turtle-dove!
  I'd soar on my pinions so high;
Slap bang to the arms of my Polly-love,
  And in her sweet bosom I'd die.

Now, all you young dukies and duchesses,
  Take warning from what I do say,
Mind, all is your own as you touchesses,
  Or you'll meet us in Botany Bay.

THE WILD COLONIAL BOY (Anonymous)

'The Wild Colonial Boy' is about a mythical bushranger, but shares a chorus with "Bold Jack Donahoo", a possibly earlier ballad based on a bushranger who was shot dead by mounted troopers in 1830. "The Wild Colonial Boy" became an informal national anthem until it was replaced by A. B. Paterson's "Waltzing Matilda" in popular affection.

Paterson made these illuminating, comments in his collection *Old Bush Songs*: "All old Scotchmen, to whom Sir Walter Scott read some of his collected ballads, expressed the opinion that the ballads were spoilt by printing. And these bush songs, to be heard at their best, should be heard to an accompaniment of clashing shears when the voice of a shearer rises through the din caused by the rush and bustle of a shearing shed, the scrambling of the sheep in their pens, and the hurry of the pickers-up; or when, on the roads, the cattle are restless on their camp at night and the man on watch, riding round them, strikes up 'Bold Jack Donahoo' to steady their nerves a little. Drovers know that they must not sneak quietly about restless cattle – it is better to sing to them and let them know that someone is stirring and watching; and many a mob of wild, pike-horned Queensland cattle, half inclined to stampede, has listened contentedly to the 'Wild Colonial Boy' droned out in true bush fashion till the daylight began to break and the mob was safe for another day. Heard under such circumstances as these the songs have quite a character of their own. A great deal depends, too, on the way in which they are sung. The true bushman never hurries his songs. They are designed expressly to pass the time on long journeys or slow, wearisome rides after sheep or tired cattle; so the songs are sung conscientiously through – chorus and all – and the last three words of the song are always spoken, never sung."

The Wild Colonial Boy

'Tis of a wild Colonial boy, Jack Doolan was his name,
Of poor but honest parents he was born in Castlemaine.
He was his father's only hope, his mother's only joy.
And dearly did his parents love the wild Colonial boy.

Chorus

Come, all my hearties, we'll roam the mountains high,
Together we will plunder, together we will die.
We'll wander over valleys, and gallop over plains,
And we'll scorn to live in slavery, bound down with iron chains.

He was scarcely sixteen years of age when he left his father's home,
And through Australia's sunny clime a bushranger did roam.
He robbed those wealthy squatters, their stock he did destroy,
And a terror to Australia was the wild Colonial boy.

In sixty-one this daring youth commenced his wild career,
With a heart that knew no danger, no foeman did he fear.
He stuck up the Beechworth mail coach, and robbed Judge McEvoy,
Who trembled, and gave up his gold to the wild Colonial boy.

He bade the Judge "Good morning," and told him to beware,
That he'd never rob a hearty chap that acted on the square,
And never to rob a mother of her son and only joy,
Or else you may turn outlaw, like the wild Colonial boy.

One day as he was riding the mountain side along,
A-listening to the little birds, their pleasant laughing song,
Three mounted troopers rode along – Kelly, Davis, and FitzRoy.
They thought that they would capture him – the wild Colonial boy.

"Surrender now, Jack Doolan, you see there's three to one.
Surrender now, Jack Doolan, you daring highwayman."
He drew a pistol from his belt, and shook the little toy.
"I'll fight, but not surrender," said the wild Colonial boy.

He fired at Trooper Kelly, and brought him to the ground,
And in return from Davis received a mortal wound.
All shattered through the jaw he lay still firing at FitzRoy,
And that's the way they captured him – the wild Colonial boy.

BARNETT LEVY (?)

This sparkling theatrical song was published in Australia's first newspaper, the *Sydney Gazette*, on 14 July 1832 "as it ought to be sung in the Theatre Royal, Sydney, by Mr Bert Levy, in the character of the Ticket-of-leave Holder". His actual name as reported in Stewart and Keesing's edition of *Old Bush Songs* was Barnett Levy. Stage personalities often performed material they wrote themselves. If he is the author, Levy is the first of a line of stage versifiers in Australia, extending through Charles Thatcher to Barry Humphries.

There was a shortage of sterling currency in the early days of the colony, and various alternatives were used as currency, such as rum. Those born in Australia came to be known as "currency lads and lasses", and the British-born were sometimes "sterling people". Female convicts who offended were punished at the "Female Factory".

Botany Bay Courtship

The Currency Lads may fill their glasses,
And drink to the health of the Currency Lasses;
But the lass I adore, the lass for me,
Is a lass in the Female Factory.

O! Molly's her name, and her name is Molly,
Although she was tried by the name of Polly;
She was tried and was cast for death at Newry,
But the judge was bribed and so were the jury.

She got "death recorded" in Newry town,
For stealing her mistress's watch and gown;
Her little boy Paddy can tell you the tale,
His father was turnkey of Newry jail.

The first time I saw the comely lass
Was at Parramatta, going to Mass;
Says I, "I'll marry you now in an hour,"
Says she, "Well, go and fetch Father Power."

But I got into trouble that very same night!
Being drunk in the street I got into a fight,
A constable seized me – I gave him a box –
And was put in the watch-house and then in the stocks.

O! it's very unaisy as I may remember,
To sit in the stocks in the month of December;
With the north wind so hot, and the hot sun right over,
O! sure, and it's no place at all for a lover!

"It's worse than the treadmill," says I, "Mr Dunn,
To sit here all day in the hate of the sun!"
"Either that or a dollar," says he, "for your folly,"
But if I'd a dollar I'd drink it with Molly.

But now I am out again, early and late
I sigh and I cry at the Factory gate,
"O! Mrs R---, late Mrs F---n,
O! won't you let Molly out very soon?"

"Is it Molly McGuigan?" says she to me,
"Is it not?" says I, for she knowed it was she.

"Is it her you mean that was put in the stocks
For beating her mistress, Mrs Cox?"

"O! yes and it is, madam, pray let me in,
I have brought her a half-pint of Cooper's best gin,
She likes it as well as she likes her own mother,
O! now let me in, madam, I am her brother."

So the Currency Lads may fill their glasses,
And drink to the health of the Currency Lasses;
But the lass I adore, the lass for me,
Is a lass in the Female Factory.

FRANCIS McNAMARA ("Frank the Poet")
c. 1810–1861+

Francis McNamara is entered in convict records as both Catholic and Protestant, and accounts differ as to where he came from in Ireland. But when tried at Kilkenny in January 1832 and sentenced to seven years transportation for smashing a shop window and stealing a bolt of cloth, he was reported to be "a real Corkonian" in his speech. He entertained the court with an extempore epigram to celebrate his sentence to Botany Bay.

He reached Sydney in September 1832 and over the next eight years received fourteen floggings (650 lashes), was put in an ironed gang for three months, served three and a half years in road gangs, spent three months on the treadmill and thirteen days in solitary confinement. He was assigned in 1838 to the Australian Agricultural Co. in Calala and then was moved to Stroud where he worked as a shepherd. When the company decided he was to work in its underground mines in Newcastle, he refused to be treated as slave labour, and was transferred to an ironed gang working in Woolloomooloo. He wrote a long poem of protest at the proposal to send him down the mine, ending:

> When the quick and the dead shall stand in array
> Cited at the trumpet's sound,
> Even then, damn me if I'd work a day
> For the Company underground.
>
> Nor over ground.

In 1842, after joining a gang of bushrangers, he was sentenced to seven months transportation to Van Diemen's Land (Tasmania). He received his ticket of leave in 1847 and a full pardon in 1849. The only subsequent record of him is an appearance on the Mudgee goldfields in 1861.

The poem "A Convict's Lament on the Death of Captain Logan" is generally regarded by experts as having been written by "Frank the Poet", but it exists in various forms under various titles. Because there appears to be no clearly authentic original version, we have used the liveliest one, which appears in Russel Ward's *The Penguin Book of Australian Ballads*, but with one significant change. The first four lines of the version below are lines 13 to 16 in the version he reproduces. However, the more popular, simplified version (which is less interesting and is known as "Moreton Bay") has these lines at the start of the poem. This is clearly where they belong, creating a single coherent narrative, rather than two stories of transportation, one of which has no ending and the other no start. By following the narrative sequence of the popular version, the line "Twelve years transportation to Moreton Bay!" moves from line twelve in Ward's version to line 16 at the end of the second verse, where it marks the first appearance of what becomes an ominous refrain.

McNamara did not write for the printed page and probably lacked the opportunity to revise and improve his poetry. "A Convict's Lament on the Death of Captain Logan" is probably one of many ballads he originated and is more polished than the poetry that survives in his own handwriting, so that it was most likely improved by anonymous singers and reciters.

A Convict's Lament on the Death of Captain Logan

Early one morning as I carelessly wandered,
  By the Brisbane waters I chanced to stray,
I heard a prisoner sadly bewailing,
  Whilst on the sunny river-banks he lay:
"I am a native of Erin's island,
  But banished now from my native shore,
They tore me from my aged parents,
  And from the maiden I adore.

In transient storms as I set sailing,
  Like mariner bold my course did steer,
Sydney Harbour was my destination –
  That cursed place at length drew near.
I then joined banquet in congratulation
  On my safe arrival from the briny sea;
But alas! alas! I was mistaken –
  Twelve years transportation to Moreton Bay!

I have been a prisoner at Port MacQuarie,
  At Norfolk Island and Emu Plains,
At Castle Hill and cursed Toongabbie –
  And at all those places I've worked in chains.
But of all the places of condemnation,
  In each penal station of New South Wales,
To Moreton Bay I found no equal,
  For excessive tyranny each day prevails.

Early in the morning as the day is dawning,
  To trace from heaven the morning dew,
Up we are started at a moment's warning,

Our daily labour for to renew.
Our overseers and superintendents –
These tyrants' orders we must obey,
Or else at the triangles our flesh is mangled –
Such is our wages at Moreton Bay!

For three long years I've been beastly treated;
Heavy irons each day I wore,
My poor back from flogging has been lacerated,
And oftimes painted with crimson gore.
Like the Egyptians and ancient Hebrews,
We were oppressed under Logan's yoke,
Till kind providence came to our assistance
And gave this tyrant his mortal stroke.

Yes, he was hurried from that place of bondage
Where he thought he would gain renown;
But a native black, who lay in ambush,
Gave this monster his fatal wound.
My fellow prisoners be exhilarated –
That all such monsters such a death may find:
For it's when from bondage we are extricated
Our former sufferings will fade from mind."

CHARLES HARPUR 1813–1868

Harpur, the first important Australian-born poet, grew up at Windsor on the Hawkesbury River, the third child of emancipated convicts, his Irish father having been transported for complicity in an armed robbery. His parents were not formally married until the year after he was born. Harpur's first seventeen years were happy and he became widely read in English literature. His father had been made schoolmaster of the Windsor Government School and parish clerk, and Harpur is likely to have had access to the Reverend Samuel Marsden's extensive library, which was made available to convicts.

In about 1828 his father lost his land, the family left Windsor and the children dispersed. During much of the 1830s Harpur lived in Sydney, working in a number of occupations, including four years as a clerk in the Post Office. During these years he struggled for recognition as a poet and to be part of the colony's intellectual elite. Elizabeth Perkins in her introduction to *The Poetical Works of Charles Harpur* commented: "Harpur was not a 19th-century democrat, and he believed in an aristocracy of the intellect to which he felt he belonged." He was discriminated against because he was the son of emancipists, rather than free-born settlers. Nor did he seek commercial success, to compensate for his origins, like some emancipists and their children.

The *Sydney Monitor* of 18 December 1833 has a comical report of a failed legal action against "Levey", the proprietor of the Theatre Royal, by a plaintiff Harpur, apparently the 21-year-old poet. Harpur, "a soft-bearded native youth", had sued Levey for £3 for breaching a contract to employ him as an actor. Levey alleged that Harpur "understood as much of theatricals as the candle-snuffer's apprentice" and Harpur responded that he could "tear a passion to rags with any gentleman of the *corps*." When Levey proposed that he would pay up if Harpur stood on the table and recited a portion of any play to the applause of the court, Harpur "threw himself into 'attitude', amidst roars of laughter, and shouted, 'Do you take me for an ass?' Mr Levey politely told him that the opera of *Midas* was in rehearsal, which would afford him an opportunity of shewing off." At this stage the Commissioner had some difficulty in restoring order in the court.

During the 1830s Harpur was able to publish a number of poems and extracts from a blank-verse tragedy in local journals. However he attracted the enmity of James Martin, later Premier and Chief Justice: Martin, then eighteen years old, published in 1838 an *Australian Sketch-Book* with a chapter on "The Pseudo-Poets" of the colony, which described Harpur as a "tall, bleary-eyed, pert-looking, cockscombish person ... The vanity of this man was beyond all conception." Martin poured scorn on Harpur's blank-verse tragedy *The Thieves of Attica, or the Depredation of a Robber* as coarse and ridiculous.

In the early 1840s Harpur moved to the Hunter River region. He did farm-work, undertook local government duties and was a school teacher. He fell in love with Mary Doyle in 1842, but it was not until 1850 that Harpur was able to satisfy her father, a respectable settler, that he had the means to marry her. Their long and difficult courtship was the subject of many poems. In the 1850s Harpur tried to set himself up as a farmer and grazier, and was rebuffed when he sought a loan from Henry Parkes, (later "the Father of Federation"), with whom he had been friendly in his Sydney years. In 1859 Harpur was appointed a Gold Commissioner, which involved visiting mining sites in an area south of Sydney. Henry Kendall began corresponding with him, encouraging and critiquing the older Harpur and helping him publish in newspapers. In 1866 Harpur's position as Gold Commissioner was abolished, prompting letters of protest to his former friend Parkes, who was Colonial Secretary under James Martin.

Harpur received some monetary compensation for his loss of employment. He suffered flood losses in 1867, and in the same year the death of his thirteen-year-old second son from a shooting accident. The reception of his poetry was another cause for bitterness. While preparing a manuscript of his major poems, for what he hoped would be an English edition, he died of consumption in the winter of 1868.

For the century or so after his death Harpur's reputation was overshadowed by Kendall and Gordon, who are his inferiors. Until the publication in 1984 of Elizabeth Perkins' *The Poetical Works of Charles Harpur* of more than 1000 pages, Harpur's status could not be fully appreciated. His posthumous *Poems*, published in 1883 after much devoted effort by his widow, gave a distorted picture of his work as its editor omitted many of the best poems, and amended and cut others, sometimes transposing lines. "A Coast View" was truncated to the opening verse paragraph. "Dawn and Sunrise in the Snowy Mountains" was presented in a wordier, differently titled version, including deadening lines about "that greater soul/Which makes all nature". Harpur's technical tour de force "A Flight of Wild Ducks" was missing, as were "A Basket of Summer Fruit", "Lost in the Bush" and many other significant poems.

What is rewarding for the contemporary reader are Harpur's long, intricate, acutely observed and detailed descriptions of the eastern coast of Australia with its vast, primaeval forests, then barely disturbed by white settlement. They allow us a glimpse into a majestic, if primitive and frightening, lost Eden. According to Harpur, we should read Wordsworth for his "simple power", something he also achieved.

Dawn and Sunrise in the Snowy Mountains

A few thin strips of fleecy clouds lie long
And motionless above the eastern steeps,
Like shreds of silver lace: till suddenly,
Out from the flushing centre to the ends
On either hand, their lustrous layers become
Dipt all in crimson streaked with pink and gold;
And then, at last, are edged as with a band
Of crystal fire. And now, even long before
The sun himself is seen, off tow'rds the west
A range of mighty summits, more and more,
Blaze, each like a huge cresset, in the keen
Clear atmosphere. As if the Spirit of Light,
Advancing swiftly thence, and eastward still,
Kept kindling them in quick succession; – till
The universal company of cones
And pyramidal peaks, stand burning all
With rosy fires, like a wide ranging circ
Of God-great altars, – and even so announce
The Sun that now, with a vast flash, is seen
Pushing his rim above yon central height.

A Mid-Summer Noon in the Australian Forest

Not a bird disturbs the air,
There is quiet everywhere;
Over plains and over woods
What a mighty stillness broods.

Even the grasshoppers keep
Where the coolest shadows sleep;
Even the busy ants are found
Resting in their pebbled mound;
Even the locust clingeth now
In silence to the barky bough:
And over hills and over plains
Quiet, vast and slumbrous, reigns.

Only there's a drowsy humming
From yon warm lagoon slow coming:
'Tis the dragon-hornet – see!
All bedaubed resplendently
With yellow on a tawny ground –
Each rich spot nor square nor round,
But rudely heart-shaped, as it were
The blurred and hasty impress there,
Of a vermeil-crusted seal
Dusted o'er with golden meal:
Only there's a droning where
Yon bright beetle gleams the air –
Gleams it in its droning flight
With a slanting track of light,
Till rising in the sunshine higher,
Its shards flame out like gems on fire.

Every other thing is still,
Save the ever wakeful rill,
Whose cool murmur only throws
A cooler comfort round Repose;
Or some ripple in the sea
Of leafy boughs, where, lazily,
Tired Summer, in her forest bower
Turning with the noontide hour,
Heaves a slumbrous breath, ere she
Once more slumbers peacefully.

O 'tis easeful here to lie
Hidden from Noon's scorching eye,
In this grassy cool recess
Musing thus of Quietness.

Lost in the Bush

Lost in the Bush! the night approaching fast,
And around loudening a cold-breathing blast!
Fancy the thing! Then mark how settler Will,
There, in the pathless Forest, stands stock-still,
With keen heed questioning yon peculiar hill,
Only to learn from it this answer – "Yea,
I tell thee, stranger, thou hast gone astray!"
Thus answered, back he turns, intent to find
Some prospect more familiar to his mind;

But vainly! for the farther back he goes,
The backward scene itself yet stranger grows!
So that he mutters, while he scans the ground,
"By Jove! the very world seems twisted round!
And yon red gleam on the horizon yet
Is where, methinks, the sun should *rise* – not *set!*"
Then with a sudden spin, the anxious Swain
Turns, just to question yon blunt hill again,
Which was the first to tell him that for once
His shrewd bush-instinct had turned out a dunce.
But which is which? A dozen summits lie
As like as eggs against the twilight sky
And it amongst them! With a blank surprise
His mouth drops open and wide stare his eyes!
Then squats he on his hams, intent to gain
Yet clearer views: but clearer views are vain!
The pleasant fact abides through every test:
And drawing a long breath, he mutters "Well, I'm blest!"

In short, he's lost. And seeing that the night
Will be a wild one, he (as well he might)
Scratches his head and much that member loads
With execrations: "What! forgo the roads
For shorter cuts so near the day's decline,
'Mongst hills and bushes! – Drat this head o' mine!
The dark is settling round as thick as mire!
The Bush too's roaring like a world on fire!
I am not one much given to foolish tirrits,
And far too knowing to believe in Spirits;
But such a night in such a cursèd place
Might almost put one in a raving case:
And somewhere here for certain it is said
There's a Blacks' grave ground! O this silly head!
Besides Peg may forget to bed the sow,
Big Bess, that is so near her pigging now;
Nor can she by herself, with all her care,
Secure the stack from that downdacious mare!
Or pen those rascal calves up from the kine –
I *must* regain the road! O this thick head o' mine!"

Thus grimly summarising his distresses,
On, dogged and desperate, he at random presses.
Ah, Will! dame Fortune owes thee some shrewd spite

Thy blazing hearth shall know thee not to-night!
In vain thy Peg now watches for her Will
To heave in sight upon the 'customed hill,
Saying the while, with a most wifely frown,
"He's boozing somewhere – but I'll comb him down!"
And just as vainly dost thou onward plod,
Dismally *cooeying* almost every rod,
And wishing, 'tween whiles, thou hadst there with thee
Thy neighbor Wilson – *just for company!*
But honest Wilson would himself no doubt
Be rather *in* on such a night than *out*,
Though with his crony Will, – and through a drinking bout.

Now thickest glooms blank every forest path,
And like a large Cyclopic eye in wrath,
One only star glares redly down, as seen
Up through a rent in heaven's dun cloudy screen:
Which gap, slow crossing, like a dim-drawn streak,
The owl pours forward his funereal shriek
Sounds of strange waters through the turmoil vast
Of the wide dark woods, dash over in the blast;
Or the lank dingo's long and weary cry
Comes wildly wailing from some covert nigh.
Rocked high in some old gum, the opossum sways,
A nest-like lump amid the hanging sprays,
Or craning outward through the gusty dark,
Croons to his mate there in the ironbark.
Or the spare curlews that from all points meet
In nightly gatherings fugitive and fleet –
That half ubiquitous appear to be,
Now near, now distant, interthrongingly –
Send suddenly upward in the hollow gale
Cries dismal, – drear as those of Spectres pale
That round some scene of wholesale murder wail!
Startlingly near, and phantom-like to see,
The sharp-voiced, bidawong *streams* from tree to tree!
Or the wild cat, with breath-suspending rush,
Whisks, imp-like, from some goblin-featured bush!
Or startled kangaroos, dark bounding high,
String like a troop of shadowy devils by!
Ah, Will! such hour may well thy spirit grieve –
Most woe-begone, most luckless son of Eve!

Worn out at last, he settles down, – and Sleep
There finds him, coiled beside that bleaching heap
Of leaves and sprays, whose sere accessions fast
Patter about him, dropping from the blast,
While laden with its over-rushing might,
Wide sway the huge dark trees above the unconscious wight.

But now, when negress Night her denser shades
Had westward drawn, and grey had grown the glades,
Stung into partial consciousness 'twould seem
By the increasing cold, he dreams a dream.
A banished man, 'neath Polar skies he fares,
On all hands menaced by dread herds of bears!
Enormous fellows! shaggy, icy, – grim
With hunger, and all bent on tasting him!
Begins the onslaught! horrible his affright!
Great his despair! Yet he maintains the fight!
But just as in the strife an arm is lost,
(That luckless arm least sheltered from the frost,
From whence no doubt the dream-suggestion came
That worked about him this strange Queen-Mab game)
Sweating and wild, he wakes! – relieved, 'tis true,
Yet in a strait that ferrets him anew.
So sitting up, he first his face long drawn
Rubs hard, then looks, and hails the wished-for dawn:
Next scans the unknown scene with rueful eyes,
And folds his arms, and shakes his head, and sighs.
When hark! distinctly, although far away,
He hears some watch-dog's thrice-repeated bay –
Starts from his huddled posture at a bound,
And briskly pushes for the grateful sound.
Nor long his search: for now some morning star
Wheels from the eastern steeps her shining car,
In whose so pallid but effectual sheen
A rude Lodge, dim and picture-like, is seen,
There where a clearing from yon hill spreads out,
With stumps all dotted, not yet fenced about;
Thither he hastens, and is welcomed there,
Consoled and fed with hospitable care,
And when the sun shall crown the wintry day,
His host can set him on his homeward way.

A Coast View

High 'mid the shelves of a grey Cliff, that yet
Hangeth in bluffs enormously above,
In a benched cleft, as in the mouldered chair
Of grey-beard Time himself, I sit alone,
And gaze with a keen wondering happiness
Out o'er the Sea. Immensely rolling forth,
See how it stretches to the circling bend
That verges Heaven, a vast luminous plain
Of waters, changeful as a lover's dream –
Into great spaces mapped by light and shade
In constant interchange – or under clouds
The billows darken, or they shimmer bright
In sunny scopes of measureless expanse!
'Tis Ocean dreamless of a stormy hour,
Calm, or but gently heaving; – yet, O God!
What a blind fate-like mightiness lies coiled
In slumber, under that wide-shining face!
While o'er the watery gleam – there where its edge
Banks the dim vacancy, the topmost sails
Of some tall Ship, whose hull is yet unseen,
Hang as if clinging to a cloud that still
Comes rising with them from the void beyond,
And bellying over – like to a heavenly net,
Drawn slowly upward by ethereal hands.
  And if I look aloft, how deep the sky,
That arches Ocean! – deeper far, it seems,
Than elsewhere. See how delicately rare
Are those sky colors that keep flickering up
From the remote horizon! Beautiful
Those lucid traceries of woven cloud
That float about the sun; and lustrous too
Are the white masses overhead, that move
And gather inland tow'rds the verdant hills.

  Withdrawing now the eye from heaven, behold
The Coast how wonderful. Proportions strange,
And unimaginable forms, more quaint,
More wild and wayward than were ever dreamt
By a mad architect, keep crowding out,
As runs the eye along it. Semblances
Of pyramidic structures vague and rent,

Hunch ledging stairwise from the general range,
Of dark time-wasted columns, leaning out
Under the bluffs, and in their seeming such
As old Assyrian trowels might have reared,
Support fantastic arches. Rugged domes,
And minarets in ruin, freak the sides
Of chasms spann'd by crude and haggard bridges;
Or overhanging Cliffs like this whose shelf
Sustains me, rest on buttresses of more
Than Babylonian vastness; – while below
Against their bases everlastingly
Beats the white wrath of the relentless surge.

Yet even 'mid these rugged forms the warm
And gentle ministry of Spring hath wrought
Its work of love. Most sparingly indeed,
But thence most gratefully, a nameless shrub
With flame-bright blossom, tufts each guttered ledge
That holds a scanty soil; and rarer still,
Green runners from some sheltering crevice throw
Their tendrils o'er the shelves, and trailing thence
Touch the stern faces of the rocks with beauty.

Nor wants the scene its meet inhabitants.
Below the porpoise breaches, and the crab
Waits for his prey amid the wave-washed stones
That glisten to the sun, – gleaming himself
Whene'er he moves, as if his wetted shell
Were breaking into flames; or more remote,
Out in the watery spaces may be seen
Some solitary diver's shining back.
Sea gulls go clanging by, and overhead
Sits the white-breasted hawk, with many a sleek
And silver pinioned wanderer in the winds
That furrow the great visage of the Deep,
And who, in conjugal convention met,
Hoard here their mottled eggs and rear their young
Amid the jags and fissures of the crags.

How nourishing is Nature to the soul
That loves her well! Not only as she acts
In instant contact with its quickened powers,
But as she tempers all its after-moods

Through distant memories and remotest tokens.
And hence, when thus beloved, not only here
By the great Sea, or amid forests wild,
Or pastures luminous with lakes, is she
A genial Ministress: – but everywhere!
Whatever testifies of her is good,
However common; fresh, however known.
Dead city walls may pen us in, but still
Her influence seeks, to find us, – even there,
Through many a simple means. A vagrant mass
Of sunshine, falling into some void place,
Shall warm us to the heart, and trade awhile,
Though through some sorrowful reminiscence,
With instincts which, regenerated thus,
Make us child-happy. A stray gust of wind,
Pent in and wasting up the narrow lanes,
Shall breathe insinuations to our age
Of youth's fresh promise. Even a bird, though caged,
Shall represent past freedom, and its notes
Be spirited with memories that call
Around us the fresh fumes of bubbling brooks
And far wild woods. Nay, even a scanty vine,
Trailing along some backyard wall, shall speak
Love's first green language; and (so cheap is truth)
A bucket of clear water from the well
Be in its homely brightness beautiful.

A Basket of Summer Fruit

First see those ample melons – brinded o'er
With mingled green and brown is all the rind;
For they are ripe, and mealy at the core,
And saturate with the nectar of their kind.

And here their fellows of the marsh are set,
Covering their sweetness with a crumpled skin;
Pomegranates next, flame-red without, and yet
With vegetable crystals stored within.

Then mark these brilliant oranges, of which
A bygone Poet fancifully said,
Their unplucked globes the Orchard did enrich
Like golden lamps in a green night of shade.

With these are lemons that are even more

Golden than they, and which adorn our Rhyme,
As did rough pendants of barbaric ore
Some pillared Temple of the olden time.

And here are peaches with their ruddy cheeks
And ripe transparency. Here nectarines bloom,
All mottled as with discontinuous streaks.
And spread a fruity fragrance through the room.

With these are cherries mellow to the stone;
Into such ripeness hath the Summer nursed them,
The velvet pressure of the tongue alone
Against the palate were enough to burst them.

Here too are plums, like edible rubies glowing –
The language of lush summer's Eden theme:
Even through the skin how temptingly keeps showing
Their juicy comfort – a rich-clouded gleam!

Here too are figs, pears, apples (plucked in haste
Our Summer treat judiciously to vary)
With apricots, so exquisite in taste,
And yellow as the breast of a canary.

And luscious strawberries all facetëd
With glittering lobes, and all the lovelier seen
In contrast with the loquat's duller red,
And vulgar gooseberry's unlustrous green.

And lastly, bunches of rich-blooded grapes
Whose vineyard bloom even yet about them clings.
Though ever in the handling it escapes
Like the fine down upon a moth's bright wings.

Each kind is piled in order in the Basket,
Which we might well imagine now to be
Transmuted into a great golden casket
Entreasuring Pomona's jewelry.

A Flight of Wild Ducks

Far up the River – hark! 'tis the loud shock
Deadened by distance, of some Fowler's gun:
And as into the stillness of the scene
It wastes now with a dull vibratory boom,
Look where, fast widening up at either end
Out of the sinuous valley of the waters,
And o'er the intervenient forest, – up

Against the open heaven, a long dark *line*
Comes hitherward stretching – a vast Flight of Ducks!
Following the windings of the vale, and still
Enlarging lengthwise, and in places too
Oft breaking into solitary dots,
How swiftly onwards comes it – till at length,
The River, reaching through a group of hills,
Off leads it, – out of sight. But not for long:
For, wheeling ever with the water's course,
Here into sudden view it comes again
Sweeping and swarming round the nearest point!
And first now, a swift airy rush is heard
Approaching momently; – then all at once
There passes a keen-cutting, gusty tumult
Of strenuous pinions, with a streaming mass
Of instantaneous skiey streaks; each streak
Evolving with a lateral flirt, and thence
Entangling as it were, – so rapidly
A thousand wings outpointingly dispread
In passing tiers, seem, looked at from beneath,
With rushing intermixtures to involve
Each other as they beat. Thus seen o'erhead
Even while we speak – ere we have spoken, – lo!
The living cloud is onward many a rood.
Tracking as 'twere in the smooth stream below
The multifarious shadow of itself
Far coming – present – and far gone at once!
The senses vainly struggle to retain
The impression of an Image (as the same)
So swift and manifold: For now again
A long dark *line* upon the utmost verge
Of the horizon, steeping still, it sinks
At length into the landscape; where yet seen
Though dimly, with a wide and scattering sweep
It fetches eastward, and in column so
Dapples along the steep face of the ridge
There banking the turned River. Now it drops
Below the fringing oaks – but to arise
Once more, with a quick circling gleam, as touched
By the slant sunshine, and then disappear
As instantaneously, – there settling down
Upon the reedy bosom of the water.

THE OLD BULLOCK DRAY (Anonymous)

We have used the version in Russel Ward's *The Penguin Book of Australian Ballads*, which is generally similar to the version in A. B. Paterson's *Old Bush Songs*, except that Paterson does not have the third verse. Ward commented that this is the most popular of all the ballads from the first half of the 19th century and that: "An Aboriginal woman was the only kind of 'wife' most bush-workers of the period could realistically hope for." Paterson provided these explanations: "A paddy-melon is a small and speedy marsupial, a sort of poor relation of the great kangaroo family. 'Calling at the depot to get an offsider.' – Female immigrants were housed at the depot on arrival, and many found husbands within a few hours of their landing. The minstrel, therefore, proposes to call at the depot to get himself a wife from among the immigrants. An offsider is a bullock-driver's assistant – one who walks on the off-side of the team and flogs the bullocks on that side when occasion arises. The word afterwards came to mean an assistant of any kind. 'Jack Robertson.' – Sir John Robertson, as he afterwards became, was a well-known politician, who believed in Australians doing their best to populate their own country. 'Budgery you' – good fellow you."

The Old Bullock Dray

Oh! the shearing is all over, and the wool is coming down,
And I mean to get a wife, boys, when I go down to town.
Everything that's got two legs presents itself to view,
From the little paddy-melon to the bucking kangaroo.

> *Chorus*
> So it's roll up your blankets, and let's make a push,
> I'll take you up the country and show you the bush.
> I'll be bound you won't get such a chance another day,
> So come and take possession of my old Bullock dray.

Now, I've saved up a good cheque and I mean to buy a team,
And when I get a wife, boys, I'll be all-serene;
For, calling at the depot, they say there's no delay
To get an off-sider for the old Bullock-dray.

I'll teach you the whip, and the bullocks how to flog,
You'll be my off-sider when we're stuck in a bog:
Lashing out both left and right and every other way,
Making skin, hair and blood fly round the old Bullock-dray.

Oh! we'll live like fighting-cocks, for good living I'm your man.
We'll have leather-jacks, johnny-cakes, and fritters in the pan;
Or if you want some fish, why, I'll catch you some soon;
For we'll bob for barramundies round the banks of a lagoon.

Oh! yes, of beef and damper I make sure we have enough,
And we'll boil in the bucket such a whopper of a duff;

And our friends will dance to the honour of the day,
To the music of the bells, around the old Bullock-dray.

Oh! we'll have plenty girls, we must mind that.
There'll be "Buck-jumping Maggie" and "Leather-belly Pat."
There'll be "Stringbark Peggy" and "Green-Hide Mike",
Yes, my Colonials, just as many as you like!

Now we'll stop all immigration, we don't need it any more;
We'll be having young natives, twins by the score.
And I wonder what the devil Jack Robertson would say
If he saw us promenading round the old Bullock-dray.

Oh! it's time I had an answer, if there's one to be had,
I wouldn't treat that steer in the body half as bad;
But he takes as much notice of me, upon my soul,
As that old blue stag off-sider in the pole.

Oh! to tell a lot of lies, you know, it is a sin,
But I'll go up the country and marry a black gin.
"Baal gammon white feller"; that is what she'll say,
"Budgery you and your old Bullock-dray!"

CHARLES THATCHER 1831–1878

Charles Thatcher was born in Bristol, England, and went on to play in London theatrical orchestras. Hearing about the gold discoveries, he arrived in Melbourne in 1852 aged 21. With some companions he set out for Bendigo on foot. After a run of bad luck at the diggings, they had a lucky strike. Thatcher's share was £1000. He gave up digging, to sing and entertain on stage. He was large and broad-shouldered, weighing 14 stone (89 kilos), and was handsome, with a drooping moustache. What he lacked in voice he made up for with his sense of humour and love of the absurd. Collections of his songs included the *Victorian Songster* (1855), *Thatcher's Colonial Songster* (1857) and *Thatcher's Colonial Minstrel* (1859). He remained in Victoria until 1861, when he set out for the New Zealand goldfields with his bride, Annie Vitelli, a singer. He published some New Zealand songs. He came back to Australia on a couple of occasions, touring with a painted diorama "Life on the Gold Fields". In 1870 with his wife and two daughters he returned to England and became a London curio dealer. He died of cholera in 1878, in Shanghai.

Thatcher wanted his songs to be "regarded as a popular history of the time". There is more life and sharply observed detail in Thatcher than in many "serious" poets. "The Queer Ways of Australia" refers to a "cabbage-tree": this is a broad-brimmed hat plaited out of cabbage-tree palm leaves. An early record of the term "coo-ey" is in a 1789 report of Captain Hunter on the exploration of the Hawkesbury River: "In the woods we frequently saw fires, and sometimes heard the natives ... We called to them in their own manner by repeating the word co-wee, which signifies 'come here'."

Gold-fields Girls

What a rum lot the girls are out here:
  They jolly soon get colonized, sirs,
I twig their rum capers sometimes,
  And feel not a little surprised, sirs.
As regards love and marriage out here,
  I'm fairly licked clean off my perch, sirs;
One day they pick up a chap,
  The next day he's walked off to church, sirs.

If at home you should flirt with a girl,
  In a twinkling the old bloke, her father,
Asks what your intentions may be,
  And isn't he down on you rather!
The mother leads you in a string,
  And sticks to you like bricks and mortar,
For she's always talking to you
  About her accomplished daughter.

The courtship lasts some little time,
  And then of course you pop the question,
She immediately bursts into tears,
  And calls it a cruel suggestion;
She falters out "Ask my papa,"
  When you beg her to be your dear wife, sirs,
And in two or three weeks from that time,
  You find that you're tied up for life, sirs.

But things are far different here:
  The girls don't consult their relations.
What's father or mother to them?
  They follow their own inclinations.
If you name the day here to a gal,
  Don't think off her perch it will lick her,
For nine out of ten will reply
  "Lor, Sammy, can't it be done quicker?"

The best of this colony is,
  The brides have no fine affectation:
In saying "I will" they're "all there",
  And they don't faint upon the occasion.
A bottle lots of 'em will use,
  And it seems to come in very handy,
You might think that it's Preston salts,
  No fear! the smell tells you it's brandy.

The bride's mother, too, will be there,
  She's not overcome by emotion,
Her spirits you find she keeps up
  By Old Tom or some other lotion;
And sometimes her voice will grow thick.
  In her speech there's a wond'rous obstruction,
But her friends are to blame for it all;
  For they ought to allowance her suction.

But some brides upon their wedding night,
  In colonial parlance get "tight", sirs,
And then in that state they evince
  A strong inclination to fight, sirs.
They've been known to take tumblers up
  And shy them in every direction,
But bless their dear hearts, we all know
  It's proof of colonial affection!

The Queer Ways of Australia

Dick Briggs, a wealthy farmer's son,
To England lately took a run,
To see his friends, and have some fun,
For he'd been ten years in Australia.
Arrived in England, off he went
To his native village down in Kent
'Twas there his father drew his rent,
And many happy days he'd spent.
No splendid, fine clothes on had he,
But jumper'n boots up to the knee,
With dirty Sydney "cabbage-tree"
The costume of Australia.

Chorus
Now when a fellow takes a run
To England for a bit of fun,
He's sure to 'stonish everyone
With the queer ways of Australia.

Now Dick went home in this array;
His sister came out and did say,
"No, we don't want anything today,"
To her brother from Australia.
Cried he, "Oh, don't you know poor Dick?"

They recognized him precious quick;
The "old man" hugged him like a brick.
And there was feasting there that night,
For Richard was a welcome sight,
For each one hailed with great delight
The wanderer from Australia.

The blessed cattle on the farm
Regarded Dick with great alarm;
His swearing acted like a charm
When he gave them a "touch" of Australia.
He could talk "bullock" and "no flies",
And when he blessed poor Strawberry's eyes,
She looked at him with great surprise
As out of her he "took a rise".
"Fie, fie," his mother said one day,
"What naughty, wicked words you say."
"Bless you, mother, that's the way
We wake 'em up in Australia."

Dick went to London for a spree,
And got drunk there most gloriously;
He gave them a touch of "Coo-oo-ee"
The bush cry of Australia.
He took two ladies to the play,
Both so serene, in dresses gay,
He had champagne brought on a tray
And said, "Now girls, come fire away."
They drank till they could drink no more,
And then they both fell on the floor.
Cried Dick, as he surveyed them o'er,
"You wouldn't do for Australia!"

THE OLD KEG OF RUM (Anonymous)

We have used Russel Ward's version from *The Penguin Book of Australian Ballads*, with additions. His version was missing the third last verse, which is the logical climax of the song. We have taken this verse and the preceding one from A. B. Paterson's version, in *Old Bush Songs* (1905). The author of this haunting and memorable song in the voice of an elderly and nostalgic alcoholic, might have been the veterinary surgeon, William Perrie, as the structure of the song is strikingly similar to "The Old Bark Hut", which has been attributed to him.

The Old Keg of Rum

My name is old Jack Palmer and I once dug for gold,
And the song I'm going to sing you recalls the days of old,
When I'd plenty mates around me and the talk would fairly hum
As we all sat together round the old keg of rum.

> *Chorus*
> The old keg of rum! the old keg of rum!
> As we all sat together round the old keg of rum!

There was Bluey Watt, the breaker, and old Tom Hines,
And Jimmy Doyle, the ringer, who now in Glory shines,
And many more hard doers, all gone to Kingdom Come,
We were all associated round the old keg of rum.

> *Chorus*
> The old keg of rum! the old keg of ruml!
> We were all associated round the old keg of rum!

When shearing time was over at the sheds on the Bree,
We'd raise a keg from somewhere and we'd all have a spree.
We'd sit and sing together till we got that blind and dumb,
We couldn't find the bunghole of the old keg of rum.

> *Chorus*
> The old keg of rum! the old keg of rum!
> We couldn't find the bunghole of the old keg of rum!

It's jovially together boys – we'd laugh, we'd chat, we'd sing;
Sometimes we'd have a little row some argument would bring,
Till often in the scrimmage, I've corked it with my thumb
To keep the life from leaking from the old keg of rum!

> *Chorus*
> The old keg of rum! the old keg of rum!
> To keep the life from leaking from the old keg of rum!

But when our spree was ended, boys, and waking from a snooze,
For to give another drain the old keg would refuse,
We'd rap it with our knuckles. – If it sounded like a drum,
We'd know the life and spirit had left the old keg of rum.

> *Chorus*
> The old keg of rum! the old keg of rum!
> We'd know the life and spirit had left the old keg of rum.

Those happy days have passed away, I've seen their pleasures fade,
And many of our good old mates have with old times decayed.

But still, when on my travels, boys, I meet with an old chum,
We will sigh in conversation of the grand old keg of rum.

Chorus
The old keg of rum! the old keg of rum!
We will sigh in conversation of the old keg of rum!

And now my song is ended, I've got to jog along,
An old buffer skiting of days dead and gone;
But you young coves who hear me will, perhaps, in years to come
Remember old Jack Palmer and his old keg of rum.

Chorus
The old keg of rum! the old keg of rum!
Remember old Jack Palmer and his old keg of rum!

WILLIAM PERRIE 19th century

We have used the version of "The Old Bark Hut" in A. B. Paterson's *Old Bush Songs* (1905), except for the third last verse and chorus which is a composite of Paterson's and another version. Will Lawson, in his *Australian Bush Songs and Ballads*, attributed this song to William Perrie, commenting, "These verses were written in the shepherding days – when fences were few and far between – at Dungog, NSW. William Perrie was a veterinary surgeon in practice there."

The Old Bark Hut

Oh, my name is Bob the Swagman, before you all I stand,
And I've had many ups and downs while travelling through the land.
I once was well-to do, my boys, but now I am stumped up,
And I'm forced to go on rations in an old bark hut.

Chorus
In an old bark hut. In an old bark hut.
I'm forced to go on rations in an old bark hut.

Ten pounds of flour, ten pounds of beef, some sugar and some tea,
That's all they give to a hungry man, until the Seventh Day.
If you don't be moighty sparing, you'll go with a hungry gut –
For that's one of the great misfortunes in an old bark hut.

Chorus
In an old bark hut. In an old bark hut.
For that's one of the great misfortunes in an old bark hut.

The bucket you boil your beef in has to carry water, too,
And they'll say you're getting mighty flash if you should ask for two.

I've a billy, and a pint pot, and a broken-handled cup,
And they all adorn the table in the old bark hut.

> *Chorus*
> In an old bark hut. In an old bark hut.
> And they all adorn the table in the old bark hut.

Faith, the table is not made of wood, as many you have seen –
For if I had one half so good, I'd think myself serene –
'Tis only an old sheet of bark – God knows when it was cut –
It was blown from off the rafters of the old bark hut.

> *Chorus*
> In an old bark hut. In an old bark hut.
> It was blown from off the rafters of the old bark hut.

And of furniture, there's no such thing, 'twas never in the place,
Except the stool I sit upon – and that's an old gin case.
It does us for a safe as well, but you must keep it shut,
Or the flies would make it canter round the old bark hut.

> *Chorus*
> In an old bark hut. In an old bark hut.
> Or the flies would make it canter round the old bark hut.

If you should leave it open, and the flies should find your meat,
They'll scarcely leave a single piece that's fit for man to eat.
But you mustn't curse, nor grumble – what won't fatten will fill up –
For what's out of sight is out of mind in an old bark hut.

> *Chorus*
> In an old bark hut. In an old bark hut.
> For what's out of sight is out of mind in an old bark hut.

In the summer time, when the weather's warm, this hut is nice and cool,
And you'll find the gentle breezes blowing in through every hole.
You can leave the old door open, or you can leave it shut,
There's no fear of suffocation in the old bark hut.

> *Chorus*
> In an old bark hut. In an old bark hut.
> There's no fear of suffocation in the old bark hut.

In the winter time – preserve us all ! – to live in there's a treat,
Especially when it's raining hard, and blowing wind and sleet.
The rain comes down the chimney, and your meat is black with soot –
That's a substitute for pepper in an old bark hut.

Chorus
In an old bark hut. In an old bark hut .
That's a substitute for pepper in an old bark hut.

I've seen the rain come in this hut just like a perfect flood,
Especially through that great big hole where once the table stood.
There's not a blessed spot, me boys, where you could lay your nut,
But the rain is sure to find you in the old bark hut.

Chorus
In an old bark hut. In an old bark hut.
But the rain is sure to find you in the old bark hut.

So beside the fire I make me bed, and there I lay me down,
And think myself as happy as the king that wears a crown.
But as you'd be dozing off to sleep a flea will wake you, but
'Tis useless cursing vermin in the old bark hut.

Chorus
In an old bark hut. In an old bark hut.
'Tis useless cursing vermin in the old bark hut.

Faith, such flocks of fleas you never saw, they are so plump and fat,
And if you make a grab at one, he'll spit just like a cat.
Last night they got my pack of cards, and were fighting for the cut –
I thought the devil had me in the old bark hut.

Chorus
In an old bark hut. In an old bark hut.
I thought the devil had me in the old bark hut.

So now, my friends, I've sung my song, and that as well as I could,
And I hope the ladies present won't think my language rude,
And all ye younger people, in the days when you grow up,
Remember Bob the Swagman, and the old bark hut.

Chorus
In an old bark hut. In an old bark hut.
Remember Bob the Swagman, and the old bark hut.

ADAM LINDSAY GORDON 1833–1870

Adam Lindsay Gordon was a descendant of Robert Gordon, a Scotsman who invested a large fortune from growing wine in France into the Scottish Barony of Esslemont, which he entailed to his eldest male heir, an action that was to set the trap for the poet's suicide a century and a quarter later. Gordon was born in the Azores, where his family had moved in the hope of restoring his mother's mental health, after she succumbed to "religious mania". On the family's return to England, Gordon became a day boy at Cheltenham College, where his father was a professor of oriental languages, after a military career in India. Gordon was an adept boxer and devotee of Latin verse but left school under a cloud. Nor did he distinguish himself at a military academy.

In 1853 he sailed for South Australia. On his arrival, just twenty years old, he applied to join the mounted police. He successfully discharged his duties for two years, being involved in several notable police exploits; however when asked to shine the boots of a sergeant who was his superior, Gordon resigned and took up horse-breaking. This was dangerous, particularly for Gordon, who was short-sighted. In wild gallops through the bush he was often knocked out of the saddle by branches. He was a fanatical steeple chaser and in 1862 suffered multiple fractures from a bad fall. He was nursed by a cheerful eighteen-year old, Maggie Park, barely five feet high, who shared his love of horsemanship but (she said) "I didn't take much notice of his poetry". While convalescing, he suggested they marry the following week, which they did. They must have been a comical pair, the tall, almost cadaverous bridegroom, with his short, brisk bride.

Two years later, there was an unexpected windfall. Gordon had disappeared from his family's ken, but was tracked down by a persevering executor, and inherited £7000 from the estate of his mother, already five years dead. He speculated in land and livestock and became a member of parliament. Distracted by adventures in horse racing, his investments went bad and he resigned from his parliamentary seat. His interest in literature had been rekindled and by 1866 Gordon had begun publishing poetry. His long philosophical poem, "Ye Wearie Wayfarer" contained a verse ("Life is mostly froth and bubble …") which was to become for a time one of the most famous in English literature. However his first book of poems, *Sea Spray and Smoke Drift*, published in 1867, received generally dismissive reviews and he did not recover his publication costs.

Gordon bought some livery stables in Ballarat, then famous for its gold mining. He got a dent in his skull in a riding accident, and his baby daughter died – events that led to long-term depression. Moving with his wife to the Melbourne seaside suburb of Brighton, he scored some notable riding victories. Although he had difficulty seeing where he was going, he had "that absolute sympathy with the horse which few riders possess: he knew just how to train and just how to get every pound at the dangerous pinch out of his mount." (Frank Maldon Robb, Oxford edition of *Poems of Adam Lindsay Gordon*, 1923). Robb speculated that suicidal tendencies may also have prompted him to ride so fearlessly. Gordon got to know the novelist, Marcus Clarke, who was to write a famous preface in a posthumous collection of Gordon's poems.

Gordon was advised by a leading Melbourne law firm that under the law of entail, the Barony of Esslemont was rightly his. He only became interested when he discovered that the present owner, a Mrs Wooldridge, was independently wealthy. He began litigation and borrowed from moneylenders, accumulating yet more liabilities, confident he was about to become a wealthy man. However, news arrived that his lawyers had been wrong. His book *Bush Ballads and Galloping Rhymes*, which was to make him famous in Britain and Australia, was about to be published, but Gordon was deeply depressed about his situation. He had injuries from yet another bad racing accident. On the morning of publication, Gordon saw the proofs of a glowing review by Henry Kendall. That afternoon he applied to a friend for a loan of £100 and was knocked back. The following morning he rose early, kissed his half-conscious wife, who remembered his beard brushing her face, and went walking on Brighton Beach, where he shot himself.

After his death Gordon was overrated as a poet for some years. In 1934 his memorial bust was unveiled by the Duke of York in the Poets' Corner of Westminster Abbey – on a pillar near Lord Tennyson's bust. He is the only Australian poet honoured in this way. His reputation faded during the 20th century. He is sometimes left out of anthologies and is now seriously underrated. Gordon's poetry was popular with bushmen and recited by drovers and in shearing sheds, with "The Sick Stockrider" being the first "literary" bush ballad to become widely known. "From the Wreck" has rarely, if ever, been anthologised. Robb has a long note on this poem. It relates to an incident in 1859 when Gordon had left the police force and the steamship *Admella* was driven ashore on the rocky South Australian coast near Cape Northumberland. Passengers were being swept to their death into the wild seas, but two seamen succeeded in sailing to a lighthouse to give an alert. In turn, a local station was alerted; hence the Browningesque ride to the nearest telegraph station of the two station hands, which Gordon describes.

from Ye Wearie Wayfarer

"There's something in this world amiss
Shall be unriddled by-and-bye." – Tennyson.

Boot and saddle! See, the slanting
  Rays begin to fall,
Flinging lights and colours flaunting
  Through the shadows tall.
Onward! onward! must we travel?
  When will come the goal?
Riddle I may not unravel,
  Cease to vex my soul.

Harshly break those peals of laughter
  From the jays aloft,
Can we guess what they cry after?
  We have heard them oft;
Perhaps some strain of rude thanksgiving
  Mingles in their song,
Are they glad that they are living?
  Are they right or wrong?
Right, 'tis joy that makes them call so,
  Why should they be sad?
Certes! we are living also,
  Shall not we be glad?
Onward! onward! must we travel?
  Is the goal more near?

Riddle we may not unravel,
  Why so dark and drear?

Yon small bird his hymn outpouring,
  On the branch close by,
Recks not for the kestrel soaring
  In the nether sky,
Though the hawk with wings extended
  Poises over head,
Motionless as though suspended
  By a viewless thread.
See, he stoops, nay, shooting forward
  With the arrow's flight,
Swift and straight away to nor'ward
  Sails he out of sight.
Onward! onward! thus we travel,
  Comes the goal more nigh?
Riddle we may not unravel,
  Who shall make reply?

* * * *

Eastward! in the pink horizon,
  Fleecy hillocks shame
This dim range dull earth that lies on,
  Tinged with rosy flame.
Westward! as a stricken giant
  Stoops his bloody crest,
And tho' vanquished, frowns defiant,
  Sinks the sun to rest.
Distant, yet approaching quickly,
  From the shades that lurk,
Like a black pall gathers thickly,
  Night, when none may work.
Soon our restless occupation
  Shall have ceas'd to be;
Units! in God's vast creation,
  Ciphers! what are we?
Onward! onward! oh! faint-hearted;
  Nearer and more near
Has the goal drawn since we started,
  Be of better cheer.

* * * *

Hark! the bells on distant cattle
  Waft across the range;
Through the golden-tufted wattle,
  Music low and strange;
Like the marriage peal of fairies
  Comes the tinkling sound,
Or like chimes of sweet St. Mary's
  On far English ground.
How my courser champs the snaffle,
  And with nostril spread,
Snorts and scarcely seems to ruffle
  Fern leaves with his tread;
Cool and pleasant on his haunches
  Blows the evening breeze,
Through the overhanging branches
  Of the wattle trees:
Onward! to the Southern Ocean,
  Glides the breath of Spring.
Onward! with a dreamy motion,
  I, too, glide and sing –
Forward! forward! still we wander –
  Tinted hills that lie
In the red horizon yonder –
  Is the goal so nigh?

Whisper, spring-wind, softly singing,
  Whisper in my ear;
Respite and nepenthe bringing,
  Can the goal be near?
Laden with the dew of vespers,
  From the fragrant sky,
In my ear the wind that whispers
  Seems to make reply –

"Question not, but live and labour
  Till yon goal be won,
Helping every feeble neighbour,
  Seeking help from none;
Life is mostly froth and bubble,
  Two things stand like stone,
Kindness in another's trouble,
  Courage in your own."

Courage! comrades, this is certain,
  All is for the best –
There are lights behind the curtain –
  Gentles, let us rest.
As the smoke-rack veers to seaward,
  From "the ancient clay",
With its moral drifting leeward,
  Ends the wanderer's lay.

The Sick Stock Rider

Hold hard, Ned! Lift me down once more, and lay me in the shade.
    Old man, you've had your work cut out to guide
Both horses, and to hold me in the saddle when I sway'd,
    All through the hot, slow, sleepy, silent ride.
The dawn at "Moorabinda" was a mist rack dull and dense,
    The sunrise was a sullen, sluggish lamp;
I was dozing in the gateway at Arbuthnot's bound'ry fence,
    I was dreaming on the Limestone cattle camp.
We crossed the creek at Carricksford, and sharply through the haze,
    And suddenly the sun shot flaming forth;
To southward lay "Katawa", with the sandpeaks all ablaze,
    And the flush'd fields of Glen Lomond lay to north.
Now westward winds the bridle path that leads to Lindisfarm,
    And yonder looms the double-headed Bluff;
From the far side of the first hill, when the skies are clear and calm,
    You can see Sylvester's woolshed fair enough.
Five miles we used to call it from our homestead to the place
    Where the big tree spans the roadway like an arch;
'Twas here we ran the dingo down that gave us such a chase
    Eight years ago – or was it nine? – last March.

'Twas merry in the glowing morn, among the gleaming grass,
    To wander as we've wandered many a mile,
And blow the cool tobacco cloud, and watch the white wreaths pass,
    Sitting loosely in the saddle all the while.
'Twas merry 'mid the blackwoods, when we spied the station roofs,
    To wheel the wild scrub cattle at the yard,
With a running fire of stockwhips and a fiery run of hoofs;
    Oh! the hardest day was never then too hard!

Aye! we had a glorious gallop after "Starlight" and his gang,
    When they bolted from Sylvester's on the flat;
How the sun-dried reed-beds crackled, how the flint-strewn ranges rang

To the strokes of "Mountaineer" and "Acrobat".
Hard behind them in the timber, harder still across the heath,
Close beside them through the tea-tree scrub we dash'd;
And the golden-tinted fern leaves, how they rustled underneath!
And the honeysuckle osiers, how they crash'd!

We led the hunt throughout, Ned, on the chestnut and the grey,
And the troopers were three hundred yards behind,
While we emptied our six-shooters on the bushrangers at bay,
In the creek with stunted box-tree for a blind!
There you grappled with the leader, man to man and horse to horse,
And you roll'd together when the chestnut rear'd;
He blazed away and missed you in that shallow watercourse –
A narrow shave – his powder singed your beard!
In these hours when life is ebbing, how those days when life was young
Come back to us; how clearly I recall
Even the yarns Jack Hall invented, and the songs Jem Roper sung;
And where are now Jem Roper and Jack Hall?

Aye! nearly all our comrades of the old colonial school,
Our ancient boon companions, Ned, are gone;
Hard livers for the most part, somewhat reckless as a rule,
It seems that you and I are left alone.

There was Hughes, who got in trouble through that business with the cards,
It matters little what became of him;
But a steer ripp'd up MacPherson in the Cooraminta yards,
And Sullivan was drown'd at Sink-or-Swim.
And Mostyn – poor Frank Mostyn – died at last a fearful wreck,
In "the horrors", at the Upper Wandinong,
And Carisbrooke, the rider, at the Horsefall broke his neck,
Faith! the wonder was he saved his neck so long!

Ah! those days and nights we squandered at the Logans' in the glen –
The Logans, man and wife, have long been dead.
Elsie's tallest girl seems taller than your little Elsie then;
And Ethel is a woman grown and wed.

I've had my share of pastime, and I've done my share of toil,
And life is short – the longest life a span;
I care not now to tarry for the corn or for the oil,
Or for the wine that maketh glad the heart of man.
For good undone and gifts misspent and resolutions vain,
'Tis somewhat late to trouble. This I know –
I should live the same life over, if I had to live again;
And the chances are I go where most men go.

The deep blue skies wax dusky, and the tall green trees grow dim,
The sward beneath me seems to heave and fall;
And sickly, smoky shadows through the sleepy sunlight swim,
And on the very sun's face weave their pall.
Let me slumber in the hollow where the wattle blossoms wave,
With never stone or rail to fence my bed;
Should the sturdy station children pull the bush flowers on my grave,
I may chance to hear them romping overhead.

From the Wreck

"Turn out, boys" – "What's up with our super. to-night?
The man's mad – Two hours to daybreak I'd swear –
Stark mad – why, there isn't a glimmer of light."
"Take Bolingbroke, Alec, give Jack the young mare;
Look sharp. A large vessel lies jamm'd on the reef,
And many on board still, and some wash'd on shore.
Ride straight with the news – they may send some relief
From the township; and we – we can do little more.

You, Alec, you know the near cuts; you can cross
'The Sugarloaf' ford with a scramble, I think;
Don't spare the blood filly, nor yet the black horse;
Should the wind rise, God help them! the ship will soon sink.
Old Peter's away down the paddock, to drive
The nags to the stockyard as fast as he can –
A life and death matter; so, lads, look alive."
Half-dress'd, in the dark, to the stockyard we ran.

There was bridling with hurry, and saddling with haste,
Confusion and cursing for lack of a moon;
"Be quick with these buckles, we've no time to waste;"
"Mind the mare, she can use her hind legs to some tune."
"Make sure of the crossing-place; strike the old track,
They've fenced off the new one; look out for the holes
On the wombat hills." "Down with the slip rails; stand back."
"And ride, boys, the pair of you, ride for your souls."

In the low branches heavily laden with dew,
In the long grasses spoiling with deadwood that day,
Where the blackwood, the box, and the bastard oak grew,
Between the tall gum-trees we gallop'd away –
We crash'd through a brush fence, we splash'd through a swamp –
We steered for the north near "The Eaglehawk's Nest" –

We bore to the left, just beyond "The Red Camp",
  And round the black tea-tree belt wheel'd to the west –

We cross'd a low range sickly scented with musk
  From wattle-tree blossom – we skirted a marsh –
Then the dawn faintly dappled with orange the dusk,
  And peal'd overhead the jay's laughter note harsh,
And shot the first sunstreak behind us, and soon
  The dim dewy uplands were dreamy with light;
And full on our left flash'd "The Reedy Lagoon",
  And sharply "The Sugarloaf" rear'd on our right.
A smothered curse broke through the bushman's brown beard,
  He turn'd in his saddle, his brick-colour'd cheek
Flush'd feebly with sundawn, said, "Just what I fear'd;
  Last fortnight's late rainfall has flooded the creek."

Black Bolingbroke snorted, and stood on the brink
  One instant, then deep in the dark sluggish swirl
Plunged headlong. I saw the horse suddenly sink,
  Till round the man's armpits the waves seemed to curl.
We follow'd, – one cold shock, and deeper we sank
  Than they did, and twice tried the landing in vain;
The third struggle won it; straight up the steep bank
  We stagger'd, then out on the skirts of the plain.

The stockrider, Alec, at starting had got
  The lead, and had kept it throughout; 'twas his boast
That through thickest of scrub he could steer like a shot,
  And the black horse was counted the best on the coast.
The mare had been awkward enough in the dark,
  She was eager and headstrong, and barely half broke;
She had had me too close to a big stringy-bark,
  And had made a near thing of a crooked sheoak.

But now on the open, lit up by the morn,
  She flung the white foam-flakes from nostril to neck,
And chased him – I hatless, with shirt sleeves all torn
  (For he may ride ragged who rides from a wreck) –
And faster and faster across the wide heath
  We rode till we raced. Then I gave her her head,
And she – stretching out with the bit in her teeth –
  She caught him, outpaced him, and passed him, and led.
We neared the new fence, we were wide of the track;
  I look'd right and left – she had never been tried

At a stiff leap; 'twas little he cared on the black.
  "You're more than a mile from the gateway," he cried.

I hung to her head, touched her flank with the spurs
  (In the red streak of rail not the ghost of a gap);
She shortened her long stroke, she pricked her sharp ears,
  She flung it behind her with hardly a rap –
I saw the post quiver where Bolingbroke struck,
  And guessed that the pace we had come the last mile
Had blown him a bit (he could jump like a buck).
  We galloped more steadily then for a while.

The heath was soon pass'd, in the dim distance lay
  The mountain. The sun was just clearing the tips
Of the ranges to eastward. The mare – could she stay?
  She was bred very nearly as clean as Eclipse;
She led, and as oft as he came to her side,
  She took the bit free and untiring as yet;
Her neck was arched double, her nostrils were wide,
  And the tips of her tapering ears nearly met –
"You're lighter than I am," said Alec at last;
  "The horse is dead beat and the mare isn't blown.
She must be a good one – ride on and ride fast,
  You know your way now." So I rode on alone.

Still galloping forward we pass'd the two flocks
  At McIntyre's hut and McAllister's hill –
She was galloping strong at the Warrigal Rocks –
  On the Wallaby Range she was galloping still –
And over the wasteland and under the wood,
  By down and by dale, and by fell and by flat,
She gallop'd, and here in the stirrups I stood
  To ease her, and there in the saddle I sat
To steer her. We suddenly struck the red loam
  Of the track near the troughs – then she reeled on the rise –
From her crest to her croup covered over with foam,
  And blood-red her nostrils, and bloodshot her eyes,
A dip in the dell where the wattle fire bloomed –
  A bend round a bank that had shut out the view –
Large framed in the mild light the mountain had loom'd,
  With a tall, purple peak bursting out from the blue.

I pull'd her together, I press'd her, and she
  Shot down the decline to the Company's yard,
And on by the paddocks, yet under my knee

I could feel her heart thumping the saddle-flaps hard.
Yet a mile and another, and now we were near
The goal, and the fields and the farms flitted past;
And 'twixt the two fences I turned with a cheer,
For a green grass-fed mare 'twas a far thing and fast;
And labourers, roused by her galloping hoofs,
Saw bare-headed rider and foam-sheeted steed;
And shone the white walls and the slate-coloured roofs
Of the township. I steadied her then – I had need –
Where stood the old chapel (where stands the new church –
Since chapels to churches have changed in that town).
A short, sidelong stagger, a long, forward lurch,
A slight, choking sob, and the mare had gone down.
I slipp'd off the bridle, I slacken'd the girth,
I ran on and left her and told them my news;
I saw her soon afterwards. What was she worth?
How much for her hide? She had never worn shoes.

HENRY KENDALL 1839–1882

Kendall was born of alcoholic but well-educated parents in a slab and bark hut in Ulladulla, New South Wales. He was one of twins, both left-handed. After his father's death from tuberculosis in 1852, his mother and her children moved to her father's house in Wollongong. He joined a whaler in September 1855 as a cabin boy, and was away until March 1857. Kendall detested the whaling life – in particular being the lookout in the crow's nest. On his return he rented a house in the Sydney suburb of Newtown for his mother, brother and sisters and took a variety of jobs: as an errand boy, a shop assistant, and a clerk in a solicitor's office. Finally, he obtained a job with the Department of Lands, later transferring to the Colonial Secretary's Office in 1866.

In 1859 he began publishing poems in periodicals and newspapers. In January 1862 he sent some poems to the editor of the *Cornhill Magazine*, a prestigious London literary journal. In his accompanying letter, Kendall wrote:

> "Will you oblige me by reading this letter and the accompanying verses? Remember that they will have travelled sixteen thousand miles, and on that account will be surely worth a few moments of your time. I think that there is merit in the verses ... If one can be selected – one up to the standard of the 'Cornhill Magazine', insert it and you will be helping me practically. I do not hint of pecuniary remuneration however, for your recognition would be sufficient reward.
>
> "Let me say a few words about myself: I was born in this colony; and am now in the nineteenth year of my age [he was twenty-two] ... At present ... most of my time is occupied at an attorney's office, but I do not earn enough there to cover my expenses; considering that I have to support

my mother and three sisters. I want to rise, and if my poems are anywhere near the mark you can assist me by noticing them.

"They recognise me in this country as the 'first Australian poet'. If the men who load me with their fulsome, foolish praises, really believed in my talents, and cared a whit about fostering a native literature, they would give me a good situation, and I should not have to appeal to you.

"If one of the poems is found to be good enough, and you publish it, someone here will surely do the rest. On the other hand if nothing can be gleaned from them, let the effusions and their author be forgotten. Hoping that you will not forget to read the verses, I remain

Yours, respectfully, H. Kendall."

The *Cornhill* rejected his verses. But a similar letter to another London magazine, the *Athenaeum*, succeeded, with the poems and letter being published in September 1862. This letter gave Kendall an even later birth date of 1842.

Kendall married in 1868. In the same year he had the misfortune to win a poetry prize which encouraged him to give up his job. He was plagued by money problems, exacerbated by his mother's and sisters' improvidence and his twin brother's being a fraudster. Hoping to earn a living as a writer, he moved to Melbourne, which was more of a literary centre. He became friendly with Adam Lindsay Gordon and other Melbourne writers. Although his book *Leaves from the Australian Forests* was reviewed favourably, his publisher lost £90 over it. Even after Kendall's death thirteen years later, hundreds of copies were still for sale in Melbourne at sixpence a copy. His first child, Araluen, died. He returned to Sydney, broken in health, and drinking to excess. For a few months in 1873 he was hospitalised in an asylum for the insane.

In the mid-1870s he was befriended by two timber merchants, the Fagan brothers. They gave him work as a clerk in the Gosford area and he was reunited with his wife and children. In 1881 Sir Henry Parkes arranged for him to be appointed Inspector of Forests at £500 a year, then a very substantial income. However, like his father, he was tubercular, and in the following year on one of his long tours of inspection caught a chill, and died in his wife's arms.

Kendall and Gordon were the two most widely regarded Australian poets in the 19th century. For some decades after his death, critics rated Kendall as "a true singer", whereas Charles Harpur was "lacking vitality" and capable only of "fitful gleams of poetic fire". This judgment has now been largely reversed. Kendall, to his credit, had befriended the older poet and was deeply affected by his death. "Bellbirds" has been for many people, from the time they encountered it at school, their favourite Australian poem.

Prefatory Sonnets

I

I purposed once to take my pen and write,
  Not songs, like some, tormented and awry
  With passion, but a cunning harmony
Of words and music caught from glen and height,
And lucid colours born of woodland light

And shining places where the sea-streams lie.
But this was when the heat of youth glowed white,
And since I've put the faded purpose by.
I have no faultless fruits to offer you
Who read this book; but certain syllables
Herein are borrowed from unfooted dells
And secret hollows dear to noontide dew;
And these at least, though far between and few,
May catch the sense like subtle forest spells.

II

So take these kindly, even though there be
Some notes that unto other lyres belong,
Stray echoes from the elder sons of song;
And think how from its neighbouring native sea
The pensive shell doth borrow melody,
I would not do the lordly masters wrong
By filching fair words from the shining throng
Whose music haunts me as the wind a tree.
Lo, when a stranger in soft Syrian glooms
Shot through with sunset, treads the cedar dells,
And hears the breezy ring of elfin bells
Far down by where the white-haired cataract booms,
He, faint with sweetness caught from forest smells,
Bears thence, unwitting, plunder of perfumes.

Bellbirds

By channels of coolness the echoes are calling,
And down the dim gorges I hear the creek falling;
It lives in the mountain where moss and the sedges
Touch with their beauty the banks and the ledges.
Through breaks of the cedar and sycamore bowers
Struggles the light that is love to the flowers;
And, softer than slumber, and sweeter than singing,
The notes of the bell-birds are running and ringing.

The silver-voiced bell birds, the darlings of daytime,
They sing in September their songs of the May-time;
When shadows wax strong, and the thunder bolts hurtle,
They hide with their fear in the leaves of the myrtle;
When rain and the sunbeams shine mingled together
They start up like fairies that follow fair weather,

And straightway the hues of their feathers unfolden
Are the green and the purple, the blue and the golden.

October, the maiden of bright yellow tresses,
Loiters for love in these cool wildernesses;
Loiters knee-deep in the grasses, to listen,
Where dripping rocks gleam and the leafy pools glisten.
Then is the time when the water-moons splendid
Break with their gold, and are scattered or blended
Over the creeks, till the woodlands have warning
Of songs of the bell-bird and wings of the morning.

Welcome as waters unkissed by the summers
Are the voices of bell-birds to the thirsty far-comers.
When fiery December sets foot in the forest,
And the need of the wayfarer presses the sorest,
Pent in the ridges for ever and ever
The bell-birds direct him to spring and to river,
With ring and with ripple, like runnels whose torrents
Are toned by the pebbles and the leaves in the currents.

Often I sit, looking back to a childhood,
Mixt with the sights and the sounds of the wildwood,
Longing for power and the sweetness to fashion,
Lyrics with beats like the heart-beats of passion –
Songs interwoven of lights and of laughters
Borrowed from bell-birds in far forest-rafters;
So I might keep in the city and alleys
The beauty and strength of the deep mountain valleys,
Charming to slumber the pain of my losses
With glimpses of creeks and a vision of mosses.

The Last of His Tribe

He crouches, and buries his face on his knees,
And hides in the dark of his hair;
For he cannot look up to the storm-smitten trees,
Or think of the loneliness there –
Of the loss and the loneliness there.

The wallaroos grope through the tufts of the grass,
And turn to their coverts for fear;
But he sits in the ashes and lets them pass
Where the boomerangs sleep with the spear –
With the nullah, the sling and the spear.

Uloola, behold him! The thunder that breaks
On the tops of the rocks with the rain,
And the wind which drives up with the salt of the lakes,
Have made him a hunter again –
A hunter and fisher again.

For his eyes have been full with a smouldering thought;
But he dreams of the hunts of yore,
And of foes that he sought, and of fights that he fought
With those who will battle no more –
Who will go to the battle no more.

It is well that the water which tumbles and fills
Goes moaning and moaning along;
For an echo rolls out from the sides of the hills,
And he starts at a wonderful song –
At the sound of a wonderful song.

And he sees through the rents of the scattering fogs
The corroboree warlike and grim,
And the lubra who sat by the fire on the logs,
To watch, like a mourner, for him –
Like a mother and mourner for him.

Will he go in his sleep from these desolate lands,
Like a chief, to the rest of his race,
With the honey-voiced woman who beckons and stands,
And gleams like a dream in his face –
Like a marvellous dream in his face?

CHARLIE "BOWYANG" YORKE (?)

"Bullocky Bill" is one of Australia's most famous and contested pieces of folk poetry. There is a bronze life-size statue of a dog *sitting* on a tucker-box (food box) near Gundagai, New South Wales, unveiled in 1932 by the then Prime Minister. It was erected to raise funds for the local hospital. The statue is still a well-known tourist attraction and is *five* miles from Gundagai, which is the distance specified in some versions of the poem. However, it would appear that this distance was chosen as more convenient for tourists. The most commonly anthologised version has "Talbingo Hill" for "Conroy's Gap", "beggar" for "bugger" and "sat" for "shat". The version used here, comes from Gundagai Shire Council's own website, as at 12 June 2009. The Council states that no definitive version exists, and claims that the unexpurgated version below was what appeared in a local newspaper in 1859!

Bullocky Bill

As I was coming down Conroy's Gap
I heard a maiden cry,
"There's goes old Bill the Bullocky
He's bound for Gundagai.
A better poor old bugger
Never earnt an honest crust,
A tougher poor old bugger
Never drug a whip through dust.
His team got bogged on the Nine-mile Creek,
Bill lashed and swore and cried,
'If Nobbie don't get me out of this
I'll tattoo his bloody hide.'
But Nobbie strained and broke the yoke
And poked out the leader's eye,
Then the dog shat in the tucker-box
Nine miles from Gundagai."

JOSEPH FURPHY ("Tom Collins") 1843–1912

Joseph Furphy, one of Australia's great novelists, was born at Yerring, near Yarra Glen, in Victoria, two years after his parents had migrated from Northern Ireland. He was at first educated by his mother in the Bible and Shakespeare. In 1850 his family moved to Kangaroo Ground where he attended the local school, and in 1852 they moved to Kyneton. After some attempts at farming, he became a bullock driver in 1873, which was to be his occupation for a decade and provide much of the material for his comic masterpiece, the novel *Such is Life*, published under the pen name "Tom Collins" in 1903. Furphy was a political moralist and cracker-barrel philosopher. On the advice of A. G. Stephens, literary editor of the *Bulletin*, he omitted much of the philosophical deadwood that would have otherwise marred his great novel. Instead it mars *Rigby's Romance*: a shorter work which could have been a fine novella apart from interminable passages of political diatribe. The bohemians of the *Bulletin* regarded Furphy as naïve because he did not drink or gamble and was an optimist. He wrote a lot of poetry that is accomplished but boring because of its hortatory tone. The poem below is an exception. "The Schoolhouse on the Plain" is virtually unknown and yet to achieve its deserved classic status.

The Schoolhouse on the Plain

On the geodetic line, where the parish boundaries join
  At a level and interminable lane
You can see it there, alone, standing calmly on its own,
  Like an iceberg in a solitary main.

It's a topographic base, and each near or distant place
  Is located from the Schoolhouse on the Plain.

It lies open to the road, in the usual country mode,
  With a few old waster posts to bridge the drain;
The reserve is clean and dry, being several inches high,
  The building standing back about a chain.
Nothing could excel the stand, and it's worth its bit of land,
  That inexpensive Schoolhouse on the Plain.

It requires a lick of paint, to correct the weather-taint,
  And its windows should have here and there a pane;
The open-jointed floor swallows pencils by the score,
  And the veteran desks are inked with many a stain;
Still it's proof against the wet, and there's lots of service yet
  In that unpretentious Schoolhouse on the Plain.

Such eventual wear and tear, with contingent disrepair,
  Is appointed unto everything mundane –
Bear in mind it braves with ease the fanatic and the breeze
  Spreading influence that nothing can restrain –
Think how superstitions yield, and sectarian feuds are healed,
  In that nation-building Schoolhouse on the Plain.

All the district, far and near, has a postal centre here,
  So suitable that no one can complain;
Here the local Rechabites, on alternate Thursday nights,
  Renew their solemn davy to abstain;
Also that improvement class, called the Literary Ass,
  Holds its meetings at the Schoolhouse on the Plain.

When election time draws near, then the hayseeds rally here,
  To catechize the candidate urbane;
To demand a cockspur line, and an open port for twine,
  With reduction of the railway freight on grain.
Here on polling day they meet, to discomfort Lygon Street,
  No nonsense with the Schoolhouse on the Plain!

Here the missionary man, fresh from India or Japan,
  Unblushingly takes on him to maintain
That he labours day and night in a harvest field that's white,
  With other statements shaky and inane;
But his magic-lantern show makes the entertainment go,
  Till applauses fill the Schoolhouse on the Plain.

Every Sunday, after two, there's an old-man rendezvous,
  And the edifice becomes a sacred fane;

Then along the fence, each side, stands a line of horses tied,
  And the seats within hold all they can contain;
While some good, well-meaning man, as per local-preachers' plan,
  Holds Service in the Schoolhouse on the Plain.

And as he exhorts or prays, or the flock their voices raise
  In rendition of some Sankey-book refrain,
A dozen dogs, and more, hold possession of the floor,
  Dumbly showing how they need insectibane –
Nor are such things taken ill, for there's no superfluous frill
  At those preachings in the Schoolhouse on the Plain.

There the boys deal glances fond, and the girls, of course, respond,
  In spite of the indifference they feign;
Whilst the mothers of the youth listen to the word of truth,
  Till they feel about as innocent as Cain;
And the toddlers play bo-peep, and the rude forefathers sleep,
  Being bosses of the Schoolhouse on the Plain.

But the Monday, coming round, as by ancient usage bound,
  Sees our jossless system under way again;
Then the hopefuls mobilize, and the droning murmurs rise,
  Whilst the tree of knowledge creaks beneath the strain;
And the R's extend their roots, and the young idea shoots,
  Under cover at that Schoolhouse on the Plain.

There are stories carted here, from the Northern Hemisphere,
  And designed to cause a thrill through every vein,
Of monarchs, grave or gay, each distinguished in his day
  By being feeble-minded or insane –
But here the kids compete for the scorner's sinful seat.
  Their troubles at the Schoolhouse on the Plain!

As becometh Jim and Bill, their solicitude is nil
  Touching Mary Queen of Scots or Anne Boleyn,
But the ructions of the kings, when their docile underlings
  Made a many-figured tally of the slain,
Are considered worth review, for the sporting instinct true
  Is powerful at the Schoolhouse on the Plain.

There are lessons setting forth how an islet somewhere north
  Knocked the stuffing out of Holland, France and Spain;
How, from east to west, its drum makes our planet fairly hum,
  And the sunrise follow meekly in its train;
How that spadeful, all alone, gave us everything we own,
  Especially this Schoolhouse on the Plain.

And the lydy-teacher there, comes from heaven alone knows where,
  Like some angel they're vouchsafed to entertain.
She controls her motley drove by the gentle power of love,
  Emphasizing her affection with a cane –
True, she cavils all the while at the rough, untidy style
  Of her pupils in the Schoolhouse on the Plain.

She sets up to know a lot, but there's one defective spot
  In the dignity she struggles to sustain;
For her days are passed in fright, and her sleep's disturbed at night
  As if she had Inspector on the brain;
And her heart is in her mouth as she watches north and south
  From the windows of the Schoolhouse on the Plain.

And when she is elsewhere gone, that old school will still live on –
  Just as she herself was not the first to reign –
Since, for better or for worse, Young Australia comes in force,
  (As a reference to the Year Book will explain);
And he only leaves a place for his duplicate to grace;
  In the roll-book of the Schoolhouse on the Plain.

They mature, and off they drop, in an intermittent crop,
  Not a single soul desiring to remain;
For *they* know their road about, *they* can turn things inside out!
  But existence, as they quickly ascertain,
Is a great deal harder row than they thought they had to hoe,
  When they wagged it from the Schoolhouse on the Plain.

Many a shearer, tough and strong; many a drover, two yards long;
  Many a bullock driver, hairy and profane;
Many an innocent yahoo; many a red-hot subject too;
  Many a law-abiding devotee of gain;
Many a work-girl; many a wife – looking back upon their life,
  Cherish memories of the Schoolhouse on the Plain.

Some important changes gleam o'er the spirit of their dream
  As they blunder through their honourless campaign –
All that sense of brutal wrong has been dissipated long
  From the standard they were driven to attain;
And they wish with all their heart they could make a second start
  At the undervalued Schoolhouse on the Plain.

ADA CAMBRIDGE 1844–1926

Ada Cambridge was born at St Germans, Norfolk, in England, the second child of a gentleman farmer. She had a precocious talent and in her early twenties published *Hymns of the Litany* (1865) and *Hymns of the Holy Communion* (1866) and some stories. In 1870 she married an Anglican clergyman, the Rev. George Frederick Cross, and the couple came to live in Australia. There she was the hard-working wife of a clergyman in the Australian bush, taking part in parish activities and making her children's clothes. She lost children to whooping cough and scarlet fever, had a nearly fatal miscarriage, and was badly injured in a carriage accident. The family were not well-off and she started writing fiction partly to help make ends meet, publishing over the course of her life twenty-five works of fiction and two autobiographical works. She and her husband moved from parish to parish, seven in all, from 1870 until his retirement in 1909. They went back to England in 1913. In 1917, after his death, she returned to Australia.

Cambridge wrote three volumes of poetry (apart from her youthful hymn collections and possibly *Echoes* [1869] by "A.C."). Her first volume of secular poetry, *The Manor House; and Other Poems*, appeared in England in 1875, the same year her first novel *Up the Murray* was serialised in *The Australasian*. With her vivid phrasing and her serious and dramatic voice, often rising to a full-hearted cry of woe, the Australian poet of the late 19th century whom she most resembles is Christopher Brennan (although her poetry lacks his symbolist manner). Like Brennan, she can overbalance into melodrama and, similar to him, she also battled with a loss of religious faith.

It is conjectured that when Cambridge visited the artists' camp on Balmoral beach, Sydney, she may have fallen in love and perhaps had an affair. The "you" of "A Promise" is unidentifiable from the poem, but it does not read like a poem addressed to a clergyman husband of long-standing.

The Venetian "colour" and detail of "A Dream of Venice" may have been gleaned from visits to London galleries and museums before her marriage. The poem begins with an unnamed narrator in Venice, who is addressed by her husband as "wife". He has been previously married and may be older. The narrator falls asleep, dreaming the thousand years of Venice's history. The lyrical colour of the poem's beginning is what struck us and we have omitted the melodramatic historical material of the dream.

from A Dream of Venice

Numb, half asleep, and dazed with whirl of wheels,
And gasp of steam, and measured clank of chains,
I heard a blithe voice break a sudden pause,
Ringing familiarly through the lamp-lit night,
"Wife, here's your Venice!"
                                        I was lifted down,
And gazed about in stupid wonderment,
Holding my little Katie by the hand –
My yellow-haired step-daughter. And again

Two strong arms led me to the water-brink,
And laid me on soft cushions in a boat, –
A queer boat, by a queerer boatman manned –
Swarthy-faced, ragged, with a scarlet cap –
Whose wild, weird note smote shrilly through the dark.
Oh yes, it was my Venice! Beautiful,
With melancholy, ghostly beauty – old,
And sorrowful, and weary – yet so fair,
So like a queen still, with her royal robes,
Full of harmonious colour, rent and worn!
I only saw her shadow in the stream,
By flickering lamplight, – only saw, as yet,
White, misty palace-portals here and there,
Pillars, and marble steps, and balconies,
Along the broad line of the Grand Canal;
And, in the smaller water-ways, a patch
Of wall, or dim bridge arching overhead.
But I could feel the rest. 'Twas Venice! – ay,
The veritable Venice of my dreams.

I saw the grey dawn shimmer down the stream,
And all the city rise, new bathed in light,
With rose-red blooms on her decaying walls,
And gold tints quivering up her domes and spires –
Sharp-drawn, with delicate pencillings, on a sky
Blue as forget-me-nots in June. I saw
The broad day staring in her palace-fronts,
Pointing to yawning gap and crumbling boss,
And colonnades, time-stained and broken, flecked
With soft, sad, dying colours – sculpture-wreathed,
And gloriously proportioned; saw the glow
Light up her bright, harmonious, fountain'd squares,
And spread out on her marble steps, and pass
Down silent courts and secret passages,
Gathering up motley treasures on its way; –
Groups of rich fruit from the Rialto mart,
Scarlet and brown and purple, with green leaves –
Fragments of exquisite carving, lichen-grown,
Found, 'mid pathetic squalor, in some niche
Where wild, half-naked urchins lived and played –
A bright robe, crowned with a pale, dark-eyed face –
A red-striped awning 'gainst an old grey wall –

A delicate opal gleam upon the tide.
I looked out from my window, and I saw
Venice, my Venice, naked in the sun –
Sad, faded, and unutterably forlorn! –
But still unutterably beautiful.

For days and days I wandered up and down –
Holding my breath in awe and ecstasy, –
Following my husband to familiar haunts,
Making acquaintance with his well-loved friends,
Whose faces I had only seen in dreams
And books and photographs and his careless talk.
For days and days – with sunny hours of rest
And musing chat, in that cool room of ours,
Paved with white marble, on the Grand Canal;
For days and days – with happy nights between,
Half-spent, while little Katie lay asleep
Out on the balcony, with the moon and stars.

O Venice, Venice! – with thy water-streets –
Thy gardens bathed in sunset, flushing red
Behind San Giorgio Maggiore's dome –
Thy glimmering lines of haughty palaces
Shadowing fair arch and column in the stream –
Thy most divine cathedral, and its square,
With vagabonds and loungers daily thronged,
Taking their ice, their coffee, and their ease –
Thy sunny campo's, with their clamorous din,
Their shrieking vendors of fresh fish and fruit –
Thy churches and thy pictures – thy sweet bits
Of colour – thy grand relics of the dead –
Thy gondoliers and water-bearers – girls
With dark, soft eyes, and creamy faces, crowned
With braided locks as bright and black as jet –
Wild ragamuffins, picturesque in rags,
And swarming beggars and old witch-like crones,
And brown-cloaked contadini, hot and tired,
Sleeping, face-downward, on the sunny steps –
Thy fairy islands floating in the sun –
Thy poppy-sprinkled, grave-strewn Lido shore –
Thy poetry and thy pathos – all so strange! –
Thou didst bring many a lump into my throat,
And many a passionate thrill into my heart,

And once a tangled dream into my head.

'Twixt afternoon and evening. I was tired;
The air was hot and golden – not a breath
Of wind until the sunset – hot and still.
Our floor was water-sprinkled; our thick walls
And open doors and windows, shadowed deep
With jalousies and awnings, made a cool
And grateful shadow for my little couch.
A subtle perfume stole about the room
From a small table, piled with purple grapes,
And water-melon slices, pink and wet,
And ripe, sweet figs, and golden apricots,
New-laid on green leaves from our garden – leaves
Wherewith an antique torso had been clothed.
My husband read his novel on the floor,
Propped up on cushions and an Indian shawl;
And little Katie slumbered at his feet,
Her yellow curls alight, and delicate tints
Of colour in the white folds of her frock.
I lay, and mused, in comfort and at ease,
Watching them both and playing with my thoughts;
And then I fell into a long, deep sleep,
And dreamed.

Rialto (Rivo alto)

Despair

Alone! Alone! No beacon, far or near!
  No chart, no compass, and no anchor stay!
  Like melting fog the mirage melts away
In all-surrounding darkness, void and clear.
Drifting, I spread vain hands, and vainly peer
  And vainly call for pilot, – weep and pray;
  Beyond these limits not the faintest ray
Shows distant coast whereto the lost may steer.

O what is life, if we must hold it thus
As wind-blown sparks hold momentary fire?
What are these gifts without the larger boon?
O what is art, or wealth, or fame to us
Who scarce have time to know what we desire?
O what is love, if we must part so soon?

Influence

As in the mists of embryonic night,
  Out of the deep and dark obscurities
  Of Nature's womb, the little life-germs rise,
Pushing by instinct upward to the light;
As, when the first ray dawns on waking sight,
  They leap to liberty, and recognize
  The golden sunshine and the morning skies
Their own inheritance by inborn right; –

So do our brooding thoughts and deep desires
Grow in our souls, we know not how or why;
Grope for we know not what, all blind and dumb.
So, when the time is ripe, and one aspires
To free his thought in speech, ours hear the cry,
And to full birth and instant knowledge come.

The Physical Conscience

The moral conscience – court of last appeal –
  Our word of God – our Heaven-sent light and guide –
  From what high aims it lures our steps aside!
To what immoral deeds it sets its seal!
That beacon lamp has lost its sacred fire;
  That pilot-guide, compelling wind and wave,
  By slow, blind process, has become the slave
Of all-compelling custom and desire.

Not so the conscience of the body. This,
  Untamed and true, still speaks in voice and face,
In cold lips stiffened to the loveless kiss,
  In shamed limbs shrinking from unloved embrace,
In love-born passion, that no laws compel,
Nor gold can purchase, nor ambition sell.

A Promise

Should'st thou, in grip of dread disease,
  Foresee the day when thou must die,
With no more hope of life or ease,
  But only, lingering, to lie
  While torturing hours go slowly by;
Thy brain awake, thy nerves alive
  To thine extremest agony,

And all in vain to rave or strive: –
  O my beloved, if this should be,
    Call me – and I will set thee free.

Murder! And thou to judgment hurled –
  Cut off from some few days of grace –
Thus will it be to that hard world
  Which fits one law to every case,
  And dooms all rebels to disgrace.
But to us twain, who stand above
  Conventioned rules, unbound, unclassed,
A solemn sacrament of love,
  More true than kisses in the past –
    Love's costliest tribute, and the last.

Thy grateful hand, unclenched, shall seek
  The hand that gave thee thy release;
Thy darkening eyes shall dumbly speak
  Of scorching pangs that sink and cease –
  Of anguish drowned in rest and peace.
And I that terrible farewell,
  Despairing but content, shall take,
Knowing that I have served thee well –
  I, that would dare the rack and stake,
    The flames of hell, for thy dear sake.

The law may hang me for my crime,
  Just or unjust, I'll not complain.
'Twere better than to live my time
  Bereaved and broken, and to wane,
  Slow inch by inch, in useless pain;
Alone, unhelped, uncomforted,
  In mine own last extremity;
No faithful lover by my bed
  To do what thou would'st do for me.
    And I shall *want* to die with thee.

STRINGY-BARK AND GREEN-HIDE (Anonymous)

Green-hide is untanned hide from cattle, used for many purposes, as was stringy-bark timber. An anonymous song "Stringy-bark and Green-hide" was published in 1866, but is a rather laboured piece. Banjo Paterson does not include it in his *Old Bush Songs* (1905), except for the quatrain below which appears on the cover of his collection. This verse was apparently sometimes a toast.

Stringy-bark and Green-hide

Stringy-bark will light your fire
Green-hide will never fail yer,
Stringy-bark and green-hide
Are the mainstay of Australia.

THE BANKS OF THE CONDAMINE (Anonymous)

This version is from Vance Palmer's *Old Bush Ballads.* There is another version where "dearest Willie" joins a group of horse-breakers on the banks of the Condamine. A "ringer" is a top shearer. "Tigering" is roughing it. "Ram-stag mutton" is tough mutton. A "jumbuck" is a sheep.

The Banks of the Condamine

Oh, hark the dogs are barking, love,
I can no longer stay,
The men are all gone mustering
And it is nearly day.
And I must off by the morning light
Before the sun doth shine,
To meet the Sydney shearers
On the banks of the Condamine.

Oh Willie, dearest Willie,
I'll go along with you,
I'll cut off all my auburn fringe
And be a shearer, too,
I'll cook and count your tally, love,
While ringer-o you shine,
And I'll wash your greasy moleskins
On the banks of the Condamine.

Oh, Nancy, dearest Nancy,
With me you cannot go,
The squatters have given orders, love,
No woman should do so;
Your delicate constitution
Is not equal unto mine,
To stand the constant tigering
On the banks of the Condamine.

Oh Willie, dearest Willie,
Then stay back home with me,
We'll take up a selection
And a farmer's wife I'll be:
I'll help you husk the corn, love,
And cook your meals so fine
You'll forget the ram-stag mutton
On the banks of the Condamine.

Oh, Nancy, dearest Nancy,
Please do not hold me back,
Down there the boys are waiting,
And I must be on the track;
So here's a good-bye kiss, love,
Back home here I'll incline
When we've shore the last of the jumbucks
On the banks of the Condamine.

THOMAS E. SPENCER 1845–1910

A building contractor and industrial arbitrator, as well as a writer, Spencer was born as Thomas O'Brien at Hoxton Old Town, London, the son of a cabinet-maker. He visited the Victorian goldfields in 1863, but returned to London in the following year and, by the time he married in 1869, had jettisoned his Irish surname. A stonemason by trade, he became vice-president of the Stonemasons' Society of London at the age of 24. He migrated to Sydney in 1875, set up as a successful building contractor and was appointed an employer's representative in the Industrial Court. An active Freemason, he was buried in Sydney with full Masonic rites.

When he began contributing to the *Bulletin* in 1891 J. F. Archibald the *Bulletin*'s co-founder told him, "Your verses blew into the office like a whiff from the bush. It was a pleasure to read some lines which did not contain wattle and dead men". As well as humorous verses, and some extremely sentimental verses, which were collected and sold well, he wrote comic prose sketches, a novel and pieces attacking "socialistic rot" ("Latter day patriots") and shonky builders ("Suburban Simplicity"). "How McDougal Topped the Score" is a famous recitation piece.

How McDougal Topped the Score

A peaceful spot is Piper's Flat. The folk that live around –
They keep themselves by keeping sheep and turning up the ground;
But the climate is erratic, and the consequences are
The struggle with the elements is everlasting war.
We plough, and sow, and harrow – then sit down and pray for rain;
And then we all get flooded out and have to start again.
But the folk are now rejoicing as they ne'er rejoiced before,
For we've played Molongo cricket, and McDougal topped the score!

Molongo had a head on it, and challenged us to play
A single-innings match for lunch – the losing team to pay.
We were not great guns at cricket, but we couldn't well say no,
So we all began to practise, and we let the reaping go.
We scoured the Flat for ten miles round to muster up our men,
But when the list was totalled we could only number ten.
Then up spoke big Tim Brady: he was always slow to speak,
And he said – "What price McDougal, who lives down at Cooper's Creek?"

So we sent for old McDougal, and he stated in reply
That he'd never played at cricket, but he'd half a mind to try.
He couldn't come to practise – he was getting in his hay,
But he guessed he'd show the beggars from Molongo how to play.
Now, McDougal was a Scotchman, and a canny one at that,
So he started in to practise with a paling for a bat.
He got Mrs Mac to bowl to him, but she couldn't run at all,
So he trained his sheep-dog, Pincher, how to scout and fetch the ball.

Now, Pincher was no puppy; he was old, and worn, and grey;
But he understood McDougal, and – accustomed to obey –
When McDougal cried out "Fetch it!" he would fetch it in a trice,
But, until the word was "Drop it" he would grip it like a vice.
And each succeeding night they played until the light grew dim:
Sometimes McDougal struck the ball – sometimes the ball struck him.
Each time he struck the ball would plough a furrow in the ground;
And when he missed, the impetus would turn him three times round.

The fatal day at length arrived – the day that was to see
Molongo bite the dust, or Piper's Flat knocked up a tree!
Molongo's captain won the toss, and sent his men to bat,
And they gave some leather-hunting to the men of Piper's Flat.
When the ball sped where McDougal stood, firm planted in his track,
He shut his eyes, and turned him round, and stopped it – with his back!

The highest score was twenty-two, the total sixty-six,
When Brady sent a yorker down that scattered Johnson's sticks.

Then Piper's Flat went in to bat, for glory and renown,
But, like the grass before the scythe, our wickets tumbled down.
"Nine wickets down for seventeen, with fifty more to win!"
Our captain heaved a heavy sigh, and sent McDougal in.
"Ten pounds to one you'll lose it!" cried a barracker from town;
But McDougal said, '"I'll tak' it, mon!" and planked the money down.
Then he girded up his moleskins in a self-reliant style,
Threw off his hat and boots and faced the bowler with a smile.

He held the bat the wrong side out, and Johnson with a grin
Stepped lightly to the bowling crease, and sent a "wobbler" in;
McDougal spooned it softly back, and Johnson waited there,
But McDougal, crying *"Fetch it!"* started running like a hare.
Molongo shouted "Victory! He's out as sure as eggs,"
When Pincher started through the crowd, and ran through Johnson's legs.
He seized the ball like lightning; then he ran behind a log,
And McDougal kept on running, while Molongo chased the dog!

They chased him up, they chased him down, they chased him round, and then
He darted through the slip-rail as the scorer shouted "Ten!"
McDougal puffed; Molongo swore; excitement was intense;
As the scorer marked down twenty, Pincher cleared a barbed-wire fence.
"Let us head him!" shrieked Molongo. "Brain the mongrel with a bat!"
"Run it out! Good old McDougal" yelled the men of Piper's Flat.
And McDougal kept on jogging, and then Pincher doubled back,
And the scorer counted *"Forty"* as they raced across the track.

McDougal's legs were going fast, Molongo's breath was gone
But still Molongo chased the dog – McDougal struggled on.
When the scorer shouted *"Fifty"* then they knew the chase could cease;
And McDougal gasped out *"Drop it!"* as he dropped within his crease.
Then Pincher dropped the ball, and as instinctively he knew
Discretion was the wiser plan, he disappeared from view;
And as Molongo's beaten men exhausted lay around
We raised McDougal shoulder-high, and bore him from the ground.

We bore him to McGinniss's, where lunch was ready laid,
And filled him up with whisky-punch, for which Molongo paid.
We drank his health in bumpers and we cheered him three times three,
And when Molongo got its breath Molongo joined the spree.
And the critics say they never saw a cricket match like that,

When McDougal broke the record in the game at Piper's Flat;
And the folk are jubilating as they never did before;
For we played Molongo cricket – and McDougal topped the score!

MARCUS CLARKE 1846–1881

Marcus Clarke was born in London, the son of a barrister, and came to Victoria in 1864. After working as a clerk, and on a station, he had a frenetic career as a journalist. He held a position with the Melbourne Public Library for the last decade of his life – but not without controversy as he wrote an article in 1879 arguing that the advance of science had made Christianity moribund. He is famous for his novel *For the Term of His Natural Life*, first published in 1870 in a journal he edited, then revised and published as a book in 1874. This story of crime and punishment is regarded as the finest Australian novel of the 19th century. In his personal life Clarke was extravagant and a gadfly. After Adam Lindsay Gordon's suicide, Clarke wrote a preface for an edition of Gordon's poems, which has the once-famous passage given below where Clarke reflects on the nature of the Australian landscape and refers indirectly to Gordon's lines (which many would contest as inaccurate):

> They are rhymes rudely strung with intent less
> Of sound than of words
> In lands where bright blossoms are scentless
> And songless bright birds.

Frank Maldon Robb (a later editor of Gordon's poetry) in 1912 described this part of Clarke's preface as "the great prose poem of Marcus Clarke on the characteristics of the Australian bush". Rather than include Clarke's most well-known but rather laboured poem "The Wail of the Waiter", we reproduce this "prose poem".

from Preface to Adam Lindsay Gordon's Poems

What is the dominant note of Australian scenery? That which is the dominant note of Edgar Allan Poe's poetry – Weird Melancholy. A poem like *L'Allegro* could never be written by an Australian. It is too airy, too sweet, too freshly happy. The Australian mountain forests are funereal, secret, stern. Their solitude is desolation. They seem to stifle in their black gorges a story of sullen despair. No tender sentiment is nourished in their shade. In other lands the dying year is mourned, the falling leaves drop lightly on his bier. In the Australian forests no leaves fall. The savage winds shout among the rock clefts. From the melancholy gums strips of white bark hang and rustle. The very animal life of these frowning hills is either grotesque or ghostly. Great grey kangaroos hop noiselessly over the coarse grass. Flights of white cockatoos stream out shrieking like evil souls. The sun suddenly sinks, and the mopokes burst out into horrible peals of semi-human laughter. The natives aver that, when night comes, from out the bottomless depth of some lagoon the Bunyip rises, and, in form like a monstrous sea-calf, drags his loathsome length from out the ooze. From a corner of the silent forest rises a dismal chant, and around a fire dance natives painted like skeletons. All is fear-inspiring and gloomy. No bright fancies are linked with the memories of the mountains. Hopeless explorers have named them out of their sufferings – Mount Misery, Mount Dreadful, Mount Despair. As when among sylvan scenes in places

> Made green with the running of rivers,
>   And gracious with temperate air,

the soul is soothed and satisfied, so, placed before the frightful grandeur of these barren hills, it drinks in their sentiment of defiant ferocity, and is steeped in bitterness.

Australia has rightly been named the Land of the Dawning. Wrapped in the mist of early morning, her history looms vague and gigantic. The lonely horseman riding between the moonlight and the day, sees vast shadows creeping across the shelterless and silent plains, hears strange noises in the primeval forests, where flourishes a vegetation long dead in other lands, and feels, despite his fortune, that the trim utilitarian civilization which bred him shrinks into insignificance beside the contemptuous grandeur of forest and ranges coeval with an age in which European scientists have cradled his own race.

There is a poem in every form of tree or flower, but the poetry which lives in the trees and flowers of Australia differs from those of other countries. Europe is the home of knightly song, of bright deeds and clear morning thought. Asia sinks beneath the weighty recollection of her past magnificence, as the Suttee sinks jewel-burdened, upon the corpse of dread grandeur, destructive even in its death. America swiftly hurries on her way, rapid, glittering, insatiable even as one of her own giant waterfalls. From the jungles of Africa, and the creeper-tangled groves of the Islands of the South, arise, from the glowing hearts of a thousand flowers, heavy and intoxicating odours – the Upas-poison which dwells in barbaric sensuality. In Australia alone is to be found the Grotesque, the Weird, the strange scribblings of Nature learning how to write. Some see no beauty in our trees without shade, our flowers without perfume, our birds who cannot fly, and our beasts who have not yet learned to walk on all fours. But the dweller in the wilderness acknowledges the subtle charm of this fantastic land of monstrosities. He becomes familiar with the beauty of loneliness. Whispered to by the myriad tongues of the wilderness, he learns the language of the barren and the uncouth, and can read the hieroglyphs of haggard gum-trees, blown into odd shapes, distorted with fierce hot winds, or cramped with cold nights, when the Southern Cross freezes in a cloudless sky of icy blue. The phantasmagoria of that wild dreamland termed the Bush interprets itself, and the Poet of our desolation begins to comprehend why free Esau loved his heritage of desert sand, better than all the bountiful richness of Egypt.

MARY HANNAY FOOTT 1846–1918

Mary Hannay Foott, neé Black, was born in Glasgow and was brought by her family to Melbourne in 1853. She became a drawing teacher, and married in 1874. In 1877 her family went to live on a station, Dundoo, in south-west Queensland, but her husband died in 1884 and Foott and her father were obliged to relinquish all their interests in Dundoo in the following year. That year her book *Where the Pelican Builds and Other Poems* was published. The title poem has been anthologised many times and refers to the legend that the best land is where the pelican nests. Two brothers, Syd and Albert Prout, disappeared in the Barkly Tableland, near the Gulf of Carpentaria, looking for land, and their bodies were found in 1880, two years after their death from thirst.

Where the Pelican Builds

The horses were ready, the rails were down,
  But the riders lingered still, –
    One had a parting word to say,
  And one had his pipe to fill.
Then they mounted, one with a granted prayer,
  And one with a grief unguessed.
    "We are going" they said, as they rode away
  "Where the pelican builds her nest!"

They had told us of pastures wide and green,
  To be sought past the sunset's glow;
    Of rifts in the ranges by opal lit;
  And gold 'neath the river's flow.
And thirst and hunger were banished words
  When they spoke of that unknown West;
    No drought they dreaded, no flood they feared,
Where the pelican builds her nest!

The creek at the ford was but fetlock deep
  When we watched them crossing there;
    The rains have replenished it thrice since then
  And thrice has the rock lain bare.
But the waters of Hope have flowed and fled,
  And never from blue hill's breast

Come back – by the sun and the sand devoured –
Where the pelican builds her nest!

New Country

Condé had come with us all the way –
Eight hundred miles – but the fortnight's rest
Made him fresh as a youngster, the sturdy bay!
And Lurline was looking her very best.

Weary and footsore, the cattle strayed
'Mid the silvery saltbush well content;
Where the creeks lay cool 'neath the gidya's shade
The stock-horses clustered, travel-spent.

In the bright spring morning we left them all
Camp, and cattle, and white, and black –
And rode for the Range's westward fall,
Where the dingo's trail was the only track.

Slow through the clay-pans, wet to the knee,
With the cane-grass rustling overhead;
Swift o'er the plains with never a tree;
Up the cliffs by a torrent's bed.

Bridle on arm for a mile or more
We toiled, ere we reached Bindanna's verge
And saw – as one sees a far-off shore –
The blue hills bounding the forest surge.

An ocean of trees, by the west wind stirred,
Rolled, ever rolled, to the great cliff's base;
And its sound like the noise of waves was heard
'Mid the rocks and the caves of that lonely place.

* * *

We recked not of wealth in stream or soil
As we heard on the heights the breezes sing;
We felt no longer our travel-toil;
We feared no more what the years might bring.

ALEXANDER MONTGOMERY 1847–1922

Montgomery was born in Londonderry, Northern Ireland. He led a nomadic life, coming to Melbourne in 1870, then spending some years in the Malayan Archipelago. In 1882 he published two novels. He moved to Sydney in 1884. The strange and memorable verses below first appeared in the *Bulletin* in 1891 and have since been anthologised a couple of times. His *Five-Skull Island And Other Tales of the Malay Archipelago* was published in Australia by George Robertson & Co. in 1897, and in the last twenty or so years of his life he published numerous short stories and a handful of poems in Australian literary magazines.

A Curious Reminiscence

Of all the bloomin' awful things, the awfullest I've knowed
  In the five·and-sixty years I've bin alive,
Took place at Paddy Doolan's on the old Jerilda road,
  'Way back in 'Sixty-four or 'Sixty-five.

Old Doolan had a handy man, a useful sort o' chap,
  But a real, right-down tiger for his rum;
An', one day, bein' tipsy, why he tumbles from a trap,
  And cracks his skull, an' goes to kingdom come.

Well, they sends an' tells the trooper, an' the trooper rides across,
  "An'," says he, "I'll have to let the 'Crowner' hear;"
So they stretches out old Jerry in the place he used to doss –
  A tumbledown old shanty at the rear.

I was trampin' down from Bulga, an' had just run out of grub;
  Rainin', too, till every rag on me was soaked;
So, you bet, I wasn't sorry to pull-up at Doolan's pub
  On the evenin' of the day that Jerry croaked.

Well, I'd had my bite o' tucker an' a glass or two o' beer
  An' was sittin' there a-fillin' of my pipe,
When in comes Mad Macarthy an' Long Jim of Bundaleer,
  An' my word! but they was well upon the swipe.

Two strappin' big six-footers, an' as strong as bullocks, both;
  An' ripe for any devilment, as well;
The man that interfered with 'em, you just might take your oath,
  Stood a pretty lively chance of catchin' hell.

Well, they drank an' laughed an' shouted, an' they swaggered an' they swore,
  Till Macarthy took a notion in his head
That they'd make old Jerry drunker than he'd ever bin before;
  "Yez can't do that!" says Doolan – "Jerry's dead!"

"Dead drunk, you mean!" says Jimmy. "No," says Doolan, "no begob!
  He's as dead as he can be – without a lie!
For he tumbled out of Thompson's trap, right fair upon his nob."
  Says Macarthy, "Come, old man, that's all my eye!"

"Bedad!" says Pat, "then take a light an' go yerselves to see.
  Sure he's lyin' in the shed forninst the gate."
So my nobles gets a candle an' they tips a wink to me,
  An' out they goes to see if it was straight.

Well, sir, back they comes directly an' a-laughin' fit to split,
  And behind 'em Mother Doolan cryin' "Shame!"
And well she might for there, between the pair of 'em, was *it* –
  The clay that used to answer Jerry's name.

With its head a-hangin' forward and its legs a-draggin' loose,
  You can bet it was a dreadful sight to see!
And I started up to stop 'em, but says Doolan, "Where's the use?
  They could smash a dozen chaps like you an' me!"

So they humped their fearsome burden to a corner of the bar,
  And propped it on a cask agin the wall;
"What will *Jerry* drink?" says Jimmy, and Macarthy says, "Three-star
  For we won't be mean with Jerry – damn it all!"

Well, sir, Doolan fills three nobblers, an' Macarthy collars one,
  And slaps it down before the senseless clay;
Then they bobs their heads to Jerry, an' says they, "Old man, here's fun!"
  And punishes their liquors right away.

Then 'twas, "Fill 'em up again, Pat – fill 'em right up to the brim!"
  Till they'd swallered half a dozen drinks a head;
Then Macarthy stares at Jerry's glass, an' then he stares at Jim –
  "By the Lord!" says he, "old Jerry *must* be dead!

"For it's five-an'-twenty minutes he has had his pizen there,
  And he's never tried to touch a bloomin' drop!
So you're right for once, old Doolan! Have a drink, an' let us square.
  For it's nearly gettin' time for us to hop."

So they humped old Jerry back again to where he was before –
  Mother Doolan still a-scoldin' them in vain;
Then they staggers to their horses that was standin' at the door
  An' gallops off like madmen through the rain.

JOHN FARRELL 1851–1904

John Farrell, born of Irish parents in Buenos Aires, came to Australia in the year after his birth. Farrell had little schooling. Growing up on his parents' farm he read poetry and took part in recitation evenings. He became a brewer, and in the early 1880s began contributing verse to the *Bulletin*. He turned to journalism and was editor of a leading Sydney daily, *The Telegraph*. He also became an ardent follower of Henry George who advocated land tax as the only tax, and Farrell wrote on "The Philosophy of the Single Tax" and accompanied George on a lecture tour. He had a modest view of his own abilities as a poet – when asked about visitations by the muse, he said, "I can't say I ever knew the lady." At the time of his death he was revising his poems for a book that appeared posthumously and went through two editions. Survived by his wife, four sons and three daughters, he was remembered as a rotund Irishman with a "rich seducing brogue" and a pipe in his mouth, usually unlit.

Farrell wrote some competent narrative poems about life in the outback that are of interest, although melodramatic. While Kenneth Slessor was not an admirer of the verse of Paterson and Lawson, he had a high regard for Farrell's "My Sundowner", which he spoke of as a minor masterpiece. This sardonic poem maintains a tricky rhyme scheme over many stanzas with great ingenuity and has no passages we would wish to omit. The sundowner (swagman or itinerant worker) who turns up at sundown, too late to be given any jobs, was an archetypal figure of Australian poetry of the second half of the 19th century. Farrell managed in his symbol of Ned Flynn's macabre tree to encapsulate an era of Australian history – of boom and bust – in a way that is not matched by any other 19th-century Australian poet.

My Sundowner

Just as the bell at the men's hut had tinkled
  For tea he came – well, sundowners must eat!
A back-block face he had, a visage wrinkled
  With lines of villainy and small deceit,
A stock of hair upon his head, just sprinkled
  With iron-grey; upon his ample feet
Were weighty bluchers, each with common string tied –
Bluchers that long ago had passed their spring tide.

"Good evenin', boss! Got any work to do?" he
  Inquired, as on the dusty earth he flung
His swag, the orthodox horse-collar "bluey";
  "I've tramped these fifteen days; I've been among
The squatters, damn 'em! Old Black Sugar Toohey
  The" – here the wanderer's up-country tongue
Tripped off expressions which may not be quoted
In pages that make claim to be devoted

To blameless literature, but on stations
  Are much affected – "offered me a job
At ringbarking – ten bob a week and rations
  I wouldn't take it under fifteen bob;
I've followed some (blank) rummy occupations
  With some queer bosses, but a one-horse swab
Like that I never work for when I know him;
A pretty thing to offer a man – blow him!"

His indignation all at once subsided
  When I (full Super) in plain language said,
If Toohey knew his sort as well as I did
  He must have been a trifle off his head
To offer even ten; I rather prided
  Myself on knowing men. "To yonder shed,"
I added, "your time-honoured bluey take down
And make yourself before it's dark a shakedown;

"Thence to the hut repair – you'll get some damper,
  And mutton, and plum duff. Tomorrow's sun
Must find you further on. I will not hamper
  Your movements by insisting that this run
Shall quite monopolize you! Now then, scamper
  And fix your doss, and when you've got it done
And had your tea and duff – the latter rich with
Rare spices – you'll find lots of chaps to pitch with

About your wrongs." An hour or so thereafter,
  Being close beside the dimly lighted hut
(Lit by a slush lamp from a smoky rafter
  Hung by a wire), through the old door half shut
I heard excessive bursts of mighty laughter
  And cries of "Go it, stranger! that's a cut
Above you, Billy! you're a (bad word) duffer
Beside this cove at pitchin' of a cuffer!"

I stood to listen, and, 'mid noisy plaudits
  I heard my sundowner asseverate
With earnest voice, "No, boys, so help me God! it's
  The solemn truth – the man was my own mate:
The thing is rather odd, but though it's odd, its
  Not half so strange as what I'll now relate —
This yarn, you'll find, will knock the other silly;
I'm thirsty, though; just shove along the billy!

"Tea's poor swill, anyway, compared to swankey,
  But still one must lap something! What d'ye think?
Your Super – who looks like a sheep-dipped Yankee" –
  (He little thought I watched him through a chink
Between the slabs) – "he says to me, 'Why, blank ye,
  My man' – you know his style – 'I fear that drink
Has been your trouble, or else how the devil
Could you – a man like you – have reached the level

"'Of seeking manual toil, while I, much younger,
  As you'll observe, have been made Super here? —
Go, fellow, to the hut; appease your hunger;
  Assuage your thirst!'" At this, from ear to ear,
The shearers grinned, and Sam, the Billabonger,
  Whose noted points were ribaldry and beer,
Exclaimed, when after a protracted laugh he
Could speak, "The Super, to an ephigraphy!"

"Well! twenty years ago I was with Dawson
  Of Murragumbalong, away out West;
You've heard of him? No! Strange! He made me boss on
  The station. 'Edward,' says he, 'all the rest
Are sodden fools! This place has been a cross on
  My back for years, and I'll give bossing best;
I'll make you manager and go you whacks on
The profits.' Ah, he was a white-skinned Saxon!

"Of course I closed with him and fixed in writin'
  The terms. It wasn't such a big chuck in
As you might think; the look of things would frighten
  An ordinary cove; the stock was thin
The paddocks hardly had a bloomin' bite in,
  And on the run you could have seen a pin
A dozen yards away. They prayed for rain for
Three months, but that you never get by prayin' for

"Out West – I couldn't tell you what's the reason,
  But from the first they never seemed to care
For Murragumbalong in Heaven. The season
  Was terrible; the land was brown and bare,
Without a blade of grass, and lots of trees on
  The ranges died. The water everywhere
Was turned to puddle and our sheep got stuck in
The dams by scores. Well, boys! once more, here's luck! in

"Black tea! If your imported Super's peeper
  Could spot me now, he'd say (his high-flown mag!)
'As I surmised, this wretched man drinks deeper
  Than wisdom prompts, so has to bear a swag.'
He shouldn't be about without a keeper
  That swell! just chuck across the sugar bag!
You don't call this tea sweet enough, boys, do ye?
They're meaner here than old Black Sugar Toohey!

"Well! things were bad enough out West that summer,
  And ruin seemed to stare us in the face;
From day to day each squatter's mug grew glummer;
  Even I began to think it was a case
When a rum thing (I never knew a rummer)
  Turned up to save us. I had gone to chase
Some brumbies off the run with Wall-Eyed Abel,
A rouseabout who hung around the stable;

"A mooney sort of chap, who used to study
  Theology and all such stuff as that;
Could tell you of some Indian cove call Buddy
  Who squatted cross-legged on a bit o' mat
And saved his people, but at bustin' wood he
  Was a poor rouseabout. We crossed the flat
Behind the homestead and struck out. 'Twas fully
Seven miles ahead of us to Simpson's Gully

"Where we'd to go. It was a fierce day well in
  December, and the horses soon were blown;
The perspiration from their tired flanks fell in
  A perfect stream. My colt was but half-grown,
So I proposed that we should take a spell in
  The shade of a big tree that stood alone
Upon a strip of plain, and helter-skelter
We both crammed on the pace to reach its shelter.

"I got there first. My horse seemed rather shy of
  The tree and snorted and played up a bit!
But Abel! boys, even now I'm like to die of
  The buster he got when I think of it!
He didn't fall, he simply seemed to fly off
  The horse's back; you could have heard him hit
The ground a mile off, while his nag skedaddled
Like blazes, bridled as it was and saddled.

"With spurs and curses and a good few lashes
  I quieted my moke – I always could
Do that. Poor Abel rose again; from gashes
  About his head there trickled rills of blood,
And all at once his face grew white as ashes —
  With pointed hand and shaking knees he stood;
And then I knew what ailed the nags. Beside him
A man hung by a piece of cord which tied him

"To a low branch! 'By ghost! a suicide, as
  I breathe!' I cried to Abel. 'Look, old man,
His swag lies over there! his hands are tied as
  A safeguard against struggling! What's our plan?
I think I'll scoot towards the town and ride as
  My neck depended on it: Jim M'Cann,
The trooper's there – I'll fetch him. As you're shaken
A bit you'd best stop here. I'm much mistaken

"'If I'm not back within three hours. I'll fetch you
  Another horse. However did you fall
Like that? It served you right, you stupid wretch! You
  Will be more careful after this, that's all:
Now, Disraeli (my colt), I bet I'll stretch you
  Across the plain.' I just drew rein to call
At Armstrong's with the news, then rode like thunder
Into the little one-horse township. Under

"The pub veranda, tossing Bull-necked Cooper,
  The publican, for drinks, I found the trap –
A stuck-up half-grown kid, who thought a trooper
  Was God Almighty almost, and his cap
A crown of glory – something like your Super,
  A 'haw-haw-my-good-fellow' sort of chap,
Though if you reckoned the slop fairly up he
Was hardly such a milk-and-water puppy.

"As your damned lunatic! I didn't stay there
  Too long – got horses, told the story straight,
Then started off to show M'Cann the way there,
  And reached the tree as it was getting late.
And what d'ye think? You think that Abel lay there
  Just as I left him? No; as sure as fate –
As sure as I'm the son of my own mother,
He hung there stiff and stark beside the other!

"Yes! there they hung, the two of them together,
  And almost touching! Jim M'Cann turned pale,
And me – if you had hit me with a feather
  Just then, it would have floored me like a flail;
But I rode up and cut poor Abel's tether
  And let him drop. I tried without avail
To bring him round. Then Jim and I kept staring
At one another. Jim was reckoned daring

"Round Murragumbalong; to perfect strangers
  He liked to skite; you should have heard him blow
About the way he'd hunted down bushrangers,
  And collared private stills, and high and low
Played up old Nick; of his escapes and dangers
  And all the bullet marks that he could show,
Then seen him running in two drunken shearers
To prove himself a hero to his hearers;

"But he was scared just then if ever man was
  And in the saddle (for he still sat there)
I saw him shake. His face was ghastlier than was
  The corpses which yet dangled in the air;
That face of his told straight that Jim M'Cann was
  A coward out and out. 'A strange affair,'
I said at last, 'one would have been enough for
One day, without this half-demented duffer

"'Improving the occasion! What's your notion
  Of who's to be the next? What's to be done
With this lot, anyhow? Propose a motion,
  I'll second it; you see, old man, the sun
Is down. Was ever upon earth or ocean
  A game like this? Now that it has begun,
Where will it end? Rouse up, mate, do, and tell us
What's best; will I ride down for Johnson's fellows?'

"'No! no! I'll go!' was his wild exclamation,
  'I'll not stop here – the living I can face,
But not the dead! How far's it to the station?
  Let me away from this infernal place!'
'You'd never get to it in the creation
  Of cats! Besides, just look at the disgrace
If people get to know you were afraid of
Two corpses! Stop and show them what you're made of,'

"I answered. 'You could never find out Johnson's
  From here; you'd beat about the bush all night;
What ails you? You must have a guilty conscience;
  God knows my own's not anything too white,
And yet *I'd* stay. Drop this old woman's nonsense,
  And tie your horse up here – he'll be all right –
Then build a thundering fire, that I can see it
Far off – I'll soon be back, I'll guarantee it.'

"So I rode off. M'Cann still sat there shaking
  And staring at the tree; the last I saw
Of him alive was that. My jaws are aching
  With all this talk; I'm not much good at jaw;
Who's got tobacco? – thanks! I'll shove this cake in
  My pocket, so that I can have a draw
Tomorrow on the tramp; I must be stirring
From here, or who knows what might be occurring?

"Your Super might endeavour to detain me
  (As he would put it) as a sort of sub;
And you can understaud how it would pain me
  To have to boss you! So I'll pack some grub
Tonight – don't speak, boys, nothing can restrain me –
  I'm quite resolved! This place will have to rub
Along without me. Though the Super may break
His heart about it, I am off at daybreak.

"Well, as I rode the night came on as black as
  The ace of spades, and even *I* got lost,
Although I thought I knew as well the track as
  The Ten Commandments. Several times I crossed
M'Nalley's Creek, and blundered like a jackass;
  But still I said, 'Whatever is the cost,
I'll find the place if it is under Heaven!' –
And so I did, but not till past eleven.

"I roused them up and told my yarn, but no one
  Would come that night. 'What good is it, they said,
'To turn out now and saddle up, and go on
  A hunt like this? If both of them are dead
We can't well bring them back to life – and so on;
  So I had a cold feed and went to bed,
And early in the morning off we started –
Three of us, mounted well and cheerful-hearted

"As crickets. By and by we came in sight of
  The tree; and there was Jim M'Cann's horse tied
To a small sapling. In the growing light of
  The sun, just risen, all at once we spied
Two dead men hanging! Well, I fainted right off
  When my two mates at the same moment cried,
'The trooper's done it!' As they had no brandy
Or any stimmylant whatever handy,

"I soon came round again. There hung the second
  Of the two victims the accursed tree
Before my very eyes, it seemed, had beckoned
  Over the brink into eternity;
So, without thinking the thing out, I reckoned
  It time to go. 'No more of this for me!
Let us away!' I yelled, 'this very minute
From here; I dread this Tree, the devil's in it!'

"I jumped upon my horse and jammed my hat down
  Across my eyes and galloped like the wind
Until I got away upon the flat down
  Below the tree, then stopped to look behind
And this was what I saw: Old Johnson sat down
  Upon a log, and (this is Gospel, mind,
As sure as that I build my firmest hope on
The Book) was fastening a halter rope on

"His neck! His man had just commenced to climb up
  The stem! And then I felt almighty queer
And thought, 'I'll just see Johnson off, then *I'm* up;
  Am I less game than one of them? No fear!
Though I'd go through it pluckier could I prime up
  With rum, or even a good fill of beer –
I *must* get out my bit of cord and twist it;
The Tree is drawing me, I can't resist it!'

"I turned my horse's head and came back slowly
  Across the plain. I saw old Johnson kneel
And pray a bit, (he hadn't been too holy
  Before – I knew the beggar used to steal
Our lambs), then start to climb. Half up the bole he
  Saw me and called, 'Ye tried to cheat the Deil;
Ye canna do 't – I tell ye, lad, ye canna –
I'm thinkin' ye'll no sup the nicht on manna!

"'I've been a sinner and I've stown the young of
 Your yowies, but I've cleansed my saul wi' prayer;
I'll reach the haven that yon Psalmist sung of –
 Farewell! I'll no meet ony Papists there!'
Just then the other fellow gently swung off
 And kicked his legs a moment in the air,
Then hung quite lifeless, with the end of rope in
His hand clutched tightly, and his mouth half open!

"Old Johnson looked, and seemed much interested;
 Then firmly fixed his rope upon the limb,
And prayed another spell, and then divested
 Himself of his old coat. To look at him
Just then for all the funk he manifested
 You'd think he was preparing for a swim;
Then in he went – no *off* he went, like winking
While I stood plaiting up my cord, and thinking

"How strange the whole thing was! I'd somewhere read of
 A tree that poisoned all who came within
Its shade, but not a word at all was said of
 A tree that made you hang yourself. 'Ned Flynn,'
I thought, 'the dance that the strange swagman led off
 You've got to join in, so you'd best begin;
Your partner's waiting – you'll just make the set up
Of three dead couples, so look sharp and get up.'

"Well, up I shinned and off I lurched! The cord broke,
 And down I came on top of Abel slap!
'I said I'd do it, and when was my word broke?'
 I thought. I went again. The cord went snap
Again! I went again, but no – the third broke
 And then I sat and thought like this: 'Old chap,
It's not to be; whatever Fate may bring you,
One thing is sure – no rope will ever swing you!'

"And then I turned my back upon the dead ones –
 Four swinging in a row, one on the ground –
The notion never came into my head once
 To try again. Whatever spell had bound
Me to the tree was broke; and so I fled once
 Again, and never stopped to look around,
Nor for my horse had much consideration
Until he brought me to our own home station.

"I'd lost my hat – a seventeen-bob soft beaver —
  In galloping, and, as the sun was hot,
I felt the rays of it as if a cleaver
  Had split my head; and by the time I got
The saddle off I had a raging fever
  Upon me. Then they had a doctor brought,
Who told them that, but for his pills and doses,
In one day more I'd be as dead as Moses.

"Three weeks I lay before they were quite sure I
  Would live, but I came round all right by then,
And all was told to me. They'd had a jury
  And held an inquest on the five dead men.
(Now, Slushy, I can see you winking your eye;
  I tell the truth.) Out of twelve, but ten
Lived through it (must I say to you once more, man,
I never told a falsehood yet!). The foreman,

"It seems, had, while the rest deliberated,
  Hid in his shirt a clothes-line, so's to be
Quite ready, and then jawed away and waited,
  And when his chance came slithered up the tree
And went! Another cried, 'He's emigrated! –
  I'll cut him down; just leave the thing to me!'
And up he went to do so, but instead of
Attempting it, swung too, and jerked his head off!

"The coroner that same night suicided
  Upon the Tree, and on the following day
Four of the jurymen came back and tried it,
  But one of them came down the very way
(Only he came down wrong end first) that I did
  And broke his neck. It went on like a play
For days, until the jury were all laid out;
And even then the Tree did not seem played out!

"Odd stragglers now and then had patronized it
  And worked themselves off, bowing to their fate;
And all these deaths so much had advertised it
  That in the end there came a magistrate
To see it – and he swung! Then they advised it
  Should be cut down. But all at once a great
Idea struck my mind, and I commenced in
The morning with two men to have it fenced in.

"I had to shepherd them, though. Bill, from Wagga,
  Who dug the post-holes, once chucked down the bar
And started, but – at that time I could slog a
  Real perisher – before he had got far
I stretched him. And that day I brought a dog, a
  Great wolf of mine – I'd christened him 'Three Star',
Because he'd killed a man (when quite a pup, too)
And got a good long chain and chained him up to

"The Tree, and by knock-off time we'd completed
  The fence, and built a humpy close beside
The gate for me, where, on a gin-case seated
  Beside the fire, I watched till I could bide
No longer, then turned in. Well – I was cheated,
  For, while I was asleep, 'Three Star' untied
His chain, climbed up the Tree, and there he hung out
On a dry branch, quite brazen, with his tongue out!

"And very close to him there hung as coolly
  A perfect stranger, comfortably dead!
'Well I *am* damned!' I cried. Now, as a rule, I
  Don't use strong talk, but I was off my head
With rage, and said, 'Now, what a blasted fool I
  Have been! While I was snoring in my bed
This swine got at me with the utmost cleanness;
Who ever heard of such infernal meanness?'

"That dog, though, turned up trumps. Flash Dick, the Ringer
  From Wilson's shed, where they had just cut out,
Came down to look at it. I saw him linger,
  Then go away, come back, and dodge about,
Then draw his diamond ring from off his finger
  And bring it over. This is good to spout
For fifteen quid,' he said. I answered 'Is it?
I'm sorry you can pay me but one visit!'

"And then the shearers came in any number
  To see *him* hang, and I stood at the gate
And said, 'Ten quid!' as cool as a cucumber.
  They planked 'em down like men, and twenty·eight
Swung before dark. I had no chance of slumber
  That night – coves came along and wouldn't wait
Till morning – in the dark I sent a score off
And before breakfast launched eleven more off!

"All day I had a better class of custom –
  Selectors and the like – and, coming on
To noon, one cockie wanted me to trust him,
  Though him and me had been at daggers drawn;
I wouldn't, and it seemed to so disgust him
  That off he went and hanged himself upon
Another tree – just walked with a grim smile off
And patronized a gum about a mile off.

"I saw at once that it might burst my bubble
  If this got known; that it might take away
Good business from my Tree, and cause me trouble;
  But no one twigged him. I took coin all day
And, after dusk (though he was nearly double
  My weight) I dropped him, and from where he lay,
Dragged him across, and had the satisfaction
Of hanging him again! Well, the attraction

"Of the infernal Tree did not diminish
  At all; the public came from far and near;
Some days, perhaps, the gathering was thinnish
  (As times were hard, some thought ten quid too dear),
But there were others when I couldn't finish
  My work. Upon an average I could clear
Five hundred sovereigns a day, or slightly
Above it, and I banked my stuff fortnightly.

"My game was watched, you may depend. Two fellows
  One night when sleepiness had grown too strong
For me, stole in and grabbed some bags of yellows
  And scooted off; but they did not stay long;
They might have hanged themselves at first as well as
  When they had done a fellow-creature wrong.
That gold – you know how wrong it is to pilfer –
Brought them to death, as did Iscariot's silver!

"There drooped the two of them at dawn, well weighted
  With my hard earnings! So, for many a week
I raked the bullion in. I estimated
  That I had netted by this single streak
Of business, thirty thousand quid, or stated
  More accurately – mostly when I speak
I like to be exact, it is a gift I
Had always – thirty thousand and odd fifty!

“When without any warning fortune played me
  A dirty trick, although it must be said
I was in fault. I found the goose that laid me
  The golden eggs one morning lying dead!
This was the way of it – a party paid me
  An extra figure, fifty quid a head
To be select, to let them go to *the* top
And hang (thirteen there were) right at the tree-top.

“Well, I consented. They were stylish jokers,
  Rich squatters and bank clerks, and all like that,
And two or three had dress suits and white chokers,
  And there they dangled gorgeous to look at,
Rigged out like lords and dukes, and stiff as pokers
  Right up aloft. For quite an hour I sat
At sunset in admiring contemplation
My Tree just then aroused my admiration

“It fairly drooped with men, the corpses swaying
  In the light wind, from scores and scores of strings,
And ropes, and hides; the poorer classes staying
  Down low; the richer up above, like kings.
I felt quite proud, but, boys, you know the saying
  That pride will have a fall. All human things
Must end; but in the morning it took *me* down
When I looked down and saw my priceless Tree down.

“The last thirteen had done it. Hanging high up
  They made the Tree top-heavy, and a squall
Had blown it over. I could only dry up
  My tears – at first I let a good few fall –
And shut the humpy door for good, and tie up
  The gate, and cart away my little haul
Quite sorrowful, but not at all unthankful
With notes and cheques I had the local bank full!

“That was a year for us! Deserted stations
  For miles and miles around, and not a man
Left living; storehouses with lots of rations,
  And stone cold fire-places, with pot and pan
Just as the suicides had left them! Lashin’s
  Of all that one could want. Our cattle ran
On all the runs, our sheep mixed all the flocks with
And no one came to claim those they might box with.

"In twelve months' time the pair of us had sold out
  For half-a-million; and I went home then
To England! and shed my Colonial gold out
  And got returned to Parliament; but, men,
I gave such sprees, my sugar couldn't hold out
  For ever, and – well, here I am again!
Good night, boys! Slushy, my important buck! ere
I go just fill this bag of mine with tucker."

* * *

Such was my Sundowner. At early dawn he
  Went lightly off, and George, a shearer, who
Was loud and large, though, all the same, a "Sawney",
  Found that his watch guard had been cut in two,
And Tom from Wellington, alert and brawny –
  The very kind of man you couldn't "do" –
Found that his Waltham, with gold chain and locket,
Had gone, like George's, into Ned Flynn's pocket.

VICTOR DALEY 1858–1905

Daley was born at Navan, County Armagh, Ireland. His father's family were all Fenians, dedicated to the establishment of an Irish republic, and he claimed often as a child to have "cast bullets at night". His father died when he was three, and after his mother remarried he was educated at a Christian Brothers' school at Devonport in England for about a year in his teens. After three years as a railway company clerk in Plymouth, he emigrated to Australia in 1878. While working as a correspondence clerk in Adelaide, he accidentally enclosed a love lyric in an envelope which should have contained a business letter and was sacked. He began writing for newspapers and publishing poetry.

In 1882 the co-founder of the *Bulletin*, J. F. Archibald, spoke of Daley "as the rising poet of this country. For a long time we have not had more melodious and imaginative verses from an Australian writer". Daley's first collection of poetry *At Dawn and Dusk* was published in 1898 to warm reviews in Australia, among them the entire "Red Page" of the *Bulletin*, but did not get the overseas attention that Daley craved. Daley had difficulty holding down a regular job and drifted into a bohemian existence, liberally oiled with alcohol, although by this stage he had a wife and children. A. G. Stephens wrote: "At times Daley touched the mire yet he remained unsoiled; for he was clean at heart, and, apart from the irregularities of Bohemia, he had no vices." Daley presided as "symposiarch" over a club of writers and artists, including Henry Lawson and Norman Lindsay, named the "Dawn and Dusk Club" in honour of his book. The club's rules were written in Chinese. He suffered from tuberculosis, and a testimonial fund was set up to send him on a sea voyage for his health. In a "curious lapse of taste", as H. J. Oliver has called it, while Daley was away on the voyage Stephens published a mock report in the

Bulletin about his death "under harrowing circumstances" in the Solomon Islands. Daley was furious. He did die two years later aged 47 of tuberculosis, cared for at the end by the Sisters of Mercy. His widow died the following year, survived by four children.

He was a prolific poet, earning him the nickname "Dozen Daily". For several years after his death his previously unpublished poems appeared on a regular, sometimes weekly, basis in the *Bulletin* – for example "Omarism" (a reference to Omar Khayyam) which appeared in 1911 and contains a self portrait:

> With pen in hand and pipe in mouth,
> And claret iced to quench my drouth,
> I sit upon my balcony
> That overlooks the sparkling sea,
> Serenely gay, and cool, and bland –
> With pipe in mouth and pen in hand ...
>
> The red-faced neighbors townward go;
> The air is in a furnace glow.
> I watch them scorching as they pass,
> Like flies beneath a burning glass –
> Each clutching at the red-hot hour
> For coin; their folly turns me sour.

Norman Lindsay wrote: "Though I illustrated much of his verse in the *Bulletin*, it was to me only that kind of poetry which is derived from poetry, not life." "Dreams" is Daley's most highly regarded poem. Anacreon (570–488 B.C.) was a Greek poet who wrote drinking songs and hymns.

Dreams

I have been dreaming all a summer day
Of rare and dainty poems I would write;
Love-lyrics delicate as lilac-scent,
Soft idylls woven of wind, and flower, and stream,
And songs and sonnets carven in fine gold.

The day is fading and the dusk is cold;
Out of the skies has gone the opal gleam,
Out of my heart has passed the high intent
Into the shadow of the falling night –
Must all my dreams in darkness pass away?

I have been dreaming all a summer day:
Shall I go dreaming so until Life's light
Fades in Death's dusk, and all my days are spent?
Ah, what am I the dreamer but a dream!
The day is fading and the dusk is cold.

My songs and sonnets carven in fine gold
Have faded from me with the last day-beam

That purple lustre to the sea-line lent,
And flushed the clouds with rose and chrysolite,
So days and dreams in darkness pass away.

I have been dreaming all a summer day
Of songs and sonnets carven in fine gold;
But all my dreams in darkness pass away
The day is fading, and the dusk is cold.

Anacreon

We bought a volume of Anacreon,
  Defaced, mishandled, little to admire,
And yet its rusty clasps kept guard upon
  The sweetest songs, the songs of young desire
Like that great song once sung by Solomon.

My sweetheart's cheeks were peonies on fire:
  We saw by the bright message of his eyes
  That Eros served us in bookseller's guise.
I keep the volume still, but She has gone ...
  Ah, for the poetry in Paradise!

There's Honey still and Roses on the earth,
And lips to kiss, and jugs to drain with mirth;
And lovers walk in pairs: but She has gone ...
            Anacreon! Anacreon!

ALICE WERNER 1859–1935

Alice Werner was born in Trieste of an English mother and German father. In the year of her birth, the family emigrated to New Zealand. Becoming a student at Newham College, Cambridge University (1878–80), she later studied native languages in South Africa and returned to London in 1896 to become Professor of Zulu at King's College, London. She published several works on African philology and mythology. It is debatable whether Werner should be treated as an Australian poet. However her "Bannerman of the Dandenong", written in 1891, was included in anthologies of Australian poetry and ballads in the early part of the 20th century, together with another Australian ballad she wrote and it has a decidedly Australian subject.

Bannerman of the Dandenong

I rode through the Bush in the burning noon,
  Over the hills to my bride, –
The track was rough and the way was long,

And Bannerman of the Dandenong,
  He rode along by my side.

A day's march off my Beautiful dwelt,
  By the Murray streams in the West; –
Lightly lilting a gay love-song
Rode Bannerman of the Dandenong,
  With a blood-red rose on his breast.

"Red, red rose of the Western streams"
  Was the song he sang that day –
Truest comrade in hour of need, –
Bay Mathinna his peerless steed –
  I had my own good grey.

There fell a spark on the upland grass –
  The dry Bush leapt into flame; –
And I felt my heart go cold as death,
And Bannerman smiled and caught his breath, –
  But I heard him name Her name.

Down the hill-side the fire-floods rushed,
  On the roaring eastern wind; –
Neck and neck was the reckless race, –
Ever the bay mare kept her pace,
  But the grey horse dropped behind.

He turned in the saddle – "Let's change, I say!"
  And his bridle rein he drew.
He sprang to the ground, – "Look sharp!" he said
With a backward toss of his curly head –
  "I ride lighter than you!"

Down and up – it was quickly done –
  No words to waste that day! –
Swift as a swallow she sped along,
The good bay mare from Dandenong, –
  And Bannerman rode the grey.

The hot air scorched like a furnace blast
  From the very mouth of Hell: –
The blue gums caught and blazed on high
Like flaming pillars into the sky; ...
  The grey horse staggered and fell.

"Ride, ride, lad, – ride for her sake!" he cried; –
  Into the gulf of flame

Were swept, in less than a breathing space
The laughing eyes, and the comely face,
  And the lips that named *Her* name.

She bore me bravely, the good bay mare; –
  Stunned, and dizzy and blind,
I heard the sound of a mingling roar –
'Twas the Lachlan River that rushed before,
  And the flames that rolled behind.

Safe – safe, at Nammoora gate,
  I fell, and lay like a stone.
O love! thine arms were about me then,
Thy warm tears called me to life again, –
  But – O God! that I came alone! –

We dwell in peace, my beautiful one
  And I, by the streams in the West, –
But oft through the mist of my dreams along
Rides Bannerman of the Dandenong,
  With the blood-red rose on his breast.

JACK MOSES (?) 1861–1945

This song, made famous by Burl Ives in 1952, was a highlight of the musical *Reedy River* in the following year, and A. L. Lloyd sang it in a 1955 album. It was first "collected" in the early 1940s by Dr Percy Jones from Jack Moses, at an encounter in Tyrrell's bookshop in George Street, Sydney, and published by Jones in 1946. Before that there is no compelling evidence of its existence. Keith McKenry (*Quadrant*, March 2009) suggested Jack Moses himself wrote the song, which is a parody of "Ring the Bell, Watchman", a Civil War era piece by the American composer Henry Clay Work (1832–84). We agree with the attribution to Moses. Jack Moses was a travelling wine salesman, who was famous as a reciter and published two books of bush verse (1923 and 1938). In a manner that was typical for a popular reciter, he was happy to rework in his own style existing material. Moses' best-known poem "Nine Miles from Gundagai", based on Charlie "Bowyang" Yorke's "Bullocky Bill", is an example of such a reworking. Moses kept Henry Lawson supplied with hats and Lawson refers to him in "Joseph's Dreams and Reuben's Brethren" in the line "my best friend was a Yid". The "ringer" is the top shearer. The "colonial experience man" is a young Englishman sent to the colony by his well-to-do family, who will go home to England after gaining some knowledge of life.

Click Go the Shears

Out on the board the old shearer stands,
Grasping his shears in his long, bony hands,

Fixed is his gaze on a bare-bellied "joe"
Glory if he gets her, won't he make the ringer go.

Chorus
Click go the shears boys, click, click, click,
Wide is his blow and his hands move quick,
The ringer looks around and is beaten by a blow,
And curses the old snagger with the blue-bellied "joe".

In the middle of the floor in his cane-bottomed chair
Is the boss of the board, with eyes everywhere;
Notes well each fleece as it comes to the screen,
Paying strict attention if it's taken off clean.

The colonial experience man, he is there, of course,
With his shiny leggin's, just got off his horse,
Casting round his eye like a real connoisseur,
Whistling the old tune, "I'm the Perfect Lure".

The tar-boy is there, awaiting in demand,
With his blackened tar-pot, and his tarry hand,
Sees one old sheep with a cut upon its back,
Hears what he's waiting for, "Tar here, Jack!"

Shearing is all over and we've all got our cheques,
Roll up your swag for we're off on the tracks;
The first pub we come to, it's there we'll have a spree,
And everyone that comes along it's "Come and drink with me!"

Down by the bar the old shearer stands,
Grasping his glass in his thin bony hands;
Fixed is his gaze on a green-painted keg,
Glory, he'll get down on it, ere he stirs a peg.

There we leave him standing, shouting for all hands,
Whilst all around him every "shouter" stands;
His eyes are on the cask, which is now lowering fast,
He works hard, he drinks hard, and goes to hell at last!

W. T. GOODGE 1862–1909

William Thomas Goodge was born in London, the son of a law courts clerk. He worked his way to Australia on *The Cathay* as a steward at the age of eighteen. He left the ship at Sydney and took a job at Windagee Station, in western New South Wales. He then roamed outback New South Wales for twelve years before working as a journalist for regional newspapers, and becoming editor and then part-owner of the *Orange Leader*. While he was in Orange, he was a prolific contributor of light verse to the *Bulletin*, which published a 197-page collection of his verse *Hits! Skits! And Jingles!* in 1899 with illustrations by Norman Lindsay. For the last nine years of his life, Goodge wrote a weekly column in the Sydney newspaper *Truth*, about an imaginary group of characters he called the Gimcrack Club.

Apart from a reprint of *Hits! Skits! And Jingles!* in 1972, and the occasional inclusion in anthologies of "The Great Australian Adjective", he has largely been forgotten. Yet Kenneth Slessor was of the view that Goodge ranked with W. S. Gilbert as the greatest writer of light verse in the English language. This was not a view which was lightly held by Slessor, as for many years he was himself a contributor of light and topical verse on a weekly basis to *Smith's Weekly*: his admiration for Goodge was that of a professional working in the same field.

Goodge's genius as a writer of comic verse was his economy of language. In "A Matter of a Knack", he tells in less than a page, a story that an accomplished light verse writer such as C. J. Dennis would have padded out over two or three pages. Goodge is also a master of surprise. It is only at the end of "Who Stole the Ponies?" that one discovers the identity of the speaker. There is something almost sinister about this poem. In the final verse of "The Shearer's Cook" there is a surprising darkening of tone when we find out that the cook is not joking, but really is disenchanted with life.

Goodge is able to get a lot of the real world into his light verse, and it is not a very reassuring place for readers looking for comfort and warm sentiment. The shanty in "Mulligan's Shanty", where even a wealthy landowner, "the squatter", is driven to drinking furniture polish, is a shanty from Hell and captures the appalling conditions under which alcohol could be consumed in the outback, no doubt experienced by Goodge. However, the world that Goodge's verses inhabit is not the physical world of trees, wind and changing light that most of us live in; it is a world of the mind, of Chinese puzzles and conundrums, where artful larrikins lay traps for the unwary. Goodge was a technical master. "How We Drove the Trotter" should be in every book of verse prosody as a demonstration model, to show what can be done with different metres.

Goodge's most popular poem is "The Spider by the Gwydir". In the past (and until now, so far as we are aware) this has been attributed to "Anon." However, it is clearly by Goodge. The poem was published anonymously at that time, because of the risqué ending. The extreme economy of language, the deftness of the rhyming and metre point to one author alone. Goodge's poem, "The Spielers and the Girl", shares elements in common with "The Spider by the Gwydir", further supporting his authorship.

How We Drove the Trotter

Oh, he was a handsome trotter, and he couldn't be completer,
He had such a splendid action and he trotted to this metre,
Such a pace and such a courage, such a record-killing power,
That he did his mile in two-fifteen, his twenty in the hour.
When he trotted on the Bathurst road the pace it was a panter,
But he broke the poet's rhythm when he broke out in a canter –

As we were remarking the pace was a panter,
But just as we liked it he broke in a canter,
And rattled along with a motion terrific,
And scattered the sparks with a freedom prolific;
He tugged at the bit and he jerked at the bridle,
We pulled like a demon, the effort was idle,
The bit in his teeth and the rein in the crupper,
We didn't much care to get home to our supper.

Then we went
Like the wind,
And our hands
They were skinned,
And we thought
With a dread
To go over his head,
And we tugged
And we strove,
Couldn't say
That we drove
Till we found
It had stopped
And the gallop was dropped!

Then he dropped into a trot again as steady as a pacer,
And we thought we had a dandy that was sure to make a racer
That would rival all the Yankees and was bound to beat the British,
Not a bit of vice about him though he was a trifle skittish;
Past the buggies and the sulkies on the road we went a-flying,
For the pace it was a clinker, and they had no chance of trying,
But for fear he'd start a canter we were going to stop his caper
When he bolted like a bullet at a flying piece of paper –

Helter skelter,
What a pelter!
Such a pace to win a welter!
Rush,
Race,
Tear!
Flying through the air!
Wind a-humming,
Fears benumbing,
Here's another trap a-coming!

Shouts!
Bash!
Crash!
Moses, what a smash!

Who Stole the Ponies?

Away down the Darling by the Callewatta Forks
In the dreary, weary desert where the stone is
On the right you find the region of the Raffertys and Rorkes;
On the left you see the Learys and Maloneys.
We were always pretty careful when the steamer anchored there,
It was well indeed for strangers to be chary,
For the Learys and Maloneys held the belt from County Clare,
And the Raffertys and Rorkes from Tipperary!

They were all of them selectors on the Steelandummie run,
And the owner of the run was named McPherson,
He was Scotch and he was clannish (and his clan was Number One)
A sedate and very sober-sided person!
And he ran a lot of stock around adjacent to the Forks,
And he lost, he said, a half-a-dozen ponies,
And he swore they had been stolen by the Raffertys and Rorkes,
If they had'nt by the Learys and Maloneys !

Then the Learys and Maloneys said the men from County Clare
Wouldn't even steal a pansy from the prairie!
And the Raffertys and Rorkes they quite accorded with them there,
"But they often stole the pigs from Tipperary!"
Then the row it fairly started; there was murther at the Forks
From the minute that McPherson lost the ponies
It was dangerous to come betwixt the Raffertys and Rorkes
When they waited for the Learys and Maloneys!

When the Learys crossed the river there was "wigs upon the green"
And diversion for the men from Tipperary!
When a Rafferty or Rorke upon the other side was seen,
He would find things just as willing and as scary!
But as you are not agoin' to the Callewatta Forks
I can sell you half-a-dozen decent ponies,
But you hadn't better show them to the Raffertys and Rorkes,
Nor McPherson, nor the Learys and Maloneys!

A Bad Break!

The preacher quoted, and the cranks
  Among his congregation smiled,
"How sharper than a serpent's thanks
  It is to have a toothless child."

He saw he erred, his eye grew wild,
  He frowned upon the mirthful ranks:
"How toothless than a serpent's child
  It is to have a sharper's thanks!"

The Shearers' Cook

Now, shearers' cooks, as shearers know,
Are very seldom wont to blow;
But when I took to dabbing tar
And "picking up" on Blaringar,
The cook, when "barbers" came at morn
To get a snack, would say, with scorn:
        "Tea on the left,
        Coffee on the right,
Brownie on the bunk, and blast yez!"

The "bunk" or slab was in the hut,
And on it "brownie" ready cut;
Two buckets o'er the fire would be –
One filled with coffee, one with tea;
And when the chaps came filing in
The cook would say, with mirthless grin:
        "Tea on the left,
        Coffee on the right,
Brownie on the bunk, and blast yez!"

Peculiar man, this shearers' cook,
And had a very ugly look.
To me – a new-chum rouseabout,
Said he, one day when all were out:
"There's nothing in this world, my lad,
That's worth your worry, good or bad;
        Grief on the left,
        Sorrow on the right,
Trouble on the bunk, but blast it!"

Mulligan's Shanty

Things is just the same as ever
On the outer Never-Never,
And you look to find the stock of liquor scanty;
But we found things worse than ordin'ry,
And in fact a bit extraordin'ry,
When myself and Bill the Pinker struck the shanty.
"Shanty?" says you. "What shanty?"
Why, Mulligan's shanty!

I says "Whisky"; Bill says "Brandy";
But there wasn't either handy,
For the boss was out of liquor in that line.
"Well, I'll try a rum," says Billy.
"Got no rum," he answers, chilly,
"But I'll recommend a decent drop o' *tine*."
"Tine?" says Bill; "what tine?"
"Why, turpentine!"

"Blow me blue!" says Bill the Pinker,
"Can't yer give us a deep-sinker?
Ain't yer got a cask o' beer behind the screen?"
Bill was getting pretty cranky,
But there wasn't any swanky.
Says the landlord, "Why not try a drop o' *sene?*"
"Sene?" says Bill; "what sene?"
"Why, kerosene!"

Well, we wouldn't spend a tanner,
But the boss's pleasant manner
All our cursing couldn't easily demolish.
Says he, "Strike me perpendic'lar
But you beggars *are* partic'lar,
Why, the squatter in the parlour's drinking polish!"
"Polish?" says Bill; "what polish?"
"Why, furniture-polish!"

A Matter of Knack

Jock M'Pherson was a person who was boastful in conversin',
But respectable and ponderous and dignified withal!
Con M'Carty was a party who was something of a smarty,
And beside the big M'Pherson looked particularly small;
But Cornelius M'Carty, he was artful, after all!

When Cornelius M'Carty thought M'Pherson was his dart, he
  Made a wager he could carry him a mile along the track;
Which, considering M'Pherson was a very weighty person,
  Was a risky undertaking for M'Carty's little back.
  But Cornelius protested it depended on the knack!
"Take yer coat off!" called M'Carty, and M'Pherson gave a start, he
  Hadn't bargained for proceedings the reverse of dignified!
But he felt he had the best of the arrangement. "Take yer vest off!"
  Said M'Carty; and M'Pherson very graciously complied.
  It was in the private parlor, and the crowd was all outside.

"Take yer boots off!" said M'Carty in a cheerful tone and hearty,
  But M'Pherson he objected that the crowd would see his toes.
Said M'Carty, "See, M'Pherson, there ain't any sense in cursin',
  Take yer boots off, I don't reckon to be handicapped with those!
  I am not the sort of Juggins you apparently suppose!"
This M'Pherson's wrath arouses. "But," said he, "I'll keep me trousers!"
  "Not a trouser!" said M'Carty, "or to me the wager goes.
  The conditions you're reversin'; I will carry *you*, M'Pherson,
  But the wager doesn't say a blessed word about yer *clothes!*"
  That was how the small M'Carty had M'Pherson by the nose!

The Spider by the Gwydir

  By the sluggish River Gwydir
  Lived a wicked red-backed spider,
Who was just about as vicious as could be:
  And the place that he was camped in
  Was a rusty Jones's jam-tin
In a paddock by the show-grounds at Moree.

    Near him lay a shearer snoozin':
  He had been on beer and boozin'
All through the night and all the previous day;
  And the rookin' of the rookers,
  And the noise of showtime spruikers,
Failed to wake him from the trance in which he lay,

    Then a crafty-lookin' spieler
  With a dainty little sheila
Came along collecting wood to make a fire.
  Said the spieler, "He's a boozer
  And he's goin' to be a loser:
If he isn't, you can christen me a liar.

"Hustle round and keep nit honey,
While I fan the mug for money,
And we'll have some little luxuries for tea."
She answered, "Don't be silly:
You go back and boil the billy.
You can safely leave the mug to little me!"

So she circled ever nearer,
Till she reached the dopey shearer
With his pockets bulgin', fast asleep and snug:
But she did not see the spider
That was ringin' close beside her,
For her mind was on the money and the mug.

The spider sighted dinner.
He'd been daily growing thinner;
He'd been fasting and was hollow as an urn.
As she eyed the bulging pocket,
He just darted like a rocket
And he bit that rookin' sheila on the stern.

Then the sheila raced off squealin',
And her clothes she was un-peelin':
To hear her yells would make you feel forlorn.
One hand the bite was pressin',
While the other was undressin',
And she reached the camp the same as she was born!

Then the shearer, pale and haggard,
Woke, and back to town he staggered,
Where he caught the train and gave the booze a rest:
And he'll never know the spider,
That was camped beside the Gwydir,
Had saved him sixty smackers of the best!

A. B. PATERSON ("The Banjo") 1864–1941

"Banjo" Paterson was born at Narambla, New South Wales, the son of an unsuccessful Scottish-born grazier and an Australian-born mother. His first ten years were spent in the bush. Aged eight, when his father was absent, he was taken to the Bogolong races by an eighteen-year-old station hand. This encounter with the race track was a love that was to last for the rest of his life (even cherishing the memory of the ginger beer). In 1874 he went to Sydney Grammar School, living with his widowed grandmother in Sydney. His vacations were spent at the station where his father had remained as a manager, after the mortgagee took possession. Paterson matriculated, aged sixteen, but did not win a university bursary since he had failed English grammar. After serving as an articled clerk, he was admitted as a solicitor in 1886 and for more than a decade practised as a lawyer. He was an outstanding polo player and amateur horse rider, competing at Randwick and Rosehill, and played tennis and rowed, remembered by the artist Norman Lindsay as a "tall man ... moving with the ease of perfectly co-ordinated reflexes. Black hair, dark eyes, a long, finely articulated nose, an ironic mouth ..."

In February 1885 he gained his first publication in the *Bulletin*. Paterson adopted the pen name "The Banjo", "after a so-called racehorse we had at the station" and his first bush ballads began to appear under that name. The novelist, Rolf Boldrewood, hailed "Clancy of the Overflow" as "the best bush ballad since Gordon" when it was published in 1889. The identity of "The Banjo" was revealed with the 1895 publication of *The Man from Snowy River and Other Verses*, the success of which was described in the London *Literary Yearbook* as "without parallel in colonial literary annals".

Paterson did not become part of the drinking set of *Bulletin* writers. The poet and bohemian, Roderick Quinn, recalled, "Banjo was never one of us ..." Paterson spent less than a decade and a half of his life in the bush, and chose to be a solicitor, then a journalist, because "there wasn't a livelihood to be gained on the land. Everyone who goes in for farming right out comes to grief sooner or later. At best it is only a continual struggle ... So while I was in the thick of the bush I didn't let it get such a hold on me that I couldn't leave it." Unlike Lawson, Paterson loved the bush, but his love was that of a disappointed lover.

Paterson's view of the bush was coloured by his father's struggles and eventual death in 1889 from an "accidental" overdose of opium. In the year of his father's death he published under the name "A. B. Paterson Solicitor" a polemic *Australia for the Australians. A Political Pamphlet Showing the need for Land Reform combined with Protection*. This pamphlet (of which this rather private man was later to say "I blush every time that I think of it") attacked the "rotten and absurd system" of land tenure which locked up land for absentee landlords, "left the present generation to the wilderness" and drove people into squalor in the cities. He suggested readers "take a night walk round the poorer quarters of our large colonial cities ... They will see vice and sin and misery ... people herded into wretched little shanties".

"The Boss's Wife" usually ascribed to Anon. is so clearly by Paterson we have included it under his name. The voice and details of this poem match "Saltbush Bill": the vivid description of natural events – the drought and arrival of the ibis in "The Boss's Wife" and the saltbush plains in "Saltbush Bill"; the determination of the boss and the guile of his wife, which match Saltbush Bill's determination and guile; and the slow and deliberate unfolding of the narrative. The risqué ending explains why Paterson published this poem anonymously.

With the Boer War, Paterson gave up the law and became a war journalist, and supported himself, usually not very well, by journalism for much of the rest of his life. He married, had a son and daughter. But the second half of his life was an anticlimax. His later poetry lacked the impact of his earlier ballads. He wrote two unsuccessful novels, never owned his own house and died, leaving barely

£300. Patrick White as a child was introduced by his father to a man in a tobacco-coloured suit, with a gold watch chain, stiff collar and trilby hat whom his father called "Mr Banjo Paterson". The older Paterson impressed White as "the driest kind of gentleman, his face like a sooty lemon."

In addition to his own verse, a significant part of Paterson's literary heritage is his collection of folk ballads, *Old Bush Songs* (1905), later revised and expanded. This book is the foundation collection of the anonymous Australian ballad and bush songs from the 19th century.

Paterson may be the most popular poet Australia has produced. But how good is his poetry? Paterson said, "I am not a poet. I am a versifier." Kenneth Slessor dismissed Paterson as "an accomplished writer of light or sentimental ballads and as such, considerably less adroit than Frederick Locker Lampson or Austin Dobson or even G. K. Chesterton." (*Bread and Wine*, 1970). Douglas Stewart, in his introduction to *Australian Bush Ballads*, pointed out that although Australian bush balladists lack the elevated tone of the Border ballads (since humour, rather than tragedy is at their heart), they should not be characterised as "light":

> What distinguishes these ballads from merely light, merely comic verse is the impression they all convey of an underlying reality, a significance. The red earth is in them; the Australian national character; and, I think, the foundation for a distinctively Australian poetry of a higher quality ... The king of them all was Paterson, widest in range, most fertile in the creation of national types whether humorous or heroic, as deft as any in versification though not as musical as Ogilvie, most typical of the proud, robust and sardonic spirit of his age, surest in his instinctive understanding that the first thing a balladist should do is tell a story.

A note on "Waltzing Matilda": This poem, as a song, has long been the unofficial national anthem of Australia. A swagman was an itinerant or tramp in the Australian bush, who occasionally worked. He carried on his back a swag or "Matilda", usually a blue blanket (hence "humping bluey") in which he bundled his possessions. "Waltzing Matilda" was another phrase for carrying the swag, and derives from "auf der Waltz", literally "on the waltz", a phrase used for itinerant German craftsmen. A "billabong" is formed by a meander in a river. A "jumbuck" is a sheep. A "tucker bag" is a bag for food. A "billy" is a metal can for boiling water for tea.

We have used Paterson's original version, which he wrote in 1895, while holidaying in outback Queensland. It was prompted by a shearers' strike which had led to violence at Dagworth station, where he was staying. Paterson sold the copyright (with some other pieces) to his publishers Angus & Robertson for £5. James Inglis & Co, who marketed "Billy Tea" then bought the copyright and had the words changed to make them more suitable for marketing their product. The "swagman" became a "jolly swagman" and he "waited till his 'Billy' boiled" (making it clear which tea he was boiling). Paterson's three "Policemen" became three "troopers" reminding listeners of the "three mounted troopers" in the song "The Wild Colonial Boy", and instead of reacting to their arrival by wordlessly jumping into the billabong and drowning himself, the Billy Tea Company's swagman reaction was: "'You'll never catch me alive,' said he." In effect he became another defiant "wild colonial boy". Even "the jumbuck" became "that jolly jumbuck". This injection of jollity and heroism into Paterson's grim lyrics by Marie Cowan, the wife of one of the tea company's directors, together with strong marketing by the company, allowed "Waltzing Matilda" to replace "The Wild Colonial Boy" as the unofficial national anthem.

The Man from Snowy River

There was movement at the station, for the word had passed around
  That the colt from old Regret had got away,
And had joined the wild bush horses – he was worth a thousand pound,
  So all the cracks had gathered to the fray.
All the tried and noted riders from the stations near and far
  Had mustered at the homestead overnight,
For the bushmen love hard riding where the wild bush horses are,
  And the stock-horse snuffs the battle with delight.

There was Harrison, who made his pile when Pardon won the cup,
  The old man with his hair as white as snow;
But few could ride beside him when his blood was fairly up –
  He would go wherever horse and man could go.
And Clancy of the Overflow came down to lend a hand,
  No better horseman ever held the reins;
For never horse could throw him while the saddle-girths would stand –
  He learnt to ride while droving on the plains.

And one was there, a stripling on a small and weedy beast;
  He was something like a racehorse undersized,
With a touch of Timor pony – three parts thoroughbred at least –
  And such as are by mountain horsemen prized.
He was hard and tough and wiry – just the sort that won't say die –
  There was courage in his quick impatient tread;
And he bore the badge of gameness in his quick and fiery eye,
  And the proud and lofty carriage of his head.

But still so slight and weedy, one would doubt his power to stay,
  And the old man said, "That horse will never do
For a long and tiring gallop – lad, you'd better stop away,
  These hills are far too rough for such as you."
So he waited, sad and wistful – only Clancy stood his friend –
  "I think we ought to let him come," he said;
"I warrant he'll be with us when he's wanted at the end,
  For both his horse and he are mountain bred.

"He hails from Snowy River, up by Kosciusko's side,
  Where the hills are twice as steep and twice as rough;

Where a horse's hooves strike firelight from the flintstones every stride,
  The man that holds his own is good enough.
And the Snowy river riders on the mountains make their home,
  Where the river runs those giant hills between;
I have seen full many horsemen since I first commenced to roam,
  But nowhere yet such horsemen have I seen."

So he went: they found the horses by the big mimosa clump,
  They raced away towards the mountain's brow,
And the old man gave his orders, "Boys, go at them from the jump,
  No use to try for fancy riding now.
And, Clancy, you must wheel them, try and wheel them to the right.
  Ride boldly lad, and never fear the spills,
For never yet was rider that could keep the mob in sight,
  If once they gain the shelter of those hills."

So Clancy rode to wheel them – he was racing on the wing
  Where the best and boldest riders take their place,
And he raced his stock-horse past them and he made the ranges ring
  With the stockwhip, as he met them face to face.
Then they halted for a moment, while he swung the dreaded lash,
  But they saw their well-loved mountain full in view,
And they charged beneath the stockwhip with a sharp and sudden dash,
  And off into the mountain scrub they flew.

Then fast the horsemen followed, where the gorges deep and black,
  Resounded to the thunder of their tread,
And the stockwhips woke the echoes, and they fiercely answered back
  From cliffs and crags that beetled overhead.
And upward, ever upward, the wild horses held their way,
  Where mountain ash and kurrajong grew wide;
And the old man muttered fiercely, "We may bid the mob good day,
  No man can hold them down the other side."

When they reached the mountain's summit, even Clancy took a pull –
  It well might make the boldest hold their breath;
The wild hop scrub grew thickly, and the hidden ground was full
  Of wombat holes, and any slip was death.
But the man from Snowy River let the pony have his head,
  And he swung his stockwhip round and gave a cheer,
And he raced him down the mountain like a torrent down its bed,
  While the others stood and watched in very fear.

He sent the flint-stones flying, but the pony kept his feet,
  He cleared the fallen timber in his stride,

And the man from Snowy River never shifted in his seat –
It was grand to see that mountain horseman ride.
Through the stringybarks and saplings, on the rough and broken ground,
Down the hillside at a racing pace he went;
And he never drew the bridle till he landed safe and sound
At the bottom of that terrible descent.

He was right among the horses as they climbed the farther hill,
And the watchers on the mountain, standing mute,
Saw him ply the stockwhip fiercely; he was right among them still,
As he raced across the clearing in pursuit.
Then they lost him for a moment, where two mountain gullies met
In the ranges – but a final glimpse reveals
On a dim and distant hillside the wild horses racing yet,
With the man from Snowy River at their heels.

And he ran them single-handed till their sides were white with foam;
He followed like a bloodhound on their track,
Till they halted, cowed and beaten; then he turned their heads for home,
And alone and unassisted brought them back.
But his hardy mountain pony he could scarcely raise a trot,
He was blood from hip to shoulder from the spur;
But his pluck was still undaunted, and his courage fiery hot,
For never yet was mountain horse a cur.

And down by Kosciusko, where the pine-clad ridges raise
Their torn and rugged battlements on high,
Where the air is clear as crystal, and the white stars fairly blaze
At midnight in the cold and frosty sky,
And where around the Overflow the reed-beds sweep and sway
To the breezes, and the rolling plains are wide,
The Man from Snowy River is a household word today,
And the stockmen tell the story of his ride.

Clancy of the Overflow

I had written him a letter which I had, for want of better
Knowledge, sent to where I met him down the Lachlan years ago;
He was shearing when I knew him, so I sent the letter to him,
Just on spec, addressed as follows, "Clancy, of The Overflow."

And an answer came directed in a writing unexpected
(And I think the same was written with a thumb-nail dipped in tar);
'Twas his shearing mate who wrote it, and verbatim I will quote it:
"Clancy's gone to Queensland droving, and we don't know where he are."

. . . .

In my wild erratic fancy, visions come to me of Clancy
  Gone a-droving "down the Cooper" where the Western drovers go;
As the stock are slowly stringing, Clancy rides behind them singing,
  For the drover's life has pleasures that the townsfolk never know.

And the bush has friends to meet him, and their kindly voices greet him
  In the murmur of the breezes and the river on its bars,
And he sees the vision splendid of the sunlit plains extended,
  And at night the wondrous glory of the everlasting stars.

. . . .

I am sitting in my dingy little office, where a stingy
  Ray of sunlight struggles feebly down between the houses tall,
And the foetid air and gritty of the dusty, dirty city,
  Through the open window floating, spreads it foulness over all.

And in place of lowing cattle, I can hear the fiendish rattle
  Of the tramways and the buses making hurry down the street;
And the language uninviting of the gutter children fighting
  Comes fitfully and faintly through the ceaseless tramp of feet.

And the hurrying people daunt me, and their pallid faces haunt me
  As they shoulder one another in their rush and nervous haste,
With their eager eyes and greedy, and their stunted forms and weedy,
  For townsfolk have no time to grow, they have no time to waste.

And I somehow rather fancy that I'd like to change with Clancy,
  Like to take a turn at droving where the seasons come and go,
While he faced the round eternal of the cash-book and the journal
  But I doubt he'd suit the office, Clancy, of The Overflow.

The Travelling Post Office

The roving breezes come and go, the reed-beds sweep and sway,
The sleepy river murmurs low, and loiters on its way,
It is the land of lots o' time along the Castlereagh.

. . . .

The old man's son had left the farm, he found it dull and slow,
He drifted to the great North-west, where all the rovers go.
"He's gone so long," the old man said, "he's dropped right out of mind,
But if you'd write a line to him I'd take it very kind;
He's shearing here and fencing there, a kind of waif and stray –
He's droving now with Conroy's sheep along the Castlereagh.

"The sheep are travelling for the grass, and travelling very slow;
They may be at Mundooran now, or past the Overflow,

Or tramping down the black-soil flats across by Waddiwong;
But all those little country towns would send the letter wrong.
The mailman, if he's extra tired, would pass them in his sleep;
It's safest to address the note to 'Care of Conroy's sheep,'
For five and twenty thousand head can scarcely go astray,
You write to 'Care of Conroy's sheep along the Castlereagh.'"

. . . .

By rock and ridge and riverside the western mail has gone
Across the great Blue Mountain Range to take the letter on.
A moment on the topmost grade, while open fire-doors glare,
She pauses like a living thing to breathe the mountain air,
Then launches down the other side across the plains away
To bear that note to "Conroy's sheep along the Castlereagh,"

And now by coach and mailman's bag it goes from town to town,
And Conroy's Gap and Conroy's Creek have marked it "Further down."
Beneath a sky of deepest blue, where never cloud abides,
A speck upon the waste of plain the lonely mail-man rides.
Where fierce hot winds have set the pine and myall boughs asweep
He hails the shearers passing by for news of Conroy's sheep.
By big lagoons where wildfowl play and crested pigeons flock,
By camp-fires where the drovers ride around their restless stock,
And pass the teamster toiling down to fetch the wool away
My letter chases Conroy's sheep along the Castlereagh.

Saltbush Bill

Now this is the law of the Overland that all in the West obey –
A man must cover with travelling sheep a six-mile stage a day;
But this is the law which the drovers make, right easily understood,
They travel their stage where the grass is bad, but they camp where the grass is good;
They camp, and they ravage the squatter's grass till never a blade remains.
Then they drift away as the white clouds drift on the edge of the saltbush plains;
From camp to camp and from run to run they battle it hand to hand
For a blade of grass and the right to pass on the track of the Overland.
For this is the law of the Great Stock Routes, 'tis written in white and black –
The man that goes with a travelling mob must keep to a half-mile track;
And the drovers keep to a half-mile track on the runs where the grass is dead,
But they spread their sheep on a well-grassed run till they go with a two-mile spread.

So the squatters hurry the drovers on from dawn till the fall of night,
And the squatters' dogs and the drovers' dogs get mixed in a deadly fight.
Yet the squatters' men, though they hunt the mob, are willing the peace to keep,
For the drovers learn how to use their hands when they go with the travelling sheep;
But this is the tale of a Jackaroo that came from a foreign strand,
And the fight that he fought with Saltbush Bill, the King of the Overland.

Now Saltbush Bill was a drover tough as ever the country knew,
He had fought his way on the Great Stock Routes from the sea to the big Barcoo;
He could tell when he came to a friendly run that gave him a chance to spread,
And he knew where the hungry owners were that hurried his sheep ahead;
He was drifting down in the Eighty drought with a mob that could scarcely creep
(When the kangaroos by the thousand starve, it is rough on the travelling sheep),
And he camped one night at the crossing-place on the edge of the Wilga run;
"We must manage a feed for them here," he said, "or half of the mob are done!"
So he spread them out when they left the camp wherever they liked to go,
Till he grew aware of a Jackaroo with a station-hand in tow.
They set to work on the straggling sheep, and with many a stockwhip crack
They forced them in where the grass was dead in the space of the half-mile track;
And William prayed that the hand of Fate might suddenly strike him blue
But he'd get some grass for his starving sheep in the teeth of that Jackaroo.
So he turned and cursed the Jackaroo; he cursed him, alive or dead,
From the soles of his great unwieldly feet to the crown of his ugly head,
With an extra curse on the moke he rode and the cur at his heels that ran,
Till the Jackaroo from his horse got down and went for the drover-man;
With the station-hand for his picker-up, though the sheep ran loose the while,
They battled it out on the well-grassed plain in the regular prize-ring style.

Now, the new chum fought for his honour's sake and the pride of the English race,
But the drover fought for his daily bread with a smile on his bearded face;
So he shifted ground, and he sparred for wind, and he made it a lengthy mill,
And from time to time as his scouts came in they whispered to Saltbush Bill –

"We have spread the sheep with a two-mile spread, and the grass it is something grand;
You must stick to him, Bill, for another round for the pride of the Overland."
The new chum made it a rushing fight, though never a blow got home,
Till the sun rode high in the cloudless sky and glared on the brick-red loam,
Till the sheep drew in to the shelter-trees and settled them down to rest;
Then the drover said he would fight no more, and gave his opponent best.

So the new chum rode to the homestead straight, and told them a story grand
Of the desperate fight that he fought that day with the King of the Overland;
And the tale went home to the Public Schools of the pluck of the English swell –
How the drover fought for his very life, but blood in the end must tell.
But the travelling sheep and the Wilga sheep were boxed on the Old Man Plain;
'Twas a full week's work ere they drafted out and hunted them off again;
A week's good grass in their wretched hides, with a curse and a stockwhip crack
They hunted them off on the road once more to starve on the half-mile track.
And Saltbush Bill, on the Overland, will many a time recite
How the best day's work that he ever did was the day that he lost the fight.

How Gilbert Died

There's never a stone at the sleeper's head,
  There's never a fence beside,
And the wandering stock on the grave may tread
  Unnoticed and undenied;
But the smallest child on the Watershed
  Can tell you how Gilbert died.

For he rode at dusk with his comrade Dunn
  To the hut at the Stockman's Ford;
In the waning light of the sinking sun
  They peered with a fierce accord.
They were outlaws both – and on each man's head
  Was a thousand pounds reward.

They had taken toll of the country round,
  And the troopers came behind
With a black who tracked like a human hound
  In the scrub and the ranges blind:
He could run the trail where a white man's eye
  No sign of track could find.

He had hunted them out of the One Tree Hill
  And over the Old Man Plain,
But they wheeled their tracks with a wild beast's skill,
  And they made for the range again;
Then away to the hut where their grandsire dwelt
  They rode with a loosened rein.

And their grandsire gave them a greeting bold:
  "Come in and rest in peace,
No safer place does the country hold –
  With the night pursuit must cease,
And we'll drink success to the roving boys,
  And to hell with the black police."

But they went to death when they entered there
  In the hut at the Stockman's Ford,
For their grandsire's words were as false as fair –
  They were doomed to the hangman's cord.
He had sold them both to the black police
  For the sake of the big reward.

In the depth of night there are forms that glide
  As stealthily as serpents creep,
And around the hut where the outlaws hide
  They plant in the shadows deep,
And they wait till the first faint flush of dawn
  Shall waken their prey from sleep.

But Gilbert wakes while the night is dark –
  A restless sleeper aye.
He has heard the sound of a sheep-dog's bark,
  And his horse's warning neigh,
And he says to his mate, "There are hawks abroad,
  And it's time that we went away."

Their rifles stood at the stretcher head,
  Their bridles lay to hand;
They wakened the old man out of his bed,
  When they heard the sharp command:
"In the name of the Queen lay down your arms,
  Now, Dunn and Gilbert, stand!"

Then Gilbert reached for his rifle true
  That close at hand he kept;
He pointed straight at the voice, and drew,
  But never a flash outleapt,

For the water ran from the rifle breech –
  It was drenched while the outlaws slept.

Then he dropped the piece with a bitter oath,
  And he turned to his comrade Dunn:
"We are sold," he said, "we are dead men both! –
  Still, there may be a chance for one;
I'll stop and I'll fight with the pistol here,
  You take to your heels and run."

So Dunn crept out on his hands and knees
  In the dim, half-dawning light,
And he made his way to a patch of trees,
  And was lost in the black of night;
And the trackers hunted his tracks all day,
  But they never could trace his flight.

But Gilbert walked from the open door
  In a confident style and rash;
He heard at his side the rifles roar,
  And he heard the bullets crash.
But he laughed as he lifted his pistol-hand,
  And he fired at the rifle-flash.

Then out of the shadows the troopers aimed
  At his voice and the pistol sound.
With rifle flashes the darkness flamed –
  He staggered and spun around,
And they riddled his body with rifle balls
  As it lay on the blood-soaked ground.

There's never a stone at the sleeper's head,
  There's never a fence beside,
And the wandering stock on the grave may tread
  Unnoticed and undenied;
But the smallest child on the Watershed
  Can tell you how Gilbert died.

A Bush Christening

On the outer Barcoo where the churches are few,
  And men of religion are scanty,
On a road never cross'd 'cept by folk that are lost,
  One Michael Magee had a shanty.

Now this Mike was the dad of a ten-year-old lad,
  Plump, healthy, and stoutly conditioned;

He was strong as the best, but poor Mike had no rest
  For the youngster had never been christened,
And his wife used to cry, "If the darlin' should die
  Saint Peter would not recognise him."
But by luck he survived till a preacher arrived,
  Who agreed straightaway to baptise him.

Now the artful young rogue, while they held their collogue,
  With his ear to the keyhole was listenin',
And he muttered in fright while his features turned white,
  "What the divil and all is this christenin'?"

He was none of your dolts – he had seen them brand colts.
  And it seemed to his small understanding,
If the man in the frock made him one of the flock,
  It must mean something very like branding.

So away with a rush he set off for the bush,
  While the tears in his eyelids they glistened –
" 'Tis outrageous," says he, "to brand youngsters like me,
  I'll be dashed if I'll stop to be christened!"

Like a young native dog he ran into a log,
  And his father with language uncivil,
Never heeding the "praste" cried aloud in his haste,
  "Come out and be christened, you divil!"

But he lay there as snug as a bug in a rug,
  And his parents in vain might reprove him,
Till his reverence spoke (he was fond of a joke)
  "I've a notion," says he, "that'll move him."

"Poke a stick up the log, give the spalpeen a prog;
  Poke him aisy – don't hurt him or maim him,
'Tis not long that he'll stand, I've the water at hand,
  As he rushes out this end I'll name him.

"Here he comes, and for shame! ye've forgotten the name –
  Is it Patsy or Michael or Dinnis?"
Here the youngster ran out, and the priest gave a shout –
  "Take your chance, anyhow, wid 'Maginnis'!"

As the howling young cub ran away to the scrub
  Where he knew that pursuit would be risky,
The priest, as he fled, flung a flask at his head
  That was labelled "Maginnis's Whisky!"

And Maginnis Magee has been made a J.P.,
  And the one thing he hates more than sin is
To be asked by the folk who have heard of the joke,
  How he came to be christened "Maginnis"!

Waltzing Matilda

Oh! there once was a swagman camped in a Billabong,
  Under the shade of a Coolabah tree,
And he sang as he looked at his old billy boiling,
  "Who'll come a-waltzing Matilda with me?"

> *Chorus*
> Who'll come a-waltzing Matilda, my darling,
>   Who'll come a-waltzing Matilda with me?
> Waltzing Matilda and leading a water-bag –
>   Who'll come a-waltzing Matilda with me?

Down came a jumbuck to drink at the water-hole,
  Up jumped the swagman and grabbed him in glee,
And he sang as he stowed him away in the tucker-bag,
  "You'll come a-waltzing Matilda with me."

Down came the Squatter a-riding his thoroughbred;
  Down came Policemen – one, two, and three.
"Whose is the jumbuck you've got in the tucker-bag?
  You'll come a-waltzing Matilda with me."

But the swagman, he up and he jumped in the waterhole,
  Drowning himself by the Coolabah tree;
And his ghost may be heard as it sings in the Billabong,
  "Who'll come a-waltzing Matilda with me?"

Santa Claus in the Bush

It chanced out back at the Christmas time,
  When the wheat was ripe and tall,
A stranger rode to the farmer's gate –
  A sturdy man and a small.

"Rin doon, rin doon, my little son Jack,
  And bid the stranger stay;
And we'll hae a crack for Auld Lang Syne,
  For the morn is Christmas Day."

"Nay noo, nay noo," said the dour guidwife,
  "But ye should let him be;

He's maybe only a drover chap
  Frae the land o' the Darling Pea.

"Wi' a drover's tales, and a drover's thirst
  To swiggle the hail nicht through;
Or he's maybe a life assurance carle
  To talk ye black and blue."

"Guidwife, he's never a drover chap,
  For their swags are neat and thin;
And he's never a life assurance carle,
  Wi' the brick-dust burnt in his skin.

"Guidwife, guidwife, be nae sae dour,
  For the wheat stands ripe and tall,
And we shore a seven-pound fleece this year,
  Ewes and weaners and all.

"There is grass tae spare, and the stock are fat.
  Where they whiles are gaunt and thin,
And we owe a tithe to the travelling poor,
  So we maun ask him in.

"Ye can set him a chair tae the table side,
  And gi' him a bite tae eat;
An omelette made of a new-laid egg,
  Or a tasty bit of meat."

"But the native cats have taen the fowls,
  They havena left a leg;
And he'll get nae omelette at a'
  Till the emu lays an egg!"

"Rin doon, rin doon, my little son Jack,
  To whaur the emus bide,
Ye shall find the auld hen on the nest,
  While the auld cock sits beside.

"But speak them fair, and speak them saft,
  Lest they kick ye a fearsome jolt.
Ye can gi' them a feed of thae half-inch nails
  Or a rusty carriage bolt."

So little son Jack ran blithely down
  With the rusty nails in hand,
Till he came where the emus fluffed and scratched
  By their nest in the open sand.

And there he has gathered the new-laid egg –

'Twould feed three men or four –
And the emus came for the half-inch nails
Right up to the settler's door.

"A waste o' food," said the dour guidwife,
As she took the egg, with a frown,
"But he gets nae meat, unless ye rin
A paddy-melon down."

"Gang oot, gang oot, my little son Jack,
Wi' your twa-three doggies sma';
Gin ye come nae back wi' a paddy-melon,
Then come nae back at a'."

So little son Jack he raced and he ran,
And he was bare o' the feet,
And soon he captured a paddy-melon,
Was gorged with the stolen wheat.

"Sit doon, sit doon, my bonny wee man,
To the best that the hoose can do –
An omelette made of the emu egg
And a paddy-melon stew."

"'Tis well, 'tis well," said the bonny wee man;
"I have eaten the wide world's meat,
And the food that is given with right good-will
Is the sweetest food to eat.

"But the night draws on to the Christmas Day
And I must rise and go,
For I have a mighty way to ride
To the land of the Esquimaux.

"And it's there I must load my sledges up,
With the reindeers four-in-hand,
That go to the North, South, East, and West,
To every Christian land."

"Tae the Esquimaux," said the dour guidwife,
"Ye suit my husband well!
For when he gets up on his journey horse
He's a bit of a liar himsel'."

Then out with a laugh went the bonny wee man
To his old horse grazing nigh,
And away like a meteor flash they went
Far off to the Northern sky.

. . . .

When the children woke on the Christmas morn
  They chattered with might and main –
For a sword and gun had little son Jack,
  And a braw new doll had Jane,
And a packet o' screws had the twa emus;
  But the dour guidwife gat nane.

The Boss's Wife

The warm winds crossed from the eastern coast,
Grew hot through the mountain passes
And picked up the breath of the burning plains
And touched on the station grasses.

And the grasses shrivelled, all dry and brown,
And shrunk to a dusty grey,
And the brown earth cracked, and the fiery drought
Came down on the land to stay.

The waters in on the homestead holes
Sank down to the blue-clay rim,
And the ibis came in their circling flocks
To feast on the bony bream.

'Twas shift all stock to the breeders' run,
With never the slightest doubt –
For the station boss 'twas a total loss
If the breeders' run gave out.

And the boss must wrestle and scheme and toil
And stick to the uphill job,
And battle it out with the fiery drought
For the sake of the starving mob.

And at night he'd go to the stockmen's hut,
For word of the day's work done,
And he'd stay for a smoke, or a yarn and a joke,
And talk of the outside run.

But it seemed somehow to the boss's wife,
A deep and rankling slight
That his plans were made with outside aid
When it came to an uphill fight.

And at night when he'd gone she'd wait and watch
In loneliest contemplation

Of the lot and life of a station wife
And the ways of an outback station.

And she'd gaze at the stockmen's huts below,
And across to the servant's light,
And she'd wait and brood in the doleful mood
That comes with the silent night.

And out of the darkness a notion grew,
A dim little gleaming dart,
It grew and flashed like a fiery sword,
And struck at the wifely heart.

'Twas a notion founded on logic's rites,
And womanly intuition,
By the housemaid's light when it sank at night,
And a shadowy apparition.

She gave no sign, but she watched each night,
Till there wasn't much room for doubt,
And she timed when the boss came in at night,
From the time that the lights went out.

And she hid the hurt with a woman's skill,
And she studied the housemaid's lighting;
To be betrayed for an artless maid –
'Twas time to be up and fighting.

When the boss was gone to the stockmen's hut
She lost no time in the going,
With a friendly smile and a bit of guile,
Would the maid come and help with the sewing?

And the maid agreed with a ready nod,
She'd nothing much to do,
She went with a smile, and fell for a pile
Would last for an hour or two.

And the wife, when the work was well in swing,
Slipped off to the housemaid's room,
And safe in the camp she blew the lamp,
And waited there in the gloom.

Till the footsteps soft on the beaten track
Turned in at the darkened door,
With scarce a rap, or the slightest tap,
For he'd been there oft before.

She spoke no word, and the darkened room
No change in the form betrayed,
Nor the greeting kiss with the meeting miss,
'Twas much as the melting maid.

'Twas a woman's style and a wifely wile.
To play the maid of the quarters,
She played with the skill and the strength of will,
And the guile of Eve's own daughters.

She played, and sudden she flashed a torch,
One horrified glance he took;
She dropped the light and she fainted quite,
'Twas Chin-ti, the Chinese cook!

MARY GILMORE 1865–1962

Mary Gilmore, whose face as a young woman appears on the current Australian $10 note (with William Dobell's notorious portrait of her as an old woman in the background), was born Mary Cameron at Cotta Walla, New South Wales, to Gaelic-speaking parents. She finished her schooling as a student teacher in various inland towns around the state. While working at a mining settlement near Broken Hill her life-long devotion to the militant Labour movement was aroused.

In 1896 she went to Paraguay to join a utopian socialist community called New Australia, and there married a shearer, William Gilmore and had a son. The community failed and the small family came back to an isolated farming existence at Casterton in western Victoria. In 1908 while continuing to live in Casterton, she became initial editor of the women's page of the Sydney *Worker.* In 1910 she collected her poems in a first book, much of which is about the joys of married life; however in 1912 she and her husband separated, he going to work in northern Queensland, and she keeping their child. In 1914, with her agreement, the youth went to join his father. He died in 1945, the same year as his father, a double blow for Gilmore.

Sympathetic commentators on her poetry, such as Les Murray and James McAuley, while valuing her directness and strong feeling, have remarked on her tendency to lapse into romantic rhetoric, her traces of Victorian diction and occasional awkwardness. Bearing this in mind, we have included just the first part of "Swans at Night", using only those verses that H. M. Green included in his path breaking *Modern Australian Poetry.*

Australian swans are black, and the flight of swans was linked in Gilmore's mind with the fate of the Aboriginal tribes, frequently referred to in the literature of her era as the "lost tribes". In a note, Gilmore wrote: "When I was a child, 'trumpeter' and 'trumpeters' were familiar words. Not every swan was called a trumpeter. The aboriginals, regarding the wild birds and animals as their flocks and herds, had provision made for their preservation. The great leaders of the flight were known, and never killed. The wisdom of the centuries was with them. And I remember well the disgust expressed by my own people when a man who was either a 'new-chum' from overseas, or a 'green-horn' from the city, shot, and boasted of shooting a trumpeter. The act was reprobated by everybody. As my father said, he might as well have killed an albatross. Everyone thought the bird should have been hung around his neck."

With "The Hunter of the Black" she included this note: "Called in those days a sharp-shooter; today he would be a sniper. I remember this man well ... He had a large family and many grandchildren, and as a paid killer of the black, he was but one of many."

Throughout her life Gilmore campaigned on behalf of the working class, children, Aborigines, and the aged. Her eight books of verse express this passionate concern. Nostalgic domesticity is another recurring theme. Her poetry is often simplistic, in both technique and content, but the commitment and strong, plain lyricism of her best work prefigure much in the poetry of Judith Wright. Her prose, *Old Days: Old Ways* and *More Recollections*, preserves her childhood in the bush and gathers pioneer lore and memories of the Aborigines (or "myalls" as she often calls them in her poems, "myall", now largely obsolete, apparently referring to wild, as opposed to assimilated, Aborigines). Mary Gilmore wrote some of her best poetry into her late eighties.

When she separated from her husband, she continued to refer to him as "my husband" and it would seem formed no other relationships. Despite a tendency to self-righteousness, one of her great virtues is her sympathy with outcasts and the inarticulate. When she died in 1962, aged 98, having long peered down and commented on the spiritual condition of the country from a tiny flat above Kings Cross, she was given a state funeral through the streets of Sydney – a Dame Commander of the Order of the British Empire who had regularly written for a communist newspaper, the *Tribune*.

Eve Song

I span and Eve span
A thread to bind the heart of man;
But the heart of man was a wandering thing
That came and went with little to bring:
Nothing he minded what we made,
As here he loitered, and there he stayed.

I span and Eve span
A thread to bind the heart of man;
But the more we span the more we found
It wasn't his heart but ours we bound.
For children gathered about our knees:
The thread was a chain that stole our ease.
And one of us learned in our children's eyes
That more than man was love and prize.
But deep in the heart of one of us lay
A root of loss and hidden dismay.

He said he was strong. He had no strength
But that which comes of breadth and length.
He said he was fond. But his fondness proved
The flame of an hour when he was moved.
He said he was true. His truth was but
A door that winds could open and shut.

And yet, and yet, as he came back,
Wandering in from the outward track,
We held our arms, and gave him our breast,
As a pillowing place for his head to rest.
I span and Eve span,
A thread to bind the heart of man!

Dedicatory

(In Memory of My Father)

I have known many men, and many men
In the quick balance of the mind have weighed,
And even as Abram found his score was ten,
His ten was one, so was my hope betrayed.
But though the tale is told, and fallen spent
Is the first fiction of a great man's name,
Eminent amid the uneminent
He still stands tall; a lonely mark for fame.
So, too, where truth sweeps out time's dusty floor
I have seen names, long praised, flung out as naught;
And I have seen one, whom the world called poor,
Walking amid the mountains of his thought.

from Swans at Night

Within the night, above the dark,
I heard a host upon the air,
Upon the void they made no mark,
For all that they went sailing there.

And from that host there came a cry,
A note of calling strange and high;
I heard it blown against the sky,
Till naught there seemed but it and I.

A long and lonely wraith of sound,
It floated out in distance wide,
As though it knew another bound,

A space wherein it never died.

I heard the swans, I heard the swans,
I heard the swans that speed by night;
That ever, where the starlight wans,
Fly on unseen within the height.

I never knew how wide the dark,
I never knew the depth of space,
I never knew how frail a bark,
How small is man within his place,

Not till I heard the swans go by,
Not till I marked their haunting cry,
Not till, within the vague on high,
I watched them pass across the sky.

The Hunter of the Black

Softly footed as a myall, silently he walked,
All the methods of his calling learned from men he stalked;
Tall he was, and deeply chested, eagle-eyed and still,
Every muscle in his body subject to his will.

Dark and swarthy was his colour; somewhere Hampshire born;
Knew no pity for the hunted, weakness met his scorn;
Asked no friendship: shunned no meetings, took what life might bring;
Came and went among his fellows something like a king;

Paid each debt with strict exactness, what the debt might be;
Called no man employed him master; master's equal, he;
Yet there was not one who sought him, none who held his hand;
Never father calling, bid him join the family band.

Tales and tales were told about him, how, from dawn till dark,
Noiselessly he trailed his quarry, never missed a mark,
How the twigs beneath his footstep "moved but never broke",
How the very fires he kindled "never made a smoke".

Men would tell with puzzled wonder, marked on voice and brow,
How he'd stand a moment talking, leave, and none knew how;
"He was there!" and then had vanished, going as he came,
Like the passing of a shadow, like a falling flame.

Once (I heard it when it happened,) word was sent to him,
Of a lone black on Mimosa – O the hunting grim!
Through three days and nights he tracked him, never asking sleep;
Shot, for him who stole the country, him who killed a sheep.

Tomahawk in belt, as only adults needed shot,
No man knew how many notches totalled up his lot;
But old stockmen striking tallies, rough and ready made.
Reckoned on at least a thousand, naming camps decayed.

Time passed on, and years forgotten whitened with the dust;
He whose hands were red with slaughter sat among the just,
Kissed the children of his children, honoured in his place,
Turned and laid him down in quiet, asking God his grace.

The Myall in Prison

Lone, lone, and lone I stand,
  With none to hear my cry,
As the black feet of the night
  Go walking down the sky.

The stars they seem but dust
  Under those passing feet,
As they, for an instant's space,
  Flicker and flame, and fleet.

So, on my heart, my grief
  Hangs with the weight of doom,
And the black feet of its night
  Go walking through my room.

The Waradgery Tribe

Harried we were, and spent,
Broken and falling,
Ere as the cranes we went,
Crying and calling.

Summer shall see the bird
Backward returning;
Never shall there be heard,
Those, who went yearning.

Emptied of us the land;
Ghostly our going;
Fallen, like spears the hand
Dropped in the throwing.

We are the lost who went,
Like the cranes, crying;
Hunted, lonely, and spent;
Broken and dying.

Nurse No Long Grief

Oh, could we weep,
And weeping bring relief!
But life asks more than tears
And falling leaf.

Though year by year
Tears fall and leaves are shed,
Spring bids new sap arise,
And blood run red.

Nurse no long grief,
Lest the heart flower no more;
Grief builds no barns; its plough
Rusts at the door.

The Brucedale Scandal

Himself and me put in the trap
  And daundered into town,
And there we found a whirlygig,
  A circus and a clown;
We took a ticket for the two,
  Without a thought of shame,
And never knew till we got home
  The loss of our good name.

'Twas Mrs Dinny met us first;
  Says she, "What's this I hear?
Ye're gaddin' round like young gossoons
  Instid of sixty year!"
Says she, "I heard a shockin' thing
  About a horse ye rid! ..."
Says I, "The divel take your ears
  I don't care if ye did!"

Says she, "I've had respect for you;
  I've held ye up to all;
And now my heart is broke in two
  To think ye've had a fall
For sure I never thought to find
  The frivolous in you ..."
Says I, for I was feelin' warm,
  "I don't care if ye do!"

We turned and left her where she stood,

A poor astonished thing,
Whose wildest dissipation was
A sober Highland Fling;
But when we came to Kelly's gate
We got another knock,
For there was John O'Brien's Joe,
Who looked his naked shock!

Says he (to Dan he whispers it)
"They say – " says he, "they say ..."
"Be damned to what they say," says Dan;
Says I, "Do asses bray?"
The poor misfortune stared at me
As if he thought me daft,
But, me, I looked him eye for eye,
Until he felt a draught.

The next was Mrs Tracy's Mick;
Who said, "I'm hearin' things!"
Says I, "We'd never need to ride
If gossipin' was wings!"
Says he, "There's decency you know;
Ye mustn't go too far.
I'm that much shocked ..." "Tut, tut," says I,
"I don't care if ye are!"

But dear old Gran O'Shaughnessy
She met us at the door,
And said, "Since first I heard the news
My foot's wore out the floor!
I never laughed so much," says she,
"Not once in all me days,
As when I heard that you and Dan
Was took to shameless ways.

"I'm keepin' up the fire," she said,
"Through all this blessed day.
My wan eye on the kittle, and
Me other up the way;
And when I heard ye on the road,
And thought of what ye'd done,
I felt me longest years slip off
For thinkin' of your fun!"

"Sure then," says I, "it's not myself
That would begrudge the tale,

And jokes, like butter on the shelf,
  If left too long grow stale."
I told her how I rid the horse
  In that there jig-ma-gee,
And when I said how I fell off,
  "A-w-w, did ye now!" says she.

I told her of the circus clown,
  And all the things he did.
She said, "He wasn't half the fun
  Of that there horse ye rid;
And though my bones is eighty-six,
  I wisht I was wi' ye!"
Says I, "Myself, I wisht it, too!"
  "I bet ye did!" says she.

"Aw, girl," she said, "ye've had your day,
  If Brucedale has the talk;
Ye've ate the apple to the core,
  So let them chew the stalk!"
They chewed the stalk from Rapley's gate
  To Cartwright's on the hill –
"Bedad," says Dan, "though years is gone,
  There's some that's chewin' still!"

Nationality

I have grown past hate and bitterness,
I see the world as one;
But though I can no longer hate,
My son is still my son.

All men at God's round table sit,
And all men must be fed;
But this loaf in my hand,
This loaf is my son's bread.

HARRY MORANT ("The Breaker") 1865–1902

"Breaker" Morant is famous as the subject of a film of that name. Born in Bridgewater in England, he later claimed to be the son of Admiral Sir George Digby Morant, but more likely was the son of Edwin Murrant, Master of the Union Workhouse. Arrived in Queensland in 1883, he was well-educated and polished, a flamboyant brawler, a hard-drinking womaniser and a lover of stunts. As an expert horseman and horse-breaker, he picked up the nickname, "The Breaker". In 1884 he married a governess at Fanning Downs, who was later to became Daisy Bates, Commander of the British Empire and a "Travelling Protector" of Aboriginal tribes, whose languages and cultures she studied. Bates (her later surname was from the first of two subsequent bigamous marriages) quickly threw Morant out when he failed to pay for the marriage and was charged with stealing pigs and a saddle. They never divorced. For the next 15 years Morant made a precarious living, droving and not paying his bills. He published a number of poems in *The Bulletin* as "The Breaker" and became a friend of Henry Lawson, Banjo Paterson and Will Ogilvie. (See Ogilvie's poem "Harry Morant".)

When the Boer War broke out, he enlisted in 1900 with the South Australian Mounted Rifles. He was in his element as a soldier, and rose to be a sergeant. His one-year term over, he briefly returned to England, then re-enlisted as a lieutenant in the Bushveldt Carbineers, who were mainly Australians. His local commander and best friend, Captain Frederick Percy Hunt, was captured by the Boers, mutilated and murdered. Morant was later court-martialled for shooting Boer prisoners and a German missionary. He was acquitted of the murder of the German missionary, but convicted of the other deaths and, together with another Australian, was shot by firing squad on 27 February 1902. Both men refused a blindfold. There is controversy as to whether he was acting under orders.

Morant wrote a number of romantic verses, but there is a hardness about them, and the sentiment seems self-conscious and skin-deep (unlike his friend Ogilvie, who was a genuine romantic). He was able to express genuine emotion only in his poems about horses. The horse Harlequin is lovingly portrayed in the second of his poems here, and appears in another poem. More famous as a man than as a poet, Morant's verse at its best has a clean, illusionless quality that is uniquely his own. No blindfold.

In "West by North Again": "boko" was a name given to an old stock horse; the "rabbit-proof" is a rabbit-proof fence; Tyson was a pastoralist whose wealth was legendary; there would be no guilt about feeding their animals at his expense. In "Who's Riding Old Harlequin Now?": "cutting out-camp" was a base for cutting out horses from a mob of wild horses or brumbies; "wheeling a piker" is a flanking manoeuvre around a wild horse; "gidgee" are small, thickly growing trees.

West by North Again

We've drunk our wine, we've kissed our girls, and funds are sinking low,
The horses must be thinking it's a fair thing now to go;
Sling the swags on Condamine and strap the billies fast,
And stuff a bottle in the bags and let's be off at last.

What matter if the creeks are up – the cash, alas, runs down!
A very sure and certain sign we're long enough in town –
The nigger rides the boko, and you'd better take the bay,
Quart Pot will do to carry me the stage we go today.

No grass this side the Border fence! and all the mulga's dead!
The horses for a day or two will have to spiel ahead;
Man never yet from Queensland brought a bullock or a hack

But lost condition on that God-abandoned Border track.

When once we're through the rabbit-proof – it's certain since the rain –
There's whips o' grass and water, so, it's West by North again!
There's feed on Tyson's country – we can "spell" the mokes a week
Where Billy Stevens last year trapped his brumbies on Bough Creek.

The Paroo may be quickly crossed – the Eulo Common's bare.
And, anyhow, it isn't wise, old man! to dally there.
Alack-a-day! far wiser men than you and I succumb
To woman's wiles, and potency of Queensland wayside rum.

Then over sand and spinifex and on, o'er ridge and plain!
The nags are fresh – besides, they know they're westward-bound again.
The brand upon old Darkie's thigh is that upon the hide
Of bullocks we must muster on the Diamantina side.

We'll light our camp-fires where we may, and yarn beside their blaze;
The jingling hobble-chains shall make a music through the days.
And while the tucker-bags are right, and we've a stick of weed,
A swagman shall be welcome to a pipe-full and a feed.

So, fill your pipe! and, ere we mount, we'll drink another nip –
Here's how the West by North again may prove a lucky trip;
Then back again – I trust you'll find your best girl's merry face,
Or, if she jilts you, may you get a better in her place.

Who's Riding Old Harlequin Now?

They are mustering cattle on Brigalow Vale
  Where the stock-horses whinny and stamp,
And where long Andy Ferguson, you may go bail,
  Is yet boss on a cutting-out camp.
Half the duffers I met would not know a fat steer
  From a blessed old Alderney cow.
Whilst they're mustering there I am wondering here –
  Who is riding brown Harlequin now?

Are the pikers as wild and the scrubs just as dense
  In the brigalow country as when
There was never a homestead and never a fence
  Between Brigalow Vale and The Glen?
Do they yard the big micks 'neath the light of the moon?
  Do the yard-wings re-echo the row
Of stockwhips and hoof-beats? And what sort of coon
  Is there riding old Harlequin now?

There was buckjumping blood in the brown gelding's veins,
  But, lean-headed, with iron-like pins,
Of Pyrrhus and Panic he'd plentiful strains,
  All their virtues, and some of their sins.
'Twas the pity, some said, that so shapely a colt
  Fate should with such temper endow;
He would kick and would strike, he would buck and would bolt –
  Ah! who's riding brown Harlequin now?

A demon to handle! a devil to ride!
  Small wonder the surcingle burst;
You'd have thought that he'd buck himself out of his hide
  On the morning we saddled him first.
I can mind how he cow-kicked the spur on my boot,
  And though that's long ago, still I vow
If they're wheeling a piker no new-chum galoot
  Is a-riding old Harlequin now!

I remember the boss – how he chuckled and laughed
  When they yarded the brown colt for me:
"He'll be steady enough when we finish the graft
  And have cleaned up the scrubs of Glen Leigh!"
I am wondering today if the brown horse yet live,
  For the fellow who broke him, I trow,
A long lease of soul-ease would willingly give
  To be riding brown Harlequin now!

"Do you think you can hold him?" old Ferguson said –
  He was mounted on Hornet, the grey;
I think Harlequin heard him – he shook his lean head,
  And he needed no holding that day.
Not a prick from a spur, nor a sting from a whip
  As he raced among deadwood and bough
While I sat fairly quiet and just let him rip –
  But who's riding old Harlequin now?

I could hear 'em a-crashing the gidgee in front
  As the Bryan colt streaked to the lead
Whilst the boss and the niggers were out of the hunt.
  For their horses lacked Harlequin's speed;
The pikers were yarded and skies growing dim
  When old Fergie was fain to allow:
"The colt's track through the scrub was a knocker" to him –
  But who's riding brown Harlequin now?

From starlight to starlight – all day in between
  The foam-flakes might fly from his bit,
But whatever the pace of the day's work had been,
  The brown gelding was eager and fit.
On the packhorse's back they are fixing a load
  Where the path climbs the hill's gloomy brow;
They are mustering bullocks to send on the road,
  But – who's riding old Harlequin now?

BARCROFT BOAKE 1866–1892

Barcroft Boake was born in the Sydney suburb of Balmain. When he left school he took up surveying and also worked as a stockman. In 1888 he and a friend "hanged" themselves from a beam at Rocklands station in the Monaro one evening as a prank. There were nearly fatal consequences for Boake, who, unlike his friend, had used a slip knot. In 1891 he began publishing poems in *The Bulletin*. Arriving back at his parents' house at the end of that year, he found his father was almost bankrupt and his eldest sister's marriage had failed. A letter arrived in which he heard about the forthcoming marriage of "his best girl" (the phrase he used to one of his sisters). Boake submitted to the depression that had stalked him for much of his life. He was unable to find a job and one day he walked out of the house and disappeared. His body was found eight days later at Folly Point on Sydney's Middle Harbour – he, having hanged himself with his stockwhip from a branch, and leaving a note: "Write to Miss McKeahnie". After his death, A. G. Stephens, the literary editor of the *Bulletin*, published a collection of Boake's poetry with a memoir.

At Devlin's Siding

What made the porter stare so hard? what made the porter stare
And eye the tall young woman and the bundle that she bare?

What made the tall young woman flush, and strive to hide her face,
As the train slid past the platform and the guard swung in his place?

What made her look so stealthily both up and down the line,
And quickly give the infant suck to still its puny whine?

Why was the sawmill not at work? why were the men away?
They might have turned a woman from a woeful deed that day.

Why did the pine-scrub stand so thick? why was the place so lone
That nothing but the soldier-birds might hear a baby moan?

Why doth the woman tear the child? why doth the mother take
The infant from her breast, and weep as if her heart would break?

Why doth she moan, and grind her teeth, and weave an awful curse
To fall on him who made of her a harlot – ay, and worse?

Why should she fall upon her knees and, with a trembling hand,
Clear off the underbrush and scrape a cradle in the sand?

Why doth she shudder as she hears the buzz of eager flies,
And bind a handkerchief across the sleeping infant's eyes?

Why doth she turn, but come again and feverishly twine,
To shield it from the burning sun, the fragrant fronds of pine?

Why, as she strides the platform, does she try hard not to think
That somewhere in the scrub a babe is calling her for drink?

Why, through the alleys of the pine, do languid breezes sigh
A low refrain that seems to mock her with a baby's cry?

Seek not to know! but pray for her, and pity, as the train
Carries a white-faced woman back to face the world again.

Where the Dead Men Lie

Out on the wastes of the Never Never –
  That's where the dead men lie!
There where the heat-waves dance forever –
  That's where the dead men lie!
That's where the Earth's loved sons are keeping
Endless tryst: not the west wind sweeping
Feverish pinions can wake their sleeping –
  Out where the dead men lie!

Where brown Summer and Death have mated –
  That's where the dead men lie!
Loving with fiery lust unsated –
  That's where the dead men lie!
Out where the grinning skulls bleach whitely
Under the saltbush sparkling brightly;
Out where the wild dogs chorus nightly –
  That's where the dead men lie!

Deep in the yellow, flowing river –
  That's where the dead men lie!
Under the banks where the shadows quiver –
  That's where the dead men lie!
Where the platypus twists and doubles,
Leaving a train of tiny bubbles.
Rid at last of their earthly troubles –
  That's where the dead men lie!

East and backward pale faces turning –
  That's how the dead men lie!
Gaunt arms stretched with a voiceless yearning –
  That's how the dead men lie!
Oft in the fragrant hush of nooning
Hearing again their mother's crooning,
Wrapt for aye in a dreamful swooning –
  That's how the dead men lie!

Only the hand of Night can free them –
  That's when the dead men fly!
Only the frightened cattle see them –
  See the dead men go by!
Cloven hoofs beating out one measure,
Bidding the stockmen know no leisure –
That's when the dead men take their pleasure!
  That's when the dead men fly!

Ask, too, the never-sleeping drover:
  He sees the dead pass by;
Hearing them call to their friends – the plover,
  Hearing the dead men cry;
Seeing their faces stealing, stealing,
Hearing their laughter, pealing, pealing,
Watching their grey forms wheeling, wheeling
  Round where the cattle lie!

Strangled by thirst and fierce privation –
  That's how the dead men die!
Out on Moneygrub's farthest station –
  That's how the dead men die!
Hard-faced greybeards, youngsters callow;
Some mounds cared for, some left fallow;
Some deep down, yet others shallow.
  Some having but the sky.

Moneygrub, as he sips his claret,
  Looks with complacent eye
Down at his watch-chain, eighteen carat –
  There, in his club, hard by:
Recks not that every link is stamped with
Names of the men whose limbs are cramped with
Too long lying in grave-mould, cramped with
  Death where the dead men lie.

HENRY LAWSON 1867–1922

Henry Lawson was born in a tent on the Grenfell goldfields, the son of Louisa Lawson neé Albury, who was to become a recognised poet herself, and a Norwegian-born miner, Niels Larsen. Over the next six years, the family moved several times, following new goldfields as they opened up. Henry was a sensitive small child, who played with dolls. Eventually his father took up a selection at Pipeclay, now Eurunderee, near Mudgee. A school was opened there in 1876, following a campaign by his mother, and Lawson attended school for the first time that year. One morning he woke up slightly deaf after a night of sickness and ear ache. Increasing deafness was to be a life-long burden. In 1879 he began attending a Catholic school at Mudgee, but did not get on with his school mates as he was attending a Protestant Sunday school. Meanwhile he was reading Dickens and Marryat, *Robbery under Arms* and *For the Term of His Natural Life*. In 1880 Lawson completed his meagre schooling and began working with his father on building jobs. He became a house painter by trade.

In 1883 Lawson's parents separated and Louisa moved to Sydney. She started a boarding house, formed associations with the radical left, as a feminist, and was involved in running a small paper, the *Republican*. His mother's literary and political interests helped to mould Lawson. He had a number of manual jobs in Sydney which he hated, and took night-classes to matriculate, but failed the examinations. Of this period in the mid-1880s he wrote: "I knew what it was to drift about the streets in shabby and patched clothes and feel furtive and criminal-like. I knew all that ... before I was twenty. I knew what it was to go home to a cold, resentful, gloomy and unbelieving welcome, and blind unreasoning reproaches at the very least."

In 1887 at the age of 20, his poem "A Song of the Republic" appeared in the *Bulletin* – his first publication. Over the next twelve years he published all of the poems which are arguably significant. He was precocious and prolific, with thirty poems listed for 1890 in Pip Wilson's Lawson chronology. This was the year in which he proposed marriage to Mary Cameron (later Gilmore). Much of what Lawson published was occasional verse, and facile. He began publishing short stories, including the famous "The Drover's Wife" in 1892.

In a few short years Lawson was to become a celebrity, then a derelict. His best collection of short stories, *Where the Billy Boils*, characterised by a great economy of language, was published in 1896, the year when he married Bertha Bredt, who was nine years younger. Marriage did not help him to settle down. After a period in a home for inebriates in 1898, he had a spell from alcohol and was industrious. With help from patrons, including the Governor, Earl Beauchamp, Lawson and his family (there were now two children) set out for London in 1900 to conquer the literary world. He had some successes, but there were strains on the marriage, living in an unfamiliar city. Bertha spent three months in a London mental asylum. They came back to Sydney in mid-1902 and Lawson attempted suicide. In 1903 Bertha divorced him and was to pursue him in the years to come through the courts for maintenance payments.

Notwithstanding his older landlady Mrs Isabel Byers' devoted care and advocacy over many years the rest of his life was a disaster. He became a familiar figure haunting the streets of Sydney, cadging money from strangers. One of his epigrams was: "Beer makes you feel as you ought to feel without beer." To earn drinking money, he continued to be a prolific writer of prose and verse between spells in mental asylums and prison for unpaid maintenance. But what he wrote (both prose and verse) was melodramatic and sentimental, a vain attempt to revive past themes and successes. Nevertheless when he died in 1922, he was given a state funeral attended by the Prime Minister and State Premier and thousands of mourners.

Lawson's major achievement lies in his short stories, a genre in which he is one of the masters. However, his poetry has had an immense popular appeal, and in his earlier poems had real emotion and vivid observation. We have used the later, trimmed-back versions of Lawson's poems, with the exception of "Sweeney" where we have used the earlier longer version: this retains the fifth verse, almost a self-portrait of the future Lawson; also retained is the prophetic second-last verse, omitted in later versions. Written in 1893, when Lawson was in his mid-twenties, this verse predicts Lawson's own future as an alcoholic derelict. In "The Lights of Cobb & Co" "Home" means the British Isles. In "Sweeney" the "army" is the Salvation Army. In "The Captain of the Push": a "push" is a gang of ruffians; the "Rocks" is a waterfront area in Sydney that was notorious for its slums and crime; "kerlonial" is "colonial".

Andy's Gone with Cattle

Our Andy's gone with cattle now –
  Our hearts are out of order –
With drought he's gone to battle now
  Across the Queensland border.

He's left us in dejection now;
  Our hearts with him are roving.
It's dull on this selection now,
  Since Andy went a-droving.

Who now shall wear the cheerful face
  In times when things are slackest?
And who shall whistle round the place
  When Fortune frowns her blackest?

Oh, who shall cheek the squatter now
  When he comes round us snarling?
His tongue is growing hotter now
  Since Andy crossed the Darling.

Oh, may the showers in torrents fall,
  And all the tanks run over;
And may the grass grow green and tall
  In pathways of the drover;

And may good angels send the rain
  On desert stretches sandy;

And when the summer comes again
  God grant 'twill bring us Andy.

The Roaring Days

The night too quickly passes
  And we are growing old,
So let us fill our glasses
  And toast the Days of Gold!
When finds of wondrous treasure
  Set all the South ablaze,
And you and I were faithful mates
  All through the roaring days.

Then stately ships came sailing
  From every harbour's mouth,
And sought the Land of Promise
  That beaconed in the South;
Then southward streamed their streamers
  And swelled their canvas full
To speed the wildest dreamers
  E'er borne in vessel's hull.

Their shining Eldorado,
  Beneath the southern skies,
Was, day and night, for ever
  Before their shining eyes.
The brooding bush, awakened,
  Was stirred in wild unrest,
And all the year a human stream
  Went pouring to the West.

The rough bush roads re-echoed
  The bar-room's noisy din,
When troops of stalwart horsemen
  Dismounted at the inn.
And oft the joyful greetings,
  And hearty clasp of hands,
Would tell of sudden meetings
  Of friends from other lands.

And when the cheery camp-fire
  Explored the bush with gleams,
The camping-grounds were crowded
  With caravans of teams;

Then home the jests were driven,
  And good old songs were sung,
And choruses were given
  The strength of heart and lung.

Oft when the camps were dreaming,
  And fires began to pale,
Through rugged ranges gleaming,
  Swept on the Royal Mail.
Behind six foaming horses,
  And lit by flashing lamps,
Old Cobb and Co., in royal state,
  Went dashing past the camps.

Oh, who would paint a goldfield,
  And limn the picture right,
As old Adventure saw it
  In early morning's light?
The yellow mounds of mullock
  With spots of red and white,
The scattered quartz that glistened
  Like diamonds in light;

The azure line of ridges,
  The bush of darkest green,
The little homes of calico
  That dotted all the scene,
The flat, straw hats with ribands,
  That old engravings show –
The dress that still reminds us,
  Of sailors long ago.

I hear the fall of timber,
  From distant flats and fells,
The pealing of the anvils,
  As clear as little bells,
The rattle of the cradle,
  The clack of windlass-boles,
The flutter of the crimson flags
  Above the golden holes.

Ah, then their hearts were bolder,
  And if Dame Fortune frowned
Their swags they'd lightly shoulder
  And tramp to other ground.

Oh! they were lion-hearted,
  Who gave our country birth,
Stout sons of stoutest fathers born,
  From all the lands of earth.

Those golden days are vanished,
  And altered is the scene;
The diggings are deserted,
  The camping-grounds are green;
The flaunting flag of progress
  Is in the West unfurled,
The mighty Bush with iron rails
  Is tethered to the world.

Ballad of the Drover

Across the stony ridges,
  Across the rolling plain,
Young Harry Dale, the drover,
  Comes riding home again.
And well his stock-horse bears him,
  And light of heart is he,
And stoutly his old packhorse
  Is trotting by his knee.

Up Queensland way with cattle
  He's travelled regions vast;
And many months have vanished
  Since home-folk saw him last.
He hums a song of someone
  He hopes to marry soon;
And hobble-chains and camp-ware
  Keep jingling to the tune.

Beyond the hazy dado
  Against the lower skies
And yon blue line of ranges
  The station homestead lies.
And thitherward the drover
  Jogs through the lazy noon,
While hobble-chains and camp-ware
  Are jingling to a tune.

An hour has filled the heavens
  With storm-clouds inky black;
At times the lightning trickles

Around the drover's track;
But Harry pushes onward,
His horses' strength he tries,
In hope to reach the river
Before the flood shall rise.

The thunder, pealing o'er him
Goes rumbling down the plain;
And sweet on thirsty pastures
Beats fast the plashing rain;
Then every creek and gully
Sends forth its tribute flood –
The river runs a banker,
All stained with yellow mud.

Now Harry speaks to Rover,
The best dog on the plains,
And to his hardy horses,
And strokes their shaggy manes;
"We've breasted bigger rivers
When floods were at their height,
Nor shall this gutter stop us
From getting home to-night!"

The thunder growls a warning,
The blue forked lightnings gleam;
As the drover turns his horses
To swim the fatal stream.
But, oh! the flood runs stronger
Than e'er it ran before;
The saddle-horse is failing,
And only half-way o'er!

When flashes next the lightning,
The flood's grey breast is blank,
A cattle dog and packhorse
Are struggling up the bank.
But in the lonely homestead
The girl shall wait in vain –
He'll never pass the stations
In charge of stock again.

The faithful dog a moment
Lies panting on the bank,
Then plunges through the current

To where his master sank.
And round and round in circles
He fights with failing strength,
Till, gripped by wilder waters,
He fails and sinks at length.

Across the flooded lowlands
And slopes of sodden loam
The packhorse struggles bravely,
To take dumb tidings home;
And mud-stained, wet, and weary,
He goes by rock and tree,
With clanging chains and tinware
All sounding eerily.

The Teams

A cloud of dust on the long white road,
And the teams go creeping on
Inch by inch with the weary load;
And by the power of the green-hide goad
The distant goal is won.

With eyes half-shut to the blinding dust,
And necks to the yokes bent low,
The beasts are pulling as bullocks must;
And the shining tires might almost rust
While the spokes are turning slow.

With face half-hid by a broad-brimmed hat
That shades from the heat's white waves,
And shouldered whip, with its green-hide plait,
The driver plods with a gait like that
Of his weary, patient slaves.

He wipes his brow, for the day is hot,
And spits to the left with spite;
He shouts at Bally, and flicks at Scot,
And raises dust from the back of Spot,
And spits to the dusty right.

He'll sometimes pause as a thing of form
In front of a settler's door,
And ask for a drink, and remark "It's warm,"
Or say "There's signs of a thunder-storm";
But he seldom utters more.

The rains are heavy on roads like these;
  And, fronting his lonely home,
For days together the settler sees
The waggons bogged to the axletrees,
  Or ploughing the sodden loam.

And then, when the roads are at their worst,
  The bushman's children hear
The cruel blows of the whips reversed
While bullocks pull as their hearts would burst,
  And bellow with pain and fear.

And thus – with glimpses of home and rest –
  Are the long, long journeys done;
And thus – 'tis a thankless life at the best –
Is Distance fought in the mighty West,
  And the lonely battle won.

Middleton's Rouseabout

Tall and freckled and sandy,
  Face of a country lout;
This was the picture of Andy,
  Middleton's Rouseabout.

Type of a coming nation,
  In the land of cattle and sheep,
Worked on Middleton's station,
  Pound a week and his keep;

On Middleton's wide dominions
  Plied the stockwhip and shears;
Hadn't any opinions,
  Hadn't any "idears".

Swiftly the years went over,
  Liquor and drought prevailed;
Middleton went as a drover,
  After his station had failed.

Type of a careless nation,
  Men who are soon played out,
Middleton was: – and his station
  Was bought by the Rouseabout.

Flourishing beard and sandy,
  Tall and solid and stout;

This is the picture of Andy,
  Middleton's Rouseabout.

Now on his own dominions
  Works with his overseers;
Hasn't any opinions,
  Hasn't any "idears".

The Captain of the Push

As the night was falling slowly down on city, town and bush,
From a slum in Jones's Alley sloped the Captain of the Push;
And he scowled towards the North, and he scowled towards the South,
As he hooked his little fingers in the corners of his mouth.
Then his whistle, loud and piercing, woke the echoes of the "Rocks",
And a dozen ghouls came sloping round the corners of the blocks.

There was nought to rouse their anger; yet the oath that each one swore
Seemed less fit for publication than the one that went before.
For they spoke the gutter language with the easy flow that comes
Only to the men whose childhood knew the gutters and the slums.
Then they spat in turns, and halted; and the one that came behind,
Spitting fiercely on the pavement, called on Heaven to strike him blind.

Let us first describe the captain, bottle-shouldered, pale and thin:
He was just the beau-ideal of a Sydney larrikin;
E'en his hat was most suggestive of the place where Pushes live,
With a gallows-tilt that no one, save a larrikin, can give;
And the coat, a little shorter than the fashion might require,
Showed a (more or less uncertain) lower part of his attire.

That which tailors know as "trousers" – known by him as "blooming bags" –
Hanging loosely from his person, swept, with tattered ends, the flags;
And he had a pointed sternpost to the boots that peeped below
(Which he laced up from the centre of the nail of his great toe),
And he wore his shirt uncollared, and the tie correctly wrong;
But I think his vest was shorter than should be on one so long.

Then the captain crooked his finger at a stranger on the kerb,
Whom he qualified politely with an adjective and verb,
And he begged the Gory Bleeders that they wouldn't interrupt
Till he gave an introduction – it was painfully abrupt –
"Here's the bleedin' push, my covey – here's a (something) from the bush!
Strike me dead, he wants to join us!" said the captain of the push.

Said the stranger: "I am nothing but a bushy and a dunce;
But I read about the Bleeders in the *Weekly Gasbag* once;

Sitting lonely in the humpy when the wind began to whoosh,
How I longed to share the dangers and the pleasures of the push!
Gosh! I hate the swells and good 'uns – I could burn 'em in their beds;
I am with you, if you'll have me, and I'll break their blazing heads."

"Now, look here," exclaimed the captain to the stranger from the bush,
"Now, look here – suppose a feller was to split upon the push,
Would you lay for him and down him, even if the traps were round?
Would you lay him out and kick him to a jelly on the ground?
Would you jump upon the nameless – kill, or cripple him, or both?
Speak? or else I'll – SPEAK!" The stranger answered, "My kerlonial oath!"

"Now, look here," exclaimed the captain to the stranger from the bush,
"Now, look here – suppose the Bleeders let you come and join the push,
Would you smash a bleedin' bobby if you got the blank alone?
Would you stoush a swell or Chinkie – split his garret with a stone?
Would you have a 'moll' to keep yer – like to swear off work for good?"
"Yes, my oath!" replied the stranger. "My kerlonial oath! I would!"

"Now, look here," exclaimed the captain to the stranger from the bush,
"Now, look here – before the Bleeders let yer come and join the push,
You must prove that you're a blazer – you must prove that you have grit
Worthy of a Gory Bleeder – you must show your form a bit –
Take a rock and smash that winder!" and the stranger, nothing loth,
Took the rock – and smash! The Bleeders muttered, "My kerlonial oath!"

So they swore him in, and found him sure of aim and light of heel,
And his only fault, if any, lay in his excessive zeal.
He was good at throwing metal, but I chronicle with pain
That he jumped upon a victim, damaging the watch and chain,
Ere the Bleeders had secured them; yet the captain of the push
Swore a dozen oaths in favour of the stranger from the bush.

Late next morn the captain, rising, hoarse and thirsty from his lair,
Called the newly-feathered Bleeder, but the stranger wasn't there!
Quickly going through the pockets of his bloomin' bags, he learned
That the stranger had been through him for the stuff his moll had earned;
And the language that he uttered I should scarcely like to tell.
(Stars! and notes of exclamation! blank and dash will do as well).

That same night the captain's signal woke the echoes of the Rocks,
Brought the Gory Bleeders sloping through the shadows of the blocks;
And they swore the stranger's action was a blood-escaping shame,
While they waited for the nameless – but the nameless never came.
And the Bleeders soon forgot him; but the captain of the push
Still is laying round, in ballast, for the stranger "from the bush."

Sweeney

It was somewhere in September, and the sun was going down,
When I came, in search of copy, to a Darling-River town;
"Come-and-Have-a-Drink" we'll call it – 'tis a fitting name, I think –
And 'twas raining, for a wonder, up at Come-and-Have-a-Drink.

Underneath the pub verandah I was resting on a bunk
When a stranger rose before me, and he said that he was drunk;
He apologised for speaking; there was no offence, he swore;
But he somehow seemed to fancy that he'd seen my face before.

"No erfence," he said. I told him that he needn't mention it,
For I might have met him somewhere; I had travelled round a bit,
And I knew a lot of fellows in the Bush and in the streets –
But a fellow can't remember all the fellows that he meets.

Very old and thin and dirty were the garments that he wore,
Just a shirt and pair of trousers, and a boot, and nothing more;
He was wringing-wet, and really in a sad and sinful plight,
And his hat was in his left hand, and a bottle in his right.

His brow was broad and roomy, but its lines were somewhat harsh,
And a sensual mouth was hidden by a drooping, fair moustache;
(His hairy chest was open to what poets call the "wined",
And I would have bet a thousand that his pants were gone behind).

He agreed: "You can't remember all the chaps you chance to meet,"
And he said his name was Sweeney – people lived in Sussex-street.
He was camping in a stable, but he swore that he was right,
"Only for the blanky horses walkin' over him all night."

He'd apparently been fighting, for his face was black-and-blue,
And he looked as though the horses had been treading on him, too;
But an honest, genial twinkle in the eye that wasn't hurt
Seemed to hint of something better, spite of drink and rags and dirt.

It appeared that he mistook me for a long-lost mate of his –
One of whom I was the image, both in figure and in phiz –
(He'd have had a letter from him if the chap were living still,
For they'd carried swags together from the Gulf to Broken Hill.)

Sweeney yarned awhile and hinted that his folks were doing well,
And he told me that his father kept the Southern Cross Hotel;
And I wondered if his absence was regarded as a loss
When he left the elder Sweeney – landlord of the Southern Cross.

He was born in Parramatta, and he said, with humour grim,
That he'd like to see the city ere the liquor finished him,

But he couldn't raise the money. He was damned if he could think
What the Government was doing. Here he offered me a drink.

I declined – *'twas* self-denial – and I lectured him on booze,
Using all the hackneyed arguments that preachers mostly use;
Things I'd heard in temperance lectures (I was young and rather green),
And I ended by referring to the man he might have been.

Then a wise expression struggled with the bruises on his face,
Though his argument had scarcely any bearing on the case:
"What's the good o' keepin' sober? Fellers rise and fellers fall;
What I might have been and wasn't doesn't trouble me at all."

But he couldn't stay to argue, for his beer was nearly gone.
He was glad, he said, to meet me, and he'd see me later on;
He guessed he'd have to go and get his bottle filled again,
And he gave a lurch and vanished in the darkness and the rain.

And of afternoons in cities, when the rain is on the land,
Visions come to me of Sweeney with his bottle in his hand,
With the stormy night behind him, and the pub verandah-post –
And I wonder why he haunts me more than any other ghost.

Still I see the shearers drinking at the township in the scrub,
And the army praying nightly at the door of every pub,
And the girls who flirt and giggle with the Bushmen from the west –
But the memory of Sweeney overshadows all the rest.

Well, perhaps, it isn't funny; there were links between us two –
He had memories of cities, he had been a jackeroo;
And, perhaps, his face forewarned me of a face that I might see
From a bitter cup reflected in the wretched days to be.

I suppose he's tramping somewhere where the Bushmen carry swags,
Dragging round the wretched stations with his empty tucker-bags;
And I fancy that of evenings, when the track is growing dim,
What he "might have been and wasn't" comes along and troubles him.

The Lights of Cobb & Co

Fire lighted; on the table a meal for sleepy men;
A lantern in the stable; a jingle now and then;
The mail-coach looming darkly by light of moon and star;
The growl of sleepy voices; a candle in the bar;
A stumble in the passage of folk with wits abroad;
A swear-word from a bedroom – the shout of "All aboard!"
"Tckh tchk! Git-up!" "Hold fast, there!" and down the range we go;
Five hundred miles of scattered camps will watch for Cobb and Co.

Old coaching towns already decaying for their sins;
Uncounted "Half-way Houses," and scores of "Ten-Mile Inns;"
The riders from the stations by lonely granite peaks;
The black-boy for the shepherds on sheep and cattle creeks;
The roaring camps of Gulgong, and many a "Digger's Rest;"
The diggers on the Lachlan; the huts of Farthest West;
Some twenty thousand exiles who sailed for weal or woe –
The bravest hearts of twenty lands will wait for Cobb and Co.

The morning star has vanished, the frost and fog are gone.
In one of those grand mornings which but on mountains dawn;
A flask of friendly whisky – each other's hopes we share –
And throw our top-coats open to drink the mountain air.
The roads are rare to travel, and life seems all complete;
The grind of wheels on gravel, the trot of horses' feet,
The trot, trot, trot and canter, as down the spur we go –
The green sweeps to horizons blue that call for Cobb and Co.

We take a bright girl actress through western dust and damps,
To bear the home-world message, and sing for sinful camps,
To stir our hearts and break them, wild hearts that hope and ache –
(Ah! When she thinks again of these her own must nearly break!)
Five miles this side the gold-field, a loud, triumphant shout:
Five hundred cheering diggers have snatched the horses out:
With "Auld Lang Syne" in chorus, through roaring camps they go
That cheer for her, and cheer for Home, and cheer for Cobb and Co.

Three lamps above the ridges and gorges dark and deep,
A flash on sandstone cuttings where sheer the sidlings sweep,
A flash on shrouded wagons, on water ghastly white;
Weird brush and scattered remnants of "rushes in the night;"
Across the swollen river a flash beyond the ford:
Ride hard to warn the driver! He's drunk or mad, good Lord!
But on the bank to westward a broad and cheerful glow –
New camps extend across the plains new routes for Cobb and Co.

Swift scramble up the sidling where teams climb inch by inch;
Pause, bird-like, on the summit – then breakneck down the pinch;
By clear, ridge-country rivers, and gaps where tracks run high,
Where waits the lonely horseman, cut clear against the sky;
Past haunted half-way houses – where convicts made the bricks –
Scrub-yards and new bark shanties, we dash with five and six;
Through stringy-bark and blue-gum, and box and pine we go –
A hundred miles shall see to-night the lights of Cobb and Co!

The Slip Rails and the Spur

The colours of the setting sun
  Withdrew across the Western land
He raised the sliprails, one by one,
  And shot them home with trembling hand;
Her brown hands clung – her face grew pale –
  Ah! quivering chin and eyes that brim! –
One quick, fierce kiss across the rail,
  And, "Good-bye, Mary!" "Good-bye, Jim!"

    Oh, he rides hard to race the pain
      Who rides from love, who rides from home;
    But he rides slowly home again,
      Whose heart has learnt to love and roam.

A hand upon the horse's mane,
  And one foot in the stirrup set,
And, stooping back to kiss again,
  With "Good-bye, Mary! don't you fret!
When I come back" – he laughed for her –
  "We do not know how soon 'twill be;
I'll whistle as I round the spur –
  You let the sliprails down for me."

She gasped for sudden loss of hope,
  As, with a backward wave to her,
He cantered down the grassy slope
  And swiftly round the dark'ning spur.
Black-pencilled panels standing high,
  And darkness fading into stars,
And blurring fast against the sky,
  A faint white form beside the bars.

And often at the set of sun,
  In winter bleak and summer brown,
She'd steal across the little run,
  And shyly let the sliprails down.
And listen there when darkness shut
  The nearer spur in silence deep;
And when they called her from the hut
  Steal home and cry herself to sleep.

    And he rides hard to dull the pain
      Who rides from one that loves him best;

And he rides slowly back again,
  Whose restless heart must rove for rest.

The Shakedown on the Floor

Set me back for twenty summers –
  For I'm tired of cities now –
Set my feet in red-soil furrows
  And my hands upon the plough,
With the two Black Brothers trudging
  On the home stretch through the loam,
While, along the grassy siding,
  Come the cattle grazing home.

And I finish ploughing early,
  And I hurry home to tea –
There's my black suit on the stretcher,
  And a clean white shirt for me;
There's a dance at Rocky Rises,
  And, when they can dance no more,
For a certain favoured party
  There's a shake-down on the floor.

You remember Mary Carey,
  Bushmen's favourite at The Rise?
With her sweet small freckled features,
  Red-gold hair, and kind grey eyes;
Sister, daughter, to her mother,
  Mother, sister, to the rest –
And of all my friends and kindred,
  Mary Carey loved me best.

Far too shy, because she loved me,
  To be dancing oft with me;
(What cared I, because she loved me,
  If the world were there to see?)
But we lingered by the slip rails
  While the rest were riding home,
Ere the hour before the dawning,
  Dimmed the great star-clustered dome.

Small brown hands that spread the mattress
  While the old folk winked to see
How she'd find an extra pillow
  And an extra sheet for me.

For a moment shyly smiling,
  She would grant me one kiss more –
Slip away and leave me happy
  By the shake-down on the floor.

Rock me hard in steerage cabins,
  Rock me soft in first saloons,
Lay me on the sand-hill lonely
  Under waning Western moons;
But wherever night may find me –
  Till I rest for evermore –
I shall dream that I am happy
  In the shake-down on the floor.

THE BASTARD FROM THE BUSH

(Anonymous, possibly Henry Lawson)

"The Bastard from the Bush" is a famous, obscene version of Henry Lawson's "The Captain of the Push". Whether Lawson wrote the obscene version first and cleaned it up to make it fit for publication, as "The Captain of the Push", or whether an anonymous author or authors made an obscene parody of the Lawson's "The Captain of the Push" is unclear. H. A. Lindsay (*Quadrant*, Summer, 1957–59) favoured the first view and claimed that Lawson "wrote the obscene version himself and circulated copies among his friends". One argument against Lawson being the author is that he was something of a puritan. On the whole we favour H. A. Lindsay's view: "The Bastard from the Bush" is far more than a parody; it is a better poem than "The Captain of the Push". It has more action, and less description of clothing and physical appearances that arguably Lawson inserted as padding to compensate for his deletions. There are variations among the published versions. We use what has come to be accepted as the best from the collection *Snatches and Lays*, published by Sun Books, 1973, edited by Sebestian Hogbotel and Simon ffuckes. Hogbotel and ffuckes also moonlighted under the pseudonyms Ian Turner and Stephen Murray-Smith. Before it was published by Sun Books, their collection circulated for a decade in a roneoed edition. "The Rocks" is a waterfront area of Sydney, notorious in Lawson's era, and "the 'Loo" is the inner-city waterfront suburb of Woolloomooloo, which was also of ill repute.

The Bastard from the Bush

As the night was falling slowly over city, town and bush,
From a slum in Jones's Alley came the Captain of the Push,
And his whistle loud and piercing woke the echoes of the Rocks,
And a dozen ghouls came slouching round the corners of the blocks.

Then the Captain jerked a finger at a stranger on the kerb
Whom he qualified politely with an adjective and verb.

Then he made the introduction: "Here's a covey from the bush –
Fuck me blind, he wants to join us – be a member of the Push."

Then the stranger made this answer to the Captain of the Push,
"Why, fuck you dead, I'm Foreskin Fred, the Bastard from the Bush.
I've been in every two-up school from Darwin to the 'Loo,
I've ridden colts and black gins – what more can a bastard do."

"Are you game to smash a window?" asked the Captain of the Push.
"I'd knock a fucking house down," said the Bastard from the Bush.
"Would you take a maiden's baby?" said the Captain of the Push.
"I'd take a baby's maiden," said the Bastard from the Bush.

"Would you dong a bloody copper if you caught the cunt alone,
Would you stoush a swell or Chinkee, split his garret with a stone?
Would you have a moll to keep you, would you swear off work for good?"
Said the Bastard: "My fucking silverplated oath I would!"

"Would you care to have a gasper?" said the Captain of the Push.
"I'll take the bloody packet," said the Bastard from the Bush.
Then the Pushites all took counsel, saying, "Fuck me, but he's game.
Let's make him our star basher, he'll live up to his name."

So they took him to their hideout, that Bastard from the Bush,
And they granted him all privileges appertaining to the Push.
But soon they found his little ways were more than they could stand,
And finally the Captain thus addressed his little band.

"Now listen here, you buggers, we've caught a fucking Tartar,
At every kind of bludging, that bastard is a starter,
At poker and at two-up, he's shook our fucking rolls,
He swipes our fucking liquor, and he robs our fucking molls."

So down in Jones's Alley all the members of the Push
Laid a dark and dirty ambush for the Bastard from the Bush.
But against the wall of Riley's pub, the Bastard made a stand,
A nasty grin upon his dial, a bike-chain in each hand.

They sprang upon him in a bunch, but one by one they fell,
With crack of bone, unearthly groan, and agonising yell,
Till the sorely-battered Captain, spitting teeth and gouts of blood,
Held an ear all torn and bleeding in a hand bedaubed with mud.

"You low polluted bastard," snarled the Captain of the Push,
"Get back to where your sort belong, that's somewhere in the bush:
And I hope heaps of misfortune may soon tumble down on you,
May some lousy harlot dose you till your ballocks turn sky-blue.

"May the pangs of windy spasms through your bowels dart,
May you shit your bloody trousers every time you try to fart,
May you take a swig of gin's piss, mistaking it for beer,
May the next push you impose on toss you out upon your ear.

"May the itching piles torment you, may corns grow on your feet,
May crabs as big as spiders attack your balls a treat,
Then when you're down and outed, to a hopeless bloody wreck,
May you slip back through your arsehole, and break your fucking neck."

MARY FULLERTON ("E") 1868–1946

Mary Eliza Fullerton was born in Glenmaggie, Victoria, and educated at home by her mother, and at a local state school. She stayed on her parents' farm after leaving school. Her childhood is recalled in a memoir, *Bark House Days* (1921). She moved to Melbourne in her early twenties, was active in the suffrage movement and involved with the Victorian Socialist Party and Women's Political Association, of which she was an office bearer, and through which in 1909 she met Mabel Singleton. Aged 41, she fell in love with Singleton, and spent the rest of her life with her, following her to England in 1922. She addressed a number of unpublished poems to Singleton ("You say that violets fade upon your breast,/I'd rather dearest that mine perished there ..."). Their relationship, which may not have been physically consummated, is discussed by Sylvia Martin (*Hecate*,Vol. 23, No. 2, 1997). She became a close friend of the novelist Miles Franklin. As well as four books of poetry, she published three novels. She wrote many aphoristic short poems influenced by Emily Dickinson.

Emus

My annals have it so:
A thing my mother saw,
Nigh eighty years ago,
With happiness and awe.

Along a level hill –
A clearing in wild space,
And night's last tardy chill
Yet damp on morning's face.

Sight never to forget:
Solemn against the sky
In stately silhouette
Ten emus walking by.

One after one they went
In line, and without haste:
On their unknown intent,

Ten emus grandly paced.

She, used to hedged-in fields
Watched them go filing past
Into the great Bush Wilds
Silent and vast.

Sudden that hour she knew
That this far place was good,
This mighty land and new
For the soul's hardihood.

For hearts that loved the strange,
That carry wonder;
The Bush, the hills, the range,
And the dark flats under.

E. J. BRADY 1869–1952

Edwin James Brady was born at Carcoar, New South Wales, of Irish parents. He was educated at Catholic schools and matriculated, but went to only a few evening lectures at the University of Sydney. His interest in sailing ships was sparked while working as a time-keeper on the Sydney wharves. He was dismissed when he refused to be sworn in as a special constable in the maritime strike of 1890, became secretary of the Australian Socialist League, and an active member of labour unions. Brady had an energetic and turbulent business life. He was half-owner of a country newspaper, which he edited, then he set up a press agency. He tried farming, was a reporter for the sensationalist *Truth* newspaper, and started a literary monthly which published Katherine Mansfield's first short stories. He tried a range of ventures from growing medicinal plants to selling a voting machine. In 1909 he set up a writers' and artists' camp at Captain's Point, Mallacoota, which was his home for the rest of his life and famous for its views of the sunset over the waters. He was a friend of Shaw Neilson, and provided a retreat for Henry Lawson at Mallacoota after Lawson had a breakdown. In 1918 his survey of Australia's primary industries, *Australia Unlimited*, was published – his only commercially successful book. His marital life was turbulent. He divorced his first wife for adultery, remarried and separated, and was refused a divorce by his second wife. Eventually in 1942, he married his third wife. Brady's lasting achievement was as a balladist. His sea ballads were admired by John Masefield. He began publishing verse in the *Bulletin* in 1891 and produced two volumes.

The Whaler's Pig

We shipped him at the Sandwich Isles
  'Fore God, he's mostly nose –
We've fetched him full eight thousand miles
  To fatten in the floes.

The Arctic wind may whistle down
  The ice-strewn Baffin Sea,
Our "passenger" don't care a darn –
  A whaler's pig is he.

The blubber which the brute devours
  Hard fruit of our harpoon –
He merely holds in trust; 'tis ours,
  Fresh pork! God send it soon!

Now, when her sloppy deck's amuck
  With stale cetacean spoil,
The glutton wallows in the ruck,
  His paunch a-drip with oil.

When from the crow's-nest rings the shout,
  Clean-echoed, "There she blows!"
"Jeff Davis" lifts his grizzled snout
  To let us know *he* knows.

The white ash blades drop down and rise,
  The royal chase begins,
He watches with his wicked eyes,
  And multiplies his sins.

With critic squint he stands beside,
  The harpooner prepares,
And, if the erring steel goes wide
  In swinish tongue he swears
(Great Heavens! how he swears!)

But when we strike her good and fair,
  Before the line runs hot,
He'll lift a hoarse hog cheer out there
  With all the strength he's got.

And when he sees the steerer take
  The bold boat-header's place,
A gourmand smile will slowly break
  Like sunrise round his face.

Around the loggerhead that line
  Grows taut as taut may be –
Three turns to hang your life and mine
  High o'er Eternity!

Who thinks of that? Not I, not you,
  Not he who most complains;

When like hell's fire the blood swirls through
  Our thumping hearts and veins,

'Tis "Fast she is" – "Now! Let her go."
  Our college stroke-oar yells;
This hour is worth a life to know;
  'Tis now the *savage* tells.

They maybe shared (ere progress rose)
  Who sired first earls and dukes,
A kindred ecstacy with those
  Who dodge a "fighter's" flukes.

So felt our simian sires who tied
  Their sheet-o'-bark canoes
To some mosasaur's slimy hide
  With only life to lose.

But this Kanaka hog will see
  The whetted lance succeed;
Glad epicure, he grunts in glee,
  Fore-knowledged of his feed.

Thus will his belly teach his tongue
  What eloquence it may
(Some noble songs by poets sung
  Have been inspired that way).

So will he squeal approval when
  Our six-hour fight is done,
And lord it bravely in his pen
  O'er quarry chased and won.

So will he join the chanty free
  That echoes as she tows,
To add his porcine jubilee
  And glad his adipose.

It is not clean or nice of taste,
  This episode of trade,
That lurches with indecent haste
  Towards the blubber spade.

But still it goes that man made sail,
  Invented rig on rig,
And God Almighty made the whale
  That feeds the whaler's pig.

This sorry beast which might have drowned,
  As hogs and human can,
He also made, so runs the round,
  To feed the whaler-man.

The whaler-man will get his "lay",
  The whaler's pig his share –
First whale, then pig, then man, some day
  The worm will make it square.

WILL OGILVIE 1869–1963

Ogilvie was born near Kelso, Roxburghshire, Scotland. His father's family had managed estates in the Scottish Border country for three centuries. His love of horses and Adam Lindsay Gordon's ballads drew him to Australia and his father agreed to his coming to this country in 1889, to get the benefit of "colonial experience". For twelve years Ogilvie roamed from the far north to the south of Australia, droving, horse-breaking and camping out. He soon became a prolific writer of ballads and poems, many of which were published in *The Bulletin*. He was a loyal friend of the later infamous Harry ("the Breaker") Morant.

In 1901 Ogilvie returned to Scotland and became a country gentleman. He never returned to Australia, but continued sending poetry to *The Bulletin* for some years. Much of his later poetry does not concern Australia and has not made an impact in his homeland. Ogilvie's romantic lyricism and charm were unique among the bush balladists. "The Death of Ben Hall" does not appear in any of the books published during his lifetime and has been attributed to Anon. It was published in *Smith's Weekly* under Ogilvie's name on 27 September 1924 at a time when both Alice Werner, a candidate for authorship, and Ogilvie were still alive.

A Bush Night

I remember the tilt of the deep canvas chairs, and the men sitting idle,
And out in the paddock a hoof going past and the click of a bridle,
And everywhere else the weird silence that lay upon sandhill and clearing,
Till the hum of a questing mosquito beat loud like a drum on our hearing.
I remember the pale summer lightning that flashed on the purple horizon,
Full sweep like the sword-play of giants, the dark to bedeck and bedizen
With gold for the path of the planets; and far by the creek I remember
A red fire that leapt and lay down, and died out in disconsolate ember;
The camp of some lonely wayfarer. The heat of the night hovered o'er us;
Then loud from the marge of the distant lagoon came the clamouring chorus
Of bull-frogs that moaned to a waterless sky for the rain cloud denied them.
Shrivelled and shamed stood the sunflowers, and prayed to the shadows to
  hide them.
The stars like cut gems in the darkness above the dim pepper-tree twinkled,

And somewhere beyond the burnt sandhill a cowbell incessantly tinkled.
The heat laid a garment about us, no wind set the vine leaves a-quiver
That fenced the broad-boarded verandah, no breeze blown across from the river
Brought coolness or comfort or promise; the bull-frogs ceased suddenly singing;
Then sounded the creak of a cane chair, and one from among us up-springing
Woke the wide boards with a jangle of loose-budded spur-rowels trailing,
And clanked to the water-bag hung from the roof by the vine-trellised railing,
Clinked the tin pannikin, dipped it, and holding it brimmingly lofted,
Murmured, "The Lord send us rain and fat horses!" then tipped up and quaffed it.

A Wildflower by the Way

The sun-rays burned like brands a-fire,
And, with a half-mile spread,
In blue grass to their heart's desire
The big Windorahs fed.

I rode the wing – a frail pretence;
What trick doth Love disdain? –
And halted at the split-rail fence
And fastened Gauntlet's rein.

She stood before her cottage home,
A maid of dimpled charms,
And churned the suds to snow-white foam
Across her nut-brown arms.

Then flashed those splendid orbs of brown:
She whispered soft and low,
"I'd love to see this Sydney town
Where all the cattle go!"

I took her sun-kissed hand and said
(And half believed it true):
"No lady there has lips so red
Or arms so soft as you –

"Or eyes one-half so bright!" I chaffed
To pass dull time away;
But Brown Eyes of the Barwon laughed,
"So all you drovers say!"

I had no longer need to speak –
Chained by those eyes of brown,
I kissed her once for Barwon Creek
And twice for Sydney town;

Then gathered bridle-rein once more
And heard a heart-beat say,
"The drover's life were dull but for
The wildflowers by the way!"

Solitude

As we drove one day through the lignum swamp
Where the spelling horses ran,
A loose horse broke from the noonday camp
And trotted beside our van.

We knew him then as a favourite steed,
A beautiful dappled dream,
The grey that went in the near-side lead
In the Boss's showyard team.

He swung in front of our station pair
And kept in the near-side place,
And trotted on with his beauty bare
Of bridle or rein or trace.

He led them away on the Woolshed track
As a harnessed leader would,
And we had not the heart to turn him back
The old grey Solitude.

He slowed and stood at the paddock gate,
Then guided the others through,
And whinnied once for his absent mate,
Then took up his task anew.

He was the pick of the four good greys
That had won three Cups in Bourke;
His poise in the ring was past all praise,
And his pluck on the road at work.

He held his place to a measured inch,
Left room for his swingle-bar,
And quickened pace at the sandhill pinch
And slowed where the deep ruts are.

So he showed the way to the Five-mile tank

With never a trace or tie,
Lifting his feet with a showyard swank
And his lean grey head held high.

And whenever I think of the brave bush teams
And their leaders staunch and good,
The horse of them all that haunts my dreams
Is the old grey Solitude.

The Township Lights

With laughter and love-spells and witch-eyes of blue
A girl in the township is waiting for you.
There is nothing that thrills like a handclasp of hers,
So bridle your best horse and buckle your spurs;
We'll wait not for moonlight, but saddle and ride
With the lights of the township our goal and our guide.

There are glasses to empty and yarns to be spun;
There are cards to be handled and coin to be won;
There are light-footed dancers that wait in the hall
For the boys from the station to open the ball,
With its waltzes for wooing and lancers for love
While the lights of the township are dancing above.

The day has been long in the dust and the heat,
But the way will be short with a guerdon so sweet;
The songs of the rover will shorten the miles
That the queen of our fancy makes bright with her smiles;
And stirrup to stirrup we'll sing as we ride
To the lights of the township that glimmer and guide.

We'll welcome old faces, our glasses we'll fill
Till the silver moon drops on the crest of the hill;
The words of our love to the night shall be borne,
Our song to the dawnwind, our laughs to the morn;
We'll dance till the sunbeams are out in the sky
And the lights of the township gleam faintly and die.

The world may despise us, and parsons disprove
That the night is for dancing and drinking and love,
But we'll saddle our horses and ride to the dance
And drink to the beauty that kills at a glance;
We'll hold to our loves and we'll stick to our creed
As long as the lights of the township may lead!

Harry Morant

Harry Morant was a friend I had
In the years long passed away,
A chivalrous, wild and reckless lad,
A knight born out of his day.

Full of romance and void of fears,
With a love of the world's applause,
He should have been one of the cavaliers
Who fought in King Charles's cause.

He loved a girl, and he loved a horse,
And he never let down a friend,
And reckless he was, but he rode his course
With courage up to the end.

"Breaker Morant" was the name he earned,
For no bucking horse could throw
This Englishman who had lived and learned
As much as the bushmen know.

Many a mile have we crossed together,
Out where the great plains lie,
To the clink of bit and the creak of leather –
Harry Morant and I.

Time and again we would challenge Fate
With some wild and reckless "dare",
Shoving some green colt over a gate
As though with a neck to spare.

At times in a wilder mood than most
We would face them at naked wire,
Trusting the sight of a gidyea post
Would lift them a half-foot higher.

And once we galloped a steeplechase
For a bet – 'twas a short half-mile
While one jump only, the stiffest place
In a fence of the old bush style.

A barrier built of blue-gum rails
As thick as a big man's thigh,
And mortised into the posts – no nails –
Unbreakable, four foot high.

Since both our horses were young and green
And had never jumped or raced,

Were we men who had tired of this earthly scene
We could scarce have been better placed.

"Off" cried "The Breaker", and off we went
And he stole a length of lead,
Over the neck of the grey I bent
And we charged the fence full speed.

The brown horse slowed and tried to swerve,
But his rider with master hand
And flaming courage and iron nerve
Made him lift and leap and land.

He rapped it hard with every foot
And was nearly down on his nose;
Then I spurred the grey and followed suit
And, praise to the gods – he rose!

He carried a splinter with both his knees
And a hind-leg left some skin,
But we caught them up at the wilga trees
Sitting down for the short run-in.

The grey was game and he carried on
But the brown had a bit to spare;
The post was passed, my pound was gone,
And a laugh was all my share.

"The Breaker" is sleeping in some far place
Where the Boer War heroes lie,
And we'll meet no more in a steeplechase –
Harry Morant and I.

The Death of Ben Hall

Ben Hall was out on the Lachlan side
With a thousand pounds on his head;
A score of troopers were scattered wide
And a hundred more were ready to ride
Wherever a rumour led.

They had followed his track from the Weddin heights
And north by the Weelong yards;
Through dazzling days and moonlit nights
They had sought him over their rifle-sights,
With their hands on their trigger-guards.

The outlaw stole like a hunted fox
Through the scrub and stunted heath,
And peered like a hawk from his eyrie rocks
Through the waving boughs of the sapling box
On the troopers riding beneath.

His clothes were rent by the clutching thorn
And his blistered feet were bare;
Ragged and torn, with his beard unshorn,
He hid in the woods like a beast forlorn,
With a padded path to his lair.

But every night when the white stars rose
He crossed by the Gunning Plain
To a stockman's hut where the Gunning flows,
And struck on the door three swift light blows,
And a hand unhooked the chain –

And the outlaw followed the lone path back
With food for another day;
And the kindly darkness covered his track
And the shadows swallowed him deep and black
Where the starlight melted away.

But his friend had read of the Big Reward,
And his soul was stirred with greed;
He fastened his door and window-board,
He saddled his horse and crossed the ford,
And spurred to the town at speed.

You may ride at a man's or a maid's behest
When honour or true love call
And steel your heart to the worst or best,
But the ride that is ta'en on a traitor's quest
Is the bitterest ride of all.

A hot wind blew from the Lachlan bank
And a curse on its shoulder came;
The pine-trees frowned at him, rank on rank,
The sun on a gathering storm-cloud sank
And flushed his cheek with shame.

He reined at the Court; and the tale began
That the rifles alone should end;
Sergeant and trooper laid their plan
To draw the net on a hunted man
At the treacherous word of a friend.

False was the hand that raised the chain
And false was the whispered word:
"The troopers have turned to the south again,
You may dare to camp on the Gunning Plain."
And the weary outlaw heard.

He walked from the hut but a quarter-mile
Where a clump of saplings stood
In a sea of grass like a lonely isle;
And the moon came up in a little while
Like silver steeped in blood.

Ben Hall lay down on the dew-wet ground
By the side of his tiny fire;
And a night-breeze woke, and he heard no sound
As the troopers drew their cordon round –
And the traitor earned his hire.

And nothing they saw in the dim grey light,
But the little glow in the trees;
And they crouched in the tall cold grass all night,
Each one ready to shoot at sight,
With his rifle cocked on his knees.

When the shadows broke and the dawn's white sword
Swung over the mountain wall,
And a little wind blew over the ford,
A sergeant sprang to his feet and roared:
"In the name of the Queen, Ben Hall!"

Haggard, the outlaw leapt from his bed
With his lean arms held on high.
"Fire!" And the word was scarcely said
When the mountains rang to a rain of lead –
And the dawn went drifting by.

They kept their word and they paid his pay
Where a clean man's hand would shrink;
And that was the traitor's master-day
As he stood by the bar on his homeward way
And called on the crowd to drink.

He banned no creed and he barred no class,
And he called to his friends by name;
But the worst would shake his head and pass
And none would drink from the bloodstained glass
And the goblet red with shame.

And I know when I hear the last grim call
And my mortal hour is spent,
When the light is hid and the curtains fall
I would rather sleep with the dead Ben Hall
Than go where that traitor went.

CHRISTOPHER BRENNAN 1870–1932

Born in Sydney in 1870, the son of an Irish brewer, Brennan was educated by Jesuits as a scholarship boy and at the University of Sydney. He was expected to enter the priesthood, but he began to have religious doubts at nineteen. He obtained an MA with honours in philosophy at 22, and went on a fellowship to the University of Berlin. There he became engaged to his landlady's daughter and also fell in love, more lastingly, with the poetry of Mallarmé. On returning to Sydney he could only find work as a cataloguer in the public library. His German fiancée, who was awaited with expectations of mystical experience, delayed coming to Australia for four years because of his lack of income. Eventually Elisabeth Werth arrived and they married and settled in Newport, on Sydney's northern beaches. She has been remembered for her golden hair and blue eyes, and for singing songs of "haunting sweetness" at the piano.

Brennan's scholarship was such that "he could have graced the chairs of philosophy, classics or modern languages" in any institution, but it was more than a decade before he was appointed to a lectureship at the University of Sydney. This was because of his "immoral" poems and his already noticeable drunkenness. Ultimately he became an associate professor of German and comparative literature, although by this time he was so much an alcoholic that his notoriously erratic lectures, to which people flocked from outside the university, had to be scheduled for early in the day. Christina Stead was among those inspired by hearing him speak.

Brennan's wife was unsympathetic to his interests. He in turn neglected and tyrannised his household, which eventually included four children and a mother-in-law (recruited by her daughter as an ally in domestic war). Outside his family, in Sydney's bohemia, Brennan was fêted for his wit, erudition and ebullience – quoting from, and conversing in, six languages. He was a massive figure, with his great hooked nose complemented by a meerschaum pipe. The student introduced into his study at the university would often find the room in darkness, lit only by the red glow of a beaker of claret over a flame. Brennan was dismissed from the university in 1925 when it became known that he had been living with a much younger woman, Violet Singer. The sacking occurred three months after she had been killed by a tram. Brennan had ceased living at his home some years before, staying at sailors' hotels and cheap boarding houses around the city. His daughter, Anne, the only one of his family to share any of his intellectual interests, was an habitué of this world also. She became a prostitute for a time. With the "fun-loving" Vi Singer Brennan had discovered a capacity for love, and he degenerated rapidly after her death, becoming more and more gross. Brennan was supported by subscriptions, was bought meals and drinks for his often still brilliant conversation, and moved between the prostitutes and the nuns in Kings

Cross. He completed a gradual return to the Church as he was dying in 1932.

Brennan is essentially a poet of the 1890s; by 1902 the main body of his work had been written. The last poem selected here, "I said this misery must end" is from 1908. He is a main gateway to modern Australian poetry; his influence reflected in poets as diverse as A. D. Hope and Roland Robinson. Despite his archaisms and portentous generalising, which are everywhere in his work, there is a real grandeur at times, as in his masterpiece "The Wanderer", which is based on his restless trampings at night along the then isolated coastal heath beyond Newport, north of Sydney. We have reproduced here the slightly abbreviated version of this poem used by H. M. Green in his 1946 anthology *Modern Australian Poetry*. R. G. Howarth made this translation of the Latin epigraph that Brennan wrote:

> Since I have yearned after the hidden heart
> I am become the wanderer among the stars of this revelation:
> And the term of my journeying afar
> is as that of the viewless winds.

In his theory, Brennan was a disciple of Mallarmé, with whom he corresponded, and who admired his work ("*Mon cher Brennan, poète merveilleux*"). His work records his Symbolist quest for an absolute reality – at first through sexual love and, after disillusionment there, through turning inwards, away from the world, to a pure poetic state. "The years that go to make me man" depicts this struggle as "magian". James McAuley was to characterise such a quest by poets and intellectuals as "the Magian Heresy". Brennan claimed that a poem is "not a way of saying something but a mode of that something's being". Claims such as this – that artists experience a super-reality – were later rejected in "The Wanderer". Chastened by the philosophy of F. C. S. Schiller and other pragmatists, he accepted that the quest, in itself, is all there is. All of Brennan's earlier search may be seen as an endeavour to create an intellectual substitute for the Catholicism of his youth: Symbolism can be seen as Catholicism theosophised, his Lilith as an inverted Maryology. Stylistically, too, Brennan's poetry is imbued with Catholicism, in its sonorous and theatrical quality. The bardic robes he drew on had always a touch of the purple.

Aubade

We woke together on a gusty dawn
in the dim house amid the level waste
and stared in anguish on the stretch of years
filled with grey dawn and ever-weeping wind.

for as the hour hung still 'twixt night and day
we whom the dark had drawn so close together
at that dead tide as strangers saw each other
strangers divided by a sea of years.

we might not weep out our passion of despair
but in lorn trance we gazed upon each other

and wonder'd what strange ways had brought our hands
together in that chamber of the west.

we felt the dumb compulsion of the hour
to wander forth in spirit on the wind
and drift far apart in undiscover'd realms
of some blank world where dawn for ever wept.

The grand cortège ...

The grand cortège of glory and youth is gone
flaunt standards, and the flood of brazen tone:
I alone linger, a regretful guest,
here where the hostelry has crumbled down,
emptied of warmth and life, and the little town
lies cold and ruin'd, all its bravery done,
wind-blown, wind-blown, where not even dust may rest.
No cymbal-clash warms the chill air: the way
lies stretch'd beneath a slanting afternoon,
the which no piled pyres of the slaughter'd sun,
no silver sheen of eve shall follow: Day,
ta'en at the throat and choked, in the huge slum
o' the common world, shall fall across the coast,
yellow and bloodless, not a wound to boast.
But if this bare-blown waste refuse me home
and if the skies wither my vesper-flight,
'twere well to creep, or ever livid night
wrap the disquiet earth in horror, back
where the old church stands on our morning's track,
and in the iron-entrellis'd choir, among
rust tombs and blazons, where an isle of light
is bosom'd in the friendly gloom, devise
proud anthems in a long forgotten tongue:
so cozening youth's despair o'er joy that dies.

Let us go down, the long dead night is done

Let us go down, the long dead night is done,
the dolorous incantation has been wrought;
soul, let us go, the saving word is won,
down from the tower of our hermetic thought.

See – for the wonder glimmers in the gates,
eager to burst the soundless bars and grace

the wistful earth, that still in blindness waits,
perfect with suffering for her Lord's embrace.

The spaces of the waters of the dawn
are spiritual with our transfigured gaze;
the intenser heights of morning, far withdrawn,
expect our dream to shine along their ways.

But speak the word! and o'er the adoring whole
straight from the marge of the perfected hours
sudden, large music through the vast, shall roll
a sea of light foaming with seedless flowers;

lilies that form on some ethereal wave,
still generate of the most ancient blue,
burst roses, rootless, knowing not the grave
nor yet the charnel thought by which they grew.

So we shall move at last, untortured powers,
and in white silence hear, as souls unborn,
our hymn given back by the eternal hours
singing together in the eternal morn.

The years that go to make me man

The years that go to make me man
this day are told a score and six
that should have set me magian
o'er my half-souls that struggle and mix.

But wisdom still remains a star
just hung within my aching ken,
and common prudence dwells afar
among contented homes of men.

In wide revolt and ruin tost
against whatever is or seems,
my futile heart still wanders lost
in the same vast and impotent dreams.

On either hand life hurries by
its common joy, its common mirth;
I reach vague hands of sympathy
a ghost upon this common earth.

The Wanderer

Quoniam cor secretum concupivi
  factus sum vagus inter stellas huius revelationis:
Atque annus peregrinationis meae
  quasi annus ventorum invisibilium.

When window-lamps had dwindled, then I rose
and left the town behind me; and on my way
passing a certain door I stopt, remembering
how once I stood on its threshold, and my life
was offer'd to me, a road how different
from that of the years since gone! and I had but
to rejoin an olden path, once dear, since left.
All night I have walk'd and my heart was deep awake,
remembering ways I dream'd and that I chose,
remembering lucidly, and was not sad,
being brimm'd with all the liquid and clear dark
of the night that was not stirr'd with any tide;
for leaves were silent and the road gleam'd pale,
following the ridge, and I was alone with night.
But now I am come among the rougher hills
and grow aware of the sea that somewhere near
is restless; and the flood of night is thinn'd
and stars are whitening. O, what horrible dawn
will bare me the way and crude lumps of the hills
and the homeless concave of the day, and bare
the ever-restless, ever-complaining sea?

* * *

Each day I see the long ships coming into port
and the people crowding to their rail, glad of the shore:
because to have been alone with the sea and not to have known
of anything happening in any crowded way,
and to have heard no other voice than the crooning sea's
has charmed away the old rancours, and the great winds
have search'd and swept their hearts of the old irksome thoughts:
so, to their freshen'd gaze, each land smiles a good home.
Why envy I, seeing them made gay to greet the shore?
Surely I do not foolishly desire to go
hither and thither upon the earth and grow weary
with seeing many lands and peoples and the sea:
but if I might, some day, landing I reck not where
have heart to find a welcome and perchance a rest,

I would spread the sail to any wandering wind of the air
this night, when waves are hard and rain blots out the land.

* * *

I am driven everywhere from a clinging home,
O autumn eves! and I ween'd that you would yet
have made, when your smouldering dwindled to odorous fume
close room for my heart, where I might crouch and dream,
of days and ways I had trod, and look with regret
on the darkening homes of men and the window-gleam,
and forget the morrows that threat and the unknown way.
But a bitter wind came out of the yellow-pale west
and my heart is shaken and fill'd with its triumphing cry:
You shall find neither home nor rest; for ever you roam
with stars as they drift and wilful fates of the sky!

* * *

Once I could sit by the fire hourlong when the dripping eaves
sang cheer to the shelter'd, and listen, and know that the woods drank full,
and think of the morn that was coming and how the freshen'd leaves
would glint in the sun and the dusk beneath would be bright and cool.

Now, when I hear, I am cold within: for my mind drifts wide
where the blessing is shed for naught on the salt waste of the sea,
on the valleys that hold no rest and the hills that may not abide:
and the fire loses its warmth and my home is far from me.

* * *

How old is my heart, how old, how old is my heart,
and did I ever go forth with song when the morn was new?
I seem to have trod on many ways: I seem to have left
I know not how many homes; and to leave each
was still to leave a portion of mine own heart,
of my old heart whose life I had spent to make that home
and all I had was regret, and a memory.
So I sit and muse in this wayside harbour and wait
till I hear the gathering cry of the ancient winds and again
I must up and out and leave the embers of the hearth
to crumble silently into white ash and dust,
and see the road stretch bare and pale before me: again
my garment and my home shall be the enveloping winds
and my heart be fill'd wholly with their old pitiless cry.

* * *

You, at whose table I have sat, some distant eve
beside the road, and eaten and you pitied me
to be driven an aimless way before the pitiless winds,
how much ye have given and knew not, pitying foolishly!
For not alone the bread I broke, but I tasted too
all your unwitting lives and knew the narrow soul
that bodies it in the landmarks of your fields,
and broods dumbly within your little seasons' round,
where, after sowing, comes the short-lived summer's mirth,
and, after harvesting, the winter's lingering dream,
half memory and regret, half hope, crouching beside
the hearth that is your only centre of life and dream.
And knowing the world how limitless and the way how long,
and the home of man how feeble and builded on the winds,
I have lived your life, that eve, as you might never live
knowing, and pity you, if you should come to know.

* * *

I cry to you as I pass your windows in the dusk;

Ye have built you unmysterious homes and ways in the wood
where of old ye went with sudden eyes to the right and left;
and your going was now made safe and your staying comforted,
for the forest edge itself, holding old savagery
in unsearch'd glooms, was your houses' friendly barrier.
And now that the year goes winterward, ye thought to hide
behind your gleaming panes, and where the hearth sings merrily
make cheer with meat and wine, and sleep in the long night,
and the uncared wastes might be a crying unhappiness.
But I, who have come from the outer night, I say to you
the winds are up and terribly will they shake the dry wood:
the woods shall awake, hearing them, shall awake to be toss'd and riven,
and make a cry and a parting in your sleep all night
as the wither'd leaves go whirling all night along all ways.
And when ye come forth at dawn, uncomforted by sleep,
ye shall stand at amaze, beholding all the ways overhidden
with worthless drift of the dead and all your broken world:
and ye shall not know whence the winds have come, nor shall ye know
whither the yesterdays have fled, or if they were.

* * *

Come out, come out, ye souls that serve, why will ye die?
or will ye sit and stifle in your prison-homes

dreaming of some master that holds the winds in leash
and the waves of darkness yonder in the gaunt hollow of night?
nay, there is none that rules: all is a strife of the winds
and the night shall billow in storm full oft ere all be done.
For this is the hard doom that is laid on all of you,
to be that whereof ye dream, dreaming against your will.
But first ye must travel the many ways, and your close-wrapt souls
must be blown thro' with the rain that comes from the homeless dark:
for until ye have had care of the wastes there shall be no truce
for them nor you, nor home, but ever the ancient feud;
and the soul of man must house the cry of the darkling waves
as he follows the ridge above the waters shuddering towards night,
and the rains and the winds that roam anhunger'd for some heart's warmth.
Go: tho' ye find it bitter, yet must ye be bare
to the wind and the sea and the night and the wail of birds in the sky;
go: tho' the going be hard and the goal blinded with rain
yet the staying is a death that is never soften'd with sleep.

* * *

Dawns of the world, how I have known you all,
so many, and so varied, and the same!
dawns o'er the timid plains, or in the folds
of the arm'd hills, or by the unsleeping shore;
a chill touch on the chill flesh of the dark
that, shuddering, shrinks from its couch, and leaves
a homeless light, staring, disconsolate,
on the drear world it knows too well, the world
it fled and finds again, its wistful hope
unmet by any miracle of night,
that mocks it rather, with its shreds that hang
about the woods and huddled bulks of gloom
that crouch, malicious, in the broken combes,
witness to foulnesses else unreveal'd
that visit earth and violate her dreams
in the lone hours when only evil wakes.

* * *

What is there with you and me, that I may not forget
but your white shapes come crowding noiselessly in my nights,
making my sleep a flight from a thousand beckoning hands?
Was it not enough that your cry dwelt in my waking ears
that now, seeking oblivion, I must yet be haunted

by each black maw of hunger that yawns despairingly
a moment ere its whitening frenzy bury it?
O waves of all the seas, would I could give you peace
and find my peace again: for all my peace is fled
and broken and blown along your white delirious crests!

* * *

O desolate eves along the way, how oft,
despite your bitterness, was I warm at heart!
not with the glow of remember'd hearths, but warm
with the solitary unquenchable fire that burns
a flameless heat deep in his heart who has come
where the formless winds plunge and exult for aye
among the naked spaces of the world,
far past the circle of the ruddy hearths
and all their memories. Desperate eves,
when the wind-bitten hills turn'd violet
along their rims, and the earth huddled her heat
within her niggard bosom, and the dead stones
lay battle-strewn before the iron wind
that, blowing from the chill west, made all its way
a loneliness to yield its triumph room;
yet in that wind a clamour of trumpets rang,
old trumpets, resolute, stark, undauntable,
singing to battle against the eternal foe,
the wronger of this world, and all his powers
in some last fight, foredoom'd disastrous,
upon the final ridges of the world:
a war-worn note, stern fire in the stricken eve,
and fire thro' all my ancient heart, that sprang
towards that last hope of a glory won in defeat,
whence, knowing not sure if such high grace befall
at the end, yet I draw courage to front the way.

* * *

The land I came thro' last was dumb with night,
a limbo of defeated glory, a ghost:
for wreck of constellations flicker'd perishing
scarce sustain'd in the mortuary air,
and on the ground and out of livid pools
wreck of old swords and crowns glimmer'd at whiles;
I seem'd at home in some old dream of kingship:

now it is clear grey day and the road is plain,
I am the wanderer of many years
who cannot tell if ever he was king
or if ever kingdoms were: I know I am
the wanderer of the ways of all the worlds,
to whom the sunshine and the rain are one
and one to stay or hasten, because he knows
no ending of the way, no home, no goal,
and phantom night and the grey day alike
withhold the heart where all my dreams and days
might faint in soft fire and delicious death:
and saying this to myself as a simple thing
I feel a peace fall in the heart of the winds
and a clear dusk settle, somewhere, far in me.

O white wind, numbing the world

O white wind, numbing the world
to a mask of suffering hate!
and thy goblin pipes have skirl'd
all night, at my broken gate.

O heart, be hidden and kept
in a half-light colour'd and warm,
and call on thy dreams that have slept
to charm thee from hate and harm.

They are gone, for I might not keep;
my sense is beaten and dinn'd:
there is no peace but a gray sleep
in the pause of the wind.

I said, This misery must end

I said, This misery must end:
Shall I, that am a man and know
that sky and wind are yet my friend,
sit huddled under any blow?
so speaking left the dismal room
and stept into the mother-night
all fill'd with sacred quickening gloom
where the few stars burn'd low and bright,
and darkling on my darkling hill
heard thro' the beaches' sullen boom
heroic note of living will

ring trumpet-clear against the fight;
so stood and heard, and rais'd my eyes
erect, that they might drink of space,
and took the night upon my face,
till time and trouble fell away
and all my soul sprang up to feel
as one among the stars that reel
in rhyme on their rejoicing way,
breaking the elder dark, nor stay
but speed beyond each trammelling gyre
till time and sorrow fall away
and night be wither'd up, and fire
consume the sickness of desire.

"BELLERIVE" (Joseph Tishler) 1871–1957

In an article on the Red Page of *The Bulletin* on 19 September 1912, the naïve poet Joseph Tishler, who chose the name of a Hobart suburb as his nom-de-plume, told some of his life story: "I first saw the light in Dunedin, New Zealand. And rank among the middle members of a large and respected family. My parents having located in vic. when I was an infant. I remembered nothing of My native land. I was sent to a State school at an early age, and although slow at learning, I evinced poetic signs, and would often visit the melbourne Cemetery to witness a pathetic burial. And read the inscriptions on the various Headstone's …

"Having read in *The Bulletin* and other journals stray verses by the Renowned Henry Lawson, Paterson And Lindsay Gordon, I recognised 'twould be folly and waste of time on my part to follow on the same trails as such clever Writer's of knowledge and Bush experience, and my ambition was to try to break new literary ground … I became a Wanderer, and carried the bluey throughout the backblocks of vic … being an Expert accordion player, I became popular with the Larrikin class, and to feed the pen, I attended their rowdy picnics and parties. I studied their sayings and style, was an eye witness to their Arguments and Brawls, and reconciled Em in trouble. under the veil of rorty Disguise I became acquainted with the Inhabitants of the city slums, and had the honour bestowed on me to mingle in their society."

During this vagabond phase of his life Bellerive "had a strong will power against evil temptation, and learned what ere I could under the veil of disguise, and withheld the honor of my parents name." He "wearied at last of roughish experience," and began selling shell necklaces to tourists in Hobart, but was ordered out of Launceston by the police "whom seemed to regard a poor starved human Being as a wild beast at large … As God's my witness, towards the close of the second week of my sufferings, a Melb. showman took pathetic compassion on Me, and shipped me Back to vic." where, at the time of the 1912 article, he was running a fancy goods stall (which he continued to do for many years in Melbourne's Queen Victoria Markets). His life "as taught me the bitter lesson – That half a loaf is better than none."

Bellerive sold brooms from door to door without much success, was treed by a bull, worked in a jam factory, was a wanderer, and eventually found happiness after a life of

> ... battle and struggle
> Like a sheep in the whirl of a flood,
> When I was clasped by the hand of affection
> By a daughter of Italian blood.

Bellerive and his wife then lived happily together:

> The pen in spare time is my hobby,
> While hers is the needle and thread.

Bellerive has been described by Douglas Stewart, who edited the only book of his poems, *The Book of Bellerive*, published in 1961 after Bellerive's death, as "the famous Poet Laureate of the Sydney *Bulletin*'s 'Answer to Correspondents'." This was a column of shame where the Literary Editor of the *Bulletin* made cutting comments about poets and others (identified by their initials or pseudonyms) who had submitted material that was rejected. Sometimes a particularly horrible verse or paragraph from the correspondent would be quoted and held up to ridicule. Bellerive's submissions were usually printed in full in the column, and – this was exceptional – he was paid. Bellerive's contributions began in 1908 (as "the Wasp") and ceased in 1953 and numbered over 300.The first nine poems in our Bellerive selection are from *The Book of Bellerive* and the remainder we took direct from the pages of the *Bulletin*. In "A Poet's Reply", "jackass" is a reference to the "laughing jackass" or kookaburra.

A Balloon Tragedy

As a balloon sailed thro' space
An aeronaut star
Attacked a student friend in
The swaying car
While above the clouds the
Huge balloon sailed
A fearful struggle between
The aeronauts prevailed
You've robbed me hissed the assailant
Of the woman I love
And I'll hurl you to eternity
By the saints above
Overpowered by the student
Was the aeronaut star
And hurled into space
From the swaying car.

The St. Singer

A wealthy bachelor was seated before a fire
In an hotel sitting room,
When the sound of a woman singing
Wafted out thro' the still night gloom;
Marble Halls was the song she sung
In the face of the drifting sleet,
And the bachelor listened with a saddened heart
To the poor singer in the street.
He opened the window of his cosy room,
And gazed down at the singer Below,
Whom sweetly rendered her pathetic song
And fell prostrate upon the snow.
He hurried down the stairs of the grand hotel
Where the lights did glitter and glare,
And made his way to the homeless girl
Shut out in the freezing air;
Fascinated by the outcast's charms
He rescued her from her piteous life,
Procured her comforts in the grand hotel
And made his lawful Wife.

Outcast Glue-Pot

Upon the refuge of a dust-bin
  In a narrow lane,
Lay a little glue-pot,
  Rusty from the rain.
I carried home the glue-pot,
  Not that I was mean,
To put it through a process
  With rag and kerosene.
I laid aside the glue-pot,
  For use some future time;
Then sat me down at twilight
  To pen my simple rhyme.

The Yachts of Hobart

The sailing yachts of Hobart,
  In beauteous array,
Present a charming picture
  On a summer day.

Tossing o'er the bosom
  Of the Derwent wide and free,
Followed by the prancing gulls,
  Bird rovers of the sea.
The sailing yachts of Hobart,
  In beauteous array,
Danceth o'er the waters
  Till the close of day.

A Rough Restaurant

A encounter ensued twixt –
  The cook and a waiter
I was struck on the neck
  With a hard-baked potatoe –
When a big pug –
  Waded into the brawl.
"Murder" and "police" an –
  Old woman did bawl.
A table went up and –
  Crockery went down
The proprietor did rave –
  With a diabolical frown,
From my chair I arose,
  With dignity quiet.
Disliking to be
  Mixed up in a riot.

Jam Factory

To try and earn an honest crust
  I was never known to shirk;
Storking plums and apricots
  In the factory was my work.
The pickers had their arguments,
  But remained the best of chums,
In the absence of the foreman
  Would skylark with the plums;
I was promoted from a picker
  To juggle greasy bins,
Assist in stacking cases
  And washing juicy tins;
Though humble were my wages,

I drifted on life's way,
And always had a shilling
For a concert or a play.

The Flying Rat

When the aeroplane reached
A height from the ground
The aviators were startled
By a gnawing sound.
When from their food
A rat did appear
Which realized danger
And trembled with fear.
From the edge of the 'plane,
In frantic despair,
With a squeak it leaped out
Into the misty air.

An Aged Man's Hideous Escapade

At the Victorian Home for the Aged and the Poor, Royal Park, April 8, 1909

A veteran sailor climbed up
On the garbled roof of the Home,
And along the parapets and tiles
Like cat did roam.
The warders endeavoured to capture
The daring climber bold,
Clad only in his nightshirt –
Upon the roof in the cold.
Letting forth a loud yell, like
A wild animal in pain,
The eccentric old joker
Scrambled down again.
He had not forgotten
His rough, dare devil ways
When afloat on the deep –
In his hardy young days.

Behind the Curtain of My Art

I dippeth my pen in silence,
My verses no longer are seen
Weekly as they were in the answers,

For years in The Bulletin.
A victim of fierce speculation
In defence I could only dare,
But never weakened nor trembled
In the thraldom of sad despair,
A mirthful clown of a circus
Who capers and rolls he's eyes
Wins more friends than a poet,
Be him ever so clever and wise.
I jotteth down verse in silence,
I'm snug in my little den,
Master of my gift from the cradle,
Wizard of ink, paper and pen.

Tumbler Pigeons

Acrobat birds of
Beauty and grace
Are tumbler pigeons, the
Wonder of space.
Attractive to view is
Their skyward flight
And aerial feats in
The evening light.
In clusters they circle,
And cloudward ascend,
Tumble and prance
And downward descend.
Acrobats birds of
Beauty and grace,
They frolic and float
Through boundless space.

Lines on a Jam Tin

Made by machinery for factory jam,
Label'ed and packed for sale
Sold by grocers for household use
Such is the jam tin's tale,
At a circus show some years ago
In a well-known country town
Music was played on old jam tins
By a clever eccentric clown.

The Dog Car

Weekly in our district wafts
  A shrill and yelling sound;
There's captures' wails and exits
  When the dog-car goes its round;
The council from its revenue
  Have motors up to date;
Only frail and mangy dogs
  Doth meet a tragic fate;
Feeling men and women dread
  The shrill and yelping sound,
Wafting from the captured brutes
  In the dog-car on its round.

A Poet's Reply

At a picnic party
  One Boxing Day
A sarcastic youth to
  Your humble did say,
"Lord Byron the Second,
  I know you won't fail,
Please write me a poem
  On a nightingale."
Realizing he wished to
  Be heard and seen,
I replied, "A jackass
  Is what you mean."

The Posey Queen

I require no stool to rest my feet
  Nor desk in my little Den;
I puff my pipe, or whistle a tune
  To the strokes of my common pen.
The past is dead, but memories live
  As the days did come and go,
I battled my way to the literary gate
  Like a sledge-dog through the snow.
I never muse in a doleful way,
  With my hands pressed to my head;
I can always write a poem or two
  Before I go to Bed.

I never await the posey queen
  To wave her wand o'er me.
I can scribble a verse on anything
  From an elephant to a Flea.
I have no fad for dainty words;
  My task I never shirk –
There's always a chance in a col. for the
  Poet who knows he's work.

JOHN SHAW NEILSON 1872–1942

John Shaw Neilson's parents were Scots, his father an immigrant. The eldest of five children, Neilson was born in South Australia in 1872. The family was always poverty-stricken, struggling to make a living on various selections in the Wimmera and Mallee regions of Victoria, hampered by poor soil, dust storms, rabbit plagues and drought. Neilson spent two and a half years at school before becoming an itinerant labourer. From the age of thirteen, his life was one of backbreaking work, as a road-mender, ditch-digger, quarryman, farmhand or fruit-picker, moving about Victoria. A congenital sight defect meant that, after his early thirties, he was unable to read for himself. Due to his poverty and his shyness, he never married, nor had any close relationships, although he always admired women.

As a boy, Neilson was influenced to write by his father, a self-educated poet. Most of Neilson's early work was destroyed in a mice plague that swept through Victoria in the 1890s. His later poetry had to be dictated to his brother or sisters, or to sometimes incredulous workmates, of an evening. Devaney's biography of Neilson has a story, recounted by the poet, of this kind of session: of a quarryman who had agreed to act as amanuensis, exclaiming "Jesus!" at regular intervals throughout the task, and warning, with real concern, that Jock was "off his onion".

Neilson's way of life contrasts utterly with the delicate, musical poetry he wrote, about children and colour, girls and light, and of some seemingly numinous thing, manifested through nature. He is a rare example in the modern world of a genuine primitive poet of quality – in the tradition of Burns, Clare and W. H. Davies. He was perhaps even more handicapped than they were and further removed from the stream of literature. It is claimed that Neilson knew from his youth only some old Scots and Irish songs, the poems of Burns and Hood, a little Coleridge, and *The Rubaiyat of Omar Khayyam* (the scepticism of which was to become more and more attractive to him as he grew older). Later, he heard or read isolated 19th-century poems and the bush balladists. More controversial is his possible exposure to the work of Emily Dickinson, some of which was very occasionally reprinted in the *Bulletin* at about the turn of the century. Also accessible to him from the *Bulletin*, which he and his father read whenever they could afford it, were essays about the French Symbolists, and examples of their work in translation. Neilson did not speak of these possible influences, and some admirers have claimed that his use of synaesthesia and colour symbolism, common in French Symbolist poetry, is entirely independent. This is not at all clear.

From the 1890s, when he began sending poems to the *Bulletin*, Neilson came under the mentorship of the paper's literary editor, A. G. Stephens, who published his work, edited it (though not always well, encouraging him to continue in his worst habits of archaism and sentimentality), brought it out in book form, and campaigned on its behalf. Their relationship lasted for nearly forty years. Neilson met "A. G." only once, in 1926, on a visit to Sydney. He was also introduced to Brennan during this time, and to other leading literary personalities of the city, at a dinner given for him. He recounted later how impressed he was that most of the conversation was in French, and remarked, innocently, that it seemed he was the only one present who did not understand the language. Neilson suffered several nervous breakdowns, as did other members of his family, in his case caused not only by the poverty, deaths and illnesses among them, but by his crises of religious belief. In 1928, when his health was failing, a position was found for him as a messenger with a government department in Melbourne. He died in 1942.

In this selection we have removed one poor stanza from "You, and Yellow Air" and another from "Eva Has Gone".

Neilson is admired above all other Australian poets by writers as remote from him as Peter Porter; for many, as for A. D. Hope, he has been "one of the beacons".

The Sundowner

I know not when this tiresome man
With his shrewd, sable billy-can
And his unwashed Democracy
His boomed-up Pilgrimage began.

Sometimes he wandered far outback
On a precarious Tucker Track;
Sometimes he lacked Necessities
No gentleman would like to lack.

Tall was the grass, I understand,
When the old Squatter ruled the land.
Why were the Conquerors kind to him?
Ah, the Wax Matches in his hand!

Where bullockies with oaths intense
Made of the dragged-up trees a fence,
Gambling with scorpions he rolled
His Swag, conspicuous, immense.

In the full splendour of his power
Rarely he touched one mile an hour,
Dawdling at sundown, History says,
For the Pint Pannikin of flour.

Seldom he worked; he was, I fear,
Unreasonably slow and dear;

Little he earned, and that he spent
Deliberately drinking Beer.

Cheerful, sorefooted child of chance,
Swiftly we knew him at a glance;
Boastful and self-compassionate,
Australia's Interstate Romance.

Shall he not live in Robust Rhyme,
Soliloquies and Odes Sublime?
Strictly between ourselves, he was
A rare old Humbug all the time.

In many a Book of Bushland dim
Mopokes shall give him greeting grim;
The old swans pottering in the reeds
Shall pass the time of day to him.

On many a page our Friend shall take
Small sticks his evening fire to make;
Shedding his waistcoat, he shall mix
On its smooth back his Johnny-cake.

'Mid the dry leaves and silvery bark
Often at nightfall will he park
Close to a homeless creek, and hear
The Bunyip paddling in the dark.

Break of Day

The stars are pale.
Old is the Night, his case is grievous,
His strength doth fail.

Through stilly hours
The dews have draped, with Love's old lavishness,
The drowsy flowers.

And Night shall die;
Already, lo! the Morn's first ecstasies
Across the sky.

An evil time is done.
Again, as someone lost in a quaint parable,
Comes up the Sun.

10 Limericks

An old lady at Tarranginnie
Took her son, most uncommonly skinny,
To the local M. D.
Who said, "Let me see,
Feed him up a bit, ma'm – half a guinea!"

Said a girl in the choir at Brim,
I know that the church lights are dim;
But there's not enough chaps,
That's the reason perhaps
I am so long in finding a hymn.

There was a young girl at McArthur
Who said to a man, Would you rather
Kiss me or my sister,
The mean wretch? – Oh Mister,
You mustn't – He's coming – That's Father.

There was an old Celt named McPhee
Who was drunk as an old Celt could be.
He would wear a kilt
And he wasn't well built.
If you look for yourself you can see.

A charming young lady named Brewster
Trimmed her hat with the head of a rooster.
When they asked, Can it crow?
She smiled and said, No –
It can't do that now, but it used to.

They were hanging a man up at Bright;
He had been a Temperance light.
When they showed him the rope
He said, I do hope
That it isn't inclined to get tight.

A cooking class girl at Sea Lake
Showed her father her very first cake.
When she pressed him to eat
He replied, No my sweet,
I must try and live on, for your sake.

A certain old maid at Port Victor
Had many strange pets to afflict her;
The kangaroos fought
With the emus she caught
And when she protested they kicked her.

There was a young lady named Gault
Exuberance was her main fault
If she came to church late
She would shock the sedate
By turning a swift somersault.

(Frank Neilson and Shaw Neilson)

There was a young lady named Dicker,
She gave the glad eye to the vicar.
She said, My dear friend!
Let us have a week-end
And both go away on the shicker!

You, and Yellow Air

I dream of an old kissing-time
  And the flowered follies there;
In the dim place of cherry-trees,
  Of you, and yellow air.

It was an age of babbling,
  When the players would play
Mad with the wine and miracles
  Of a charmed holiday.

Bewildered was the warm earth
  With whistling and sighs,

And a young foal spoke all his heart
  With diamonds for eyes.

You were of Love's own colour
  In eyes and heart and hair;
In the dim place of cherry-trees
  Ridden by yellow air.

It was the time when red lovers
  With the red fevers burn;
A time of bells and silver seeds
  And cherries on the turn.

Out of your eyes a magic
  Fell lazily as dew,
And every lad with lad's eyes
  Made summer love to you.

It was a reign of roses,
  Of blue flowers for the eye,
And the rustling of green girls
  Under a white sky.

I dream of an old kissing-time
  And the flowered follies there;
In the dim place of cherry-trees,
  Of you, and yellow air.

Love's Coming

Quietly as rosebuds
  Talk to the thin air,
Love came so lightly
  I knew not he was there.

Quietly as lovers
  Creep at the middle moon,
Softly as players tremble
  In the tears of a tune;

Quietly as lilies
  Their faint vows declare
Came the shy pilgrim:
  I knew not he was there.

Quietly as tears fall
  On a warm sin,

Softly as griefs call
  In a violin;

Without hail or tempest,
  Blue sword or flame,
Love came so lightly
  I knew not that he came.

Nimitybelle

Nimitybelle is a dear little town;
  Its trees are green and its homes are cosy;
The lads grow up and their dads grow down,
  The dames wax stout, and the girls are rosy.
The rest of the world is all very well,
But not important to Nimitybelle.

The cows are sleepy; the goats go slow;
  The horses know that nothing can matter;
Even the cocks have a careless crow,
  And one day dies and the next seems flatter.
The grocer casually hopes to sell
But no one worries in Nimitybelle.

Yet things do happen – they always will;
  The windmill works in the windy weather;
The lad with the shanghai loves to kill;
  The belle and her beau go out together.
The old men fish – and they sometimes tell
The tale of fishes in Nimitybelle.

A story of Love you ask … ah, yes!
  She was as bright as a dog-wood blossom
(She did the courting, I must confess);
  Her eyes were the eyes of a pert opossum.
I made a Madame of Mademoiselle,
And we rented a cottage in Nimitybelle.

May

Shyly the silver-hatted mushrooms make
  Soft entrance through,
And undelivered lovers, half awake,
  Hear noises in the dew.

Yellow in all the earth and in the skies,
  The world would seem

Faint as a widow mourning with soft eyes
  And falling into dream.

Up the long hill I see the slow plough leave
  Furrows of brown;
Dim is the day and beautiful; I grieve
  To see the sun go down.

But there are suns a many for mine eyes
  Day after day:
Delightsome in grave greenery they rise,
  Red oranges in May.

The Hour of the Parting

Shall we assault the pain?
  It is the time to part:
Let us of Love again
  Eat the impatient heart.

There is a gulf behind
  Dull voice and fallen lip,
The blue smoke of the mind,
  The gray light on the ship.

Parting is of the cold
  That stills the loving breath,
Dimly we taste the old
  The pitiless meal of Death.

The Orange Tree

The young girl stood beside me. I
  Saw not what her young eyes could see:
– A light, she said, not of the sky
  Lives somewhere in the Orange Tree.

– Is it, I said, of east or west?
  The heartbeat of a luminous boy
Who with his faltering flute confessed
  Only the edges of his joy?

Was he, I said, borne to the blue
  In a mad escapade of Spring
Ere he could make a fond adieu
  To his love in the blossoming?

– Listen! the young girl said. There calls
  No voice, no music beats on me;
But it is almost sound: it falls
  This evening on the Orange Tree.

– Does he, I said, so fear the Spring
  Ere the white sap too far can climb?
See in the full gold evening
  All happenings of the olden time?

Is he so goaded by the green?
  Does the compulsion of the dew
Make him unknowable but keen,
  Asking with beauty of the blue?

– Listen! the young girl said. For all
  Your hapless talk you fail to see
There is a light, a step, a call
  This evening on the Orange Tree.

– Is it, I said, a waste of love
  Imperishably old in pain,
Moving as an affrighted dove
  Under the sunlight or the rain?

Is it a fluttering heart that gave
  Too willingly and was reviled?
Is it the stammering at a grave,
  The last word of a little child?

– Silence! the young girl said. Oh, why,
  Why will you talk to weary me?
Plague me no longer now, for I
  Am listening like the Orange Tree.

Schoolgirls Hastening

Fear it has faded and the night:
  The bells all peal the hour of nine:
The schoolgirls hastening through the light
  Touch the unknowable Divine.

What leavening in my heart would bide!
  Full dreams a thousand deep are there:
All luminants succumb beside
  The unbound melody of hair.

Joy the long timorous takes the flute:
  Valiant with colour songs are born:
Love the impatient absolute
  Lives as a Saviour in the morn.

Get thou behind me, Shadow-Death!
  Oh ye Eternities, delay!
Morning is with me, and the breath
  Of schoolgirls hastening down the way.

The Evening is the Morning

To make my love more delicate
  I say into her eyes
The evening is the morning, dear,
  but in a sweet disguise.
The morning was too loud with light
  and the many birds would sing
Who but the thoughtless would exchange
  the Autumn for the Spring?

To make my love more beautiful
  I sing into her ear
'Tis not the morning that I love,
  it is the evening, dear:
No sweets of all the sweets we knew
  are sweet as those we know,
And tho' she sighs most heavily
  she says 'tis even so.

To make my love think happily
  I say the morning wine
Did much disturb thy maiden's heart
  and put a storm in mine:
The sunlight did so play with us
  what strength or sight had we?
And tho' her tears will come, she says
  I speak most faithfully.

I say to make my sweetheart laugh
  now all our work is done,
The evening is the morning, dear,
  we shall deceive the sun!
Her hair that once was summer heat
  is but a bloom in gray,

Still she will tell me Evening is
  the Morning that I say.

Love in Absence

When thou art gone but a little way
  I am in a cold fear:
The day like a long sickness is,
  And I count the moon a year.

When thou art gone but a little way
  I am in a deep alarm:
I cry, Oh God! her dear body,
  If it should come to harm!

When thou art gone and light is gone
  I fiercely wish thee near:
The day like a long sickness is,
  And I count the moon a year.

Now mournfully I dream I fall
  Where the uncouth shadows be:
I foot it on the mist – the heart
  Renounces liberty.

Eva Has Gone

The women they tell how it all began,
And the men that her face was sunny.
Eva has gone with the sailor-man;
She has taken the ready money.

She said "I am off in a leaky boat;
What a fool was I to marry!
But the ten-pound note and the five-pound note
Are easy enough to carry."

Her husband toiled as a slow man can
To put those notes together.
He had stuck to his work when many a man
Would never have faced the weather.

The sailor-man he was six foot high
And of the salt sea smelling.
On earth or in hell there was never a lie
That he was not proud of telling.

Some dark things out on the line she hung;
'Twas a fine warm day for drying.
Oh, cruel was she, for her child was young,
And the neighbours found it crying.

"Now," they said, "she has lost her all;
Not even her God can pity."
And they heavily talked of her dreadful fall
And her open shame in the city.

"She might have gone by the night," said they,
"When the lovers creep together.
'Twas a shameful way that she went by day,
Like a wild thing off the tether."

The women they speak of her laziness,
And the men that her mouth was honey.
Eva has gone with a sailor-man;
She has taken the ready money.

The women they say that her eyes were hard,
The men that her mouth was pretty;
And some will say they have gone to the Bush,
And some say into the City.

Her husband said as he worked one day
With his old mate in the quarry,
"The women, they make the worst of it;
And the sailor will soon be sorry."

Concerning Little Waitresses

As glad they are as butterflies,
Who walk upon the blue;
They come from heaven but I know not
Where they journey to.

They are as light as thistle-tops
That far above us blow;
I see – I see not – waitresses,
I know not where they go.

The Winter Sundown

They falter, they stay not
  To your eyes and mine,
The boatmen in violet
  On bays of wine.

Calm without sorrow,
  The peace without prayer:
All fear is folly in
  That country out there.

Many we mourn are out
  Seaward away;
Tears did they leave us
  As players who play.

The highlands, the hilltops,
  They make the heart bare,
Burned out with wishing
  For the country out there.

***

They stay not, they stay not,
  But your eyes and mine
Have boatmen in violet
  On bays of wine.

The Birds Go By

Westward at even ... yet never, never to die!
Surely they live as ever the laugh and the sigh:
After the fight and the fall, the defeat of the pilgrim,
    The birds go by.

No, not for dying like all the sweet flowers are they,
– Flowers giving hope to mankind on their little stay,
Failing only as love fails at the end of the day.

Green earth and water have gladdening out of their cry,
Lifting the eyes of the heart to the height of the sky:
I dream that they bear to the dead the thoughts of the living ...
    The birds go by.

The Diver

Each night I am diving;
'Tis a blue floor;
The dead men come lightly
And walk not ashore.

Each night I go diving.
I speak with dead men

But at sunrise come up to
The fields again.

I love the good light
More than the dim,
And there is scarlet
In the birds' hymn.

But at night I go diving.
Women walk there,
Yet no colour bides on
Old eyes and hair.

The strange, the unseemly
Wrap me around;
Old summer walks up
On the blue ground.

I who go diving
Talk with dead men;
At the sunrise I come up
To the fields again.

***

But I shall go diving
Someday in some year;
Shall I be listening then
Dead men to hear?

I shall look into
Great eyes of dead men,
But no more at sunrise
The fields again.

Sunday Evening

Homeward, still homeward
  The calm folk ride,
And the unsoiled children
  In dreams abide.

Homeward, still homeward
  Fond arms display
Flowers and calm children – 'tis
  A holy day.

The love will uphold them:
  Softly they bear

Green leaves and children with
  The falling hair.

As stars on the darkness
  Console the eye,
So do the deep children
  Bring down the sky.

As flowers at the nightfall
  Give silence fair,
So give the white children
  With falling hair.

The Ways of the Wildflower

It is but a wildflower untamed by man;
It is one of all outcasts of the berry clan.

It will not be staying where the good flowers abide;
It will be burning and crying on the bare hillside.

In the hopeless desert it will strive to grow;
It will not be the servant in a quiet row.

In the sweet garden it will make the moan;
It will be crying and crying to go out alone.

It will go to the dark lane, it will live in woe;
It will be in places where the weeds are ashamed to grow.

It will turn bitter all the heart of man;
It is the wild thing that grows with the berry clan.

Say This for Love

Say this for love, when the great summer time
Is gone, and only winter wisdoms blow:
Fiercely he burned, like some imperious rhyme,
Burned, and he burned, but would not let me go.

Say this: His ominous riddlings were so deep
I could not see, I knew not where he trod.
He did from out a thousand centuries creep,
As some insurgent enemy of God.

Say this for love: You who did smite to kill,
And you did lie, it was my soul to soil;
Dressed as a hatred you did flog me still,
Chained to the last insanities in toil.

Say this for love: Oh fire of love delay;
Love me and tell me all the lies you told,
When, a reproach to love, I feel my way
Dark to the springboard, whimpering at the cold.

JACK MATHIEU 1873–1949

Jack Mathieu was born in the Goulburn Valley, Victoria. He was a sailor, drover, digger and shearer, and lost his eyesight in north-west Queensland. He then lived in Brisbane for many years until his death. His published literary output is small: a few short stories and *Backblock Ballads and Lignum Lyrics*, an undated 58-page pamphlet of ballads (usually with a twist in the plot) and sentimental verses. "That Day at Boiling Downs" first appeared in *The Bulletin* in 1899. "Driving Irish tandem" means walking.

That Day at Boiling Downs

He was driving Irish tandem, but perhaps I talk at random –
I'd forgotten for a moment you are not all mulga bred;
What I mean's he had his swag up through his having knocked his nag up;
He had come in off the Cooper – anyhow that's what he said.

And he looked as full of knowledge as a thirty-acre college
As he answered to the question – "How's things look the way you come?"
"Well, they *were* a trifle willing for a bit. There's been some killing;
In fact, *I*'m the sole survivor of the district ... mine's a rum!"

Then we all got interested in the chap as he divested
Himself of a fat puppy that he carried in his shirt;
But he said no more until he had put down his swag and billy,
And had taken off his bluchers just to empty out the dirt.

Bits of cork were tied with laces round his hat in many places,
Out of which he gave the puppy some refreshment, and began –
"Sammy Suds was boundary-riding, quite content and law-abiding,
Till he bought some reading-matter one day off a hawker man.

"Then he started to go ratty, and began to fancy that he
Was an Injun on the warpath; so he plaited a lassoo,
Shaved and smeared his face with raddle, and knocked up a greenhide saddle,
After creeping on his belly through the grass a mile or two.

"Then he decked himself in feathers, and went out and scalped some wethers –
Just to give himself a lesson in the sanguinary art;

Sammy then dug up the hatchet, chased a snake but couldn't catch it,
Killed his dog, lassooed a turkey, scalped the cat and made a start.

"And he caused a great sensation when he landed at the station;
And the boss said, 'Hullo! Sammy, what the devil's up with you?'
'I am Slimy Snake the Snorter! Wretched pale-face, crave not quarter!'
He replied, and with a shot-gun nearly blew the boss in two.

"Next, the wood-and-water joey fell a victim to his bowie,
And the boss's weeping widow got a gash from ear to ear;
And you should have seen his guiver when he scalped the bullock-driver
And made openings for a horse-boy, servant-maid, and overseer.

"Counting jackeroos and niggers, he had put up double figures,
When ensued his awful combat with a party of new-chums,
All agog to do their duty, with no thought of home or beauty –
But he rubbed them out as rapid as a schoolboy would his sums.

"Out across the silent river, with some duck-shot in his liver,
Went the store-man, and a lassooed lady left in the same boat.
Sam then solved the Chinese question – or at least made a suggestion –
For he dragged one from a barrel by the tail and cut his throat.

"But, with thus the job completed, Sammy he got overheated
And dropped dead of apoplexy: I felt better when he did!
For I'd got an awful singeing while I watched this mulga engine
Doing all that I've related – through a cracked brick oven lid.

"And when now I find men strangled, or I come across the mangled
Corpses of a crowd of people or depopulated towns,
Or even a blood-stained river, I can scarce repress a shiver,
For my nerves were much affected that day out on Boiling Downs."

"RITA SUNYASEE"

"Rita Sunyasee" published this poem in the *Bulletin* on 17 November 1904. She – if it is a she, which is most likely – published another poem in the *Bulletin* earlier in the year entitled "Dad's Cheque" (28 January 1904), also "Our Jim" on 16 May 1918. Her gem-like "Bush Courtin'" prefigures C. J. Dennis, but "Rita Sunyasee" has a lighter touch.

Bush Courtin'

When the milkin' music's ended, and the big cans stacked away,
An' the poddies have done drinkin', an' the neddies chew their hay,
Then I eat my snack while dressin', for Dad's always on the growl,
An' the cow-hairs from my love-lock brush, ere to my tryst I prowl.

Through my doss-room windy leavin', for the old man's ears are cocked,
I negotiate the pickets as the garden gate is locked;
For I hear the bittern's boomin' from the lily beds afar,
And my heart-strings are a tingle to old Cupid's sweet guitar.

Jake is waitin' in the timber, where the lace-like shadows fall;
'Tis his signal that is stealin' like the mopoke's croakin' call;
Then he clasps me to his shirt-front with a bushman's brawny squeeze,
An' his whiskers sweep my freckles like soft tangles off the trees!

We discuss the price of sorghum; will there be a rise in wheat?
(Just a crumb or two of love-talk, for this fare is awful sweet!)
An' Jake's gettin' in his taters – half a patch a day he digs –
While his paddies feed themselves now; an' he's goin' to sell his pigs!

Then we let the world go hang there, as together close we cling
An' swear we'll love each other whate'er prices Fate may bring
(Jake's old trusty dog is watchin' where the shadows dim the track),
An' into Life's old, grey portmanteau a thousand joys we pack.

How the saucy moonbeams mock us, an' the grey bats tauntin' fly –
Seems they know that we are wanted, that we're courtin' on the sly;
We'll be married "after harvest" if the wheat will only rise,
An' Dad will get what he's expectin' – that's a mighty big surprise!

C. J. DENNIS 1876–1938

C. J. Dennis was born in Auburn, South Australia, but was to become, like Barry Humphries, a quintessential Melbourne poet. As a small boy, he was superintended by four prim and pious maiden aunts. Alec Chisholm, in the introduction to *Selected Verse*, describes the aunts as "developing a rural edition of Lord Fauntleroy. They dressed the boy in a starchy suit, with Eton collar, peaked cap, and patent leather shoes, rounded off with brown gloves and a cane, and they trained him to raise that cap to every woman about the place." This made Dennis a target for the lads of the village, and the experience "may well have been soul-searing." Chisholm sees Dennis's love of larrikins and his later apotheosis as "Australia's Laureate of the Larrikin" as a reaction to these early experiences. He discarded his "stately" Christian name "Clarence" and called himself "Den". Dennis's education was at Catholic colleges. He began publishing poetry at 19. Following a number of occupations, including clerk and barman, Dennis depended for most of his life on journalism to support him and his wife when the income from his popular verse was insufficient.

His first book, *Backblock Ballads and Other Verses* (1913), was published when he was very poor and living in an abandoned timberman's hut. The book was not a success. However overnight he became a household name with *The Songs of a Sentimental Bloke*, published in 1915. This is a vernacular verse novel, comprising 14 poems and a glossary. The "Bloke" is the narrator and tells the simple story of falling in love with Doreen, who plays coy at first; the Bloke has to give up his roughhouse ways. They court, marry and have a son. We have chosen the second poem, "The Intro", and the fifth, "The Play", Dennis's most famous piece. In a preface to the book, Henry Lawson wrote of its "exquisite humour" and "brilliance", and how when episodes from *The Bloke* were run in the *Bulletin* they "brightened up many dark days for me." "The Play" was written by Dennis after he saw a young couple holding hands at a performance of *Romeo and Juliet*. They were out of their element, but were obviously swept away by the emotion. Dennis spoke with the young man during the interval. By 1976, 57 editions of *The Bloke* had been published in the English-speaking world, with 285,000 copies sold. It has been filmed (twice), made into a stage play (1922) and a musical (1961).

Dennis published a sequel to *The Sentimental Bloke* and a number of other books of popular verse, including some children's poetry. Many anthologists either leave Dennis out, or represent him with less characteristic poems. Often there is too much sugar in the tea. But Dennis had an expert ear for the vernacular and was a brilliant verse technician. In *The Sentimental Bloke* the rhymes and rhythm are perfect, there are no inversions and the narrative flows naturally through a variety of demanding stanza patterns, as easily as eating cake.

Dennis struggled with asthma later in life, and was a small man, described as having a "slight but enduring physique". In "An Old Master" the enfeebled old bullock driver, Dad McGee, who lived in a hut, may be an unwitting self-portrait. We leave readers to decode some more obvious items of the Bloke's argot in "The Intro" and "The Play". However Dennis's glossary to *The Sentimental Bloke* is a treasure-house of linguistic curios, and is a poem in itself. Dennis, like Dad McGee, loved language, and this love is at the heart of his achievement as a poet. We therefore reproduce those parts of the glossary to *The Sentimental Bloke* that are relevant and less obvious.

Back the barrer. – To intervene without invitation.

Block. – The head. **To lose** or **do in the block.** – To become flustered; excited; angry; to lose confidence.

Bloke. A male adult of the genus homo.

Bonzer, boshter, bosker. – Adjectives expressing the superlative of excellence.

Brums. – Tawdry finery (from Brummagen – Birmingham).

Bundle, to drop the. – To surrender; to give up hope.

Cheque, to pass in one's. – To depart this life.

Chuck off. – To chaff; to employ sarcasm. [Dennis does not explain "like a phonergraft" which follows this expression. The implication is that the Bloke is in the habit of employing sarcasm on women repeatedly as though he is a disc spinning around on a phonograph or gramophone.]

Click. – A clique; a "push".

Cliner. – A young unmarried female.

Dash, to do one's dash. – To reach one's Waterloo.

Dawg (dog.) – A contemptible person. **To put on dawg.** – To behave in an arrogant manner.

Duck, to do a. – To depart in haste.

Fluff, a bit of. – A young female person.

Gazob. – A fool; a blunderer.

Glarssy. – The glassy eye; a glance of cold disdain. **The Glassey Alley.**

– The favourite; the most admired.

Gorspil-cove. – A Minister of the Gospel.

Guy, to do a. – To retire.

Guyver. – Make-believe.

Intro. – Introduction; knock-down. q.v.

Joes. – Melancholy thoughts.

Lash. – Violence.

Lid. – The hat. **To dip the lid.** – To raise the hat [a sign of politeness or approbation when Dennis was writing].

Little Lon. – Little Lonsdale Street, Melbourne, Australia [a street with an evil reputation when Dennis was writing].

Lurk. – A plan of action; a regular occupation.

Maul. – To lay hands upon, either violently or with affection.

Moniker. – A name; a title; a signature.

Orfis (office). – A warning; a word of advice; a hint.

Oricle (oracle), to work the. – To secure desired results.

Peach. – A desirable young woman; "fresh as a peach."

Pot, the old. – The male parent (from "Rhyming Slang," the "old pot and pan" – the "old man.").

Push. – A company of rowdy fellows gathered together for ungentle purposes.

Rabbit, to run the. – To convey liquor from a public-house.

Ribuck. – An interjection signifying assent.

Smooge.– To flatter or fawn; to bill and coo.

Sprag. – To accost truculently.

'Struth. – An emaciated oath.

Tart. – A young woman (contraction of sweetheart).

Toff. – An exalted pers.

Treat, a. – Excessively, abundantly.

Tom. – A girl.

Tug. – An uncouth fellow; a hardy rogue.

Wet, to get. – To become incensed; ill-tempered.

The Intro

'Er name's Doreen ... Well, spare me bloomin' days!
You could 'a' knocked me down wiv 'arf a brick!
  Yes, me, that kids meself I know their ways,
  An' 'as a name for smoogin' in our click!
I jist lines up an' tips the saucy wink.
But strike! The way she piled on dawg! Yer'd think
  A bloke was givin' back-chat to the Queen ...
    'Er name's Doreen.

I seen 'er in the markit first uv all,
Inspectin' brums at Steeny Isaacs' stall.
  I backs me barrer in – the same ole way
  An' sez, "Wot O! It's been a bonzer day.

'Ow is it fer a walk?" ... Oh, 'oly wars!
The sorter *look* she gimme! Jest becors
  I tried to chat 'er, like you'd make a start
    Wiv *any* tart.

An' I kin take me oaf I wus perlite,
An' never said no word that wasn't right,
  An' never tried to maul 'er, or to do
  A thing yeh might call crook. Ter tell yeh true,
I didn't seem to 'ave the nerve – wiv 'er.
I felt as if I couldn't go that fur,
  An' start to sling off chiack like I used ...
    Not intrajuiced!

Nex' time I sighted 'er in Little Bourke,
Where she was in a job. I found 'er lurk
  Wus pastin' labels in a pickle joint,
  A game that – any'ow, that ain't the point.
Once more I tried ter chat 'er in the street,
But, bli'me! Did she turn me down a treat!
  The way she tossed 'er 'ead an' swished 'er skirt!
    Oh, it wus dirt!

A squarer tom, I swear, I never seen,
In all me natchril, than this 'ere Doreen.
  It wer'n't no guyver neither; fer I knoo
  That any other bloke 'ad Buckley's 'oo
Tried fer to pick 'er up. Yes, she wus square.
She jist sailed by an' lef' me standin' there
  Like any mug. Thinks I, "I'm out o' luck,"
    An' done a duck.

Well, I dunno. It's that way wiv a bloke.
If she'd ha' breasted up ter me an' spoke,
  I'd thort 'er jist a commin bit er fluff,
  An' then fergot about 'er, like enough.
It's jist like this. The tarts that's 'ard ter get
Makes you all 'ot to chase 'em, an' to let
  The cove called Cupid get an 'ammer-lock,
    An' lose yer block.

I know a bloke 'oo knows a bloke 'oo toils
In that same pickle found-ery. ('E boils
  The cabbitch storks or somethink.) Anyway,
  I gives me pal the orfis fer to say

'E 'as a sister in the trade 'oo's been
Out uv a job, an' wants ter meet Doreen;
  Then we kin get an intro, if we've luck.
    'E sez, "Ribuck."

O' course we worked the oricle; you bet!
But, struth, I ain't recovered frum it yet!
  'Twas on a Saturdee, in Colluns Street,
  An' – quite be accident, o' course – we meet.
Me pal 'e trots 'er up an' does the toff –
'E allus wus a bloke fer showin' off.
  "This 'ere's Doreen," 'e sez. "This 'ere's the Kid."
    I dips me lid.

"This 'ere's Doreen," 'e sez. I sez "Good day."
An', bli'me, I 'ad nothin' more ter say!
  I couldn't speak a word, or meet 'er eye.
  Clean done me block! I never been so shy
Not since I wus a tiny little cub,
An' run the rabbit to the corner pub –
  Wot time the Summer days wus dry an' 'ot –
    Fer my ole pot.

I dunno 'ow I done it in the end.
I reckerlect I arst ter be 'er friend;
  An' tried ter play at 'andies in the park,
  A thing she wouldn't sight. Aw, it's a nark!
I gotter swear when I think wot a mug
I must 'a' seemed to 'er. But still I 'ug
  That promise that she give me fer the beach.
    The bonzer peach!

Now, as the poit sez, the days drag by
On ledding feet. I wish't they'd do a guy.
  I dunno 'ow I 'ad the nerve ter speak
  An' make that meet wiv 'er fer Sundee week!
But, strike! It's funny wot a bloke'll do
When 'e's all out ... She's gorn, when I come-to.
  I'm yappin' to me cobber uv me mash ...
    I've done me dash!

'Er name's Doreen .... An' me – that thort I knoo
The ways uv tarts, an' all that smoogin' game!
  An' so I ort; fer ain't I known a few?
  Yet some'ow ... I dunno. It ain't the same.

I carn't tell wot it is; but, all I know,
I've dropped me bundle – an' I'm glad it's so.
  Fer when I come ter think uv wot I been ....
    'Er name's Doreen.

The Play

"Wot's in a name?" – she sez ... An' then she sighs,
An' clasps 'er little 'ands, an' rolls 'er eyes.
"A rose," she sez, "be any other name
Would smell the same.
Oh, w'erefore art you Romeo, young sir?
Chuck yer ole pot, an' change yer moniker!"

Doreen an' me, we bin to see a show –
The swell two-dollar touch. Bong tong, yeh know.
A chair apiece wiv velvit on the seat;
A slap-up treat.
The drarmer's writ be Shakespeare, years ago,
About a barmy goat called Romeo.

"Lady, be yonder moon I swear!" sez 'e.
An' then 'e climbs up on the balkiney;
An' there they smooge a treat, wiv pretty words
Like two love-birds.
I nudge Doreen. She whispers, "Ain't it grand!"
'Er eyes is shining an' I squeeze 'er 'and.

"Wot's in a name?" she sez. 'Struth, I dunno.
Billo is just as good as Romeo.
She may be Juli-er or Juli-et –
'E loves 'er yet.
If she's the tart 'e wants, then she's 'is queen,
Names never count ... But ar, I like "Doreen!"

A sweeter, dearer sound I never 'eard;
Ther's music 'angs around that little word,
Doreen! ... But wot was this I starts to say
About the play?
I'm off me beat. But when a bloke's in love
'Is thorts turns 'er way, like a 'omin' dove.

This Romeo 'e's lurkin' wiv a crew –
A dead tough crowd o' crooks – called Montague.
'Is cliner's push – wot's nicknamed Capulet –
They 'as 'em set.

Fair narks they are, jist like them back-street clicks,
Ixcep' they fights wiv skewers 'stid o' bricks.

Wot's in a name? Wot's in a string o' words?
They scraps in ole Verona wiv the'r swords,
An' never give a bloke a stray dog's chance,
An' that's Romance.
But when they deals it out wiv bricks an' boots
In Little Lon., they're low, degraded broots.

Wot's jist plain stoush wiv us, right 'ere to-day,
Is "valler" if yer fur enough away.
Some time, some writer bloke will do the trick
Wiv Ginger Mick,
Of Spadger's Lane. *'E'll* be a Romeo,
When 'e's bin dead five 'undred years or so.

Fair Juli-et, she gives 'er boy the tip.
Sez she: "Don't sling that crowd o' mine no lip;
An' if you run agin a Capulet,
Jist do a get."
'E swears 'e's done wiv lash; 'e'll chuck it clean.
(Same as I done when I first met Doreen.)

They smooge some more at that. Ar, strike me blue!
It gimme Joes to sit an' watch them two!
E'd break away an' start to say good-bye,
An' then she'd sigh
"Ow, Ro-me-o!" an' git a strangle-holt,
An' 'ang around 'im like she feared 'e'd bolt.

Nex' day 'e words a gorspil cove about
A secret weddin'; an' they plan it out.
'E spouts a piece about 'ow 'e's bewitched:
Then they git 'itched ...
Now, 'ere's the place where I fair git the pip!
She's 'is for keeps, an' yet 'e lets 'er slip!

Ar! but 'e makes me sick! A fair gazob!
E's jist the glarsey on the soulful sob,
'E'll sigh and spruik, a' 'owl a love-sick vow –
(The silly cow!)
But when 'e's got 'er, spliced an' on the straight
'E crools the pitch, an' tries to kid it's Fate.

Aw! Fate me foot! Instid of slopin' soon
As 'e was wed, off on 'is 'oneymoon,

'Im an' 'is cobber, called Mick Curio,
They 'ave to go
An' mix it wiv that push o' Capulets.
They look fer trouble; an' it's wot they gets.

A tug named Tyball (cousin to the skirt)
Sprags 'em an' makes a start to sling off dirt.
Nex' minnit there's a reel ole ding-dong go –
'Arf round or so.
Mick Curio, 'e gets it in the neck,
"Ar rats!" 'e sez, an' passes in 'is check.

Quite natchril, Romeo gits wet as 'ell.
"It's me or you!" 'e 'owls, an' wiv a yell,
Plunks Tyball through the gizzard wiv 'is sword,
'Ow I ongcored!
"Put in the boot!" I sez. "Put in the boot!"
"'Ush!" sez Doreen ... "Shame!" sez some silly coot.

Then Romeo, 'e dunno wot to do.
The cops gits busy, like they allwiz do,
An' nose around until 'e gits blue funk
An' does a bunk.
They wants 'is tart to wed some other guy.
"Ah, strike!" she sez. "I wish that I could die!"

Now, this 'ere gorspil bloke's a fair shrewd 'ead.
Sez 'e "I'll dope yeh, so they'll *think* yer dead."
(I tips 'e was a cunnin' sort, wot knoo
A thing or two.)
She takes 'is knock-out drops, up in 'er room:
They think she's snuffed, an' plant 'er in 'er tomb.

Then things gits mixed a treat an' starts to whirl.
'Ere's Romeo comes back an' finds 'is girl
Tucked in 'er little coffing, cold an' stiff,
An' in a jiff,
'E swallows lysol, throws a fancy fit,
'Ead over turkey, an' 'is soul 'as flit.

Then Juli-et wakes up an' sees 'im there,
Turns on the water-works an' tears 'er 'air,
"Dear love," she sez, "I cannot live alone!"
An' wiv a moan,
She grabs 'is pockit knife, an' ends 'er cares ...
"*Peanuts or lollies!*" sez a boy upstairs.

An Old Master

We were cartin' laths and palin's from the slopes of Mount St Leonard,
  With our axles near the road-bed and the mud as stiff as glue;
And our bullocks weren't precisely what you'd call conditioned nicely,
  And meself and Messmate Mitchell had our doubts of gettin' through.

It had rained a tidy skyful in the week before we started,
  But our tucker-bag depended on the sellin' of our load;
So we punched 'em on by inches, liftin' 'em across the pinches,
  Till we struck the final section of the worst part of the road.

We were just congratulatin' one another on the goin',
  When we blundered in a pot-hole right within the sight of goal,
Where the bush-track joins the metal. Mitchell, as he saw her settle,
  Justified his reputation at the peril of his soul.

We were in a glue-pot, certain – red and stiff and most tenacious;
  Over naves and over axles – waggon sittin' on the road.
"'Struth," says I, "they'll never lift her. Take a shot from Hell to shift her.
  Nothin' left but to unyoke 'em and sling off the blessed load."

Now, beside our scene of trouble stood a little one-roomed humpy,
  Home of an enfeebled party by the name of Dad McGee.
Daddy was, I pause to mention, livin' on an old-age pension
  Since he gave up bullock-punchin' at the age of eighty-three.

Startled by our exclamations, Daddy hobbled from the shanty,
  Gazin' where the stranded waggon looked like some half-foundered ship.
When the state o' things he spotted, "Looks," he says, "like you was potted,"
  And he toddles up to Mitchell. "Here," says he, "gimme that whip."

Well! I've heard of transformations; heard of fellers sort of changin'
  In the face of sudden danger or some great emergency;
Heard the like in song and story and in bush traditions hoary,
  But I nearly dropped me bundle as I looked at Dad McGee.

While we gazed he seemed to toughen; as his fingers gripped the handle
  His old form grew straight and supple, and a light leapt in his eye;
And he stepped around the waggon, not with footsteps weak and laggin',
  But with firm, determined bearin', as he flung the whip on high.

Now he swung the leaders over, while the whip-lash snarled and volleyed;
  And they answered like one bullock, strainin' to each crack and clout;
But he kept his cursin' under till old Brindle made a blunder;
  Then I thought all Hell had hit me, *and the master opened out.*

And the language! Oh, the language! Seemed to me I must be dreamin';
  While the wondrous words and phrases only genius could produce

Roared and rumbled, fast and faster, in the throat of that Old Master –
  Oaths and curses tipped with lightning, cracklin' flames of fierce abuse.

Then we knew the man before us was a Master of our callin';
  One of those great lords of language gone for ever from Outback:
Heroes of an ancient order; men who punched across the border;
  Vanished giants of the sixties; puncher-princes of the track.

Now we heard the timbers strainin', heard the waggon's loud complainin',
  And the master cried triumphant, as he swung 'em into line,
As they put their shoulders to it, lifted her, and pulled her through it:
  "That's the way we useter do it in the days o' sixty-nine!"

Near the foot of Mount St Leonard lives an old, enfeebled party
  Who retired from bullock-punchin' at the age of eighty-three.
If you seek him folk will mention, merely, that he draws the pension;
  But to us he looms a Master – Prince of Punchers, Dad McGee!

Hist!

Hist! . . . . . . Hark!
The night is very dark,
And we've to go a mile or so
Across the Possum Park.

Step . . . . . . light,
Keeping to the right;
If we delay, and lose our way,
We'll be out half the night.
The clouds are low and gloomy. Oh!
It's just begun to mist!
We haven't any overcoats
And – Hist! . . . . . . Hist!

(Mo . . . . . . poke!)
Who was that that spoke?
This is not a fitting spot
To make a silly joke.

Dear . . . . . . me!
A mopoke in a tree!
It jarred me so, I didn't know
Whatever it could be.
But come along; creep along;
Soon we shall be missed.
They'll get a scare and wonder where
We – Hush! . . . . . . Hist!

Ssh! . . . . . . Soft!
I've told you oft and oft
We should not stray so far away
Without a moon aloft.

Oo! . . . . . . Scat!
Goodness! What was that?
Upon my word, it's quite absurd,
It's only just a cat.
But come along; haste along;
Soon we'll have to rush,
Or we'll be late and find the gate
Is – Hist! . . . . . . Hush!

(Kok! . . . . . . Korrock!)
Oh! I've had a shock!
I hope and trust it's only just
A frog behind a rock.

Shoo! . . . . . . Shoo!
We've had enough of you;
Scaring folk just for a joke
Is not the thing to do.
But come along, slip along –
Isn't it a lark
Just to roam so far from home
On – Hist! . . . . . . Hark!

Look! . . . . . . See!
Shining through the tree,
The window-light is glowing bright
To welcome you and me.

Shout! . . . . . . Shout!
There's someone round about,
And through the door I see some more
And supper all laid out.
Now, Run! Run! Run!
Oh, we've had such splendid fun –
Through the park in the dark,
As brave as anyone.

Laughed, we did, and chaffed, we did,
And whistled all the way,
And we're home again! Home again!
Hip . . . . . . Hooray!

HUGH McCRAE 1876–1958

Hugh McCrae was born in Melbourne. His father was a high civil servant, a poetaster, and a person of apparently great charm who entertained in his home all the leading literary figures of the day. McCrae, after leaving school early, decided on a career as a freelance writer and illustrator and became a member of the artists' club, the Prehistoric Order of Cannibals. At 21 he met Norman Lindsay, then an art student. Lindsay, three years the junior, always acknowledged the debt of his graphic art and painting to McCrae's verse, with its historical pantomime and whimsical caricatures of Greek mythology. McCrae and Lindsay can each be seen as influenced by the *fin de siècle* paganism of the *Yellow Book*, but with the strange addition of an Australian healthiness; of a jaunty, larrikin quality.

At about the same time as Lindsay, McCrae moved to Sydney in 1901, immediately after marrying. He settled with his wife's parents, wealthy graziers who had recently sold their country property. Lindsay remembered visiting him at that time: "We usually found him lolling on the back veranda, very hearty and gay, but suffering, he assured us, from a peculiar physical infirmity. If he ventured beyond the front gate, he lost his equilibrium and fell down ... Nearly all the *Satyrs and Sunlight* poems were written in a burst of inspiration at that Wahroonga home." Lindsay saw in McCrae what he called "a gift, the capacity of idleness without the stress of thought." McCrae and his wife later shared a house with the Lindsays in Lavender Bay, on Sydney Harbour.

With no money or work in Australia, McCrae went to the United States in 1914, and barely survived in New York, taking minor roles in plays and selling his illustrations. Returning to Melbourne, he played the lead in the silent film *The Life's Romance of Adam Lindsay Gordon* (1916). In 1922 McCrae and his family went back to Sydney, where he remained for the rest of his life, except for the early 1930s when he lived in Camden, outside the city.

McCrae had a family of three daughters. His constant womanising, at least in his younger days, is said to have given his wife "a worn and worried look". McCrae's preferred occupation between his brief outbursts of inspiration was practical joking. His contribution to the First World War, while employed as a decoder at the censor's office, was to spend "most of his time driving its officials distracted, by devising evidence of German espionage", with fake telephone calls in Teutonic accents, messages in coded gibberish, and letters arranging assignations after midnight. Unworldly, always impecunious, McCrae was immensely popular amongst his friends. Douglas Stewart remembered him visiting the *Bulletin* offices and standing in the room "tall and handsome as the sunlight".

McCrae and Lindsay (the latter as theorist) were the source of the Sydney school of Nietzschean "vitalists", associated with the magazine *Vision*. Both insisted that poetry should only deal in clear images, which embody life-enhancing emotions, uncontaminated by abstract thought. McCrae's work was an affront to the wowsers, the conventional, the narrowly mercantile in the society of his time. His sensuousness, his "pure poetry", prepared the way for the acceptance of modernity in his main disciple, Kenneth Slessor. Slessor has written of "I Blow My Pipes" as "that shout of joy ... an uprush of clamour and elation" marred only by the abstract adjective "splendid" in the fourth line (*Bread and Wine*, 1970). He pointed out that McCrae must be imagined against "the bagatelle blown up and overvalued and enshrined of *Lays from an Austral Lyre* and *Warblings from the Bush* and *Dewdrops from the Manse*" [actual book titles] and for contemporary readers "the sudden apparition of *Satyrs and Sunlight* in 1909 ... must have seemed like the passage of a flight of fiery parakeets." The Catholic poet Vincent Buckley was to adopt a severer view of Sydney vitalism as "anti-tragic, anti-spiritual and ultimately anti-human" and described the last three lines of "I Blow My Pipes" as "McCrae's inane shout" (*Essays on Poetry*, 1969).

Song of the Rain

Night,
And the yellow pleasure of candle-light ...
Old brown books and the kind, fine face of the clock
Fogged in the veils of the fire – its cuddling tock.

The cat,
Greening her eyes on the flame-litten mat;
Wickedly, wakeful she yawns at the rain
Bending the roses over the pane,
And a bird in my heart begins to sing
Over and over the same sweet thing –

Safe in the house with my boyhood's love
And our children asleep in the attic above.

Colombine

Exit the ribald clown –
  Enter like bubbling wine,
Lighter than thistledown,
  Sweet little Colombine.

Whisht! and behold the game,
  Long eyes and pointed chin
Paler than candleflame,
  At her feet Harlequin.

Look how their shadows run,
  Swift as she flies from him! –
Moths in the morning sun,
  Out of a garden dim.

Faint through the fluttering
  Fall of a flute divine,
Softly the 'cellos sing
  "Colombine, Colombine."

. . . . . .

Softly the 'cellos sing:
"Colombine" ...
"Colombine" ...

I Blow My Pipes

I blow my pipes, the glad birds sing,
The fat young nymphs about me spring,
The sweaty centaur leaps the trees
And bites his dryad's splendid knees;
The sky, the water, and the earth
Repeat aloud our noisy mirth ...
Anon, tight-bellied bacchanals,
With ivy from the vineyard walls,
Lead out and crown with shining glass
The wine's red baby on the grass.

. . . . . .

I blow my pipes, the glad birds sing,
The fat young nymphs about me spring,
I am the lord,
I am the lord,
I am the lord of everything!

June Morning

The twisted apple, with rain and magian fire
  Caught in its branches from the early dawn,
I, from my bed, through the fogged pane see and desire
  Of its sharp sweetness, something. Green the lawn
And stiff with pointed spears of daffodils run wild:
  The sluggard sun draws the drowned daphne back to life –
And all the drowsy doves, brown sparrows, husband, wife,
  Are stirring on the housetops – child to early child
Cooeeing and calling; blind windows open eyes,
  And in the air the bitter fragrance floats
Of someone's gardener's pipe. I will arise
  And in the stinging shower forget gold motes,
Thick pillows, blankets, books; travel the wholesome road
  And give my body to the sun.

The Watchers

We sat beside the water
  And we saw the ringdoves fly

Against the cloudy castles
  Of the Genie in the sky ...

And, from the hazel copses,
  Where the night was coming in,
We heard the sound of voices
  And of harp and violin ...

We saw the hounds and huntsmen
  Go in couples past the moon,
With giant shadows waving
  On the motionless lagoon.

They went into the distance,
  Through faded flower and tree,
Like thin transparent phantoms,
  On an ancient tapestry.

. . . . . .

Then, silver-sweet and flowing
  Across the sleeping corn
We heard their bugles blowing
  Amid the stars at morn.

The Mouse

All Christmas night upon the shelf;
  Among the apples yellow-faced,
There played a pretty maiden mouse
  Divinely slim and very chaste.

Who, when I held my candle up,
  Did twink her little eyes at me ...
So mad, so bright, so mischievous;
  I thought of *you*, dear Dorothy!

Ambuscade

Or the black centaurs, statuesquely still,
  Whose moving eyes devour the snuffling mares,
And watch with baneful rage their nervous strides
  Whip the dark river white, lest unawares
Some danger seize them ... Statuesquely still,
  Behind the waving trellises of cane,
The centaurs feel their hearts – besieged with blood –
  Stagger like anvils when the sled-blows rain

Shower on shower in persistent flood ...

Now Cornus, he, the oldest of the group,
  With many wounds, strong arms, and clay-rolled hair,
Coughs for a signal to his dreadful troop,
  And springs, wide-fingered, from the crackling lair.
Loudly the victims neigh, they thrash the stream,
  They tear their foemen's beards with frothy teeth,
And fill the banks with sparkling spires of steam
  That heavenward roll in one tumultuous wreath.

Within the branches of an ancient oak,
  A mother-satyr, sleeping with her young,
Smit by a sudden stone, upbraids the stroke,
  Then turns to see from whence it has been flung.
Scarce does she view the cursed centaur-pack,
  Than, standing clear, she blows a whistle shrill,
Which, like an echo, straight comes flying back
  Louder and louder down the empty hill.

A roar of hooves, a lightning-view of eyes
  Redder than fire, of long, straight whistling manes,
Stiff crests, and tails drawn out against the skies,
  Of angry nostrils webbed with leaping veins,
The stallions come ...

Enigma

I watch her fingers where they prance
Like little naked women, tango-mad,
Along the keys, a cup-shot dance –
Music, who'll say, more joyous or more sad?

A mystery ... but not so strange
As she, Enigma is her pretty name;
And though she smiles, her veiled eyes range
Through tears of melancholy and shame.

She laughs and weeps ... Is it because
Only tonight she gave herself to me?
The new bud frightened to be glad ...
The child's first vision of the insatiate sea.

P. J. HARTIGAN ("John O'Brien") 1878–1952

Monsignor Patrick Hartigan was born in Yass, New South Wales, the fourth of nine children of parents who came from County Clare, Ireland. His early schooling was in Yass, where his father had a transport business. He studied for the priesthood at St Patrick's College, Manly, a vast stone palace of a seminary, overlooking the southern end of Manly beach. Ordained in 1903, Hartigan was appointed to Albury, where, ahead of his time, he demonstrated a sympathy with other faiths. In 1910 he was appointed Inspector of Schools for Goulburn Diocese, and moved to a hamlet, Thurgoona.

The next year Father Pat, as he was known, began a sustained love affair with the motor car. He purchased a second-hand Renault – the first of nine cars he owned at various times, including two Hudsons, a Buick and a Packard. Not long after he bought the Renault, a dying Irishman, Jack Riley was brought forty miles across the mountains to Hickey's Hut near Khancoban. Riley asked for a priest. Because Father Pat had the Renault, the parish priest at Albury asked him to make the hundred-mile journey, which would otherwise have taken a week. After two days of driving, opening and shutting gates, Hartigan and John (Joker) Byrne, whom he had taken along, located the hut. Once the last rites had been administered, Hartigan, to be friendly, recited Banjo Paterson's "The Man from Snowy River". There was a moment of silence, and Hartigan asked if he'd been offensive. The bushmen who were present said no. It was an exploit of the dying man, Jack Riley, on which the famous ballad was based.

Hartigan became parish priest at the inland town of Narrandera in 1917, where he remained until 1944. The local milkman, named O'Brien, was reputed to water down his milk. Hartigan joked that his own poetics efforts were watered-down too, so he took "John O'Brien" as his pen name. His book, *Around the Boree Log and Other Verses*, was first published in 1921 and reprinted many times. A posthumous volume of later verse was published. "Said Hanrahan" is one of the most famous poems written in Australia.

Said Hanrahan

"We'll all be rooned," said Hanrahan
In accents most forlorn
Outside the church ere Mass began
One frosty Sunday morn.

The congregation stood about,
Coat-collars to the ears,
And talked of stock and crops and drought
As it had done for years.

"It's lookin' crook," said Daniel Croke;
"Bedad, it's cruke, me lad
For never since the banks went broke
Has seasons been so bad."

"It's dry, all right," said young O'Neil,
With which astute remark
He squatted down upon his heel
And chewed a piece of bark.

And so around the chorus ran
"It's keepin' dry, no doubt."
"We'll all be rooned," said Hanrahan,
"Before the year is out.

"The crops are done; ye'll have your work
To save one bag of grain;
From here way out to Back-o'-Bourke
They're singin' out for rain.

"They're singin' out for rain," he said,
"And all the tanks are dry."
The congregation scratched its head,
And gazed around the sky.

"There won't be grass, in any case,
Enough to feed an ass;
There's not a blade on Casey's place
As I came down to Mass."

"If rain don't come this month," said Dan,
And cleared his throat to speak –
"We'll all be rooned," said Hanrahan,
"If rain don't come this week."

A heavy silence seemed to steal
On all at this remark;
And each man squatted on his heel,
And chewed a piece of bark.

"We want an inch of rain, we do,"
O'Neil observed at last;
But Croke "maintained" we wanted two
To put the danger past.

"If we don't get three inches, man,
Or four to break this drought,
We'll all be rooned," said Hanrahan,
"Before the year is out."

In God's good time down came the rain;
And all the afternoon

On iron roof and window-pane
It drummed a homely tune.

And through the night it pattered still,
And lightsome, gladsome elves
On dripping spout and window-sill
Kept talking to themselves.

It pelted, pelted all day long,
A-singing at its work,
Till every heart took up the song
Way out to Back-O'-Bourke.

And every creek a banker ran,
And dams filled overtop;
"We'll all be rooned," said Hanrahan,
"If this rain doesn't stop."

And stop it did, in God's good time:
And spring came in to fold
A mantle o'er the hills sublime
Of green and pink and gold.

And days went by on dancing feet,
With harvest-hopes immense,
And laughing eyes beheld the wheat
Nid-nodding o'er the fence.

And, oh, the smiles on every face,
As happy lad and lass
Through grass knee-deep on Casey's place
Went riding down to Mass.

While round the church in clothes genteel
Discoursed the men of mark,
And each man squatted on his heel,
And chewed his piece of bark.

"There'll be bush-fires for sure, me man,
There will, without a doubt;
We'll all be rooned," said Hanrahan,
"Before the year is out."

FRANK WILMOT ("Furnley Maurice")
1881–1942

Frank Wilmot was born in the Melbourne suburb of Richmond, the son of a pioneer of the Australian socialist movement. He became a printer, bookseller and in his last decade the manager of Melbourne University Press. He adopted the pen name "Furnley Maurice" to disguise his identity from the editor of the literary "Red Page" of the *Bulletin*, A. G. Stephens, who was set against him. Wilmot was on the fringe of the Victorian Socialist Party. He campaigned against conscription in World War I and his heavily rhetorical 15-part poem "To God: From the Warring Nations" expresses his pacifism. A tendency to 19th-century bombast may reflect his admiration for his mentor, the poet Bernard O'Dowd. A more constructive influence was modern English and American poetry. As a bookseller, Wilmot had access to contemporary poets such as Yeats and the Georgians, e. e. cummings, Pound and Sandburg.

Wilmot was stranded between the Victorian romanticism of his youth and modernism. His best longer poem, "The Victoria Markets Recollected in Tranquility" shows the influence of T. S. Eliot's "Prufrock". While Eliot was preoccupied with the spiritual decay of the West, Wilmot's concerns were more immediate: disparities of wealth worried him and he had an aesthetic preoccupation about the deadening effect of modern materialism. We have omitted some of Part II and the entirety of III, IV and V of this poem, as in them he casts aside modernist influences to make pronouncements such as "Grace is the power:/ Only vision can flower/ Into immortal song." To clarify some references in this poem: John Batman founded Melbourne in 1835 and entered into a "treaty" with local Aboriginals to lease their land, quickly repudiated by the colonial authorities; the butcher's old-style scales have a large circular face with a "finger-point" indicating the weight; "turksheads" are pumpkins; "two-toothed lamb" is a lamb so young it has only its first two teeth; "Plymouth Rocks" are a breed of poultry.

Some may think the last line of "1914" "But pity to the hearts of men no more" an exaggeration, but it must have felt that way to many observers after the optimism of the *belle époque*.

1914

The sparrow has gone home into the tree;
And the belled cattle, vague and pensive-eyed,
Drowse in the twilight; to the red cliffside
Comes but a faded murmur of the sea.
Comes down the night; comes down reluctantly
The mist upon the hill whence soon shall glide
A pale and bashful moon; with arms spread wide
Affrighted pixies seek the dark from me.

These shall return: the mountains and the haze,
The blue lobelias ledging all the lawns,
The pixies, the lost roads and the sun-blaze,
These waters surge to-morrow to this shore –

All these things shall return with other dawns
But pity to the hearts of men no more.

from The Victoria Markets Recollected in Tranquility

I

Winds are bleak, stars are bright,
Loads lumber along the night:
Looming, ghastly white,
A towering truck of cauliflowers sways
Out of the dark, roped over and packed tight
Like faces of a crowd of football jays.

The roads come in, roads dark and long,
To the knock of hubs and a sleepy song.
Heidelberg, Point Nepean, White Horse,
Flemington, Keilor, Dandenong,
Into the centre from the source.

Rocking in their seats
The worn-out drivers droop
When dawn stirs in the streets
And the moon's a silver hoop;
Come rumbling into the silent mart,
To put their treasure at its heart,
Waggons, lorries, a lame Ford bus,
Like ants along the arms of an octopus
Whose body is all one mouth; that pays them hard
And drives them back with less than a slave's reward.

When Batman first at Heaven's command
Said, "This is the place for a peanut-stand."
It must have been grand!

II

"Cheap to-day, lady; cheap to-day!"
Jostling water-melons roll
From fountains of Earth's mothering soul.
Tumbling from box and tray
Rosy, cascading apples play
Each with a glowing auriole
Caught from a split sun-ray.
"Cheap to-day, lady, cheap to-day."
Hook the carcases from the dray!

(Where the dun bees hunt in droves
Apples ripen in the groves.)

An old horse broods in a Chinaman's cart
While from the throbbing mart
Go cheese and celery, pears and jam
In barrow, basket, bag or pram
To the last dram the purse affords –
Food, food for the hordes.

Shuffling in the driven crush
The souls and the bodies cry,
Rich and poor, skimped and flush,
"Spend or perish, buy or die!"

Food, food for the hordes!
Turksheads tumble on the boards.

There's honey at the dairy produce stall
Where the strung saveloys festooning fall;
Yielding and yellow, the beautiful butter blocks
Confront the poultryman's plucked Plymouth Rocks.
The butcher is gladly selling,
Chopping and slaughtering, madly yelling.
A bull-like bellow for captured sales;
A great crowd surges around his scales.

Slap down the joint!
The finger-point
Wobbles and comes alive,
Springs round to twenty and back to five.

No gracious burbling, nor arts to please,
No hypocritical felicities.
Buy and be damned to you! Sell and be damned also!
Decry the goods, he'll tell you where to go!

To him Creation's total aim
Is selling chops to a doubting dame.
And what will matter his steaks and joints,
The underdone and the overdone,
On the day when the old Earth jumps the points
And swings into the sun?

Along the shadows furtive, lone,
The unwashed terrier carries his week-end bone.
An old horse with a pointed hip

And dangling disillusioned under-lip
Stands in a harvest-home of cabbage leaves
And grieves.
A lady by a petrol case,
With a far-off wounded look in her face
Says, in a voice of uncertain pitch,
"Muffins" or "crumpets," I'm not sure which.
A pavement battler whines with half a sob,
"Ain't anybody got a bloody bob?"
Haunted by mortgages and overdrafts
The old horse droops between the shafts.
A smiling Chinaman upends a bag
And spills upon the bench with thunder-thud
(A nearby urchin trilling the newest rag)
Potatoes caked with loamy native mud.

Andean pinnacles of labelled jam.
The melting succulence of two-toothed lamb.
The little bands of hemp that truss
The succulent asparagus
That stands like tiny sheaves of purple wheat
Ready to eat!
Huge and alluring hams and rashered swine
In circular repetitive design.
Gobbling turkeys and ducks in crates,
Pups in baskets and trays of eggs;
A birdman turns and gloomily relates
His woes to a girl with impossible legs.

When Batman first at Heaven's command
Stuck flag-staffs in this sacred strand ...
We'll leave all that to the local band.

Rabbits skinned in a pink nude row,
Little brown kidneys out on show;
"Ready for the pot, mum, ready to bake!"
Buy them, devour them for pity's sake –

. . . .

"Cheap to-day, lady, cheap to-day."
Slimy fish slide off the tray.
Women pondering with a sigh –
"Spend or perish, buy or die!"
Packed with babies and Brussels sprouts,

It's a ricketty pram for a woman to shove –
But tell me, lady, whereabouts
Is the long leisure of love?

Winterlight

Oft have I seen at evening by the lake
The swans sail past the willow-hooded boat,
Where broken light and spreading ripples make
A comet-train behind them as they float.

I have absorbed great artistry; song has wrought
Its magic upon me; often I have come
Out of a trance of passionate reading fraught
With power of vision to draw the faint hills home.

These and their company take me, magic, immense;
Yet in the morning equivalent wonders unfold
When the sun pours through the breaks in a paling fence
To stencil a frosted pavement with jagged gold.

Whenever I have ...

Whenever I have, in all humility, moved
Amid dire forests of fact, unproved and overproved,
Then only the incomprehensible thing has vividness of hue
And only the unutterable is true.

There's weariness in the columned and tabular shame
Of elaborate amplification of law half-discerned
Which from their thrones of authority the hooded doctors declaim.
So I light my path with a candle lit from the altar that burned
In the deep arbours of vision, remote and untended.
And there I return for solace to things only apprehended,
The uncapturable, the indefinable thing, the unlearned.

FREDERIC MANNING 1882–1935

Frederic Manning was born in Sydney, into a wealthy Australian Catholic family of Irish origin, the son of a politician, Sir William Patrick Manning. He was asthmatic and educated at home. In 1898 Manning went to England with his tutor, who became a vicar in South Lincolnshire. Manning came back to Australia in 1900 and finally settled in England in 1903. He became known in literary circles and was friendly with figures such as William Rothenstein, Max Beerbohm, Richard Aldington and Ezra Pound. Pound praised his poetry highly and the two were close. Manning was a reviewer for *The Spectator*. When war began, his first attempts to enlist were rejected for medical reasons. He was finally accepted into the King's Light Shropshire Infantry and fought as a private at the Somme in 1916. The following year he was posted to Ireland where he was court-martialled for drunkenness. He resigned from the army in 1918, his reason being "dislike of the pretensions of the officer class". Much of his remaining life he spent in the Bull Hotel, Bourne. When he travelled in Europe, his asthma required that he take along two oxygen cylinders and an aide. In 1932, in poor health, he returned to Australia. Two years later he went back to England and died not long afterwards. Manning was an aesthete, in manner, in the '90s style; an "exquisite" who served in the trenches with the common soldiers.

In 1929 Manning published his literary masterpiece, *The Middle Parts of Fortune*, in a limited edition anonymously because of concerns about obscenity. Now one of the most famous novels to come out of World War I – Ernest Hemingway called it "the greatest novel of modern warfare" – it was written reluctantly and with much effort. In 1930 an expurgated version, *Her Privates We*, was published. The eight poems selected here show an ability to cut to the quick of the experience described, demonstrating the influence of Imagism. Pound thought "Kore" a better work than anything by his friend W. C. Williams.

"Kore" is another name for Persephone, an earlier title of the poem, the goddess of fertility. She was abducted by Hades (Pluto), the King of the Underworld, returning to the upper world in the warm seasons, and with winter descending again to become Queen of the Underworld. One of the meanings of "garth" is a hedge and "stack" is a haystack. A "limber" is the dismantled frame of a gun carriage, with an axle and two wheels.

Kore

Yea, she hath passed hereby, and blessed the sheaves,
And the great garths, and stacks, and quiet farms,
And all the tawny, and the crimson leaves.
Yea, she hath passed with poppies in her arms,
Under the star of dusk, through stealing mist,
And blessed the earth, and gone, while no man wist.

With slow, reluctant feet, and weary eyes,
And eye-lids heavy with the coming sleep,
With small breasts lifted up in stress of sighs,
She passed, as shadows pass, among the sheep;
While the earth dreamed, and only I was ware
Of that faint fragrance blown from her soft hair.

The land lay steeped in peace of silent dreams;
There was no sound amid the sacred boughs.
Nor any mournful music in her streams:
Only I saw the shadow on her brows,
Only I knew her for the yearly slain,
And wept, and weep until she come again.

Grotesque

These are the damned circles Dante trod,
Terrible in hopelessness,
But even skulls have their humour,
An eyeless and sardonic mockery:
And we,
Sitting with streaming eyes in the acrid smoke,
That murks our foul, damp billet,
Chant bitterly, with raucous voices
As a choir of frogs
In hideous irony, our patriotic songs.

The Face

Out of the smoke of men's wrath,
The red mist of anger.
Suddenly,
As a wraith of sleep,
A boy's face, white and tense,
Convulsed with terror and hate,
The lips trembling …

Then a red smear, falling …
I thrust aside the cloud, as it were tangible,
Blinded with a mist of blood.

The face cometh again
As a wraith of sleep:
A boy's face, delicate and blonde,
The very mask of God,
Broken.

Relieved

(Guillemont)

We are weary and silent;
There is only the rhythm of marching feet
Though we move tranced to keep it,
As clockwork toys.

But each man is alone in this multitude;
We know not the world in which we move,
Seeing not the dawn, earth pale and shadowy,
Level lands of tenuous grays and greens,
For our eyeballs have been seared with fire.

Only we have our secret thoughts,
Our sense floats out from us delicately apprehensive
To the very fringes of our being,
Where light drowns.

The Sign

We are here in a wood of little beeches:
And the leaves are like black lace
Against a sky of nacre.

One bough of clear promise
Across the moon.

It is in this wise that God speaketh unto me.
He layeth hands of healing upon my flesh,
Stilling it in an eternal peace,
Until my soul reaches out myriad and infinite hands
Towards him,
And is eased of its hunger.

And I know that this passes:
This implacable fury and torment of men,
As a thing insensate and vain:
And the stillness hath said unto me,
Over the tumult of sounds and shaken flame,
Out of the terrible beauty of wrath,
I alone am eternal.

One bough of clear promise
Across the moon.

Transport

(Courcelles)

The moon swims in milkiness,
The road glimmers curving down into the wooded valley,
And with a clashing and creaking of tackle and axles
The train of limbers passes me, and the mules
Splash me with mud, thrusting me from the road into puddles,
Straining at the tackle with a bitter patience,
Passing me …
And into a patch of moonlight,
With beautiful curved necks and manes,
Heads reined back, and nostrils dilated,
Impatient of restraint,

Pass two grey stallions,
Such as Oenetia bred;
Beautiful as the horses of Hippolytus
Carven on some antique frieze.
And my heart rejoices seeing their strength in play,
The mere animal life of them,
Lusting,
As a thing passionate and proud.

Then again the limbers and grotesque mules.

The Trenches

Endless lanes sunken in the clay,
Bays, and traverses, fringed with wasted herbage,
Seed-pods of blue scabious, and some lingering blooms;
And the sky, seen as from a well,
Brilliant with frosty stars.
We stumble, cursing, on the slippery duck-boards.
Goaded like the damned by some invisible wrath,
A will stronger than weariness, stronger than animal fear,
Implacable and monotonous.

Here a shaft, slanting, and below
A dusty and flickering light from one feeble candle
And prone figures sleeping uneasily,
Murmuring,
And men who cannot sleep,
With faces impassive as masks,
Bright, feverish eyes, and drawn lips,
Sad, pitiless, terrible faces,
Each an incarnate curse.

Here in a bay, a helmeted sentry
Silent and motionless, watching while two sleep,
And he sees before him
With indifferent eyes the blasted and torn land
Peopled with stiff prone forms, stupidly rigid,
As tho' they had not been men.

Dead are the lips where love laughed or sang,
The hands of youth eager to lay hold of life,
Eyes that have laughed to eyes,
And these were begotten,
O Love, and lived lightly, and burnt

With the lust of a man's first strength: ere they were rent,
Almost at unawares, savagely; and strewn
In bloody fragments, to be the carrion
Of rats and crows.

And the sentry moves not, searching
Night for menace with weary eyes.

Leaves

A frail and tenuous mist lingers on baffled and intricate branches;
Little gilt leaves are still, for quietness holds every bough;
Pools in the muddy road slumber, reflecting indifferent stars;
Steeped in the loveliness of moonlight is earth, and the valleys,
Brimmed up with quiet shadow, with a mist of sleep.

But afar on the horizon rise great pulses of light,
The hammering of guns, wrestling, locked in conflict
Like brute, stone gods of old struggling confusedly;
Then overhead purrs a shell, and our heavies
Answer, with sudden clapping bruits of sound,
Loosening our shells that stream whining and whimpering precipitately,
Hounding through air athirst for blood.

And the little gilt leaves
Flicker in falling, like waifs and flakes of flame.

"BRIAN VREPONT" (B. A. Truebridge) 1882–1955

Brian Vrepont (his pseudonymous surname is a French-sounding adaptation of his actual surname) was born Benjamin Arthur Truebridge in Melbourne and became a music teacher, at first privately, and then with the Conservatorium at the University of Melbourne, where his instrument was the violin. He left Melbourne in 1920 and became a goldminer in Queensland, a masseur, a busker and in the early 1940s an employee at Angus & Robertson's bookshop in Sydney. While he was in Brisbane, he was a member of the group, including Clem Christesen, which in 1940 founded the magazine *Meanjin*. He was a tall, lean, suntanned man. There is an appealing restless, discontented, romantic tone to his poetry, as he argues with himself.

The Net Menders

I came upon them by a strip of sea,
In a drizzle of rain mending their fishing-net,
Four swift brown hands, and lean with industry,
Shuttling the thin twine skilfully in–out, repairing the fret
Of rock-jag, shark-tooth and thresh;

He, tense as a mackerel, strong and agile,
Sea-eyed and grim as a rock, turned, and his smile
Was as the wonder of sunshine on sea-rock,
His fingers harping the net-mesh;
She on the sea-side, facing the land, took stock
Of me leisurely nearing, through half-shut eyes.
"Defence," I thought; but her mouth relaxed, went sweet
And soft as a sea-flower, her hands' enterprise
On the sea-side of the breaks in the net
Rippling the strings of the two-sided harp o' the sea,
And I thought, "Here is where sea-melodies meet,
Mending the breakage of earth-and-sea-fret,"
And the strange great grace of simplicity came on me.

If they had angers in them, these two by the sea,
Not in the two days dwelt with them,
Watching the shuttle flying, the flat corks tied,
And the strong boat pitch-caulked for battle with the sea,
Was flaw apparent in the gem;
Their poverty, too real for pride to hide,
Gave them no envy, not even in the lamp-light
And shadows of our talk,
Not when the net was trailed and netted nought
Save weed, nor when I spoke, that unforgettable night
We fought the tide, and drifted home star-caught,
And I spoke of the hawk
Now in the dark vanished, that all day long
Circled and soared and plunged on innocence; "Cruel life!" I cried
But my cry crossed over the woman's song,
Over the zither of the boat cutting the brine, and died,
And the man said, "It is life,"
And the boat gritted the waiting sand
With sound of a cleansing knife,
And we slept, at life's command.

ETHEL ANDERSON 1883–1958

Ethel Anderson was born in Warwickshire, England, the eldest child of two Australians. Her father was a "squatter", the holder of a large tract of pastoral land. She was brought up in Sydney and on her grandfather's station, near Picton, New South Wales. "At Rangamatty", a series of "Bucolic Eclogues", recalls her childhood, and we have included two of these, "The Household" and "Mariana's Dairy". Aged 21, she married 36-year-old Major Austin Anderson in 1904, in

Bombay, India. They lived there until 1914 and "adored many things about India. She accompanied Austin (usually riding) – whether he was shooting bears or marching with his battery – from the remote North-West Frontier to the Himalayan foothills" (*The Australian Dictionary of Biography*). In 1907 their daughter was born.

With the outbreak of war in 1914, her husband went to serve in France. He survived the war and the family remained in England for ten years, where she attended drawing classes and began painting murals in tempera. In 1924 her husband, now a Brigadier, retired from the army and they settled on Sydney's North Shore. Her husband was private secretary to a succession of governors. She became friendly with modernist painters of that era and promoted their work. A group of which she was a member painted jewel-like murals on the wall of the Children's Chapel in the crypt of St James, King Street, Sydney. Ethel Anderson wrote that their aim was to "give the tiny room the brilliance of a page from the *Book of Kells*". As well as her activities as a writer and artist, Anderson was a member of the general council of the Girl Guides' Association. When her husband died in 1949, she was left with very little means, which is hinted at in some of her later poems, but managed to support herself with her writing.

She published two volumes of verse, *Squatter's Luck* (Melbourne, 1942, and a second enlarged edition, 1954) and *Sunday at Yarralumla* (1947) as well as four collections of essays and short stories, which drew on her life in India, England and Australia. Her work appeared in venues such as the *Spectator*, *Punch* and the *Cornhill Magazine* in England, in the American *Atlantic Monthly*, and in the *Sydney Morning Herald* and *Bulletin*.

Ethel Anderson is one of Australia's most underrated poets. She is absent from many anthologies (including our previous Heinemann anthology). One reason for her neglect is that she did not write a large volume of poetry. Another may be the range of her activities. Some admirers of her art and stories are unaware of her poetry. Another reason is that unlike Patrick White and Judith Wright, who were also both from the squattocracy, she did not reject her family background and wrote happily about it.

In the preface to the first edition of *Squatter's Luck* she wrote: "In these poems I write of life as an Australian sees life ... The Australian system of ethics is more closely allied to that of the ancient Greeks than to the beliefs and practices of the British stock in which this country originated ... Australians are, at heart, half-pagan ... They have ... a short memory and an Epicurean delight in the present – all attributes more Attic than English!"

She wrote poetry like a painter, with vividly coloured images, and often using a large canvas. Like the painters of her era, who were trained in life classes, her poetry is that of someone who was classically educated. It uses a variety of verse forms: for instance, "Flood" is in sapphics. She could also write exquisite miniatures, such as the tiny elegy for her husband "Sleeping Soldier". In her very deaf widowhood she used a large silver ear-trumpet, around which she twined a scarf of coloured silk to match her dress.

Afternoon in the Garden

Put the sun a thought below his prime
Shake the light across the apple-tree.

Let the shadow lengthen on the lawn.

Dent a dimple in a passing cloud.
Show a flight of field-fares on the wing.
Fling a wedge-tailed swallow in the height.

Run an azure ribbon through the wheat.
Where the willows linger by the stream
Dip their weeping tendrils in the blue.

Right beyond the hazy rim of sight
Swathe the amber grasses on the plain.
Lie the folded mountains in a ring.

Hark! The happy tap of bat and ball!
Beat of flitting feet across the court.
Laughter in the precincts of the sun.

See! bright figures flit between the trees!
One picks apples. Someone pats a horse.
Eight play tennis. (Let the Navy win.)

Time, you rogue, be still a little while,
Space, be kind, a moment keep your place,
Call King Joshua, let the sun stand still.

Good King Joshua's dead and turned to clay.
I, evoking pictures from the past,
Do again what lordly Joshua did.

Flood (*from* Squatter's Luck)

From thick clouds over the black Warrumbungles,
And wracked, far-travelling Tambourine Mountains,
Red-earthed Jugiongs, steep Picton Razorbacks,
Rock-pierced, ice-weathered, snow-tossed Kosciusko,
        Autumnal sharp rains inundate the paddocks;

Infect with mildew the silk-tasselled maize-cobs,
Hurt more than seven years' drought the pastures,
Defile with seepage the claypanned waterholes;
Soon sluice down contours in the unsown fallows;
        Soon silt up creeks with alluvial wastage.

The water-hyacinth, treacherous, beautiful,
Mauve and merciless foe of fishermen,
The Creeping-Judas of soaks and billabongs,
Chokes up the channels, its tough seeds and stolons
        Increased by prolific multiplication.

Eroded then the buff shelved banks of Logan,
Lachlan, blue Hunter or swift-flowing Murray,
Denuded of oaks and grey eucalyptus,
Feathery sour-sapped bent-boughed melaleucas,
        Cave in; let spread the loud-snarling flood waters.

Waking, child while you slept

Waking child, while you slept, your mother took
Down from its wooden peg her reaping-hook,
Rustless with use, to cut (her task when dawn
With nervous light would bead the dusky leaves)
From the cold wheat-paddock's shivering fringe, two sheaves;
Against a block she'd thrash the golden grain,
Then winnow corn and husk, and toss again,
And yet again, her dish, and frisk the chaff
Wide to the wind;
Then grind,
Her new steel hand-mill being still the pride
Of the astonished country-side.
Her meal cooked, she'd call men and children in;
With bustling care, in genial haste, not late
Her cows she'd milk, her butter churn and set
Fresh cream in scalded pans. Her hens she'd feed
With hot scraps, stirred in pollard from the bin;
Then give her dribbling calves what drink they need;
Or drive with flowery staff
Meek stragglers through the gate;
Or on her youngest-born
Impose the fret,
The letter'd tyranny, of the alphabet.

        Yet in this daily round
        She nothing trivial found.
        A little love to earn
        She, but a girl, did learn;

To dig, to delve, to drive wild cattle in,
("Ester, ley thou thy mekeness al a-doun")
To scour, to sweep, to wash and iron, to spin;
("Penalopee and Marcia Catoun
Make of your wifehood no comparisoun,")
To sew, to darn, to cook, to bake, to brew,
To bear, to rear, to nurse her children, too;

("And Cleopatre, with al thy passioun
Hyde ye your trouthe of love, and your renoun.")

Though, child, your mother, trembling, smiled at fear,
Fears had she; the blackfellow's cruel spear,
White desperadoes. When to the open well
She crept at nightfall, being all alone,
The well, with she-oaks ringed, where dark and slow
Stole east-going, prostrate shades; where one would go,
Sometimes, bolt upright, darker and less slow –
But noiseless, too – her warlike bandolier
And bell-mouthed blunderbuss (all else disown
Having new flintlocks) would her terrors tell.

For comfort, then, she'd watch her frugal rush,
The only gleam in all that virgin bush,
Cheer the unshutter'd, distant, window-pane;
Then hoist her twirling bucket yet again;
Or, set beyond the tassell'd corn-cobs, see
Her chimney's sepia plume
For Hesperus make room;
Or, through the peppermint-tree,
A crescent, coasting moon a reef of stars
Skirt; or a dangerous Jupiter, or Mars;
As on that happy night when in her pride
Quickening, she felt her son stir in her side.

When in a drought the waterholes ran dry
And of "dry-bible" half the herds would die,
And others in their agony creep to lie
About the homestead, moaning piteously,
Or, famished, on the deadly purple weed,
Or poisonous variegated thistle, feed,
– The purple weed that lames – or in the creek,
Among dead frogs, dead ferns, water would seek;
The men being absent, then, to give release,
She brought to every suffering brute death's peace;
        Who never heard the rain
        Fall, but she heard again
        The cattle in their pain.

But in a lucky year your mother's care
Was all to save the wealth her orchard bore;
Apples and plums, peach, apricot and pear,

Mandarins, nectarines, tangerines, a score
Of rosy berries, currants and their kind;
Drying these last, through muslin she would squeeze
Damson or apple cheese;
Quinces, conserve; bottle black mulberries;
Sweet cherries and strawberries in honey seal;
Float cumquats in syrup; candy lemon-peel;
Or, versed in the housewife's alchemy once more,
Jams in her pantry stack – a round fourscore.

She for her cellar with a cheerful mind
Would brew in tubs peach-beer,
Sparkling and clear,
Rub pears, and trinities of apples bruise
To perry and cider in a wooden cruse.
Of keeving and pomace then gossip ran,
One servant assigned her being a Devon man,
Whose convict clothes and homely face – so kind –
Smiling, you may remember, musing on
The knight, his grandson and the judge, his son.

Sleeping Soldier

Dear love, I've seen you fast asleep,
  Twitched the green blind that screens the sun,
And sheathed the sword, once bright to reap
  The little sheaf your virtue won;

Your narrow bed's not made so strait
  That there's no room for me when, too,
I plumb the darkness where you wait,
  I go to lie night long by you.

The Garden in June

When in June cobwebs star the elms, the grass,
The gardening ant retires before St. Elmo's fires
And on the gravel path centipedes pass.

Smaller than little finger-nails
Whole colonies of new-born snails
Trail agate skeps across the red-ripe guava rind,

Gone are the wasps, the bees; the children find
Mushrooms; leaves falter, flushing, falling, dews
Invade the shade.

Papery, the moths lie
Ambushed by winter. Twinkling, the humorous
Stars, Aldebaran, far Betelgeux,
Perhaps, even, the winking Gemini,
See less of us – the fireside claims us –
While in the first sharp frost the dahlias die.

The Household (*from* At Rangamatty)

Who first wakes up? Why, Craddock and his wife!
Black-bearded Craddock, ear-rings in his ears,
Gold ear-rings! The story was he had won
The Grand Prix once (it would be once) upon
– Minting? The jockey sick, he rode, being stable-lad,
And took the jockey's name. Certainly Craddock had
A gold watch, French-inscribed. He orders life
For all the farm. Godlike, his words give birth
To calves, to foals, to pigs. In time of dearth
He deals out death or market; sometimes both.

Ike Peachy, then, a tousled sandy thatch
Tears from the straw, and, groping, finds the latch
Of the stable door. (At three o'clock he'd come
Back from a Picton social, walking twelve miles home.)

Mariana, next, will lift a lovely head
From an uneasy pillow, sip her tea – in bed –
Choose something starched to wear, then bravely dare
The windswept verandah, bathe, six pannikins her share
Of water. Burnished her bright hair,
Soon she'll survey her kingdom – *what to do?*

The notes in Conington's Virgil, all she knew
Of farming, as sole guide were not much use;
She turns the page, to sigh, to smile, to muse;

"The old drudging sun from his long-beaten way
Shall hear thy voice, start, and disorient day"

Whose voice? She listens. Reads – "Oh, Caesar's" –
"Plough
When winter's gone". "I did. Sowed corn. Came frost!
– A black frost out of season. All was lost."

She steals a glance at the far-distant gate,
Another at the glass; continues to translate;

"Is the Bull in the east?" Virgil says "Beans
Must be sown". Do the Pleiades set?
Westward where the moon's sickle gleans?
He says "Plough in the stars, fast, fast sow your wheat."
Does a crane alight? He promises yet
More rain, and – "when the wind is red" –

"Now, about that red wind? What was it Virgil said?"

Mariana's Dairy (*from* At Rangamatty)

The Dairy, facing south, as clean as cold,
Woke to the daily round when first the gold
Noose of the sun caught the veiled hills with light,
While far away the Appin mists gleamed bright.

The milk being warmed, then, cooled the wrinkled cream,
The sanded churn, scrubbed sweet as hazel-nuts,
Was then her toy. A wooden box might seem
Archaic – so it was! The handle turned
(And turned and turned) until the cream was churned.

Washed, salted, washed, pressed dry with butter-pats,
Coloured with saffron (one must live) in rounds
Stamped with her crown and thistle, quite ten pounds
Of butter went to market in the dray,
To gain, in Picton, perhaps, five shillings a day.

Roses jet black tapped at her window-panes,
Birds sang. Trees flowered. Her orchard gains,
Ripe peaches, cherries, strawberries, at her door,
She did not once imagine she was poor.

VANCE PALMER 1885–1959

At the time of his greatest influence, in the 1930s and '40s, Vance Palmer was the most influential man of letters in Australia. He was an essayist, playwright, poet, reviewer, broadcaster, editor, writer of short stories, and a prolific novelist. He was aided and complemented in seeking to promote an authentically Australian literature by his wife Nettie, also a freelance literary journalist, whose autobiographical record *Fourteen Years* remains, if undervalued, a classic. In it she writes that Palmer, through over-work, was neglectful of her and their two daughters. Nettie Palmer, like her husband, produced a vast amount of critical writing, much of which is not collected. She learned to read in French, German, Greek and Spanish, and wrote the first full-length study of the outstanding novelist Henry Handel Richardson. The family lived for some years in the small fishing village of Caloundra in Queensland, but returned to Melbourne, the place with which the Palmers are particularly associated.

Vance Palmer's literary ideas were much influenced by those of Henry Lawson: he was a realist concerned with "the spirit of place" (the phrase is from D. H. Lawrence, but applicable here). He thought the "Australian spirit" first became apparent in the 1890s, and wrote a book on the period in relation to the *Bulletin* magazine. His best work, still highly readable, is the novel *The Passage*, set in a Queensland coastal town. He published two books of poetry, but only the piece collected here has survived in esteem. Relevant to it, Palmer was an impassioned critic of conscription for the First World War, but then late in the conflict volunteered, although he did not see active service.

His father was a school teacher, but Palmer had no higher education. In his early years, he travelled widely, spending time in Spain and working in London, in "Grub Street"; he journeyed to Russia, unsuccessfully attempting to meet Tolstoy, and came home via Japan. He also visited the United States and Mexico. He travelled again later in Europe, with his wife. His became a familiar voice on publically owned radio, giving talks on literature and reviewing books.

The Farmer Remembers the Somme

Will they never fade or pass!
The mud, and the misty figures endlessly coming
In file through the foul morass,
And the grey flood-water ripping the reeds and grass,
And the steel wings drumming.

The hills are bright in the sun:
There's nothing changed or marred in the well-known places;
When work for the day is done
There's talk, and quiet laughter, and gleams of fun
On the old folks' faces.

I have returned to these:
The farm, and the kindly Bush, and the young calves lowing;
But all that my mind sees
Is a quaking bog in a mist – stark, snapped trees,
And the dark Somme flowing.

DOROTHEA MACKELLAR 1885–1968

Dorothea Mackellar was born in her family's home at Point Piper, overlooking Rose Bay on Sydney Harbour, where she would have watched the lights of the trams passing at night, described in her poem "Magic". The only daughter of a physician and parliamentarian, Sir Charles Kinnaird Mackellar, she was privately tutored in painting, fencing and languages. While not enrolled as a student, she attended lectures at the University of Sydney. Mackellar spoke French, German, Italian and Spanish fluently and acted as an interpreter for her father when they travelled overseas. The Mackellar family owned properties, including "The Rampadells" near Gunnedah, which is the subject of "Burning Off". She was an expert horsewoman. There is a story that, while in London, she fell in love with an English poet, Patrick Chalmers, but her letters to him were lost during World War I, so that Chalmers married someone else. However, Beverley Kingston says in her foreword to *A Poet's Journey* (a 2002 collection of Dorothea Mackellar's work) that this "clichéd story of romance blighted by war" has no substance.

Her poem, "My Country" was written in England at a time of homesickness. On her return to Australia it was rewritten several times. She continued writing and travelling until the early 1930s and her work appeared overseas in the *Spectator*, *Harper's Magazine* and in Australia in the *Bulletin*. She published four volumes of poetry during this period. Later in life she suffered increasing ill health and stopped writing.

Perhaps ranking only after Paterson's "Waltzing Matilda" and "The Man from Snowy River", as one of Australia's most loved poems, Mackellar's "My Country" is a full technicolour *Gone with the Wind* picture of Australia, and thrilling because of that. Nor is she a one-poem poet. In "Magic" her image of a tram passing at night, flaming red, green and orange, lives up to the title of the poem. We have deleted two uninspired final verses. Her charming "Dusk in the Domain" refers to a large open park with huge, gloomy Moreton Bay and Port Jackson fig trees, which is adjacent to Woolloomooloo, a suburb notorious at that time for its slums and unsavoury characters.

As she left youth behind, her poems are coloured by an increasing bitterness. Some overbalance into self-pity, but the best have a restrained power. "The Fire in the Laurel Bush", with its reflected fire that does not burn, and "Heritage" hint at a life that is unfulfilled.

My Country

The love of field and coppice,
Of green and shaded lanes.
Of ordered woods and gardens
Is running in your veins,
Strong love of grey-blue distance
Brown streams and soft dim skies –
I know but cannot share it,
My love is otherwise.

I love a sunburnt country,
A land of sweeping plains,
Of ragged mountain ranges,
Of droughts and flooding rains.
I love her far horizons,
I love her jewel-sea,
Her beauty and her terror –
The wide brown land for me!

The stark white ring-barked forests
All tragic to the moon,
The sapphire-misted mountains,
The hot gold hush of noon.
Green tangle of the bushes,
Where lithe lianas coil,
And orchids deck the tree-tops
And ferns the warm dark soil.

Core of my heart, my country!
Her pitiless blue sky,
When sick at heart, around us,
We see the cattle die –
But then the grey clouds gather,
And we can bless again
The drumming of an army,
The steady, soaking rain.

Core of my heart, my country!
Land of the Rainbow Gold,
For flood and fire and famine,
She pays us back threefold.
Over the thirsty paddocks,
Watch, after many days,
The filmy veil of greenness
That thickens as we gaze ...

An opal hearted country,
A wilful, lavish land –
All you who have not loved her,
You will not understand –
Though earth holds many splendours,
Wherever I may die,
I know to what brown country
My homing thoughts will fly.

Magic

Crawling up the hillside,
  Swinging round the bay,
With a ceaseless humming,
  Ply the trams all day.

When it's dark I linger
  Just to see the sight:

All those jewelled beetles
  Flashing through the night!

Anything more lovely
  I have never seen
Than the sparks above them,
  White and blue and green;

Sometimes they are tiny:
  In a storm they shine,
Dragons' tongues that follow
  All along the line!

When the wind has fallen,
  And the bay's like glass,
Would you see some magic?
  Watch what comes to pass:

There is just a ripple
  Where the water breaks,
All the lamps reflected
  Show like golden snakes:

Wait, the tram is coming
  Round the curving shore,
And its humming changes
  To a hollow roar:

There's a flaming glory
  On the bay at last,
Red and green and orange –
  It has come; and passed.

Nothing breaks the stillness,
  All is as before,
And the golden serpents
  Quiver near the shore …

Burning Off

They're burning off at the Rampadells,
The tawny flames uprise,
With greedy licking around the trees;
The fierce breath sears our eyes.

From cores already grown furnace-hot –
The logs are well alight!
We fling more wood where the flameless heart

Is throbbing red and white.

The fire bites deep in that beating heart,
The creamy smoke-wreaths ooze
From cracks and knot-holes along the trunk
To melt in greys and blues.

. . . . . .

The young horned moon has gone from the sky,
And night has settled down;
A red glare shows from the Rampadells,
Grim as a burning town.

Full seven fathoms above the rest
A tree stands, great and old,
A red-hot column whence fly the sparks,
One ceaseless shower of gold.

All hail the king of the fire before
He sway and crack and crash
To earth – for surely tomorrow's sun
Will see him white fine ash.

The king in his robe of falling stars,
No trace shall leave behind,
And where he stood with his silent court,
The wheat shall bow to the wind.

Dusk in the Domain

Elf light, owl light,
Elfin-green sky;
Under the fig trees
Bats flit by;

Under the fig trees
Sprawl in a ring
Slim-limbed courtiers,
Brown Elf King.

Crowned with autumn's
Tawny gold,
Lizard-eyed, cricket-thighed,
Neither young nor old:

Like the fig-leaves'
Broad yellow wreath
Round each forehead – like
The waves beneath

Lipping the weed-hung
Low sea-wall
Ageless, careless
Lords of all!

Grey rock-monsters
Out of the grass
Heaved, lie staring;
Moths drift past

On their business –
None have the elves,
Who hold high festival
By themselves.

. . . . .

So I saw them
Very plain,
Green-dusky Elfland,
Their Domain.

So I saw them
As I went through:
Seven slum children from
Woolloomooloo!

Heritage

Though on the day your hard blue eyes met mine
  I did not know I had a heart to keep,
All the dead women in my soul
  Stirred in their shrouded sleep.

There were strange pulses beating in my throat,
  I had no thought of love: I was a child:
But the dead lovers in my soul
  Awoke and flushed and smiled;

And it was years before I understood
  Why I had been so happy at your side
With the dead woman in my soul
  Teaching me what to hide.

For it was not the springtime that had come,
  Only one strong flower thrusting through the snows,
But the dead women in my soul
  Knew all that summer knows.

The Fire in the Laurel Bush

The nursery fire was crackling gold,
The nursery tea was set,
Joan turned from both to where a fire
Was burning in the wet;
Outside the window's streaming glass
Where rain was driving hard,
It flamed within the laurel-bush
And not a leaf was charred.

Within the laurel's sumptuous green
It leapt and danced, while Joan
Watching its live ethereal light,
Stood like a child of stone,
A stolid little statue, till
Old Nurse said "Drat the child,
She's seen reflections there before.
She'd drive a body wild.

"Come, don't you want your tea?" But no,
Joan had not that desire,
For all her small soul fed itself
In gazing at the fire.
She knew as well as Nurse that this
Was but the ghost of flame
And yet she whispered "Burning Bush!"
And gloated on the name.

Rain slanted down unceasingly
But yet the golden plumed
Flame danced within a shrine of green
That never was consumed.
The burning bush, the laurel bush!
No earthly warmth it shed;
That evening's fire will burn until
Old wrinkled Joan is dead.

HARLEY MATTHEWS 1889–1968

Harley Matthews was born in Sydney and educated at Sydney Boys High School. He was an articled clerk in a solicitor's office when he enlisted in the Australian Infantry Forces in 1914. Matthews was among the Anzacs who landed at Gallipoli beach in a campaign against the Turks, which became a legendary disaster. He was wounded and mentioned in dispatches. On leave from service in France in 1916,

Matthews was spotted on a London street by Jacob Epstein who used him for his bronze bust of a steel-helmeted soldier "Spirit of Anzac", now in the Imperial War Museum in London. After the war Matthews worked for a Sydney afternoon newspaper, and in 1920 went to the United States, where he was a freelance writer for two years. On returning he established a vineyard at Moorebank, outside Sydney, with his wife, Barbara Goode. This became a weekend meeting-place for writers, and is referred to by Slessor in "Five Bells", when he recalls "The night we came to Moorebank in slab-dark".

In 1942 Matthews was arrested after midnight and interned in an army prison camp for six months because of his association with members of the Australia First movement (an isolationist, anti-British, quasi-Fascist organisation), although he himself was not a member. During this time his elderly mother died (of a heart attack, possibly prompted by her son's fate), and his vineyard was ruined through neglect. Later he was cleared and awarded compensation of £700 by a Royal Commission. Divorced in 1940, he established another rural property near Sydney, where he lived until he died in 1968.

"The Return of the Native" exists in two versions. The earlier, which we have used here, can be read as a love poem, and may refer to his return from World War I or from the United States. The capitalised "You" of this version is most probably his wife, or it could be the poet's native land. The second version of the poem is tidier, less radiant, and has a quite different opening: "I have come back again:/ And should never have been away from you." The "you" in this version is impersonal. The bleaching out of the loved "You" from the second version may have been prompted by his divorce, which Matthews initiated in an era of fault divorce and is the subject of an extraordinarily bitter poem, "Decree Absolute".

"Decree Absolute" and the second version of "The Return of the Native" both appear in *Patriot's Progress*, which was published in 1965, three years before his death. Our copy of this volume has an inscription, handwritten by the ex-wife, who was excoriated in "Decree Absolute": "To Mrs Wentworth – In memory of a gracious hostess in happy surroundings – from Barbara Goode Matthews February 1966".

Two Brothers

We laughed. Those two were with us still.
Always in camp, on shipboard, they had held
Themselves apart from us. Packed in the boat
Just now, they had sat staring, beyond reach
Of every joke we made to keep our dread
Down. Then we had forgotten them. Instead,
Grinding of keels. Shouts ... "Over with you!" The swill
Of water round your body. Your feet jarred
Against stones. Stumblings. Breaths coming hard,
This pack pushing you down. Blankness ...
                                        Half-afloat
A dead sailor lay sprawled upon the beach.
But no rest for us. On. On. In a cleft

Between the hills the wounded lay or sat.
Some cheered. But most were still. "Give it to them
For us," a gash that was a mouth once wailed.
On. Up. Legs, feet heavy – this pack – Up still ...
Now we lay waiting on the hill,
And with us were those two. They were two brothers.
They kept aloof there even from us others.

In front, over the ridge some rifles spat;
Beyond, the battle came to life. It rushed
Along unvisioned valleys at a stride,
Roaring its challenge out for us to pit
Our strength against it. Then grew sullen, hushed;
Once more, louder than ever, as over it
The seaplane sailed.
"We'll soon be in it," someone said. The air
Cracked open over us. Smoke swooped down.
Things fell, fell, fell. A man screamed: "I'm hit."
More, more shells shrieked their coming. We lay flat,
But never flat enough. Run! Down the slope.
No. No. Where then? "Earth take and hide
Me," all my being cried.
That will fall here. Run! Which way? Too late. "Earth –"
No. There is no escape from the machine;
Unseeing it picks us out, and strikes unseen.
You are the one hope, Earth. Only a hope ...
Then one shell passed us by. Now they all burst
Behind us, spattering the sea below –
Like a storm gone over. The sun shone again,
And slender grasses leaned and swayed.
Patches of ocean toyed with glints and gleams,
Ships swung at anchor unafraid.
We saw men come unhurrying, and go
This way and that down on the beach. "It seems
More like a holiday," one brother said.
"Somewhere at home, some seaside place – the sun,
The boats, and all that passing to and fro."
The other laughed. "Colour is all it lacks –
Some women's dresses here and there." No one
Spoke for a while. We lay against our packs,
Each watching what he saw. "A prisoner,
Look!" Halfway down the hill

A man stood up. He screamed. "Kill him! Kill. Kill.
There, bayonet him. Shoot him. Our orders were
Not to take one of them."
Not an arm lifted. None took up that shout.
The prisoner shambled round the hill. "He's out
Of it," we were all thinking.
"He seemed glad
To have been taken," someone's voice broke in.
"Who could have shot a man like that? Not me."

The world had grown to only sky and sea,
To only murmurs from beyond the blue.
"Their orders cannot make us beasts, blood-mad,"
That was the older brother speaking. "And I say,
The man who took that prisoner, he won
For us the greatest victory to-day."
No word more. Sprawl, eyes shut against the sun.
The wind brought rumors up. Deep-stained the glare
Into that inner world of ours pierced through.
"You wait till we advance and they begin
To shoot at you." It was the old soldier's voice.
At things it hinted that could not be told,
But only learnt, each for himself. The air
Settled about us. Unseen shadows came
And touched our hearts with cold.
"That will not make me want to kill." That cry
Rippled across our thoughts.
"You'll have no choice
When the order comes to open fire."
"No! No!
I will not. I will not. I will shoot high."
New voices crowded out all else. "Then why
Did you enlist?" ... "Traitor to waste
Good ammunition!" ... "Let us shoot him here,
Ourselves." ... "Think of the wounded men below."

Quick! Flat! Words died. Thought stopped. From out to sea
It came. There. Our own battleships again.
Guns. Guns. Their dark din
Trailed through the sky; then shattered itself on hills
Far over. Earth shuddered. Yes, men embraced
You there, too, Earth; and cried out in the pain
Of their fear, men we called the enemy.

"The bastards!" a man shouted. "That shell kills
A hundred of them." The air beat out and in
As though great doors were slammed and opened.
"Boys,
I know." The voice laughed. "Both came to the war
To please some girl." We laughed too. In that noise
And tremor we remembered them once more.
We talked, laughed, listened. Still there stirred that thought.
Stories of places, women, men.
Nothing could dull the ache of waiting. How long? When?
Then all at once the word –
And over that hillside there were heard
Hands kissing rifles as they caught
Them up. "Advance." Men rising, packs being eased;
It was as though Earth had herself been stirred
To action. "We are advancing."
We were going
Along the beach again. But now we turned
Into a valley, banked with bushes growing
So furtive in the sun;
And pools quivered, where water had now ceased
For heaviness to run.
The path forked. We halted. Now which way
To the edge of this world? Did they both lead there
Sooner or later? Left or right?
Our captain muttered: "Orders do not say
Which track we are to take." He turned about.
"At least let us go light.
Quick, men, off with these packs and leave them here.
And now I want two men to volunteer
To stay and guard them." Me! I cannot. Out
At last two men stepped. At this chance they smiled.
We moved off. Up that right-hand track we filed,
Disdainful, at heart envious
Of two men made so sure of living. They
Were not those brothers. They went on with us.

How near were we now? Would we find it there
In the next valley? Yet it was aware
Of our coming. We heard its anger grow.
Up on the left it stamped, stamped, and the track
Was barred with smoke and noise.

Bullets snarled by, or flicked off leaves. A man
Stumbled ... "He's only wounded. Come on, boys,
We can't stop. He must find his own way back."
  We ran. We crawled. We ran,
And that unseen eye followed all the way;
Always the shells kept bursting just ahead.
Look! Over there. Four men down at once. "Spread
Out more, you fools." Spread out? There is no room.
Into the bushes then ... They clutch and tear,
The ground gives underfoot.
Up! Help me, twig, bough, root.
  Under the ridge at last. Rest. Breathe. The air –
How quiet here. A flower is in bloom.
  And then they came, our own men, over the crest,
Bleeding and limping, babbling out their news:
"We've chased them miles ahead" ... "They won't
Stand up and fight like us" ... "They're just in front."
They led one who kept crying: "I could see
No one. Only green bushes and a hill."
He would never see so much again. Breathe. Rest.
  "Fix bayonets," the word comes. "Charge!" Charge. Kill.
Now go and kill the man who has to wait
For you down there. Legs, bring me to him straight.
Do not falter. All along this had to be,
And just this way. Where is he hiding?
Only green bushes and a hill.
                    Suppose
There is no man at all. Yes, but there is.
I feel his eye on me, He knows. He knows
I'm on this ridge; I'm crawling through this wheat,
There is no hiding from him anywhere.
"Take cover, men. Lie down. Here in this dip."
  Behind this bush. Already bullets strip
Off one by one the leaves above me – his.
Dig, fingers, scratch deep in that earth. Down there
Is shelter. See – this root,
The way it goes. And stones know it, too.
"I'm shot," a man cries. "Oh! Don't touch me. No,
I can't bear it." Bullets come, more and more;
Nothing may stir. Fingers, only grip
The ground tighter. He is calling still:
"Don't leave me to them. Shoot me first. Shoot ..."

The air is turned to lead,
Its weight presses me down and holds me flat.
Now he is crying only to himself.
  "Fire!" The word runs. "On that ridge ahead."
Fire. Fire. Shoot. Shoot. Something at last to do,
If only it is to kill.
But no man shows himself. Shoot. Shoot. What at?
Nothing – only green bushes and a hill.

We were back on the ridge again.
At nightfall we'd come in; the crest was lined
With men already digging to entrench.
Not a face there we knew. They cried "Dig here,
They'll attack soon." And as we worked they told
Of Turks who'd stood, and Turks who'd run,
Of Turks they'd killed, of men they'd left behind
In fights on far high hills they could not hold.
  We all knew one another now. One fear
Brought us together, made all work as one.
There was no officer to see it done.

The trench was to our knees when it began.
In front, sparks pricked the darkness. Bullets whined
Again above us. The old soldier took
Command. "Don't fire. Not yet. Wait till they come."
Those sparks kept creeping down. Crackling, they ran
Ripping the darkness through from end to end.
The air is combed deeper. I dare not look
Upward. I press my face against this heap
Of earth, and only listen. Rifles crash.
Over me, I could touch that rushing sound.

"Up! Up! Here they come. Fire!" I see a flash,
I press my finger. There leaps out a flame
From my own rifle. Shouts, flame, crashings smash
The night to pieces. Fire, Re-load. Fire. "Keep
It up, lads," Hot. My rifle burns my hand –
"Cease fire." Is it all over? "Stop!" Men aim
And shoot into the darkness just the same.
"Cease fire, you fools. Don't waste another round."
The clamour dies away, to leave at last
Only a whimper on the left, The night
Draws in together. "Dig," is the command,

And sometimes words from man to man are passed –
"More stretcher-bearers wanted on the right,"
Or, "Stand to arms. Stand-to." We rise and stand .

We heard them gathering on the hills again.
They called and whistled, bugles blew.
"Allah!" they cried. Then feet came thudding on.
"Allah!" Up on the left the firing grew,
In one gust it came down to us. "Stand-to!
Here they come. Fire!" Once more
We fire at shouts and shadows – and then … gone.
They are gone now, all melted as before.
"Dig!" Now we dig to keep
The cold back. One time it began to rain.
For how long? Did we sleep?
"Stand-to. They're coming." It was that all night.
We stood-to, waiting for the dawn.
They would attack before it came, we thought,
But the darkness held only darkness. We heard
No foot stumbling, out on the hills no call.
Far-off a rifle spluttered – that was all.
At last there came the light,
The hills showed motionless. A stray air caught
A bush nearby; its rain-drops kissed the earth.
"Stand down! Some men may sleep." The word
Passed gladly on. We saw the day's slow birth,
We who were left to watch. We hoped anew.
The trench was to our breasts. Out came the sun,
And now this glow to warm our tired limbs through;
This stillness made for sleep … But we must dig.

A rifle broke the quiet. A man cried out,
Along the trench a little way.
Now he lay on its floor –
One of those brothers. He gasped, gasped and then was still
It was the younger one;
The other kneeled by him. We heard him say:
"Come, Tom. We have to dig now. Only wait,
And we can all sleep soon." The old soldier said,
"Yes, dig, man. Can't you see that he is dead?"

He got up. From his eyes had gone all doubt.
He threw his rifle up to fire; to shout:

"Kill! Kill them all!" There showed upon the hill
No one. But we knew then that, for a war,
Love they enlisted too, as well as Hate.

Women are not Gentlemen

They said there was a woman in the hills
Behind us. All day long she watched for when
A man's head showed.
Some knew that she was young
And beautiful. And some that she was old,
Mad with a hate of men.
"Each shot she fires she kills,"
They said. "She never misses. Then at night
She comes and takes their money from the dead."
She would not even leave them with their names.
Her hiding place was hung
With paper, silver, gold;
Her neck with all the things that would have told
Who a man was when we must bury him.
"Here lies an unknown soldier," we would write.
Oh, we'd be bitter when we turned and left
Him pushed out of men's sight, and mind. Bereft
Of body and of name. For all time more,
In the one world we knew, nothing. And all
Through an old woman's spite,
Or young girl's whim.

Those weeks we moved in fear of her all day.
Up in the trenches we crouched low. "Stand-to!"
The word would come. "They're forming to attack.
UP! Watch!" And there again the dead men lay,
Sharing the sunlight and the flowers that grew
In the old places. Often nothing stirred
Beyond. Then in the trench a man would fall,
Shot in the back.
"Down! Quick!" There, kneeling on that gritty floor,
We'd watch him sob his life out. Some men swore
From her had come the word,
Sent through a spy amongst us – "And I'll bet
The bastard sleeps with her.
One night I'll find her burrow. He'll die first."
None laughed at the old soldier's boasting now.

But sometimes there would gleam a bayonet
Then others. On the left firing. Bombs burst.
In front the ground heaves men up, up, and out
Into the open. On they come. The shout
To see at last these men set on to kill
Us. "Fire!" Still they come running. "Get out, boys,
And meet them." I am up here. My legs take
Me forward. Faces rush in. And hurt eyes.
Steel flashes. Impacts. Bodies struggle, strive
In big gasps. A red darkness. Thrust. I break
Up through it. I see men's backs running. Cries:
Cheers all around. A dry mouth. My own voice
At last cheering. Sunlight. I am alive.
A whistle blows: "Retire.
Get back before they open fire."
Run. Run. Here is our trench. Breathless we drop
Into it safe. "We're coming through the wire,"
A voice calls. "Help me down with him. Take care."
Two feet show first, feeling the air. They stop.
That shot was from behind.
Down! "There! She fires again." No voice on top
Calls for help now. Past help, those feet hang there –
"She's got them both." We know they both are dead.

Machine guns stutter. Rifles start up. Lead
Weighs down the air above.
"They're coming soon, again," a man cries. "No,
You fool, they think that we'll attack instead.
Hear how afraid of us they are." High, low,
The bullets come and go.
We lie back, glad to know that there is dread
Out there, too. With that woman still in mind,
Pity, almost a love.
We feel for those men in the trench ahead.

Then someone would want water. There'd not be
A drop in any bottle. Straightway thirst
Came into every mouth.
Water – It was behind our talk of guns.
Guns – Why we heard guns drumming in the south?
Slaughter by battleships –
Mines blowing up advancing battalions –
Of generals' new schemes to have more killed.

Through it all we would see
A corner of the valley road. There lay
Water – a muddied pool where tins were filled.
But no one dared start down. We sat and cursed
That woman with set lips.

We did not watch the sun, those evenings, sink
Behind the ships, the day
Plunge from the headlands. There would come a star
Into our strip of sky. Then could we stand
And see the lights afloat off-shore, afar.
Along the paths they laid,
Homeward we wandered from the gloomy land –
"Go down, you two, to fill them. Come
Back quick."
"It is like home. Off for a drink
While she's not looking."
The old soldier laughed.

You know that you are near it by the hum
Of talk. But not a word
You hear until you drink that long, first draught.
"They got into our trench to-day. We had
To bomb them out of it." You break the scum.
There is your form beneath you in the pool,
Deep down. Dipping and filling, it grows blurred.
"Who says the navy is no help? The fool."
"I do. And our artillery is as bad.
They've killed more of our own than Turks." By some
Fresh fit of firing stirred
Your form down there is breaking
Into strange shapes. "I say, that's near Lone Pine.
Hear the destroyer on our right join in?"
Shadows, not of your making,
Trouble the water. Fires into it come
And pass, and go. "Our colonel has gone mad;
They're taking him away."
"I wish they'd take ours, too. He's drunk all day.
Fewer of us get killed. But it's our rum."
"A soldier, you? To talk
Of officers like that. Why, ours all say
We'll be across to Maidos in a week."
"Yes, if the battleships go overland."

More men crowd in. Lights shine.
The pool mirrors it all, not right, not wrong.
"She shot my mate to-day." "Here, that's my tin."
"I tell you it is mine."
"Clean out behind his eyes the bullet came – "
"Stop fighting, there. No war's down here. Get back,
You two, where you belong."
New faces show as matches flame.
The cigarettes glow and the pool turns black.
"We buried him just now."

    All the way back it seemed the earth were waking
To a new life from some day-dream of Death's.
The slopes were deafening with fiery flowers,
Winds of all colours blew.
Forests of smoke rode by on unfelt breaths.
Lights crashed. Flames strode along the ridges, making
A world where nought was fixed, but all was true:
A time that had no hours,
No days, nor years;
A world where, a time when
Height called to height and kindred ears,
And, without speaking, men could speak to men.
Pallor bloomed dim as shapes came, carried by,
Towards ease at last. No moan was heard, no cry
Of pity. Pain was here an ecstasy
That held lips mute, made eyes too wide for tears.
And figures passed, heads high,
Walking as men should walk the earth,
Proud, without pride of birth,
Gentle, though unbeset by fears.

    And in the morning still was Beauty there.
We lived. We could stand up and watch the sea,
Telling its dream. Then how
The wind would have it told another way:
See how the first light found
A new cape, a fresh tree;
The mist still hid a hollow, until now
Unguessed at.
                    We would hear again the sound
Of silence settling in from everywhere:

Then voices floating strangely in. Far-off
In front behind their lines the same cock crew.
And still his brother lived beneath the hill
To answer. Closer in the dog barked still.
We'd listen, straining towards the trench out there
To catch the same man's laugh, his comrade's cough.
We'd call good morning, then. And they'd call, too.

    Deep in the hush somewhere
A rifle whispers, a spent bullet whirs
Past us. "That is not hers.
It is too early for her yet. She knows
We'd see her rifle smoking in this light."
The left is waking. As it stretches, stirs
Its limbs, things crash. It mutters now in fear
Of the time coming – "That is where the fight
Will be to-day. There – " Its full roar we hear
Of rifle, bomb, rifle. "Look!
It's our men attacking. See the way
They're going over?" "Here, let me
Up! Why, you'd think they're walking out to play
A game of football." The rifle fire rushes
All to one spot, to one noise. In the trench
We crowd together, clambering up to see.
"Get down, men. It will be
Her time, soon." Arms, heads, bodies drop to stay
Down. Every voice hushes.

    And still the battle shouts. The hill behind
Mimics it shrilly. "They are never done,
Women, spoiling our fun,"
The old soldier mutters. "I came here to get
Away from one.
For King and country, I told her. She swore
I went because I was a coward. True,
That was, truer than she knew.
Now here is this one saying the same thing yet:
'Sneak! Liar! Coward! You won't see the war.'"
A youngster down the trench says: "And I am here
Because a girl said I'm a coward, too.
She never even came to wave good-bye."
  The firing stops for breath. Only the shout,

Shout from men's throats, strikes on that other ear
Of ours. "You have an eye for women, son,
I have a way with them. Point this one out
And I'll soon show her it is not
Her war." Bombs. Up there rifles snarl.
Leashes are slipped. New packs give tongue. "They've got
Our fellows on the run."

And then, one morning, the young soldier raised
His rifle up. He cried: "I've got her. Look!
There is her rifle lying beneath that bush.
I saw the sun shine on it when she took
Aim at somebody." "Get down. Quick!
You young fool. You shoot her? It's just a trick
Of hers."
  Still he stood there and no shot came.
Then men began to push
Hats up on bayonets. Their arms grew tired
And let them fall while we looked on amazed.
A man stood up, and then another. Soon
We were all standing, and no rifle fired
At us. "There, see it lying shining there."
There was a wrinkled smile upon the sea.
The leaves across the valley gleamed. Below,
Uncringing, men went on their ways, as though
They knew already. "It makes a man feel
The War is almost over." "God! For me
It is all over," the old soldier said.
"What is there now to be afraid of?" "Her!"
Our sergeant told him, "We are going across
To-night to see if she is really dead."
"What for? If she stays quiet I don't care."
"The sergeant wants to get that money. Share
And share alike, I say."
"But it's the boys' here."
                    "God! I wouldn't touch
The bloody stuff. Yes, yes, there's too much
Blood on it."
                    "We can play
For it, then."
                    Someone found
Two pennies. "Let the sergeant toss."

"Heads! Tails!" It went. "Heads!"
The old soldier won.

We felt our way down; up. Our best guide was
To keep the uproar of the fight
Behind us. Bushes clutched, leaves felt our faces,
Then whispered us to pass.
Eyes told but little, blind with all the light
Of one bright instant, then the sudden dark.
Like that for hours we went. Our whispers grew
To mutterings – "We've long lost our landmark,
Sergeant. Let us go back."
"Come on! The place is
Somewhere between that hump there and that star."
We crept behind him still, sick of it all,
Cold, tired. "We can't be far
From it now. This way!"
Then we heard him fall,
Snapping wood, cursing. "Help me out of this.
Stop laughing up there. God, there's something soft
Under my foot. It's her.
Give me that torch. Yes, here she is."
We leaned over. Then a man laughed. He coughed
With laughing, still –
"Sergeant, she grew a strong
Beard, did that woman there."
"God," a voice gasped,
"It was a man, poor bastard, all the time."

"What," the old soldier cried. "But what about
My money? Turn the pockets out."
"Here you are. Look!" There were
Some copper coins, a charm, a crust of bread.

Nobody spoke till we began the climb
Back to the trench. Then the old soldier said,
"My luck with women never lasted long."
Another laughed: "Well, anyway, she's dead."
Someone was humming to himself a song:
"And my thoughts back there fly,
To where I said good-bye.
To my land, my own land, where the sky
Is always blue,

And blue her eyes are, too.
Oh, I love her true,
And she loves – "

The young soldier's tawdry song
Told us that she would never die.

The Return of the Native

I have come back again.
Back to the one thing I have met
Worth loving – You.
Yes, I know that now, hearing
That bird who, just returned at this time, too,
Cries out there in the clearing.
The rain-bird he is called by farmers: Yet
It's not because he brings
Even a drizzle when, year after year
He comes and prophesies the springs.
But they remember how they hear
His voice complaining,
Full of some brighter place he can't forget
Perched alone on a fence-post when it's raining.

And we will hear him in the night
Too, crying for his distant sun,
"Me. Me. Poor me. Me." – His notes run
On, on to a sad silence.
When he's gone
Hence, at our summer's end, will his song be
Still in that minor key,
Voicing the same nostalgic pain?
Do not ask me.
The answer's in a land from us remote.
All I can say, and on a major note
Is – I am home again.

JAMES DEVANEY 1890–1976

James Devaney was born in Bendigo, Victoria, and educated at St Joseph's College in Sydney. Entering the juniorate of the Marist Brothers in 1904 and taking his final vows in 1915, his religious name was Brother Fabian. He taught in a number of outback stations, but left the order when his health broke down in his early 30s. Devaney's most influential book is *The Vanished Tribes* (1929). This is a book of Aboriginal stories, including five poems, of which two are represented here. Brian Elliott, in his introduction to *The Jindyworobaks* (1979), related how Devaney told him that as a young man "he had gone among the northern blacks as a teacher and had sat with the elders and learned from them. It would appear that most of the material in his book was drawn from tribal talk … He gathered no particularly sacred narrative, and had no anthropological pretensions, but cared a great deal for the stories as stories". Elliott traces the etymology of the word "Jindy-worabak". It first appears in *The Vanished Tribes*. Devaney's glossary lists it as meaning: "To annex; to join". It is used in a story: "'That fellow close up finish," said Broken Face, speaking the Jindy-worabak words which sounded strange to her." The word was later borrowed and its spelling altered by Rex Ingamells when he founded the literary movement known as "the Jindyworobaks". As well as being a foundation text for the Jindyworobaks, a line of influence can be traced from the five poems in *The Vanished Tribes* to T. G. H. Strehlow's translations of poems of the Aranda people, *Songs of Central Australia*, and to Ronald M. Berndt's translations of Arnhem Land song cycles, and ultimately to Les Murray's "Buladelah-Taree Holiday Song-Cycle". In particular one of Devaney's handful of "Aboriginal" poems, "Dirrawan, the Song-Maker" showed it was technically possible to translate the concepts of Aboriginal poetry into English that reads like real poetry. The relaxed free verse of this poem and its use of the Aboriginal word followed by an English explanation, in effect a rhythmic doubling, have provided a formal template for successors translating from Aboriginal languages, or doing white-man homage to Aboriginal poetic concepts, as in the "Buladelah-Taree Holiday Song-Cycle".

Devaney may have undervalued his "Aboriginal" poems and not been fully conscious of the breakthrough he had achieved, as they were unrhymed and irregular in form and almost all of his *Poems* (1950) are in regular, rhymed verse. The five "Aboriginal" poems in *The Vanished Tribes* were an aberration and only two of them, but not "Dirrawan, the Song-Maker" were included in his *Poems*. For some years Devaney corresponded with the poet, John Shaw Neilson and finally met him in Melbourne in 1934, calling in at the Country Roads Board office where Neilson was working as a messenger. A friendship developed quickly and Devaney effectively became Neilson's editor and champion. In 1941 Neilson visited for a time with the Devaneys in their house on the Brisbane River.

Dirrawan, the Song-maker

Dirrawan went into the bush to spear waat,
But he forgot about waat the red wallaby.
He thought about dirridirri the small bird and deereeree the wagtail,
He thought about wonning the lightning and tumberumba the thunder,
He did not spear anything at all.

Dirrawan went down to the Long Brown Water to catch makora.
He thought about balleballea the silence of the night,
He thought about ballanda the long time ago.
He did not catch any fish, he brought back a new song to the gunyahs.

Song of the Captured Woman

I did not cry at all
Till I went down by the white edges of the lake.
I watched the wild swans rising from the lake
With sweet wild cries;
They went away, away to the south to my Murrawal River country,
And I to remain here in this place!
Ah, I could not follow the wild swans.

The women here are kind to the captured woman,
The lake men are straight and tall ones,
But their songs are strange to me, and their ways are not my ways,
The emu to the great brown plains,
The swamp-hen to her native reed-beds,
The eaglehawk to his own wide empty skies;
But I am a Murrawal River woman
And my country is down by the Murrawal River,
The talking Murrawal where my own people sit down.

I saw the wild black swans, wild and free
Rise out of the reeds and go;
Now they are there, down on the shady Murrawal River, the bends I know,
And I to remain here in this place!
It was then I sat down and cried,
For I would be again with my own people,
My own poor laughing people down by the Murrawal River,
The singing Murrawal, the Voice-that-does-not-cease.

LESBIA HARFORD 1891–1927

Lesbia Harford (neé Keough) was born in a Melbourne suburb, Brighton, with a congenital heart defect. This made her life more than usually exhausting, precarious and short, but she also had extraordinary willpower, and lived fully and self-sacrificingly before she died at the age of 36.

Nettie Palmer, who was six years older, remembers her at a children's party as "the dark-eyed little girl who sat quite still, looking on, her dark hair waving round her like a cape ..." (as quoted in Drusilla Modjeska's introduction to *The Poems of Lesbia Harford* (1985), p. 15). Her family's circumstances were comfortable at first: "There were maids and nurses", her brother Esmond remembered. Then her father became bankrupt and in about 1900 left his wife and children without a house or income. Her mother was determined her children would be educated and supported them by working at menial jobs. Lesbia Keough was educated at convents, and in 1912 became one of the few female law students at Melbourne University, graduating in 1916. She did not practice law, and became an articled clerk only in the last year of her life.

In 1912 she fell in love with Katie Lush, a philosophy tutor, with whom she remained friends to the end of her life. Lush was remembered by Professor Boyce Gibson as "a very tall rather dominating woman with red hair and a mind like a knife ..." (Modjeska, p. 20). The sexual relationship of the two women seems to have been brief.

Harford became a political radical and in her March 1915 sermon to the Free Religious Fellowship she said, "The life of a typist, the life of a clerk, the life of a merchant, a doctor, a lawyer, seem to some of us pretty well immoral." She put this belief into practice at the end of that year by going to work in a sewing factory (strenuous labour that strained her frail physique to the limit) and by joining the International Workers of the World (the "Wobblies"). Mixed emotions and an essential irony which is characteristic of her poetry explain why it was not taken up by the Wobblies in the pages of their *Direct Action*. Modjeska (p. 29) mentions that Guido Baracchi (Harford's lover and a Wobbly who was gaoled) regarded her as a "romantic revolutionary".

In 1918 she moved to Sydney, living with the wife of one of the dozen Wobblies on long gaol sentences. Then in 1920 she unexpectedly married Pat Harford, an unsuccessful working-class artist, remembered as "charming", but who was an alcoholic and sometimes violent. The marriage failed after a short period of happiness, and in 1921 she returned to Melbourne. She drifted away from organised politics and worked as a school teacher among working-class children. She wrote a novel, *The Invaluable Mystery*, about the treatment of Germans and radicals in Australia during World War I, which was lost until it was published in 1987. She returned to living with her mother. In 1927 exhausted by her year as an articled clerk, she became ill with pneumonia and died in St Vincent's Hospital, Melbourne, from a bacterial infection of her damaged heart valves.

Only with the 1985 edition of her poems, edited by Drusilla Modjeska and Marjorie Pizer, which included material from three thick exercise books lent to Pizer by Guido Baracchi, has it been possible to appreciate Harford's poetry for its true worth. In 1941 a slim edition of some poems appeared. During the half century after her death she was typically represented in anthologies by well-made but conventionally wrought poems such as "Beauty and Terror" and "I have golden shoes". But Harford's poetry is not always well-made. One of its attractions is that her voice is naked and hesitant, as in "Why does she put me to many indignities".

After her death, her poetry was too personal to be of interest to the literary or political left. Her revolutionary ardour, sexual candour and her plain and sometimes awkward language also meant she was not attractive to literary conservatives. The late poem, "Pruning Flowering Gums" may be seen as an expression of her later political philosophy with its quiet mockery of authority and its spectacle of spontaneous mass action by children, the "child bees" clearing away all the flowering branches lopped by Council employees. Harford said she was "not a Bolshevist in verse" (Modjeska, p. 33). She rejected classical music as elitist, preferring brass bands, and composed music for some of her poems, no scores of which have survived.

"We climbed that hill" may be Harford's masterpiece. Written in about 1917, it is perhaps the first poem by a non-Aboriginal that depicts an Australian landscape in all its individuality, without an overlay of 19th-century romanticism. The lines "Ruddy,/As zinnias and paint-water and a flood/ Of heavy auburn hair ..." indicate that the "you" of the poem may have been the philosopher Katie Lush. There is a point and counterpoint between the Katie-like "you" in the poem who has "eyes on the line/The sweep and curve of fields against the sky" and "liked the whole/Broad sweep of things" and Harford, who is intrigued by "small/Jewel incidents". This "argument" is unresolved at the end of the poem as "You still proclaim the far/Eternal unity of things that are/Like Plato and the mountains" compared with the more modest Harford who says "I prefer/inchoate beauty, for my part aver/Plurality essential, am content/To find a gain in difference". The only resolution is their union as friends and agreement about the loveliness of the walk.

Summer Lightning

Just now, as warm day faded from our sight
Hosts of archangels, fleet
On lighting-wingéd feet
Passed by, all glimmering in the busy night.

Sweet angels, bring no blinding truth to birth
Give us no messages
From heavenly palaces;
Leave us our dark trees and our starlight earth.

Day's End

Little girls,
You are gay,
Little factory girls,
At the end of your day.

There you stand,
Huddled close,
On the back of a tram,
Having taken your dose.

And you go
Through the grey
And the gold of the streets
At the close of the day,

Blind as moles.
You are crude,
You are sweet, little girls,
And amazingly rude,

But so fine
To be gay.
Gentle people are dull
At the end of the day.

Why does she put me to many indignities

Why does she put me to many indignities,
Shifts to prevent myself thinking upon her,
My golden Katie, who loveth not kisses?

I wear my new dresses and put on silk stockings,
All to prevent myself thinking upon her,
Who is more lovely than fair river-lilies.

Law Student and Coach

Each day I sit in an ill-lighted room
To teach a boy;
For one hour by the clock great words and dreams
Are our employ.

We read *St Agnes' Eve* and that more fair
Eve of St Mark
At a small table up against the wall
In the half-dark.

I tell him all the wise things I have read
Concerning Keats,
"His earlier work is overfull of sense
And sensual sweets."

I tell him all that comes into my mind
From God-knows-where,
Remark, "In English poets Bertha's type
Is jolly rare.

She's a real girl that strains her eyes to read
And cricks her neck.
Now Madeline could pray all night nor feel
Her body's check.

And Bertha *reads*, p'rhaps the first reading girl
In English rhyme."
It's maddening work to say what Keats has said
A second time.

The boy sits sideways with averted head.
His brown cheek glows.
I like his black eyes and his sprawling limbs
And his short nose.

He, feeling, dreads the splendour of the verse,
But he must learn

To write about it neatly and to quote
These lines that burn.

He drapes his soul in my obscuring words,
Makes himself fit
To go into a sunny world and take
His part in it.

"Examiners' point of view, you know," say I,
"Is commonsense.
You must sift poetry before you can
Sift Evidence."

Machinist Talking

I sit at my machine,
Hour long beside me Vera aged nineteen,
Babbles her sweet and innocent tale of sex.

Her boy, she hopes, will prove
Unlike his father in the act of love,
Twelve children are too many for her taste.

She looks sidelong, blue-eyed
And tells a girlish story of a bride
With the sweet licence of Arabian queens.

Her child, she says, saw light
Minute for minute, nine months from the night
The mother first lay in her lover's arms.

She says a friend of hers
Is a man's mistress who gives jewels and furs
But will not have her soft limbs cased in stays.

I open my small store
And tell of a young delicate girl, a whore,
Stole from her mother many months ago.

Fate made the woman seem
To have a tiger's loveliness, to gleam
Strong and fantastic as a beast of prey.

I sit at my machine.
Hourlong beside me, Vera, aged nineteen,
Babbles her sweet and innocent tale of sex.

The Invisible People

When I go into town at half past seven
Great crowds of people stream across the ways,
Hurrying, although it's only half past seven.
They are the invisible people of the days.

When you go in to town about eleven
The hurrying, morning crowds are hid from view.
Shut in the silent buildings at eleven
They toil to make life meaningless for you.

Closing Time: Public Library

At ten o' clock the great gong sounds its dread
Prelude to splendour. I push back my chair,
And all the people leave their books. We flock,
Still acquiescent, down the marble stair
Into the dark where we can't read. And thought
Swoops down insatiate through the starry air.

Periodicity

My friend declares
Being woman and virgin she
Takes small account of periodicity.

And she is right.
Her days are calmly spent
For her sex-function is irrelevant.

But I whose life
Is monthly broke in twain
Must seek some sort of meaning in my pain.

Women I say,
Are beautiful in change
Remote, immortal, like the moon they range.

Or call my pain
A skirmish in the whole
Tremendous conflict between body and soul.

Meaning must lie,
Some beauty surely dwell
In the fierce depths and uttermost pits of hell.

Yet still I seek,
Month after month in vain,
Meaning and beauty in recurrent pain.

We climbed that hill

We climbed that hill,
The road flushed red in pride
At being beauty's boundary. Either side
Stretched beauty, beauty ever, beauty still.

For on the left
Rose sandhills bound together by the deft
Long fingers of sea-grass
Humped like the Punch and Judy of a farce,
Comical, cleft
With gaps for wind to pass
Spotted
With dark
Clumped tea-tree, stark
With rushes, fierce with burrs,
Blotted
With purple earth,
Stains, remnants, marks of birth
On too-exuberant beauty.

On the right
Long paddocks stooped under a cloudy sky.

"They're lovely paddocks. Look at them," you said.
I turned my head.
What I'd thought gray
Was seen
To be the young beginning of live green
Under a spray
Of ghostly weed-stalks – lilacs, mauves and blues
At interplay –
A delicate tracery of shadow hues.

"There's colour," I began
And straightway knew
I saw what you
Saw not, and yet your vision was not mine.
Your eyes were on the line
The sweep and curve of the fields against the sky.
You'd heard
My poor beginning of a word.
I had no more to praise
An unfamiliar loveliness. To gaze
Was all my praise.

At the hilltop it was your turn to say
"There's colour." You had found
Silver and gold on my Tom Tiddler's ground.
At the roadside
A clump of grasses, all
Caught round a little bush and tangled, tied
With unimagined colours people call
Green when they see them. This was treasure spied
By your eyes with my soul.
You'd liked the whole
Broad sweep of things, had scarcely seen such small
Jewel incidents until
I showed you, who had never watched a hill
Remote in contemplation 'neath far, far skies,
Except with eyes
That had no mind to see
A present beauty, only what might be
If distance were annihilate.

And then,
Where the road crossed the creek we could not cross,
We found again
Our power of sight redoubled by the loss
Of what I'd planned.
You said it was no sense
To pull off shoes and fasten up a skirt
And plunge through dirt
And mud
And water, water
Muddy,
Ruddy,
As zinnias and paint-water and a flood
Of heavy auburn hair. We'd better go
Round by the beach,
Not by the cliffs, to reach
That farthest cliff
I wanted to see tower
Above the waves in colour and in power,
More solid than the sky.
And so
We turned
Seaward among the sea-grass. I had learned

Some of your alien sense of beauty, line
Preferred to colour, distance to the near.
For it was I
Who saw
The lovely curve of the creek.
But the whole shore
Yellow, untrodden, (more
The loveliest thing of our whole lovely week
For subtle curve, unbroken surface, than
For colour) this wide shore
Was yours and mine
And yours and mine the foam
When it would shine
Flower-coloured in a glint of sun. But mine
The hurry
And swift scurry
Of wind-blown tea-tree up the cliff.

We gave
A double dower
Of beauty to each wave
That trailed its hair in the wind before it broke.
For all the power
Of alien philosophies awoke
Our power of sight.
You still proclaim the far
Eternal unity of things that are
Like Plato and the mountains. I prefer
Inchoate beauty, for my part aver
Plurality essential, am content
To find a gain in difference, in a while
Admit there's gain in union. Argument
Recurs. Oh well, at any rate we know
That walk was lovely;
Ecstasies of mind
And subtle mysteries of sight combined
With the dear love of friends to make it so.

An Improver

Maisie's been holding down her head all day,
Her little red head. And her pointed chin
Rests on her neck that slips so softly in

The square-cut low-necked darling dress she made
In such a way, since it's high-waisted too,
It lets you guess how fair young breasts begin
Under the gentle pleasant folds of blue.

But on the roof at lunchtime when the sun
Shone warmly and the wind was blowing free
She lifted up her head to let me see
A little rosy mark beneath her chin –
The mark of kisses. If her mother knew
She'd be ashamed, but a girl-friend like me
Made her feel proud to show her kisses to.

Revolution

She is not of the fireside,
My lovely love;
Nor books, nor even a cradle,
She bends above.

No, she is bent with lashes,
Her flesh is torn.
From blackness into blackness
She walks forlorn.

But factories and prisons
Are far more fair
Than home or palace gardens
If she is there.

When I get up to light the fire

When I get up to light the fire,
And dress with all the speed I may
By candlelight, I dread the hours
That go to make a single day.

But then I leave my room, and see
How brightly, clearly darkness shines,
When stars ten thousand miles away
Are caught in our veranda vines.

And I am almost glad that fires
Have to be lit, before the day
Comes up between the trees and drives
The strange familiar dark away.

Pruning Flowering Gums

One summer day, along the street,
Men pruned the gums
To make them neat.
The tender branches, white with flowers,
Lay in the sun
For hours and hours,
And every hour they grew more sweet,
More honey-like
Until the street
Smelt like a hive, withouten bees.
But still the gardeners
Lopped the trees.

Then came the children out of school,
Noisy and separate
As their rule
Of being is. The spangled trees
Gave them one heart:
Such power to please
Had all the flowering branches strown
Around for them
To make their own.
Then such a murmuring arose
As made the ears
Confirm the nose
And give the lie to eyes. For hours
Child bees hummed
In the honey flowers.

They gathered sprigs and armfuls. Some
Ran with their fragrant
Burdens home,
And still returned; and after them
Would drag great boughs.
Some stripped a stem
Of rosy flowers and played with these.
Never such love
Had earthly trees
As these young creatures gave. By night,
The treasured sprays
Of their delight
Were garnered every one. The street
Looked, as the council liked it, neat.

LEON GELLERT 1892–1977

Leon Gellert was born in Adelaide and enlisted in the Australian Imperial Force in 1914, 18 days after Britain had declared war on Germany. He fought at Gallipoli and after nine weeks in action came down with dysentery, was evacuated to Malta, where he caught typhoid, and convalesced in England. He was discharged in 1916 as medically unfit after collapsing in a coma, with suspected epilepsy. He re-enlisted four months later and was promptly discharged, when his medical record emerged. Returning to Australia he became a journalist, edited the journal, *Art in Australia*, and later was a columnist with *The Sydney Morning Herald*. His *Songs of a Campaign*, published in 1917, made him at the time the outstanding Australian poet of World War I, but the quality of these poems was not matched by his later romantic, domestic and light verse, most of which is fairly uninteresting. Many of Gellert's war poems were written in 1915, while the campaign in Gallipoli was under way. He is an example of a man shocked into poetry by war, and then perhaps struck dumb by the experience.

A Night Attack

Be still. The bleeding night is in suspense
  Of watchful agony and coloured thought,
And every beating vein and trembling sense,
  Long-tired with time, is pitched and overwrought.
And for the eye, the darkness holds strange forms,
  Soft movements in the leaves, and wicked glows
That wait and peer. The whole black landscape swarms
  With shapes of white and grey that no one knows;
And for the ear, a sound, a pause, a breath,
  A distant hurried footstep moving fast.
The hand has touched the slimy face of death.
  The mind is raking at the ragged past.
. . . . A sound of rifles rattles from the south,
  And startled orders move from mouth to mouth.

Rendezvous

Long before the dawn breaks
With a bird's cry,
I'll be hustling on the wind
Out to where you lie –
Hurrying to our rendezvous
Under the April sky.

I'll step from out the sea again
To the shoulder of the land,
And pass the dead boy where he lies

Prone on the tideless strand,
Treading lightly lest I move
His fingers in the sand.

Do you remember how you stopped
After the sudden climb,
Sniffing the air as one who comes
On a holy thing sublime?
I'll meet you where the breeze brought
The first sent of thyme.

I'll meet you where we yarned that morn.
Under the April sky,
Waiting on our bellies there
For the battle cry.
I'll meet you where I left you there
Lying all awry.
You said, "We will continue the
Discussion by and by."

. . . . .

If I could but remember what
We spoke of, you and I!

Before Action

We always had to do our work at night.
I wondered why we had to be so sly.
I wondered why we couldn't have our fight
Under the open sky.

I wondered why I always felt so cold.
I wondered why the orders seemed so slow,
So slow to come, so whisperingly told,
So whisperingly low.

I wondered if my packing-straps were tight,
And wondered why I wondered. Sound went wild ...
An order came ... I ran into the night
Wondering why I smiled.

In the Trench

Every night I sleep,
And every night I dream
That I'm strolling with my sheep
By the old stream.

Every morn I wake,
And every morn I stand
And watch the shrapnel break
On the smashed land.

Some night I'll fall asleep,
And will not wake at dawn.
I'll lie and feed my sheep
On a green Lawn.

These Men

Men moving in a trench, in the clear noon,
  Whetting their steel within the crumbling earth;
Men, moving in a trench 'neath a new moon
  That smiles with a slit mouth and has no mirth;
Men moving in a trench in the grey morn,
  Lifting bodies on their clotted frames;
Men with narrow mouths thin-carved in scorn
  That twist and fumble strangely at dead names.

. . . . .

These men know life – know death a little more.
  These men see paths and ends, and see
Beyond some swinging open door
  Into eternity.

"RICKETY KATE" (Minnie Agnes Filson)
1898–1971

Mrs Minnie Agnes Filson was born in Wyalong in New South Wales, educated at Cleveland Street High School, Sydney, and at a business college and did secretarial work. For nine years she was manager of *The Church Standard*. The composer Richard Charlton relates that she was "an accomplished pianist, singer and dancer until she was struck down by rheumatoid arthritis early in life". An invalid for most of her life, she distributed the small jewels of her poems under the humorous pen name which she gave herself.

Waratah

How many dawns and sunsets came
Across the valley of the years
Before your heart of sculptured flame
Blazed through its galaxy of spears?

Green spears that lift with one desire
To shield your heart of chiselled fire.

Affinity

I wonder if the cabbage knows
He is less lovely than the rose,
Or if he squats in snug content,
A source of noble nourishment.
And if he pities for her sins
The rose, who has no vitamins,
Or, if one thing his green heart knows ...
That same Fire that warms the rose.

Via the Bridge

If you come often to Sydney via the Bridge
And have studied the racing notes
And scanned the headlines,
You may glance at the Cables
Or the crimson pointed nails
Of the woman opposite.
But, if you have not passed that way before,
You will look at the Pylons
And you will say to yourself:
"How regular these pinnacles are,
And
How alien!"
And, when they are behind,
"I am treading upon the smoke
Of a ship that perhaps
Sailed out from Brazil;"
Or you will whisper to yourself:
"This is the way the winds walk
Above the sea.
Where the gulls flicker like silver moths."
Then you will want to put your hands
Out of the window
And let them flutter
With all the things
That move above the waters.
And, when you are in the centre –
That enormous centre
Moulded of concrete and steel,

And the sweat of hands
And the labour of minds –
And there is nothing beneath
But the wind and the smoke and the gulls –
Nothing to the East and nothing to the West
But the miraculous web of the skies
Spun from the four horizons,
"This is a great wonder,"
Your spirit will sing:
"I shall not pass
This way again, too soon,
That I may keep
This vast astonishment."

KENNETH SLESSOR 1901–1971

Kenneth Slessor was born in Orange, New South Wales, the elder son of Robert Schloesser, a German Jewish mining engineer, who Anglicised the family name during the First World War. His mother was the daughter of Scottish immigrants. Slessor was brought up at Chatswood in Sydney, and after leaving school, went into a lifetime career in journalism. He worked for the *Sun* and *Smith's Weekly* (which he joined in 1927, and of which he was editor from 1935 to 1939, and editor-in-chief 1939–40). From 1940 to 1944 he was official war correspondent accompanying the Australian Infantry Forces in Greece, Crete, Syria, North Africa, and New Guinea, an assignment he regarded as a great honour. His reporting was distinctive and acid, and he resigned his commission in a controversy over army censorship of correspondents' dispatches. After his resignation he rejoined the Sydney *Sun*, a mass-circulation afternoon newspaper, becoming its editor, then in 1957 moved to the *Telegraph*, a right-wing "popular" morning newspaper, where he was leader writer and chief book reviewer almost until his death in 1971.

Slessor was the president of the Sydney Journalists' Club from 1956 to 1965, and brought his courtly style (bow ties, waistcoats, portliness) to a scene of hard drinking and poker machines above the railway yards in south Sydney. Frank Hardy, the well-known Communist novelist (until he left the Party after 1956), had a story of this period of Slessor's life, which shows the low profile Slessor's poetry had among a section of his friends. Hardy was talking to one of Slessor's drinking mates from the Journalists' Club – a man with whom, on Hardy's estimate, Slessor would have had a casual drink two or three times a week. Hardy mentioned to this man that he, together with Slessor, was about to go to a writers' conference at the University of New England. "Old Ken, eh?" Slessor's friend replied, "What's he doing up there?"

Slessor was, with Douglas Stewart, responsible for government grants to Australian writers, on the Commonwealth Literary Fund, from 1953. He was co-editor with John Thompson and Guy Howarth of *The Penguin Book of Australian Verse* (1958), later revised as *The Penguin Book of Modern Australian Verse* (1961), an anthology that was influential for many years and deliberately left the 19th century behind. Slessor had a low regard for the poetry of Gordon and Kendall and the balladists such as Paterson and Lawson. Although the anthology included some poets with birth dates earlier than Hugh McCrae, the editors said of McCrae's poetry "there can be no doubt that it marks a turning point between the mass of shoddy second-rate writing in verse-form which went before it and the development of the higher technical standards which have been achieved in genuine poetry since *Satyrs and Sunlight* [McCrae's first book] was published in 1909."

For most of his adult life Slessor lived around the bohemian Kings Cross area of Sydney. He rented for a long period one half of a "minor mansion" overlooking Sydney Harbour, which he kept shadowy, dusty and filled with curios: heavy cedar furniture, hefty silver, china and glassware, pewter tankards, old maps, etchings, tarot cards, watercolours by Norman Lindsay, and a library of antique books.

Slessor's first wife, Noëlla Senior, whom he married when he was 21 and she 28, died in 1945 of cancer, an event which was devastating for him. They were childless. He remarried and had a son, Paul, by his second wife, Pauline Wallace (née Bowe), and won custody of their son when they divorced. In his final years, Pauline moved back as a housekeeper into his house, which was now at Chatswood. He died suddenly of a myocardial infarction in 1971 and was cremated without religious ceremony. His ashes were placed next to those of his first wife.

One of the mysteries of Slessor's life is the poetic silence of his last thirty years. He was already recognised as Australia's finest poet, but in the ten years after 1937, the year of "Five Bells", he wrote only three poems that he retained, then nothing further. Depression does not entirely explain this poetic silence. In his last years, Slessor, according to accounts like that of Hal Porter in *The Extra*, was privately and stoically depressed; yet despite "his gout giving him hell, and with his haemorrhoids aflame", he maintained his immaculate manners, his dandyism, and his generosity to young writers. In any event, depression does not stop poets writing. "Five Bells" is infused with a great wave of regret and pessimism.

Another explanation is that Slessor had written himself out, exhausted by the daily grind of journalism and the demands of producing light ephemeral verse for *Smiths Weekly*. He wrote for *Smiths* more than seventy-five pieces of light verse over ten years, starting in 1928. (Excellent as they are, we have included only one example, "Streamer's End".) The introduction by Julian Croft to Slessor's posthumous volume of light verse, *Backless Betty from Bondi*, tells the story of Robert D. FitzGerald's surprise when he met Slessor in Sydney's Martin Place, with a bag of golf clubs on his shoulder – a game Slessor did not play. FitzGerald became "even more surprised" when Slessor announced he was giving up serious poetry to write only humorous verse. Croft points out that although FitzGerald did not take him seriously, Slessor was serious about light verse, even preparing "piles of rhymes stacked like roulette chips, and lists of brand names, foods, clothing, in unlikely but rhyming combination." The period of Slessor's maturity as a poet and his greatest poems coincides with his versifying for *Smiths*. His light verse enhanced the virtuoso technique of his major poems, and unlike Lawson he did not let the two streams of his poetic activity mix and become turbid.

Slessor is an example of a poet who peaked early – other Australian examples are Brennan, Stowe and Wright. He was unable to reinvent his style and was too exacting merely to repeat himself. FitzGerald recalled that John Betjeman, when visiting Australia "innocently expressed disappointment at no recent Slessor poems having come his way; and Ken answered to the effect that he had no wish to dilute what he had finished saying. Then he kept on talking engagingly." (*Robert D. FitzGerald*, UQP, 1987, p. 57).

Slessor's supreme importance to Australian poetry lies in the visual and auditory richness of his style. He brought a European ornateness to a country that had seemed to rebuff such sensuality. Slessor's language is the most original and individual of any Australian poet. The associative daring of this language is present in his earliest published poems, his youthful fantasias, exotic scenes and allegories that derive from Hugh McCrae and from a fascination with European high culture. He related that he once tried to write a novel, but could not get past the first 50 pages (perhaps fewer than that) as he got stuck on physical details.

Slessor was co-editor of the briefly flaring *Vision* magazine, which was a vehicle for the philosophy of Norman Lindsay. Of the Lindsay credo, he said, "A lot of it I never agreed with. I did agree on one point of dogma ... our insistence on the concrete image in art, and our hatred of the abstract." The most significant development in Slessor's work is his movement away from Lindsay's Nietzschean vitalism to an attitude that permitted pessimism and pity. All of his poetry is obsessed with the flux of things, with meaninglessness and death. His strategy for dealing with "the tunnels of nothingness" between the stars, with "Infinity's trapdoor, eternal and merciless", was to savour the finest pleasures of life – wine and friends, odes and curries, billiards, girls, metaphors, metres, "every dish that passes", as he puts it in "To a Friend".

The Night-Ride

Gas flaring on the yellow platform; voices running up and down;
Milk-tins in cold dented silver; half-awake I stare,
Pull up the blind, blink out – all sounds are drugged;
The slow blowing of passengers asleep;
Engines yawning; water in heavy drips;
Black, sinister travellers, lumbering up the station,
One moment in the window, hooked over bags;
Hurrying, unknown faces – boxes with strange labels –
All groping clumsily to mysterious ends,
Out of the gaslight, dragged by private Fates.
Their echoes die. The dark train shakes and plunges;
Bells cry out; the night-ride starts again.
Soon I shall look out into nothing but blackness,
Pale, windy fields. The old roar and knock of the rails
Melts in dull fury. Pull down the blind. Sleep. Sleep.
Nothing but grey, rushing rivers of bush outside.
Gaslight and milk-cans. Of Rapptown I recall nothing else.

Streamer's End

Roses all over the steamer,
  Paper all over the sky,

And You at the end of a streamer
  Smiling goodbye, goodbye.
It isn't to me you dangle,
  It isn't to me you smile,
But out of the rainbow tangle
  Our lines have crossed for a while.

Somebody's benediction
  Pitches a streamer – whizz! –
Under the firm conviction
  You're on the end of his.
Others may claim attention,
  Rolling away to sea,
But nobody's there to mention
  The cove at this end is ME!

Don't you consider the danger
  Of setting a heart on fire
By tossing a perfect stranger
  Your 10,000 volt live-wire?
I'm only a face on the skyline,
  Something the wharf obscures –
But you're on the end of my line,
  And I'm on the end of yours!

Off in the vast *Orsova*,
  Soon you will wave in vain;
I could be Casanova,
  You could be Queen of Spain –
I must go back to the city,
  You must go back to the King.
Blow me a kiss for pity,
  Girl at the end of the string!

Wild Grapes

The old orchard, full of smoking air,
Full of sour marsh and broken boughs, is there,
But kept no more by vanished Mulligans,
Or Hartigans, long drowned in earth themselves,
Who gave this bitter fruit their care.

Here's where the cherries grew that birds forgot,
And apples bright as dogstars; now there is not
An apple or a cherry; only grapes,

But wild ones, Isabella grapes they're called,
Small, pointed, black, like boughs of musket-shot.

Eating their flesh, half-savage with black fur,
Acid and gipsy-sweet, I thought of her,
Isabella, the dead girl, who has lingered on
Defiantly when all have gone away,
In an old orchard where swallows never stir.

Isabella grapes, outlaws of a strange bough,
That in their harsh sweetness remind me somehow
Of dark hair swinging and silver pins,
A girl half-fierce, half-melting, as these grapes,
Kissed here – or killed here – but who remembers now?

Dutch Seacoast *(from* The Atlas*)*

"Toonneel der Steden van vereenighde Nederlanden met hare Beschrijvingen uytgegeven by Joan. Blaeu."

No wind of Life may strike within
This little country's crystal bin,
Nor calendar compute the days
Tubed in their capsule of soft glaze.

Naked and rinsed, the bubble-clear
Canals of Amsterdam appear,
The blue-tiled turrets, china clocks
And glittering beaks of weathercocks.

A gulf of sweet and winking hoops
Whereon there ride 500 poops
With flying mouths and fleeting hair
Of saints hung up like candles there –

Fox-coloured mansions, lean and tall,
That burst in air but never fall
Whose bolted shadows, row by row,
Float changeless on the stones below –

Sky full of ships, bay full of town,
A port of waters jellied brown:
Such is the world no tide may stir,
Sealed by the great cartographer.

O, could he but clap up like this
My decomposed metropolis,

Those other countries of the mind,
So tousled, dark and undefined!

Captain Dobbin

Captain Dobbin, having retired from the South Seas
In the dumb tides of 1900, with a handful of shells,
A few poisoned arrows, a cask of pearls,
And five thousand pounds in the colonial funds,
Now sails the street in a brick villa, "Laburnum Villa",
In whose blank windows the harbour hangs
Like a fog against the glass,
Golden and smoky, or stoned with a white glitter,
And boats go by, suspended in the pane,
Blue Funnel, Red Funnel, Messageries Maritimes,
Lugged down the port like sea-beasts taken alive
That scrape their bellies on sharp sands,
Of which particulars Captain Dobbin keeps
A ledger sticky with ink,
Entries of time and weather, state of the moon,
Nature of cargo and captain's name,
For some mysterious and awful purpose
Never divulged.
For at night, when the stars mock themselves with lanterns,
So late the chimes blow loud and faint
Like a hand shutting and unshutting over the bells,
Captain Dobbin, having observed from bed
The lights, like a great fiery snake, of the *Comorin*
Going to sea, will note the hour
For subsequent recording in his gazette.

But the sea is really closer to him than this,
Closer to him than a dead, lovely woman,
For he keeps bits of it, like old letters,
Salt tied up in bundles
Or pressed flat,
What you might call a lock of the sea's hair,
So Captain Dobbin keeps his dwarfed memento,
His urn-burial, a chest of mummied waves,
Gales fixed in print, and the sweet dangerous countries
Of shark and casuarina-tree,
Stolen and put in coloured maps,
Like a flask of seawater, or a bottled ship,

A schooner caught in a glass bottle;
But Captain Dobbin keeps them in books,
Crags of varnished leather
Pimply with gilt, by learned mariners
And masters of hydrostatics, or the childish tales
Of simple heroes, taken by Turks or dropsy.
So nightly he sails from shelf to shelf
Or to the quadrants, dangling with rusty screws,
Or the hanging-gardens of old charts,
So old they bear the authentic protractor-lines,
Traced in faint ink, as fine as Chinese hairs.

Over the flat and painted atlas-leaves
His reading-glass would tremble,
Over the fathoms, pricked in tiny rows,
Water shelving to the coast.
Quietly the bone-rimmed lens would float
Till, through the glass, he felt the barbéd rush
Of bubbles foaming, spied the albicores,
Thee blue-finned admirals, heard the wind-swallowed cries
Of planters running on the beach
Who filched their swags of yams and ambergris,
Birds' nests and sandalwood, from pastures numbed
By the sun's yellow, too meek for honest theft;
But he, less delicate robber, climbed the walls,
Broke into dozing houses
Crammed with black bottles, marish wine
Crusty and salt-corroded, fading prints,
Sparkle-daubed almanacs and playing cards,
With rusty cannon, left by the French outside,
Half-buried in sand,
Even to the castle of Queen Pomaree
In the Yankee's footsteps, and found her throne-room piled
With golden candelabras, mildewed swords,
Guitars and fowling-pieces, tossed in heaps
With greasy cakes and flung-down calabashes.

Then Captain Dobbin's eye,
That eye of wild and wispy scudding blue,
Voluptuously prying, would light up
Like mica scratched by gully-suns,
And he would be fearful to look upon
And shattering in his conversation;

Nor would he tolerate the harmless chanty,
No *"Shenandoah"*, or the dainty mew
That landsmen offer in a silver dish
To Neptune, sung to pianos in candlelight.
Of these he spoke in scorn,
For there was but one way of singing *"Stormalong"*,
He said, and that was not really singing,
But howling, rather – shrieked in the wind's jaws
By furious men; not tinkled in drawing-rooms
By lap-dogs in clean shirts.
And, at these words,
The galleries of photographs, men with rich beards,
Pea-jackets and brass buttons, with folded arms,
Would scowl approval, for they were shipmates, too,
Companions of no cruise by reading-glass,
But fellows of storm and honey from the past –
"The Charlotte, Java, '93,"
"Knuckle and Fred at Port au Prince,"
"William in his New Rig,"
Even that notorious scoundrel, Captain Baggs,
Who, as all knew, owed Dobbin Twenty Pounds
Lost at fair cribbage, but he never paid
Or paid "with the slack of the tops'l sheets"
As Captain Dobbin frequently expressed it.

There were their faces, grilled a trifle now,
Cigar-hued in various spots
By the brown breath of sodium-eating years,
On quarter-decks long burnt to the water's edge,
A resurrection of the dead by chemicals.
And the voyages they had made,
Their labours in a country of water,
Were they not marked by inadequate lines
On charts tied up like skins in a rack?
Or his own Odysseys, his lonely travels,
His trading days, an autobiography
Of angles and triangles and lozenges
Ruled tack by tack across the sheet
That with a single scratch expressed the stars,
Merak and Alamak and Alpherat,
The wind, the moon, the sun, the clambering sea
Sails bleached with light, salt in the eyes,
Bamboos and Tahiti oranges,

From some forgotten countless day,
One foundered day from a forgotten month,
A year sucked quietly from the blood,
Dead with the rest, remembered by no more
Than a scratch on a dry chart –
Or when the return grew too choking bitter-sweet
And laburnum-berries manifestly tossed
Beyond the window, not the fabulous leaves
Of Hotoo or canoe-tree or palmetto,
There were the wanderings of other keels,
Magellan, Bouganville and Cook,
Who found no greater a memorial
Than footprints over a lithograph.

For Cook he worshipped, that captain with the sad
And fine white face, who never lost a man
Or flinched a peril; and of Bougainville
He spoke with graceful courtesy, as a rival
To whom the honours of the hunting-field
Must be accorded. Not so with the Spaniard,
Sebastian Juan del Cano, at whom he sneered
Openly, calling him a fool of fortune
Blown to a sailors' abbey by chance winds
And blindfold currents, who slept in a fine cabin,
Blundered through five degrees of latitude,
Was bullied by mutineers a hundred more,
And woke and found himself across the world.

Coldly in the window,
Like a fog rubbed up and down the glass
The harbour, bony with mist
And ropes of water, glittered; and the blind tide
That crawls it knows not where, nor for what gain,
Pushed its drowned shoulders against the wheel,
Against the wheel of the mill.
Flowers rocked far down
And white, dead bodies that were anchored there
In marshes of spent light.
Blue Funnel, Red Funnel,
The ships went over them, and bells in engine-rooms
Cried to their bowels of flaring oil,
And stokers groaned and sweated with burnt skins,
Clawed to their shovels.

But quietly in his room,
In his little cemetery of sweet essences
With fond memorial-stones and lines of grace,
Captain Dobbin went on reading about the sea.

Five Visions of Captain Cook

I

Cook was a captain of the Admiralty
When sea-captains had the evil eye,
Or should have, what with beating krakens off
And casting nativities of ships;
Cook was a captain of the powder-days
When captains, you might have said, if you had been
Fixed by their glittering stare, half-down the side,
Or gaping at them up companionways,
Were more like warlocks than a humble man –
And men were humble then who gazed at them,
Poor horn-eyed sailors, bullied by devils' fists
Of wind or water, or the want of both,
Childlike and trusting, filled with eager trust –
Cook was a captain of the sailing days
When sea-captains were kings like this,
Not cold executives of company-rules
Cracking their boilers for a dividend
Or bidding their engineers go wink
At bells and telegraphs, so plates would hold
Another pound. Those captains drove their ships
By their own blood, no laws of schoolbook steam,
Till yards were sprung, and masts went overboard –
Daemons in periwigs, doling magic out,
Who read fair alphabets in stars
Where humbler men found but a mess of sparks,
Who steered their crews by mysteries
And strange, half-dreadful sortilege with books,
Used medicines that only gods could know
The sense of, but sailors drank
In simple faith. That was the captain
Cook was when he came to the Coral Sea
And chose a passage into the dark.

How many mariners had made that choice
Paused on the brink of mystery! "Choose now!"
The winds roared, blowing home, blowing home,

Over the Coral Sea. "Choose now!" the trades
Cried once to Tasman, throwing him for choice
Their teeth or shoulders, and the Dutchman chose
The wind's way, turning north. "Choose, Bougainville!"
The wind cried once, and Bougainville had heard
The voice of God, calling him prudently
Out of a dead lee shore, and chose the north.
The wind's way. So, too, Cook made choice,
Over the brink, into the devil's mouth,
With four months' food, and sailors wild with dreams
Of English beer, the smoking barns of home.
So Cook made choice, so Cook sailed westabout,
So men write poems in Australia.

II

Flowers turned to stone! Not all the botany
Of Joseph Banks, hung pensive in a porthole,
Could find the Latin for this loveliness,
Could put the Barrier Reef in a glass box
Tagged by the horrid Gorgon squint
Of horticulture. Stone turned to flowers
It seemed – you'd snap a crystal twig,
One petal even of the water-garden,
And have it dying like a cherry-bough.
They'd sailed all day outside a coral hedge,
And half the night. Cook sailed at night,
Let there be reefs a fathom from the keel
And empty charts. The sailors didn't ask,
Nor Joseph Banks. Who cared? It was the spell
Of Cook that lulled them, bade them turn below,
Kick off their sea-boots, puff themselves to sleep,
Though there were more shoals outside
Than teeth in a shark's head. Cook snored loudest himself.

One day, a morning of light airs and calms,
They slid towards a reef that would have knifed
Their boards to mash, and murdered every man.
So close it sucked them, one wave shook their keel.
The next blew past the coral. Three officers,
In gilt and buttons, languidly on deck
Pointed their sextants at the sun. One yawned,
One held a pencil, one put eye to lens:
Three very peaceful English mariners

Taking their sights for longitude.
I've never heard
Of sailors aching for the longitude
Of shipwrecks before or since. It was the spell
Of Cook did this, the phylacteries of Cook.
Men who ride broomsticks with a mesmerist
Mock the typhoon. So, too, it was with Cook.

III

Two chronometers the captain had,
One by Arnold that ran like mad,
One by Kendal in a walnut case,
Poor devoted creature with a hangdog face.

Arnold always hurried with a crazed click-click
Dancing over Greenwich like a lunatic,
Kendal panted faithfully his watch-dog beat,
Climbing out of Yesterday with sticky little feet.

Arnold choked with appetite to wolf up time,
Madly round the numerals his hands would climb,
His cogs rushed over and his wheels ran miles,
Dragging Captain Cook to the Sandwich Isles.

But Kendal dawdled in the tombstoned past,
With a sentimental prejudice to going fast,
And he thought very often of a haberdasher's door
And a yellow-haired boy who would knock no more.

All through the night-time, clock talked to clock,
In the captain's cabin, tock-tock-tock,
One ticked fast and one ticked slow,
And Time went over them a hundred years ago.

IV

Sometimes the god would fold his wings
And, stone of Caesars turned to flesh,
Talk of the most important things
That serious-minded midshipmen could wish,

Of plantains, and the lack of rum
Or spearing sea-cows – things like this
That hungry schoolboys, five days dumb,
In jolly-boats are wonted to discuss.

What midshipman would pause to mourn
The sun that beat about his ears,

Or curse the tide, if he could horn
His fists by tugging on those lumbering oars?

Let rum-tanned mariners prefer
To hug the weather-side of yards;
"Cats to catch mice" before they purr,
Those were the captain's enigmatic words.

Here, in this jolly-boat they graced,
Were food and freedom, wind and storm,
While, fowling-piece across his waist,
Cook mapped the coast, with one eye cocked for game.

V

After the candles had gone out, and those
Who listened had gone out, and a last wave
Of chimney-haloes caked their smoky rings
Like fish-scales on the ceiling, a Yellow Sea
Of swimming circles, the old man,
Old Captain-in-the-Corner, drank his rum
With friendly gestures to four chairs. They stood
Empty, still warm from haunches, with rubbed nails
And leather glazed, like agèd serving-men
Feeding a king's delight, the sticky, drugged
Sweet agony of habitual anecdotes.
But these, his chairs, could bear an old man's tongue,
Sleep when he slept, be flattering when he woke,
And wink to hear the same eternal name
From lips new-dipped in rum.

"Then Captain Cook,
I heard him, told them they could go
If so they chose, but he would get them back,
Dead or alive, he'd have them,"
The old man screeched, half-thinking to hear "Cook!
Cook again! Cook! It's other cooks he'll need,
Cooks who can bake a dinner out of pence,
That's what he lives on, talks on, half-a-crown
A day, and sits there full of Cook.
Who'd do your cooking now, I'd like to ask,
If someone didn't grind her bones away?
But that's the truth, six children and half-a-crown
A day, and a man gone daft with Cook."

That was his wife,
Elizabeth, a noble wife but brisk,
Who lived in a present full of kitchen-fumes
And had no past. He had not seen her
For seven years, being blind, and that of course
Was why he'd had to strike a deal with chairs,
Not knowing when those who chafed them had gone to sleep
Or stolen away. Darkness and empty chairs,
This was the port that Alexander Home
Had come to with his useless cutlass-wounds
And tales of Cook, and half-a-crown a day –
This was the creek he'd run his timbers to,
Where grateful countrymen repaid his wounds
At half-a-crown a day. Too good, too good,
This eloquent offering of birdcages
To gulls, and Greenwich Hospital to Cook,
Britannia's mission to the sea-fowl.

It was not blindness picked his flesh away,
Nor want of sight made penny-blank the eyes
Of Captain Home, but that he lived like this
In one place, and gazed elsewhere. His body moved
In Scotland, but his eyes were dazzle-full
Of skies and water farther round the world –
Air soaked with blue, so thick it dripped like snow
On spice-tree boughs, and water diamond-green,
Beaches wind-glittering with crumbs of gilt,
And birds more scarlet than a duchy's seal
That had come whistling long ago, and far
Away. His body had gone back,
Here it sat drinking rum in Berwickshire,
But not his eyes – they were left floating there
Half-round the earth, blinking at beaches milked
By suck-mouth tides, foaming with ropes of bubbles
And huge half-moons of surf. Thus it had been
When Cook was carried on a sailor's back,
Vengeance in a cocked hat, to claim his price,
A prince in barter for a longboat.
And then the trumpery springs of fate – a stone,
A musket-shot, a round of gunpowder,
And puzzled animals, killing they knew not what
Or why, but killing ... the surge of goatish flanks

Armoured in feathers, like cruel birds:
Wild, childish faces, killing; a moment seen,
Marines with crimson coats and puffs of smoke
Toppling face-down; and a knife of English iron,
Forged aboard ship, that had been changed for pigs,
Given back to Cook between the shoulder-blades.
There he had dropped, and the old floundering sea,
The old, fumbling, witless lover-enemy,
Had taken his breath, last office of salt water.

Cook died. The body of Alexander Home
Flowed round the world and back again, with eyes
Marooned already, and came to English coasts,
The vague ancestral darknesses of home,
Seeing them faintly through a glass of gold,
Dim fog-shapes, ghosted like the ribs of trees
Against his blazing waters and blue air.
But soon they faded, and there was nothing left,
Only the sugar-cane and the wild granaries
Of sand, and palm-trees and the flying blood
Of cardinal-birds; and putting out one hand
Tremulously in the direction of the beach,
He felt a chair in Scotland. And sat down.

The Country Ride

"... Of all the Journeys that ever I made, this was the merriest, and I was in a strange mood for mirth." – Samuel Pepys, 11 April, 1661.

Earth which has known so many passages
Of April air, so many marriages
Of strange and lovely atoms breeding light,
Never may find again that lost delight.

In the sharp sky, the frosty deepnesses,
There are still birds to barb the silences,
There are still fields to meet the morning on,
But those who made them beautiful have gone.

Diamonds are flung by other smoking springs,
But where is he that cropped their offerings –
The pick-purse of enchantments, riding by,
Whistling his "*Go and Be Hanged, That's Twice Good-bye*"?

Who such a frolic pomp of blessing made
To kiss a little pretty dairymaid ...

And country wives with bare and earth-burnt knees,
And boys with beer, and smiles from balconies ...

The greensleeve girl, apprentice-equerry,
Tending great men with slant-eye mockery:
"Then Mr Sam says, 'Riding's hot,' he says,
Tasting their ale and waving twopences ..."

Into one gaze they swam, a moment swirled,
One fiery paintbox of the body's world –
Into Sam's eye, that flying bushranger –
Swinging their torches for earth's voyager.

And how the blood sang, and the senses leapt,
And cells that under tents of horn had slept
Rose dancing, at the black and faceless bale
Of gallows-flesh that had not girl nor ale!

Country Towns

Country towns, with your willows and squares,
And farmers bouncing on barrel mares
To public houses of yellow wood
With "1860" over their doors,
And that mysterious race of Hogans
Which always keeps the General Stores ...

At the School of Arts, a broadsheet lies
Sprayed with the sarcasm of flies:
"The Great Golightly Family
Of Entertainers Here To-night" –
Dated a year and a half ago,
But left there, less from carelessness
Than from a wish to seem polite.

Verandas baked with musky sleep,
Mulberry faces dozing deep,
And dogs that lick the sunlight up
Like paste of gold – or, roused in vain
By far, mysterious buggy-wheels,
Lower their ears, and drowse again ...

Country towns with your schooner bees,
And locusts burnt in the pepper-trees,
Drown me with syrups, arch your boughs,
Find me a bench, and let me snore,

Till, charged with ale and unconcern,
I'll think it's noon at half-past four!

North Country

North Country, filled with gesturing wood,
With trees that fence, like archers' volleys,
The flanks of hidden valleys
Where nothing's left to hide

But verticals and perpendiculars,
Like rain gone wooden, fixed in falling,
Or fingers blindly feeling
For what nobody cares;

Or trunks of pewter, bangled by greedy death,
Stuck with black staghorns, quietly sucking,
And trees whose boughs go seeking,
And trees like broken teeth

With smoky antlers broken in the sky;
Or trunks that lie grotesquely rigid,
Like bodies blank and wretched
After a fool's battue,

As if they've secret ways of dying here
And secret places for their anguish
When boughs at last relinquish
Their clench of blowing air –

But this gaunt country, filled with mills and saws,
With butter-works and railway-stations
And public institutions,
And scornful rumps of cows,

North Country, filled with gesturing wood –
Timber's the end it gives to branches,
Cut off in cubic inches,
Dripping red with blood.

Last Trams

I

That street washed with violet
Writes like a tablet
Of living here; that pavement
Is the metal embodiment

Of living here; those terraces
Filled with dumb presences
Lobbed over mattresses,
Lusts and repentances,
Ardours and solaces,
Passions and hatreds
And love in brass bedsteads
Lost now in emptiness
Deep now in darkness
Nothing but nakedness,
Rails like a ribbon
And sickness of carbon
Dying in distances.

II

Then, from the skeletons of trams,
Gazing at lighted rooms, you'll find
The black and Röntgen diagrams
Of window-plants across the blind

That print their knuckleduster sticks,
Their buds of gum, against the light
Like negatives of candlesticks
Whose wicks are lit by fluorite;

And shapes look out, or bodies pass,
Between the darkness and the flare,
Between the curtain and the glass,
Of men and women moving there.

So through the moment's needle-eye,
Like phantoms in the window-chink,
Their faces brush you as they fly,
Fixed in the shutters of a blink;

But whose they are, intent on what,
Who knows? They rattle into void,
Stars of a film without a plot,
Snippings of idiot celluloid.

Out of Time

I

I saw Time flowing like the hundred yachts
That fly behind the daylight, foxed with air;

Or piercing, like the quince-bright, bitter slats
Of sun gone thrusting under Harbour's hair.

So Time, the wave, enfolds me in its bed,
Or Time, the bony knife, it runs me through.
"Skulker, take heart," I thought my own heart said.
"The flood, the blade go by – Time flows, not you!"

Vilely, continuously, stupidly,
Time takes me, drills me, drives through bone and vein,
So water bends the seaweeds in the sea,
The tide goes over, but the weeds remain.

Time, you must cry farewell, take up the track,
And leave this lovely moment at your back!

II

Time leaves the lovely moment at his back,
Eager to quench and ripen, kiss or kill;
To-morrow begs him, breathless for his lack,
Or beauty dead entreats him to be still.

His fate pursues him; he must open doors,
Or close them, for that pale and faceless host
Without a flag, whose agony implores
Birth to be flesh, or funeral, to be ghost.

Out of all reckoning, out of dark and light,
Over the edges of dead Nows and Heres,
Blindly and softly, as a mistress might,
He keeps appointments with a million years.

I and the moment laugh, and let him go,
Leaning against his golden undertow.

III

Leaning against the golden undertow,
Backward, I saw the birds begin to climb
With bodies hailstone-clear, and shadows flow,
Fixed in a sweet meniscus, out of Time,

Out of the torrent, like the fainter land
Lensed in a bubble's ghostly camera,
The lighted beach, the sharp and china sand
Glitters and waters and peninsula –

The moment's world it was; and I was part,
Fleshless and ageless, changeless and made free.

"Fool, would you leave this country?" cried my heart,
But I was taken by the suck of sea.

The gulls go down, the body dies and rots,
And Time flows past them like a hundred yachts.

Five Bells

Time that is moved by little fidget wheels
Is not my time, the flood that does not flow.
Between the double and the single bell
Of a ship's hour, between a round of bells
From the dark warship riding there below,
I have lived many lives, and this one life
Of Joe, long dead, who lives between five bells.

Deep and dissolving verticals of light
Ferry the falls of moonshine down. Five bells
Coldly rung out in a machine's voice. Night and water
Pour to one rip of darkness, the Harbour floats
In air, the Cross hangs upside-down in water.

Why do I think of you, dead man, why thieve
These profitless lodgings from the flukes of thought
Anchored in Time? You have gone from earth,
Gone even from the meaning of a name;
Yet something's there, yet something forms its lips
And hits and cries against the ports of space,
Beating their sides to make its fury heard.

Are you shouting at me, dead man, squeezing your face
In agonies of speech on speechless panes?
Cry louder, beat the windows, bawl your name!

But I hear nothing, nothing ... only bells,
Five bells, the bumpkin calculus of Time.
Your echoes die, your voice is dowsed by Life,
There's not a mouth can fly the pygmy strait –
Nothing except the memory of some bones
Long shoved away, and sucked away, in mud;
And unimportant things you might have done,
Or once I thought you did; but you forgot,
And all have now forgotten – looks and words
And slops of beer; your coat with buttons off,
Your gaunt chin and pricked eye, and raging tales
Of Irish kings and English perfidy,

And dirtier perfidy of publicans
Groaning to God from Darlinghurst.
Five bells.

Then I saw the road, I heard the thunder
Tumble, and felt the talons of the rain
The night we came to Moorebank in slab-dark,
So dark you bore no body, had no face,
But a sheer voice that rattled out of air
(As now you'd cry if I could break the glass),
A voice that spoke beside me in the bush,
Loud for a breath or bitten off by wind,
Of Milton, melons, and the Rights of Man,
And blowing flutes, and how Tahitian girls
Are brown and angry-tongued, and Sydney girls
Are white and angry-tongued, or so you'd found.
But all I heard was words that didn't join
So Milton became melons, melons girls,
And fifty mouths, it seemed, were out that night,
And in each tree an Ear was bending down,
Or something had just run, gone behind grass,
When, blank and bone-white, like a maniac's thought,
The naphtha-flash of lightning slit the sky,
Knifing the dark with deathly photographs.
There's not so many with so poor a purse
Or fierce a need, must fare by night like that,
Five miles in darkness on a country track,
But when you do, that's what you think.
Five bells.

In Melbourne, your appetite had gone,
Your angers too; they had been leeched away
By the soft archery of summer rains
And the sponge-paws of wetness, the slow damp
That stuck the leaves of living, snailed the mind,
And showed your bones, that had been sharp with rage,
The sodden ectasies of rectitude.
I thought of what you'd written in faint ink,
Your journal with the sawn-off lock, that stayed behind
With other things you left, all without use,
All without meaning now, except a sign
That someone had been living who now was dead:
"At Labassa. Room 6 x 8

On top of the tower; because of this, very dark
And cold in winter. Everything has been stowed
Into this room – 500 books all shapes
And colours, dealt across the floor
And over sills and on the laps of chairs;
Guns, photoes of many differant things
And differant curioes that I obtained …"

In Sydney, by the spent aquarium-flare
Of penny gaslight on pink wallpaper,
We argued about blowing up the world,
But you were living backward, so each night
You crept a moment closer to the breast,
And they were living, all of them, those frames
And shapes of flesh that had perplexed your youth,
And most your father, the old man gone blind,
With fingers always round a fiddle's neck,
That graveyard mason whose fair monuments
And tablets cut with dreams of piety
Rest on the bosoms of a thousand men
Staked bone by bone, in quiet astonishment
At cargoes they had never thought to bear,
These funeral-cakes of sweet and sculptured stone.

Where have you gone? The tide is over you,
The turn of midnight water's over you,
As Time is over you, and mystery,
And memory, the flood that does not flow.
You have no suburb, like those easier dead
In private berths of dissolution laid –
The tide goes over, the waves ride over you
And let their shadows down like shining hair,
But they are Water; and the sea-pinks bend
Like lilies in your teeth, but they are Weed;
And you are only part of an Idea.
I felt the wet push its black thumb-balls in,
The night you died, I felt your eardrums crack,
And the short agony, the longer dream,
The Nothing that was neither long nor short;
But I was bound, and could not go that way,
But I was blind, and could not feel your hand.
If I could find an answer, could only find
Your meaning, or could say why you were here

Who now are gone, what purpose gave you breath
Or seized it back, might I not hear your voice?

I looked out of my window in the dark
At waves with diamond quills and combs of light
That arched their mackerel-backs and smacked the sand
In the moon's drench, that straight enormous glaze,
And ships far off asleep, and Harbour-buoys
Tossing their fireballs wearily each to each,
And tried to hear your voice, but all I heard
Was a boat's whistle, and the scraping squeal
Of seabirds' voices far away, and bells,
Five bells. Five bells coldly ringing out.

Five bells.

Beach Burial

Softly and humbly to the Gulf of Arabs
The convoys of dead sailors come;
At night they sway and wander in the waters far under,
But morning rolls them in the foam.

Between the sob and clubbing of the gunfire
Someone, it seems, has time for this,
To pluck them from the shallows and bury them in burrows
And tread the sand upon their nakedness;

And each cross, the driven stake of tidewood,
Bears the last signature of men,
Written with such perplexity, with such bewildered pity,
The words choke as they begin –

"*Unknown seaman*" – the ghostly pencil
Wavers and fades, the purple drips,
The breath of the wet season has washed their inscriptions
As blue as drowned men's lips,

Dead seamen, gone in search of the same landfall,
Whether as enemies they fought,
Or fought with us, or neither; the sand joins them together,
Enlisted on the other front.

El Alamein

R. D. FITZGERALD 1902–1987

Robert D. FitzGerald was born at Hunters Hill, a Sydney suburb, where he lived most of his life. He abandoned a science course at the University of Sydney and became a surveyor, working in Fiji for five years, and eventually was the senior surveyor for the New South Wales State Government. Influenced by the cultural theories of the painter and novelist Norman Lindsay, he published his early work in the Lindsayite journal *Vision*.

Geoffrey Lehmann reviewed *Robert D. FitzGerald* (ed. Julian Croft, 1987, UQP) for the Australian Broadcasting Commission's "First Edition". As a schoolboy he met FitzGerald at a function in a teacher's sitting room: "FitzGerald was a serious, lean man with long legs; in his early fifties, soberly suited, with glasses and balding. He looked very much the senior surveyor, whose job it was to survey the site of future aerodromes. I remember FitzGerald saying that the worst thing about being a poet was the dry periods. It must have been a winter night – he pointed at the radiator – and said that if you hadn't written for a while, you had to get yourself started by writing about anything – whatever was available – about a radiator for instance ..."

For many years FitzGerald and Slessor were spoken of in tandem, as Australia's outstanding modern poets. More recently FitzGerald's reputation has declined. His qualities are still admirable: his hard-won optimism; his insistence that activity, despite death and eventual obliteration, is worthwhile for its own sake; and his ability to deal with large philosophical problems. But his language is usually unmusical and awkward. FitzGerald laboured to come to terms with modernism; something which came easily to Slessor. "1918–1941" is one of his first poems to sound as though it was written well into the 20th century. Also, and this is unusual for FitzGerald, it expresses personal emotion, as the poet in bewilderment holds up a child to watch the soldiers marching off to World War II. The poet realises that the peace between the two world wars was a delusion. FitzGerald was to write other anti-war poems, and became an opponent of the war in Vietnam.

"The Face of the Waters" is exceptional amongst FitzGerald's work in its freedom of form and unhampered movement. He successfully gives an imaginative, sensory form to his preoccupation with the philosopher Whitehead's metaphysical system. "Fifth Day" has a liveliness, a lightness of touch, a mixture of viewpoints and sharp observation that marks it out among his narrative poems, more so than "The Wind at Your Door", which, fine as it is, has become his classic anthology piece mainly because it deals with Australia's convict past. Vincent Buckley (*Essays in Poetry* (1957)) wrote perceptively about "Fifth Day":

> It is rather like the first scene of a film scenario, written in verse. We see Hastings, the victim: Edmund Burke, the prosecutor; Francis, the informant; the two Houses of Parliament assembled; the fashionable onlookers, eaten with curiosity. We see all this, now through the eyes of Joseph Gurney, a clerk whose only part in the proceedings is to record them, and who is quite relieved when Burke collapses under the strain, because it gives him the opportunity to go home early ...
>
> "Fifth Day" is a very intelligent, beautifully balanced and mature poem. One could understand, however, if the bulk of modern readers found it arid and boring; its value is not guaranteed by any staple in their reading;

> it is in fact, a completely new mode in contemporary poetry. FitzGerald's theme [as espoused in his early abstract philosophical poems] has not really changed, except in depth and complexity. His basic method, however has altered entirely ... he is concerned with a poetry of statement, a poetry of ideas; and his method is to take an historical character, place him in some imaginative context which has possibilities for his dramatic development and ... to show the philosophical significance of the adventure in which he is engaged.

1918–1941

Not those patient men who knocked and were unheeded
where ignorance impeded like a flat panel swung
before the tower-stair to the dark mind of the young:
another moved beside them on the dais, at the desk –
War in a square cap, gowned and grotesque.

This was the master whose tongue did the talking;
then time became a chalking-off of dates upon the wall –
for no lad chose a calling who heard instead a call,
and just beyond a boy's years (so the lesson ran)
the one work waited fitting for a man.

None grew so tiptoe as to see the plain road, yonder,
at the hour's edge dip under to the leagues of calm before.
It was odd to break step and shamble from the door,
to plough the broad peace, and be older, and learn pride
from the day's task met and the morrow still defied.

Distant the guns are, and no wind veering
has brought them into hearing, nor yet in these lands
do they bawl between hills as between a pair of hands;
but there's what we were bred to ... and strange it is then
to be lifting our sons up to watch the marching men.

Tattered the bewilderment I pull across my shoulders,
and shamed before beholders in this torn shirt,
like a slave to my shoes I wander unalert,
with eyes but no thought in them to mark the way I tread
and a thought without eyes that runs lost in my head.

The Face of the Waters

Once again the scurry of feet – those myriads
crossing the black granite; and again
laughter cruelly in pursuit; and then
the twang like a harpstring or the spring of a trap,

and the swerve on the polished surface: the soft little pads
sidling and skidding and avoiding; but soon caught up
in the hand of laughter and put back ...

There is no release from the rack
of darkness for the unformed shape,
the unexisting thought
stretched half-and-half
in the shadow of beginning and that denser black
under the imminence of huge pylons –
the deeper nought;
but neither is there anything to escape,
or to laugh,
or to twang that string which is not a string but silence
plucked at the heart of silence.

Nor can there be a floor to the bottomless;
except in so far as conjecture must arrive,
lungs cracking, at the depth of its dive;
where downward further is further distress
with no change in it; as if a mile and an inch
are equally squeezed into a pinch,
and retreating limits of cold mind
frozen, smoothed, defined.

Out of the tension of silence (the twanged string);
from the agony of not being (that terrible laughter
tortured by darkness); out of it all
once again the tentative migration; once again
a universe on the edge of being born:
feet running fearfully out of nothing
at the core of nothing:
colour, light, life, fearfully
becoming eyes and understanding: sound becoming ears ...

For eternity is not space reaching
on without end to it; not time without end to it,
nor infinity working round in a circle;
but a placeless dot enclosing nothing,
the pre-time pinpoint of impossible beginning,
enclosed by nothing, not even by emptiness –
impossible: so wholly at odds with possibilities
that, always emergent and wrestling and interlinking
they shatter it and return to it, are all of it and part of it.

It is your hand stretched out to touch your neighbour's,
and feet running through the dark, directionless like darkness.

Worlds that were spun adrift re-enter
that intolerable centre;
indeed the widest-looping comet
never departed from it;
it alone exists.
And though, opposing it, there persists
the enormous structure of forces, laws,
as background for other coming and going,
that's but a pattern, a phase, no pause,
of ever-being-erected, ever-growing
ideas unphysically alternative
to nothing, which is the quick. You may say hills live,
or life's the imperfect aspect of a flowing
that sorts itself as hills; much as thoughts wind
selectively through mind.

The egg-shell collapses
in the fist of the eternal instant;
all is what it was before.
Yet is that eternal instant
the pinpoint bursting into reality,
the possibilities and perhapses,
the feet scurrying on the floor.
It is the suspense also
with which the outward thrust
holds the inward surrender –
the stresses in the shell before it buckles under:
the struggle to magpie-morning and all life's clamour and lust;
the part breaking through the whole;
light and the clear day and so simple a goal.

Fifth Day

In William Rufus's hall the galleries reached
half to the rafters like a roost for lords,
perching the fashion of England; back seats fetched
more than a nabob's bribe. The season affords
nothing so sought as these hard boards;
so rustling ladies, crush your muslin frocks ....
There's Mrs Fitzherbert in the royal box.

Scarlet and ermine judges, wigs, gold laces,
canopies, woolsacks, drapings in red and green
for Peers' benches and Commons' – the culprit faces
a canvas not a court, a painted scene;
and from the obsolete frame there lean
figures trapped for tomorrow: history hooks
the observer into its foreground while he looks.

The proclamation for silence! Silence lies deep
under two hundred years. Almost you would say
the heralds are varnished over, standing asleep,
and the voice demanding silence has echoed away
far into silence. As if that day
were flat, still surface at last. But there survives
a hand in the midst, turning old thoughts, old lives.

Quill-marks migrate across a writing-block –
it is Joseph Gurney's hand. He heads his page:
"Fifth day: it wants a quarter of twelve o'clock:
the Chancellor presides"; so sets a stage
where words must jostle and engage
and die on utterance. But as they pass
paper shall catch their breaths like fog on glass.

"Warren Hastings Esquire, come forth in court
to save thee and thy bail" … Seven years shall run;
but a verdict will not end it – would a report
settle affairs in India, cool that sun
that policies well and ill begun
curve about since da Gama? Britain was built
round India and on Hastings – prove his guilt!

"Charges of misdemeanours and high crimes" –
prove – if proved, share them! Long ago, far hence,
they are drowned under the influx of new times.
What's done goes on for ever as consequence;
but there's some blurring of evidence
by happenings more at elbow. Why try this man?
Hastings is no concern of Pakistan.

But it concerns all men that what they do
remains significant unbroken thread
of the fabric of our living. A man spoke so,
and acted so; and everything done or said
is superseded and overlaid

by change of time and pattern. Be that as it may,
there was need he lift his finger, say his say.

Attitude matters: bearing. Action in the end
goes down the stream as motion, merges as such
with the whole of life and time; but islands stand:
dignity and distinctness that attach
to the inmost being of us each.
It matters for man's private respect that still
face differs from face and will from will.

It is important how men looked and were.
Infirm, staggering a little, as Hastings was,
his voice was steady as his eyes. Kneeling at the bar
(ruler but late of millions) had steeled his poise;
he fronted inescapable loss
and thrown, stinking malice and disrepute,
calmly, a plain man in a plain suit.

Undersized, spare, licked dry by tropic heat;
one, with severe forehead and hard lips,
who had taken age's shilling and complete
grey uniform though not its grey eclipse –
with movements like commands, like whips:
here is the centre, whether for applause or loathing,
when evidence and acquittal alike mean nothing.

But the eye strays from centre. The axle's part
is just to endure the play and spin of the spokes.
It is another figure rouses the heart,
a scholar loving his nation above his books,
who, pushed by a conscience that provokes
past reason or discretion, steps, half blind,
to darkness of anger from great light of his mind.

A compact, muscular man warms to the work
which will embitter him in another's feud,
his own mission and error. Edmund Burke
for right's clear sake is hounding his pursued,
inveterate, through this seven years' cloud
where subtle poison – Francis – steeps him whole;
he stands at the middle of the floor and twists his scroll.

"My lords, the gentlemen whom the Commons appoint
to manage this prosecution direct me thus
to inform your lordships" ... The cool phrases joint

one into other, and clause links on clause
wrought arguments whereby the cause
of justice and upright dealing may extend
from Westminster to India, and beyond.

Pitt sits near Fox and the managers, listens and learns.
Burke's heavy features liven with that magic
under them and their spectacles, which turns
knowledge to vision, and vision to strategic
marshalling of words and march of logic
through illustrations like landscapes and up steep
Quebec heights of statistics. Fox is asleep.

Francis is awake – behind the mask of his face,
inscrutable ... as Junius. "I have found,"
Hastings had said, "in private as in his place,
he is void of truth and honour." But cards go round;
brilliant, elegant as unsound,
he is one to hold them craftily, lead them well;
Hastings is now his victim, Burke his tool.

Something is eternal in the tugging of minds
which is not in mountains or monuments maturing
through day and darkness of centuries; something that binds
life into tensions and balances enduring
amid flowers withering and years flowering;
whereby in the instant of contest men outlive
upshots that melt in hot hands that achieve.

The fifth day wore to its close. On his feet still,
Burke was become tired body, who was cold brain
of impersonal Accusation. Suddenly ill,
he suddenly was himself, forcing through pain
words that seemed far off and in vain –
empty things scattered about by someone else,
a child dressed up in a bob-wig, playing with shells.

That moment swallows everything, like the gulf
two hundred years are hushed in: the fatigues
that buzzed like sickness in his brain; the trial itself
which was a swarming of motives and intrigues.
All the antagonisms, leagues,
plots and pamphlets are folded up, collapse;
but still the persons move, the drama shapes.

Here is displayed failure. Though there ensues
a recovery, a tomorrow that shall atone –
another hour, when Burke's voice shall cry: "Choose!"
and he shall stand in England almost alone,
weighing a guillotine and a throne –
results mean little; they cancel and coalesce.
A gesture will outweigh them, a trick of dress.

The common work outweighs them – the anonymous gift
to the future, living, widening. What indeed
of that old struggle matters or would be left
but for an ordinary fellow's simple need,
who had a family to feed
and liked going to church looked up to, known
as a man with a tidy business of his own?

Fox hurried to Burke's aid. The court adjourned.
Gurney stoppered his inkhorn, wiped his pen ...
Poor Mr Burke! But it was money earned
lightly and sweetened labour, for lesser men,
to go home early now and then.
Tuck today under an arm – though Hastings bent
that frown, there remained but shorthand. He bowed and went.

The Wind at Your Door

(to Mary Gilmore)

My ancestor was called on to go out –
a medical man, and one such must by law
wait in attendance on the pampered knout
and lend his countenance to what he saw,
lest the pet, patting with too bared a claw,
be judged a clumsy pussy. Bitter and hard,
see, as I see him, in that jailhouse yard.

Or see my thought of him: though time may keep
elsewhere tradition or a portrait still,
I would not feel under his cloak of sleep
if beard there or smooth chin, just to fulfil
some canon of precision. Good or ill
his blood's my own; and scratching in his grave
could find me more than I might wish to have.

Let him then be much of the middle style
of height and colouring; let his hair be dark

and his eyes green; and for that slit, the smile
that seemed inhuman, have it cruel and stark,
but grant it could be too the ironic mark
of all caught in the system – who the most,
the doctor or the flesh twined round that post?

There was a high wind blowing on that day;
for one who would not watch, but looked aside,
said that when twice he turned it blew his way
splashes of blood and strips of human hide
shaken out from the lashes that were plied
by one right-handed, one left-handed tough,
sweating at this paid task, and skilled enough.

That wind blows to your door down all these years.
Have you not known it when some breath you drew
tasted of blood? Your comfort is in arrears
of just thanks to a savagery tamed in you
only as subtler fears may serve in lieu
of thong and noose – old savagery which has built
your world and laws out of the lives it spilt.

For what was jailyard widens and takes in
my country. Fifty paces of stamped earth
stretch; and grey walls retreat and grow so thin
that towns show through and clearings – new raw birth
which burst from handcuffs – and free hands go forth
to win tomorrow's harvest from a vast
ploughland – the fifty paces of that past.

But see it through a window barred across,
from cells this side, facing the outer gate
which shuts on freedom, opens on its loss
in a flat wall. Look left now through the grate
at buildings like more walls, roofed with grey slate
or hollowed in the thickness of laid stone
each side the court where the crowd stands this noon.

One there with the officials, thick of build,
not stout, say burly (so this obstinate man
ghosts in the eyes) is he whom enemies killed
(as I was taught) because the monopolist clan
found him a grit in their smooth-turning plan,
too loyally active on behalf of Bligh.
So he got lost; and history passed him by.

But now he buttons his long coat against
the biting gusts, or as a gesture of mind,
habitual; as if to keep him fenced
from stabs of slander sticking him from behind,
sped by the schemers never far to find
in faction, where approval from one source
damns in another clubroom as of course.

This man had Hunter's confidence, King's praise;
and settlers on the starving Hawkesbury banks
recalled through twilight drifting across their days
the doctor's fee of little more than thanks
so often; and how sent by their squeezed ranks
he put their case in London. I find I lack
the hateful paint to daub him wholly black.

Perhaps my life replies to his too much
through veiling generations dropped between.
My weakness here, resentments there, may touch
old motives and explain them, till I lean
to the forgiveness I must hope may clean
my own shortcomings; since no man can live
in his own sight if it will not forgive.

Certainly I must own him whether or not
it be my will. I was made to understand
this much when once, marking a freehold lot,
my papers suddenly told me it was land
granted to Martin Mason. I felt his hand
heavily on my shoulder, and knew what coil
binds life to life through bodies, and soul to soil.

There, over to one corner, a bony group
of prisoners waits; and each shall be in turn
tied by his own arms in a human loop
about the post, with his back bared to learn
the price of seeking freedom. So they earn
three hundred rippling stripes apiece, as set
by the law's mathematics against the debt.

These are the Irish batch of Castle Hill,
rebels and mutineers, my countrymen
twice over; first, because of those to till
my birthplace first, hack roads, raise roofs; and then
because their older land time and again

enrolls me through my forbears; and I claim
as origin that threshold whence we came.

One sufferer had my surname, and thereto
"Maurice", which added up to history once;
an ignorant dolt, no doubt, for all that crew
was tenantry. The breed of clod and dunce
makes patriots and true men: could I announce
that Maurice as my kin I say aloud
I'd take his irons as heraldry, and be proud.

Maurice is at the post. Its music lulls,
one hundred lashes done. If backbone shows
then play the tune on buttocks! But feel his pulse;
that's what a doctor's for; and if it goes
lamely, then dose it with these purging blows –
which have not made him moan; though, writhing there,
"Let my neck be," he says, "and flog me fair."

One hundred lashes more, then rest the flail.
What says the doctor now? "This dog won't yelp;
he'll tire you out before you'll see him fail;
here's strength to spare; go on!" Ay, pound to pulp;
yet when you've done he'll walk without your help,
and knock down guards who'd carry him being bid,
and sing no song of where the pikes are hid.

It would be well if I could find, removed
through generations back – who knows how far? –
more than a surname's thickness as a proved
bridge with that man's foundations. I need some star
of courage from his firmament, a bar
against surrenders: faith. All trials are less
than rain-blacked wind tells of that old distress.

Yet I can live with Mason. What is told,
and what my heart knows of his heart, can sort
much truth from falsehood, much there that I hold
good clearly or good clouded by report;
and for things bad, ill grows where ills resort:
they were bad times. None know what in his place
they might have done. I've my own faults to face.

J. A. R. McKELLAR 1904–1932

John Alexander Ross McKellar was born at Dulwich Hill, educated at the selective state school, Sydney Boys' High School, and became an employee of the Bank of New South Wales (now Westpac Banking Corporation), where he was rapidly promoted and at the time of his death was being groomed as the possible CEO. In 1930 he was a member of the Randwick Rugby Union 1st XV which won the New South Wales Premiership. He was also a keen cricketer. In January 1932 a volume of his verse, *Twenty-six*, was published. In the following month he fell ill with pneumonia, apparently recovered, then suddenly collapsed and died on 8 March, having only three months earlier turned twenty-seven. His posthumous editor, J. W. Gibbes, a friend, struggled for a decade and a half to get the collected poems published. Writing in 1946, Gibbes stated that Mackellar had "a remarkably wide and accurate knowledge of the literatures of France and England, as well as a critical appreciation of Greek and Latin poetry through the medium of French and English translation". McKellar's adherence to classical values and shapeliness may be one reason why his poetry has fallen into neglect over the last forty years.

Written in the Year of His Bi-centenary

1727–1927

And if no drowsy apple fell, what then?
Be it in street, or quiet room, or field,
Somewhere in England, loved by Englishmen,
The rule to Isaac Newton was revealed.

So let me think it was when summer shuts
He wandered homeward down a country lane,
Worn by the harvest waggons into ruts,
The starry secret burning in his brain.

The world was his, at his command to move
In calculated paths – but as he trod
The lumbering road, he stumbled in a groove,
And warned by chance, resigned the stars to God.

Over the hill and homeward Isaac went,
But as he passed them, who in England saw
A new authentic Moses in descent,
Bearing the sacred tablets of the Law?

The Retreat from Heaven

The armies joined; I saw the Prince of Peace
Desert his Staff of twelve, and then advance,
Beneath the swirling snow that would not cease,
To greet the waiting Emperor of France.

The soldiers laughed, unloosing belt and pack;
Now was the fighting done, the end in sight.
For comrades left to wolves along the track
They sighed, who'd rest in Heaven's beds that night.

The leaders now agreed upon their plan,
And to the Gates of Heaven turned their feet.
First to regain the citadel of man,
Their footsteps echoed down the hollow street.

All was deserted; walls gave back the sound
Of nothing but their voices, rising shrill
In wonderment at this, the holy ground,
This skeleton of cities, frozen still.

Bare were the windows, and the doors were wide,
The rooms were empty as a stranded shell.
Each drew the other closer to his side ....
Deep in the soundless city clanged a bell.

Napoleon shivered; blanched was Jesus' cheek,
And coldly glistened sweat upon each brow;
Dry lips refused, but eyes remained, to speak
The question voiceless: Master, whither now?

Napoleon turned, and Jesus called his name;
They paused, and then fled headlong down the street ....
The waiting armies marked a distant flame,
Then heard the bugles sounding the retreat.

They saw their leaders' carriage thunder past,
And Rumour whispered, until Panic cried;
A musket cracked; defiant, scornful, last
Stood Michel Ney, with Peter at his side.

Twelve O'Clock Boat

Only the creaking murmur of the wheel,
The trembling of the engines as they turn;
The ferry glides upon an even keel,
And Pinchgut squats in shadow hard astern ....

The lips of ocean murmur at delay.
The lovely moon no longer will refuse,
And from the arms of darkness slips away
To tryst with young Ephesians on Vaucluse,

Naked as when some mercenary Greek
The galleys bore to Carthage stared the sky,
Feeling a wind Sicilian on his cheek,
And fell asleep with no more hope than I

Of life eternal, love, or length of days,
Dreaming he saw his Macedonian home;
Awoke, and duly went his ordered ways
To die at Zama, on the swords of Rome.

But what was moon to him, and what was sea
Two thousand years before myself was born,
Are sickle moon and silver yet to me,
Though Scipio should wait upon Cremorne.

Res Publica

They bled a bullock, and stripped the hide,
Cast to the dogs what they could not use;
Tanned the skin that the sun had dried,
And made the leather for Caesar's shoes.

A shivering lamb was shorn in Spain;
The wool was teased and combed and dressed.
They washed it clean of the pasture stain,
And wove the toga for Caesar's breast.

A pig that rooted acorns saw
The shrub resent as they plucked the bough,
And watched the shadows of men withdraw
Bearing the laurel for Caesar's brow.

They dug the metal to fill the mould,
And fed the flame in a place apart;
Ground the edge when the steel was cold,
And made the dagger for Caesar's heart.

A. D. HOPE 1907–2000

Alec Derwent Hope was born at Cooma, New South Wales, son of a Presbyterian minister, and spent most of his childhood at a manse in rural Tasmania. He was schooled at home in his earlier years, his mother having been a teacher, his father taking him for Latin. At the University of Sydney he won the university medal in both English and philosophy and went on a scholarship to Oxford, but he was unhappy there and was awarded third-class honours – the equivalent of failure. Returning to Australia in the Great Depression, he camped at first on some land of his father's at Bungan Head on the peninsula north of Sydney Harbour. His father paid him the equivalent of the dole and Hope enjoyed himself editing Marlowe's *Doctor Faustus*, a project finally published in 1982.

He studied at the Sydney Teachers' College and became a school teacher, married in 1937 and in 1938 became a lecturer at Sydney Teachers' College within the University of Sydney, where he formed a close friendship with James McAuley, ten years his junior. McAuley stayed with the Hopes who were renting an abandoned house that overlooked Sydney Harbour. They were strong influences on each other's work, but when McAuley converted to Catholicism their interests began to diverge. Hope moved to the English department at the University of Melbourne and then became professor of English at the Australian National University in Canberra, where he remained until his retirement in 1968. He and his wife had three children.

Hope's first book of poetry was published in 1955, when he was 48 and had been writing for many years. The delay is attributable to the explicitly sexual content of much of his early work. Although he quickly became part of the literary "establishment", when *The Wandering Islands* appeared, Hope was long regarded as a "wild man" and an outsider, even though a professor. He was also making a reputation as a particularly acerbic reviewer, determined to disrupt the self-cosseting standards of the Australian literary world of the time. He deplored any social purpose in literature, insisting literary values alone should be applied. He was suspicious of the obscurity of experimental modes, believing a good mind can make itself understood, and opposed surrealism and dissociation as self-indulgence. These ideas – shared with McAuley – were influenced by the classicism of John Anderson of the University of Sydney, the leading philosopher in Australia of that era. Most notorious of all Hope's criticism was his attack on Patrick White's novels; he also wrote a post-mortem on free verse. Both these positions were rather ruefully modified.

Hope acknowledged a difficulty in writing about his homeland and directly of his own experience, since his work typically has an intellectual origin and is written "to illuminate an idea". Mythology, the classics and European culture often provide the catalyst or reference point for his poems.

The most profound influence on Hope's attitudes has been Nietzsche. A theme is his disgust with those who may be identified as Nietzsche's "last men": the self-indulgent, suburban, vicariously experiencing, technologically protected modern citizen. Hope's *Übermensch* is the scientist or intellectually daring artist who challenges conventional ideas and easy solutions. Poetry is the subjective, value-creating response to a rational, objective picture of the world. Celebration, the proper concern of poetry, includes for him "an intellectual assent to the causes that make the natural world an order and system, and an imaginative grasp of … its processes". He was an addict, he said, of popularised science. He saw the natural world as being entirely physical processes, and humans as continuous with this, as literally beasts, though not necessarily to be despised because of that. We are noble in our capacity to witness to the truth, and to create "new orders of being" through the imagination, through art.

Though never of Norman Lindsay's circle, it is Hope who best conveys in poetry many of Lindsay's ideas – the individualism, the "healthy" lustfulness, the admiration for strenuous achieving, the paganism, the caricatured "classicism". His women are often only their primary sexual characteristics (yet Hope wrote in "Advice to Young Ladies" one of the outstanding Australian feminist poems, though it is perhaps too rhetorical which is why we have passed it over). Particularly in his poems written up to the late 1950s women are visualised as in Lindsay's art: great Wagnerian nudes, white and pink, and dolloped like meringues with their sexual attributes. Most likely Hope found his affinity with Lindsay's "vision" through admiration for the poetry of Hugh McCrae. There is a similar boisterous, vulgarly energetic quality, a similar neo-classical theatre and caricature. The difference is the much wider scope and intelligence of Hope.

The Damnation of Byron

When the great hero, adding to the charms
Of genius and his scandals, left the light
Stamped with the irresistible trade of arms,
The Hell of Women received him as their right.

Through the Infernal Fields he makes his way
Playing again, but on a giant stage.
His own Don Juan: pursuing day by day
Childe Harold's last astonishing pilgrimage.

It is the landscape of erotic dreams:
The dim, brown plains, the country without air
Or tenderness of trees by hidden streams,
But cactus or euphorbia here and there

Thrusts up its monstrous phallus at the sky.
And moving against this silvered, lustrous green
Like a pink larva over the whole dry
Savannah of hell, the bodies of women are seen.

And at his coming all their beauties stir
Mysterious, like the freshening of a rose
As, the incomparable connoisseur,
Pale and serene across their world he goes,

Always there rises glowing in his path,
Superb and sensual, in the light that pours
A tarnished glory on the soil of death,
This leafless nakedness of tropic flowers;

The female body's impersonal charm, the curves
Of a young head poised on its gracious stalk.
The idiom of her gesture he observes,
That tender dislocation of her walk.

Held in his brain's deep lupanar they float,
The tapering trunk, the pure vase of the hips,
The breasts, the breasts to which the hands go out
Instinctive, the adoring finger-tips,

The thighs incurved, the skin misted with light,
The mouth repeating its own rich circumflex ...
At first he moves and breathes in his delight
Drowned in the brute somnambulism of sex.

He is a kind of symbol of the male:
As a great bull, stiffly, deliberately
Crosses his paddock, lashing his brutal tail,
The sullen engine of fecundity,

So, in his first youth and his first desire,
His air of pride and the immortal bloom,
Once more he sets the feminine world on fire,
Passing in his romantic blaze of gloom.

Prodigious vigour flowers new in him:
Each morning nerves him with heroic lust.
His thoughts are women, he breathes, is clothed with them,
He sinks on something female in the dust.

He has them all, all the menagerie
Of race, the subtle stimulus of shapes:
Negresses in their first nubility
With the sad eyes and muzzles of young apes,

Vast Scandinavian divinities
Superbly modelled, for all their cowlike air,
The pale bread of their bellies' magnificent rise
From the blond triangle of pubic hair,

And slender girls with delicate golden shanks
And elongated skulls from lost Peru ...
The sensual emphasis of the Spaniard's flanks,
And the callipygous haunches of the Jew ...

Dancers and whores, blue-stockings, countesses,
Types of La Fornarina and Caroline Lamb,
All the seductions of all mistresses,
The savage, the sentimental and the sham ...

And yet he is alone. At first he feels
Nothing above the tumult of his blood,
While through his veins like the slow pox there steals
The deep significance of his solitude.

And from this feeling without haste or pause
Vengeance predestined sharpens, bit by bit;
As lust its anaesthesia withdraws

The force of his damnation grows from it.

Grows as the mind wakes inexorably
The critic, the thinker, the invincible
Intelligence at last detached and free
Wakes, and he knows … he knows he is in hell.

And there begins in him that horrible thing,
Clairvoyance, the cruel nightmare of escape:
He seeks companions: but they only bring
Wet kisses and voluptuous legs agape …

He longs for the companionship of men,
Their sexless friendliness. He cannot live
"Like the gods in Lucretius once again"
Nor ever in woman's wit and charm forgive

The taint of the pervading feminine
Yet always to this nausea he returns
From his own mind – the emptiness within
Of the professional lover. As he learns

How even his own society has become
A horror, a loneliness he cannot bear,
The last stage of Don Juan's martyrdom,
The last supreme resources of despair

Appear, and brutally lucid he descends
Simply to treat them as The Enemy.
His lust becomes revenge, his ardour lends
Insatiable pleasure to his insanity.

As he exhausts himself in the delights
Of torture, gourmandising in their pain,
Hate eats his features out: it seethes and bites
Like a slow acid. It destroys his brain.

Yet this resource betrays him, even this,
For like tormented demons, they adore
Their torment. They revere like savages
The god's ferocity with lascivious awe.

Until, neurotic, hounded by strange fears,
At last his journey changes to a flight.
Delirious, broken, fugitive, he hears
Marching and countermarching in the night,

The panic of vague terrors closing in:
Whichever way he turns he hears them come.

Far off immeasurable steps begin,
Far off the ominous mumble of a drum,

And from the bounds of that dim listening land
Approaches with her grave incessant tread
The Eternal Goddess in whose placid hand
Are all the happy and all the rebellious dead.

Before her now he stands and makes his prayer
For that oblivion of the Second Death ...
When suddenly those majestic breasts all bare
Riding the tranquil motion of her breath

Reveal the body of her divinity:
The torso spread marmoreal, his eyes
Downwards uncover its mighty line and see
Darkness dividing those prodigious thighs.

There as she stares, slowly she smiles at him ...
And the great hero, mad with the terrible
Madness of souls, turns fleeing, while the dim
Plains heave with the immense derision of Hell.

The Return from the Freudian Islands

When they heard Sigmund the Saviour in these coasts
The islanders were very much impressed;
Abandoned the worship of their fathers' ghosts
And dedicated temples to their guest,

Shocked and delighted as the saint revealed
The unacknowledged body and made them see,
Suppressed by corsets, morbidly concealed
In cotton combinations, neck to knee,

How it bred night-sweats, the disease of shame,
Corns, fluxions, baldness and the sense of sin,
How clothes to the Analytic Eye became
Fantasies, furtive symbols of the skin.

At first the doctrine took them all by storm;
Urged to be stark, they peeled as they were told;
Forgetting their rags had also kept them warm,
For the island climate is often extremely cold.

And if the old, the wry, the ugly shared
Some natural reluctance to begin it,

Enthusiasts all, the young at once declared
Their Brave Nude World, that had such people in it.

Till some discovered that stripping to the buff
Only exposed the symbol of The Hide:
Its sinister pun unmasked, it must come off,
The saint must preach The Visible Inside!

The saint, though somewhat startled at this view,
Trapped by the logic of his gospel, spent
Some time in prayer, and in a week or two,
To demonstrate the new experiment,

Breastless and bald, with ribbed arms, lashless eyes,
In intricate bandages of human meat,
With delicate ripple and bulge of muscled thighs,
The first skinned girl walked primly down the street.

Though there were many to admire her charms:
The strappings and flexures of twig-like toes, the skeins
And twisted sensitive cables of her arms,
The pectoral fans, the netting of nerves and veins:

Yet those who followed her example found
One lack – till Sigmund undertook to prove
How much their late behaviour centred round
A common skin disease they had called love.

And for a time they thoroughly enjoyed
The brisk intolerance of the purified,
In sects and schisms before The Holy Freud
Self-torn – while lesser saints were deified.

Till Faith, which never can let well alone,
From heresy and counter-heresy
Prompted the saint to bare beneath the bone
The Ultimate Visceral Reality.

Long time he mused before The Sacred Id,
Long prayed, before he finally began
And, purged, impersonal, uninhibited,
Produced at last The Basic Freudian Man.

At the Fertility Festival that year
The skinned men blushed to see the skeleton,
A bone-cage filled with female guts appear
Tottering before them in the midday sun.

Its slats and levering rods they saw, the full
Cogged horseshoe grin of two and thirty teeth,
The frantic eyeballs swivelling in the skull,
The swagging human umbles underneath,

The soft wet mottled granite of the lung
Bulge and collapse, the liver worn askew
Jauntily quiver, the plump intestines hung
In glistening loops and bolsters in their view,

And clear through gut and bowel the mashy chyme
Churn downward; jelled in its transparent sheath
The scowling foetus tethered, and the time-
Bomb tumour set unguessed its budded death.

And while for them with mannequin grace she swayed
Her pelvis, Sigmund, so that none should miss
The beauty of the new world he had made,
Explained The Triumph of Analysis:

Pimples and cramps now shed with pelt and thews,
No dreams to fright, no visions to trouble them,
For, where the death-wish and self-knowledge fuse,
They had at last The Human L.C.M ....

Here the saint paused, looked modestly at the ground
And waited for their plaudits to begin.
And waited ... There was nothing! A faint, dry sound
As first a poet buttoned on his skin.

Three Ecclesiastical Limericks

The elderly Rabbi of Joppa
Said, "I think circumcision improper
        If the organ is small,
        But I don't mind at all
About cutting a slice off a whopper."

The Bishop of Alexandretta
Loved a girl and couldn't forget her,
        So he thought he'd enshrine her
        As the Holy Vagina
In the Church of the Sacred French Letter.

Said St Joseph, "Although I'm not vain
I regard your condition with pain
        And the neighbours all snigger

As they look at your figure,
'Is the Holy Ghost at it again?' "

The Pleasure of Princes

What pleasures have great princes? These: to know
Themselves reputed mad with pride or power;
To speak few words – few words and short bring low
This ancient house, that city with flame devour;

To make old men, their father's enemies,
Drunk on the vintage of the former age;
To have great painters show their mistresses
Naked to the succeeding time; engage

The cunning of able, treacherous ministers
To serve, despite themselves, the cause they hate,
And leave a prosperous kingdom to their heirs
Nursed by the caterpillars of the state;

To keep their spies in good men's hearts; to read
The malice of the wise, and act betimes;
To hear the Grand Remonstrances of greed,
Led by the pure; cheat justice of her crimes;

To beget worthless sons and, being old,
By starlight climb the battlements, and while
The pacing sentry hugs himself for cold,
Keep vigil like a lover, muse and smile,

And think, to see from the grim castle steep
The midnight city below rejoice and shine:
"There my great demon grumbles in his sleep
And dreams of his destruction, and of mine."

Death of the Bird

For every bird there is this last migration:
Once more the cooling year kindles her heart;
With a warm passage to the summer station
Love pricks the course in lights across the chart.

Year after year a speck on the map, divided
By a whole hemisphere, summons her to come;
Season after season, sure and safely guided,
Going away she is also coming home.

And being home, memory becomes a passion
With which she feeds her brood and straws her nest,
Aware of ghosts that haunt the heart's possession
And exiled love mourning within the breast.

The sands are green with a mirage of valleys;
The palm tree casts a shadow not its own;
Down the long architrave of temple or palace
Blows a cool air from moorland scarps of stone.

And day by day the whisper of love grows stronger;
That delicate voice, more urgent with despair,
Custom and fear constraining her no longer,
Drives her at last on the waste leagues of air.

A vanishing speck in those inane dominions,
Single and frail, uncertain of her place,
Alone in the bright host of her companions,
Lost in the blue unfriendliness of space.

She feels it close now, the appointed season;
The invisible thread is broken as she flies;
Suddenly, without warning, without reason,
The guiding spark of instinct winks and dies.

Try as she will, the trackless world delivers
No way, the wilderness of light no sign,
The immense and complex map of hills and rivers
Mocks her small wisdom with its vast design.

And darkness rises from the eastern valleys,
And the winds buffet her with their hungry breath,
And the great earth, with neither grief nor malice,
Receives the tiny burden of her death.

Easter Hymn

Make no mistake; there will be no forgiveness;
No voice can harm you and no hand will save;
Fenced by the magic of deliberate darkness
You walk on the sharp edges of the wave;

Trouble with soul again the putrefaction
Where Lazarus three days rotten lies content.
Your human tears will be the seed of faction,
Murder the sequel to your sacrament.

The City of God is built like other cities:
Judas negotiates the loans you float;
You will meet Caiaphas upon committees;
You will be glad of Pilate's casting vote.

Your truest lovers still the foolish virgins,
Your heart will sicken at the marriage feasts
Knowing they watch you from the darkened gardens
Being polite to your official guests.

Moschus Moschiferus

A song for St Cecilia's Day

In the high jungle where Assam meets Tibet
The small Kastura, most archaic of deer,
Were driven in herds to cram the hunter's net
And slaughtered for the musk-pods which they bear;

But in those thickets of rhododendron and birch
The tiny creatures now grow hard to find.
Fewer and fewer survive each year. The search
Employs new means, more exquisite and refined:

The hunters now set out by two or three;
Each carries a bow and one a slender flute.
Deep in the forest the archers choose a tree
And climb; the piper squats against the root.

And there they wait until all trace of man
And rumour of his passage dies away.
They melt into the leaves and, while they scan
The glade below, their comrade starts to play.

Through those vast, listening woods a tremulous skein
Of melody wavers, delicate and shrill:
Now dancing and now pensive, now a rain
Of pure, bright drops of sound and now the still

Sad wailing of lament; from tune to tune
It winds and modulates without a pause;
The hunters hold their breath; the trance of noon
Grows tense; with its full power the music draws

A shadow from a juniper's darker shade;
Bright-eyed, with quivering muzzle and pricked ear,
The little musk-deer slips into the glade
Led by an ecstasy that conquers fear.

A wild enchantment lures him, step by step
Into its net of crystalline sound, until
The leaves stir overhead, the bowstrings snap
And poisoned shafts bite sharp into the kill.

Then, as the victim shudders, leaps and falls,
The music soars to a delicious peak,
And on and on its silvery piping calls
Fresh spoil for the rewards the hunters seek.

But when the woods are emptied and the dusk
Draws in, the men climb down and count their prey,
Cut out the little glands that hold the musk
And leave the carcasses to rot away.

A hundred thousand or so are killed each year;
Cause and effect are very simply linked:
Rich scents demand the musk, and so the deer,
Its source, must soon, they say, become extinct.

Divine Cecilia, there is no more to say!
Of all who praised the power of music, few
Knew of these things. In honour of your day
Accept this song I too have made for you.

On an Engraving by Casserius

for Dr John Z. Bowers

Set on this bubble of dead stone and sand,
Lapped by its frail balloon of lifeless air,
Alone in the inanimate void, they stand,
These clots of thinking molecules who stare
Into the night of nescience and death,
And, whirled about with their terrestrial ball,
Ask of all being its motion and its frame:
This of all human images takes my breath;
Of all the joys in being a man at all,
This folds my spirit in its quickening flame.

Turning the leaves of this majestic book
My thoughts are with those great cosmographers,
Surgeon adventurers who undertook
To probe and chart time's other universe.
This one engraving holds me with its theme:
More than all maps made in that century

Which set true bearings for each cape and star,
De Quiros' vision or Newton's cosmic dream,
This reaches towards the central mystery
Of whence our being draws and what we are.

It came from that great school in Padua:
Casserio and Spiegel made this page.
Vesalius, who designed the *Fabrica*,
There strove, but burned his book at last in rage;
Fallopius by its discipline laid bare
The elements of this humanity,
Without which none knows that which treats the soul;
Fabricius talked with Galileo there:
Did those rare spirits in their colloquy
Divine in their two skills the single goal?

"One force that moves the atom and the star,"
Says Galileo; "one basic law beneath
All change!" "Would light from Achernar
Reveal how embryon forms within its sheath?"
Fabricius asks, and smiles. Talk such as this,
Ranging the bounds of our whole universe,
Could William Harvey once have heard? And once
Hearing, strike out that strange hypothesis,
Which in *De Motu Cordis* twice recurs,
Coupling the heart's impulsion with the sun's?

Did Thomas Browne at Padua, too, in youth
Hear of their talk of universal law
And form that notion of particular truth
Framed to correct a science they foresaw,
That darker science of which he used to speak
In later years and called the Crooked Way
Of Providence? Did *he* foresee perhaps
An age in which all sense of the unique,
And singular dissolves, like ours today,
In diagrams, statistics, tables, maps?

Not here! The graver's tool in this design
Aims still to give not general truth alone,
Blue-print of science or data's formal line:
Here in its singularity he has shown
The image of an individual soul;
Bodied in this one woman, he makes us see

The shadow of his anatomical laws.
An artist's vision animates the whole,
Shines through the scientist's detailed scrutiny
And links the person and the abstract cause.

Such were the charts of those who pressed beyond
Vesalius their master, year by year
Tracing each bone, each muscle, every frond
Of nerve until the whole design lay bare.
Thinking of this dissection, I descry
The tiers of faces, their teacher in his place,
The talk at the cadaver carried in:
"A woman – with child!"; I hear the master's dry
Voice as he lifts a scalpel from its case:
"With each new step in science, we begin."

Who was she? Though they never knew her name,
Dragged from the river, found in some alley at dawn,
This corpse none cared, or dared perhaps, to claim;
The dead child in her belly still unborn,
Might have passed, momentary as a shooting star,
Quenched like the misery of her personal life,
Had not the foremost surgeon of Italy,
Giulio Casserio of Padua,
Bought her for science, questioned her with his knife,
And drawn her for his great *Anatomy*;

Where still in the abundance of her grace,
She stands among the monuments of time
And with a feminine delicacy displays
His elegant dissection: the sublime
Shaft of her body opens like a flower
Whose petals, folded back expose the womb,
Cord and placenta and the sleeping child,
Like instruments of music in a room
Left when her grieving Orpheus left his tower
Forever, for the desert and the wild.

Naked she waits against a tideless shore,
A sibylline stance, a noble human frame
Such as those old anatomists loved to draw.
She turns her head as though in trouble or shame,
Yet with a dancer's gesture holds the fruit
Plucked, though not tasted, of the Fatal Tree.
Something of the first Eve is in this pose

And something of the second in the mute
Offering of her child in death to be
Love's victim and her flesh its mystic rose.

No figure with wings of fire and back-swept hair
Swoops with his: Blessed among Women!; no sword
Of the spirit cleaves or quickens her; yet there
She too was overshadowed by the Word,
Was chosen, and by her humble gift of death
The lowly and the poor in heart give tongue,
Wisdom puts down the mighty from their seat;
The vile rejoice and rising, hear beneath
Scalpel and forceps, tortured into song,
Her body utter their magnificat.

Four hundred years since first that cry rang out:
Four hundred years, the patient, probing knife
Cut towards its answer – yet we stand in doubt:
Living, we cannot tell the source of life.
Old science, old certainties that lit our way
Shrink to poor guesses, dwindle to a myth.
Today's truths teach us how we were beguiled;
Tomorrow's how blind our vision of today.
The universals we thought to conjure with
Pass: there remain the mother and the child.

Loadstone, loadstar, alike to each new age,
There at the crux of time they stand and scan,
Past every scrutiny of prophet or sage,
Still unguessed prospects in this venture of Man.
To generations, which we leave behind,
They taught a difficult, selfless skill: to show
The mask beyond the mask beyond the mask;
To ours another vista, where the mind
No longer asks for answers, but to know:
What questions are there which we fail to ask?

Who knows, but to the age to come they speak
Words that our own is still unapt to hear:
"These are the limits of all you sought and seek;
More our yet unborn nature cannot bear.
Learn now that all man's intellectual quest
Was but the stirrings of a foetal sleep;
The birth you cannot haste and cannot stay

Nears its appointed time; turn now and rest
Till that new nature ripens, till the deep
Dawns with that unimaginable day."

Hay Fever

Time, with his scythe honed fine,
Takes a pace forward, swings from the hips; the flesh
Crumples and falls in wind-rows curving away.
Waiting my turn as he swings – (Not yet, not mine!)
I recall the sound of the scythe on an earlier day:
Late spring in my boyhood; learning to mow with the men;
Eight of us mowing together in echelon line,
Out of the lucerne patch and into the hay,
And I at the end on the left because I was fresh,
Because I was new to the game and young at the skill –
As though I were Time himself, I remember it still.

The mild Tasmanian summer; the men are here
To mow for my minister father and make his hay.
They have brought a scythe for me. I hold it with pride.
The lucerne is up to my knee, the grass to my waist.
I set the blade into the grass as they taught me the way;
The still dewy stalks nod, tremble and tilt aside,
Cornflowers, lucerne and poppies, sugar-grass, summer-grass, laced
With red-stemmed dock; I feel the thin steel crunch
Through hollow-stalk milk thistle, self-sown oats and rye;
I snag on a fat-hen clump; chick-weed falls in a bunch,
But sorrel scatters; dandelion casts up a golden eye,
To a smell of cows chewing their cuds, the sweet hay-breath:
The boy with the scythe never thinks it the smell of death.

The boy with the scythe takes a stride forward, swings
From the hips, keeping place and pace, keeping time
By the sound of the scythes, by the swish and ripple, the sigh
Of the dying grass like an animal breathing, a rhyme.
Falling pat on the ear that matches the steel as it sings
True through the tottering stems. Sweat runs into my eye.
How long to a break? How long can I hold out yet?
I nerve my arms to go on; I am running with, flooding with, sweat.

How long ago was it? – Why, the scythe is as obsolete now
As arrows and bow. I have lived from one age to another;
And I have made hay while I could and the sun still shone.
Time drives a harvester now: he does not depend on the weather.

Well, I have rolled in his hay, in my day, and now it is gone;
But I still have a barn stacked high with that good dry mow,
Shrivelled and fragrant stems, the grass and the flowers together
And a thistle or two in the pile for the prick of remorse.
It is good for a man when he comes to the end of his course
In the barn of his brain to be able to romp like a boy in the heap …
To lie still in well-cured hay … to drift into sleep.

The Mayan Books

Diego de Landa, archbishop of Yucatan
– The curse of God upon his pious soul –
Placed all their Devil's picture-books under ban
And piling them in one sin-heap, burned the whole;

But took the trouble to keep the calendar
By which the Devil had taught them to count time.
The impious creatures had tallied back as far
As ninety million years before Eve's crime.

That was enough: they burned the Mayan books,
Saved souls and kept their own in proper trim.
Diego de Landa in heaven always looks
Towards God: God never looks at him.

EVE LANGLEY 1908–1974

Born in Forbes, New South Wales, Eve Langley is known for one novel, *The Pea-Pickers*, although she also published a sequel, *White Topee*. Langley went to New Zealand, married there, and had three children by her husband and one illegitimately. She spent several years in New Zealand in a mental hospital. Returning to Australia, she tried to enter the Sydney literary scene, but soon withdrew to a shack in the bush of the Blue Mountains and worked on what eventually amounted to another eleven novels. Despite the sympathy of editors at Angus & Robertson, such as Beatrice Davis and Douglas Stewart, who regarded *The Pea-Pickers* as a classic, these later novels could not be published, because of the uncontrolled elaborateness of their style and their illegibility. It seems Langley continued to type long after her typewriter ribbons had worn out. At the age of 50 Langley adopted the name "Oscar Wilde" by deed poll, and something of his persona and dress. She always wore men's clothes, to which she added a sheath knife in her belt, and a white topee, and she was obsessed with guns. When she died her house was found to be full of brown paper parcels which contained only folded chicken wire, stones or feathers. Steve, the boisterous heroine of her two published novels discovers, in *White Topee*, that "What I really wanted to be was a man." Langley wrote a number of poems, some published in the *Bulletin* and some in the Mitchell Library in manuscript.

Native Born

In a white gully among fungus-red
Where serpent logs lay hissing at the air,
I found a kangaroo. Tall dewy, dead,
So like a woman, she lay silent there.
Her ivory hands, black-nailed, crossed on her breast,
Her skin of sun and moon hues, fallen cold.
Her brown eyes lay like rivers come to rest
And death had made her black mouth harsh and old.
Beside her in the ashes I sat deep
And mourned for her, but had no native song
To flatter death, while down the ploughlands steep
Dark young Camelli whistled loud and long,
"Love, liberty and Italy are all."
Broad golden was his breast against the sun.
I saw his wattle whip rise high and fall
Across the slim mare's flanks, and one by one
She drew the furrows after her as he
Flapped like a gull behind her, climbing high,
Chanting his oaths and lashing soundingly,
While from the mare came once a blowing sigh.
The dew upon the kangaroo's white side
Had melted. Time was whirling high around,
Like the thin woomera, and from heaven wide
He, the bull-roarer, made continuous sound
Incarnate lay my country by my hand:
Her long hot days, bushfires, and speaking rains,
Her mornings of opal and the copper band
Of smoke around the sunlight on the plains.
Globed in fire-bodies the meat-ants ran
To taste her flesh and linked us as we lay,
Forever Australian, listening to a man
From careless Italy, swearing at our day.
When, golden-lipped, the eagle-hawks came down
Hissing and whistling to eat of lovely her,
And the blowflies with their shields of purple brown
Plied hatching to and fro across her fur,
I burnt her with the logs, and stood all day
Among the ashes, pressing home the flame
Till woman, logs and dreams were scorched away,
And native with night, that land from whence they came.

RONALD McCUAIG 1908–1993

Ronald McCuaig was born at Newcastle, New South Wales, and was an only child. His "Berceuse de Newcastle" (cradle song of Newcastle) evokes the red glow and relentless noise of the steelworks at night that haunted his childhood. McCuaig's mother, who is the subject of "Mrs Agnes McCuaig at the Piano" (along with "Five Bells", one of the greatest Australian elegies) died when he was seven years old. Her "afternoon-at-home" is recalled achingly in "L'Après-midi d'une fille aux Cheveux de Lin".

McCuaig's father, John (portrayed as a quiet, laconic man in "Au Tombeau de mon Père"), then reared young Ron. The father arranged for his son to be given elocution lessons, which Peter Kirkpatrick, in the introduction to *Selected Poems* (1992), says "laid the foundations of an interest in poetry" as "those were the days of parlour entertainments where recitation was extremely popular". (Note the reference to his "elocution" in McCuaig's elegy to his mother.) McCuaig went to school in Newcastle and then in Sydney, and his father, who was an ironmonger, decided he should become a commercial traveller. But this did not work out. Except for a short period after leaving school, and an overseas trip with his wife in 1939, McCuaig was a journalist all his working life, employed by *Wireless Weekly* from 1928 to 1938, and later by the Australian Broadcasting Commission, *Smith's Weekly*, *The Sydney Morning Herald* (then a stuffy organisation which he quickly left as he was afraid "they were about to appoint prefects"), the *Bulletin* (for which he was short-story editor and wrote light verse under the name "Swilliam"), and the Department of Information. McCuaig and his wife had two sons. Toward the end of his life, he lived with one of his sons in Sydney (in the backyard and possibly in a caravan, if our memory of a comment by McCuaig is correct).

McCuaig became a "professional" poet early. In 1927, working as an office boy, he heard that a radio station wanted a nightly "Topical Chorus" – a piece of light verse, that could be set to music and sung. So he produced about fifty of these pieces, some of which were printed in the *Bulletin* and later appeared in *The Wanton Goldfish* (1941). McCuaig burned the rest of them. The "Topical Choruses" were the beginning of McCuaig's career as a professional poet, and, as Kirkpatrick points out, the writing of light verse honed his technical skills and steered him away from the Victorian clichés that were then still prevalent among Australian poets. Kirkpatrick reports that "the great breakthrough for McCuaig came in 1932 when he read F. R. Leavis's *New Bearings in English Poetry* and was introduced to the modernism of Eliot, Pound and Hopkins."

The result of this exposure to modernism was the 20 poems of his first book, *Vaudeville*, written according to Kirkpatrick, in two months between November 1933 and January 1934. The sexually explicit nature of some of these poems and the public prudishness that prevailed in Australia at that time meant that when approached by McCuaig to print the book, seven printers refused, afraid of going to gaol. Frustrated by these refusals, McCuaig himself printed 150 copies of *Vaudeville* in 1938, on a galley press in a bedroom of his Potts Point flat. The first four poems in our selection of McCuaig come from that volume.

McCuaig was a friend of Slessor, who admired his acerbic love poems, written from the viewpoint of a clerk living in the high-rise dilapidation of Sydney's Kings

Cross during the 1930s. But in more recent years his work has tended to be forgotten and he is either omitted from anthologies or represented sparingly. McCuaig's "serious" poetry, which is light in tone, is far more successful than his topical verse. His own modesty may also have contributed to his oversight – it caused him in his later years to introduce himself to fellow writers, seemingly without irony, as a public servant. One was approached by a thin, tallish, grey, self-effacing man in a grey suit, with hand extended, announcing he was "McCuaig from Information".

Except for "Mrs Agnes McCuaig at the Piano", the last four poems of our selection are from a group of poems written between 1953 and 1959, which are given the title "Childhood Scenes" in his *Selected Poems*. His years of writing very pedestrian light verse meant that he was able to apply to these works of art an extraordinarily supple technique, arguing with himself in different voices and flipping effortlessly from one metre to another. Unaccountably, the elegy for his mother does not appear in his *Selected*, deleted apparently at McCuaig's request. These four poems represent the acme of McCuaig's achievement, "light" as puff pastry and yet profound at the same time, virtuoso pieces with the power to hurt as they gaze back at a world that has vanished.

The Passionate Clerk to his Love

Live with me; be my wife;
  We'll end flirtations;
You'll find it a slow life,
  But with compensations.

And we'll get a flat
  Of two witty
Rooms, a bath and kitchenette,
  High over the city,

Where, in the evening
  When dinner's over,
We'll wash up everything
  And I'll be your lover,

And tie knot after knot
  Of flesh aching,
Then cut the lot,
  And without waking

You'll sleep till sunrise,
  And we'll rise early,
And through each other's eyes
  We'll see things clearly,

And never be dismayed
  To find them shoddy,
And never be afraid

Of anybody;

And on Sunday afternoon
About three or four
I'll play the gramophone
While you pour

Afternoon tea
Into my soul,
And bending to me
With the sugar bowl

You'll be a priestess
Swaying the sheathing
Of a flower-stained dress
With even breathing

And in this atmosphere
Charmed from your breast
Half we shall hear
And feel the rest

As we talk scandal and
A kind of wit
We alone understand,
Or maybe just sit

Quiet while the clock chimes
Patient tomorrows,
And smile sometimes
At old sorrows.

The Surfer

The breakers crash on the sands
In a white line of roar
Over the mumble of thousands
Stretched on the shore:

A cliff reared at the sky
Southwards, holds on its back
Little red roofs that defy
The wind's wrack:

In and out of the sea run
Boys cutting capers;
Young girls lie down for the sun;
Old men read newspapers;

And out to the skyline
  My soul made new
Sings, like an old violin
  For a genius Jew,

Of her, poised on an edge
  Of great sloping water
Like a rose in a hedge
  That has risen and caught her

Up high; as it curves,
  Her body, brown and lean,
Swoops down and swerves,
  Breasts keeling the green:

Like an impatient bride
  Grudging her lover sleep,
Shaking speed from his side
  In a long sweep,

Whose wakening kiss
  Flakes, flashes and smoulders
In white ashes that hiss
  On lips, eyes and shoulders:

She is rushed to the beach,
  And stands, and the sea
Sags out of reach
  Wearily,

And the clean sky shines above her
  Like a benediction,
And her wily old lover
  With slavering tongue

Coaxes her feet again
  To his lecherous bed,
And the sea floods in my brain
  And goes red:

Sun-dazzled and numb
  I feel half dead;
I must go home
  To my lecherous bed;

In the morning I shall rise
  Red-raw and aching

From memories of bronzed thighs
  And stupid sunbaking.

The Commercial Traveller's Wife

I'm living with a commercial traveller;
He's away, most of the time.
Most I see of him's his wife; as for her:
I'm just home from a show,
And there I am undressing, in my shirt.
I hear midnight chime,
And up flares the curtain at the window.
The door's opened. It's Gert –
That's the wife. Her hair's hanging down.
She's only got her nightgown
Blowing up against her in the wind.
She's fat, and getting fatter.
I said, "What's the matter?"
"Jack," she said, "now's your chance."
"What chance?" I said. "You out of your mind?"
She goes over to the bed.
I grab my pants.
"That's enough of that," I said. "Now go on; you get out."
"But Jack," she said, "don't you love me?"
"I don't know what you're talking about,"
I said; "Besides, Jim –
What about him?"
"Yes; Jim," she said; "there's always Jim, but he's
Always away; and you don't know
What it's like. I can't stand it. And anyhow,
Jack, don't you want me?"
                                        "Oh, don't be an ass,"
I said; "Look at yourself in the glass."

She faced the mirror where she stood
And sort of stiffened there.
Her eyes went still as knots in a bit of wood,
And it all seemed to sigh out of her:
"All right," she said; "all right, all right, good night,"
As though she didn't know if I heard,
And shuffled out without another word.

Well, I was tired; I went to bed and slept.
In the morning
I thought I'd dreamt the whole thing,

But at breakfast, I could have wept:
Poor Gert, clattering the dishes
With a dead sort of face
Like a fish's.
I'll have to get a new place.
I'm going out today to have a look.
Trouble is, she's a marvellous cook.

The Letter

Dear, as I write and think of you,
And several other people too,
The flooring of the flat above,
Creaking with aged, illicit love,
Reminds me, when I was trying to write
These very words the other night,
He spoke from three till half past four
Merely repeating she was a whore.
The boy below has just begun
To find it not precisely fun;
The trouble is, as he explained
The Thursday evening when it rained
To a judicial prig of a friend
(I thought their talk would never end),
The girl is really not the kind
Of girl he really had in mind.
But still he keeps her on, for fear
Of hurting her. And now I hear
The lovely girl who loves to dwell,
And dwells to love, across the well,
Saying, since he is married, he
Should be considerate, in that she
Is taking risks. As for the rent,
She fears, it has been otherwise spent.
The opposite flat is dark and dumb,
Yet I feel certain he will come
Home to his love as drunk as ever
And, in a slowly rising fever,
Noting the whisky bottle gone,
Will trip and curse and stumble on
Into the bathroom, pull the chain,
Fumble the cabinet, curse again;
Will ask the slut where she has hid

His toothbrush; blunder back to bed,
Find his pyjamas tied in knots
And give her, as he puts it, what's
Coming to her. She won't escape
Her deeply meditated rape.
But I must write of love, and all
That once was high, and had a fall,
And how I burn; and I confess
It gives me little happiness:
Encompassed so, my rooms become
A kind of lovers' vacuum,
Dear, as I write, and ache for you,
And dream of all that we could do
If these delights thy mind might move
To live with me and be my love.

Love Me and Never Leave Me

Love me, and never leave me,
Love, nor ever deceive me,
And I shall always bless you
If I may undress you:
        This I heard a lover say
        To his sweetheart where they lay.

He, though he did undress her,
Did not always bless her;
She, though she would not leave him,
Often did deceive him;
        Yet they loved, and when they died
        They were buried side by side.

Berceuse de Newcastle

It's always sunset in the east
    With a *roddle-toddle-toddle*,
When the night furnace is in blast
    With a *roddle-toddle-toddle*
And all night long the rolling-mill
    Goes *roddle-toddle-toddle*;
A minute's pause when all is still,
    Then: *roddle-toddle-toddle*,
Shaking the windows in their frames
    With *roddle-toddle-toddle*,

Blurring the contours of my dreams
    With *roddle-toddle-toddle*,
But if the windows didn't shake
    With the *roddle-toddle-toddle*
Would I sleep sounder, or awake
    From the *roddle-toddle-toddle*?

        The *roddle-toddle-toddle*

          Roddle-toddle-toddle.

Mrs Agnes McCuaig at the Piano

(Etudes, Op. 25, No. 2: Chopin)

Fluttering like leaves, the flickering triplets
Replace the hands that play with hands that played
In music's kinematic light and shade.
Creating you, the music begets
Chopin, your composer, for me, your composition,
Muttering, "These young women fill me with contrition,
Studying my studies without thought of recognition
Endlessly, endlessly, endlessly, endlessly ...."

"No, no, no, Chopin. This time you are mistaken.
I shall avenge her, I am a poet. She had me taught to speak,
And I shall use my elocution in praise of her technique:
The grave will open! The dead will awaken!"
"She is well-spared your second-rate critique.
What had she that biographers might seek?"
        "She read me books, she gave me toys,
        She sang of comical negro boys;
        She cried and cried when Judy died
        With a broken back
        On a book bush-track;
If she turned you could see the flames of her brilliant eyes –"
"Let her face the keys. We die when music dies.
Elusive as my music she will soon be gone,
Wavering on and on, and on and on ..."

Ghost of gaiety, guest of grief,
I have grown older, now, because of you
Than you, because of me, could manage to;
Soon you will be beyond belief,
And no one left who knew you, or could say
How you threw all that ecstasy away:

Enchant me with the void where we belong,
My mother of memory,
My man of melody,
My child of song.

L'Après-midi d'une Fille aux Cheveux de Lin

(Homage to Debussy)

Bearing their birds and gardens on their hats
The ladies of suburbia have come,
Fresh in their sweeping skirts from sweeping mats,
To grace my mother's afternoon at-home.

For each, a delicately different china cup;
For all, the scandal and the price of eggs;
For me, my bright white sailor-suit starched up,
Its pinked seams chafing me between my legs,

And the white-frocked Renoir child with the flaxen hair
Tied in those chocolate-boxy bows he makes –
I am to take her to play in the open air,
Leaving her mother to the tea and cakes:

Into the stare of the afternoon sun at the grass
Wandering out in silence, hand in hand,
I, her diminutive and dutiful Pelléas,
She, my mysterious, miniature Mélisande,

I see us yet, a portrait lost to tense,
Rapt in the heat as flowers in their aroma,
Fixed by the master's gaze of innocence …
But life shakes rudely at pictorial coma:

The sweep has left behind his tin of soot –
These things must happen; why, I cannot tell:
For every Adam, his forbidden fruit,
For every Mélisande, her destined well:

"Put in your head." The summer air is cursed
As Eden's with the scented breath of sin.
The fig-tree shudders. "You put yours in first."
The bamboo stirs and sighs. My head goes in.

My sailor-suit, the glow of Renoir's paint,
Become our weekly charwoman's despair,
Life's evil critic, throwing off restraint,
Empties his inkpot on the flaxen hair.

Golliwogs, now, we
Run in to show the
People what we have done.
We cause a creaking of the tight-laced sitters.
Somebody shrieking,
Everyone speaking,
One of them drops her bun.
They all seek hiding-places for their titters.

And we are trapped in passion's aftermath,
Prophecy and prototype of others –
The double expiation of the bath,
The hissings of the geyser and the mothers,

Conclude this formal afternoon at-home.
I wonder would she think me past all shame,
Rejoicing in the roses of her small, spanked bottom,
A lover of Renoirs who has forgotten her name?

Au Tombeau de mon Père

I went on Friday afternoons
Among the knives and forks and spoons
Where mounted grindstones flanked the floor
To my father's office door.

So serious a man was he,
The Buyer for the Cutlery …
I found him sketching lamps from stock
In his big stock-records book,

And when he turned the page to me:
"Not bad for an old codger, eh?"
I thought this frivolous in him,
Preferring what he said to them:

They wanted reparations paid
In German gold and not in trade,
But he rebuked such attitudes:
"You'll have to take it out in goods."

And what they did in time was just,
He said, what he had said they must:
If Time had any end in sight
It was, to prove my father right.

The evening came, and changed him coats,

Produced a rag and rubbed his boots,
And then a mirror and a brush
And smoothed his beard and his moustache;

A sign for blinds outside to fall
On shelves and showcases, and all
Their hammers, chisels, planes and spades,
And pocket-knives with seven blades.

Then, in the lift, the patted back:
"He's growing like you, Mr Mac!"
(The hearty voices thus implied
A reason for our mutual pride.)

And so the front-door roundabout
Gathered us in and swept us out
To sausage, tea in separate pots,
And jellies crowned with creamy clots.

And once he took me on to a
Recital, to hear Seidel play,
And Hutchens spanked the piano-bass,
Never looking where it was.

When I got home I practised this,
But somehow always seemed to miss,
And my cigar-box violin,
After Seidel's, sounded thin.

And once he took me to a bill
Of sporadic vaudeville.
A man and woman held the stage;
She sneered in simulated rage,

And when he made a shrewd reply
He'd lift his oval shirt-front high
And slap his bare and hairy chest
To celebrate his raucous jest.

Then, as the shout of joy ensued,
Uniting mime and multitude,
And mine rang out an octave higher,
A boy-soprano's in that choir,

My father's smile was half unease,
Half pleasure in his power to please:
"Try not to laugh so loudly, Ron;
Those women think you're catching on."

But far more often it was to
The School of Arts we used to go;
Up the dusty stairway's gloom,
Through the musty reading-room

And out to a veranda-seat
Overlooking Hunter Street.
There in the dark my father sat,
Pipe in mouth, to meditate.

A cake-shop glowed across the way
With a rainbow-cake display;
I never saw its keeper there,
And never saw a customer,

And yet there was activity
High in the south-western sky:
A bottle flashing on a sign
Advertising someone's wine.

So, as my father thought and thought
(Considering lines of saws he'd bought,
Or, silence both his church and club,
Feeling close to Nature's hub,

Or maybe merely practising
Never saying anything,
Since he could go, when deeply stirred,
Months, at home, without a word,

Or pondering the indignity
Of having to put up with me),
I contemplated, half awake,
The flashing wine, the glowing cake:

The wine that no one can decant,
And the cake we didn't want:
As Mr Blake's Redeemer said,
"This the wine, and this the bread."

SONGS OF CENTRAL AUSTRALIA (T. G. H. Strehlow) 1908–1978

Theodor (Ted) George Henry Strehlow was born at Hermannsburg, in central Australia, the son of Pastor Carl Strehlow, a Lutheran missionary. After graduating with Honours in English from the University of Adelaide, he returned to Hermannsburg on a grant to study the culture of the Arrernte (Aranda) people. Aboriginal elders became concerned that there were no younger men to whom they could confide the secrets of their ceremonies and, at their invitation in 1933, he began recording their beliefs and songs. He waited until all his informants were dead before publishing his monumental *Songs of Central Australia* in 1971, which is the source of the translations here.

Even in translation, on the page, unsupported by the rituals and performance of which they were a part, the force of these songs can be shocking. The words have a purpose beyond entertainment. For example "Women's Verses of Execration" (and the accompanying ritual) were intended to kill the woman being cursed. The songs use parallelism, like the Hebrew psalms. Although not epic in their length, songs such as "Song of the Termite Women of Iloata" achieve an epic, timeless quality by their repetition of phrases with small variations. Strehlow compared the songs he collected with Greek drama and Anglo-Saxon poetry, such as *Beowulf*.

We have inserted titles at the start of each song, based on titles Strehlow supplied, usually in his accompanying text. He numbered each verse; we have deleted these numbers. We have also deleted the complicated accents he inserted above letters, to denote a particular pronunciation. Finally, he placed square brackets around a word that he was inserting and that was implied. In general we have deleted these brackets. We have deleted some verses, where, although there were slight differences from previous verses, the effect became excessively repetitive for a poem on the page. These deletions are indicated by three dots. With some of the songs, Strehlow re-ordered the verses to follow the sequence of a narrative. He extracted some of his songs from longer works. Except as indicated, we have not altered Strehlow's text.

These notes on each song follow in abbreviated form Strehlow's comments:

"Women's Verses of Execration": A wronged wife and woman-friend might intone these verses to punish a rival woman. The two women cut off their own locks and pubic hair and work this into plaits and tie these plaits to two digging sticks, to which kangaroo leg bones and teeth have been fastened by porcupine [echidna] resin. The sticks now represent plait women (tjimbarkna). A large fire is lit and the sticks are pushed into the ground close to the fire. The two women dance, the sticks are pulled up and down and rubbed with lime, the outlines of a snake are drawn, and the verses are intoned.

"Ndapa Song": This describes how a group of dancing ancestresses from Areiltjara (the Dreamtime) passed through Thata on their way to the distant Loritja territory, creating the parallel ridges of the hills. Strehlow explained that they advance in a line by hooking their little fingers into the little fingers of the companions on either side.

"Song of the Termite Women of Iloata": This song describes the ranges and bluffs near Mt Conway (Iloata) in the Central MacDonnell Ranges as seen by sisters sitting on their isolated mountain, which they cannot leave. One of the sisters sees bandicoot tailtips at Urumuna, twenty miles away, suspended from the pole of an ancestress, who is beckoning to her, and she bursts into tears, because she cannot accept the invitation. Another sister gazes towards Alkneutjata, which is fifty miles away, and exchanges glances with an ancestress there. The second sister begins to weep. The final verse is spoken by the ancestress who also weeps at the sight of her descendant weeping on the mountain. We have added the italic indications of who is speaking.

Women's Verses of Execration

The tjimbarkna plaits are lying there:
She is continually wasting away without hope.

With bleaching teeth she is lying there,
With shrivelling brain she is lying there.

Her eyeballs are projecting from their sockets;
Her head has grown too large for her.

The plait woman keeps on crying and crying;
In her loneliness she keeps on crying and crying.

The tjimbarkna plaits are breaking her life;
The avenging woman is breaking her life.

Ndapa Song

Yonder women from Areiltjara
Come dancing along, in glistening lines.

The little youthful maidens
Are tripping away, tossing their feet.

Girls and maidens, young and mature,
Are tripping away, tossing their feet.

Each holding her stick before her,
They are tripping away, tossing their feet.

The girls move in a pair of rows, –
One row to the left and one to the right.

Leave in your tracks lines of hills!
Leave in your tracks parallel ridges!

The legs of the girls are moving ceaselessly;
The heads of the girls are waving with tailtips.

Song of the Termite Women of Iloata

"Among the boulders of the peak we shall ever sit, –
A band of sisters we shall ever sit."

"Among the boulders of the peak we shall ever sit;
Sisters all, let us recline here!"

From the north the wind is blowing fiercely;
The east wind is blowing fiercely.

The north wind blows incessantly;
The east wind blows incessantly ...

The mountain hawks scream as they come swooping down.
In the vault of the sky they scream as they come swooping down ...

The mountain hawks are descending with whirring wings;
From the vault of the sky they are descending with whirring wings.

They come swooping lower and lower;
With hoarse cries they are settling on the ground.

The mountain bluffs are rising in parallel ridges;
The mountain valleys are running in parallel grooves.

The mountain bluffs are rising in parallel ridges;
The mountain bluffs are falling down in sharp precipices.

Towards the foothills they are descending tier by tier,
Into the depths below they are descending tier by tier ...

Banks of kangaroo grass are descending tier by tier, –
Into the depths below they are descending tier by tier.

Thick stands of mountain grasses are descending tier by tier, –
Towards the foothills they are descending tier by tier.

Both sisters:
"The holly trees are standing with intertwined branches;
Our own fruit trees are standing with intertwined branches."

First sister:
"With bandicoot tips she beckons me to come;
With furry tailtips she beckons me to come."

On the edge of the precipice she bows low her head;
The tear drops are chasing each other down her cheeks.

Second sister:
"From Alkneutjata her eyes are staring at me unflinchingly;
Under half-closed lids her eyes are staring at me unflinchingly."

The tear drops are chasing each other down her cheeks;
Searing her brain, they are chasing each other down her cheeks.

The tears are chasing each other down her cheeks,
Tears upon tears, bitter with grief.

Ancestress:
"From the crest of her mountain she causes me to weep, –
A flood of tears she causes me to weep."

ELIZABETH RIDDELL 1910–1998

Elizabeth Riddell was born in New Zealand, and came to Australia immediately she left school, invited by a Sydney newspaper editor to work as a journalist on the strength of some schoolgirl verses published in a magazine. "They thought that a poet might make a journalist ... It was terrible poetry." Her fare was paid, and her rent for two weeks, and she immediately had to produce a theatre page. She became one of Australia's most respected journalists, a career in which she felt she had "done everything", and which brought her the prestigious Walkley Award. During World War II she was a correspondent in New York and London. After her return to Australia in 1945, she continued to work as a journalist into her retirement. She was married to the journalist Edward "Blue" Greatorex, whom she met on Bondi Beach. They had no children, and "never meant to". He died in 1964. Her poetry, she has said, has been strongly influenced both in style and content by her career. Her work has, in tension with its spareness, a very unjournalistic aestheticism, and in her later poems she is able to reflect on a life of considerable emotional intensity.

Wakeful in the Township

Barks the melancholy dog,
Swims in the stream the shadowy fish.
Who would live in a country town
If they had their wish?

When the sun comes hurrying up
I will take the circus train
That cries, cries once in the night
And then not again.

In the stream the shadowy fish
Sleeps below the sleeping fly.
Many around me straitly sleep
But not I.

Near my window a drowsy bird
Flickers its feathers against the thorn.
Around the township's single light

My people die and are born.

I will join the circus train
For mangy leopard and tinsel girl
And the trotting horses' great white haunches
Whiter than a pearl.

When to the dark blue mountains
My captive pigeons flew
I'd no heart to lure them back
With wheat upon the dew.

When the dog at morning
Whines upon the frost
I shall be in another place.
Lost, lost, lost.

Suburban Song

Now all the dogs with folded paws
Stare at the lowering sky.
This is the hour when women hear
Their lives go ticking by.

The baker's horse with rattling hooves
Upon the windy hill
Mocks the thunder in the heart
Of women sitting still.

The poppies in the garden turn
Their faces to the sand
And tears upon the sewing fall
And on the stranger's hand.

Flap flap the washing flies
To meet the starting hail.
Close the door on love and hang
The key upon the nail.

Patrick White, His Day

That morning he felt not too old
to go to the double window and watch the birds.

Later he telephoned to report
a spotted pardalote impetuously had left the nest
and spiralled down, drifting on indifferent air
discovering flight too soon,

to fall bewildered in the small shade of windflowers
while above the community chattered,
before it levitated back laboriously
from branch to branch
into the nest. Then all quietened.

Last week he had read in a magazine that in Costa Rica
they do not kill the birds.
Instead they kill the people, he observed.

That afternoon he sat at a table on the flagstones
and drank lemon tea. Manoly walked the dogs
around the drowsy park.
A friend came. He signed a book with a bold flowing hand.
The Jack Russell shifted on its haunches,
scratched, muttered and appealed.

He wore a sweater of a certain dashing green
and a fisherman's woollen tasselled cap
a traveller had brought him from Cascais.
He gave the terrier a biscuit
and when the sun paused behind a calligraphy of leaves
he read its message and rose and walked inside
and as he walked a great wracking cough
risen from the humid pastures
and lake shore of his youth seized him
and shook him in its jaws.

The day was almost over. In the glimmer of mahogany
and the profound presence of enormous paintings
the light was gradually dimmed and then went out.

The man sought sleep.

Below his bed the terrier twitched and snored.

W. HART-SMITH 1911–1990

Born in England, William Hart-Smith emigrated to New Zealand with his parents in 1924 at the age of thirteen, and first came to Australia when he was 25. After serving with the Australian army within Australia during World War II, he returned to New Zealand in 1946 staying there until the early '60s, then settled back in Australia. He worked mainly in advertising or as a radio broadcasting technician in this country, and in adult education in New Zealand. His main poetry collections were published here. In 1978 after a nervous collapse and hospitalisation in Perth, where he had taught creative writing, Hart-Smith returned once more to live in

New Zealand. He died in Auckland of a stroke, aged 79, leaving a dozen books of poetry and four children.

Although only a phase in his career, Hart-Smith was one of the principal contributors to the nationalist Jindyworobak movement, out of his fascination with Aboriginal culture and the outback, where he travelled during his war service. In technique Hart-Smith's imagist free verse shows the influence of D. H. Lawrence – although nowhere more than in "Nullarbor", which remains a genuinely personal poem – and of William Carlos Williams, in its tightly controlled, improvised rhythms, and its expressive use of enjambment. Hart-Smith's is the earliest application of the Williams poetic in Australia. Unlike Williams he often makes use of impromptu rhyming. He admired Ezra Pound, and did not like Eliot.

Barbara Petrie in her foreword to Hart-Smith's posthumous collection *Hand to Hand: A Garnering* wrote: "I believe Bill practised the Gurdjieff method [based on the sufi-influenced teachings of G. I. Gurdjieff] for many years … One of the effects of Bill's involvement with Gurdjieff's teachings was his reluctance to express negative emotions, in life and in his art. Not only did he consciously try to avoid the expression of negative emotions in his poetry, at one stage he went so far as to avoid the use of words such as 'no'." Hart-Smith was a conchologist and ardent conservationist, who collected the shells of dead organisms from beaches and rock-pools. He had a large, carefully catalogued collection and in 1967 a variety was named after him – *Notadusta Hartsmithi Schilder.*

Hart-Smith was a prolific poet. His estimate of his total output was about 4000 poems, many of which were not preserved. Like a photographer who takes many photographs and chooses only a few images, many of his poems have a hit-or-miss quality. The "hits" can be both attractively casual and austere and isolate images of great refinement. The "misses" may be marred by whimsy and triviality.

Nullarbor

Here earth and sky are reduced to an ultimate simplicity,
The earth to a completely flat circle,
An ocean-circle of red soil with flecks of white limestone,
Patches of dead brown grass and stiff dead bushes
And tuft-like clumps and knots of dwarf bushes
That look dead,
But really grip their lives tightly away from the sun,
Grip hold of their lives with little hard fists.
The leaves
Are leathery tongues with a small spittle of salt in them.
And the sky is a pure thing,
A flawless cover of glass,
An inverted glass cover upon a table.

When the train stopped I swung my legs over the side,
jumped down from the roped truck and sat on the dry hot boards of the
flat-top,
My feet dangling over, idly swinging, my hands behind me,

The palms taking a print from the rough wood
And the cinders and grit,
Making up my mind to take the next jump, the leap to the track,
And curiously examining a reluctance to do so …
Sleepers, a slope of cinders and metal, then
The desert, the miraculous, empty, utterly pure desert,
The clean desert and the clean bright wind,
The rim out there
Not abruptly ending, but broken,
An undercutting and a flowing into,
The sky running into the earth and the earth running into the sky,
Long liquid lines of sky, opaque, making inroads into the rim,
The edge of the world,
And long low islands floating …
Mirage.
It is the hot air rising,
The air becoming hot and beginning to tremble and throb and dance,
Destroys the abruptness, the clean cut-off.

And then you appeared. There you were, suddenly there in the desert
Beyond the train, beyond the line of waiting trucks,
As if you had suddenly appeared out of nothing,
With your black body, your brush of sun-bleached hair
And the stick stuck in your belt
Behind you, sticking out like a tail.
You were not looking at us. You were walking away from us when you appeared,
Walking away in a queer loping fashion
Going off at an angle with your back to us.
My legs stopped swinging and I stared at you, fascinated,
Looked into your back and wondered what it was you were after,
You, boy …
I saw you were a boy.
You stopped then, turned back and ran a little distance,
Then turned again and walked straight towards me,
Closer and closer, till I could see into your eyes,
Closer, without stopping; then you swung yourself up onto the flat-top beside me
And sat there looking out over the desert.

How long did we sit there? How long was it we sat there saying nothing?
Perhaps an eternity. Sat there saying nothing.
I could hear your breathing. Your body had a familiar strong smell,

An earth smell, a special earth smell;
And I thought of the leaves with the taste of brine in them,
The spicy tang of them, the gnarled old bushes,
Life bunched up in their fists.

I changed. Slowly I changed. I became a grotesque thing.
I became white-skinned, a human being with a white skin …
Grotesque!
A thin being with a sharp nose and a strong reek,
Huddled into myself, covered up, cowering away from life,
A distorted thing with my senses only half awake,
My eyes only half opened, my nostrils clogged with a numbing deadness,
My ears with a pressure on the drums,
Only partly sensitive.

It was an eternity. I know it was.

Did you break it because of me? Did you speak at last because you knew
 what was happening to me?
Did you do it to save me?
You moved,
You pointed upward with your finger at a bird, a solitary great bird with
 white wings tipped with brown,
Spiralling, making circles, great wide circles and spirals with motionless
 huge wings
High over our heads.
"Eaglehawk," you said. "Eaglehawk."

It's funny, but you accepted me then. We used the code of stranger
 approaching stranger.
You came and sat down beyond the limits of my camp,
The camp of my personality and the small fire of my heart,
Waiting with your back to it before my thoughts sent out their women
With food and drink, went out and brought you in. We talked.
You asked for a cigarette. I gave you one and lit it for you.
I can see my white hands cupped against the brown skin of your face.
The deep ridge of brows as you bent over my hands and sucked in the flame;
 the tuft of beard on your chin.
A boy.
I remarked to myself on the rich body quality of your voice
And unconsciously deepened the tones of my own.
You talked as you smoked, the cigarette looking silly and pathetic in your
 fingers,
Held between ball of thumb and forefinger.

Then my own world broke in. It came
Out of the future, out of the future from a terrible distance,
Roared down on me and shrieked, and pounded fists on my heart.
The clash of jerked couplings shattered something in my head.
You jumped down. I heard above the noise the soft crunch of your feet as
they hit the ground
And you looked at me over your shoulder, then turned away.
Turned your back on me and walked away
With that queer loose-swinging lope of yours,
That straight-backed, loose-limbed walk full from the hips.
You walked away and never looked back.

I sat there as the train moved
And the ground began to slide sideways under my feet,
Sideways under my boots,
Until the blur made me giddy and sick.
And when I looked up you had gone.
I looked back, but you had gone.
The desert was flowing away to the left
Bringing the clean wind strong on the right side of my head;
And the stones and low bushes were flowing away, faster and faster,
Faster. Only the desert remained itself, remained unchanged,
Flowing away from itself,
Yet continually renewing itself from right to left, faster, faster,
And the wind a gale,

And under me a grind and clatter of wheels.

Burning Off

Don't heed them. Those fires are tame
burning over the hill. The tethered dogs
lie with chain slack, sleeping. The smoke
is invisible, it is something in the air
makes all day's colours sombre, a fragrance,
subtle, nameless. And you may have noticed
the early stars are not of the purest water
and do not twinkle. The grass, the grass is dry,
the roof metal shines like steel
under a paring of moon. Like a procession
of torchbearers going on some pilgrimage,
the lines of flame on the hilltop.
Leave the door open. Come inside.
The night grows cold. Light the lamp.

Cyclone

The first rain in months
drops
drops
splash on the roadway
from a clear blue sky
overhead

Footprints of the Spirit Dog

spatter on the asphalt
of the desert road
in the ominous stillness
in the looming darkness

They print their pawmarks
on the dry road
on the windscreen dust

From the wide desert
the kangaroos come out
bend down on their huge haunches
go down on their hands
to
to lap the road
to lap the drops

lick from the road
the raindrops

the first rain.

from Man into Trees

for Caroline Kalmar

Here, nothing is ever folded
and put away:

leaf, stick, twig, shards
of bark, like shed garments,

are simply dropped when finished with,
and turn to compost where they lie.

Pollen is spilled upon the glass
of a dressing-table top;

earring petals drop
and rust where they are fallen.

The floors and walls are damp,
tier upon tier of shelves of stone descend

scattered with gritty pebbles
and glittering sand.

But not a tidy notion troubles
the innocent conscience of this land,

a sweet, sweet odour rises,
a lovely fragrance comes

of spilled unguents, spices,
and aromatic gums.

Notes in Pencil

Sea touches land where …
and the newly-sharpened pencil snaps

at a too-finely-razored
tip, making a scar

and scumble of black grains. One intended
tracing the longest reach

of a breaking wave, noticing
how like a mantle it is

extended from a living mollusc
deliberately, purposefully

up the camber of the beach
and then withdrawn.

One would have recorded
a fringe of sea-mucous, thin

as a strand of flotsam thread.
But this blunted stub

serves better as a rod now
to probe a knot of sundried weed,

releasing a spray of sand-hoppers
that pepper hands, face

with pellets of sensation.
Notice also how these newly-dead

shells pour a libation of sand,
a trickle of golden

treasure
in the palm of the hand.

Wetlands, Perth

The black marshlands are streaked with moon water
donk donk

waruk

The sky is too luminous
with moonlight for stars

Only the pinhole of Venus
for the moon's companion

waruk waruk

Night a still night
donk

in Spring Paperbark trees
those most silent of drinkers
taking their fill towards summer

donk waruk waruk

donk

Watercolour

The stillness is full of menace and foreboding.
It is hard to say whether it is thunder one hears
or the rumble of car-wheels approaching
over the wooden bridge.

The sky behind the river-gums
is a wall, a screen
a perpendicular barrier, blue-black.

A long late sun
cannot penetrate the barrier,
the light hits the white trunks of the trees
and bounces back.

The shapes of the trunks are frozen lightning
which blazes on the black screen.

The green of the leaves of the river-gums
is incredibly intensified: it burns.

And the cockatoos that swarm, and scream insanely
as the storm approaches,
cannot bear the intensity of their own whiteness.

HAL PORTER 1911–1984

Hal Porter grew up in Bairnsdale, Victoria, worked as a journalist, teacher and librarian, was a major Australian short-story writer and wrote two highly praised volumes of memoirs, *The Watcher on the Cast-Iron Balcony* and *The Paper Chase*. In the course of writing a respectful biography of Porter, whom she regarded as her friend and a major writer, Mary Lord discovered that he had sexually violated her ten-year-old son.

Porter had a high-camp prose style that was astonishing in its virtuosity, resembling the description of the golf-bag in his comic story "Say to Me Ronald!" in which his alter ego, Perrot, has been given a set of golf clubs by an Asian student he has coached: "Good God! thought Perrot ... The golf-bag was the biggest he had ever seen. The biggest in the world? ... the golf-bag totemically stood, its effect admonitory. It had, too, the quality of a menhir, albeit composed of a circus-red species of leather, and fleur-de-lis-ed, gusseted, gored and belted with whitest white. Buckles and nodules of nickel ratified its Maya-like power. From its well protruded uncountable ... weapons? ... virile insignia? ... surely not golf-clubs? ... of some surely Venusian alloy."

Porter's poetry is not at the same level as his prose. His first two books of poetry, *The Hexagon* and *Elijah's Ravens* are almost unreadable, the metaphors, similes and consonance so thickly encrust the poems. They read like Slessor (whose unreliable friend he was) on steroids. The feverish excitement of language had abated with his final book of verse *In An Australian Country Graveyard – And Other Poems* (1974) from which "Alexandra Tea-room" comes.

Alexandra Tea-room

(A Provincial City, 1968)

An East-of-Suez ceiling-fan, stopped dead
some hot, F. Scott Fiztgerald afternoon,
says ten-to-nevermore above your head
while you, you bitch, and I do good-bye's deed,
stir stillborn tea with an unsilver spoon.

One other patron (naice) who's overheard
our nitric-acid truths, art nouveau lies
(two haters parting spare no hurting word),
in genteel autumn cocoa strives to hide
her White Queen's Church-of-England-coloured eyes.

If you and I were Alice we could climb
this nervy marble table-top and pass

into that other tea-room's Proustian time,
the Jabberwocky lovescape we disclaim,
the mimsy vistas through the looking-glass.

The White Queen there, all tousled shawl and hair,
would shrill that pins had pricked before they had,
and waste some grief on us who do not care
that love has cured to loathing, There to Here:
"I wish that you could manage to be glad."

"Consider what o'clock it is," she'd plead.
Near shut-up time, the storm-chipped cups drunk dry
(too Tenniel for tears), things run to seed.
Each city's full of cities. Hell's deployed.
All abysses are shallow. So am I.

"I must first hurt if I am to forgive."
Who says it? You. You fool! I'm silent stone
not snarling, "I'm indifferent that you live,"
and "I don't feel the wound you think you give,"
or "So *that's* how you look when you're alone!"

ROLAND ROBINSON 1912–1992

Born in Ireland of English parents, Roland Robinson was nine years old when he came to Australia. At fourteen he was already working on a sheep station in outback New South Wales, first as a houseboy and then as a rouseabout and boundary rider. Later he was a horse-trainer, jockey, fencer, dam builder, factory worker, railway fettler, cleaner, art school model, ballet dancer (as a member of the Kirsova Ballet), dance critic for the *Sydney Morning Herald* in the 1950s and 1960s, caught crocodiles and snakes for a menagerie; and in his last job, over many years, was the greenkeeper on a golfcourse in Rose Bay, Sydney. During World War II, as a conscientious objector, he had to labour on railway lines in the Northern Territory. It was here that he had his first contact with tribal Aborigines, having already sought out detribalised blacks on the south coast of New South Wales. After James Devaney, he was the first white poet to listen to, and collect, the anecdotes and oral traditions of these people, which he set down in verse and prose.

Intensely attracted by the Australian landscape and the bushman's ethos, always a radical, Robinson joined whole-heartedly from its beginning in the Jindyworobak program – to write out of the uniqueness of the Australian environment and to incorporate Aboriginal culture – after meeting the group's founder, Rex Ingamells, in Adelaide. He has come to be seen as the Jindyworobaks' most successful poet.

Robinson wrote eight small volumes of poetry, five prose works on Aboriginal myths and legends, a book of stories about the relationships of Aborigines and whites, and three volumes of autobiography. These last reveal an extremely emotional, driven nature. He regularly fled to the bush to escape routine, or what he felt as emotional demands. A man of striking looks, his relationships with women were difficult and twice ended tragically. The anguished third volume of his autobiography, *A Letter to Joan*, is addressed to the poet Joan Maas, who walked into the sea, when he was away from her with another woman. He was a fine performer and recited his poetry without reference to the written text in an oracular voice. He had no children and was keen to make contact with younger poets.

Robinson was devoted to the poetry of Edward Thomas, for the purity of its impulse and style, and he valued Brennan's "The Wanderer" above all other Australian poems. These influences show as both naturalness and elevation in his work. But he had an intensity that is all his own – his best poems burn with the colours of the outback and of the coastal bush. His work has been undervalued because it is small in scope and lacks any intellectual scheme, but its vividness and emblematic force amply compensate.

Drifting Dug-out

Now that the fig lets fall her single stars
of flowers on these green waters I would be
withdrawn as Gul-ar-dar-ark the peaceful dove
sending his callings over the many springs,
over the fountains and the jets of song
of Nin the finch and Geek-keek the honeyeater.
I would be withdrawn as Gul-ar-dar-ark calling
out of the distant sky and tresses of the leaves,
now that the fig lets fall her single flowers
like stars to pass beyond my trailing hand.

To a Mate

He was a man who, with his hand,
would make the language of the sand
that showed where piccaninny walked,
where emu trod or dingo stalked.

Euro's pad or writhe of snake,
or brolga's imprint he could make.
And he was one to booze and brawl
and lie beside the fire asprawl.

He was a man, when moved, who spoke
of how at Innaminka soak,
when the molten west grew dim,
the creatures from the desert's rim

came in to drink and play as he
lay watching by a hakea tree,

where stars and dingo howls, he swore
were solitude not known before.

Wherever now with swag outspread
he camps by soak or river-bed,
would that I saw his camp-fire's sparks
and hailed him through the paper-barks.

Would I might find my country

Would I might find my country as the blacks
come in and lean their spears up in the scrub,
and crouch and light their flickering fires and spread
their mission blankets on the ground beneath
the dark acacia and bauhinia trees.
Would I might find my people as the blacks
sit with their lubras, children, and tired dogs,
their dilly-bags, their bundles of belongings
tied up in scraps of some old coloured dress,
and pass the long straight smoking pipe around,
and talk in quiet calling voices while
the blood deep crimson flower of sunset burns
to smouldering ash and fume behind the trees,
behind the thin grassed ridges of their land.

The Drovers

Over the plains of the whitening grass
and the stunted mulga the drovers pass,
and in the red dust cloud, each side
of the cattle, the native stockmen ride.

And day after day lays bare the same
endless plains as the way they came,
and ever the cloven ranges lie
at the end of the land and the opal sky.

With creak of pack and saddle leather,
and chink of chain and bit together,
with moan of the herd, with hobble and bell
they come to the tanks at the tea-tree well.

And through corroding blood-red hills,
by sanded rivers the Gulf rain fills,
far, where the morning star has shone
and paled above, their tracks are gone.

Casuarina

The last, the long-haired casuarina
stands upon the hillside where
against the turquoise night of those first
yellow stars, she shakes her hair.

She shakes her hair out in her singing
of cliffs and caves and waterfalls,
and tribes who left the lichened sandstone
carved in gods and animals.

This is her country: honeyeaters
cry out its Aboriginal name
where on her ridges still the spear
tall lilies burn in flame and flame.

I listen, and our legend says not
more than this dark singing tree,
although her golden flowering lover
lies slain beside the winter sea.

The Prisoners

After our labouring train had passed
through those red sandridges at last
and, straightening out, went racing for
dark mountains in the desert's floor,
I saw, in that red-purple land,
the bearded Italian prisoners stand
beside the line until our train
should pass to let them toil again.
Then, clinging to the rushing car,
I leaned out, shouting: *Come sta!*
And, from blurred faces by the track,
heard: *Bene! Bene!* shouted back.
I looked and saw them where they stood
against those ridges red as blood,
looked and saw them lessen and
be lost in spinifex and sand.
There, we were carried northward while
my vision stayed and shared exile
with those men whom, I believed,
the blood deep desert had received.

Northern Oriole

The tumult ends, the downpour stops.
On broad palm leaves the large warm drops
cling. That bird calls out again
as though his throat were filled with rain.
From tree to tree he glides among
the dripping leaves and makes his song.
Now from the poinciana's bough
sounds his echoing song, and now
deep within the banyan's shade,
that bell like, flute cool call is made.
High in the orange flowering gum
his voice is heard, but where I come
he makes no more that blended note
as though the rain had filled his throat.
Swooping, with folded wings he goes
over the far tree tops for those
mountains of the clouds and where
the storms let down their purple hair.

Deep Well

I am at Deep Well where the spirit trees
writhe in cool white limbs and budgerigar
green hair along the watercourse carved out
in deep red earth, a red dry course that goes
past the deep well, past the ruined stone
homestead where the wandering blacks make camp
(their campfire burning like a star at rest
among dark ruins of the fallen stone)
to find the spinifex and ochre red
sandhills of a land inhabited by those
tall dark tribesmen with long hair and voices
thin and far and, deepening, like a sea.
I am at Deep Well where the fettlers' car
travels towards the cool blue rising wave
that is the Ooraminna Range, and starts
those pure birds screaming from the scrub to swerve,
reveal their pristine blush in wings and breasts,
to scatter, settle and flower the desert-oak.
Here I have chosen to be a fettler, work
to lay the red-gum sleepers, line and spike

the rails with adze and hammer, shovel and bar,
to straighten up and find my mates, myself
lost in the spinifex flowing down in waves
to meet the shadow-sharpened range and know
myself grown lean and hard again with toil.
Here, in the valley camp where hills increase
in dark blue depths, the desert hakea stands
holding the restless finches and a single star.

Kimberley Drovers

I am drained out. All day I have driven
through a barbaric country of burning colour.
Fire-red mountains, fissured and caverned,
lilac-hazed ranges, red-purple ravines,
have reared round, receded and reappeared
all day through my vision. This is the region
of the baobab trees, of monstrous, obese
baobabs squatting in the chaos of sun-fired,
sun blackened boulders in the ranges' ravines.

I set down my swag. Against the sunset
an amber red dust cloud is rising. I rest
camped close to drovers settling their cattle
down for the night. Out of the haze comes
the muted, mingled moan of the mob.
I hear from behind me the sharp "Crack-crack"
sound of stockwhips. Stockmen come driving
their horses, donkeys, and mules with hobbles
and jangling horse-bells back from the bore.

It is after sunset. A star burns above
the bush fire haze from the bellowing beasts.
Whistles, shouts of stockmen unseen
ring out as they ride round the restless mob.
My campfire blazes among the baobabs.
A mopoke calls from the stars. Crickets sing;
clear on the night, an Aboriginal stockman
ceaselessly sings, as he rides round the mob,
his savage songs. And I cannot sleep.

I crouch by the glowing coals and the cattle
bellow, scream hoarsely. The horsemen shout,
whistle. The Aboriginal sings. Does the mob
feel a blind, brute impulse to break

back to the solitudes of sun-fired ranges,
plains and paper-bark shaded pools,
sensing the drovers send them to slaughter?
Out of the stars, the mist of the moonlight,
a savage song soothes the cattle to sleep.

The Fitzroy River Crossing

Camped above the Fitzroy River Crossing
under white limbed river-gums, I'm gathering
firewood this evening, walking through
graves and headstones lost in the dust and grass.
A red, protruding boulder is inscribed:
"James Lennon. Prospector. Died 14-9-08."
I stand there with the firewood under my arm
and a voice is speaking to me out of the dust:
"It was wild country when first I came here.
I searched for gold. The Aborigines were wild.
They circled my camp, dragging their spears,
gripped between their toes, through the grass.
A black woman was my mate. She eased loneliness
and terrors. You who see the sun and stars,
hear the crescendos of the cockatoos, you wonder
at this grave and at that grave. You search for poetry.
Most search for wealth or love or fame;
leave children behind them that they may live on.
You, who stand listening to the whispered speech
of the dead, your words may be remembered, or forgotten.
You'll neither know nor care, as I do not now
care if ever I found gold or love or fame."
It is a name, cut into a boulder. My campfire's
leaping and flowing on the wind. Summoned
out of the darkness, muscle rippling torsos fling
fork lightning limbs against the stars.
Turn in. Lie down. Those other sleepers will
not trouble you. Earth's deep blanket covers them
from the stars' cold blaze, the merciless suns.

The Cradle

A corrugated iron shack. One room.
Tree-posts its uprights, saplings, axe-
trimmed, its beams and rafters. It stands

fast, no matter how the huge hands
of mountain winds grasp it. Rain
is tumult, deafening peace on the roof.

Rain-forest rises behind it, a maze
of cicada-sound. Tonight you will hear
the creek like rain as, just on dark,
the cat-bird meows and yowls from the edge
of the jungle-forest. Your eyes will daze,
close in lamplight over your book.

The kettle sings on the "Waratah" stove.
Pots and pans gleam on their ledge
above. You will wish dawn not to come.
You will sleep, a child, as the hoarse wind
cradles you in the trees, as the arm
of the mountain holds the light of the farm.

Yoola and the Seven Sisters

related by Minyanderri

Yoola, always wanting women,
women run from him,
sees seven women, seven sisters,
and chases after them.

The seven sisters are frightened.
Whirring, they leave the ground.
They travel down the sky and at
a rock-hole come down.

From that place the seven women
look back and see that man
coming still, and to another
waterhole they run.

Yoola walks all round that place.
Steep cliffs rise
all round the sisters. The cliffs
echo their cries.

Through the only gap comes Yoola.
At him the sisters run.
Yoola, grasping at the sisters,
misses every one.

The sisters run into the desert.
Among waterless sands,
they make ritual with song and
dance and clapping hands.

Yoola, tired in the desert,
drags his spear along
behind him. Sandhills rise
at his ritual song.

Yoola camps. There, he stands
his spear upright.
In that place a sacred gum-tree
grows up in the night.

Yoola camps. He lays his spear
down on the ground.
In that place he leaves a
stone spear behind.

From waterhole to waterhole
the seven sisters run.
Yoola, carrying his spear,
thinks of them one by one.

The seven sisters are running
between two ranges' walls.
Yoola, on a rearing cliff,
sings his rituals.

The sisters rest beside a soak.
Yoola comes again.
The sisters scatter, come together
far out on the plain.

At Wankareenga waterhole
cliffs rise all about
the seven sisters. Yoola comes.
There is no way out.

"The waterhole," the sisters shriek.
They plunge, and swimming down,
with Yoola swimming after them,
one by one they drown.

The spirits of the sisters
went up into the sky.

And Yoola followed after
running hard close by.

The sisters are those seven stars
running away in fright.
Yoola is the big star close
beside them in the night.

Mapooram

related by Fred Biggs, Ngeamba Tribe

Go out and camp somewhere. You're lying down.
A wind comes, and you hear this "Mapooram".
"What's that?" you say. "Why, that's a 'Mapooram' "
You go and find that tree rubbing itself.
It makes all sorts of noises in the wind.
It might be like a sheep, or like a cat,
or like a baby crying, or someone calling,
a sort of whistling-calling when the wind
comes and swings and rubs two boughs like that.

A Wirreengun, a clever-feller, sings
that tree. He hums a song, a "Mapooram":
a song to close things up, or bring things out,
a song to bring a girl, a woman from that tree.
She's got long hair, it falls right down her back.
He's got her for himself. He'll keep her now.

One evening it was sort of rainy-dark.
They built a mia-mia, stripping bark.
You've been out in the bush sometime and seen
them old dry pines with loose bark coming off.
You get a lot of bark from them dry pines,
before they rot and go too far, you know.
That woman from the tree, she pulled that bark.
It tore off, up and up the tree. It pulled
her up into the tree, up, up into the sky.
Well, she was gone. That was the end of it.
No more that Wirreengun could call her back.

"Mapooram. Mapooram." "What's that?" you say.
Why, that's two tree boughs rubbing in the wind.

The Star-tribes

related by Fred Biggs, Ngeamba tribe

Look, among the boughs. Those stars are men.
There's Ngintu, with his dogs, who guards the skins
of Everlasting Water in the sky.
And there's the Crow-man, carrying on his back
the wounded Hawk-man. There's the Serpent, Thurroo,
glistening in the leaves. There's Kapeetah,
the Moon-man, sitting in his mia-mia.

And there's those Seven Sisters travelling
across the sky. They make the real cold frost.
You hear them when you're camped out on the plains.
They look down from the sky and see your fire
and, "Mai, mai, mai!" they sing out as they run
across the sky. And, when you wake, you find
your swag, the camp, the plains all white with frost.

The Bunyip

related by Percy Mumbulla, Wallaga Lake

Old Billy Poddam was a real bugeen, a clever
old-man. He used to have half-a-crown. He'd go
an' play cards, go through all his silver, an' then
he'd play his half-a-crown. He'd lose it, but
next day he'd have it back in his hand again.
No one could get that half-a-crown from him.

This old feller had a bunyip. It was his power,
his moodjingarl. This bunyip was high in front,
an' low at the back, like a hyena, like a lion.
It had a terrible big bull-head an' it was
milk-white. This bunyip could go down into the ground
an' take the old man with him. They could travel
under the ground. They could come out anywhere.
They could come out of that old tree over there.

Old Billy Poddam never did no harm to no one
all the time he was at Wallaga Lake.
He went out to Brungle, the home of his tribe,
an' did something wrong an' hurt his sister's feelings.
His sister caught him with the guneena stones.
She was as clever as he was. So, when he knew,

he caught his own sister with the guneena stones.
"Well," he said, "you'll die; I'll die too."

That bunyip, he went away back to the swamp. If he
was comin' out of the swamp you'd see the water
bubblin' an' boilin'. He'd make the water all milky.

My old dad was smokin' his pipe by the chimney.
Mum heard this bunyip comin', roarin'. The ground
started to shake. He was comin' closer. He came
out of the ground underneath the tank-stand, he went
over to the chimney an' started rubbin' himself
against it. He started to get savage. He started to roar.
Mum told Dad to go out an' talk to him in the language.

Dad went out an' spoke to him in the language.
He talked to him, "We are all right. No one
doing any harm. You can go away." Dad followed him
across the road, talkin' to him in the language.

That's when I saw the bunyip. I looked out through
the window. He was milk-white. He had terrible eyes,
an' they were glarin' an' rollin' about. Every time
Dad spoke to him he'd roar. My old man was talkin',
"Everything is all right. Don't get savage here."

The bunyip went down into the hill an' down into
the salt water. I've never seen that bunyip since.
It was the last people of the tribe who left him there.
He only shows himself to certain fellers.
You can hear him comin', pantin' "Hah-hah-hah."

He travels around, up an' down the coast
as far as Kempsey, lookin' for anyone who has
done anything wrong. When he bites you, you die. He's
even been seen in Victoria, at Lake Tyers Mission.

The Sermon of the Birds

related by Alec Vesper, Gullibul tribe

I was clearing thirty or forty acres once
out on the western range near Nightcap Mountain.
And as I was working I heard a gathering of crows
singing out in a jungle gully. Their clamorous cries
drawed the attention of all the other birds,
jackass and butcher bird, soldier bird, sparrow bird,

scrub robin, magpie, the black and the while cockatoo,
they all flew down to the crows in the jungle gully.

And I followed their clamour, and in the midst
of all the splendid excitement of all the birds,
I heard one fellow was singing above them all.
It was the lyrebird, the mimic of all the scrub.
And they held this beautiful sermon for half an hour.
The birds would stop and listen awhile, but still
that beautiful voice, the lyrebird, would keep on singing
and draw them and join them all to a chorus again.

As I stood there and listened, the Scriptures was
hitting me all the time. That sermon seemed
like the prophecy when Christ shall come and summon
the birds, the valleys and the hills, the mountains and ocean
to sing in praise of the grace and the reckoning day,
and the beauty of the earth in the splendour that He created.
And I went back and told my people of what I had seen,
of the sermon of praise I heard on the mountain range.

JOHN BLIGHT 1913–1995

John Blight spent almost all his life in Queensland. His father was the steward of the property of Sir Harry Chauvel (of Light Horse fame) in southern Queensland and the young Blight was able to read widely in the extensive Chauvel library. In the 1930s during the Great Depression he tramped the coastline of his home state looking for work. In 1939 he took up an accountant's job in Bundaberg. For a while during World War II he was a prices inspector for the Commonwealth Government, and later became part-owner of a timber mill at Maryborough. He married and had two daughters. In 1968 he went to live in Brisbane, working as a purchasing officer for the public hospital system, and in 1973 became a full-time writer.

Blight was widely appreciated when he began to publish his remarkable and profound "sea sonnets", which were collected in two volumes, his third and fourth books, *A Beachcomber's Diary* (1963) and *My Beachcombing Days* (1968). The sonnet, inventively manhandled, was the ideal form to concentrate Blight's sinewy, untidy, flashing and wry meditations on life, and these poems were organised further by their concentration on a single (but multifaceted) subject: the sea. His sonnets, as they strain to break out of their framework, are about the mind being as rich and strange as the ocean. Some of these sonnets exist at the edge of language, for example "Voices of the Sea". We have chosen the original untidy version of this poem, not the tidied-up one in the 1992 *Selected Poems*.

After his move to Brisbane in 1968, Blight wrote prolifically, mainly on urban subjects. Martin Duwell commented that "retirement in the mid-1970s produced a freedom to write and a freedom to satisfy the desire to look at the public world" and that "the output of poems in this period is enormous", with the works published in his four volumes during this phase being only a sample of what he was writing then. These unpublished poems are held in the Fryer Library at the University of Queensland. Apart from a few sonnets, which he continued to produce, he rejected fixed form. His intention is often obscure. The lines of these later poems routinely end on a preposition or an article – a device used so reiteratively it loses any expressive function. Disgust about urban humanity, anger at old age, and lust are recurring themes. Never complacent, Blight became more uncomfortable over time. In general this late flowering, although voluminous, is not rewarding. Much of the individuality of Blight's best poems comes from his eking an awkward meaning out of the parsimonious and obdurate sonnet form. He seems to have needed this tension.

Blight corresponded with Judith Wright, as they shared a passionate environmentalism and a concern about urbanisation, but he was less sophisticated than Wright at a personal level, and his attempt to reinvent his style, unlike his near contemporary, David Campbell, was not successful.

Noddies

Sad to remember such obsolete gadgets
as pulley-wires flying their monies and dockets
in small wooden buckets to cashiers in heaven
– or, so my eyes said, when I was eleven;
loving the big store, where mother went shopping.
But all of that childhood's long since gone hopping.
Yet noddies at sunset, to the island homing,
have reminded me life doubles back in the gloaming.
For me, then, the noddies are money and dockets
seeking that haven of small wooden buckets;
on wires, for a surety, so safe and securely
each homes to the island. Oh, surely! oh, surely,
each sea bird's known shopping, as did those small buckets
from far-off departments, white breasted with dockets.

Seaweed

There is the brown dress, tattered, in shreds,
from the ocean's mermaid-flats; from paddocks under
that vast drifting heaven of water, wave-flash and thunder.
In pockets, still, a red string of berries bleeds,
and little trinkets of fish unnaturally silver.
Kick at that sodden mass, and turn it over,
just like a drowned dress, ruined stook of clover,
or some shabbiness brought here by death: this elver-
refuge from the angry sea! Do not doubt me;
it is death's own gown, thrown down by storm

and anticlimax, the ugly revolt of the sea.
Thrust in a foot and feel it yet body-warm.
It is not long torn asunder; search it with care:
you may kick it some day to find a body there.

Nor'-easter

The straw broom of the nor'-east sweeps the beach.
Yellow, raking straws of sand, stinging, cleansing, scratch
my raw legs; but no woman can I see,
my head hung low, while she is ranting at me.
Not my day; not a day for dogs, or gulls,
or canvas flapping. Cleaning the beach, squalls
threatening, cumulus cumbersome in the hills
of the sea-littoral; this wind kills
all joy of the beach, is a steamroller wife
of a man by the sea. All my life
I have been sullenly subdued when she blows.
Only some little good in all her bluster shows:
she cleans the beach, sweeps, beats the sand.
For the white strand of her morning, I once took her hand.

Death of a Whale

When the mouse died, there was a sort of pity:
the tiny, delicate creature made for grief.
Yesterday, instead, the dead whale on the reef
drew an excited multitude to the jetty.
How must a whale die to wring a tear?
Lugubrious death of a whale: the big
feast for the gulls and sharks; the tug
of the tide simulating life still there,
until the air, polluted, swings this way
like a door ajar from a slaughterhouse.
Pooh! pooh! spare us, give us the death of a mouse
by its tiny hole; not this in our lovely bay.
– Sorry we are, too, when a child dies;
but at the immolation of a race who cries?

Crab

Shellfish and octopus, and all the insane
thinking of the undersea, to us is lost;
at most is food, in our higher plane.

But, what of this submarine ghost-
life, without its meddling monkey? Can
the crab regenerate into prototype merman?
Sea, of nightmare pressure and mask-
green faces in the gloom – what is your task
in creation; or is it over? Has space
such aquariums of planets trapped? Was
Eden thus? Oh, pressures which the lace-
sponge of the brain survives. What has
the life of the sea of my ignorance,
but such creatures; much of this wild-shaped chance?

Ghost Crabs

(For Miss Lenore Smith)

Ghost crabs, their fleetness, have made me
desperate to delineate the norm
of the effacing creatures. I must
describe nothing less ephemeral than dust;
and you who read must barely hope to see
a creature, an image, but a mere scrabble of form.
It is on these sticks of letters, like the legs
of ghost crabs scurrying across a page
– rustling vellum sounds, on a dry beach –
that your eyes must follow and teach
themselves the trick of seeing the cage
of limbs, the bedouin band which drags
behind horses of sand the eyes on a pole:
the only Christian sign betraying a soul.

Fisherman and Jetty

Old jetty, wade with me out into the sea
and there let us watch ship and shag pass;
knee-deep I, thigh-deep you. We
with our reasons to be there: standing in the glass
sea, rod in hand, crane on deck;
each under scrutiny, looking a wreck,
yet part of the scene which people on shore
come here, long hours, to gaze at …
"Will he catch a fish?" "The jetty is more
like Japanese torii with that
missing wood decking." They're speaking of us.

If we were on land, they'd never discuss
two such old derelicts. So – the sea honours all,
the quick and the dead, that age in its thrall.

Voices of the Sea

Voices of the sea – of its infinite forest voice,
soft interminable hush of calm. Choice
of no birdsong, but a seabird's cry
– scream or screech we may call it. Try
to define it. Try, try, and the
very endeavour stultifies. Not sob, not sigh,
not wail, not growl, not howl … not this,
nor any sound performed with our epiglottis,
our voicebox. Noisy, alien sea,
peopled by wraiths that cannot speak to us;
only its crushing voice, or silence: mus-
ic of a ship's bell (little enough sweet-
ness); unintelligible gurglings; offbeat
slough, slur; Echo unwilling to repeat.

Plankton

I have watched plankton over reefs float by
in rivers wide as seas that strained belief;
but, most, the shapes so intimate that I
could think that children drew them. Sheaf on sheaf
of comic drawings, unspoiled primitives
that couldn't live, yet represented lives
so simply limned; and, yet, seen here alive
too difficult to understand, so make-believe
and yet alive. Have you seen plankton float,
barely an outline round transparent space?
It can here represent whatever crayons trace
extravagantly wild. No nature note
has chronicled such shapes. Only a child's quick mind
has realised this life so naively designed.

Sea-Level

Over this flat-pan sea, this mud haven,
this shelf of the sea-floor, sea birds paddle
and the red mud raddles the sea.
You are on creation's level. Proven

your lowly origin, where, in one puddle,
sea-snails and your toes agree –
the same spasms and rhythms. Stub
on a rock, or a sharp stab of a beak:
they draw in. Pain is the one language
spoken to them. You, in the sky, snub
your feet. Impediments! But can you take
your brain's cloud and drift, disengage
those "body's worms"? Try: disconnect
the thought from their feeling, and soon the soul is wrecked.

The Shark

There, in the first breaker, was the shark's shape
trailing the pilchards black in their escape;
so tightly packed, they blacked out the sea
just as a storm cloud does the blue sky.
But, ignorantly, the immigrant waded right in.

"Get out! Get out, you fool!" some bawled above the din
and train-noise of the rolling surf.

Unheard of, in Poland, any danger from a wolf
in the water. Why were they crying, trying to divert
the surfer from his pleasure? In a sea-girt
country he was living now. No warring Prussia,
no fear, ancient fear, of old steam-roller Russia.

In a sea-girt country he was living without fear,
and now they must tell him death loiters near.

The Coral Reef

In the baroque style of coral, India,
Java, your conglomerate gods assemble.
Having just walked the reef at low water,
I have a fear of their numbers, a psychic tremble,
a mental numbness at my failure to describe
their Nirvana, their inscrutable jungle of peace
– a peace that is death in stone. As though a rib
were stolen from every mortal, each piece
cemented in place a monument to mankind – a reef?

I walked it – walked on the faces of its gods,
on their many visages ... on my own belief,
I fear, exhausted my many moods,

my paucity of words – a failure at expression
by this mass of death; unable to follow its vast progression.

Shells and Skulls

Death leaves them strewn on the shore, embedded in rocks
which were once mud of the seafloor.
Yet women and children gather shells. It never shocks
them to pick up shells. Skulls? Say no more.
Shells and skulls do not look alike
except that both are white. On a background of black
shells look like gems, while skulls, bones, strike
terror in our hearts – insignia for no Union Jack,
but the Jolly Roger, pirates' flags! Why that
distinction of grace which death strangely saves
to bestow upon shells? Shells are the outlines of life,
its final shape; bones, like a hateful knife,
hide in its innards, sheathed in dissembling fat.
Shells tell us of life's pride – skulls, frightfully, of its graves.

Stingray Bay

I live at a place where the seasons change each day,
where the tide comes in, goes out, in Stingray Bay:
where there's sunshine, rain-shower, storm, and calm;
green mangrove, pine-tree, she-oak, coconut palm.
There's mud crab, sand crab, shark, and crocodile;
and mudflat, sandbank. A reef runs out a mile
to sea in Stingray Bay. On any old day here,
the sandflies will prove even giants fear;
and, if you choose to wade in Stingray Bay,
there's poisonous stonefish, cone-shells, so they say.
And yet it is a place where children play
and swim and paddle, much to the dismay
of the occasional tourist who comes here, astray,
misguided by the map to Stingray Bay.

In the Wake of the Ship

The sailors passed and the ocean vanished,
the fair blue day of the sea became
a vibration of atoms. Banished
were all thoughts of mermaids and sirens. Some
fish and lowly life of plankton remained,

but such life did not intelligently
register the fair blue day of the sea.
As a matter of fact, if it rained
and thundered, if the hurricane blew,
there might be a little loss, but such life
seemed to burgeon from the elemental strife,
the vibration of atoms. Nothing knew
it was a fair blue day at sea. It was
all lost in the wake of the ship, because …

And About Phosphorescence

The round tank of the ocean reaches far
as the eye can see, and contains every star
and the image of the moon. They are
constantly filling it with light. Swirl an oar
and their phosphorus glows. Step ashore
and slap the wet sand, and, once more,
a repetition of stars. They have been filling the ocean
with light all their light-years. A potion
of time and starshine the sea is. The notion
of night at sea as dismally black is a joke.
Not since Phosphorus, the morning star, first woke
has there been any cessation of light
pouring into the ocean. It is just as bright
in its fastest deeps, where the fish seem alight.

DOUGLAS STEWART 1913–1985

Douglas Stewart was born in Eltham, New Zealand, the son of a lawyer who had emigrated from Melbourne. Stewart, one of Australia's most nationalistic poets, first came to this country in 1933, for a short stay, and then returned in 1938. He felt that his Australian father made him a native of his adopted country. He became editor of the *Bulletin*'s literary section, "the Red Page", in 1940, a position he held for over 20 years. Under Stewart's editorship, the Red Page regained its position as the central forum for Australian literature, particularly poetry, but this could not save the rest of the magazine from dwindling in relevance. He joined Angus & Robertson, the largest, most established Australian publisher, as editor of the prestigious poetry list, and remained there until 1971.

Stewart was married to Margaret Coen, the watercolourist, who had modelled for Norman Lindsay when she was young. He was the closest disciple of Lindsay, and the artist responded to the younger poet with equal enthusiasm. Stewart sympathised with Lindsay's anti-modernism, but not his Dionysian streak.

As an editor and publisher, Stewart championed the young Francis Webb, and regularly published Judith Wright, R. D. FitzGerald, Rosemary Dobson, John Blight, David Campbell, Roland Robinson, William Hart-Smith and many others. He encouraged Australian poets to write accessibly, without obscure experiment or academicism, particularly about the country's landscape. He preferred poems in fixed form, but was less dogmatic about this than Hope and McAuley. He and the communist poet John Manifold independently helped revive interest in the bush ballads. He also contributed to a fashion for the poem-as-sequence, celebrating the early maritime and outback explorers, which Slessor had begun with "Five Visions of Captain Cook". One of his own contributions to this genre is "Terra Australis", in which the Spanish explorer Ferdinand De Quiros, who led an expedition eastward looking for Terra Australis in 1605–06, is imagined as meeting in the mid-Pacific William Lane, a pioneer of the Australian labour movement, who in 1893 sailed westward with a group of idealists in the *Royal Tar* to found the colony of New Australia in Paraguay. The tone of the poem reflects Stewart's religious and political scepticism.

His poetry written in New Zealand looked towards the current 1930s English style. Many of these early poems use a language which is notably vigorous and contemporary, compared with the language of his later Australian work. "Mending the Bridge" shows a willingness to embrace modernity that he later eschewed.

In Australia his style grew closer to the English Georgian poets of earlier in the century. He directed his energies to creating a larger market for his own poetry and poetry generally – possibly hoping for a revival of the wide audience that Australian poetry had in the 1890s and early 1900s. Reflecting the attempts of Eliot, Auden and Fry to revive the verse drama, he wrote six verse plays. One play for radio, *The Fire on the Snow*, celebrating Scott's tragic Antarctic expedition, was frequently performed and prescribed as a school text. Stewart's verse stage play *Ned Kelly* (1940), about the famous bushranger, achieved acclaim, with Leo McKern (later of "Rumpole" fame) taking the role of Kelly in a production in the late 1950s. Stewart led the way in mythologising Kelly. Sidney Nolan's Kelly paintings soon followed, and Kelly has since become a preoccupation of Australian novelists and film makers.

In his non-dramatic poetry, Stewart tried to revive the popular ballad. James McAuley (*A Map of Australian Verse*, 1975) disliked the "whimsy and pseudo-popular idiom" of these balladic poems. However McAuley saw Stewart's narrative sequence *Glencoe* (1947) as a turning point, and felt that the next volume *Sun Orchids* (1952) displayed a "mastery of the things he does best: the short, often lyrical nature poems, and now and then a longer poem in which an aspect of the human condition is caught and examined ... In some poems the metaphysical is present simply in a special sense of being, a sheer awareness of a thing's act of existence: it is this that ... comes ... in the concentrated vision of 'Sun Orchids' ... the image of the flower is exact, precise, yet in the last lines subtly transfigured."

The freezing of Stewart's tastes in a Georgian style of poetry and his lack of sympathy for the Vietnam War generation (unlike his friend David Campbell) possibly contributed to the decline in his poetic output in the last decade and a half of his life. This is not to undervalue the high quality of his poetry written in the middle period identified by McAuley.

Mending the Bridge

Burnished with copper light, burnished,
The men are brutal: their bodies jut out square
Massive as rock in the lanterns' stormy glare
Against the devastation of the dark.
Now passionate, as if to gouge the stark
Quarry of baleful light still deeper there
With slow gigantic chopping rhythm they hack,
Beat back and crumple up and spurn the black
Live night, the marsh-black sludgy air.

And clamour the colour of copper light
Swings from their hammering, and speeds, and breaks
Darkness to clots and spattering light, and flakes
Oily, like dazzling snow and storms of oil.
The night that never sleeps, quickens. The soil,
The stones and the grass are alive. The thrush awakes,
Huddles, and finds the leaves gone hard and cool.
The cows in the fields are awake, restless; the bull
Restless. The dogs. A young horse snorts and shakes.

Beneath the square of glaring light
The river still is muttering of flood,
The dark day when thick with ugly mud,
Swirling with logs and swollen beasts (and some
Still alive, drowning) it had come
Snarling, a foul beast chewing living cud,
And grappled with the bridge and tried to rend it,
So now these stronger brutes must sweat to mend it
Labouring in light like orange blood.

Men labour in the city so,
With naked fore-arms singed with copper light
And strangeness on them as with stone they fight,
Each meet for fear, and even the curt drill
Mysterious as trees and a dark hill.
But these are stronger, these oppose their might
To storm and flood and all the land's black power.
Burnished with sweat and lanterns now they tower
Monstrous against the marshes of the night.

Terra Australis

I

Captain Quiros and Mr William Lane,
Sailing some highway shunned by trading traffic
Where in the world's skull like a moonlit brain
Flashing and crinkling rolls the vast Pacific,

Approached each other zigzag, in confusion.
Lane from the west, the Spaniard from the east,
Their flickering canvas breaking the horizon
That shuts the dead off in a wall of mist.

"Three hundred years since I set out from Lima
And off Espiritu Santo lay down and wept
Because no faith in men, no truth in islands
And still unfound the shining continent slept;

"And swore upon the Cross to come again
Though fever, thirst and mutiny stalked the seas
And poison spiders spun their webs in Spain,
And did return, and sailed three centuries,

"Staring to see the golden headlands wade
And saw no sun, no land, but this wide circle
Where moonlight clots the waves with coils of weed
And hangs like silver moss on sail and tackle,

"Until I thought to trudge till time was done
With all except my purpose run to waste;
And now upon this ocean of the moon,
A shape, a shade, a ship, and from the west!"

II

"What ship?" "The *Royal Tar*!" "And whither bent?"
"I seek the new Australia." "I, too, stranger;
Terra Australis, the great continent
That I have sought three centuries and longer;

"And westward still it lies, God knows how far,
Like a great golden cloud, unknown, untouched,
Where men shall walk at last like spirits of fire
No more by oppression chained, by sin besmirched."

"Westward there lies a desert where the crow
Feeds upon poor men's hearts and picks their eyes;
Eastward we flee from all that wrath and woe
And Paraguay shall yet be Paradise."

"Eastward," said Quiros, as *San Pedro* rolled,
High-pooped and round in the belly like a barrel,
"Men tear each other's entrails out for gold;
And even here I find that men will quarrel."

"If you are Captain Quiros you are dead."
"The report has reached me; so is William Lane."
The dark ships rocked together in the weed
And Quiros stroked the beard upon his chin:

"We two have run this ocean through a sieve
And though our death is scarce to be believed
Seagulls and flying-fish were all it gave
And it may be we both have been deceived."

III

"Alas, alas, I do remember now;
In Paradise I built a house of mud
And there were fools who could not milk a cow
And idle men who would not though they could.

"There were two hundred brothers sailed this ocean
To build a New Australia in the east
And trifles of money caused the first commotion
And one small cask of liquor caused the last.

"Some had strange insects bite them, some had lust,
For wifeless men will turn to native women,
Yet who could think a world would fall in dust
And old age dream of smoke and blood and cannon

"Because three men got drunk?" "With Indian blood
And Spanish hate that jungle reeked to Heaven;
And yet I too came once, or thought I did,
To Terra Australis, my dear western haven,

"And broke my gallows up in scorn of violence,
Gave land and honours, each man had his wish,
Flew saints upon the rigging, played the clarions:
Yet many there were poisoned by a fish

"And more by doubt; and so deserted Torres
And sailed, my seamen's prisoner, back to Spain."
There was a certain likeness in the stories
And Captain Quiros stared at William Lane.

IV

Then "Hoist the mainsail!" both the voyagers cried,
Recoiling each from each as from the devil;
"How do we know that we are truly dead
Or that the tales we tell may not be fable,

"Surely I only dreamed that one small bottle
Could blow up New Australia like a bomb,
A mutinous pilot I forbore to throttle
From Terra Australis send me demented home?

"The devil throws me up this Captain Quiros,
This William Lane, a phantom not yet born,
This Captain Quiros dead three hundred years,
To tempt me to disaster for his scorn –

"As if a blast of bony breath could wither
The trees and fountains shining in my mind.
Some traveller's tale, puffed out in moonlit weather,
Divert me from the land that I must find!

"Somewhere on earth that land of love and faith
In Labour's hands – the Virgin's – must exist,
And cannot lie behind, for there is death,
So where but in the west – but in the east?"

At that the sea of light began to dance
And plunged in sparkling brine each giddy brain;
The wind from Heaven blew both ways at once
And west went Captain Quiros, east went Lane.

Sun Orchids

Again next spring when the heath blows white and pink
And ants come out of their holes and run on the rock
Those clear blue flowers will stand on the blue sky's brink
And close in rain and open in sun and look
Except for the cup at the centre, some flecks like sand,
More like a distillation of sapphire air
Than anything out of the earth; and when they stand,
So clear, so candid, somebody else can peer
As I once did in that deep silky cup
Whose seed of light would drown in a drop of rain,
For there's no orchid of gully or mountain top
But holds some secret knowledge best left alone;

And small as it was, blue on that sandstone spur,
Once was enough: it held the sun in there.

The Sunflowers

"Bring me a long sharp knife for we are in danger;
I see a tall man standing in the foggy corn
And his high, shadowy companions." – "But that is no stranger,
That is your company of sunflowers; and at night they turn
Their dark heads crowned with gold to the earth and the dew
So that indeed at daybreak, shrouded and silent,
Filled with a quietness such as we never knew,
They look like invaders down from another planet.
And now at the touch of light from the sun they love" –
"Give me the knife. They move."

Mahony's Mountain

If there's a fox, he said, I'll whistle the beggar;
And shrill the counterfeit cry of the rabbit's pain
Rang out in the misty clearing; so soon to be lost
In the stony spurs and candlebarks darker and huger
Where Mahony's mountain towers in drifts of rain.
No sharp wild face out of burrow or hollow stump,
No rustle shaking the raindrops from rushes or flowers
– Greenhood and bulbine lily lighting the swamp –
Nothing but bush and silence; so on and up
Tramping through moss where so many violets cluster
You cannot help but crush them; and still more steep
The sheep-track winds through the dripping leaves and the rocks,
And still no fox, no bandicoot's tiny fluster,
No flurry of green rosellas flashing past,
Nothing but the huge grey silence, the trees and – look;
There where the mountain breaks on its granite peak,
The doubletail orchid, O like some fairy tale fox,
Whistled from earth by a wilder call than ours,
Pricks up its yellow ears and stares through the mist.

The Last of Snow

It is the last of the snow
Under a bush on the heath
Like a little white calf forgotten
While sunlight bares its teeth;

And still where Bullock's Head Creek
Spills down to the Eucumbene
And the granite highlands sprawl
Without one shoot of green,

That broken briar, that heath
Flattened and crushed and tramped
Show as if in vast shadows
The place where the cattle camped,

Drowsing all winter through
In a dream with their mild eyes full
Of blizzard and flying starlight,
The cow lying down by the bull.

And they pressed their mighty forms
On the rough green rug below,
And they swayed their horns of ice:
The wild white cattle of snow.

Little white calf, stand up
And follow the wild mob
Far over Bullock's Head Creek,
Over Kiandra's top.

Spider-gums

Where winter's snow and crashing rains
Have forced the snow-gums to their knees,
High in the sky on Kelly's Plains
These frail and delicate spider-trees:

As though some pigtailed fossicker here
Now bleached as quartz on Dead Man Range
Had drawn a Chinese sketch on air
To speak for him when all should change;

Or high from where the Murrumbidgee's
Tussocky rapids flash and race
A flying swarm of water-midges
Hangs in a mist of light and lace.

As though through summer's huge hot noon
Lost drifts of winter linger still
And twenty flakes of snow are blown
All dark against the granite hill;

Or light winds silvery with frost
Have breathed upon the sky's blue glass
To make a tree that seems half ghost
And melts into the russet grass.

As though in earth's deep dream of stone
Some leafy thought was taking form
And fled before the dream was done,
Half-finished out to sun and storm;

Or some tall tree not there at all
Has flecked the sunlight with its shadow
And shadows' shadows glide and fall
Dark green upon air's crystal hollow;

As though, as though – but now I see
The white clouds covering the blue,
A chill breeze beating on the tree
That hardly shakes as it goes through,

And know how earth took deepest thought
In this cold kingdom of the winter
To make some shape of grace to float
On high while snow-gums crack and splinter,

And made this phantom tree at last,
A thing more air than leaf or bough,
That slips clean through the killing blast
And dances clear from all the snow.

The Silkworms

All their lives in a box! What generations,
What centuries of masters, not meaning to be cruel
But needing their labour, taught these creatures such patience
That now though sunlight strikes on the eye's dark jewel
Or moonlight breathes on the wing they do not stir
But like the ghosts of moths crouch silent there.

Look it's a child's toy! There is no lid even,
They can climb, they can fly, and the whole world's their tree;
But hush, they say in themselves, we are in prison.
There is no word to tell them that they are free,
And they are not; ancestral voices bind them
In dream too deep for wind or word to find them.

Even in the young, each like a little dragon
Ramping and green upon his mulberry leaf,

So full of life, it seems the voice has spoken:
They hide where there is food, where they are safe,
And the voice whispers, "Spin the cocoon,
Sleep, sleep, you shall be wrapped in me soon."

Now is their hour, when they wake from that long swoon;
Their pale curved wings are marked in a pattern of leaves,
Shadowy for trees, white for the dance of the moon;
And when on summer nights the buddleia gives
Its nectar like lilac wine for insects mating
They drink its fragrance and shiver, impatient with waiting,

They stir, they think they will go. Then they remember
It was forbidden, forbidden, ever to go out;
The Hands are on guard outside like claps of thunder,
The ancestral voice says Don't, and they do not.
Still the night calls them to unimaginable bliss
But there is terror around them, the vast, the abyss,

And here is the tribe that they know, in their known place,
They are gentle and kind together, they are safe for ever,
And all shall be answered at last when they embrace.
White moth moves closer to moth, lover to lover.
There is that pang of joy on the edge of dying –
Their soft wings whirr, they dream that they are flying.

B Flat

Sing softly, Muse, the Reverend Henry White
Who floats through time as lightly as a feather
Yet left one solitary gleam of light
Because he was the Selborne naturalist's brother

And told him once how on warm summer eves
When moonlight filled all Fyfield to the brim
And yearning owls were hooting to their loves
On church and barn and oak-tree's leafy limb

He took a common half-a-crown pitch-pipe
Such as the masters used for harpsichords
And through the village trod with silent step
Measuring the notes of those melodious birds

And found that each one sang, or rather hooted,
Precisely in the measure of B flat.
And that is all that history has noted;
We know no more of Henry White than that.

So, softly, Muse, in harmony and conformity
Pipe up for him and all such gentle souls
Thus in the world's enormousness, enormity,
So interested in music and in owls;

For though we cannot claim his crumb of knowledge
Was worth much more than virtually nil
Nor hail him for vast enterprise or courage,
Yet in my mind I see him walking still

With eager ear beneath his clerical hat
Through Fyfield village sleeping dark and blind,
Oh surely as he piped his soft B flat
The most harmless, the most innocent of mankind.

Two Englishmen

Far, far from home they rode on their excursions
And looked with much amusement and compassion
On Indians and Africans and Persians,
People indeed of any foreign nation
Who milled in mobs completely uninhibited
In the peculiar lands that they inhabited.

But in their own small island crowded thickly,
Each with his pride of self and race and caste,
They could not help but be a little prickly
And in their wisdom they evolved at last
This simple code to save them from destruction –
One did not speak without an introduction.

So naturally when Kinglake on his camel,
Mounted aloft to see the world or take it,
Saw faint against the sky's hard blue enamel
A solar topee, then a shooting jacket,
Then all too clear an Englishman appearing
He found the prospect anything but cheering.

Merely because the distances were wider
One could not speak with every Dick or Harry,
For all he knew some absolute outsider,
Who trotted up upon his dromedary,
And yet he felt, alone and unprotected
On these bare sands some talk might be expected.

Of course, he thought, with spirits briefly lightened,
Though ten to one he did not know the fellow

He might be quite all right; but then he mightn't;
And on he came by sandy hill and hollow –
It was a bit too thick thus to arrive at
The desert's core and then not find it private.

For if for one's own reasons one had ridden
By camel through the empty wastes to Cairo
From Gaza in the distance back there hidden
One did not do the thing to play the hero
Or have some chap come dropping from the sky
To ask what one was doing there, and why.

The sweat lay on his camel dank and soapy
And Kinglake too broke out in perspiration
For close and closer in his solar topee
The stranger came with steady undulation;
One could not hide, for shelter there was none,
Nor yet, however tempting, cut and run.

No, if they met, as meet it seemed they must,
Though heartily he wished him at the devil,
Kinglake decided, halting in the dust,
That if the fellow spoke he must be civil;
But then observed, in ultimate dismay,
He could not think of anything to say.

But he, as it fell out, need not have worried.
It was an English military man
Long years in Burma boiled, in India curried,
Who riding home on some deep private plan
Now sat his camel equally embarrassed
To find himself thus hunted out and harassed;

And while their Arab servants rushed together
With leaps and yells to suit the glad occasion
Each Englishman gazed coolly at the other
And briefly touched his hat in salutation
And so passed by, erect, superb, absurd,
Across the desert sands without a word.

But when they'd passed, one gesture yet endures;
Each turned and waved his hand as if to say,
"Well, help yourself to Egypt" – "India's yours,"
And so continued grandly on his way;
And as they went, one feels that, truth to tell,
They understood each other pretty well.

DAVID CAMPBELL 1915–1979

Born at Ellerslie, the family sheep station in the rolling Monaro country beyond Canberra, the son of a doctor, David Campbell was educated at The King's School, in Sydney, and at Cambridge University. He was an outstanding sportsman: at King's, captain of the rugby and rowing teams; at Cambridge, winner of a rugby blue against Oxford in 1936, and of two international caps for England in 1937. The poet, John Manifold, who was at Cambridge with him, remembered Campbell striding late into an examination room, then clasping his head theatrically as he read the paper. With every eye upon him, he drew from his pocket a bottle of whisky, which he drank straight off, before proceeding to work, the room left floundering in his wake. Manifold later learned that the bottle had contained cold tea.

At Cambridge, he read widely, including most importantly, the poetry of W. B. Yeats. From boyhood, Campbell knew the works of Banjo Paterson and other bush balladists; at Cambridge he discovered the Elizabethan lyricists, and saw a way of creating something of his own in combining these two styles. He wrote his first poems at university, and was surprised at the praise his efforts received, having seen himself until then as "a pretty dumb footballer".

Campbell graduated on the outbreak of war, returned to Australia to join the Royal Australian Air Force, and married. He was to have two sons and a daughter. He flew in New Guinea against the Japanese, becoming a Squadron Leader, and later Wing Commander. In 1942, while on reconnaissance over Rabaul, he and his co-pilot and gunner were attacked, in a twin-engined Hudson, by two Japanese fighters. Despite receiving more than 250 bullet holes in his plane, having his crew badly wounded, and being shot through the left hand and wrist himself, Campbell eluded the attackers, and flew back 500 miles through bad weather, "the instrument panel falling apart", to land in Port Moresby on one engine and with one tyre shot away. He was awarded the DFC. Later he received the decoration a second time, after bombing raids and supply drops he made in Timor.

Following the war, Campbell took up sheep farming near Canberra, and wrote poetry in whatever time he could find from "hard work and harsh seasons". In 1973 he divorced, and in 1974 remarried. On another, smaller "run", he began to write in free verse, while still producing characteristically brief and short-lined poems. His ideal was always that poetry should have the clarity and economy of a theorem. He suggested that his change in style, and in subject, as he now ranged beyond pastoral and love poems into politics, fantasy, classical myth and family history, had much to do with the disruptive effects on him of the Vietnam War, to which he was actively opposed.

Campbell's poetry has a recurring theme: his feeling that the robust appearance of things, which he enjoys so much, is really an illusion. He responds to this intuition positively. Ideas about the cosmos being ultimately only a dance of energy preoccupied him, particularly in his later work. "What's matter but a hardening of the light?" he wrote, and concluded that "Matter is thought" – although in what sense this totalising conception is to be understood is not defined. His poem "The End of Exploring" is one of his most successful "philosophical" lyrics. But what is profound about Campbell's work is his appetite for life. His poetry has great warmth and openness to experience. It was this openness that allowed him to move so successfully from being the most typical member of Douglas Stewart's group of *Bulletin* poets (even more typical than Stewart himself whose way of life was urban) into a more contemporary idiom.

Campbell maintained as the motto of his work Rilke's words (which echo Nietzsche): "I praise". With his friend Douglas Stewart he consciously makes a second generation of the Vitalist school. Campbell's flamboyance, broken-nosed good looks, enjoyment of drink, and of the company of women and artists, made him an attractive figure. He was devastated towards the end of his life by the death of his daughter, electrocuted by a washing machine. He died at what seemed the surprisingly early age for him of 64, from lung cancer.

Men in Green

There were fifteen men in green,
Each with a tommy-gun,
Who leapt into my plane at dawn;
We rose to meet the sun.

Our course lay to the east. We climbed
Into the break of day
Until the jungle far beneath
Like a giant fossil lay.

We climbed towards the distant range,
Where two white paws of cloud
Clutched at the shoulders of the pass.
The green men laughed aloud.

They did not fear the ape-like cloud
That climbed the mountain crest
And rode the currents of the air
And hid the pass in mist.

They did not fear the summer's sun
In whose hot centre lie
A hundred hissing cannon shells
For the unwatchful eye.

And when at Dobadura we
Set down, each turned to raise
His thumb towards the open sky
In mockery and praise.

But fifteen men in jungle green
Rose from the kunai grass
To come aboard and my green men
In silence watched them pass:

It seemed they looked upon themselves
In a prophetic glass.

There were some leaned on a stick
And some on stretchers lay,
But few walked on their own two feet
In the early green of day.

They had not feared the ape-like cloud
That climbed the mountain crest;
They had not feared the summer's sun
With bullets for their breast.

Their eyes were bright, their looks were dull;
Their skin had turned to clay.
Nature had met them in the night
And stalked them in the day.

And I think still of men in green
On the Soputa track,
With fifteen spitting tommy-guns
To keep a jungle back.

Spring Hares

There is a stranger on the stock route.
See his red beard and eyes of flame!
The sky's his swag; the magpies shout
Across the continent his name:
It is the sun! It is the dawn!–
Bless the day that I was born.

There are two boxers through the gum-trees;
Their shadows spar on the far hill,
Counter and close. What giants are these?
Surprised, a pair of hares stand still.
It's a fine thing at your front gate
To see such angry lovers mate.

Bill is out on the red stallion;
His piebald mob crops blades of fire.
Trees burn, leaves melt; in conflagration
The big buck hare has his desire
Where the red ridge meets the spring sky,
Locked in the sun's irradiant eye.

The End of Exploring

See! down the red road by the brown tree
The gate leans wide like morning. Here's winter's green;
Here are summer's bleached affairs; and here between
Rain work and wind work, the road winds free.

The shed is slabbed with shimmer. Fence-posts go
Hill-high for shadows. Ben's on his bright chain:
And it's the dog's limit, the green cock's strain;
And the road lies hard and open towards the snow.

But why go? The time waits deep for summer
With the grain, for the ringed shade and sheep
Cropping the silence while the swagmen sleep,
Though on the height the ice-etched symbols glimmer.

And the road? Go then; and smothered in the snow,
Or on the violet ridge where the ice-trees burn,
Trust to your lucky heart you may return
With love to dog-bark, gate, and sweet cock-crow.

Hogan's Daughter

Clancy saddles his narrow mare
For frosts have come before the rain,
And he's away with Conroy's sheep
To drove them on the western plain.

He whistles an old dog to the lead,
A roan kelpie to crowd the rear;
And whistles a song to suit himself
As rose-hips dance on the winter brier.

And they string along a drover's mile
And dust is ringing from the shale
When lightning skins the bony ridge
And green as opal falls the hail.

And they string along a drover's mile
When granite heights stand up on air;
The lightning lights on Hogan's pub
And a long girl knitting behind the bar.

"O what is the web you weave, girl?
What is the net you knit so thin
That blows with the lamp and your yellow hair?"
"It's a web to catch a drover in.

"The winds are loose in the mountain sky
And tear the fleece from the fleeing storm;
Tether your mare or ride on by,
Here's a fire to wrap your spirit warm."

His mare is hitched to the veranda rail;
In long green paddocks stray the sheep,
The dogs are barking in the hall –
And he has kissed her underlip.

"Is it mirage-water brims your eye
Or a spring where a man may drink his fill?"
The lightning clove the cliffs of sky;
He stood alone upon the hill.

Then good-bye to his dark lank wife
And his shack and his shears and his family;
And drought or the devil take Conroy's sheep
And the hips that dance on the brier-tree.

For he rolled a swag of his saddle-cloth
And called his kelpie dogs to heel,
Fixed his eye on the glinting storm;
And he has gone across the hill.

Pallid Cuckoo

Alone the pallid cuckoo now
Fills his clear bottles in the dew:
Four five six seven – climb with him!
And eight brings morning to the brim.

Then from green hills in single file
My ewes and lambs come down the scale:
Four three two one – the matrons pass
And fill their bellies up with grass.

But in the evening light the lambs
Forget their hillward-munching dams;
To cuckoo pipes their dances start
And fill and overflow the heart

On Frosty Days

On frosty days, when I was young,
I rode out early with the men
And mustered cattle till their long

Blue shadows covered half the plain;

And when we turned our horses round,
Only the homestead's point of light,
Men's voices, and the bridles' sound,
Were left in the enormous night.

And now again the sun has set
All yellow and a greening sky
Sucks up the colour from the wheat –
And here's my horse, my dog and I.

Mothers and Daughters

The cruel girls we loved
Are over forty,
Their subtle daughters
Have stolen their beauty;

And with a blue stare
Of cool surprise,
They mock their anxious mothers
With their mothers' eyes.

The Australian Dream

The doorbell buzzed. It was past three o'clock.
The steeple-of-Saint-Andrew's weathercock
Cried silently to darkness, and my head
Was bronze with claret as I rolled from bed
To ricochet from furniture. Light! Light
Blinded the stairs, the hatstand sprang upright,
I fumbled with the lock, and on the porch
Stood the Royal Family with a wavering torch.

"We hope," the Queen said, "we do not intrude.
The pubs were full, most of our subjects rude.
We came before our time. It seems the Queen's
Command brings only, 'Tell the dead marines!'
We've come to you." I must admit I'd half
Expected just this visit. With a laugh
That put them at their ease, I bowed my head.
"Your Majesty is most welcome here," I said.
"My home is yours. There is a little bed
Downstairs, a boiler-room, might suit the Duke."
He thanked me gravely for it and he took

Himself off with a wave. “Then the Queen Mother?
She’d best bed down with you. There is no other
But my wide bed. I’ll curl up in a chair.”
The Queen looked thoughtful. She brushed out her hair
And folded up *The Garter* on a pouf.
“Distress was the first commoner, and as proof
That queens bow to the times,” she said, “we three
Shall share the double bed. Please follow me.”

I waited for the ladies to undress –
A sense of fitness, even in distress,
Is always with me. They had tucked away
Their state robes in the lowboy; gold crowns lay
Upon the bedside tables; ropes of pearls
Lassoed the plastic lampshade; their soft curls
Were spread out on the pillows and they smiled.
“Hop in,” said the Queen Mother. In I piled
Between them to lie like a stick of wood.
I couldn’t find a thing to say. My blood
Beat, but like rollers at the ebb of tide.
“I hope your Majesties sleep well,” I lied.
A hand touched mine and the Queen said, “I am
Most grateful to you, Jock. Please call me Ma’am.”

Le Wombat

Voyage de Découvertes Aux Terres Australes
(Atlas par MM. Lesueur et Petit)

Le wombat inhabits the Ile King
Of Terre Napoléon
En Nouvelle Hollande.

L’ile de l’artiste M. Lesueur
Is a scrubby cloud where
Le wombat bleu watches
La femelle rousse watching
While four enfants wombats terribles
Climb out of her pouch. Voilà!

Les wombats mère et père
Have the innocence of a magician
Producing un lapin blanc
From le chapeau noir.

If le père wombat bleu
Were to burrow in the shallow cloud
They would tumble tout de suite
Into le Golfe Joséphine. Les pauvres!

At l'ouverture du Golfe Joséphine
Is un pied-à-terre circumnavigated
By la corvette le *Géographe* in 1803,
Le capitaine, M. Baudin.

Ah l'Ile Decrés! where le casoar
Displayed his petites jambes bleues
And fine blue mutton-chops
Before his harlequin poulets. Hélas!
The dwarf emus of Kangaroo Island
Are only to be found today
Dans l'oeuvre de l'artiste M. Lesueur.

And la ville de Sydney
En Nouvelle Galles du Sud
With her moulins et boulangeries,
Her magasin de liqueurs fortes et de salaisons,
Mr Palmer's Wooloomooloo habitation,
Mr Campbell's débarcadère,
And the black Première Potence en Activité
Dans le Village de Brick-field,
The natives blowing coals
Among the stacked up merchandise
By the Route de Parramatta?

Lunching above cloud
Above the murmur of the turning city
And the geographical outlines of
La ville de Sydney 1802 preserved
Dans l'atlas de l'artiste M. Lesueur,
We are moved by the innocence of the penal colony
As by le wombat français de l'Ile King
And les travaux executés dans le Golfe Bonaparte
A bord de la corvette le *Géographe*.
"Au fond de l'Inconnu pour trouver du *nouveau!*"

Head of the River

Four of us in the river: Mal,
My youngest son, fourteen,

And the French girl, as good as naked,
Who chickened us in;

And me, of course, game to the last,
Sea-lion among green weed
Bubbling a call of lust.
She and Mal swarm off.

All afternoon the eights and fours
Stroked the long river
Like coloured dragonflies; and younger
Than youth, I tumbled for her:

For the woman of Lawes. Her ancestors
Brewed beer in Flanders and
Drank wine in Paris. She was cool and curved
As Chateau Yquem. Faint bubbles rose.

"Your Strine wine does not give!"
Mal's smile was slow as summer. "I rowed once;
And then I saw the morning." Eights
Walked on the water and were gone.

They've stacked the shells in tiers
For another year. White counterpanes
Cover the beds of the Mens' ward
Where I ferment with fever, chill as wine.

The Little Grebe

When moved in age to share a varied life
With his unworldly son
My father backed a horse between the shafts
Of an old gig – "Whoa back!" – and off we spun.

He reined beside the rushes of a dam
But his eyes travelled on
Beyond the misted city to the range.
Late snow lay on Franklin.

And while he yarned, I watched the little grebe
Appear and disappear.
The dam filled up with clouds, and when the bird
Bobbed there again, the sky and dam were clear.

So I half-listened to my father's life,
Considering the grebe
And how it fed its feathers to its young

On rafts amongst the reeds.

Those floating incubators hatched the eggs.
Father, I did not know
Your shapely tales would wake in me in age
And fill my mind with distances and sorrow.

Duchesses

A mob of dressing-tables is grazing
The pile of the plain
Under paper blue mountains.

Now and then one will pause
And raise its mirror
Reflecting the white sunlight.

Little cupboards
Hop in and out of the drawers
And suck at the crockery knobs.

The only sounds are the snip, snip,
Of grazing furniture
And the rattle of wooden droppings.

A truck is hurrying over the plain.
The mob raises its mirrors,
Little cupboards hop back in the drawers.

The dressing-tables head for the paper hills,
But the truck is upon them.
Pom pom! Corks fly from swivel guns.

Pomeranians snap
At the heels of wheeling dressing-tables.
They snarl in mirrors, savaging the doilies.

The furniture is surrounded.
Men rope the younger pieces
And load them squealing onto the truck.

Now solitary in bedrooms
Dressing-tables look back at women
Who question them with rouge lips.

Sometimes through windows
They glimpse the paper blue mountains,
And the tears of the women fall on the doilies.

The Secret Life of a Leader

I was born in a wire house
They wrapped me in the wind's blanket
My mother's breasts were cans

On my birthday they gave me a rifle
My first love was a dead man's thought
Colours drained to black and white

My first duty was to my parents
They were shuffled away
For my second lesson
I shot a close friend and the music master
They looked younger in death

My third task was at peak hour
Percussion
Hammered the subway
The gutters
Ran with a red ketchup

They said I was ready
My vision spread like a virus
A crippled man blessed me

The city was gay with white flags
Skeletons
Cheered from the sidewalks
A schoolgirl presented a sheaf
Of spring flowers and fainted

When they unveiled the statue
I lost all movement in my right side
At my guarded chateau
Resting
the trees kept rustling
They lopped the branches

I fished in a red river
And caught a beer can
At a farmhouse I rested

The farmer's wife curtsied
It was my mother
I picked up a hen egg
It blew my hand off
In the yellow nursery

I said I'd begin again

Mother tucked me in
And blew out the candle
Shh! she said
What dreams you have!

JOHN MANIFOLD 1915–1985

John Manifold was born to a wealthy pastoralist family from the Western District of Victoria. He was educated at Geelong Grammar and then at Jesus College, Cambridge, where he joined the Communist party. In a preface to Manifold's *On My Selection* (1983), A. D. Hope wrote that Manifold's career at Jesus College combined "rowing and fencing and poetry with equal distinction ... to cap it all, he played the trombone!" In 1939 Manifold enlisted in the British army and served in Europe and West Africa in intelligence. A *Selected Verse* was published in New York (1946) and London (1948). He was the first Australian poet of his generation to gain an international reputation. When he returned to Australia in 1949 with his English wife Katharine, family disapproval of his politics caused him to settle in Queensland, and for many years he lived in the outer Brisbane suburb of Wynnum in a spacious old weatherboard house on stilts, where he held weekly music nights. He was active in collecting and recording bush songs and ballads, and edited books about Australian folk songs, as well as writing two scholarly works on Elizabethan music.

Manifold was an impressive and handsome man, who spoke with an upper-class English accent, his conversation interspersed with words like "dinkum" (his ultimate cachet of approval). He travelled widely in communist countries during the heyday of the Soviet Union and was a faithful Stalinist to the end of his life. He visited Hungary in 1956 a few weeks after a large Soviet force invaded Budapest and forcibly reimposed communist rule. His conclusion was there had been no spontaneous popular uprising. More than a decade later his comment was: "I can tell you they were counter-revolutionaries."

His dogmatic political views are echoed in his poetry by his simple and somewhat heavy verse form and rhymes. But his work is always good-humoured and civilised. He remained the gentleman scholar, his writing shapely and never careless, and having pungency and panache. The poet that he most resembled in poetic style was Roy Campbell, who fought on the side of Franco in the Spanish Civil War. Manifold wrote to A. D. Hope: "I met Roy Campbell too. In spite of his being on the wrong side of the political fence, he was a good bloke."

One of the mysteries about Manifold is why, after a promising international debut, he chose to live in obscurity on the outskirts of Brisbane, then one of Australia's more provincial state capitals (although a circle of younger admirers, including Rodney Hall, David Malouf and Judith Rodriguez and folk musicians was to gather about him). Jamie Grant, writing in *The Oxford Companion to Twentieth Century Literature*, relates that Manifold, at the age of eighteen, was told by his father that he would not inherit the family property, and it would be bequeathed to his younger brothers, as they were not as gifted intellectually and less assured of earning a living.

Manifold wrote the following note for "Makhno's Philosophers": "The *tachanka*, a light, four-wheeled cart mounting a machine-gun, was a characteristic weapon of the Russian Civil War ... In the Ukraine the straightforward warfare between Red and White armies was complicated by the existence of 'Green' bands who fought and plundered with some lack of discrimination. Makhno's Greens professed to be Anarchists, having learned the word, no doubt, from the academics whom they did in fact capture and cart around with them. See Sholokhov's *Don* trilogy."

Fencing School

White to the neck he glides and plunges
But black above, no human foe
Pity for whom could rob my lunges
Of their direction. Faceless, so,

He is no fellow but a show
Of motion purposed to withstand
The blade that sets my nerves aglow
And sings exultant in the hand.

Thus each withdrawn and wide alert,
Focussed on self from hilt to heel,
Nothing breaks in to controvert

The single aim. I only feel
The sinews of my wrist assert
The tremor of engaging steel.

Fife Tune

For Sixth Platoon, 308th I.T.C.

One morning in spring
We marched from Devizes
All shapes and all sizes
Like beads on a string,
But yet with a swing
We trod the bluemetal
And full of high fettle
We started to sing.

She ran down the stair
A twelve-year-old darling
And laughing and calling
She tossed her bright hair;
Then silent to stare
At the men flowing past her –

There were all she could master
Adoring her there.

It's seldom I'll see
A sweeter or prettier;
I doubt we'll forget her
In two years or three,
And lucky he'll be
She takes for a lover
While we are far over
The treacherous sea,

The Tomb of Lt. John Learmonth, A.I.F.

"At the end on Crete he took to the hills, and said he'd fight it out with only a revolver. He was a great soldier."

– One of his men in a letter.

This is not sorrow, this is work: I build
A cairn of words over a silent man,
My friend John Learmonth whom the Germans killed.

There was no word of hero in his plan;
Verse should have been his love and peace his trade,
But history turned him to a partisan.

Far from the battle as his bones are laid
Crete will remember him. Remember well,
Mountains of Crete, the Second Field Brigade!

Say Crete, and there is little more to tell
Of muddle tall as treachery, despair
And black defeat resounding like a bell;

But bring the magnifying focus near
And in contempt of muddle and defeat
The old heroic virtues still appear.

Australian blood where hot and icy meet
(James Hogg and Lermontov were of his kin)
Lie still and fertilise the fields of Crete.

* * *

Schoolboy, I watched his ballading begin:
Billy and bullocky and billabong,
Our properties of childhood, all were in.

I heard the air though not the undersong,
The fierceness and resolve; but all the same
They're the tradition, and tradition's strong.

Swagman and bush ranger die hard, die game,
Die fighting, like that wild colonial boy –
Jack Dowling, says the ballad, was his name.

He also spun his pistol like a toy,
Turned to the hills like wolf or kangaroo,
And faced destruction with a bitter joy.

His freedom gave him nothing else to do
But set his back against his family tree
And fight the better for the fact he knew

He was as good as dead. Because the sea
Was closed and the air dark and the land lost,
"They'll never capture me alive," said he.

* * *

That's courage chemically pure, uncrossed
With sacrifice or duty or career,
Which counts and pays in ready coin the cost

Of holding course. Armies are not its sphere
Where all's contrived to achieve its counterfeit;
It swears with discipline, it's volunteer.

I could as hardly make a moral fit
Around it as around a lightning flash.
There is no moral, that's the point of it,

No moral. But I'm glad of this panache
That sparkles, as from flint, from us and steel,
True to no crown nor presidential sash

Nor flag nor fame. Let others mourn and feel
He died for nothing: nothings have their place.
While thus the kind and civilised conceal

This spring of unsuspected inward grace
And look on death as equals, I am filled
With queer affection for the human race.

For Comrade Katharine

I

That moment on my mind
Etched you, with one arm raised
Tautening the breasts I praised,
Dark on the street-lit blind;

Moment and pose combined
Luxuriously appraised
Revealed to me amazed
Love's rare and perfect kind;

Not just the ornament
Of leisure and content
But sinewy and keen

To walk in the cold and share
The tang as if marine
Of hatred in the air.

II

Give me what of death you hold
In your loins and lips and hands;
Act and word are contraband
At a frontier so controlled.

So in earth and darkness rolled
Sleeps the harvest of wild lands
And again in summer stands
Vigorously manifold.

Hands from writing, lips from speech
Turn to festival with yours,
Mingle, play, and sleep, and then

Like the sailor to the beach
Fresh with our united force
Rally to our task again.

Chillianwallah Station

When his hopes of a colonelcy faded away
He retired to the colonies, still on half-pay,
Preferring to Cheltenham a Gulf-country run
And a heat of a hundred-and-ten in the sun.

His cook was a Cantonese – Asian at least! –
Who thought enough curry as good as a feast;
And his ex-soldier-servant, from Antrim, named Barney,
Used to rowse the black stockmen in bad Hindustani.

He kept the fair flag of the Empire afloat
By wearing a tunic done up to the throat;
And the style of his most conversational speeches
Had its thumbs well in line with the seam of its breeches.

He played a straight bat, and a good hand at solo,
He would ride forty miles for a chukker of polo,
So the district forgave him his finical pride
Which demurred for so long at selecting a bride.

Then the seasons got worse, and the banks took a hand,
They called in the mortgage they held on his land;
And the Major was found in the harness-room, shot
Thro' the head with his old-fashioned Webley-&-Scott.

The jury said: "Accident; no one's to blame;"
And the Major was buried, leaving only the name
"Chillianwallah" in letters some eight inches high
On the gate at the stock-route to remember him by.

Except that old Barney's the grandfather now
Of a quarter-caste family, no one knows how,
Who have never been coached since the Major passed on,
But who ride like the Ashtons and bat like the Don.

The Map

Devil take our city-minded, imitative gran'dads who
Saddled us with Warwick, Ipswich, Bloomsbury (near Yalbaroo),
Surbiton on Belyando – names like these will never do!

Mount Mistake, The Risk, The Blunder, Wilson's Downfall make a change,
But the names I like are those that show a sense of somewhere strange –
One Tree Hill and Wild Horse Mountain, Razorback and Nightcap Range –

And at sundown, when the hills are monstrous and the bunyip stirs,
I am pretty sure the native names are what the land prefers:
Murderer's Flat was our invention, but Eurunderee was hers.

Jundah, Thunda, Nocatunga, Thargomindah, Gunnewin,
Tarrewinnabar, Canungra, Tabragalba, Coolwinpin,
Ulandilla by the Maranoa where the songs begin,

Binna Burra, Bindebango, Mullumbimby – these belong! –
Bunya, Quinalow, Nanango, Tallebudgera, Durong,
Xylophones among the timber,
            Bellbirds in the border mountains,
                        Wallangarra, Woodenbong.

Elegy I

I wonder did my darling's mother mind
When I undressed her daughter from behind?
I leaning back, she forward, in the chair,
I made acquaintance with her underwear,
Detaching first her jersey, then her chaste
Blouse, from the girdle round her trousered waist,
And with Mosaic exultation felt
The silken singlet loosen from the belt.
Then, while her bent-back wrist protested, mine
Mapped the declivities of charming spine,
Shoulders and nape – reconnaissance of ground
To take and hold when zero-hour comes round.
I laid the flat of one exploring hand
On that contested still but promised land;
And so we sat till on the verge of cramp
With innocent face forward to the lamp.
Then father ceased to read, I to explore;
I tucked her shirt into her belt once more,
And mother sat with unsuspecting smile
(Or *was* it unsuspecting?) all the while.

Elegy II

Why should I hate or envy him who taught
You how to use your body as you ought?
It's long since over. Since he went away
You've never even written. All you say
Is truth itself. Yet on you, as you stand,
I trace the brushwork of another's hand;
I see how this and that and t'other whim
With which you pleasure me derive from him;
And, even naked, many a subtle sign,
Device or gesture marks you his, not mine.
First love may prosper greatly, I discover,
Or tenth, but not a woman's second lover.

Makhno's Philosophers

Back in *tachanka* days, when Red and Green
Pursued in turn each other and the White,
Out on the steppe, I'm told, there could be seen
A novel sight.

Professors of philosophy, whom war
From some provincial faculty dismissed
To seek new pasture on the Black Sea shore,
Fell in with Makhno – anarchist,

Terrorist, bandit, call him what you will –
Who spared their lives and, either for a laugh
Or from some vague respect for mental skill,
Attached them to his staff.

Their duties were not hard. For months or years,
Lacking a porch in which to hold debate,
These peripatetics, ringed by Cossack spears,
Had leisure to discuss The State.

With flashing pince-nez, while the sabres flashed,
They sat berugged in carts and deep dispute,
Or in some plundered village hashed and thrashed
The nature of The Absolute.

Bergsonians quite enjoyed it: from the first
They'd known Duration to depend on Space.
But Nietzscheans found their values arsy-versed
By Supermen of unfamiliar race.

And, whereas Platonists got mulligrubs,
Cynics were cheerful – though I'll not deny
They grumbled when obliged to share their tubs
With hogs from Epicurus' sty.

On quiet nights, bandits would form a ring
And listen with amazed guffaws
As syllogisms flew, and pillaging
Was reconciled with Universal Laws.

Symposia were held, whereat the host
(Taught by Hegelians of the Left)
In stolen vodka would propose a toast
To Proudhon's dictum: Property is Theft!

How did this idyll end? There's some confusion.

Makhno, I fear, was caught –
Perhaps he let his native resolution
Get sicklied o'er with other people's thought.

But what of his philosophers? I feel
Certain they reached an Academe at last
Where each in his own manner might conceal
His briefly bandit past.

To fool the OGPU or the C.I.A.
Would not be hard for any skilled expounder
Of Substance and Illusion, growing grey
But ever metaphysically sounder.

Yet each might feel at times old memories stir,
And know himself, as ever, set apart:
Once, among bandits, a philosopher;
Now, among academics, Green at heart.

In fact – I've wondered – take Professor X –
Mightn't his arid manner be a blind?
Are those lack-lustre eyes, behind those specs,
Truly the mirror of his mind?

Or is the real man, far away
From Kantian imperatives, once more
Roaming the steppe, not as a waif and stray
But waging revolutionary war?

Although his tongue belabours
The stony boundaries of a bloodless creed,
His soul is back again among the sabres
Yelling, "The Deed! The Deed!"

DAVID MARTIN (Lajos or Ludwig Detsinyi)
1915–1997

David Martin was born into a Jewish family in Hungary. He was educated in Berlin where he became a Communist at the age of seventeen. After experiencing the first years of Nazi rule, he worked in the Netherlands, then emigrated to Palestine, and later took part in the Spanish Civil War as a volunteer first-aid man in the International Brigade. From 1938 he worked in London for the BBC. In 1947 he went to India and finally settled in Australia in 1949. He wrote novels, short stories and plays as well as poetry. While he wrote some ostentatiously "Aussie" poems in fixed form, influenced perhaps by John Manifold and the social realist school, most of his poetry has a middle-European sensibility, playing with paradox and parables. He has a careful, mannered style that can sometimes be laboured.

"Dreams in German" is Martin's masterpiece. For a reader with a smattering of German it is a heart-stopping piece. Martin explains many of the German terms in the poem itself. However "Grunewald" means "Greenwood", a forested park in Berlin; "Weissensee" means "White Lake", a district of Berlin; "Die Schlüssel sind verloren" means "the keys are lost"; "Rosenrot" means "Rose Red"; "Deutscher Wald" means "German forest"; "Schneeweisschen" means "little Snow White"; "Schlagetot" means "Strike Dead"; "Tief aus dem Walde" means "from deep in the woods"; "Schlug alle tot" means "struck them all dead"; and "Du liebes Land" means "you dear (or beloved) land". "Buchenwald", literally "beech forest", was one of the main Nazi death camps.

Dreams in German

Undated dreams: the sea of Heringsdorf,
The Brocken behind Schierke and the snow
That falls like sugar on the Christmas trees
They're selling in the square. It's hard to know
This land in English. What is Grunewald,
And what is Weissensee and what the name
I seek for her who lies there? All my keys
Are lost. Die Schlüssel sind verloren. Do I still,
As I return to Brandenburg at night,
Declare my landmarks in the tongue I knew,
Say Deutscher Wald when I'm with Rosenrot
Deep in the forest? No, for life went ill
With all my fairies, and in nightmares only
I call by name the giant Schlagetot
Who killed my people and stays close to me
Wherever I may sleep. Yes, not until
He dies shall I go home to childhood. Say it now:
Say Rosenrot, Schneeweisschen, how they came
Tief aus dem Walde, and how Schlagetot
Schlug alle tot and took my book away …
Snow White and Rose Red, they are not the same.
Stretch out your hand and gather what is left:
The frieze upon the nursery wall, a light
Kept covered on the landing, or the face
Of Lotte in Charlottenburg that day;
But in translation, like a gazetteer.
Du liebes Land! To call my country dear
Still burns the mouth. But Buchenwald flows right
From German lips into my English ear.

JUDITH WRIGHT 1915–2000

Judith Wright came from a prominent pastoralist family which was granted land in the 1820s. She was born at Thalgarrah Station near Armidale, New South Wales, and grew up on the family property, "Wallamumbi". Her mother died when she was ten. Her father, the person in her family to whom she was closest, helped found the University of New England. He had had an Aboriginal nurse and Wright learned Aboriginal stories from him, absorbing a sympathy for Aboriginal culture. She was educated at first by correspondence and then at New England Girls' School and between 1934 and 1936 at the University of Sydney, where she studied philosophy under John Anderson. Sydney University was surrounded by what were slum suburbs at that time, and the Great Depression was under way. She witnessed poverty in the streets, which was "something new to me … poverty could actually be smelt, as a kind of dark-grey sourness … it was not possible not to wonder what had gone wrong."

On graduating from university, Wright travelled in 1937 through central Europe, when it was succumbing to totalitarianism, and the likelihood of war was obvious. After working as a stenographer in Sydney, she returned home at the outbreak of World War II, at her father's request, to help run the property. At this time she began writing her first mature poems. She wrote in the foreword of her *Collected Poems 1942–1985* with particular reference to her earlier poems: "The poems have been written out of the events, the thinking and feeling, the whole emotional climate and my own involvements of that time … Today's shifts in critical practice have begun to tear texts from their contexts. Indeed, the need to know something of the context, historical or personal, of poems has almost disappeared from critical practice. So a reader of a poem like 'The Company of Lovers' may know little of the great displacements of people during World War II, their snatching into armies and other defence forces, the desperation of lovers faced with the prospect of a separation which might last forever, and the urgency of need which drove the young into each others' arms."

From 1944 to 1948 Wright worked at the University of Queensland and at this time met J.P. (Jack) McKinney, marrying him in 1960. He was twenty-four years her senior, a farmer, drover, shearer, writer and self-taught, serious philosopher, whose neo-Kantian *The Structure of Modern Thought* appeared posthumously in 1971. McKinney's philosophy, which espoused archetypal principles, significantly influenced Wright's work. Their marriage was close, but caused Wright to be rejected by her family for a long period. She and McKinney had a daughter. Wright's concern about nuclear weapons was so great that she decided not to have more children. She and McKinney lived at Mt Tambourine, out of Brisbane, on a small property that, with its hens and vegetables, was largely self-sufficient. There was a rainforest nearby, through which she would take visitors on walks, enthusiastically identifying the different species of trees. After her husband's death in 1966, she felt an increasing sense of despair over public events in Australia and the world. She moved to a property near Braidwood outside Canberra, and made it a wildlife sanctuary, where she lived alone for much of the time, hampered by her long-term deafness.

Wright was a pioneering and militant conservationist, and was active in founding the Wildlife Preservation Society of Queensland, and became its president. She was one of the most persistent white voices supporting the Aboriginal campaign for land rights. Her wish to be engaged in public issues would have been one of the things that drew her in her later years to "Nugget" Coombs, the former Reserve Bank Governor who was heavily involved in policy decisions for Aboriginals in the 1970s. In her personal style she was forthright and direct; also modest and abstemious. In about 1970, staying for a few days in Sydney at the Rushcutter's Bay flat of a friend, she invited a group of younger people to dinner. As she served reheated meat pies to the assembled guests, she announced with aplomb, "Well, I think it's the company that counts, not the food."

Judith Wright is an iconic figure in Australian poetry, who has captured the imagination of generations of Australian readers. Her early poems have a freshness and depth, a sense of mystery, informed by her enthusiasms for psychoanalytic theory – Jung in particular – mythology and primitive cultures. Fiona Capp (*My Blood's Country* at p.37) relates a telling incident from Wright's childhood, as the older bossy sister: "Her brother, Peter Wright, later recalled that during these games on Council Rock [given that name by the children after Rudyard Kipling's *The Jungle Book*] Judith would strike the granite with a piece of iron and raise sparks, claiming she had magical powers. It is a glimpse of the very young Judith in the process of discovering the extraordinary power of language and her ability to wield it: a moment ... during which she felt that anything was possible."

These "magical powers" are strongly present in Wright's first two books of poetry and fade in her later work. Wright asks in a late poem, "At Cedar Creek": "How shall I remember the formula for poetry?" and then mocks her earlier enthusiasms for myths and the unconscious, and for "language clotted with ancient metaphor". The magic and freshness of her early poems were replaced by a toughness of thought and despair at the modern world. While lacking the transformative power she once had, these later poems speak with a strong personal voice. Donald Davie, the English poet and critic, concluded that she was among the best contemporary poets in the language.

The Company of Lovers

We meet and part now over all the world.
We, the lost company,
take hands together in the night, forget
the night in our brief happiness, silently.
We who sought many things, throw all away
for this one thing, one only,
remembering that in the narrow grave
we shall be lonely.

Death marshals up his armies round us now.
Their footsteps crowd too near.
Lock your warm hand above the chilling heart
and for a time I live without my fear.
Grope in the night to find me and embrace,
for the dark preludes of the drums begin,

and round us, round the company of lovers,
Death draws his cordons in.

South of My Days

South of my days' circle, part of my blood's country,
rises that tableland, high delicate outline
of bony slopes wincing under the winter,
low trees blue-leaved and olive, outcropping granite –
clean, lean, hungry country. The creek's leaf-silenced,
willow-choked, the slope a tangle of medlar and crabapple
branching over and under, blotched with a green lichen;
and the old cottage lurches in for shelter.

O cold the black-frost night. The walls draw in to the warmth
and the old roof cracks its joints; the slung kettle
hisses a leak on the fire. Hardly to be believed that summer
will turn up again some day in a wave of rambler roses,
thrust its hot face in here to tell another yarn –
a story old Dan can spin into a blanket against the winter.
Seventy years of stories he clutches round his bones.
Seventy summers are hived in him like old honey.

Droving that year, Charleville to the Hunter,
nineteen-one it was, and the drought beginning;
sixty head left at the McIntyre, the mud round them
hardened like iron; and the yellow boy died
in the sulky ahead with the gear, but the horse went on,
stopped at the Sandy Camp and waited in the evening.
It was the flies we seen first, swarming like bees.
Came to the Hunter, three hundred head of a thousand –
cruel to keep them alive – and the river was dust.

Or mustering up in the Bogongs in the autumn
when the blizzards came early. Brought them down; we brought them
down, what aren't there yet. Or driving for Cobb's on the run
up from Tamworth – Thunderbolt at the top of Hungry Hill,
and I give him a wink. I wouldn't wait long, Fred,
not if I was you; the troopers are just behind,
coming for that job at the Hillgrove. He went like a luny,
him on his big black horse.
                                        Oh, they slide and they vanish
as he shuffles the years like a pack of conjuror's cards.
True or not, it's all the same; and the frost on the roof

cracks like a whip, and the back-log breaks into ash.
Wake, old man. This is winter, and the yarns are over.
No one is listening.
South of my days' circle
I know it dark against the stars, the high lean country
full of old stories that still go walking in my sleep.

Woman to Man

The eyeless labourer in the night,
the selfless, shapeless seed I hold,
builds for its resurrection day –
silent and swift and deep from sight
foresees the unimagined light.

This is no child with a child's face;
this has no name to name it by:
yet you and I have known it well.
This is our hunter and our chase,
the third who lay in our embrace.

This is the strength that your arm knows,
the arc of flesh that is my breast,
the precise crystals of our eyes.
This is the blood's wild tree that grows
the intricate and folded rose.

This is the maker and the made;
this is the question and reply;
the blind head butting at the dark,
the blaze of light along the blade.
Oh hold me, for I am afraid.

The Unborn

I

I know no sleep you do not stand beside.
You footless darkness following where I go,
you lipless drinker at my drowsy breast –
yet whom I must deny I have denied.
The unpossessing is the unpossessed.

Slight is the foothold from the well of night,
the stair is broken and the keys are lost,
and you whom I have wrecked are wrecked indeed;
and yet you stand upon the edge of sight,

and I have known no path you have not crossed.

The shadow wakeful on my sleeping arm
stares from the hidden depths far under birth.
How like a diamond looks the far-off day,
that crystal that reflects your darkened dream,
that bubble of sunlight broken and blown away.
O gift ungiven. O uncreated earth.

II

Not even tears were mine,
not even death;
not even the dazzling pain
of one first breath.

I never knew the sleep
of the warm womb.
The end of my beginning
was dumb; was dumb.

Only the foot of the stair
I felt, being blind.
Then came the touch of fear
time now can never mend.

My name was a dark sound
that made no word.
Terror alone spoke it
and nothing heard.

Neither awake nor asleep
on the rack of dark I lie,
hearing my own not-voice.
"What was I? I? I?"

The Old Prison

The rows of cells are unroofed,
a flute for the wind's mouth,
who comes with a breath of ice
from the blue caves of the south.

O dark and fierce day:
the wind like an angry bee
hunts for the black honey
in the pits of the hollow sea.

Waves of shadow wash
the empty shell bone-bare,
and like a bone it sings
a bitter song of air.

Who built and laboured here?
The wind and the sea say
– Their cold nest is broken
and they are blown away.

They did not breed nor love.
Each in his cell alone
cried as the wind now cries
through this flute of stone.

Flame-tree in a Quarry

From the broken bone of the hill
stripped and left for dead,
like a wrecked skull,
leaps out this bush of blood.

Out of the torn earth's mouth
comes the old cry of praise.
Still is the song made flesh
though the singer dies –

flesh of the world's delight,
voice of the world's desire,
I drink you with my sight
and I am filled with fire.

Out of the very wound
springs up this scarlet breath –
this fountain of hot joy,
this living ghost of death.

Country Dance (*from* The Blind Man)

The dance in the township hall is nearly over.
Hours ago the stiff-handed wood-cheeked women
got up from the benches round the walls
and took home their aching eyes and weary children.
Mrs McLarty with twenty cows to milk
before dawn, went with the music stinging
like sixty wasps under her best dress.
Eva Callaghan whose boy died in the army

sat under the streamers like a house to let
and went alone, a black pot brimming with tears.
"Once my body was a white cedar, my breasts the buds on the quince-tree,
that now are fallen and grey like logs on a cleared hill.
Then why is my blood not quiet? what is the good
of the whips of music stinging along my blood?"

The dance in the township hall is nearly over.
Outside in the yard the fire like a great red city
eats back into the log, its noisy flames fallen.
Jimmy Dunn has forgotten his camp in the hills
and sleeps like a heap of rags beside a bottle.
The young boys sit and stare at the heart of the city
thinking of the neon lights and the girls at the corners
with lips like coals and thighs as silver as florins.
Jock Hamilton thinks of the bally cow gone sick
and the cockatoos in the corn and the corn ready to pick
and the wires in the thirty-acre broken.
Oh, what rats nibble at the cords of our nerves?
When will the wires break, the ploughed paddocks lie open,
the bow of the fiddle saw through the breast-bone,
the dream be done, and we waken?

Streamers and boughs are falling, the dance grows faster.
Only the lovers and the young are dancing
now at the end of a dance, in a trance or singing.
Say the lovers locked together and crowned with coloured paper,
"The bit of black glass I picked up out of the campfire
is the light the moon puts on your hair."
"The green pool I swam in under the willows
is the drowning depth, the summer night of your eyes."
"You are the death I move to." "O burning weapon,
you are the pain I long for."

Stars, leaves and streamers fall in the dark dust
and the blind man lies alone in his sphere of night.

Oh, I,
red centre of a dark and burning sky,
fit my words to music, my crippled words to music,
and sing to the fire with the voice of the fire.
Go sleep with your grief, go sleep with your desire,
go deep into the core of night and silence.
But I hold all of it, your hate and sorrow,
your passion and your fear; I am the breath

that holds you from your death.
I am the voice of music and the ended dance.

Train Journey

Glassed with cold sleep and dazzled by the moon,
out of the confused hammering dark of the train
I looked and saw under the moon's cold sheet
your delicate dry breasts, country that built my heart;

and the small trees on their uncoloured slope
like poetry moved, articulate and sharp
and purposeful under the great dry flight of air,
under the crosswise currents of wind and star.

Clench down your strength, box-tree and ironbark.
Break with your violent root the virgin rock.
Draw from the flying dark its breath of dew
till the unliving come to life in you.

Be over the blind rock a skin of sense,
under the barren height a slender dance ...

I woke and saw the dark small trees that burn
suddenly into flowers more lovely than the white moon.

Flood Year

Walking up the driftwood beach at day's end
I saw it, thrust up out of a hillock of sand –
a frail bleached clench of fingers dried by wind –
the dead child's hand.

And they are mourning there still, though I forget,
the year of flood, the scoured ruined land,
the herds gone down the current, the farms drowned,
and the child never found.

When I was there the thick hurling waters
had gone back to the river, the farms were almost drained.
Banished half-dead cattle searched the dunes; it rained;
river and sea met with a wild sound.

Oh with a wild sound water flung into air
where sea met river; all the country round
no heart was quiet. I walked on the driftwood sand
and saw the pale crab crouched, and came to a stand
thinking, A child's hand. The child's hand.

At Cooloolah

The blue crane fishing in Cooloolah's twilight
has fished there longer than our centuries.
He is the certain heir of lake and evening,
and he will wear their colour till he dies,

but I'm a stranger, come of a conquering people.
I cannot share his calm, who watch his lake,
being unloved by all my eyes delight in,
and made uneasy, for an old murder's sake.

Those dark-skinned people who once named Cooloolah
knew that no land is lost or won by wars,
for earth is spirit: the invader's feet will tangle
in nets there and his blood be thinned by fears.

Riding at noon and ninety years ago,
my grandfather was beckoned by a ghost –
a black accoutred warrior armed for fighting,
who sank into bare plain, as now into time past.

White shores of sand, plumed reed and paperbark,
clear heavenly levels frequented by crane and swan –
I know that we are justified only by love,
but oppressed by arrogant guilt, have room for none.

And walking on clean sand among the prints
of bird and animal, I am challenged by a driftwood spear
thrust from the water; and, like my grandfather,
must quiet a heart accused by its own fear.

Request to a Year

If the year is meditating a suitable gift,
I should like it to be the attitude
of my great-great-grandmother,
legendary devotee of the arts,

who, having had eight children
and little opportunity for painting pictures,
sat one day on a high rock
beside a river in Switzerland

and from a difficult distance viewed
her second son, balanced on a small ice-floe,
drift down the current towards a waterfall
that struck rock-bottom eighty feet below,

while her second daughter, impeded,
no doubt, by the petticoats of the day,
stretched out a last-hope alpenstock
(which luckily later caught him on his way).

Nothing, it was evident, could be done;
and with the artist's isolating eye
my great-great-grandmother hastily sketched the scene.
The sketch survives to prove the story by.

Year, if you have no Mother's day present planned;
reach back and bring me the firmness of her hand.

For One Dying

Come now; the angel leads.
All human lives betray,
all human love erodes
under time's laser ray;

the innocent animals
within us and without
die in corrupted hells
made out of human thought.

Green places and pure springs
are poisoned and laid bare –
even the hawk's high wings
ride on a fatal air.

But come; the angel calls.
Deep in the dreamer's cave
the one pure source upwells
its single luminous wave;

and there, Recorder, Seer,
you wait within your cell.
I bring, in love and fear,
the world I know too well

into your hands. Receive
these fractured days I yield.
Renew the life we grieve
by day to know and hold.

Renew the central dream
in blazing purity,
and let my rags confirm

and robe eternity.

For still the angel leads.
Ruined yet pure we go
with all our days and deeds
into that flame, that snow.

Halfway

I saw a tadpole once in a sheet of ice
(a freakish joke played by my country's weather).
He hung at arrest, displayed as it were in glass,
an illustration of neither one thing nor the other.

His head was a frog's, and his hinder legs had grown
ready to climb and jump to his promised land;
but his bladed tail in the ice-pane weighed him down.
He seemed to accost my eye with his budding hand.

"I am neither one thing nor the other, nor here nor there.
I saw great lights in the place where I would be,
but rose too soon, half made for water, half air,
and they have gripped and stilled and enchanted me.

"Is that world real, or a dream I cannot reach?
Beneath me the dark familiar waters flow
and my fellows huddle and nuzzle each to each,
while motionless here I stare where I cannot go."

The comic O of his mouth, his gold-rimmed eyes,
looked in that lustrous glaze as though they'd ask
my vague divinity, looming in stooped surprise,
for death or rescue. But neither was my task.

Waking halfway from a dream one winter night
I remembered him as a poem I had to write.

Finale

The cruellest thing they did
was to send home his teeth from the hospital.
What could she do with those,
arriving as they did days after the funeral?

Wrapped them in one of his clean handkerchiefs
she'd laundered and taken down.
All she could do was cradle them in her hands;
they looked so strange, alone –

utterly jawless in a constant smile
not in the least like his. She could cry no more.
At midnight she took heart and aim and threw
them out of the kitchen-door.

It rocketed out, that finally-parted smile,
into the gully? the scrub? the neighbour's land?
And she went back and fell into stupid sleep,
knowing him dead at last, and by her hand.

Small Town Dance

Two women find the square-root of a sheet.
That is an ancient dance:
arms wide: together: again: two forward steps: hands meet
your partner's once and twice.
That white expanse
reduces to a neat
compression fitting in the smallest space
a sheet can pack in on a cupboard shelf.

High scented walls there were of flapping white
when I was small, myself.
I walked between them, playing Out of Sight.
Simpler than arms, they wrapped and comforted –
clean corridors of hiding, roofed with blue –
saying, Your sins too are made Monday-new;
and see, ahead
that glimpse of unobstructed waiting green.
Run, run before you're seen.

But women know the scale of possibility,
the limit of opportunity,
the fence,
how little chance
there is of getting out. The sheets that tug
sometimes struggle from the peg,
don't travel far. Might symbolise
something. Knowing where danger lies
you have to keep things orderly.
The household budget will not stretch to more.

And they can demonstrate it in a dance.
First pull those wallowing white dreamers down,
spread arms: then close them. Fold

those beckoning roads to some impossible world,
put them away and close the cupboard door.

ABORIGINAL SONG CYCLES
(Ronald M. Berndt) 1916–1990

Ronald Berndt was born in Adelaide, the son of a jeweller, joined the Anthropological Society of South Australia in 1938 and began publishing ethnographic papers soon afterwards. In 1941 he married Catherine Helen Webb, a fellow anthropology student, and the couple worked together, mainly in Australia, but also in the Eastern Highlands of New Guinea. He was appointed professor of anthropology at the University of Western Australia in 1963. Berndt's output on a range of ethnographic issues was voluminous and diverse and he wrote or edited 35 books, 15 of them with his wife. Robert Tonkinson wrote in the Australian Dictionary of Biography: "Consummate field-workers, with an eye for detail, the Berndts cared less for anthropological theorising and cross-cultural generalisation than for the ethnographic and representational tasks they set themselves." It is humbling to realise that the two song cycles reproduced here are just two of what Berndt refers to as "a great number of song cycles. Every clan has in its possession at least two or three of these ... each cycle consists of dozens (some, several hundreds) of separate songs of varying length."

Notes on the Wonguri-Mandjikai Song Cycle of the Moon-Bone

Berndt was of the view that singing among the North-eastern Arnhem Land people "is perhaps the most highly developed of all their arts. They are not so much interested in relating a tale ... but in expressing themselves rhythmically in songs of exceptional beauty and poetic quality." Most of the songs were remarkable for being much longer than in other areas of the Northern Territory. The songs are "more than just vehicles of passing poetic expression ... Their main themes are traditional" and "symbolize the hopes and strivings of a people in relation to its own culture".

Berndt explained in his paper for *Oceania* 19 (September 1948), where the cycle was first published, that this song cycle was secular, and shorter than most (which were the two reasons for making it the subject of the paper) and it was sung "in the camp generally to the accompaniment of a wooden blow trumpet and beating sticks, and of dancing by the women." It was part however of a much longer cycle. Berndt pointed out that this song cycle assumes a knowledge of mythological events. These are that the Moon, when he was a man, lived near the clay pan of the Moonlight at the place of the Dugong by Arnhem Bay. When he died he went down to the sea, where his bones became the nautilus shell. Since this event, the Moon repeats his death, casts away the bone and is reborn.

The climax of the cycle, Song 13, Berndt explained in the following synopsis:

"The people see the Evening Star rising: they are watching it from the clay pan of the Moonlight, the place of the Dugong. It is a sign that their day's work is completed: men return from the hunt and women from collecting vegetable foods; fires are refuelled for the night, and the evening meal is cooking. At the rising of the New Moon and the Evening Star the wooden 'trumpet' is blown, the singing sticks are beaten and the songs begin; the shuffling steps of dancing women are heard, and the hum of chatter throughout the clustered camps. Little children rush along the moon-whitened beach playing, and trying vainly to reach for the Moon Bone and its Lotus Bloom, suspended so near the camp. The Evening Star 'hangs' over the places mentioned in the Song Cycle; it cannot rise too far into the heavens, for it is fastened to the end of a string held by Spirits of the West. It comes to people around Arnhem Bay from Milingimbi way, passing over the heads of people and headmen of many clans, and shining on many places.

"The Evening Star is finally revealed as a Lotus Bloom, a Lily Root, and the string attached to it is the stalk of these plants.

"The Moon himself, having made the clay-pan or billabong in which lotus and lilies grow, left his spiritual reflection upon that country, which became his 'Dreaming Centre.' Since he refuses to die, his disappearance and rebirth are likened to the sequence of the seasons, in the hope of maintaining a continual supply of edible lotus and lily roots.

"It is because of the association of the Moon with this billabong and with the Lotus that the Spirit Beings send out the Lotus Bloom (the Evening Star) attached to a string, in order to attract the Moon, as well as to provide him with food so that he may grow gradually and eventually cast his bone away."

In Song 9, line 6, Berndt inserted the word "bukelili", after "bone", "catfish", "frog" and "sacred tree" to signify that the original Wonguri word was a "power name". In the *Collins Book of Australia Poetry* (1980), which included this cycle and broke new ground by including translations from Aboriginal languages, Rodney Hall substituted "invocation" for "bukelili". We have followed Hall's precedent. In Song 13, "Wu:lamba people" is, Berndt explained, "a collective tribal term for all the clans of the region, irrespective of their linguistic grouping".

Wonguri-Mandjikai Song Cycle of the Moon-Bone

1.

The people are making a camp of branches in that country at Arnhem Bay:
With the forked stick, the rail for the whole camp, the *Mandjikai* people are making it.
Branches and leaves are about the mouth of the hut: the middle is clear within.
They are thinking of rain, and of storing their clubs in case of a quarrel,
In the country of the Dugong, towards the wide clay-pans made by the Moonlight.
Thinking of rain, and of storing the fighting sticks.
They put up the rafters of arm-band-tree wood, put the branches on to the camp, at Arnhem Bay, in that place of the Dugong.
And they block up the back of the hut with branches.
Carefully place the branches, for this is the camp of the Morning-Pigeon man,
And of the Middle-of-the-Camp man; of the Mangrove-Fish man; of two other head-men,

And of the Clay-pan man; of the *Baijini-Anchor* man, and of the Arnhem Bay country man;
Of the Whale man and of another head-man; of the Arnhem Bay Creek man;
Of the Scales-of-the-Rock-Cod man; of the Rock Cod man, and of the Place-of-the Water man.

2.
They are sitting about in the camp, among the branches, along the back of the camp:
Sitting along in lines in the camp, there in the shade of the paperbark trees:
Sitting along in a line, like the new white spreading clouds:
In the shade of the paperbarks, they are sitting resting like clouds.
People of the clouds, living there like the mist; like the mist sitting resting with arms on knees,
In here towards the shade, in this Place, in the shadow of paperbarks.
Sitting there in rows, those *Wonguri-Mandjikai* people, paperbarks along like a cloud.
Living on cycad-nut bread; sitting there with white-stained fingers,
Sitting in there resting, those people of the Sandfly clan …
Sitting there like mist, at that place of the Dugong … and of the Dugong's Entrails …
Sitting resting there in the place of the Dugong …
In that place of the Moonlight Clay Pans, and at the place of the Dugong …
There at that Dugong place they are sitting all along.

3.
Wake up from sleeping! Come, we go to see the clay pan, at the place of the Dugong …
Walking along, stepping along, straightening up after resting:
Walking along, looking as we go down on to the clay pan.
Looking for lily plants as we go … and looking for lily foliage …
Circling around, searching towards the middle of the lily leaves to reach the rounded roots.
At that place of the Dugong …
At that place of the Dugong's Tail …
At that place of the Dugong; looking for food with stalks,
For lily foliage, and for the round-nut roots of the lily plant.

4.
The birds saw the people walking along.
Crying, the white cockatoos flew over the clay pan of the Moonlight;

From the place of the Dugong they flew, looking for lily-root food; pushing the foliage down and eating the soft roots.
Crying, the birds flew down and along the clay pan, at that place of the Dugong …
Crying, flying down there along the clay pan …
At the place of the Dugong, of the Tree-Limbs-Rubbing-Together, and of the Evening Star.
Where the lily-root clay pan is …
Where the cockatoos play, at that place of the Dugong …
Flapping their wings they flew down, crying, "We saw the people!"
There they are always living, those clans of the white cockatoo …
And there is the Shag woman, and there her clan:
Birds, trampling the lily foliage, eating the soft round roots!

5.
An animal track is running along: it is the track of the rat …
Of the male rat, and the female rat, and the young that hang to her teats as she runs,
The male rat hopping along, and the female rat, leaving paw-marks as a sign …
On the clay pans of the Dugong, and in the shade of the trees,
At the Dugong's place, and at the place of her Tail …
Thus, they spread paw-mark messages all along their tracks,
In that place of the Evening Star, in the place of the Dugong …
Among the lily plants and into the mist, into the Dugong place, and into the place of her Entrails.
Backwards and forwards the rats run, always hopping along …
Carrying swamp-grass for nesting, over the little tracks, leaving their signs.
Backwards and forwards they run on the clay pan, around the place of the Dugong.
Men saw their tracks at the Dugong's place, in the shade of the trees, on the white clay;
Roads of the rats, paw-marks everywhere, running into the mist.
All around are their signs; and there men saw them down on the clay pan, at the place of the Dugong.

6.
A duck comes swooping down to the Moonlight clay-pan, there at the place of the Dugong …
From far away. "I saw her flying over, in here at the clay-pan …" [the duck speaking]
Floating along, pushing the pool into ripples and preening her feathers.

"I carried these eggs from a long way off, from inland to Arnhem Bay ..."
[the duck speaking]
Eggs, eggs, eggs; eggs she is carrying, swimming along.
She preens her feathers, and pulls at the lily foliage.
Drags at the lily leaves with her claws for food.
Swimming along, rippling the water among the lotus plants ...
Backwards and forwards: she pulls at the foliage, swimming along, floating and eating.
This bird is taking her food, the lotus food in the clay-pan,
At the place of the Dugong there, at the place of the Dugong's Tail ...
Swimming along for food, floating, and rippling the water, there at the place of the Lilies.
Taking the lotus, the rounded roots and stalks of the lily; searching and eating there as she ripples the water.
"Because I have eggs, I give to my young the sound of the water."
Splashing and preening herself, she ripples the water, among the lotus ...
Backwards and forwards, swimming along, rippling the water,
Floating along on the clay-pan, at the place of the Dugong.

7.
People were diving here at the place of the Dugong ...
Here they were digging all around, following up the lily stalks,
Digging into the mud for the rounded roots of the lily,
Digging them out at that place of the Dugong, and of the Evening Star,
Pushing aside the water while digging, and smearing themselves with mud ...
Piling up the mud as they dug, and washing the roots clean.
They saw arm after arm there digging: people thick like the mist ...
The Shag Woman too was there, following up the lily stalks.
There they saw arm after arm of the *Mandjikai* Sandfly clan,
Following the stalks along, searching and digging for food:
Always there together, those *Mandjikai* Sandfly people.
They follow the stalks of the lotus and lily, looking for food.
The lilies that always grow there at the place of the Dugong ...
At that clay-pan, at the place of the Dugong, at the place of the lilies.

8.
Now the leech is swimming along ... It always lives there in the water ...
It takes hold of the leaves of the lily and pods of the lotus, and climbs up on to their stalks.
Swimming along and grasping hold of the leaves with its head ...
It always lives there in the water, and climbs up on to the people.

Always there, that leech, together with all its clan ...
Swimming along towards the trees, it climbs up and waits for people.
Hear it swimming along through the water, its head out ready to grasp us ...
Always living here and swimming along.
Because that leech is always there, for us, however it came there:
The leech that catches hold of those *Mandjikai* Sandfly people ...

9.

The prawn is there, at the place of the Dugong, digging out mud with its claws ...
The hard-shelled prawn living there in the water, making soft little noises.
It burrows into the mud and casts it aside, among the lilies ...
Throwing aside the mud, with soft little noises ...
Digging out mud with its claws at the place of the Dugong, the place of the Dugong's Tail ...
Calling the bone invocation, the catfish invocation, the frog invocation, the sacred tree invocation ...
The prawn is burrowing, coming up, throwing aside the mud, and digging ...
Climbing up on to the lotus plants and on to their pods ...

10.

Swimming along under the water, as bubbles rise to the surface, the tortoise moves in the swamp grass.
Swimming among the lily leaves and the grasses, catching them as she moves ...
Pushing them with her short arms. Her shell is marked with designs,
This tortoise carrying her young, in the clay pan, at the place of the Dugong ...
The short-armed *Mararlpa* tortoise, with special arm-bands, here at the place of the Dugong ...
Backwards and forwards she swims, the short-armed one of the *Mararlpa*, and the *Dalwongu*.
Carrying eggs about, in the clay pan, at the place of the Dugong ...
Her entrails twisting with eggs ...
Swimming along through the grass, and moving her patterned shell.
The tortoise with her young, and her special arm-bands,
Swimming along, moving her shell, with bubbles rising;
Throwing out her arms towards the place of the Dugong ...
This creature with the short arms, swimming and moving her shell;
This tortoise, swimming along, with the drift of the water ...
Swimming with her short arms, at the place of the Dugong ....

11.
Wild-grape vines are floating there in the billabong:
Their branches, joint by joint, spreading over the water.
Their branches move as they lie, backwards and forwards,
In the wind and the waves, at the Moonlight clay pan, at the place of the Dugong ...
Men see them lying there on the clay pan pool, in the shade of the paperbarks:
Their spreading limbs shift with the wind and the water:
Grape vines with their berries ...
Blown backwards and forwards as they lie, there at the place of the Dugong.
Always there, with their hanging grapes, in the clay pan of the Moonlight ...
Vine plants and roots and jointed limbs, with berry food, spreading over the water.

12.
Now the New Moon is hanging, having cast away his bone:
Gradually he grows larger, taking on new bone and flesh.
Over there, far away, he has shed his bone: he shines on the place of the Lotus Root, and the place of the Dugong,
On the place of the Evening Star, of the Dugong's Tail, of the Moonlight clay pan ...
His old bone gone, now the New Moon grows larger;
Gradually growing, his new bone growing as well.
Over there, the horns of the old receding Moon bent down, sank into the place of the Dugong:
His horns were pointing towards the place of the Dugong.
Now the New Moon swells to fullness, his bone grown larger.
He looks on the water, hanging above it, at the place of the Lotus.
There he comes into sight, hanging above the sea, growing larger and older ...
There far away he has come back, hanging over the clans near Milingimbi ...
Hanging there in the sky, above those clans ...
"Now I'm becoming a big moon, slowly regaining my roundness ...
In the far distance the horns of the Moon bend down, above Milingimbi,
Hanging a long way off, above Milingimbi Creek ...
Slowly the Moon Bone is growing, hanging there far away.
The bone is shining, the horns of the Moon bend down.
First the sickle Moon on the old Moon's shadow; slowly he grows,
And shining he hangs there at the place of the Evening Star ...
Then far away he goes sinking down, to lose his bone in the sea;
Diving towards the water, he sinks down out of sight.
The old Moon dies to grow new again, to rise up out of the sea.

13.

Up and up soars the evening Star, hanging there in the sky.
Men watch it, at the place of the Dugong and of the Clouds, and of the Evening Star,
A long way off, at the place of Mist, of Lilies and of the Dugong.
The Lotus, the Evening Star, hangs there on its long stalk, held by the Spirits.
It shines on that place of the Shade, on the Dugong place, and on to the Moonlight clay pan ...
The Evening Star is shining, back towards Milingimbi, and over the *Wu:lamba* people ...
Hanging there in the distance, towards the place of the Dugong,
The place of the Eggs, of the Tree-Limbs-Rubbing-Together, and of the Moonlight clay pan ...
Shining on its short stalk, the Evening Star, always there at the clay pan, at the place of the Dugong ...
There, far away, the long string hangs at the place of the Evening Star, the place of Lilies.
Away there at Milingimbi ... at the place of the Full Moon,
Hanging above the head of that *Wonguri* tribesman:
The Evening Star goes down across the camp, among the white gum trees ...
Far away, in those places near Milingimbi.
Goes down among the *Ngurulwulu* people, towards the camp and the gum trees,
At the place of the Crocodiles, and of the Evening Star, away towards Milingimbi ...
The Evening Star is going down, the Lotus Flower on its stalk ...
Going down among all those western clans ...
It brushes the heads of the uncircumcised people ...
Sinking down in the sky, that Evening Star, the Lotus ...
Shining on to the foreheads of all those headmen ...
On to the heads of all those Sandfly people ...
It sinks there into the place of the white gum trees, at Milingimbi.

Notes on the Goulburn Island Cycle

This epic cycle of 27 songs was translated from Riradjingu by Berndt and appears in his *Love Songs of Arnhem Land*. Because of its length, Songs 19, 20, 23, 24 and 25 have been omitted. The following notes are based on Berndt's commentary:

Song 1: Houses are built on stilts in shallow billabongs and swamps. They are similar in construction to those of Macassan (Indonesian) visitors to the north Australian coast. The floor and roof are made of stringybark sheets, and the roof is sealed with "ant-bed" from termite mounds, which is waterproof when it dries. The sacred site of Muruwul or Miraraminar, near the mouth of the Woolen River, is where the two Wawalag sisters and their child were swallowed by Yulunggul the Rock Python (and later brought back to life).

Song 2: Huts are built on rafts which float when the rain comes or can be tied to a tree, and are like those in Song 1 except they do not have stilts.

Song 4: The people decorate their chests with "water designs" of freshwater snakes. A "fighting-bag" is a woven, padded bag stuffed with wild cotton or native string and sewn up and worn as a necklet that rests on the chest. It is used in dancing or held between the teeth during fighting or ritualized fighting. Biting them was said to help concentration.

Song 5: The uncircumcised penes of the Western Arnhem Landers were believed to be longer than circumcised penes and were a source of amusement for North Eastern Arnhem Landers, whose men were customarily circumcised.

Song 8: The first storms are over, the billabong is filled with water, people move about outside, the men hunt and fish and the women soften the leaves of the pandanus palm by heating them over fires.

Song 10: The girls making string figures have only just reached puberty and are menstruating. Eastern Arnhem Landers believed that at this time the sexual urge was particularly intense. A pigeon perched in a cabbage palm watches as the girls sit modestly with one heel pressed against the vulva. The pigeon flaps its wings and calls out when the girls move their heels and it sees the menstrual blood drip through the planks of the hut and wash away in the water below. The girls hide in the foliage of the cabbage palm, which is a tabu tree, and where, after they have arranged their assignations, they need not fear discovery during lovemaking. Wawalag theology deals with the erotic appeal of menstrual blood.

Song 14: Berndt explained the traditional belief that during intercourse the penis broke a bone at the entrance to the uterus by the force of penetration, releasing blood stored in the uterus.

Song 16: Berndt explained that when the men throw their bamboo-shafted spears they "are caught by the wind, and in their spirit form are carried to various places some distance away".

Songs 17 and 18: The clouds that bring the wet season are attracted by the pheasant in its carefully constructed nest and by the men arranging their fighting clubs like rows of clouds.

Song 21: Yulunggul, the python referred to in Song 2, and the freshwater snakes referred to in Song 4 are mythic snakes associated with thunder and lightning, and the Lightning Snake has an erotic significance as well as impelling clouds to shed rain: "North-eastern Arnhem Landers saw this as an observable progression of inevitable events: coitus among the palms; the onset of the menstrual flow; the attraction of the clouds; the arrival of the Lightning Snake, drawn by the smell of blood; and finally the coming of the monsoonal season."

Songs 26 and 27: These conclude the cycle. Wood-and-feathered-string seagulls were used as a traditional love-magic object by north-eastern Arnhem Landers. A wooden gull's head is tied to a length of feathered string: "The wooden gull's head is carved with its beak open, holding a leech (or sometimes a worm, or a mouse, or a small fish) which represents a girl 'caught' by her lover." In Song 26, the sea-gull is a real gull and also the magic love-object. In Song 27, the sea-gull is real and "the squeaking of the mouse symbolizes the cries of the girls during coitus".

The Goulburn Island Cycle

1.

Erecting forked sticks and rafters, posts for the floor, making the roof of the hut like a sea-eagle's nest:
They are always there, at the billabong of the goose eggs, at the wide expanse of water.
As they build, they think of the monsoon rains – rain and wind from the west, clouds spreading over the billabong …
They cover the sides of the hut, placing rails on the forked sticks.
We saw the heaving chests of the builders, calling invocations for the clouds rising in the west …
With heaving chests, calling the invocations …
Making the door of the hut, preparing it within …
They think of the coming rain, and the west wind … wind bringing the rain, spreading over this country.
Carefully, therefore, prepare the hut, with its roof, and its posts …
We saw the heaving chests of men of the Maiar'maiar clan, clans from the Woolen River …
They are always there at that place, that billabong edged with bamboo,
There by the wide expanse of water … carefully laying the rails.

2.

There is the framework, the rafters and door of the hut.
We saw the heaving chests of Goulburn Island men and Burara men, as they made it,
Preparing the stilted hut, like a sea-eagle's nest in a tree.
We saw their heaving chests as they invoked the Yulunggul Snakes, their coiling, and crawling …
Invoking the coiling Snakes and their entrails … and building stilted huts all over the billabong,
At the place of the Rising Western Clouds … at the place of Standing Clouds: spreading all over the sky at the place of Coloured Reflections.
Huts all around, at the Sea-Eagle place, at Milingimbi Point, and over towards the Sandspit near Goulburn Islands …
My hut is nearing completion,
With forked sticks and roof like a sea-eagle's nest, with rails and door …
They are always there at that billabong, with the wide expanse of water …
It is almost ready. We make these huts all around, and north-east of Milingimbi.
Clouds banking along the horizon, passing north-eastward over the Crocodile Islands …
Thus they were making the huts. We saw their heaving chests and the rising

clouds from the west, small clouds rising and spreading,
Saw their heaving chests, as black clouds came bringing a sheet of rain,
Sound of thunder, roaring of wind and rain ...
I am making it for myself, with forked sticks and with rails ...
Thunder leaving its noise for me, sound rolling along the bottom of the clouds,
Echoing on the billabong, across the wide expanse of water ...
I am making my sea-eagle nest to float in the rising waters of the billabong.
I am making it, and later the lightning will play on its roof and on me inside.
For its tongue flickers along the horizon, and thunder rolls along the bottom of the clouds,
Clouds rising from the place of the Wawalag sisters, from where they were swallowed ...
I am preparing for you, clouds massing along the horizon: using my posts, my forked sticks and my rails ...
You, clouds, are banking along for me ...
The wind brings clouds, of the *jiridja* moiety – clouds like penes.
A cool wind blows, easing the heat and bringing the small clouds ...
Thunder rolling along the bottom of the clouds, as the lightning flashes ...
I am making it ready for you, fixing the door and the inside:
Because I invoke the clouds rising from Goulburn Islands ...
I am making it for myself, to float across the billabong,
Across the wide expanse of water, to float like a sea-eagle's nest ...
We saw their heaving chests, as they invoked the clouds rising from Goulburn Islands ...

3.

Get the clapping sticks and the didjeridu, for we feel the urge for enjoyment.
Hear the rhythmic beat, and the singing of Goulburn Island people, clans from the Woolen River ...
Chests turned towards the cold west wind, and the sound of the didjeridu ...
Rhythmically beating, within the huts like sea-eagle nests ...
Sound from within the huts, spreading across the country ...
Clapping-sticks at the Sandspit near Goulburn Islands, at the place of Western Clouds, and of Standing Clouds, and at Milingimbi Creek ...
Opposite Milingimbi, at the place of Coloured Reflections ... sticks clapping within the huts,
Sticks clapping, for we feel the urge for enjoyment: invoking the western rain clouds ...
Sound rising like clouds, wafted across the waters to Milingimbi:
Like clouds banking up, the sound hovers over the Island of Clouds ...
Cold wind from the west, striking their chests ...

It is ours! With this singing the wind begins to blow, swaying the branches,
Cold stranger wind from somewhere, from Goulburn Islands!

4.
Take clay and coloured ochres, and put them on!
They paint chests and breasts with clay, in water-designs,
Hang round their necks the padded fighting-bags.
They paint themselves, those Goulburn Island people, and clans from the Woolen River ...
They are always there, at the wide expanse of water ...
They take more clay, for painting the fighting-sticks ...
Paint on their chests designs of water-snakes ...
And paint the boomerangs with coloured ochres ...
Painting the small boomerangs ...
Calling the invocations ... all over the country, and at the place of the Wawalag sisters ...
Painting themselves at Milingimbi Point, at the place of Standing Clouds.
At the place of the Western Clouds, at the place of Coloured Reflections ...

5.
They grasp the padded fighting-bags, holding them in their mouths ...
Come, let us dance, stepping along, biting the padded bags ...!
Swaying branches from side to side:
They are always there, at those places near Goulburn Islands.
We dance, swaying branches from side to side, like the cold west wind ...
We saw their chests, people short like new paperbark saplings:
Goulburn Island people, clans from the Woolen River, men with uncircumcised penes,
Clans of the long foreskins.
Thus they move their chests, swaying branches from side to side, around Milingimbi ...
Thus the padded ball sways from side to side on their chests at Milingimbi Point, at the place of Standing Clouds, the place of the Western Clouds ...
They dance, invoking the rising western clouds ...
They dance, calling the invocations ...
We saw their chests heave, as they called the invocations ...
Because they are always there, at the stilted huts like sea-eagles' nests ...

6.
They have thrown aside their branches: the wind flings them into the cabbage palm foliage ...
Leave the branches for me! [the wind says] The wind blows them along,

calling the water,
At that billabong, at the wide expanse of water among the bamboos ...
It blows them along, branches twisting and turning ...
Branches tossed aside, and flung back.
The voice of the wind calls the open water, in Wawalag country.
Rain streams down their chests, and the wind flings it away:
Cold west wind, flinging away the branches.
It is our wind that we feel, the cold west wind! [the people say]
And another wind is ours, the north-west *jiridja* wind swaying the branches!
We feel the north-west winds, their coolness retracting our penes,
Flinging our branches away, blowing them down.
Blowing the branches, calling the names of the country ...
Calling the names: the place of the Wawalag sisters, the place of the Python ...

7.
Hang up the basket, the padded fighting-bag: put it on to the post,
On the forked stick of the hut, or on to the rail:
Men's bodies are tired from dancing, and swinging the branches. So put away the bag ...
Take the possum fur headband, and hang it at the door of the hut ...
That headband which has been worn; hang it up on the forked stick, or on the rafter rails.
We saw them wearing it: short people like paperbark saplings, from Goulburn Islands,
Men with uncircumcised penes.
We saw them, putting the padded fighting bag on their chests,
The ball bag, hung at the door of the hut ...
They hung it up on the forked sticks ...
We saw their chests, heard them invoking the rising western clouds ...
They are always there, at the wide expanse of water ...

8.
Preparing strips of pandanus leaf, making the ball bags ...
They are always there, at the wide expanse of water, those huts like sea-eagles' nests.
We saw the breasts of the young girls, girls of the Burara tribe and of clans from the Woolen River.
Girls from Goulbum Islands, from many clans: moving their hands, as they split the pandanus leaves to weave the baskets ...
They are always there, at the place of Standing Clouds, near Milingimbi, where clouds spread all over the country ...

We saw their moving breasts as they softened the strips of pandanus, weaving the padded fighting-bags ...
Within those huts, at the wide expanse of water ...
They are always there, at the billabong edged with bamboo ...
Making them as they sit on the floor at the open doorways ...
They are always there at the wide expanse of water, at the place of Standing Clouds, the place of the Sea-Eagle,
The place of Coloured Reflections, where the western clouds arise, towards Milingimbi.

9.

Girls take up their strings, to make "cat's-cradles", girls from the Burara and Gunwinggu tribes ...
They take their breast girdles, twisting the string. We saw their breasts, young girls of Goulburn Islands ...
They are always there in that camp, at the wide expanse of water ...
Making string figures, leaning back on the forked rails of the hut, the sea-eagle nest ...
We saw their breasts, and their hands moving – Goulburn Island girls, clans from the Woolen River ...
Their breasts in the cold west wind, as they flutter their eyes at the men:
Swaying their buttocks, speaking in Goulburn Island language.
This is our string, from our breast girdles [say the girls]: always there inside the huts, at the wide expanse of water.
They saw men of the Goulburn Island people ... men with uncircumcised penes ...
They flutter their eyelids, young girls of the Burara and Gunwinggu tribes.
They are always there at the billabong edged with bamboo, the wide expanse of water.
We saw their breasts, young girls of the western clans.
We twist the string in our hands, for we feel like playing [say the girls]: twisting our breast girdles, at the wide expanse of water.
They sway their buttocks, young Gunwinggu girls, girls from the western clans ...
Thus they twist their string, watching the Goulburn Island men with their long penes ...
We flutter our eyes at them as we twist the strings [say the girls].
Sitting among the cabbage palm foliage,
Leaning back on the forked rails of the hut, the sea-eagle nest ...
They are always there at the place of Standing Clouds: clouds spreading all over the country, from near Milingimbi ...
We saw their breasts ... young girls from Goulburn Islands, girls from the

western clans …
We saw their breasts … always there, at the billabong edged with bamboo …
Saw their breasts, as they moved the string in their fingers …
Twisting the string, leaning back on the forked rails of the hut …

10.
The bird saw the young Burara girls, twisting their strings, making string figures.
Watching with head poised, the bird cries …
The pigeon saw the young Gunwinggu girls, twisting their strings …
With head poised, saw their hands moving, saw the blood as they moved their heels.
The pigeon watches them, flapping its wings and calling out as it sees the blood.
The cry goes out to Blue Mud Bay, among the new paperbark shoots …
The cry of the bird goes over to Goulburn Islands …
Perched on the topmost leaves of the cabbage palm …
Clasping the cabbage palm with its claws …
Crying out as it sees the blood.
It saw them twisting their strings, moving the string-patterns – young girls of the Gunwinggu tribe …

11.
They saw the young girls twisting their strings, Goulburn Island men and men from the Woolen River:
Young girls of the western clans, twisting their breast girdles among the cabbage palm foliage …
Stealthily creeping, the men grasp the cabbage tree leaves to search for their sweethearts.
Stealthily moving, they bend down to hide with their lovers among the foliage …
With penis erect, those Goulburn Island men, from the young girls' swaying buttocks …
They are always there, at the wide expanse of water …
Always there, at the billabong edged with bamboo.
Feeling the urge for play, as they saw the young girls of the western clans,
Saw the young girls hiding themselves, twisting the strings …
Girls twisting their breast girdles, making string figures: and men with erect penes,
Goulburn Island men, as the young girls sway their buttocks.

12.

They seize the young girls of the western tribes, with their swaying buttocks – those Goulburn Island men ...
Young girls squealing in pain, from the long penis ...
Girls of the western clans, desiring pleasure, pushed on to their backs among the cabbage palm foliage ...
Lying down, copulating – always there, moving their buttocks ...
Men of Goulburn Islands, with long penes ...
Seizing the beautiful young girls, of the western tribes ...
They are always there at that billabong edged with bamboo ...
Hear the sound of their buttocks, the men from Goulburn Islands moving their penes ...
For these are beautiful girls, of the western tribes ...
And the penis becomes erect, as their buttocks move ...
They are always there at the place of Standing Clouds, of the rising western clouds,
Pushed on to their backs, lying down among the cabbage palm foliage ...

13.

Ejaculating into their vaginas – young girls of the western tribes.
Ejaculating semen, into the young Burara girls ...
Those Goulburn Island men, with their long penes;
Semen flowing from them into the young girls ...
For they are always there, moving their buttocks.
They are always there, at the wide expanse of water ...
Ejaculating, among the cabbage palm foliage:
They cry out, those young girls of the Nagara tribe ...
He ejaculates semen for her, among the cabbage palm foliage ...
Ejaculating for the young girls of the western clans ...
From the long penes of men from Goulburn Islands ...
They are always there at the open expanse of water, at the sea-eagle nest ...
Ejaculating semen, for the young girls ...
Into the young girls of the western tribes ...
For they are ours – it is for this that they make string figures ... [the men say]
Thus we ejaculate for her – into the young girl's vagina.
Semen, among the cabbage palm foliage ...
Thus we push her over, among the foliage;
We ejaculate semen into their vaginas – young girls of the western tribes ...
Ejaculating semen, into the young Burara girls ...
For they move their buttocks, those people from Goulburn Islands.

14.
Blood is running down from the men's penes, men from Goulburn Islands ...
Blood running down from the young girls, like blood from a speared kangaroo ...
Running down among the cabbage palm foliage ...
Blood that is sacred, running down from the young girl's uterus:
Flowing like water, from the young girls of the western tribes ...
Blood running down, for the Goulburn Island men had seen their swaying buttocks ...
Sacred blood running down ...
Like blood from a speared kangaroo; sacred blood flows from the uterus ...
They are always there, at the wide expanse of water, the sea-eagle nests ...
They are sacred, those young girls of the western tribes, with their menstrual flow ...
They are always there, moving their buttocks, those Goulbum Island people ...
Sacred, with flowing blood – young girls of the western clans ...
They are always there, sitting within their huts like sea-eagle nests, with blood flowing ...
Flowing down from the sacred uterus of the young girl ...
Sacred young girls from the western tribes, clans from the Woolen River:
Blood, flowing like water ...
Always there, that blood, in the cabbage palm foliage ...
Sacred blood flowing in all directions ...
Like blood from a speared kangaroo, from the sacred uterus ...

15.
They talked together, we heard them speaking the western language:
Heard their words – men from the western clans, and from Goulburn Islands.
They are always there, in the huts like sea-eagle nests: young girls leaning against the walls ...
We heard the speech of the western clans, clans from the Woolen River ...
Heard them speaking, girls and men of the western tribes ...
Flinging their words into the cabbage palm foliage ...
They are always talking there, at the billabong edged with bamboo: their words drift over the water ...
There at the Sea-Eagle place, we heard them speaking the western language ...
Heard their words at the Sea-Eagle place – clans from the Woolen River ...
Talking there, Goulburn Island men of the long penes ...

They are always there, at the wide expanse of water ...
We heard their words, men from the western tribes, and clans from the Woolen River ...

16.
Get the spears, for we feel like playing!
They are always there, at the billabong edged with bamboo ...
They fling them one by one as they play, the bamboo-shafted spears ...
Twirling the shaft, pretending to throw, then flinging them back and forth ...
The wind catches the spear, and blows it point upwards into the cabbage palm ...
Thin shaft twisting up like a snake, as they fling it in play ...
Spears travelling to different places, and different tribes ...
We saw the spear-throwers' chests and buttocks swinging – those Goulburn Island people ...
They are always there, at the billabong edged with bamboo ...
They feel like playing, and flinging spears – Goulburn Island men, clans from the Woolen River:
Twirling the shaft, pretending to throw: the point twists up like a snake ...
They feel like play, leaning back on the forked sticks within the huts ...

17.
The pheasant cries out from the door of its nest ...
Crying out from the door, at the sound of the coming rain ...
Rain and wind from the west, spreading over the country ...
It cries out, perched on the top rails of the huts.
It is always there, at the wide expanse of water, listening for the rising wind and rain:
Wind and rain from the west, as the pheasant cries out ...
The pheasant, within its wet-season hut – for it has heard the coming rain ...
Darkness, and heavy rain falling ...
It is for me! [says the pheasant] My cry summons the wind and rain ...
Noise of the rain, and of thunder rolling along the bottom of the clouds ...
The pheasant cries out from its nest, from the door of its hut ...
It is always there, at the billabong edged with bamboo.

18.
They take the fighting clubs, standing them upright ...
We saw their chests, men of the western clans, of the rising clouds.
Carefully they stand them up in the ground, these groups of clubs ...
Carefully, assembling them in rows, like a line of clouds in the west.

They are always there, at the wide expanse of water ...
We saw their chests, men of the west, invoking the rising clouds ...
Assembling the fighting clubs, like lines of clouds ...
At the place of Standing Clouds, of the Rising Western Clouds, spreading all over the country.
They drift over the huts, the sea-eagle nests, at the billabong edged with bamboo:
Carefully they assemble the clubs in rows, like a line of clouds in the west ...
From within these rows of clubs, from the lines of clouds, comes the western rain ...
Thus we assemble the fighting clubs in rows, like lines of clouds ...

21.
The tongues of the Lightning Snake flicker and twist, one to the other ...
They flash among the foliage of the cabbage palms ...
Lightning flashes through the clouds, with the flickering tongues of the Snake ...
It is always there, at the wide expanse of water. at the place of the Sacred Tree ...
Flashing above those people of the western clans ...
All over the sky their tongues flicker: above the place of the Rising Clouds, the place of Standing Clouds ...
All over the sky, tongues flickering and twisting ...
They are always there, at the camp by the wide expanse of water ...
All over the sky their tongues flicker: at the place of the Two Sisters, the place of the Wawalag ...
Lightning flashes through the clouds, flash of the Lightning Snake ...
Its blinding flash lights up the cabbage palm foliage ...
Gleams on the cabbage palms, and on the shining semen among the leaves ...

22.
The "swallow" approaches, flying through the west wind and the rain clouds.
The "swallow" ... its feathers blown by the wind ...
It is always there, at the wide expanse of water ...
Flying through the west wind, and the dark storm clouds,
Flying through the wind, close to the clouds ...
It flies through the wind, close to the wide expanse of water ...
All over the country. the bird flies low:
To the place of the Clouds, and the Sea-Eagle place, to Goulburn Islands and Milingimbi Point,

All over the sky: to the place of Coloured Reflections, the place of the Western Clouds ...
Bird, with its feathers blown by the wind ...
The "swallow", flying through the west wind and rain clouds ...
Winds from the west calling, like sacred singing.
North-west winds of the *jiridja* moiety, clouds heavy with rain ...

26.

The seagull flaps its wings, flying along; it is always there, in the west, at the place of the Red Egg ...
The voice of the seagull, its cry, drifts all over the country ...
It circles low over the cabbage palm foliage ...
Crying out, at the place of the fresh water,
The gull swoops low, skimming the water, at the wide expanse of billabong ...
Keen beak probing, it searches for food, skimming the water ...
Circling over the billabong grass and the water-lilies ...
Circling around, in search of the freshwater leech ...
Always there in the west, the sound of its cry: at the place of the Red Egg ...
This string is mine [says the seagull], at the place of the billabong ...
String, short string, and a bird's head ...
The keen eyes of the gull search for food in the night, as a lover looks for his sweetheart ...
Flapping its wings, and crying out as it flies ...

27.

With its keen eyes, the gull saw the small tracks of the mice,
Mouse tracks, leading into the grass and the lily foliage ...
The gull circles around, flapping its wings and crying ...
It is always there, at the wide expanse of water, at the place of the Sacred Tree ...
Diving down, probing about with its beak ...
The sound of its flapping wings, as it swoops on a mouse ...
It is always there, that bird, among the western people ...
Its cry spreads over the country during the wet season, the time of the new grass ...
And the squeaking cry of the mouse ...
It is mine! [says the gull] I spear the mouse on its track, holding it in my beak ...
The squeak of the mouse, and the cry of the gull, echoing up to the sky ...

HAROLD STEWART 1916–1995

Harold Stewart, one of Australia's most undervalued poets, was born in Drummoyne, Sydney, and attended Fort Street School while James McAuley was a pupil there. He began writing poetry at school, including painful love poems about a boy, "R. M." He went to the University of Sydney in 1936, but dropped out in the first year. Early enthusiasms were the poetry of the French symbolists Mallarmé and Valéry, whom he translated, and the poetry of Americans such as Wallace Stevens and Hart Crane. His friendship with McAuley continued in the army during World War II, when they were in the same research and civil affairs unit. In 1944, before either had published a book, they concocted the famous "Ern Malley" poems, as a hoax on the *avant garde* literary magazine *Angry Penguins*. (See Ern Malley commentary.) Stewart always took great pride in the hoax but seems to have been the junior partner, with McAuley holding the pen and contributing much of the tone of voice in the poems.

After the war, Stewart worked in a bookshop in Melbourne for fifteen years. From the early 1950s, he organised Friday night discussion groups on comparative religion at his workplace. His first book of poetry, *Phoenix Wings* (1948), shows him deeply involved in Buddhist and Taoist culture. This contains the splendid "A Flight of Wild Geese". There is a revised version with Stewart's papers in the National Library of Australia; many of Stewart's revisions were not improvements, but we have adopted Stewart's changes where we thought they were better. The centrepiece of his next volume, *Orpheus and Other Poems* (1956), is a cycle of 27 poems, dealing with the myth of Orpheus and reflecting his interest in Carl Jung. The cycle is didactic, and monotonous in its versification.

Stewart's engagement with Japan was to produce his most lasting achievements, in particular his translations of Japanese haiku. He took lessons in Japanese and in 1960 published *A Net of Fireflies*, the first of his books of rhyming translations from the haiku poets. This was to remain in print for many years and became a "desert island book" for a loyal group of readers from a number of countries. Stewart made his first trip to Japan in 1962, financed by a patron. He was greatly disappointed, but decided to "obliterate modern Japan from his consciousness" and return there, which he did, again with assistance, in 1966. Determined to attach himself to the Pure Land school of Buddhism, he simply turned up at the gate of a temple in Kyoto. He was taken in, rather uncertainly, and put through a course of study. He remained for the rest of his life in that city, living in a small room lined with books.

In 1969 Stewart published a second book of haiku translations, *A Chime of Wind-bells*, which maintained the standard of his previous volume, and then in 1979 a 4350-line poem, *By the Old Walls of Kyoto*, which is a guide to the city and to Pure Land doctrine. Stewart became known in his adopted country as an expert on the culture of Kyoto and on Japanese Buddhist art. His second book-length poem (of about 5000 lines), *Autumn Landscape-Roll: A Divine Panorama*, was finished just before his death in 1995 and has not been published.

Stewart's haiku translations are often criticised negatively. It is argued that his heroic couplets have a prose explicitness and a sense of closure that destroys the most important feature of haiku, particularly from the Zen viewpoint, their suggestion of experience beyond words. Stewart came to have an interest in Eastern poetry and religion, after an intensive apprenticeship in English verse prosody. He therefore had an understanding of Western, as well as Eastern, traditions. Stewart defended the heroic couplet for English-language haiku as being a minimal form indigenous to the Western tradition in which the aural properties of the Japanese poem can be conveyed. Japanese poems do not rhyme but are richly alliterative and onomatopoeic, and Stewart regrets there is no approximation of this in the usual syllabic form of translation.

A. D. Hope was of the view that *By the Old Walls of Kyoto* was the "greatest long poem written in English this century". It has 300 pages of erudite prose commentary, and the poem is at times didactic and claustrophobic in its religious intensity. Stewart seems to have been aware that didacticism was a problem; in his manuscripts in the National Library of Australia his notations included "Too didactic". In general his later devotional poetry lacks the spontaneity and freedom of the haiku translations.

His translations present a remarkable mirror of several centuries of Japanese society, as various and rich as the great Russian novels.

NOTES: Dates supplied by Stewart for haiku poets are: Arô (b. 1879); Bashô (1644–1694); Buson (1715–1783); Chiyo ((1701–1775); Gyodai (1732–1792); Hô-ô (b. 1917); Issa (1763–1827); Izen (1646–1711); Jôsô (1662–1704); Kakei (1648–1716); Kijiro (b. 1887); Kikaku (1661–1707); Kitô (1741–1789); Kyoroku (1655–1715); Kyukoku (1719–1805); Meisetsu (1847–1926); Onitsura (1660–1738); Raizan (1653–1716); Ranko (1726–1799); Ryota (1707–1787); Seishi (b. 1868); Shiki (1866–1902); Shirao (1735–1792); Soin (1604–1682); Sôseki (1865–1915); Taigi (1709–1771); Toho (1657–1730); Yayu (1701–1783).

A Flight of Wild Geese

Wu Tao-tzŭ, the greatest of Chinese artists, was once commissioned by the Emperor Ming Huang of the T'ang Dynasty to paint a landscape-roll. Wu so entered into the spirit of the scene that he could walk about in the picture at will. One day he wandered over a distant mountain, and was never seen again.

Now Wu Tao-tzŭ, continuing his stroll
Into the landscape on the silken roll,
Comes to the misty shores around a sheet
Of broad water, reaching from his feet
To where a promontory's rocky bar
Lies in the evening sky, it is so far.
Their taper necks stretched out in line of flight,
The wild geese row over at a height;
And while they clang their long-throated cry,
Tow the full moon into an autumn sky.
Diagonals that widen from a wake
Lattice the tranquil surface of the lake
When in the lapping ebb they intervene,
And shake the level creases of its sheen:
A clear grey-green, yet in its depth opaque;

As though four ladies rolling silk should take
Layer on layer of green gauze, and of grey,
And stretch them taut across a vacant bay.

To skirt these shores, the painter has to pass
Where the long legs of flowering river-grass
Stand in the margin shallows: feathery rushes
Drawn by his most meticulous of brushes,
Their tufted tops with seed are light and loose
As the soft underdown of a grey goose.
In a flat inlet hereabouts, he sees
How, warily protruding out of these,
A narrow blackened prow nuzzles the bank:
The grasses thriving here are lush and lank.
Lulled by the idle suction of the tide,
And the slap of lapsing water against the side,
The wily poet snoozing in the stern
With chin on elbow, smiles in unconcern
As round his line a school of mullet feeds.
Under an overcoat of plaited reeds,
He wears the faded purple robe he wore;
To shade his head, a limpet-shell of straw.
His scant beard and moustaches' straggling hair
Are lightly lifted; flow along the air
Like water-weed that sways this way and that;
And the two fish-tailed ribbons from his hat
Follow them, flapping with a fugal motion.

To bait this nodding angler seems a notion
Well-timed to Wu, for judging by his creel,
Scarcity's pinch will be his evening meal.

Wu Tao-tzŭ:

"Among the Hundred Surnames, mine is Wu.
Pardon my mannerless presumption, who,
Ancient and solitary one, are you?"

The rustic archly opens up one eye
To view this doze-disturbing stranger by;
Yawns like a fox, and stretches to arouse
His cramped limbs from their pictorial drowse.

The Old Fisherman:

"I came here twenty years ago or more,
And yet these hands have never once before

Shaken themselves in salutation's hold.
Then I was Chang Chih-ho. But now the Old
Fisherman of the Waters and the Mists
Tells you of what my way of life consists."

Wu Tao-tzŭ:

"Why did you quit humanity and home
And choose this wilderness in which to roam?
Why in a humble sampan hold aloof,
Its wicker cradle as your only roof?"

Chang Chih-ho:

"I find it serves quite well to keep me dry.
After the autumn rains stop, and the sky
Clears rapidly, all space shall cover me.
The moonrise, pale and golden, on the sea
Fulfils my modest wishes for a door;
And the sea's jade pavement lays the floor.
These, with the valley walls, make up my home.
What do you mean by saying that I roam?
Here cares and creditors no more infest
The house of mind. Its poverty is rest.
Possessing nothing, I am not possessed.
The State's a monstrous and amorphous plan,
Man's mobilized insanity, and man
Believes it real. Afraid of being free,
He fights to keep his cangue, and cannot flee.
An intimate I would far rather be
Of the white gull which climbs and squalls aloud
Sailing across that black cliff of cloud,
Than have the freedom of my spirit furled
And flung upon the dust-heap of the world."

Wu Tao-tzŭ:

"From vanity of rank you may retire;
The lust to rule, that menial desire,
The web of power, possessions which degrade –
These you may shun: you cannot thus evade
Your unlived life, the fate you left unpaid."

Chang Chih-ho:

"No debts or duties did I set aside;
And one who under Su Tsung occupied
The post of minister, was no misfit:

I fled not from the world, but into it.
What other, pray, could I escape to? I'm
Still in this world. I've been here all the time."

Wu Tao-tzŭ:

"Go where you will, you take your troubled mind,
Whose fears you cannot face, nor leave behind.
In vain your doubts and sorrows you suppress;
In vain avoid society's distress:
Escape has no road from its loneliness."

Chang Chih-ho:

"An Emperor's entreaty I would spurn;
I have no inclination to return
To where the simple way is smothered in
The court's incessant fuss; where dust and din
Cover the capital, as with a pall;
Where I could have no peace of mind at all.
The case of Chuang Tzŭ doubtless you recall?
Two high officials from the State of Ch'u,
Who called upon him for an interview,
While he was fishing in the river P'u,
Announced, 'Our Prince proposes we transfer
The government to you – an office, sir,
Only your wisdom can administer.'
The Taoist did not deign to turn his head.
With rod in hand, he watched his line and said,
'In Ch'u there is a tortoise which they hold
Sacred for divination, so I'm told.
It has been dead three thousand years, and since
Kept in a covered casket by the Prince,
Who heats its shell in his ancestral shrine
And reads the cracks from which he can divine.
Given the choice when caught, which would it choose:
To stay alive, draggling its tail in ooze;
Or to be reverenced by men, but dead?'
'To be alive, of course,' the officials said.
'Off with you then, and let me,' he replied,
'Waggle my tail, too, in the muddy tide.'
And some declare the sage washed out his ears
To cleanse them of political ideas;
And that downstream a cowherd then complained
The waters were polluted and profaned."

Wu Tao-tzŭ:

"But see! The skeins of geese arriving span
The sky and write the words for 'one' and 'man'."

Chang Chih-ho:

"And yet they have been here since time began."

Down the sky in file the wild geese tack,
Slanting their obliquely angled track
To reach the estuary's banks of sand
Where basalt blocks have sunk along the strand.
The leader there comes skidding in, to sit
On a long splash, for the sheer sport of it:
His broad tail-feathers fan to brake the flight;
His webbed feet splay, and his red legs alight,
Fixed in the instant's clear aquamarine,
So still the surface-water is, and green.
To wash his travel-dusty feathers clean
He ducks, and ladles over back and head
Wingfuls of water, till its trickles spread.
Next he stands upright in the water-rings,
Throws out his breast, and flaps his wide wings;
Then sits again, and shakes his tail to shed
Stray superfluous drops that diamonded
His oily coverts; then with beak depressed,
Restoring comfort with a fluffed unrest,
And last, his bathing over, preens and grooms
Down smooth and trim his toilet-ruffled plumes.
More glide in after him. The others land
Pinions aloft, and settle on the sand,
Where flatly snapping bills hiss and contest
Scraps of aquatic weed not long possessed.
Pushing a fold of glass against the stream,
One paddles in pursuit of his own gleam.
Another stoops his pliant neck to sip
This running ripple with the glassy lip,
And cranes to swallow after every dip.
A third, whose bill tugged at the wavering weeds,
Lifts their dripping ribbons up, and feeds.
Riding its undulating ebb, the fleet
Of geese sets sail upon the glaucous sheet;
But a snapped stick startles one among
The floating flock. Instantly all are sprung!

As low over the water skims each pair:
The wing-tip beaten downward through the air
Touches its upward-beaten image there.
Once in the central sky, they travel south
Beyond the sandspit at the river's mouth,
Beyond the dim horizon. All are gone.
But, like a drift of feathers dropped upon
The refluent air after their motion has flown,
A soft flocculence of cloud is strown;
Hovering, while invisible waves of wake
Diverge, and on the mountains, sprayless, break.

Wu Tao-tzŭ:

"They have migrated toward a warmer clime."

Chang Chih-ho:

"They will be here now till the end of time."

A light breeze that springs up off the bay,
Bending the plume-topped grasses all one way
And carrying silver seeded fluff astray,
Just as suddenly drops. At once the rushes'
Thicket of dry whispers thins and hushes
To a faint rustle. Nothing stirs the brake.
Chang winds his fishing-line in from the lake.
Wu's face is lost in an astonished look,
For dangling thence is neither bait nor hook!

Wu Tao-tzŭ:

"How can you ever hope to catch a stray
Tadpole, though you angle here all day?
That is no way to get a bite! You need
A tempting bait: some juicy worm or weed
To hide the hook of cunning, if you wish
To cast the right enticement for a fish."

Chang Chih-ho:

"Ah! But that's not what I was fishing for!"

He poles his lean black punt away from shore.
The layered streaks of vapour closing in,
Leave no trace that he has ever been . . . . .

Into infinite distance, sad and clear,
Recede the miles of autumn atmosphere:

With pale citron tone, the watery light
That shines out after rain, washes their height.
The autumn mountain, swept as neat and clean
As the tidy winds can, reclines serene:
No twig is out of place; no leaf is seen
Of all that tarnished ruin of gold which lay
So densely underfoot, but yesterday.
Claimed by the earth as tribute to decay.
Upon its sides the naked forests brood,
Locked in a crystalline disquietude;
And looped with sleeping vines and beards of moss,
Despair for want of leaves, the season's loss.
Each tall, gaunt, calligraphic tree
Forked against the light's sour clarity,
Soars with static branches, sparse and bare,
In that remote and disappointed air.
An empty vast, the autumn waters lie
Merging into the open sea of sky.
Slowly the ebb goes out, and from the height
Drains away the westering tide of light.

Ah! The evening's mood is growing late.
The peasant enters now his brushwood gate.
The garden, overgrown with grass and weed,
Where spires of wilding lettuce run to seed,
Lies drenched with recent rain, and desolate.
A sulphur-coloured butterfly chases its mate
Over the fence with devious flutterings:
They are the only autumn leaves with wings.
The altered air that chills the end of day
Makes the fishing-nets and tackle sway
Gently over on their bamboo poles.
And now a temple-bell remotely tolls
The still and solemn hour; now holds its peace.
The work of men, the year's affairs decrease.
Now lamps are lit in windows far and near.
See! Through the yellow dusk their flames appear.
Within the peasant's hut two suppers wait.
Ah! The evening's mood is growing late.

A smooth moon in the laminated fog
Whose levels weave above the stagnant bog
With trails of gossamer, is hanging low

Its pallid disc, too early yet to glow.
Beside this languid marsh the artist walks.
Still to the old and withered lotus stalks
The rattling seeds in conic pods adhere;
The round leaves droop, their flounces tattered, sere;
And sere the willow leaves spin as they sift
On the despondent pond a falling drift.
There, like yellow sampans, they are thrust
Aimlessly along by a tired gust
To strand in a backwater. There some dust
Is spent, and settles, and the waste becalms
Among an undergrowth of roots with arms
For now the world of nature grows subdued
And grave with an autumnal lassitude.

Out on the lake one solitary sail
Goes home into the world. With this detail
The old recluse aboard his fishing-smack
Sketches in the landscape's only lack.
Its blind of mat, diminished, outward blown.
One last goose wings on its way alone:
A flick of ink against the silken sky,
Gone with the echo from a far high cry . . . . .

Wu Tao-tzŭ:

"A lone goose and a lone sail depart;
They do not leave the shore, they leave the heart."

Haiku Translations

from A Net of Fireflies *and* A Chime of Wind-bells *and unpublished typescripts*

SPRING

NOBODY
The long spring day: before and after reach
The footprints left along the sandy beach.

– Shiki

FROM A HILLSIDE
The rice-fields spread their flooded terracing
Of mirrors: segments in a beetle's wing.

– Hô-ô

SOWN WITH GOLD
How far these fields of flowering mustard run:
East to the moonrise, west to the setting sun!

– Buson

TRANSMIGRATION
Lighting one candle with another's flame
At dusk in spring – the same, yet not the same.

– Buson

THE BOOK-BROWSER
An open shop with picture-books in rows,
On each a paperweight: the spring wind blows.

– Kitô

AT THE CARPENTER'S SHOP
A chase of shavings which the plane has stripped
Runs down the lane, like cursive script.

– Anon

AT THE CHINESE WINDOW
The pear-tree blossoming in the moonlit night,
A lady reads her letter by its light.

– Buson

THE SPRING SEA
All day, with gently undulating swell,
The spring sea rose and fell, and rose and fell ...

– Buson

AND SO
And so the spring buds burst, and so I gaze,
And so the blossoms fall, and so my days ...

– Onitsura

ECSTASY
In high detachment from all earthly things
Above the grassland, how the skylark sings!

– Bashô

SUMMER

VIGOROUS STOCK
Red cotton carp, swimming against the air
Over a farmer's roof: ten sons live there.

– Hô-ô

THE NOON CONVOLVULUS
Ah! It will never wash its face of blue
In dew of morning or in evening dew.

– Yayu

AFTER THE HEAT
A moonlit evening: here beside the pool,
Stripped to the waist, a snail enjoys the cool.

– Issa

KYOTO IN SUMMER
Cooling on Sanjô Bridge as evening fades,
A thousand hands are on the balustrades.

– Kikaku

A CHANGE OF SERVANTS
Umbrella in hand, the housemaid due to leave
Stands gazing out: a rainy summer's eve.

– Kyoroku

THE REPLACEMENT
The new maid says: "My name is Flora, sir."
Alas! A crippled flower: no name for her.

– Sôseki

WIND, STEAM, AND SPEED
As wind-waves race across the rice field's sea,
Steam sweeps over my bowl of clear green tea.

– Hô-ô

NOCTURNE
Where is the moon? Engulfed in clouds once more.
The bell lies sunken on the deep sea-floor.

– Bashô

MORNING SERVICE
While nuns intone within the upstairs hall,
Through tall bamboo outside the raindrops fall.

– Hô-ô

THE HOUR-GLASS
The colts with frisky vigour scour the plain,
Whose sandstone cliff is crumbling, grain by grain.

– Tôhô

INTERIOR VISTAS
Hot-spring hotel: down every corridor,
Mountains in summer green abruptly soar.

– Shiki

THE OLD FOLLY
The octopus, while summer moonshine streams
Into the trap, enjoys its fleeting dreams.

– Bashô

IN THE PICTURE
Over the summer moor my horse would stroll:
I find myself inside a landscape roll.

– Bashô

WAYFARERS
Across the summer grassland, bent in waves,
Passes a single file of pilgrim-staves.

– Ishû

FRIGHTENED DELIGHT
A sudden downpour! Thunderclouds are cracking!
And round the farmhouse all the ducks run, quacking!

– Kikaku

ANOTHER DAY, ANOTHER WAY
Between the barley's bending ears of grain,
The path has narrowed since the heavy rain.

– Jôsô

WANDERER FROM THE WORLD
Deepen, O cuckoo in the wood, my mood
Of mutability, my solitude ...

– Bashô

SATORI
I bowed before the Buddha, now obscure,
Now bright with lightning, on the stormy moor.

– Kakei

AUTUMN

THE BLUE FLOWER
A flower unknown to bird or butterfly
Opens its petals: Ah, the autumn sky!

– Bashô

Stewart's note: For most of the summer, the sky in Japan is overcast with hot grey cloud, and only with the arrival of autumn does the blue sky reappear.

INITIAL CHILL
Autumn has dawned: bare feet that step abroad
First feel it on the washed veranda-board.

– Ishû

SQUARE, TRIANGLE, AND CIRCLE
Beneath the bed's mosquito-net, I tie
One corner up: the harvest moon is high.

– Chiyo

ON THE DEATH OF THE POET ISSHÔ
Shake, O desolate grave-mound, shake!
My wail of mourning is the autumn's headlong gale!

– Bashô

CHAIN-MAIL
A chestnut dropped in. A goldfish rose to drink.
Their widening rings of water interlink.

– Kijiro

LAST POEM
Though on a journey I have fallen ill,
My dreams on withered moorland wander still.

– Bashô

COLD MEMENTO
A chill runs through the bedroom where I roam,
Treading by chance upon my dead wife's comb.

– Buson

A DELICIOUS NASHI
Peeling a woody pear, sweet drops run down
The knife that cuts the skin of oil-spot brown.

–Shiki

THE TOMBS AT MUKDEN
The imperial tombs are cold. Through middle air
The sun and moon at one another stare.

– Seishi

A DYING HOUSE
The household standing by the ancestral graves
Are all white-haired, and lean upon their staves.

– Bashô

ON IZUMO CLIFF
Arching above the wild and gloomy sea,
Far out to Sado Isle – the Galaxy!

– Bashô

DOUBLE-EDGED
Into the darkness which a lightning-streak
Has slashed, recedes the wild night-heron's shriek.

– Bashô

EVOCATIVE
Closing the temple's massive double gate,
Its hinges creak: the evening grows late.

– Shiki

THE ROUND DANCE
The tide is out, and dancing in a ring
Five miles around, the sea-hawks on the wing.

– Taigi

ARROWHEAD OF SOUND
Why do the migrant geese relay their cry?
To keep in chevron through the midnight sky.

– Rankô

DESOLATE COURTSHIP
The rutting stag through drizzling autumn mist
Repeats three times his dismal call to tryst.

[Author unknown. Stewart has more than 20 different typed versions for this presumed translation]

WINTER

MONOCHROME AT NIGHTFALL
Only one monk, one woman, left to row
Over the ferry through the falling snow.
– Meisetsu

WHAT THE EAGLE SAW
Snowflakes falling, through the air for miles
Above Shisaku's bay of pine-clad isles.
– Hô-ô

SELF-ABSORBED
Chanting, beating the bowl, from place to place,
I drink the raindrops running down my face.
– Raizan

MORNING RELIEF
How round and straight the hole is that I bore
By leaking in the snow outside my door!
– Issa

UNBIDDEN DUTY
Our simple honest servant: every day
From next door, too, he sweeps the snow away.
– Issa

ON THE NIGHT BEFORE BASHÔ'S DEATH
Tugging from side to side the quilt we share,
Wryly we smile – in spite of our despair.
– Izen

ATTACK AT DAWN
Surrounding it with cries, the wild ducks lay
Siege to the castle-moat at break of day.
– Kyoroku

MIDNIGHT PILGRIMS
Winter Nembutsu: white-robed voices go
Running with bells and lanterns through the snow.
– Ryôta

DOUBT
A light that moved about the gloomy moor,
Entered a cottage: where is now unsure.

– Shiki

EMERGENCY
The rich-robed abbot, dignified and pure,
Surprised at stool amid the withered moor!

– Buson

FOREWARNING
The thatcher on the roof, as raindrops fall,
Turns and looks out to sea: a rising squall.

– Jôsô

THE SEARCH
"Oh, but he must, he must be mine! I know
That lost child's cry for help amid the snow!"

– Arô

LIVING LEGEND
"Now long ago there lived a wicked witch ..."
The withered pampas grass begins to twitch!

– Issa

DESTITUTE
They take their only son, not ten years old,
To give the monks: a night of piercing cold.

– Shiki

HOSPITALITY
Denied a lodging for the night: the row
Of lights from houses standing in the snow.

– Buson

LISTEN
Evening snowfall, with the faint dry crunch
Of straw that stabled horses twitch and munch.

– Kyukoku

from Senryu – Laughing River-willows

ANACHRONISM
Midnight: a young policeman on his beat
Carries a paper lantern down the street.

FOREIGN INTRUSION
Das Rheingold: singing as she swims with ease,
One of the maidens is a Japanese.

Lingering at the Window of an Inn after Midnight

(Part Four of By the Old Walls of Kyoto)

At the very moment when we are moved to utter the Nemhutsu by a firm Faith that our Rebirth in the Pure Land is attained solely by virtue of the unfathomable working of the Amida's Original Vow, we are enabled to share in its benefits that embrace all and forsake none.

– Shinran Shōnin, as quoted by Yuien-bō *from* Letters to Live Poets in his Tannishō

I

At Shirakawa after midnight: still
Leaning upon my upstairs window-sill
In hot oppressive darkness, I despair
Of finding even the faintest breath of air
That might relieve my sweltering distress;
But in this black humidity's excess
No leaf will stir. I wait for sleep in vain,
Though all night long the voice of water rills
In trickles channelled from the Eastern Hills;
Soliloquising in the trench of stone
That runs down every quiet street and lane,
It lulls me with an eloquent undertone,
But not to sleep. In vegetable patches
And flooded plots of rice at side and back,
The frogs that, following their cantor, quack
In flat cacophony till croaking-matches
Rapidly overlap from ditch and drain,
All stop at once; then they start up again.

So by monotonous rote I, too, repeat
Meaningless invocations, bound to fail
For lack of faith; in pious counterfeit
Telling my round of beads to no avail.

Though I recite the words, no help can come
From Jodo, for my obdurate heart is dumb.
How could a mere six syllables, so frail,
Feeble, and ineffectual, that bear
On speech vibrating briefly through the air
The Name of Amida, alone prevail
Against the infernal forces that assail
My sceptic mind with dread, dismay, despair?
How could a mythic Buddha, as the vower
Of some imagined paradise, have power
To rescue me with all my faults, enslaved
By passionate cravings, darker, more depraved,
In this degenerate age when few are saved?
And yet the Pure Land saints and sages claim,
Despite all rational dispute and doubt,
That sole reliance on the Vow and Name
Can bring miraculous Rebirth about,
Whereby my undeserving self inherits
A Bodhisattva's six perfected merits.

Though Mount Daimonji's shaven crest, for lack
Of summer's farewell Bon-fire, still is black,
Looming against the humid starless night,
On wooded slopes infrequent points of light
Amid its sash of vapour come and go,
Shooting aloft a blurred and baffled glow.
The dark mysterious house across the street
Rises two-storeyed from behind its fence,
Sequestered by the darker garden's dense
Bushes and trees. Why is it in retreat
And closely shuttered, even in this heat?
Under its rustic gateway's shingled eaves
The lantern scattering light among the leaves
Has long gone out. Now suddenly upstairs
A panel sliding open in the night
Shows through a papered lattice-work of squares
The dimly amber glow of candlelight.
On shrubberies below, obscured from sight,
Gardenias have unfurled their ivory-white
Petals in whorls, and so profusely bloom
That climbing up the wall beneath my room,
Eddies of warm delicious perfume creep
In at my window, soon inducing sleep . . . .

II

Hours later: in the huge and sultry gloom
A temple bell has tolled with solemn boom:
Its lingering overtones profoundly steep
The distant stillness, where it still resounds.
Again the heavy pole is swung, and pounds
Its tongueless dome, whose bronze vibrations vie
In their sonorous hive, and humming deep
Pervade the hush that holds the earth and sky.
The damp air breathes, lifting the slightest sigh:
A little windbell, hung beneath my eaves,
Instantly rings its lightly trilled reply.

I wake at once out of a lifelong sleep:
My being's inmost solitude receives
A summons that dissolves its sombre spell.
The Heart's reverberations rise and swell
Till lips and tongue spontaneously exclaim:
"Amida Butsu!" – Buddha's sacred Name.
At once I utter my submissive cry:
"Namu Amida Butsu!" in reply.
For while his call commands, I am not here
To doubt or disobey; my thoughts in blind
Confusion can no longer interfere:
Only his Name resounds within the mind,
And he alone is present in his Name.
So, as the Nembutsu is pronounced, I hear
The ineffable Will of Amida behind
The spoken words that momently appear
Out of the soundless Void within, and then
Into its Ground of Silence fade again.
During this call our voices sound the same,
And yet I do not call on him, but he
By my response recalls himself through me.
All his Compassion and Wisdom are enshrined
Within this one Nembutsu. It now bestows
Initiation from the Buddha's Mind
Upon my own, until it overflows
With calm inherent Light. Its sounds endow
My heart with pure and boundless Life that knows
The power of Amida's perfected Vow
To save all beings who but once proclaim

With Single-minded Faith his holy Name.
Amida's mercy need not summon twice:
After his first definitive recall,
No one falls back, no doubts remain at all
Of ultimate Rebirth in Paradise;
For which with many callings I express
My heart's devotion, praise, and thankfulness.

III

Although the stifling summer night is far
Too veiled with haze to show a single star,
Just before dawn above the mountain breaks,
A light inside a lonely farm-house wakes.
The dark by gradual shades has been withdrawn
To leave this delicate-tinted transience
Of clouds above Japan, a touch of dawn
Like rose and white hibiscus-flowers that lay
Their heads upon a weathered brushwood fence.
The dull air freshens, barely felt and brief:
I drink its fugitive coolness with relief.
Since Amida's unspoken Name united
With that dry Nembutsu which my will recited,
The same three words, calling far off and faint
Within my heart, answer its vain complaint;
His gracious consolation is transferred,
Embodied audibly, through every word.
My weakness feels the strange resistless strength
Of Faith flow in, that will prevail at length;
While all my restless questions are resigned,
And silence has absorbed the noisy mind.

Already dawn is whitening into day;
But though the early sky is overcast,
Under the clouds the morning light assures
That in this life, or when its night has passed,
However long confusion still obscures,
The radiance beyond will rise at last.
I slide my window open: from this height
Vistas of silent houses stretch away,
Not yet awakened by the clouded light
Over their undulating roofs of grey.
Shōji, removed to catch the cool, disclose
Interiors, which their paper panels screen,

With mats of rush-straw, neatly kept and clean,
Where the natural brown of woodwork shows
Their airy structure: empty, light, serene.
Kitchen gardens, edged with cypress-thickets
Tied to a trellis-fence of bamboo pickets,
Are still deserted: woven cobwebs lie
Like scraps of dusty muslin spread to dry
Over their hedges. No one comes in sight.
A storage loft with mud walls plastered white
And tiles of glistering grey is glimpsed between
Secluding maple-trees that intervene
With fanning branches, delicately green.
Sunk to the eaves among its shrubs and vines,
One isolated dwelling here declines
Into neglect and age, till almost drowned
By waves of verdure, varied in their greens.
A sagging wicket-gate that hangs aslant
Amid the weary straggling fence, whose scant
Staggering bamboo sticks enclose the ground
Still under cultivation, through its gap
Leads to a little field of aubergines,
Their leaves and fruitage dark with purple sap.
There young green sallows by a ditch surround
The fallow patches ready tilled to plant,
And lightly tousled on the returning tide
Of air, reverse their silver underside,
Fitful as faith that vacillates and veers.
But on the foot-hills, where the pines have laid
Upon their slender tilted colonnade
A roof of needles, thatching it with shade,
The tallest pine has stood a thousand years
Above the wooded ridge, with trunk and bough
As strong and straight and steadfast as the Vow
To save all beings. Looking farther down
Each leafy lane and narrow avenue
To where they end in fields beyond the town,
The rounded Kyoto hills, abruptly blue,
Misty with conifers, close in the view.

JAMES McAULEY 1917–1976

James McAuley grew up in Homebush, a working-class Sydney suburb, and went to the selective Fort Street High School, where he was school captain, and then to the University of Sydney where he took a Master's degree in English and studied philosophy and German. Although his father was born a Catholic, a critical fact alluded to in his autobiographical "Father, Mother, Son", McAuley began life as an Anglican, and was choirmaster and occasional organist at Holy Trinity, Dulwich Hill, Sydney. As an adolescent, reading James Frazer's *The Golden Bough* his "disturbed religious faith finally died ..." He became known at university as a poet and jazz pianist. One of his lecturers, the philosopher John Anderson, influenced McAuley towards classicism in art and anti-communism in politics, but failed to persuade him about a materialist ontology – McAuley was already set on a course which would make him a Catholic convert.

Donald Horne's *The Education of Young Donald* recalled through the memories of the poet and novelist Amy Witting aspects of McAuley's undergraduate days: "[She] rebuilt for me the romance of Jimmy the jazz pianist – at bottle parties, playing 'St James Infirmary', cigarette in mouth, hair falling over his forehead, glass of neat gin on top of the piano ... After a party he had once gone on to the University and played 'Rhapsody in Blue' on the carillon."

In 1942 he became a school teacher in Newcastle, and married. He and his wife were to have a daughter and four sons. His Newcastle days were later recalled in "Self-portrait, Newcastle 1942". In 1943 he was mobilised into the army. It was during this period that he and Harold Stewart (with whom he had been at school and who was a co-worker in a military directorate) concocted the "Ern Malley" hoax poems.

After the war McAuley was a lecturer at the School of Pacific Administration. He made numerous trips to New Guinea where his contact with the mission of Marie Thérèse Noblet was to influence his religious conversion in 1952. In 1956 he became, part-time, the first editor of *Quadrant*, a right-wing intellectual journal. During the 1950s McAuley was active in politics, supporting anti-communist policies.

In 1961 he was appointed a reader in poetry at the University of Tasmania, where he became professor of English, a position he held until his death in 1976. He was less involved in politics while there and his interest in poetry and literature revived. In 1970 he was diagnosed as having bowel cancer, and was cured, leading to his quip "better a semi-colon than a full stop". In 1976, the year of his death, he was diagnosed with liver cancer, an event recorded in his poem "Explicit": "Fully tested I've been found/ Fit to join the underground."

Probably more than any other Australian poet, McAuley had a formally argued philosophical position, which informed his poetry and religious and political views, and which he proselytised as poet, critic and editor and later as teacher. "The Incarnation of Sirius" from his first book, *Under Alderbaran* (1946), expresses his rejection of what he called "the Magian heresy", in which individuals propose millenarian solutions based on personal emotion and intuition. His first book demonstrates an ambivalence towards this heresy: many of the poems, although classical in form, are influenced by German Romanticism, French Symbolism, William Blake and Christopher Brennan – all infected with the Magian heresy.

The heightened excitement of language present in his first book is largely and deliberately missing in his second, *A Vision of Ceremony* (1956). His acceptance of the self-restraint imposed by classical formalism and by his puritan view of Catholicism had become complete. Following *Under Alderbaran*, during his "middle period" of almost two decades, McAuley's poetry was marked by a rigid formalism, and language that is often colourless.

We have chosen two poems from this middle period. "The Death of Chiron" has for its theme Chiron's loss of divinity. An immortal god, he was accidentally wounded by a poisoned arrow of the hero Heracles (Hercules). The pain was so intense, he agreed to give up his divinity and die, with Prometheus taking his place as a god. The replacement of Chiron, the gentle teacher and healer, by the man who stole fire from the gods and gave it to mankind, is a metaphor for the transition from an age of ceremony and traditional values ("the golden calm") into the modern era of individualism and rationalism. Chiron's tale may also be seen as a metaphor for McAuley's loss of faith at that time. Significantly Chiron says finally: "But I must go/ Unreconciled into the dark below." McAuley's search for reconciliation was life-long. The second poem from this period is "New Guinea". McAuley noted: "Archbishop de Boismenu lived in a tiny house at the subcoastal mission station called Florival, at Kubuna in Papua, from which packhorse trains used to depart to supply the mountain stations. He died in 1953."

Surprises of the Sun (1969) marked a second turning point in McAuley's poetry. Although he had earlier expressed the view that life as a literary academic was not compatible with being a poet, he took up a readership in English at the University of Hobart in 1961. This exposure to literature as a full-time profession, and most importantly to students, may have been a catalyst for McAuley's fruitful final period.

Later in his life he seems to have become more sceptical about his search for a tradition that was supposedly independent of personal feeling. In *A Map of Australian Verse* (1975), published a year before his death, McAuley wrote: "It seems that in the last decade I have come full circle back to the kind of poem I began with, but with a greater depth of experience which has brought me closer to fulfilling the persistent desire to write poems that are lucid and mysterious, gracefully simple but full of secrets, faithful to the little one knows and the much one has to feel." Although more spontaneous, and more personal, these later poems do not recapture the striking language and conceptions of his earliest book. Rather, they show, in more muted language what McAuley has referred to as "that exquisitely keen sense of life and its fragility which such experiences [illness] give."

Terra Australis

Voyage within you, on the fabled ocean,
And you will find that Southern Continent,
Quiros' vision – his hidalgo heart
And mythical Australia, where reside
All things in their imagined counterpart.

It is your land of similes: the wattle
Scatters its pollen on the doubting heart;

The flowers are wide-awake; the air gives ease.
There you come home; the magpies call you Jack
And whistle like larrikins at you from the trees.

There too the angophora preaches on the hillsides
With the gestures of Moses; and the white cockatoo,
Perched on his limbs, screams with demoniac pain;
And who shall say on what errand the insolent emu
Walks between morning and night on the edge of the plain?

But northward in valleys of the fiery Goat
Where the sun like a centaur vertically shoots
His raging arrows with unerring aim,
Stand the ecstatic solitary pyres
Of unknown lovers, featureless with flame.

The Incarnation of Sirius

In that age, the great anagram of God
Had bayed the planets from the rounds they trod,
And gathered the fixed stars in a shining nation
Like restless birds that flock before migration.

For the millennial instinct of new flight
Resolved the antinomy that fixed their light;
And, echoing in the troubled soul of Earth,
Quickened a virgin's womb, to bring to birth

What scarce was human: a rude avatar
That glistened with the enclosed wrath of a star.
The woman died in pangs, before she had kissed
The monstrous form of God's antagonist.

But at its showing forth, the poets cried
In a strange tongue; hot mouths prophesied
The coolness of the bloody vintage-drops:
"Let us be drunk at least, when the world stops!"

Anubis-headed, the heresiarch
Sprang to a height, fire-sinewed in the dark,
And his ten fingers, bracketed on high,
Were a blazing candelabrum in the sky.

The desert lion antiphonally roared;
The tiger's sinews quivered like a chord;
Man smelt the blood beneath his brother's skin
And in a loving hate the sword went in.

And then the vision sank, bloody and aborted.
The stars that with rebellion had consorted
Fled back in silence to their former stations.
Over the giant face of dreaming nations

The centuries-thick coverlet was drawn.
Upon the huddled breast Aldebaran
Still glittered with its sad alternate fire:
Blue as of memory, red as of desire.

The Death of Chiron

from "The Hero and the Hydra" 1947–49

The herdboys shout unseen among the rocks;
Autumn grows colder, and they lead their flocks
From the high pastures down into the plain.
To feel the golden calm I have dragged my pain
Outside the cavern mouth, but still inhale
The smell of sweat and sickness, dung and stale.

The wild bees know the time of dearth has come,
And signal the grim rites of harvest home,
When crumpled bodies of the drones are thrust
Out of the hive and fall into the dust.
The year sinks underground, and with it I
Put off divinity and learn to die.

A son of Time no less than Zeus, I chose
To be the friend of centaurs and all those
Who draw a harsh life from this mountain breast.
I tutored many heroes, but loved best
The hardy unheroic simple folk
Who drive their herds and put the ox to yoke.

I taught them spells and simples that could salve
Their peaceful wounds, or help their cows to calve;
Even the village girls would come for charms
To guard against lost love or freckled arms,
Leaving small gifts of honey, eggs, and fruit;
Or sometimes, laughing, would not long dispute

Among the crushed herbs of the cave to measure
What god and beast can bring to country pleasure.
Sometimes in the spring I joined the dance
With hard hooves beating, and the men would prance

In mimic masks to lead the season in;
And what was done those nights was not held sin.

In winter when the owl sat humped with cold
I came down to their firesides and told
Stories of gods and heroes; and often then
Would tell of one who brought down fire to men,
And how, before the Hero sets him free,
Some god must give his immortality

And die: not as the sacred ear of corn
Lies in darkness waiting to be reborn,
But as the dry stalk falls and vanishes.
A dear exchange it seemed – nor did I guess
What Hydra-poisoned arrow, from what bow,
Would send me willing to the shades below.

Heracles, saviour of men, sun-bright defender,
I watched your youth rise to its noon-splendour
Of clear heroic fire; but feared to see
The fitful presage of that insanity
When, blundering in the mind's eclipse, you strike
At shadows, killing friend and child alike.

So Linus died, and Eunomus, then all
Your children; and the darkness yet will fall
On others, as it did on me that day
The odorous wine-casks bred the wild affray
That drove the routed centaurs to my cave;
And I went down to stay your hand and save

The hunted. I saw blind frenzy in your soul
Like shadows wavering in a red-hot coal,
Such as the warriors of Asia feel
And quench their bodies, as men temper steel,
Hissing in the wave. Unchecked you drew
The bowstring taut, and the long arrow flew.

As the devising wasp with darting skill
Thrusts in her sting to paralyse, not kill,
The insect that survives to be the prey
Of her hatched grub when she has flown away,
So did attentive Fate spring forth to guide
The venomed stroke, then vanish satisfied.

Now when the shepherds bring their summer flocks
To the high pasture-grounds among the rocks,

They are afraid to come near where I lie.
There is no herb or spell can purify
The inherent Hydra; why should I not consent
To free the Titan from his banishment?

Never was earth more radiant than in this
Last autumn gold that I take down to Dis.
I have loved the earth alone, and had no will
To change the measures of its good and ill;
Others give laws and blame, and sit above,
But there were no conditions in my love.

Men will bewail my fate when I am gone
And in it see the pattern of their own;
Their poisoned instinct writhes incurable
Within the ancient cave of touch and smell;
They feel the Hydra-taint of guilty care
Rankle their joy and bring them to despair.

But in exchange, instead of plaited straw,
The heavy golden crown of art and law
Will press upon their brows, and in their hand
The imperial builder's dream of stone will stand;
And on the rustic year they will impose
New time that does not vary as it flows.

Yet their Promethean victories will rise
But as the smoke of nature's sacrifice
Within, without. Everywhere they tread
The beasts will sicken and the desert spread.
Their baffled hero in his turn will die
Howling in envenomed agony.

I have but little skill of forward sight,
Nor have I overheard in the still night,
As once the Titan did, the singing Fates:
The spirit alone can judge what it creates
And see it to the end. But I must go
Unreconciled into the dark below.

New Guinea

In memory of Archbishop Alain de Boismenu, M.S.C.

Bird-shaped island, with secretive bird-voices,
Land of apocalypse, where the earth dances,

The mountains speak, the doors of the spirit open,
And men are shaken by obscure trances.

The forest-odours, insects, clouds and fountains
Are like the figures of my inmost dream,
Vibrant with untellable recognition;
A wordless revelation is their theme.

The stranger is engulfed in those high valleys,
Where mists of morning linger like the breath
Of Wisdom moving on our specular darkness.
Regions of prayer, of solitude, and of death!

Life holds its shape in the modes of dance and music,
The hands of craftsmen trace its patternings;
But stains of blood, and evil spirits, lurk
Like cockroaches in the interstices of things.

We in that land begin our rule in courage,
The seal of peace gives warrant to intrusion;
But then our grin of emptiness breaks the skin,
Formless dishonour spreads its proud confusion.

Whence that deep longing for an exorcizer,
For Christ descending as a thaumaturge
Into his saints, as formerly in the desert,
Warring with demons on the outer verge.

Only by this can life become authentic,
Configured henceforth in eternal mode:
Splendour, simplicity, joy – such as were seen
In one who now rests by his mountain road.

Father, Mother, Son

From the domed head the defeated eyes peer out,
Furtive with unsaid things of a lifetime, that now
Cannot be said by that stiff half-stricken mouth
Whose words come hoarse and slurred, though the mind is sound.

To have to be washed, and fed by hand, and turned
This way and that way by the cheerful nurses,
Who joke, and are sorry for him, and tired of him:
All that is not the worst paralysis.

For fifty years this one thread – he has held
One gold thread of the vesture: he has said
Hail, holy Queen, slightly wrong, each night in secret.

But his wife, and now a lifetime, stand between:

She guards him from his peace. Her love asks only
That in the end he must not seem to disown
Their terms of plighted troth. So he will make
For ever the same choice that he has made –

Unless that gold thread hold, invisibly.
I stand at the bed's foot, helpless like him;
Thinking of legendary Seth who made
A journey back to Paradise, to gain

The oil of mercy for his dying father.
But here three people smile, and, locked apart,
Prove by relatedness that cannot touch
Our sad geometry of family love.

One Tuesday in Summer

That sultry afternoon the world went strange.
Under a violet and leaden bruise
The air was filled with sinister yellow light;
Trees, houses, grass took on unnatural hues.

Thunder rolled near. The intensity grew and grew
Like doom itself with lightnings on its face.
And Mr Pitt, the grocer's order-man,
Who made his call on Tuesdays at our place,

Said to my mother, looking at the sky,
"You'd think the ending of the world had come."
A leathern little man, with bicycle-clips
Around his ankles, doing our weekly sum,

He too looked strange in that uncanny light;
As in the Bible ordinary men
Turn out to be angelic messengers,
Pronouncing the Lord's judgments why and when.

I watched the scurry of the small black ants
That sensed the storm. What Mr Pitt had said
I didn't quite believe, or disbelieve;
But still the words had got into my head,

For nothing less seemed worthy of the scene.
The darkening imminence hung on and on,
Till suddenly, with lightning-stroke and rain,
Apocalypse exploded, and was gone.

By nightfall things had their familiar look.
But I had seen the world stand in dismay
Under the aspect of another meaning
That rain or time would hardly wash away.

Because

My father and my mother never quarrelled.
They were united in a kind of love
As daily as the Sydney Morning Herald,
Rather than like the eagle or the dove.

I never saw them casually touch,
Or show a moment's joy in one another.
Why should this matter to me now so much?
I think it bore more hardly on my mother,

Who had more generous feeling to express.
My father had dammed up his Irish blood
Against all drinking praying fecklessness,
And stiffened into stone and creaking wood.

His lips would make a switching sound, as though
Spontaneous impulse must be kept at bay.
That it was mainly weakness I see now,
But then my feelings curled back in dismay.

Small things can pit the memory like a cyst:
Having seen other fathers greet their sons,
I put my childish face up to be kissed
After an absence. The rebuff still stuns

My blood. The poor man's curt embarrassment
At such a delicate proffer of affection
Cut like a saw. But home the lesson went:
My tenderness thenceforth escaped detection.

My mother sang *Because*, and *Annie Laurie*,
White Wings, and other songs; her voice was sweet.
I never gave enough, and I am sorry;
But we were all closed in the same defeat.

People do what they can; they were good people,
They cared for us and loved us. Once they stood
Tall in my childhood as the school, the steeple.
How can I judge without ingratitude?

Judgment is simply trying to reject
A part of what we are because it hurts.
The living cannot call the dead collect:
They won't accept the charge, and it reverts.

It's my own judgment day that I draw near,
Descending in the past, without a clue,
Down to that central deadness: the despair
Older than any hope I ever knew.

Self-portrait, Newcastle 1942

First day, by the open window,
He sits at a table to write,
And watches the coal-dust settle
Black on the paper's white.

Years of breathing this grime
Show black in the lungs of the dead
When autopsies are done;
So at least it is said.

Sunset over the steelworks
Bleeds a long rubric of war;
He thinks he knows, but doesn't,
The black print of the score.

He, like that sullied paper,
Has acquired no meaning yet.
He goes for long walks at night,
Or drinks with people he's met.

In sleeping panic he shatters
The glass of a window-pane.
What will he do with his life?
Jump three storeys down in the rain?

Something – guilt, tension, or outrage –
Keeps coming in nightmare shape.
Screams often startle the house:
He leaps up blind to escape.

By day he teaches the dullest
Intermediate class;
He gets on well with them, knowing
He too has a test to pass.

With friends he talks anarchism,
The philosophical kind,
But *Briefe an einen jungen*
Dichter speaks close to his mind.

In The Huon Valley

Propped boughs are heavy with apples,
Springtime quite forgotten.
Pears ripen yellow. The wasp
Knows where windfalls lie rotten.

Juices grow rich with sun.
These autumn days are still:
The glassy river reflects
Elm-gold up the hill,

And big white plumes of rushes.
Life is full of returns;
It isn't true that one never
Profits, never learns:

Something is gathered in,
Worth the lifting and stacking;
Apples roll through the graders,
The sheds are noisy with packing.

Explicit

So the word has come at last:
The argument of arms is past.
Fully tested I've been found
Fit to join the underground.

No worse age has ever been –
Murderous, lying, and obscene;
Devils worked while gods connived:
Somehow the human has survived.

Why these horrors must be so
I never could pretend to know:
It isn't I, dear Lord, who can
Justify your ways to man.

Soon I'll understand it all,
Or cease to wonder: so my small
Spark will blaze intensely bright,
Or go out in an endless night.

Welcome now to bread and wine:
Creature comfort, heavenly sign.
Winter will grow dark and cold
Before the wattle turns to gold.

ANNE ELDER 1918–1976

Anne Elder was born in Auckland, New Zealand, the daughter of an Australian insurance-manager. She moved with her parents to Melbourne in 1921. She was dux and a prefect of St Catherine's School for Girls, Toorak, and edited the school magazine. She became a ballet dancer and was a foundation member and soloist with the Borovansky Ballet during World War II. In 1940 she married a Melbourne solicitor and they had two children. In 1966 she began to publish her poetry and in 1968 she had her first heart attack. Her health declined in later years.

"Horse and Mare" is from her first book *For the Record* (1972). The other poems here are from her posthumously published *Crazy Woman* (1976). Elder said: "I detest obscure, phantasist poetry, so I have aimed at lucidity without being mundane." This tension between lucidity and avoiding the mundane is present in much of her work. An example is the poem "Crazy Woman". The poet presents herself as an older woman lured by Euterpe, the muse of lyric poetry – probably a statue under a tree – in, one assumes, the Melbourne Botanical Gardens. She is alarmed when a foreign man sits next to her and starts admiring her aged knee. A gardener rescues her, they have a mad conversation, and he gives her a fern. Clutching this, she encounters a pair of lovers on the path. This simple story could have been a banal narrative of an event in an older woman's day. Elder entices the reader into experiencing her fears and hopes by delicate self-mockery, cleverly elevating her modest adventures into a dangerous and strange odyssey. "Singers of Renown" refers to a radio program which continued to be presented by John Cargher every Saturday for 42 years (long after Elder herself had died).

Tina Kane, for whose mother the poem "Crazy Woman" was written, recalls summer holidays shared by her mother's and Anne Elder's family at Summerlands on Philip Island: "Anne was very beautiful (exotic) with high cheek bones and eyes like a cat. I found her a tad remote. My strongest memory of her was dancing on the beach … and she was fantastic, doing grand jetés and arabesques down the length of the deserted shore."

Horse and Mare

Last week was horizontal snow driven.
Today the month turns seasonably and surely to gold.
A milky dusk calls them downhill by habit; slow
they drift in to the leaning thorn and stand,
solids unmoved by the expectation of wind,
where the old shed ribbed like a ruined boat
spells to them shelter, a hulk in the night.

In differing bulk and shape they gloom.
Molly, the barrel of all stock ponies,
sway-back, cantankerous, letting her hair go
moorland and frizzled with age. Free Kiss
who is Freaky to you and high-handed with me
drops his swan neck with a touch of Arab,
lending her an undemanding by-the-way munch
of companionship, his gelded wistfulness.

Noiseless on sweetening turf they pass
the darkening windowed room and know
me not, nor my envy of their grace and peace
beyond my firelight and, in the neutral wash
of mist before the moon erupts,
their matching equine stance in sexlessness.

In comfort or in hardship night is borne.
They ease one hoof. An elbowed branch
shifts to them. In their side no thorn.

Crazy Woman

On the first day of autumn Euterpe called to me:
I am the Muse that sits musing under the lyric tree
plucking and plaiting the thoughtful branches
deep in the heart of the public gardens
where I first saw you, a queer child with your grandfather.
It is nice here, you should be with me.
We can sit alone.
I will pluck you and suck you the fruit for a serious poem.

So I went, and sure enough it was nice;
the first leaf already fallen,
the last white daisy still crawling
in bluish dewy grass, a pair of birds
black-white and neat, no longer matey, but still friendly,
unsurprised at my feet.
But another madwoman came by
and pecked me with her smile. Aren't they tame
she said, Yes I said, What's their name
she said, A couple called Magpie Lark I said,
built last spring, now semi-detatched, it's autumn,
and she said fancy, what a shame.

I detached myself to the perfect seclusion
of the remembered grotto, the only intrusion

a fountaining cherubic boy, his little bronze spout
of Eros still delightful as when my grandfather
took pains not to point it out.
But a chap came by who was foreign.
You are zitting in vot beautiful zun, he said,
yes I said abstractedly (I was writing a serious poem)
and he went and sat tactfully
on the next seat. How lonely can you get
to be looking so slantingly
at my withering crossed knee.

For security I became engaged to the gardener
in passionately horticultural conversation
of considerable duration,
even to how the nights in the gardens of Spain
are enlivened with runnels and babbles
of conversational water, and he agreed with me
that the Spanish are gardeners of great subtlety.
What's that, I said, like a fern dotted with stars?
Oh that, that's a thing we've had for years
for which no municipal gardener cares,
but if you would like it, come into the shrubbery
and I will give you a good root
he said, with subtlety I thought,
and I jumped at it
and went off with my fern dripping good fruitful earth
down the mysterious path.

But along the misty vistas of Arcady
behold young lovers approaching, she
not beautiful but beautifully shy,
he with the true, the demented languishing eye,
swinging along wonderfully lonely
hand in hand worlds apart
by the width of the path
so that I met them where they joined, they dropped hands
for the Weird Woman gathering ferns and simples
and muttering God keep you under her breath
like a gipsy, meaning no harm.

I debated how to say it aloud,
to their alarm. Before our death
there is much to communicate that goes by the board
because it is thought unusual indeed crazy

to gather the fallen leaf and the daisy,
the magpie lark and the private lark
in the public park,
the eternal cherubic spout, the nakedness
and lovingness of loneliness
into the right word
to bless our other selves in the name of the Lord.

With coupled hands and crooked stare
and pointed smile they dance around
the poor old crazy head-in-air,
the poet, who has first to find
the spangled fern, the gift, then grow it
bedded in the heart's ground.

Singers of Renown

I listen each week to the discs
on radio, superlative voices
busting their boilers to bring us
nostalgia. Being a woman, it is the tenors
and baritones who afford me
most mellifluous pain
at the heart. Standing tonight at the door
I look over evening fields and listen
to someone's immortal heartache.
What more
can I do but watch an eagle wheeling
into night and write
this dry little verse, collapsing
the whole sexuality of men and women
via the voice into one ragged stanza.

Still, it is done, and I can go to the kitchen
having loved my little bit with a pen
and unaccompanied. Catharsis
makes bearable the frying of brains.
I thank you,
plump amorous tenor,
I thank you with tender stewed plums.

"ERN MALLEY" 1918–1943

The American poet and critic, and editor of *The Oxford Book of American Poetry* (2006), David Lehman, has described the Ern Malley hoax as "[t]he greatest literary hoax of the twentieth century".

In October 1943 James McAuley and Harold Stewart concocted in one afternoon and evening, at their army barracks in Melbourne, sixteen poems supposedly written by a garage mechanic, who had died at the Keatsian age of 25. Malley's poems were "discovered" by his sister Ethel, who sent them to the editor of *Angry Penguins*, the 22-year old Max Harris, and they were duly printed in the Autumn 1944 edition after they were considered by Harris and his partners, John and Sunday Reed and the painter Sidney Nolan. Ethel appears now in her correspondence as a slyly comic creation worthy of Barry Humphries. *Angry Penguins* was detested by the hoaxers because of the free-associational rhetoric and meaninglessness of the work it promoted. In playing their trick on the magazine, McAuley and Stewart made use of a dictionary, a collected Shakespeare, a rhyming manual, a book of quotations, and a report on the control of mosquitoes by draining swamps, from which they took lines and words at random. So as to be sure that the hoax worked, the Malley poems contain some obviously striking lines, but they are for the most part hyperbole and deliberate bathos. Each author was careful to interrupt the other's stream of consciousness, so that no unintended "profundity" could be attributed to them, and all of the poems are ultimately absurd.

Nevertheless, the brilliance of the fragments and the sheer exuberance of the best of the Ern Malley poems – that McAuley and Stewart were in a high state of excitement as they assembled them at breakneck speed is palpable – is such that they justify their inclusion in an anthology. As well, although this was accidental, technically McAuley and Stewart did something new for the time. Eliot's *Waste Land* had previously used the technique of splicing together fragments of songs, ordinary speech and other writers' phrases, but Ern Malley took this technique to an extreme. The authors' decision to interrupt each other (the "interpolations" referred to in "Documentary Film"), to use invented quotations, to deceive and to simultaneously admit in the poems that this was what they were doing, and their use of parataxis, resulted in a voice that was strikingly fractured and unique.

The hoax was artfully conducted with "Ethel" initially posting to Harris just two of Ern's poems, including "Dürer: Innsbruck". "He was very ill in the months before his death last July and it may have affected his outlook", she wrote. The letter was accompanied by a tuppence-halfpenny stamp "for reply". The other poems were submitted, together with Ern's detailed life history, after Harris asked to see more. When Harris was telephoned by the Sydney *Sun* at 3 a.m. in June 1944 with the startling news that Ern Malley was a hoax, his response "in a state of semi-somnolence" was: "'The myth is sometimes greater than its creator." Although this was the year of the Normandy invasion, the hoax attracted worldwide attention and was picked up in the London *Times* and the American news magazine *Time*.

One bizarre outcome was that Harris was charged under the Police Offences Act by a member of the South Australian police force with the Nabokovian name of Detective Vogelsang (German for bird-song) who argued that although he could not understand the poems' meaning, he believed some parts of them were obscene. Harris was found guilty, and was fined £5 with the alternative of twelve weeks in gaol.

The Ern Malley poems have continued to attract admirers in the subsequent half century. In 1960 the poet and broadcaster John Thompson interviewed some of the protagonists for an Australian Broadcasting Commission radio programme. None of them had changed their mind (although Harris himself had in the meantime become a more conventional poet). Sidney Nolan, by 1960 Australia's most celebrated painter, asserted the correctness of his original opinion: "I think they gave a grace and a new thing to Australian poetry ... Well, I liked a number of them. There is one here particularly which I like. It's called 'Young Price of Tyre' ... This seems to me a beautiful example of the English language being renewed out of Australia ... And 'The new men are cool as spreading fern' is, I think, one of the most beautiful Australian images that I've ever read."

The international reputation of the Ern Malley poems has continued. David Lehman points out: "Ern Malley has always had an honored place among the poets of the New York School. Kenneth Koch printed two Malley poems, 'Boult to Marina' and 'Sybilline,' in the 'collaborations' issue of *Locus Solus*, the avant-garde literary magazine, in 1961. At Columbia University in 1968, Koch introduced his writing students to Malley's poetry, suggesting that the hoaxer's antics were well worth imitating not for purposes of polemic but for legitimate poetic ends. In 1976 John Ashbery asked his MFA students at Brooklyn College to compare Malley's 'Sweet William' to one of Geoffrey Hill's *Mercian Hymns*. Which did they think was the genuine article? (The students were divided.) Ashbery's point – and it seems to be Malley's point – is that intentions may be irrelevant to results, that genuineness in literature may not depend on authorial sincerity, and that our ideas about good and bad, real and fake, are, or ought to be, in flux."

It is sometimes argued that the Ern Malley hoax was a setback for the Modernist movement in Australian poetry, delaying the arrival of modernism for a generation. If there is a generation *manqué* of *Angry Penguin* poets who were nipped in the bud, it is difficult to identify them apart from a couple of young poets who died in World War II and are now almost entirely forgotten. The poetry of only two of the *Angry Penguin* poets has continued to be very modestly anthologised. These are Harris himself and Geoffrey Dutton. The best poems to appear in the *Angry Penguins* magazine were Ern Malley's.

Dürer: Innsbruck, 1495

I had often, cowled in the slumberous heavy air,
Closed my inanimate lids to find it real,
As I knew it would be, the colourful spires
And painted roofs, the high snows glimpsed at the back,
All reversed in the quiet reflecting waters –
Not knowing then that Dürer perceived it too.
Now I find that once more I have shrunk
To an interloper, robber of dead men's dream.
I had read in books that art is not easy

But no one warned that the mind repeats
In its ignorance the vision of others. I am still
The black swan of trespass on alien waters.

Documentary Film

Innumerable the images
The register of birth and dying
Under the carved rococo porch
The Tigris – Venice – Melbourne – the Ch'en Plain –
And the sound track like a trail of saliva.
Dürer:
"Samson killing the Lion" 1498
Thumbs twisting the great snarl of the beast's mouth
Tail thrashing the air of disturbed swallows
That fly to the castle on the abraded hill
London:
Samson that great city, his anatomy on fire
Grasping with gnarled hands at the mad wasps
Yet while his bearded rage survives contriving
An entelechy of clouds and trumpets.
There have been interpolations, false syndromes
Like a rivet through the hand
Such deliberate suppressions of crisis as
Footscray:
The slant sun now descending
Upon the montage of the desecrate womb
Opened like a drain.
The young men aspire
Like departing souls from leaking roofs
And fractured imploring windows to
(All must be synchronized, the jagged
Quartz of vision with the asphalt of human speech)
Java:
The elephant motifs contorted on admonitory walls,
The subtle nagas that raise the cobra hood
And hiss in the white masterful face.
What are these mirk channels of the flesh
That now sweep me from
The blood-dripping hirsute maw of night's other temple
Down through the helpless row of bonzes
Till peace suddenly comes:
Adonai:

The solemn symphony of angels lighting
My steps with music, o consolations!
Palms!
O far shore, target and shield that I now
Desire beyond these terrestrial commitments.

Culture as Exhibit

"Swamps, marshes, borrow-pits and other
Areas of stagnant water serve
As breeding grounds ..." Now
Have I found you, my Anopheles!
(There is a meaning for the circumspect)
Come, we will dance sedate quadrilles,
A pallid polka or a yelping shimmy
Over these sunken sodden breeding-grounds!
We will be wraiths and wreaths of tissue paper
To clog the Town Council in their plans.
Culture, forsooth! Albert, get my gun.

I have been noted in the reading-rooms
As a borer of calf-bound volumes
Full of scandals at the Court. (Milord
Had his hand upon that snowy globe
Milady Lucy's sinister breast . .) Attendants
Have peered me over while I chewed
Back-numbers of Florentine gazettes
(Knowst not, my Lucia, that he
Who has caparisoned a nun dies
With his twankydillo at the ready? . .)
But in all of this I got no culture till
I read a little pamphlet on my thighs
Entitled: "Friction as a Social Process."
What?
Look, my Anopheles,
See how the floor of Heav'n is thick
Inlaid with patines of etcetera . .
Sting them, sting them, my Anopheles.

Colloquy with John Keats

"And the Lord destroyeth the imagination of all them that had not the truth with them." (Odes of Solomon 2418).

I have been bitter with you, my brother,
Remembering that saying of Lenin when the shadow
Was already on his face: "The emotions are not skilled workers!"
Yet we are as the double almond concealed in one shell.
I have mistrusted your apodictic strength
Saying always: Yet why did you not finish Hyperion?
But now I have learned not to curtail
What was in you the valency of speech
The bond of molecular utterance.

I have arranged the interstellar zodiac
With flowers on the Goat's horn, and curious
Markings on the back of the Crab. I have lain
With the Lion, not with the Virgin, and become
He that discovers meanings.

Now in your honour Keats, I spin
The loaded Zodiac with my left hand
As the man at the fair revolves
His coloured deceitful board. Together
We lean over that whirl of
Beasts, flowers, images and men
Until it stops . . Look! my number is up!
Like you I sought at first for Beauty
And then, in disgust, returned
As did you to the locus of sensation
And not till then did my voice build crenellated towers
Of an enteric substance in the air.
Then first I learned to speak clear; then through my turrets
Pealed that Great Bourdon which men have ignored.

CODA

We have lived as ectoplasm
The hand that would clutch
Our substance finds that his rude touch
Runs through him a frightful spasm
And hurls him back against the opposite wall.

Le Petit Testament

In the twenty-fifth year of my age
I find myself to be a dromedary
That has run short of water between
One oasis and the next mirage
And having despaired of ever
Making my obsessions intelligible
I am content at last to be
The sole clerk of my metamorphoses.
Begin here:

In the year 1943
I resigned to the living all collateral images
Reserving to myself a man's
Inalienable right to be sad
At his own funeral.
(Here the peacock blinks the eyes
of his multipennate tail.)
In the same year
I said to my love (who is living)
Dear we shall never be that bird
Perched on the sole Arabian Tree
Not having learnt in our green age to forget
The sins that flow between the hands and feet
(Here the Tree weeps gum tears
Which are also real: I tell you
These things are real)
So, I forced a parting
Scrubbing my few dingy words to brightness.

Where I have lived
The bed-bug sleeps in the seam, the cockroach
Inhabits the crack and the careful spider
Spins his aphorisms in the corner.
I have heard them shout in the streets
The chiliasms of the Socialist Reich
And in the magazines I have read
The Popular Front-to-Back.
But where I have lived
Spain weeps in the gutters of Footscray
Guernica is the ticking of the clock
The nightmare has become real, not as belief
But in the scrub-typhus of Mubo.

It is something to be at last speaking
Though in this No-Man's-language appropriate
Only to No-Man's-Land.
Set this down too:
I have pursued rhyme, image, and metre,
Known all the clefts in which the foot may stick,
Stumbled often, stammered,
But in time the fading voice grows wise
And seizing the co-ordinate of all existence
Traces the inevitable graph
And in conclusion:
There is a moment when the pelvis
Explodes like a grenade. I
Who have lived in the shadow that each act
Casts on the next act now emerge
As loyal as the thistle that in session
Puffs its full seed upon the indicative air.
I have split the infinitive. Beyond is anything.

ROSEMARY DOBSON 1920–

Born in Sydney, Rosemary Dobson, a grand-daughter of the English poet Austin Dobson, was educated as a boarder at the Frensham Girls' School, on the southern tablelands of New South Wales, where her mother became housemistress, after being widowed (when Dobson was five) and left in straitened circumstances. After leaving school, Dobson studied art, and in her early twenties joined the editorial department of the publisher Angus & Robertson. In 1952 she married Alec Bolton, who became from 1966 to 1971 the London editor for Angus & Robertson. During this period she travelled in Europe, deepening her appreciation of Renaissance painting, which has been important to much of her work as a poet. In 1972 she and her husband moved to Canberra, where her husband became director of publications at the National Library of Australia; he died in 1996, and she continues to live in that city.

Rosemary Dobson has published thirteen volumes of poetry, including selected and collected editions. Five of the poems selected here are about paintings. A. D. Hope recalled in *Quadrant* (vol. 16, no. 4, 1972), that when he first reviewed the book from which these poems come (*Child with a Cockatoo* (1955)) he "took the poet severely to task for basing her poems so often on other works of art." The problem with art works about other art is, he says, that: "we feel they are parasitic growths". However looking back on this review, he changed his mind, and said "the least I can do is now confess its inadequacy".

The best response to Hope's early criticism is some comments by Dobson herself. Writing about "The Raising of the Dead", she explained: "The starting point of the poem for me was a painting of the Siennese school called 'S. Bernadino Resuscitates a Dead Child', and yet there is very little of the painting in the poem except the rather primitive simplicity of it, the wonder of the onlookers ... In fact the painting just started the movement of the poem in my mind ... at one level, the poem is about a painting, even though the painting is largely an imagined one. At another level the poem is about miracles; at another about angels and how humans may envy them their freedom to pass from one world to another while they are themselves bound in their own limited time and space ... The poem has yet another meaning which for me is the most important one ... The young man who has been raised to life from death has my pity since, because he has come to life in a painting, he cannot die again and return to the Paradise he has glimpsed, but must stay alive for ever."

In the introduction to her *Selected Poems* (1973) Dobson wrote: "I hope it will be perceived that the poems presented here are part of a search for something only fugitively glimpsed; a state of grace which one once knew, or imagined, or from which one was turned away ... a doomed but urgent wish to express the inexpressible."

Country Press

Under the dusty print of hobnailed boot,
Strewn on the floor the papers still assert
In ornamental gothic, swash italics
And bands of printer's flowers (traditional)
Mixed in a riot of typographic fancy,
This is the *Western Star*, the Farmer's Guide,
The Voice of Progress for the Nyngle District.
Page-proofs of double-spread with running headlines
Paper the walls, and sets of cigarette-cards
Where pouter-bosomed showgirls still display
The charms that dazzled in the nineteen hundreds.
Through gaping slats
Latticed with sun the ivy tendrils fall
Twining the disused platen thrust away
Under a pall of dust in nineteen-twenty.
Draw up a chair, sit down. Just shift the galleys.
You say you have a notice? There's no one dies
But what we know about it. Births, deaths and marriages,
Council reports, wool prices, river-heights,
The itinerant poem and the classified ads –
They all come homewards to the *Western Star*.
Joe's our type-setter. Meet Joe Burrell. Joe's
A promising lad – and Joe, near forty-seven,
Peers from a tennis-shade and, smiling vaguely,
Completes the headline for the Baptist Social.
The dance, the smoke-oh, and the children's picnic
Down by the river-flats beneath the willows

They all come homewards and Joe sets them all,
Between the morning and the mid-day schooner.
Oh, *Western Star* that bringest all to fold,
The yarding sales, the champion shorthorn bull,
And Williams' pain-relieving liniment,
When I shall die
Set me up close against my fellow-men,
Cheer that cold column headed "Deaths" with flowers,
Or mix me up with Births and Marriages;
Surround the tragic statement of my death
With euchre-drives and good-times-had-by-all
That, with these warm concomitants of life
Jostled and cheered, in lower-case italics
I shall go homewards in the *Western Star.*

The Raising of the Dead

Moved by the miracles of saints –
The child restored, the leper healed –
Through the black plumes of death I watch
The intervening angels step
Down the blue sky, across the field.

To see the young man raised to life,
The soul return to shuttered eyes
They crowd in faded radiance
Where, underneath an orange-tree,
So inexplicably he lies.

They lift the hand left limp by death
And stir the stiffly painted gown,
The wind of life is on their lips,
The holy gold about their heads:
Thus has the painter set them down.

Angels are free to come and go –
My pity for the youth who lies
These seven centuries at least
Returned to Life; who once had caught
A wink, a glimpse, of Paradise.

The Bystander

I am the one who looks the other way,
In any painting you may see me stand

Rapt at the sky, a bird, an angel's wing,
While others kneel. present the myrrh, receive
The benediction from the radiant hand.

I hold the horses while the knights dismount
And draw their swords to fight the battle out;
Or else in dim perspective you may see
My distant figure on the mountain road
When in the plains the hosts are put to rout.

I am the silly soul who looks too late,
The dullard dreaming, second from the right.
I hang upon the crowd, but do not mark
(Cap over eyes) the slaughtered Innocents,
Or Icarus, his downward-plunging flight.

Once in a Garden – back view only there –
How well the painter placed me, stroke on stroke,
Yet scarcely seen: among the flowers and grass –
I heard a voice say, "Eat," and would have turned –
I often wonder who it was that spoke.

Detail from an Annunciation by Crivelli

My sisters played beyond the doorway,
My mother bade me hush and go,
I did not think that any saw me
I went so still on tip of toe.

My sisters played beneath the olives,
They called like birds from tree to tree;
I climbed the stairs and through the archway
Looked where no one else could see.

My hair hung straight beneath my cap,
My dress hung down in fold on fold,
And when the painter filled it in
He edged it round with strokes of gold.

My mother thought I played without,
My sisters thought I stayed within,
Only the painter saw me hide –
His brush held upwards to begin.

I saw the Dove, I saw the Lady
Cross her hands upon her breast.

I heard a music, and a shining
Came upon my eyes to rest.

I am twelve, but I was eight then:
No one listens when I tell –
Least of all my little sisters –
What I saw and what befell.

Look upon the painter's picture,
See, he shows you where I hid,
What I saw, and how I listened –
You believe me that I did?

The Martyrdom of Saint Sebastian

My scarlet coat lies on the ground.
You note the texture of the fur,
What miracles of art, you say,
Those Flemish painters could command,
Each brush-stroke like a single hair.

How the eye focuses upon
The archer stiffly draped in black
Cutting the foreground to the right –
Masterly, that foreshortened arm,
Skilful, the modelling of the neck.

How colour, line, and form combine
To give the painting depth and space!
Beyond the stream, beyond the hill,
The village – each receding plane
Leads to the sky the travelling glance.

And in the sky the angels throng
Like glittering birds upon a tree –
Marvellous, you say, the mind that takes
A fantasy upon the wing
And out of prose makes poetry.

I am Sebastian. While you praise
I suffer and my lips are dumb,
The arrows pierce me through and through,
Yet you admire with abstract phrase
The torment of my martyrdom.

Child with a Cockatoo

Portrait of Anne, daughter of the Earl of Bedford, by S. Verelst

"Paid by my lord, one portrait, Lady Anne,
Full length with bird and landscape, twenty pounds
And framed withal. I say received. Verelst."

So signed the painter, bowed, and took his leave.
My Lady Anne smiled in the gallery
A small, grave child, dark-eyed, half turned to show
Her five bare toes beneath the garment's hem,
In stormy landscape with a swirl of drapes.
And, who knows why, perhaps my lady wept
To stand so long and watch the painter's brush
Flicker between the palette and the cloth
While from the sun-drenched orchard all the day
She heard her sisters calling each to each.
And someone gave, to drive the tears away,
That sulphur-crested bird with great white wings,
The wise, harsh bird – as old and wise as Time
Whose well-dark eyes the wonder kept and closed.
So many years to come and still, he knew,
Brooded that great, dark island continent
Terra Australis.

To those fabled shores
Not William Dampier, pirating for gold,
Nor Captain Cook his westward course had set
Jumped from the longboat, waded through the surf,
And clapt his flag ashore at Botany Bay.
Terra Australis, unimagined land –
Only that sulphur-crested bird could tell
Of dark men moving silently through trees,
Of stones and silent dawns, of blackened earth
And the long golden blaze of afternoon.
That vagrant which an ear-ringed sailor caught
(Dropped from the sky, near dead, far out to sea)
And caged and kept, till, landing at the docks,
Walked whistling up the Strand and sold it then,
The curious bird, its cynic eyes half-closed,
To the Duke's steward, drunken at an inn.
And he lived on, the old adventurer,
And kept his counsel, was a sign unread,
A disregarded prologue to an age.

So one might find a meteor from the sun
Or sound one trumpet ere the play's begun.

Ampersand

I lie between the black & white,
The half-tone eve, the twilight grey,
Slip like a shadow, curl like a cat
After the night, before the day.

Between the sea & shore I make
My scribbled, fluent, changing line;
The earth & air would join in one
But that their meeting-place is mine.

With bell & book – a hand to each –
I banish chaos from the scene
For, think, unless I interposed,
Yellow & blue would run to green.

I stand between the left & right
Tall as a post to point the ways
For sinners & saints, who'd all unite –
But I prevent – to sing my praise.

I am the twenty-seventh child,
The last-born of the alphabet,
Yet Kings & Queens reserve a place –
Between them Ampersand is set.

Who?

Who, then, was "Auntie Molly"? No one now
Can tell me who she was: or how it was
She and my mother shared a rented house
One summer for a fortnight – we took a train
And from the station trudged a country road.
I know she worked year-long and lived alone
Somewhere with a strange name, like Rooty Hill.

Postoffice-Store-in-one sold bread and milk
Returning to our house we scuffed along
Cloth-hatted, sandalled, kicking at the stones.
Mother and Auntie Molly walked ahead
And suddenly Mother stopped, threw back her head
And laughed and laughed there in the dusty road.
We were amazed to hear our mother laugh.

The fowl-yard fence sagged with ripe passion-fruit,
We bought cream in a jug. At night we sat
Around the lamp-lit table, colouring in.
In bed, near sleep, we'd hear the rise and fall
Of their grave voices – hers, and Auntie Molly's.
Whom no one now would know; who made my mother
Laugh joyfully in the middle of the road.

The Green Years

With wandering thoughts content, never at pains
To put her mind upon the thing at hand
Careless, untouched, she moved through distant days
A green, a silly girl. Was troubled only
By small guilts of omission: by words of hers
Wounding, better not said. And still these loom
Darker with time than many an outright wrong.

A yard of pump-water. A long thin girl.
Winters at boarding-school were bright with frost,
The nights so sharp. And day and night
Her feet and fingers burned unbearably
Inflamed with chilblains.
                                        Humorous complaint,
The stuff of jokes: as gout, hiccup, and sneeze,
Hay fever, cheek swollen with aching tooth.

But Shakespeare made all right. Antonio said
The kibe would put him to his slipper. "Kibe?"
He meant the chilblain so her teacher said.
Shakespeare! Well then, that made it bearable.
I knew that girl. Knew that for her each art –
The paintings looked at and the poems read –
Ringed its own radiance round the everyday.

She, like a yard of pump-water, slipped away
But something of her still remains with me –
The magic healing power of all she read.
Chilblains have disappeared. I share no joke
At pitiful human ills. Am troubled still
By guilt for past omissions, wounding words;
Wakeful at night, recalling the green years.

from Poems of a Marriage

1. Empty Spaces

We never could walk then
Unimpeded, direct,
Through the furnished rooms
Of the house we lived in.

Cupboard and shelf
Stubbornly blocked us
We went zig-zag
By chairs and tables.

And where to put down
The children to sleep
Cots heaped over
With books and clothing?

Now the children are flown
And you, oh you
Who were always with me,
You, gone, too,

I can cross this room
From any direction
To the single chair
The single bed.

2. Reading Aloud

Low, clear and free of self your voice went on
At night you read, and for how many years
From Sterne to Kipling, Flaubert, Boswell, Proust –
Proust a whole year, and finishing you said
"One of the great experiences of my life."
And mine, and mine.

Intent to listen, quieting my hands
With plain and purl, I followed your low voice.
Knitting unmindfully long scarves for friends
Sent off as signs of that shared calm content
Still looked for in the un-shared books I choose
Reading alone.

Well, we gave up once, stalled on Chuzzlewit.
How wrong it felt. You sensed a binding need
To take books to the end. Faced with reverses said,
"We must press on."

From books to life, your thought:
"Forgive, learn from the past. Press on."
And I press on.

GWEN HARWOOD 1920–1995

Gwen Harwood (née Foster) was raised in Brisbane in a family devoted to music. She studied piano and composition, taught piano and was a church organist. Harwood began writing poetry in the early 1940s, but her first book was not published until 1963. In 1945 she married William Harwood, a linguist, and settled in Tasmania. They had four children. In the early 1960s she was made briefly notorious by newspapers as the "Tas. housewife" who had hoaxed the *Bulletin* magazine. It had printed a sonnet of hers that read acrostically "Fuck all editors", and when this was discovered the proprietor, Sir Frank Packer, recalled all unsold copies. "It was just a piece of natural mischief", Harwood explained. In the 1960s and early 1970s she published poems under a variety of pseudonyms, including Walter Lehmann, Francis Geyer and Miriam Stone.

Harwood said that she loved domestic life and raising her children, and that her poems about women's domestic *angst* do not refer to her own experience. It is of interest that "Suburban Sonnet" was originally published under the pseudonym Miriam Stone. Her earlier poems show the influence of A. D. Hope and perhaps the cerebral, academic style of the Melbourne academic poets of the '60s and '70s, who were themselves influenced by the British "Movement" poets. She wrote libretti for well-known musicians who were friends, and her interests included German language and culture, gardening and domestic animals. She found the Tasmanian landscape melancholy and chilling, but thought her poetry may have benefited from this.

The adoption of looser verse forms in Harwood's later work has freed her own voice, and *Bone Scan* (1988) is widely regarded as her best collection. When Harwood's poems first appeared, her enormous facility (the poems of her *Collected Poems 1943–1995* were to occupy 571 pages), the multiplicity of pseudonyms, her recurring characters (Eisenbart and Kröte – "toad" in German), her "blue-stocking brightness", made it difficult to identify a "true" voice.

The 2003 publication of Harwood's *Collected Poems* allows the trajectory of her poetry to be understood. Very early poems, those written in the 1940s up to the mid 1950s, were competent, but not exciting. As she moved into her forties, released from child-rearing, the poems poured forth. She had a facility with fixed forms, and experimented excitedly with voices and subject matter. "Suburban Sonnet" and "New Music" are exceptionally controlled, with almost none of the academic language (of that era) which mar other poems. Too often though, self-conscious observations such as "Nestling my cheek against/ the hollow of your thigh/ I lay cockeyed with love/ in the most literal sense" are followed by such routine ones as "Roses knocked on the glass./Wine like a running stream/ no evil could cross/ flowed round the house of touch." ("Carnal Knowledge II").

In *Bone Scan* (1988) the experience of cancer and the abandonment of rhyme (but not in the title poem) allowed her to write more directly and simply, as in "The Twins", "Bone Scan", "Crow-Call" and "Night and Dreams". This new plainness is maintained in her final book *The Present Tense* (1995), published just weeks before her death.

In "Crow-Call", "Corvo" is Portuguese for crow. "Baron Corvo" was a pseudonym of Frederick Rolfe, the strange and self-destructive late 19th-century novelist. Harwood gave his name to a particular half-tame crow she had observed.

Suburban Sonnet

She practises a fugue, though it can matter
to no one now if she plays well or not.
Beside her on the floor two children chatter,
then scream and fight. She hushes them. A pot
boils over. As she rushes to the stove
too late, a wave of nausea overpowers
subject and counter-subject. Zest and love
drain out with soapy water as she scours
the crusted milk. Her veins ache. Once she played
for Rubinstein, who yawned. The children caper
round a sprung mousetrap where a mouse lies dead.
When the soft corpse won't move they seem afraid.
She comforts them; and wraps it in a paper
featuring: *Tasty dishes from stale bread.*

New Music

to Larry Sitsky

Who can grasp for the first time
these notes hurled into empty space?
Suddenly a tormenting nerve
affronts the fellowship of cells.
Who can tell for the first time
if it is love or pain he feels,
violence or tenderness that calls
plain objects by outrageous names

and strikes new sound from the old names?
At the service of a human vision,
not symbols, but strange presences
defining a transparent void,
these notes beckon the mind to move
out of the smiling context of
what's known; and what can guide it is
neither wisdom nor power, but love.

Who but a fool would enter these
regions of being with no name?
Secure among their towering junk
the wise and powerful congregate
fitting old shapes to old ideas,
rocked by their classical harmonies
in living sleep. The beggars' stumps
bang on the stones. Nothing will change.

Unless, wakeful with questioning,
some mind beats on necessity,
and being unanswered learns to bear
emptiness like a wound that no
word but its own can mend; and finds
a new imperative to summon
a world out of unmeasured darkness
pierced by a brilliant nerve of sound.

A Music Lesson

Kröte's not well. His mood is bloody.
A pupil he can hardly stand
attacks a transcendental study.
– Lord, send me one real pianist.
Soul of a horse! He shapes her hand
and breathes apologies to Liszt.

"Reflect: in order to create
we must know how to. Think about
the balance between height and weight,
shoulder to fingertip; a hanging
bridge, resilient, reaching out
with firm supports. Let's have no banging!

"Playing begins inside your brain.
Music's much more than flesh and bone.
Relax, and listen. If you strain
your muscles *here* and *here* contract.
You get a stiff, unlovely tone."
His pupil says, "Is that a fact?"

She plays the passage louder, faster;
indeed deliberately tries
to infuriate her music master.
"The year that Liszt was born, a comet

blazed over European skies."
"Am I to draw conclusions from it?

"And, if so, what?" the tyro sneers.
– Cold heart, stiff hands. How to explain?
"When a new genius appears
it's like that fiery head of light
drawing us in its golden train.
Now, shall we try to get it right?

"Does it give you no pride to say
'My teacher's teacher learned from Liszt?'
Feel in your hands, before you play,
the body's marvellous architecture:
the muscles between hand and wrist
kept flexible; now try to picture

"the finger forming, from the point
where it rests on the key, an arc
curving through every finger-joint,
supporting the whole arm's free weight.
Now the least effort makes its mark.
The instrument can sing."
"I'm late,"

the pupil whines. The lesson's over.
The teacher pours himself a gin,
pats the piano like a lover
(– Dear mistress, we're alone once more).
Liszt, with his upper lip gone in,
beams from the cover of a score.

Abbé, forsooth! A toast to you,
old friend, old fiend in monkish dress.
I know you had your off days too.
At Schumann's, Clara said, you played
his work so badly once (confess!)
that only her good manners made

her sit in silence in that room.
– Have mercy on all pianists,
Architect of the world, of whom
I ask that I may live to see
Halley's Comet.
If God exists
then music is his love for me.

A Simple Story

A visiting conductor
  when I was seventeen,
took me back to his hotel room
  to cover the music scene.

I'd written a composition.
  Would wonders never cease –
here was a real musician
  prepared to hold my piece.

He spread my score on the counterpane
  with classic casualness,
and put one hand on the manuscript
  and the other down my dress.

It was hot as hell in the Windsor.
  I said I'd like a drink.
We talked across gin and grapefruit,
  and I heard the ice go clink

as I gazed at the lofty forehead
  of one who led the band,
and guessed at the hoarded sorrows
  no wife could understand.

I dreamed of a soaring passion
  as an egg might dream of flight,
while he read my crude sonata.
  If he'd said, "That bar's not right,"

or, "Have you thought of a coda?"
  or, "Watch that first repeat,"
or, "Modulate to the dominant,"
  he'd have had me at his feet.

But he shuffled it all together,
  and said, "That's *lovely*, dear,"
as he put it down on the washstand
  in a way that made it clear

that I was no composer.
  And I being young and vain,
removed my lovely body
  from one who'd scorned my brain.

I swept off like Miss Virtue
  down dusty Roma Street,

and heard the goods trains whistle
  WHO? WHOOOOOO? in aching heat.

Naked Vision

I was sent to fetch an eye
promised for a fresh corneal graft.
At the doctor's rooms nurse gave me
a common paper bag;
in that, a sterile jar;
in that, the disembodied eye.

I sat in Davey Street
on a low brick garden wall
and looked. The eye looked back.
It gazed, lucid and whole,
from its colourless solution.
The window of whose soul?

Trees in St David's Park
refreshed the lunchtime lovers:
riesling gold, claret dark;
late flowers flaunted all colours.
But my friend and I had eyes
only for one another.

In flawless solitude
it stared, blue as the sky.
Nothing seemed out of range
of our crystalline exchange.
The longing in that eye
will haunt me till I die.

The Secret Life of Frogs

Mr Gabriel Fur, my Siamese,
brings to the hearth a Common Toadlet,
Crinia tasmaniensis.
Mice are permitted, frogs forbidden.
It will live. I carry it outside.
Its heartbeat troubles my warm hand
and as I set it down I see
two small girls in a warmer land.

    My friend Alice and I would sit
    cradling our frogs behind the tankstand.

Other fathers would talk about
the Great War. Mine would only say,
"I used to be a stretcher-bearer."
Not seen, not heard, in childhood's earshot
of the women on the back veranda,
we knew about atrocities.
Some syllables we used as charms:
Passchendaele   Mons   Gallipoli.
We knew about Poor George, who cried
if any woman touched her hair.
He'd been inside a brothel when
the Jerries came and started shooting.
(We thought a brothel was a French
hotel that served hot broth to diggers.)
The girl that he'd been with was scalped.
Every Frog in the house was killed.

Well, that was life for frogs. At school
the big boys blew them up and spiked them.
One bully had the very knife
with which his father killed ten Germans –
twenty – a hundred – numbers blossomed.
Dad the impaler! making work
for the more humble stretcher-bearers.
In safety by the dripping tankstand
our frogs with matchstick hands as pale
as the violet stems they lived among
cuddled their vulnerable bellies
in hands that would not do them wrong.

Homage to Ferd. Holthausen

At a street bookstall in Karlsruhe, my father
bought for my schoolboy son, then starting German,
Etymologisches Wörterbuch der Englischen Sprache
by Ferd. Holthausen, Professor of Kiel.
Lovely old binding, elegant type, good paper,
printed in Leipzig, 1917.
I like to think of Ferd. Holthausen sitting
with Skeat and Sweet and part of the New Oxford
(war having cut the final letters off)
working on his Büchlein (it's pocket sized)
transcribing words while Europe raged outside:

Breviloquent, compagination, dittany,
griskin, harmel, irrision, kilderkin, nimb,
obnubilation, oleraceous, parpent –
O Holthausen, O Ferd.! O dear Professor!
Forgive me my papilionaceous mind.
Teach me to perlustrate my native language.
Let me be of your phatry. My pignoration,
see, is this smaragd, of porraceous hue.
Bless my tripudiation, stellify
my verses, Ferd., be ever at my scrutoire.

Mother Who Gave Me Life

Mother who gave me life
I think of women bearing
women. Forgive me the wisdom
I would not learn from you.

It is not for my children I walk
on earth in the light of the living.
It is for you, for the wild
daughters becoming women,

anguish of seasons burning
backward in time to those other
bodies, your mother, and hers
and beyond, speech growing stranger

on thresholds of ice, rock, fire,
bones changing, head inclining
to monkey bosom, lemur breast,
guileless milk of the word.

I prayed you would live to see
Halley's Comet a second time.
The Sister said, When she died
she was folding a little towel.

You left the world so, having lived
nearly thirty thousand days:
a fabric of marvels folded
down to a little space.

At our last meeting I closed
the ward door of heavy glass
between us, and saw your face
crumple, fine threadbare linen

worn, still good to the last,
then, somehow, smooth to a smile
so I should not see your tears.
Anguish: remembered hours:

a lamp on embroidered linen,
my supper set out, your voice
calling me in as darkness
falls on my father's house.

The Twins *(from* Class of 1927*)*

Three years old when their mother died
in what my grandmother called
accouchement, my father labour,
they heard the neighbours intone
"A mercy the child went with her."

Their father raised them somehow.
No one could tell them apart.
At seven they sat in school
in their rightful place, at the top
of the class, the first to respond
with raised arm and finger-flick.

When one gave the answer, her sister
repeated it under her breath.
An inspector accused them of cheating,
but later, in front of the class,
declared himself sorry, and taught us
a marvellous word: *telepathic.*

On Fridays, the story went,
they slept in the shed, barred in
from their father's rage as he drank
his dead wife back to his house.
For the rest of the week he was sober
and proud. My grandmother gave them
a basket of fruit. He returned it.
"We manage. We don't need help."

They could wash their own hair, skin rabbits,
milk the cow, make porridge, clean boots.

Unlike most of the class I had shoes,
clean handkerchiefs, ribbons, a toothbrush.

We all shared the schoolsores and nits
and the language I learned to forget
at the gate of my welcoming home.

One day as I sat on the fence
my pinafore goffered, my hair
still crisp from the curlers, the twins
came by. I scuttled away
so I should not have to share
my Saturday sweets. My mother
saw me, and slapped me, and offered
the bag to the twins, who replied
one aloud and one sotto voce,
"No thank you. We don't like lollies."

They lied in their greenish teeth
as they knew, and we knew.
Good angel
give me that morning again
and let me share, and spare me
the shame of my parents' rebuke.

If there are multiple worlds
then let there be one with an ending
quite other than theirs: leaving school
too early and coming to grief.

Or if this is our one life sentence,
hold them in innocence, writing
Our Father which art in Heaven
in copperplate, or drawing
(their work being done) the same picture
on the backs of their slates: a foursquare
house where a smiling woman
winged like an angel welcomes
two children home from school.

Bone Scan

Thou hast searched me and known me. Thou knowest my downsitting and mine uprising. – Psalm 139

In the twinkling of an eye,
a moment, all is changed:
on a small radiant screen
(honeydew melon green)

are my scintillating bones.
Still in my flesh I see
the God who goes with me,
glowing with radioactive
isotopes. This is what he
at last allows a mortal
eye to behold: the grand
supporting frame complete
(but for the wisdom teeth),
the friend who lives beneath
appearances, alive
with light. Each glittering bone
assures me: you are known.

Crow-Call

"He lives eternally who lives in the present" – Tractatus 6.4311

Let this be eternal life:
light ebbing, my dinghy drifting
on watershine, dead centre
of cloud and cloud-reflection –
high vapour, mind's illusion.

And for music, Baron Corvo,
my half tame forest raven
with his bad leg unretracted
beating for home, lamenting
or, possibly, rejoicing
that he saw the world at all.

Space of a crow-call, enclosing
the self and all it remembers.
Heart-beat, wing-beat, a moment.
My line jerks taut. The cod
are biting. This too is eternal:
the death of cod at twilight.
And this: food on my table
keeping a tang of ocean.

So many, in raven darkness.
Why give death fancy names?

Corvo, where have you settled
your crippled leg for the night?

Night and Dreams

I

"I come to you in a dream of ages
past", sings Crab. He swirls his velvet-
seaweed cloak. "When first we met,
and last, you will recall, I was
imprisoned in your father's house."

Sea colours on his carapace,
wave-hiss, tide-rustle in his voice.
"Some fiend had tied my fearful claws –"
– Yes, I recall. I must have been
a skinny child of eight or nine

that night my father brought you home –
"No, let *me* tell", says Crab, "this is
my aria, *my* party piece.
Grandmother, mother, father, brother
and you, went to the local theatre

leaving me bound in parching darkness.
I prayed: Redeemer Crab, release me
by your own sidelong righteousness
from these straightforward evildoers.
Take me where my transparent children

float in their manifold sea vision.
Silence. Mouse-whisper, cockroach-scuttle.
I felt, not far, the Brisbane River
ebbing to salt creek, mangrove swamp,
and burst my bonds, O yes I did!

and raged through your dark house, and hid.
That night you dared not go to bed
finding me gone when you returned.
Splintered pencils and toys proclaimed
my ocean strength. How soon forgotten

what Stan and Olly did and said!
Time, time. I felt the tide returning
far off. O Salt Redeemer, come
(I prayed) let navies drown to feed me
with rotten stump, decaying belly,

or if I am to die, allow me
one crunch bone tender-balancing foot."

– My father caught you. "Ah, he did.
'We'll cook the brute tonight', he said.
'Bring me the hatpin.' Someone put

a diamond eye on a steel stalk
into your father's hand to stab
my stalked eyes. O the blaze of pain
eclipsing light's immense mandala!
Sea green, sea blue, I raged to red.

Boiling, crab died. I became Crab."

II

Crab is dressed for the feast: on lettuce shredded
to seaweed ribbons, cracked claws reassembled,
he lies among parsley curls and radish roses.
Our starchy Sunday-snowy cloth is set
with what remains of Greatgrandmother's china,
translucent white, rimmed with a deepsea blue.
On his great serving dish Crab's at the centre
of a splendid colour wheel: cucumber slices,
tomato, celery, carrot, egg: my work,
duly admired. My grandmother says grace.
"Where would you eat like this", my father asks,
passing the homemade bread, "except in Queensland?"
A lovely room. Windows give on the garden,
rose and green panes of bubble-glass enchanting
the dullest day. The sideboard mirror offers
more light. Such light, restoring, recomposing
many who dined here. Most of them are dead.

III

"That's enough of pentameters",
says Crab, returning to my dream.
– What shall I write, I ask. He writes,
so I won't miss his fearful joke:
THE DIRE BELLY VARIATIONS!

Making himself a cairn of stones
he says, "This is my own rock group.
O I'm the original punk rocker
with a hatpin through my brain, my brain,
with a diamond hatpin through my brain."

– Your jokes are awful. "I know worse."
– Impossible. "Shall I rehearse
the names of those who've died from cancer?
O I'm the original merry prankster,
a diamond hatpin's all my eye.

Tell me, where are those who ate
my claws, my tender body meat?
Laurel and Hardy fans, long gone!
You cracked my hardware, ate my software.
Now I'm programmed in your brain."

IV

More and more of the great questions,
such as: what am I doing here
in gumboots and a summer nightdress
in a moonlit garden chasing sheep?

The sheep are out. It's not a dream.
I'll mend the broken fence tomorrow.
What's left of night? Enough to dream in.
What dreams will come? Who else but Crab.

I ate him sixty years ago.
Ocean of memory, transposing
feaster and feast. He beckons, wearing
seaweed clothes, with sidelong charm.

"Shall we go to a pirate movie?"
– You like the sea? "I like the bodies,
and 'Take the lady below and make
her comfortable', that's what I like.

I can't be bothered with the love scenes.
I've opened hearts. I know what's in them."
At interval he buys refreshments,
"Two seafood sticks. One without crab.

Come live with me and be my supper
where colours have no boundaries,
where every word is writ in water,
I'll put my arm around your waist.

I'll put my armour round your waist.
Shell after shell my soft self waxes.
Seek help! Sea kelp for drowning sailors.
Great questions all have wavering answers."

Ghosts crowd to hear. O my lost loves.
Waking to hard-edge sunlit colours,
sharp birdsong, lamb-bleat, I recall
myself among the moonlit sheep

questioning – what? Why should I care
how long ago my death began?
Am I a ghost dreaming I'm human
with herbs to plant, a fence to mend?

On Uncertainty

"Why can we not teach a cat to retrieve? Does it not understand what we require of it?" – Wittgenstein

We all know that Yeats was silly
like us; but Wittgenstein was sillier
and really not like us at all.
He said himself he wrote for men
who'd breathe, one day, a different air.
In that case, they'd need different lungs.
Never rely on metaphor.

I see him as a gifted poet
who somehow never found his way
to writing poems. "A poem can pierce us,"
he wrote. Also, "A poem is not
used in the language game of giving
information."
                        What you see
as the sun sets is not the sun:

that's down below the earth's horizon.
You see an image of the sun
refracted through earth's atmosphere.
Some poems that look as clear as air
carry an image of what's gone.
Fade like a smiling Cheshire Cat,
you orb of day! You cats, come out!

You never stumble in the dark.
Beware of Faithful Fido, fouling
the footpaths, waiting to retrieve
his master's footwear. Fido knows
what is required of him: his soul.

They say that Wittgenstein was handsome
as Lucifer before the fall.

His gestures linger. Old disciples
still screw their faces up like him.
Students of students use his tones
of voice. What made him think of cats?
It's not known that he ever had one.
Perhaps he did, and tried to teach it,
and came to grief (his usual state).

Perhaps, unwilling to admit
defeat, he thought the cat was stupid
(as were most people that he met).
Perhaps it turned its back on him
as he would turn his back on people.
It would have done him good to own one,
to sit and watch the sun set, stroking

a creature quite indifferent
to human guilt, for whom the riddle
did not exist. He might have felt
his tension crackle off and vanish,
and spared his colleagues suicidal
Austro-Hungarian-Empire grapplings
with things that never were the case.

I've read of an old chimpanzee
to whom researchers taught sign language.
He grew, not unsurprisingly,
to loathe his captors, so they shipped him
off to a zoo in San Diego
where, an Ape-Ovid in exile,
he tried to teach his fellow captives.

"If we could teach a lion to speak
how could we hope to understand it?"
That's Wittgenstein again. If only
he'd kept a cat, like Dr Johnson,
and held it in his lap, and brushed it,
and really listened to its purring,
he might have been a happier man.

A Sermon

"The way to make sense of a text is to give it a context" – Veronica Brady

Out of informing chaos, everything:
aardvark to zebra, Abelard to Zeno,
Abacus to zinc-plate, abstrips to zetalisp,

Aaron to Zog. Mostly uncatalogued
things that get on your nerves, or bite the baby,
or snap the harpstrings. God won't interfere.

As Hume observed, he well might be a spider.
In fact he's language, throned among the cherubim,
enclosing his own elementary syntax,

sole I-am-that-I-am, a thought we think
among the coloured surfaces of things
that offer us no literal understanding,

imagining a silence we must enter,
a space of pure unmediated knowledge.
Death lies between us and futurity

seeming, sometimes, "chief good and final hope" –
ague to zona in the fragile body
built of the residue of once-bright stars.

Out come the paperbacks, papaverous
on bedside tables, or papilionaceous
in bus exchanges, bright and fluttering:

extra-terrestrial consciousness, dark matter,
polyfidelity, Utopian group living,
the universe attaining self-awareness,

metapsychology, demonic influence,
the non-material entity of particles,
black holes engulfing us, karmic survival,

greenhouse cucumbers dying of rock music
while in another greenhouse cucumbers
grow splendidly, exposed to Brahms and Schubert.

God bless you all. I mean, may language bless you.
Find a lover or a favourite friend, go walking
from the Abbey to the Zoological Gardens.

There's no statue in the stone. If you want statues
transform the stone; interpret your own life;

engage in idle talk, or walk in silence.

Sibylline vacancies do no one harm.
Good poems mean what they say, good silences
mean, if you listen, what the good poems say.

Ruskin declared that characters of beauty
are stamped on everyday familiar shapes.
Cucumber made him ill. He didn't know

such flesh responded to romantic music.
But he knew leaves and flowers and Gothic arches
and read them in a true contextual structure.

Stroll in the gardens, pause by the enclosures.
Find the small lives contained in their own time.
They have value in the world, with or without you.

Imagination tires, but nature never,
said Pascal. Though you did not make the world
you can adorn it. You can say with Zeno

that commonsense is wrong, play with infinity,
or show the murmurers Aaron's blossoming rod.
If God is language, he can turn the alphabet

backwards, and write from right to left, inscribing
Know before whom thou standest and delight us
with music we have never heard before.

OODGEROO NOONUCCAL (Kath Walker)
1920–1993

Oodgeroo Noonuccal (also known as Kath Walker) was the first Aboriginal Australian to have a book of poems published: *We Are Going*, in 1964. During her lifetime her volumes of poetry enjoyed considerable popular success, probably at that time outselling any Australian poet since C. J. Dennis. She was born on North Stradbroke Island with Aboriginal parentage on both sides. Her father was a labourer and led a strike in 1935. She has written: "I was of the Noonuccal tribe of Stradbroke Island near Brisbane, my totem was the carpet snake. I was born in 1920 and arrived about a week before expected, at the home of white friends where there was a wedding in progress; and the little black baby stole the show from the star performer, the bride. They named me Kathleen Jean Mary Ruska." At school on Stradbroke she remembered her teacher, Mr A. G. McPhail, as "a fair and just man who taught me the rudiments and took as much interest in the Aborigines as he did in the white children. At thirteen I began domestic work in Brisbane at 2/6 a week" (25 cents in current Australian currency).

Two of her brothers were prisoners-of-war in Singapore during World War II, and she volunteered in 1942 to join the Army, serving as a switchboard operator. Once she was enlisted she was surprised to encounter less discrimination as an Aboriginal. She married Bruce Walker, an Aboriginal welder and boxer, but the marriage did not last. In the 1950s she became a member of the Communist Party, which was the only political party at that time opposed to the White Australia Policy. She left after a few years when she found the Party was less committed to opposing racism than she was. She wrote: "At the age of 37 I went back to school under the repatriation scholarship scheme for service men and women, and took a stenographers' course." In the 1960s she became prominent as a political activist. She lobbied for the constitutional amendment under which Aboriginal people have been given special recognition. She was a member of a number of political organisations and was Queensland state secretary of the Federal Council for the Advancement of Aboriginal and Torres Strait Islanders.

In 1972 she bought a property on North Stradbroke Island and called it Moongalba (the "sitting-down place"), and established the Noonuccal-Nughie Education and Cultural Centre. She said of her education program: "The last seventeen years I've had 26,500 children on the island. White kids as well as black. And if there were green ones, I'd like them too ..." In 1987 she changed her name to Oodgeroo (meaning paperbark) Noonuccal (her tribal name). When the bicentenary of white settlement was celebrated in 1988, she handed back her MBE (Member of the British Empire), saying that two hundred years of carnage and failure to rectify the damage done to the Aboriginal people was nothing to celebrate. She was happy to share her Aboriginality with white friends. Arriving one day at "Edge", the property of her good friend Judith Wright, outside Braidwood, Noonuccal opened an Esky (portable chiller) she had brought with her, and produced a magpie-goose – a species which was regarded as a great delicacy, but was protected, except for Aboriginals with traditional rights. Wright quickly recovered from her surprise. The two women cooked and ate an enjoyable meal.

When Noonuccal's poetry was first published, it was criticised by some as "propaganda". However her propaganda pieces are not a major part of her work, and her best poems, which are often humorous, speak passionately for Aboriginal experience.

Cookalingee

For Elsie Lewis

Cookalingee, now all day
Station cook in white man's way,
Dressed and fed, provided for,
Sees outside her kitchen door
Ragged band of her own race,
Hungry nomads, black of face.
Never begging, they stand by,
Silent, waiting, wild and shy,
For they know that in their need
Cookalingee give them feed.

Peeping in, their deep dark eyes
Stare at stove with wide surprise,
Pots and pans and kitchen-ware,
All the white-man wonders there.

Cookalingee, lubra still
Spite of white-man station drill,
Knows the tribal laws of old:
"Share with others what you hold;"
Hears the age-old racial call:
"What we have belongs to all."
Now she gives with generous hand
White man tucker to that band,
Full tin plate and pannikin
To each hunter, child and gin.
Joyful, on the ground they sit,
With only hands for eating it.
Then upon their way they fare,
Bellies full and no more care.

Cookalingee, lubra still,
Feels her dark eyes softly fill,
Watching as they go content,
Natural as nature meant.
And for all her place and pay
Is she happy now as they?
Wistfully she muses on
Something bartered, something gone.
Songs of old remembered days,
The walkabout, the old free ways.
Blessed with everything she prized,
Trained and safe and civilized,
Much she has that they have not,
But is hers the happier lot?

Lonely in her paradise
Cookalingee sits and cries.

We Are Going

For Grannie Coolwell

They came in to the little town
A semi-naked band subdued and silent,
All that remained of their tribe.
They came here to the place of their old bora ground

Where now the many white men hurry about like ants.
Notice of estate agent reads: "Rubbish May Be Tipped Here".
Now it half covers the traces of the old bora ring.
They sit and are confused, they cannot say their thoughts:
"We are as strangers here now, but the white tribe are the strangers.
We belong here, we are of the old ways.
We are the corroboree and the bora ground,
We are the old ceremonies, the laws of the elders.
We are the wonder tales of Dream Time, the tribal legends told.
We are the past, the hunts and the laughing games, the wandering camp fires.
We are the lightning-bolt over Gaphembah Hill
Quick and terrible,
And the Thunderer after him, that loud fellow.
We are the quiet daybreak paling the dark lagoon.
We are the shadow-ghosts creeping back as the camp fires burn low.
We are nature and the past, all the old ways
Gone now and scattered.
The scrubs are gone, the hunting and the laughter.
The eagle is gone, the emu and the kangaroo are gone from this place.
The bora ring is gone.
The corroboree is gone.
And we are going."

Dawn Wail for the Dead

Dim light of daybreak now
Faintly over the sleeping camp.
Old lubra first to wake remembers:
First thing every dawn
Remember the dead, cry for them.
Softly at first her wail begins,
One by one as they wake and hear
Join in the cry, and the whole camp
Wails for the dead, the poor dead
Gone from here to the Dark Place:
They are remembered.
Then it is over, life now,
Fires lit, laughter now,
And a new day calling.

Ballad of the Totems

My father was Noonuccal man and kept old tribal way,
His totem was the Carpet Snake, whom none must ever slay;
But mother was of Peewee clan, and loudly she expressed
The daring view that carpet snakes were nothing but a pest.

Now one lived inside with us in full immunity,
For no one dared to interfere with father's stern decree:
A mighty fellow ten feet long, and as we lay in bed
We kids could watch him round a beam not far above our head.

Only the dog was scared of him, we'd hear its whines and growls,
But mother fiercely hated him because he took her fowls.
You should have heard her diatribes that flowed in angry torrents,
With words you'd never see in print, except in D.H. Lawrence.

"I kill that robber," she would scream, fierce as a spotted cat;
"You see that bulge inside of him? My speckly hen make that!"
But father's loud and strict command made even mother quake;
I think he'd sooner kill a man than kill a carpet snake.

That reptile was a greedy guts, and as each bulge digested
He'd come down on the hunt at night, as appetite suggested.
We heard his stealthy slithering sound across the earthen floor,
While the dog gave a startled yelp and bolted out the door.

Then over in the chicken-yard hysterical fowls gave tongue,
Loud frantic squawks accompanied by the barking of the mung,
Until at last the racket passed, and then to solve the riddle,
Next morning he was back up there with a new bulge in his middle.

When father died we wailed and cried, our grief was deep and sore,
And strange to say from that sad day the snake was seen no more.
The wise old men explained to us: "It was his tribal brother,
And that is why it done a guy" – but some looked hard at mother.

She seemed to have a secret smile, her eyes were smug and wary,
She looked about as innocent as the cat that ate the pet canary.
We never knew, but anyhow (to end this tragic rhyme)
I think we all had snake for tea one day about that time.

Gifts

"I will bring you love," said the young lover,
"A glad light to dance in your dark eye.
Pendants I will bring of the white bone,
And gay parrot feathers to deck your hair."

But she only shook her head.

"I will put a child in your arms," he said,
"Will be a great headman, great rain-maker.
I will make remembered songs about you
That all the tribes in all the wandering camps
Will sing forever."

But she was not impressed.

"I will bring you the still moonlight on the lagoon,
And steal for you the singing of all the birds;
I will bring down the stars of heaven to you,
And put the bright rainbow into your hand."

"No," she said, "bring me tree-grubs."

Nona

At the happy chattering evening meal
Nona the lithe and lovely,
Liked by all,
Came out of her mother's gunya,
Naked like the rest, and like the rest
Unconscious of her body
As the dingo pup rolling about in play.
All eyes turned, men and women, all
Had smiles for Nona.
And what did the women see? They saw
The white head-band above her forehead,
The gay little feather-tuft in her hair
Fixed with gum, and how she wore it.
They saw the necklet of red berries
And the plaited and painted reed arm-band
Jarri had made her.
And what did the men see? Ah, the men.
They did not see armlet or band
Or the bright little feather-tuft in her hair.
They had no eye for the red berries,
They did not look at these things at all.

No more boomerang

No more boomerang
No more spear;
Now all civilised –

Colour bar and beer.

No more corroboree,
Gay dance and din.
Now we got movies,
And pay to go in.

No more sharing
What the hunter brings.
Now we work for money,
Then pay it back for things.

Now we track bosses
To catch a few bob,
Now we got walkabout
On bus to the job.

One time naked,
Who never knew shame;
Now we put clothes on
To hide whatsaname.

No more gunya,
Now bungalow,
Paid by hire purchase
In twenty year or so.

Lay down the stone axe,
Take up the steel,
And work like a nigger
For a white man meal.

No more firesticks
That made the whites scoff.
Now all electric,
And no better off.

Bunyip he finish,
Now got instead
White fella Bunyip,
Call him Red.

Abstract picture now –
What they coming at?
Cripes, in our caves we
Did better than that.

Black hunted wallaby,
White hunt dollar;

White fella witchdoctor
Wear dog-collar.

No more message-stick;
Lubras and lads.
Got television now,
Mostly ads.

Lay down the woomera,
Lay down the waddy.
Now we got atom-bomb,
End *every*body.

LEX BANNING 1921–1965

Lex Banning was afflicted from birth with cerebral palsy, and his movements were difficult and jerky. He spluttered when he spoke, usually with a twisted grin, framed by a pencil moustache. He grew up with his mother at Punchbowl in the outer suburbs of Sydney, and went to local schools. Vocational counsellors advised him to drop out of high school and work at shoe repairs. After two years of this, during which he continued to read widely, he was granted entry to the University of Sydney. He graduated with honours in arts, and became a librarian and freelance journalist. Banning's intelligence was incisive and dandified, with affinities to Slessor, though lacking Slessor's inventive genius with language. Well-known in Sydney's bohemia, appreciated as a wit, he was attractive to women, and was married for a time to a doctor. He had an admiring coterie of friends. A user of amphetamines and an enthusiastic drinker, Banning's health failed rapidly and he was dead at 44. The poet and editor Richard Appleton, who co-edited Banning's posthumous collected poems *There was a Crooked Man* (1987) recalled his first encounter with Banning, in 1949 or 1950, in a bohemian haunt of that era: "Wearing a beret, and with my overcoat collar turned up about my ears, I was descending the stairs into the Lincoln Coffee Lounge in Rowe Street, Sydney, when a voice spluttered up from the gloom below: 'Somebody should tell that young man that the Spanish Civil War is over.' " Banning distilled a painful existence in lapidary epigrams and in poems which celebrate moments of beauty while insisting on a pessimistic, materialist philosophy.

Ixion

Turning and re-turning,
  the wheel returns once more,
once more the circus-master
  beckons through the door.
Will nothing stop the shadows'
  convolutions on the floor?

Will nothing stop the shadows?
  Must I once again perform
the usual limited number
  of variations from the norm?
Though the sky seems set for thunder
  there is never any storm.

Though the sky seems set for thunder,
  rest assured it will not rain;
at least till the appropriate season
  has everything in train.
There is never any reversal
  for the slayer and the slain.

There is never any reversal,
  the axe achieves the block,
denial produces only
  the crowing of the cock.
Turning and re-turning;
  no one stops the clock.

Five

Truly to set in words,
five things are my despair;
the flower of the poinciana,
the scent of a woman's hair,

the burst of a cigarette-end
flung hard against a stone,
the arc of water falling,
the longing in the bone.

NAN McDONALD 1921–1974

Nan McDonald was born in the Sydney suburb of Eastwood. After graduating from the University of Sydney in arts, she worked for the publishing firm Angus & Robertson as an editor, during one of its most interesting periods. McDonald never married, lived always with members of her family, and died when she was 52 of cancer. Hal Porter has described her in *The Extra*, one of his volumes of autobiography: "She looks [the way] one expects a poetess to look: pale, stilled, as tall and serene as a Parmigianino Madonna. She matches her poems [and yet] within the seeming temperance of her poetry stir darkness, world-weariness, despair, civilized anguish." Porter commented that though he saw McDonald shortly before her death, and corresponded with her, she never gave any indication to him of her illness. In "Burragorang", she describes a valley about to be inundated following the construction of a dam, and in "The Barren Ground" she imagines a national park near Kiama, which she never visited. Both poems are typical of her palette, cool green and blue, with an isolated image such as an eagle as a splash of gold. Nan McDonald's poetry can remind one of Emily Brontë's, though the Englishwoman is more passionate: there is a similar exultation in cold, inhuman places; a style similarly plain, muted, and austere; and in both an undertone of stoic Protestant religion.

The Barren Ground

I think of it, that high, bare place in the mountains,
Always under a cool grey blowing sky
Where the eagle hangs black and alone – clean wind whistling
Through tussock and long low swell of scrub, and through
Hollows the rainy centuries have worn
In the huge ruinous heaps of silent stone,
I trace on the map the way from the blue-edged coast
Across green, where the rich farms lie, through the deepening brown
That marks the rising ground, till the clear road fades
And a broken track goes climbing on to that space
Empty of all but the three words standing plain,
And I think I could lie down there, and be at peace.

It was not named for a blue dog, a dead horse,
Nor for some dark tribe's thought that haunts the ear
And still eludes the brain; no bold explorer
Made record of his desperate journey there;
No settler left his name to cry when the bush
Has flowed back across the furrows and the cold hearth,
When the fruit-trees have gone wild and the children are scattered,
"By sorrow and sweat I was conqueror of this earth."
No, it was not named for glory or possession,
The foolish dreams of man, whose stiffening hand
Lets the bright coin drop and follows it down to dust,
But simply for itself – The Barren Ground.

How lovely its fall on the ear bewildered with words,
On the mind sick with the eddies of thought, for at last
The eyes are filled with the glitter of light on the leaves,
With the million-petalled flowers, and can only thirst –
Turning from life grown rank and smelling of death –
With a great thirst for the truth of barrenness.
For what is life, or what is death, who knows?
But all men know that peace is only peace.

Yet it may not be as I dream – three words on the map
Are all my knowledge, and that I have seen as well
Through a gap in the hills, rising far and strange in the evening,
The darkening ramparts of its eastern wall.
But the heart has its own routes and its journeys' ends,
And sooner or later strikes, though travelling blind,
The rocky track where the long road gives out
And comes on a grey day to its Barren Ground.

Burragorang

Coming to the farm that winter afternoon
I thought they had all died or gone away.
The river-oaks were keening, the wind blew cold
Down the long valley between mountain walls,
One with its cliffs sunward and blazing gold
And one in dark-blue shade. Late in the day
It was, late in the season. I remember
One yellow wattle danced and did not care
If it never flowered again; but the gate hung wide
And in the growing crop the weeds stood high
And at the house a pane was cracked, a door
Groaned to the wind, shifting on broken hinges.
Then a voice spoke, and someone moved inside.
That was what frightened me. They still lived there
If you could call it living. I had passed by
The churchyard where the slanting sunlight shone
On crosses and green graves of the old settlers
But the tongue of Death clamoured more loudly here
Saying, Let the thistles grow, there will be no harvest.
Let the house fall, for all this will be gone
And the waters over it, within a year.

Long ago, before the wars and the time of fear
My mother came to the valley, down the track
From the King's Tableland, a wild steep way.
They found the river running swift and clear
And crossed it, laughing, on a borrowed horse,
But for the rest they walked, sixty odd miles,
And none too long; they were young and friends together,
The mountains lifted up their hearts all day –
At morning blue through rising mist, at noon
Purple as grapes beyond the sun-bleached corn,

And deepening through the hours in fold on fold,
The wall of shadow and the wall of light,
Till the great crags stood black against the stars.
No dream troubled her sleep of what would be,
How the kind homesteads sheltering them by night,
Farms and farmers, before her children were old,
Wives, sons, cattle, would vanish utterly
As the tribes that earlier yet melted away
In dusk of river-oaks, with the songs they sang
And their dances, leaving a little ash and silence
About the sacred stones of Burragorang.

Today the wind blew up from Burragorang,
At its touch I felt my life shudder and stir,
The whole fine framework of things known and done
Slip from its centre like a broken door,
Seeing how the world could be no more than this:
Song failed and fire dead, the work begun
And left unfinished because it is no use,
A weed-grown crop that will not come to reaping,
Winter evening closing in, the end sure.
And then the stubborn flame leaps in my blood
To think how even now, above the cold
Wind-fumed water there, the mountains rise
Casting their glory on the desolate flood
That has drowned all the good years, strong as of old,
High and more fair than any earthly city,
The walls of sapphire, the towers of burning gold.

DIMITRIS TSALOUMAS 1921–

The Greek-Australian poet Dimitris Tsaloumas was born on the island of Leros, when it was under Italian rule (which was from 1912 to 1947). He was initially educated in Italian. During World War II he was a courier in the resistance. Before migrating to Australia in 1952, because of political persecution, he had already published two volumes of poetry. One of these was printed with help from the English novelist and poet Lawrence Durrell, whom Tsaloumas met on Rhodes, and who admired his poetry. When he came to Australia, Tsaloumas intended to stay only two years, to learn English. But to his surprise he remained. He studied at the University of Melbourne and became a school teacher of modern languages and English. He and his wife have four children. In more recent years he has spent much of his time on Leros. Starting in the 1970s he began publishing poetry in Greek, in Greece and Australia (which should not be surprising as Melbourne claims it has, after Athens, the largest population of Greeks in the world). In

1983 a bi-lingual edition of his selected poems, *The Observatory*, translated into English by Philip Grundy, was published by University of Queensland Press. "The Sick Barber" is taken from this book. A further volume of translations appeared and then in 1988 Tsaloumas began publishing poetry he had written in English. Tsaloumas is a poet with a rich and subtle mind, with major themes, who writes on a large scale, but much of the power of his poetry depends on densely packed language which does not translate easily.

The Sick Barber

At the top of Patmos
thirty-two years ago and more
one winter's day.

The north wind, bleak, teeth-clenching
sinks the headlands
in cataracts of spume,
falls on the breakwater and bursting forth
rushes uphill
screaming and howling
and threatening the island's lid,
thrusting the cowering sun
into bolted courtyards.
You daren't risk the sunless alleys
where women round the corners in full sail
with billowing skirts
and monks perch perilously
on the monastery's white battlements.
On days like this
drunkards' noses turn blue,
doors slam and sounds are heard
in the empty houses of the rich.
From time to time
a fishing-boat sinks
drowning captain and crew
and in the coffee-house they'd talk about the loss
amid the rising bitterness
from steaming sage-tea cups.

Days like this
drift rudderless in the mists
from sleep to murkier sleep,
but sometimes they'll stop in a clearing
where everything is seen in its place
alive as in memorial services

for drowned ships:
wan sunlight on the window
and a fly glued to the pane.
The mandolin hung from a nail
with the Palm Sunday cross,
a rickety chair and two customers
fingering their beads on the couch.
War, hunger, suffering
– have you heard any news, boys,
any news –

To one side of the mirror
Fair Genevieve with the fawn,
and a fierce battle
framed in the far-off steppes of Asia
with field-marshals in the upper corners
mustachioed and dreamy-eyed
over the merciless pounding of the guns
engulfing the world in a tornado blackness
of smoke and flame.
On the other side, a flashy calendar
in colours of unheard-of opulence –
bananas, pineapples, lotus-fruit
from Pacific orchards,
citron and apples, grapefruit and strawberries –
and amid these aromas and exotic juices
Uncle aproned at the counter
rich and stern
subject of the widow's tales to her suffering son
whose sighs at the telling
would drain the blood from your veins.

You'll say: why does time now look
for rope-ends to pick up and knots to tie,
why do the dusty hours converge
from such a distance
on the twilight doorsteps of the old.
You'll even say: my friend
there's no cure for your sadness
and the more you lean on the window-pane
the worse it gets.
If I had some wine like yours
I'd fill my pitcher
and go outside to sit in the yard

and chat with the sparrow.

I've tried that too.
I've talked with men and birds.
But the tune grows hackneyed
and talk is a facade.
If you plan to spend
the night in wakefulness,
you'd best sort out
your voices now, while it's still light,
for they get entangled in the folds of fear
and the crumbs of love are scattered.
They say that Erebus has already set sail
on the broad sea
and I can hear winds whistling
in the pale beards of constellations,
and immortal lappings of waters
on the shores where moonlight sets
and the scent of lilies withers.
Before too long the barges will glide in,
and the seagulls are restless on the beach.
Gird up your loins, lads,
spit on your palms:
God only knows
where we'll stow so much darkness.

That's my news.
No word from the Red Cross
or the decisions of the Great.
"How'd you like your sideburns, Dimitri my boy –
let's rub out the brackets so your face
can shine, seeing as you've an educated girlfriend.
Let's have a go at your neck, let it get used to the blade.
Shall we shave your nose today
Mr Sotiris" – meaning
Mr Sotiris's porous bulb that looks
like the backside of a badly-plucked chicken
with nostrils sprouting curly hairs
to tempt a man's fingers.
"I see the flies have mated on the window:
does that mean peace this year?"

Barber's jokes. Wet as water.
But with a certain mild gentleness,
humble like the gaze of martyrs

sitting half-heartedly on the coals
while an angel waits in vain
for the flame to unstitch the flesh.

"And when the days grow warmer in the spring
we'll take down the mandolin.
These north winds have shrivelled my hands" –
squeezing his right hand into a fist
the little finger protruding above the others
because of the precious long nail
which you'd hear brushing backwards
like lightning over the four strings
before the chord was smothered by the palm.
A delicate, fastidious soul.
For neither the sadness of "rebetika"
nor yearning "hasapiko" tunes would shift
the bitter knot of his nostalgia.
Exotic music, genteel melodies
would bow his shoulders
and blur his distant gaze:
stroke by stroke
Silvestri's Serenade
Tosti's Serenade
The Waves of the Danube.
Beat by beat, his heel
on the bare floorboards.

But steadily and skilfully the scissors
would discipline the customer's gaze
shutting out irrelevant observation:
clippings and dandruff on the cloth
spread over hidden hands,
the much-pressed trousers
with the yellow stain at the fly,
the spots at the bottom of the tie
and the ancestral watch-chain.
A whiff of incense would emerge
from his chest as he bent over.
But when he shook the towel
his huge puzzled eyes would nail you
over the pale edge of his nose
while the two most consumptive fingers
would stroke his small moustache,
first one side then the other,

the small cough stubbornly
suppressed in the palm –
good health to you, Mr Sotiris,
your good health.

Our good health indeed
now that a spiteful north wind
pushes us against his glass door
one day on the winter side of the world.
But we wait in vain for the stairs to creak.
The barber is laid up
curled on his bed
with wood-stiff fingers.
The barber won't get up again,
not now not in spring
however warm the days.
The pretty serenades and
the Waves of the Danube
hang now from the nail
along with the washed-out smells
above the basin-stand
with the barbers-shop debris,
dirty lather, stale bristles, cigarette butts.
Further along, on another nail,
the striped cloth, greasy
where it fastens round the neck,
and a shudder runs down the spine of time.

GEOFFREY DUTTON 1922–1998

Geoffrey Dutton was born at "Anlaby" in South Australia, a famous property with a grand house, which was the state's first sheep stud, founded by his English ancestors in 1838. He went to the elite Geelong Grammar School, and read English at the University of Adelaide. Dutton interrupted his university studies to enlist in the Royal Australian Air Force in World War II. He became a flying instructor. In 1944 he married the enamellist Ninette Trott, and they had two sons and a daughter. They were to divorce after a long marriage. In 1985 he married the writer Robin Lucas.

After World War II he followed the family tradition and went to Magdalen College, Oxford, but he disliked the British class system and later became a republican. He was Senior Lecturer in English at the University of Adelaide from 1953 to 1962. In 1957, he co-founded *Australian Letters*, a literary magazine that published out of Adelaide for more than a decade. In 1962 he was founding editor of Penguin Australia, and in 1965 was co-founder of Sun Books, an independent publisher that over time became an imprint of Macmillan. His most durable publishing venture was co-founding in 1961 the *Australian Book Review*, which continues.

As an undergraduate at the University of Adelaide, he became one of the writers associated with the avant-garde *Angry Penguins* magazine edited by Max Harris. After this brief dalliance with the avant-garde, his own writing was to become mainstream, but his taste was always open and eclectic. He published nine collections of poetry, eight novels (three for children), critical studies, biographies of Australian writers and explorers and a frank autobiography, *Out in the Open*. The unhurried, patrician and appreciative style of the two autobiographical poems we have selected is an accurate reflection of the man.

A Finished Gentleman

"In the distant desert you unexpectedly stumble on a finished gentleman" –
Captain George Grey, Journals of Two Expeditions of Discovery

Under the white silence of the great gumtree avenue
My parents taught me to be an English gentleman,
And a thousand galahs rose like petals thrown at the sunset,
Swearing like the native Australians they are. Bastards! Bastards!
Yet no one more legitimate than I, whose ancestors
Planted the trees and houses here where no one had planted
Even a seed, or penned a sheep, or dammed a creek.
No style grows out of nothingness, droughts and scabby sheep
Teach patience but not manners, and so it was 1900,
And the second generation, and there was Grandfather, gleaming,
The Squire of Anlaby, with a steam-yacht, R.Y.S.,
Fourteen gardeners, and silver-gilt candlesticks for the church he was building.

And so with Oxford, rowing, and maybe the Diplomatic in view,
I grew among grass-seeds and dust-storms and later, in the scent
Of the distillery wafting across the Eton of Corio Bay,
Being expert at coping with visiting Governors and their intolerable A.D.C.'s,
And their ladies (though once I shot one of these in the bottom with an arrow),
Could tell a Holland and Holland from a Greener, English cloth from Australian,
Knew the Wars of the Roses but had scarcely heard of Eureka,
Could decline Omnis Gallia into any number of parts,
And after chanting "Alpha Beta Gamma Delta,
Knock a lady down and belt her", learned to read
In Greek the speech of an Athenian lawyer in a dispute over drains,

Though I knew nothing of Bligh or Macarthur, Parkes or Deakin,
Could tell you the agonies of Xenophon, Livingstone, and someone up the
Amazon,
But nothing of Sturt down the Murray, or Eyre across the Nullarbor,
Knew the *Revenge* and the *Golden Hind*, but not *Sirius* or the *Endeavour.*

And yet, in the coach-house I ran my finger over the acetylene lamps
Of my father's 1908 Talbot, first car driven across Australia,
Walked through the mulgas my mother had brought back from the Territory,
Grilled chops on gum-sticks, caught yabbies, had the slippery bumps
Of a rabbit's guts often in my hand, loved Australia passionately
As did my father and mother in between reading
The Illustrated London News, The Cornhill, Britannia and Eve.

And what did it give me, to be an Austroenglish gentleman?
A torment of comparative values, nothing here so old, so rare,
So fine. Trivial despairs at people who drank sweet wine,
Sat on Genoa velvet, walked in square-capped shoes,
Talked of nothing but marks, furlongs, overs, of dagoes and reffos,
Of long-hairs and sissies, the wisdom of the ordinary, decent bloke.

Well, as I look back, I was indeed a finished gentleman.
Twenty years to learn to be one, twenty years and more
To learn what Jack or Mick knew all the time, that here
It is we live, unless we pretend, or run away.

But hold it! The galahs are thicker than they ever were,
Four thousand marvellous sunset flowers tumbling
On to the shredded upper stalks of the great white trees.
Bastards! Bastards! they scream. Yes, Jack and Mick
Were ignorant bastards in another way. Maybe they could whittle
Myall stockwhip handles and ride straight home through the maze
Of mallee, and roll their own and recite all of "The Sick Stockrider",
But this landscape was not cleared by such sweet simplicities alone,
And their bright axes would bounce off the rubbery jungle
Of ideas never thought necessary in this innocent country.
And, educated down, I still know the world's crooked hours are different
From the hands around me, raising schooners at closing time.

The Smallest Sprout

A lioness killing a Nubian in a field of lotuses,
Made of ivory, gold, lapis lazuli and cornelian,
Four inches high, found in a well at Nimrud;
This torn from *The Illustrated London News*;

From the Adelaide *Chronicle*, "How to make whitewash";
Next, a seedsman's catalogue, with "This is *no good*"
Scribbled under one highly recommended camellia.
And in the drawer itself, the scent a smallest boy
Needed no opening of eyes to prove it hers.
And now no looking in any favourite place
Will find her, no telephone ringing at the most awkward moment
Will yield her voice, no mail a letter with news
Of the dogs, or the difficulties of painting a dying rose.

But walk on earth she walked, how much still grows.
She was not one to cut a single rose
Then watch the whole vast garden die.
She died between footfalls, in her own house,
A widow for thirty years, but never afraid
Of loneliness, nor of commanding what she thought was best.
However feminine, no Little Woman she.
She knew her place, and it was at the head;
A beauty old men did not forget, and the young noticed,
Which filled them less with sorrow or lust than awe,
Since like a judge's robes it symbolized the law,
An ordered life of strenuous principle,
Distrust of ease (at seventy striding on
While grown men ran behind), and dedication
To beauty itself, in flower or art or action,
(With nothing but scorn for that self-pity
Which holds beauty irrelevant to this ugly age.)

This was a beauty that soon left mirrors empty,
However often it returned to them.
Fingers that pressed on piano or violin
Could knead the compost round the hairs of roots
Or roll out pastry on a floury board;
Eyes that burnt as cold as salt in candleflame
Watched tenderly for the first crabapple blossom.

She knew the droughts, the country where they breed,
But she had looked beyond mirages of a gibber plain
And dry creeks running like cracks in a steer's skull
Towards the homestead, where the underground tank
Always keeps the pure rain water cool.
Only the sea she did not care to touch,
Admiring a moonlit bay, or an albatross
In flight, that smooth seismograph of storms,

But safe on land that could still fight off the sea
She was not going to walk back in again.

On the sea it is only by favour anyone has control,
But on the land a man is more or less in command,
A woman even more so. Once forced to fight
The wars she hates, she wins them, beating the guerillas
Through knowing their jungles better than they do themselves.
Not only that, she lets the conquered see
That she was what they were really fighting for,
The earth itself, the swamps of intuition,
The tropic mountain snows and the fantastic butterflies,
Over which the solitary woman, trailing her beauty,
Flies like a bird of paradise to her own death,
Inviolable, no shout nor shot can halt her.

Achieved perfection is loveless, but she was loved.
Beauty, the vision vanishing beyond the trees,
Leaves a cold kiss on statues that do not change;
The mould is broken for lovers and for children.
She knew the earth was there for walking on;
It would have startled worshippers of her image
To have seen her tuck her skirts into her bloomers
And wade out laughing (rare occasion for the sea)
To scoop with a net the big blue crabs;
To hear her call a fart a fart; or flay
The snobbery of a visiting Englishwoman; or haul out
The steaming guts of a just-slaughtered fowl.

These were her robust and sometimes angry days,
But none of us could ever know her nights,
After she marked the page in Gibbon with a hairpin
And then turned off the light. The widow was a woman,
What agony for her never to be comforted;
Love's most heroic response is to the 3 a.m. despair.
Nor in such darkened moods is daylight any help;
Walking away from light one's shrinking shadow on the wall
Grows more nearly what one is, till it becomes
Nothing at all. Death eats what the self has left.

Life gone, there's left a kind of statue
That will not survive a living day, nor yet
Be beautiful uncovered in a thousand years
Like a miniature of ivory and precious stones.

It is only the taken body draws our tears;
Mortal beauty, once dragged down to earth
Is already a praise of life, the grave's no fear
For the grandchildren hunting for lizards under the crabapple trees.

Smooth ceremonies of black are suitable for strangers
And calculated for the praise of death, but for life
Any battered detail with a fingerprint will do,
Like her old car stacked full with flowers
Following behind the hearse, as someone said,
Like the General's charger. There were, in fact, on a hill
Not far from her open grave, some draught horses grazing,
A comfortable old piebald nipping and nuzzling
The big brown mare beside him. The grass around them
Showed in smallest sprouts the green of May.

DOROTHY HEWETT 1923–2002

The prolific and turbulent playwright and poet Dorothy Hewett was born in Perth and grew up on a farm in the West Australian wheatbelt, near Wickepin, where she was educated through correspondence school. At nineteen she published her first poem and joined the Communist Party of Australia. In 1948 Hewett went to live in Sydney with the communist boilermaker Les Flood. She had three sons with him. This was a period of struggle against poverty, working in factories, organising strikes, being bashed and arrested and watching Flood go mad with schizoid paranoia. In 1960 she returned to Perth. She took her degree, taught English at the University of Western Australia, and married a former merchant seaman, Merv Lilley, with whom she had two daughters. He became a writer with Hewett's encouragement. Having grown increasingly disillusioned with the Communist Party, but not causes of the Left, she published her disaffected poem "The Hidden Journey" in 1967, and resigned from the Party in 1968, following the Soviet repression in Czechoslovakia. Her critical obituary of the Gulag-denying Communist writer Katharine Susannah Prichard, and her break with the CPA, provoked a backlash from former comrades.

She became a playwright in the 1960s and this drew her back to Sydney in 1974. In the last decade of her life she lived with her husband in the Blue Mountains, near Sydney. She wrote more than 15 plays, three novels, a volume of short stories, published a dozen or so books of poetry and the first volume of an autobiography, dying of breast cancer before she could complete it.

The disciplined development and historical density of "The Hidden Journey" is remarkable. It is as though, knowing she was about to become an apostate from her cause of more than twenty years, Hewett wanted to quote every relevant verse that the faithful would recognise, before she exited.

The following notes may help readers who grew up after the end of the Cold War: *Isaac Babel* (1894–1940), one of 20th century's great short story writers, was tortured and murdered by Stalin's secret police. His signed "confession", literally stained with his blood, still exists. *Ilya Ehrenburg* (1891–1967) the Soviet poet and novelist was awarded the Stalin Peace Prize in 1952, and in 1954 published a novel *The Thaw* which sensationally described a tyrannical factory boss as a "little Stalin". The novel's title was applied to "Krushchev's Thaw" of the mid-1950s, when Stalin was personally denounced, but the regime's legitimacy was still proclaimed. *Yevgeny Yevtushenko* (b. 1933), a poet who attained pop-star status, had an ambivalent relationship with the Soviet regime. He married the poet *Bella Akhmuldina* in 1954, the first of his four wives. *Vladimir Mayakovsky* (1893–1930), a great Russian poet who regarded his work as "Communist futurism" became disillusioned with Stalinism. His play *The Bedbug* (1929) satirised Soviet bureaucracy and philistinism. In the following year he shot himself, although Hewett refers to him as "murdered". After his death he was criticised in the Soviet press, until 1935, when it became known that Stalin regarded him as "the most talented poet of our Soviet epoch". This revival of Mayakovsky's reputation by Stalin has been referred to as Mayakovsky's "second death". The mining city of Novokuznesk has a statue of Mayakovsky. *Andrey Voznesensky* (b. 1933), described by Robert Lowell as "one of the greatest living poets in any language", first published poetry in 1958. As a teenager he sent his poems to the dissident Russian poet *Boris Pasternak* (1890–1960) who is famous as the author of *Doctor Zhivago*. *Daniil Granin* (b. 1919) was a Russian novelist. The popular war-poet *Aleksei Surkov* (1899–?) became First Secretary of the Writers' Union (1954–59), after Fadeyev resigned, but was castigated by Krushchev for having disgraced the Soviet Union, in persecuting Pasternak. *Natasha Tolstoy* was the daughter of the great novelist. The trial of the writers *Sinyavsky* and *Daniel* in 1965–66 for publishing anti-Soviet material in the West under assumed names brought to an end the Krushchev Thaw. They were sentenced to prison for five and seven years forced labour respectively. In 1966 the Soviet regime allowed the republication of the poetry of the alcoholic poet *Sergei Yesenin*, who married five times and hanged himself aged 30 from the heating pipes of his room in the *Hotel Angleterre*. The novelist *Alexander Fadeyev* (1901–1956) had two lengthy stints as General Secretary of the Writers' Union, claimed Stalin was "the greatest humanist the world has ever known", and was complicit in the repression of many Soviet writers, but interceded on behalf of others. He became an alcoholic and shot himself through the heart in his villa in the Peredelkino forest, leaving a suicide note in which he castigated the "ignorant leadership of the Party" following Lenin's death: "... The best cadres of literature – in number far more than the tsarist satraps could even dream of – have been physically exterminated or have died thanks to the *criminal connivance* of those in power. The best literary people died at an unnaturally young age; all the rest who were, even to the smallest degree, capable of producing true works of value died before reaching 40–50 years of age." *Yuri Gagarin* was the first Soviet cosmonaut.

The Hidden Journey

I

In 1952, in the year of Stalin, I came to Russia,
And saw flowers growing out of the blinkers on my eyes,
Saw the statues in the squares with their heads blown off,

The stumps of their thick stone necks stuffed up with roses.
Saw the wedding cake skyscrapers toppling like ice-cream cones,
And the firecrackers dripping off Stalin's moustache in the sky.
Saw a dumb cracked girl in Stalino who would not speak,
Welding under the great ribcage of the foundry,
While the Heroes of Labor smirked in the avenue outside.
Saw a blind man standing on a village corner,
With white eyes and a tin to take the kopeks,
Under the limes and the wind shaking the bird cherries.
Saw a ragged child who ran begging by the train in winter,
While the commissars pulled their pale fur coats to their ears.
Saw a man who sat on a step in a Siberian village,
Naked to the waist in the sleet, head buried in his hands,
Saw a woman with savage eyes who sat beside him
One arm flung over his body to shield him from cold.
Was he drunk or mad or in prison, his naked flesh
Blue-veined like breakable china left out in the rain?
A town of furtive eyes and whispering mouths,
Where men jostle against me in the State Railway Store,
Smelling of sunflower seeds and unwashed footrags,
Muttering out of closed lips in an unknown language
I do not understand: but sometimes in the river of sleep
A doubt surfaced, bumping like a stone, and would not be pushed under
And I would see the prison train pulled into Moscow Station.
Who are those paper faces pressed to the bars, behind the fixed bayonets
And the sleepy young snub-nosed soldiers, behind the flowers
And the speeches, the loudspeakers sweetly bawling "Soviet Land"?

I went back to mouth my commonplaces on street corners.
We are all guilty, ignorance was as inexcusable
As the blissful cataracts that closed on our white eyes.
Eyes, it was always eyes that gave me trouble,
Eyes cannot be denied; the sullen eyes of the Ukrainian women,
The mud snuffling at the doorsteps of their wooden houses.
The wind flattened the grass on the dark steppe, three men,
Huddled and reined on horses, stared into the safe, closed world
Of the train; hermetically sealed, warmed with pink lampshades,
Central heating and silver glasses of tea, we plunged
Into Moscow, to Lenin's tomb, the black queues moved like ants,
The red stars on the Kremlin blazed through the spring rain,
And Stalin kissed the little girls on the balcony,
His moustache ends teasing and tickling their rosy cheeks.

Mayakovsky, that murdered, trousered giant, legs astride,
Shut his stone mouth on the square, and Isaac Babel,
Round-faced, bespectacled, tender, still cried from the grave,
"The Revolution has given us the gift of silence".
Who spoke the truth; the old woman bowed in a black shawl
By the Moscow River, who crossed herself and cried "Peace",
Under the gilt onion domes of the orthodox churches?
Ivan, the Party secretary, warm and sardonic,
Who worshipped the Rembrandt oils in the Hermitage,
Tamara, with the brown blown hair and the angry eyes,
Whose dream was a dacha, lost, lost in the green virgin country?
Who knocked on your doors at night? Who hid the microphone,
Behind the gold frame of your favourite painting of roses?
Who disappeared from your street, who informed, who was guilty?
Where were you when they killed Isaac Babel's uncompromising tongue?
While I walked through the streets and listened to your marvellous lies,
Ehrenburg had a secret drawer for his autobiographies,
Khrushchev was playing with fire and a Twentieth Congress,
And Yevtushenko, that marvellous schoolboy, would, one day, stand
Beneath Mayakovsky's statue and shout out poems
Pressing open the lidless eyes and inserting truth,
Yevtushenko was only sixteen: the long winter fell
On the forests of Peredelkino, Pasternak's poems lay buried
Under the snow, a boy named Voznesensky sat at his feet in the fir forest.

Why did you deceive us? There was so much joy stirring
In the lilac roots under the black banks of that winter.
Beside the Leningrad River I might have met Daniil Granin,
Shot up from the war, an ache in his gut, his gold hair
Blowing truth in his candid mouth, I might have rubbed shoulders
With young Voznesensky, dreaming of ivory skyscrapers
Spinning like clouds, Bella Akhmadulina in a white pinafore
Playing hopscotch along the banks of the Moscow River.

II

Spring, 1965, a bleached crooner in a silver dress
Sings a Yevtushenko poem in the Hotel Moskva.
Rasputin bled on the snowy tablecloth.
The janitor gently draws the long cream curtains
Against the peroxide light and the upturned chairs,
The orchestra packs up like a Hemingway story.
The lilac, the marble staircase, the ringing voices
Of the amazons in the parks in their dark blue track suits.

The cafe in the Writers' Club where Natasha once
Came swan-bosomed down the stairs to old Lev Tolstoi,
His beard blue-fired in the teardrop chandelier.
Old Surkov stiff on the platform at the poetry reading,
Heroic, while the pitiless students chant "Where were you?"
The playwright sips his cognac, fat, gone to seed:
"Ah, the bureaucrats, the bureaucrats are always with us".
The Tolstoyans and the Dostoievskians argue outside in the street,
The blossom falls in snow-white tufts on their hair,
An old, fat, sunburnt woman in a dirty dress speaks French and German
The yellow-haired journalist steers her car through the rain.

"We Russians are all romantics. Do you believe in love at first sight?
That building on the corner has a special magic for me.
I met my husband in the lift. We looked at each other, and knew."
The rosy light sparkles like a samovar in the upstairs windows,
The windscreen wipers swish, the girls in their red silk London suits,
Pressing my fingers, the pavement glistens, the spires tremble
Like Pushkin's tales, Marina cries: "We Russians are a tragic people",
And checks behind the painting of roses that hangs in my hotel bedroom.
The young men in the Youth Cafe are listening to detective stories,
The girls are pinning up pictures of President Kennedy,
Khrushchev is a little shocked man in a Moscow apartment,
The gargantuan editor rolls through the Moscow night-spots
Throwing roubles like emerald rain at the hat-check girls,
The taxi driver reads "War and Peace" in the parking lot.
"We Russians have soul. To understand us you must know the Russian soul,
Have you a soul in your country?" Irena swings her sooty eyelashes
In the back of the taxi. *Have* we a soul in my country?
The girls and boys place dark roses, gently, on Pasternak's grave.

III

1967, the Exhibition of Abstract Art is closed, the young men demonstrate
Under Pushkin's statue, Sinyavsky, Daniel, the poor demented son
Of Sergei Yesenin, are lost in a labor camp, alive or dead?
Yesenin's body dangles from a rope in the rosy twilight,
The gun goes off, the echoes roll across the city, Mayakovsky
Sprawls like a giant on the floor, the Bolshoi whirls with light?
"The Bedbug" plays to packed houses, screaming, "I am alone ... alone".
The girls in their red silk London suits trip through the Red Square
Dreaming of Paris visas, the playwright in the blue straw dacha
Of cherries and limes, puzzles his brow over questions of Trotsky, Bukharin.
"They have not been rehabilitated, therefore we cannot discuss them."

The Japanese "No" masks hang sardonic as words on his wall.
Yevtushenko washes his hands and the trial begins …
"I agree with what was done, but not with how it was done.
Should they be allowed to wash their dirty linen outside their country?"

IV

The dirty, rosy, glittering linen of Moscow,
Spreads out in a snowy meadow under the sky.
The blossom whirls in the wind from Moscow Airport,
The taxi carries me with my broken eyeglasses, dazzled
With light and pain, past Lenin's Tomb, the dismantled
Statues of Stalin, the broken iron bell in the Kremlin.
The backs of Sinyavsky and Daniel bend over the golden cupolas,
    The black backs of Satan ironically bending and bending,
    Wringing their dirty linen out in the sky.
    Seven years, five years' hard labor. Ah! slanderers,
    Cut out the silver tongues that toll black as the cracked bell.
Sinyavsky carries Pasternak's coffin shoulder high up the grassy meadow,
Mayakovsky floats like a cloud in trousers over this city,
Blessed, with a powder burn on his forehead, Yesenin's shadow swings
Back and forth on the stairs, Eisenstein's voice screams confessions
Endlessly into the amplifiers, where is Meyerholt's grave and Babel groping
Shortsightedly, shabby and plump, bespectacled, tender as blue lilacs
Shambling down Gorky Street? … I will speak with the tongue,
The iron tongue, the tongue of the bell, the gift of the dumb.
Why do I start from my sleep at Fadeyev's gun going off at midnight?
His vodka bottle stands, thick with cobwebs and dust, under the naked bulb
In the Writers' Union, the chandelier glitters, the blonde crooner sings
"Moscow Nights", holy city, Jerusalem, the janitor twitches the curtain,
Gagarin sits in the moonlight and autographs endless postcards,
The linen shroud of the snow touches the sleeping faces,
The voices cry out under the red stars like untended graves …
"We Russians have soul. Have you a soul in your country?"
Which country is mine? I dare not be dumb but must speak
With the voice of men who dream to be angels.
A fumbling at the door, short-sighted, blinking like owls –
"Is that you my friend? Come in and speak to me now,
Have you called to lend me an extra pair of your spectacles?
Look! there is nothing, nothing at all behind those monstrous roses
In the gilded frame, nothing … Isaac Babel, come in."

ERIC ROLLS 1923–2007

Eric Rolls was born at Grenfell, in western New South Wales, and his early education was mainly by correspondence. "His promise as a storyteller emerged early. Every Friday afternoon at his kindergarten in Grenfell, his teacher, Miss Postlethwaite, used to tell the class stories. But she was rather dull. So one day, five-year-old Eric put up his hand and said 'Miss Postlethwaite I'd like to tell a story'. She said 'Alright, come out here.' Eric told the story of a grain of wheat from sowing to harvesting, miming the process as he talked. He started telling stories every Friday afternoon, and adults came to hear him." (Tom Griffiths: Eric Rolls' obituary for The Australian Academy of the Humanities.)

Rolls won entry to the selective Fort Street School in Sydney and from high school went straight into the army. During World War II he served in New Guinea and Bougainville with the New Guinea Air Warning Wireless Company which reported movements of Japanese troops and aeroplanes. On his discharge he took up a Soldiers' Settlement property in the New South Wales wheat belt where he was a "full-time" farmer until 1986. He married Joan Stephenson and they had three children, one of whom, Kerry, is referred to in "Four Poems for Joan". Joan died in 1985 and he remarried in 1988.

Rolls is best known for his acclaimed non-fiction prose: works such as *They All Ran Wild* (1969), about rabbits and other pests introduced into Australia, and *A Million Wild Acres* (1981), an ecological history of the Pilliga forest near his home. He was also the leading historian of the Chinese in Australia, in his two-volume *Flowers and the Wide Sea*. Rolls commented that his feeling for poetry perhaps found its truest fulfilment in these factual books which display his eye for striking and sensuous detail and his exuberant interest in life. "Emperor Butterfly", "Bamboo", "Crossing the Surinam River" and "Dog Fight" are from *The Green Mosaic* (1977), his second volume of poems, which reflects on his World War II experiences in New Guinea.

The Hare

The long view first, the distant scene:
A moving splotch of brown on green;
A hare-because-he-must-be-hare,
For what else brown could be feeding there?

Then middle-distance hare-by-shape;
Hare by his long-eared long-legged lope;
Hare by the way he stands up straight
With forepaws bent as though he were praying
But the tilt of his head as he looks about
And the flare of his eyes at once denying
His pantomime humility;
And hare in his crouch as a hawk flies over,
Belly so low in the short white clover
That a pattern of leaves only three inches high

Breaks the line of his back to the hawk in the sky;
And hare while he crawls with his ears tucked down
To a clump of dead grass that matches his brown
Where he hides from the hawk who is out to seek
No more than a cricket to fill his beak.

And last the close-up in a squat:
Each-hair-detailed hare-by-Dürer;
And difficult now when he should be clearer
For brown unbrowns to grey and white,
Black and cream and brown, and light
So confuses tone and shadow,
And the long hairs spiked from his tidy coat
Like his whiskers tremble so,
It makes him somewhat indistinct;
And when side-on I meet his eye,
As black and full as a muscat grape,
Fixed in a deep unblinking stare,
It bears such urgent life within
That the eye rates more and the body less
Till like some ancient birth from chaos
There is one live eye in a waste of hare.

Meg's Song and Davie's Song

MEG
Yesterday I was a maid
And timidly down the paddock strayed
With one wild bluebell at my breast
That pricked me so I could not rest
To where young Davie stooked the hay.
O he was strong as the spring day.
In the shade of a stook in a hay-sweet haze
I sat and slacked my trembling knees
And laughed with Davie standing there
As I fitted wheat ears in my hair.

DAVIE
Corn plump and corn crisp
Meg has a waist to clasp
And breasts that were never kissed
And loins that had never sung
To vibrant pluck of hand and tongue:
Burning naked as the sky

We sang together Meg and I.
I speared her like a sheaf of hay
And tossed her maidenhead away.

MEG
Now today I try to work
But my arms are heavy as I sweep
And every little while I look
To Davie down amongst the hay
And through the open door I keep
Asking quietly if I may
Come to him again today
And will that he may hear, may see
And turn about and beckon me.
O quickly then I'll gladly run
And naked in the glorious sun
Kiss for love and kiss for fun
And when at last he breaks my thighs
My mother's love I will despise.

DAVIE
Corn crisp and corn plump
Meg rolls upon her rump
Like a sheaf of hay unbound
Wind teased about the ground
And darling darling are her cries
As I take her by the thighs.

The Fox

Ho, the fox; he was a cocky one, oh yes,
With a ruff that would grace the cub of a lion
And a brush as full and long as he please.
Abroad with his mate when the moon was bright
He walked as though he owned the night
And he stepped as though he stepped on stars;
And came in his pride where a tethered dog
Slept by a piece of unwanted meat.
The fox walked up and gave him the treat
Of three fox barks from six short feet.
The fat dog jumped out of sense and wit
To the end of his chain and he strained at it
And barked till his lips and the ground about
Were specked with foam and his tongue lolled out.

The fox stood off and barked again
Then circled outside the sphere of the chain.
As the dog in fury followed him round
The chain on its centre peg was wound.
When it was short enough, the fox,
Showing how often the calm are wise,
Went quietly in and claimed his prize.
Then with the piece of stolen meat
He trod as though on pointed stars
And he walked like the king to the queen of night
And dropped it down beside his mate;
And after her, he deigned to eat.

Emperor Butterfly

Beauty (and poetry) are usually misunderstood –
They are attributed to fragile origins.
Birds of paradise were said to feed on dew.

Here you can see the robust substance of beauty (and poetry).
On this path ahead, resting on mud,
Is a New Guinea Emperor.
His five-inch blue wings pulsate
While he feeds on the droppings of a cassowary.

Bamboo

I sing the quality of bamboo.
I cut a small cane and make a pipe to sing the quality of bamboo.
Bamboo is the comb in my hair.
Bamboo cut off my foreskin and pierced my nose.

I wore a toucan's wing-bone in my nose that time I hid in bamboo
And leapt from it to kill my first man.
I wrapped his head in banana leaves and bore it on a bamboo pole.

Bamboo stores the water I drink.
Bamboo made the spears I learnt to fish with.
Bamboo is the floor I stand on
Or a knife that will skin a cuscus.
Bamboo are the poisoned needles I push into the mud
So that an enemy treads himself to death.
Bamboo is the cage the foolish fish cannot swim out of
And the prop which holds open the snare for the careless wallaby.
Bamboo is a platform for the dead.

Bamboo is all these things and more
Yet one man may carry a bundle of bamboo
As big as a log of pine which many men will strain under.

Bamboo are the rafters of the house I must soon build.
Bamboo are the anklets which Sauri wears on her right leg
And the bracelets which encase her left arm
From wrist to elbow.
Bamboo strings the cowrie shells which are part of her price
And bamboo will prod the five pigs I must drive to her father's house.

What is that which is round and hollow like bamboo?
It is as small as the pipe I play
Or as big as my water-carrier.
It is a water-carrier.
It bears two waters
And of one of these Sauri will drink so deeply
Her belly will swell rounder than a bundle of water-carriers.

But I sing of the quality of bamboo.

Crossing the Surinam River

An old native, his mary and two young children
Came up the track from Kaigulin.
None of them looked at us. They went about their business
As though we were not by the Surinam River.
The mary swung a net bag of yams onto her head,
Then she put her son on top of the yams.
The old man held his daughter as high as he could reach.
And they both stepped into the Surinam River.

The surface was as bumpy as a line of boulders.
We had been trying to cross for hours.
The river came out of the Finisterre Ranges
And raced for the Ramu at fifteen knots.

They all went under, straight down under –
We gasped that they hadn't even tried to swim –
Then heads speared out of water ten feet from the bank
Then ten feet farther on in a dead straight line.
They bounced off the bottom of the Surinam River
And they held a straight line to the opposite bank.

No one had done better since Christ walked on the water
But they had no aura of miracle makers.

They behaved like people who had crossed a river.
They shook themselves dry and they combed their hair.
The mother wiped her children's noses and picked up her yams
Then they all walked gravely on.

We couldn't call them back to ask them how they did it.
We couldn't speak their tongue and they couldn't hear for rushing water.
We just felt foolish by the Surinam River.

Dog Fight

Inside
The wireless is irritable with static.
The relieving sig. turns down the volume
And strains to hear his call sign.

Outside
The relieved sig. is relieving himself.
He is trying to piss his full name in the dust.
He has been saving up for hours.
He has to concentrate to control the flow.

Overhead
Two Zeros come out of cloud.
They hope to beat the Lightnings to the take-off.

On the ground
The Lightnings are already rolling.
They have been forewarned.
The cloud was too far from the strip anyway.
One Zero turns and bolts.
The other climbs
To try to stop the Lightnings getting above him.

The sig. has finished his first Christian name neatly.
He takes two paces right and begins a capital W.

A morse signal offers an urgent weather report.
Two spotters jam each other in plain language
Reporting the Zeros
Which had already been reported.

The Lightnings are too fast for the Zero.
Only one goes in to attack.
It seems so easy:
There is a burst of smoke
And the Zero begins a slow spiral to ground.

It looks like a feather coming down.
You think about reaching up to catch it.

The sig. finds it harder near the end.
The pressure is dropping
And there is a T to be crossed.

The message about the Zeros
Has been relayed to Port Moresby
And the sig. has got down the coded weather report.
He is sending R for received.

There is another little burst of smoke
As the Zero hits the ground.
Two drops of urine
Make sufficient dent in the dust
To dot a final I.
A Morse signal sounds the end of transmission.

Four Poems for Joan

Going to Bed

She undresses unconsciously although she knows I watch her.
She ignores the sleeve turned inside out on her jumper
Like a child hurrying into bed.

The gay blouse I bought her may crumple on a chair back.
She reaches to undo the hooked elastic on her bare back
And stoops to drop her breasts free.

They swing as she straightens. Cold stiffens the nipples.
The areolae stained in pregnancy are bronze as apples.
She scratches where the cups rubbed

And huddles into a pyjama coat as shapeless as love.
She balances each foot athletically to remove
Shoes, socks and jeans.

She strips off her panties, teases her pubic hair,
Picks up the pyjama pants she decides not to wear
And drops them at the foot of the bed.

Then she crawls towards her pillow. Her coat rides out of reach
Of her buttocks and displays her cushiony arch
Framed between her thighs.

She curls under the blankets, picks up yesterday's newspaper
And props herself lightly on her side. But, a sudden sleeper,

She soon lies among crumpled pages.

And when I join her, awake or asleep
She moves to welcome me, if I am not too cold, and I keep
Aware of her integrity.

Death

Joan's laughter surely must have startled death.
What would he have been expecting at that stage?
She couldn't talk, she couldn't turn in bed;
Kerry and I had washed her wafer of flesh, we'd stroked it with oil,
Now we had to roll her free of the pain that threatened movement.
We discussed how far to bend her knees,
How to control her head, whose arm would lift her thighs.
Perhaps concern made us absurdly solemn. Joan's face crinkled,
Blue eyes glittered, she shook with laughter.
A few days later she died.

Death was disappointed with our offering, I'm confident of that.
He expected a distraught family to present him with a boxful of sad body.
All he got was two double handfuls of laughter
Covered with the bush flowers she loved, an insubstantial titbit
For his appetite. Perhaps he realised his work was waste effort:
She'd have given him all of her in thirty years time
When she was ready.

Double Bed

Hard nipple studded into my palm,
In brief wakings she fed me warmth,
Wonder, interest, excitement, comfort, need, trust:
She fed me love.

Penis hard against her buttock,
In brief wakings I emitted gratitude,
Respect, energy, curiosity, relief, expectation, lust:
I emitted love.

My nights now are commonplace.
I sleep huddled closely.
I wake sometimes with a hungry hand
Groping in cold space.

Last Kiss

Kissing her kisses to take with her, where?
Across her forehead and into her hair,

Eyebrows, eyes, and down each cheek,
Lobe of an ear and nose and neck,
On her lips I realise
She is trying to kiss me back,
Whispered kisses I barely feel.

This wondrous woman more frail than a moth –
I tell her I love her, I tell, I tell.
What can I tell her to take with her, where?
There ought to be something to comfort her with:
A word, a phrase to startle death.
We exhausted our talking this last mad year.
I stroke her, I fail her, I finger her hair.

VINCENT BUCKLEY 1925–1988

Vincent Buckley was born in Romsey, Victoria. His father was a carter, and his mother, a teacher and librarian. Buckley was to describe himself as "an Irishman born in Australia who has spent long periods in Ireland over the past thirty years." Seven of Buckley's great-grandparents were Irish. During much of the Great Depression Buckley's father was unemployed or had labouring jobs. Buckley wrote of him: "Day after day, he repeated certain Irish familial and individual patterns not only under but inside a conscious ideology of Australianness. He wanted to be Australian, even if it meant ceasing to be perceived as Irish or to feel Irish." His father loved the verse of "Banjo" Paterson. Buckley realised when he heard Paterson's lines "Where the air is clear as crystal, and the white stars fairly blaze/At midnight in the cold and frosty sky" that he wanted to be a poet.

In 1938, at the age of twelve, Buckley left Romsey and became a boarder at St Patrick's College, East Melbourne. He said: "There's nothing like a boy of poor family given a Jesuit education. They're very faithful but uncomfortable colleagues". He enlisted in the Royal Australian Air Force in 1943 and was invalided out in 1945. Enrolled in the University of Melbourne in 1946, in 1947 he married Edna Forbes in St Patricks Cathedral. In 1951 he began teaching at the University of Melbourne.

The dust jacket blurb of his first volume of poems, *The World's Flesh* (1954), was a declaration of war on the then dominant school of Australian nature poetry, stating the book "is not merely nature poetry; it represents an attempt to state in many different imaginative contexts the issues which face a modern man who is both Christian and Humanist." Buckley's attempt to be a "modern man" who combined Humanism and Christianity was to prove a source of life-long tension. But it provided the "pressure" that he believed he needed and allowed his later poetry to flourish after an over-rhetorical debut. From 1955 to 1957 he studied at Cambridge, visiting Ireland for the first time. From 1958 until 1964 he was the intermittent editor of the quarterly magazine *Prospect* produced by liberal Catholics associated with the University of Melbourne's apostolate.

In 1960 Buckley's carefully constructed world was shattered. He fell in love with Penelope Curtis. Buckley's wife Edna after many years agreed to a divorce. The relationship with Curtis had continued and was formalised in 1976. She had adopted the surname Buckley. Soon afterwards they had two daughters, one of them Grania, who is mentioned in the final section of "Hunger-strike".

In 1961 Buckley became poetry editor of *The Bulletin*. In 1967 he was appointed to a personal chair by the University of Melbourne. During the 1950s he published perceptive and pioneering critical essays collected in *Essays in Poetry: Mainly Australian* (1957) and *Poetry and Morality* (1959). His third volume of poetry, *Arcady and Other Places* (1966) largely broke free of the "high seriousness" that constricted his first two volumes. The book's centre is "Stroke", which was prompted by his father's death in 1963. Buckley published three more volumes of poetry during his lifetime. He drifted away from institutional Catholicism but remained, as he put it, an "ethnic Catholic".

A passionate involvement with Ireland replaced his lapsed Catholicism. In the 1970s and 1980s he stayed for extensive periods in that country. His love for Ireland and his anger at the long history of English repression found expression in what may be his finest poem, "Hunger-strike". This deals with the 1981 defiance, led by Bobby "Geronimo" Sands, among Provisional Irish Republican Army prisoners in the Maze prison, ten of whom died of starvation. John McLaren, Buckley's biographer, states Buckley "claimed it was not a political sequence". However one may feel about its politics, as a human document – a statement of the men's suffering and the popular support they aroused – this poem is extremely moving. The rhetorical furniture is sparse, the language undecorated. The typography, with the text indented to the right beneath each section heading, makes it read like an indictment. Among Irish-born literary figures who had a more complicated view of the events, Seamus Heaney in *Stepping Stones – Interviews with Seamus Heaney* (Faber & Faber, 2008) commented: "I realized that Vincent Buckley had an unflinching loyalty to the hunger strikers when he began a sequence of poems about them, even naming them individually. As far as I was concerned, Vincent was romanticizing the situation that pertained by then. He was caught in a time loop and was holding on to a late-1960s, early-1970s vision of 'the struggle'."

Buckley, a short man with a soft voice and patrician features, was a commanding presence, but suffered from ill-health, having had rheumatic fever when young. A few years before his death he refused heart surgery, and he died, aged 63, of a heart condition. His funeral was attended by eleven priests, with Father Peter Steele SJ delivering the homily.

Stroke

I

In the faint blue light
We are both strangers; so I'm forced to note
His stare that comes moulded from deep bone,
The full mouth pinched in too far, one hand
Climbing an aluminium bar.

Put, as though for the first time,
In a cot from which only a hand escapes,
He grasps at opposites, knowing
This room's a caricature of childhood.
"I'm done for."

"They're treating you all right?"
We talk from the corners of our mouths
Like old lags, while his body strains
To notice me, before he goes on watching
At the bed's foot
His flickering familiars,
Skehan, Wilson, Ellis, dead men, faces,
Bodies, paused in the aluminium light,
Submits his answer to his memories,
"Yes, I'm all right. But still it's terrible."

Words like a fever bring
The pillar of cloud, pillar of fire
Travelling the desert of the mind and face.
The deep-set, momentarily cunning eyes
Keep trying for a way to come
Through the bed's bars to his first home.
And almost find it. Going out I hear
Voices calling requiem, where the cars
Search out the fog and gritty snow,
Hushing its breathing under steady wheels.
Night shakes the seasonable ground.

II

Decorous for the dying's sake
The living talk with eyes and hands
Of football, operations, work;
The pussyfooting nurses take
Their ritual peep; the rule demands

I stand there with a stiff face
Ready, at a word or gleam,
To conjure off the drops of sweat.
So small a licit breathing-space
Brings each inside the other's dream.

Across the bright unechoing floors
The trolleys and attendants rove;
On tiptoe shine, by scoured walls,

The nearly speechless visitors
Skirt the precipice of love.

III

Oaks, pines, the willows with their quiet
Terror; the quiet terror of my age;
The seven-year-old bookworm sitting out
At night, in the intense cold, the horse
Tethered, the stars almost moving,
The cows encroaching on the night grass.
The frost stung my lips; my knees burned;
Darkness alone was homely. The hawthorn tree
Glimmered as though frost had turned to language
And language into sharp massy blossoms.
Once, I even scraped my father's hand
And glimpsed the white underside of poplars
That, moving, almost touched the flashing stars.
Squat, steep-browed, the Methodist Church nestled
Halfway between the distant police station
And the near barn; a whole world
Gave neither words nor heat, but merely
A geometry of the awakening sight.
I had forgotten that night, or nights;
And if I think back, there's nothing mythical:
A cross-legged kid with a brooding nose
His hands were too chilled to wipe,
A book whose pages he could hardly turn,
A silent father he had hardly learned
To touch; cold he could bear,
Though chill-blooded; the dark heat of words.
A life neither calm nor animal.
Now, in the deeper quiet of my age,
I feel thirty years
Turning my blood inwards; neither trees nor stars,
But a hush and start of traffic; spasms of sound
Loosening tram rails, bluestone foundations,
Manuscripts, memories; too many tasks;
A body shrinking round its own
Corruption, though a long way from dying.
We suit our memories to our sufferings.

IV

Every clod reveals an ancestor.
They, the spirit hot in their bodies,
Burned to ash in their own thoughts; could not
Find enough water; rode in a straight line
Twenty miles across country
For hatred jumping every wire fence;
With uillean pipes taunted the air
Ferociously that taunted them;
Spoke with rancour, but with double meanings;
Proud of muscle, hated the bone beneath;
Married to gain forty acres
And a family of bond servants; died bound.
I, their grandson, do not love straight lines,
And talk with a measured voice – in double meanings –
Remembering always, when I think of death,
The grandfather, small, loveless, sinister,
  ("The most terrible man I ever seen,"
  Said Joe, who died thin as rice paper)
Horse-breaker, heart-breaker, whose foot scorches,
Fifty years after, the green earth of Kilmore.
It's his heat that lifts my father's frame
Crazily from the wheel-chair, fumbles knots,
Twists in the bed at night,
Considers every help a cruelty.

V

Indoors and out, weather and winds keep up
Time's passion: paddocks white for burning.
As usual, by his bed, I spend my time
Not in talk, but restless noticing:
If pain dulls, grief coarsens.
Each night we come and, voyeurs of decay,
Stare for minutes over the bed's foot,
Imagining, if we think at all,
The body turning ash, the near insane
Knowledge when, in the small hours,
Alone under the cold ceiling, above
The floor where the heating system keeps its pulse,
He grows accustomed to his own sweat
And sweats with helplessness, remembering
How, every day, at eight o' clock

The Polish nurse kisses him goodnight.
His arms are bent like twigs; his eyes
Are blown to the door after her; his tears
Are squeezed out not even for himself.
Where is the green that swells against the blade
Or sways in sap to the high boughs? To the root
He is dry wood, and in his sideways
Falling brings down lights. Our breath
Mingles,
Stirs the green air of the laurel tree.

VI

The roofs are lit with rain.
Winter. In that dark glow,
Now, as three months ago,
I pray that he'll die sane.

On tiles or concrete path
The old wheeling the old,
For whom, in this last world,
Hope is an aftermath,

And the damp trees extend
Branch and thorn. We live
As much as we believe.
All things covet an end.

Once, on the Kerrie road,
I drove with him through fire.
Now, in the burnt cold year,
He drains off piss and blood,

His wounded face tube-fed,
His arm strapped to a bed.

VII

At the merest handshake I feel his blood
Move with the ebb-tide chill. Who can revive
A body settled in its final mood?
To whom, on what tide, can we move, and live?

Later I wheel him out to see the trees:
willows and oaks, the small plants he mistakes
For rose bushes; and there
In the front, looming, light green, cypresses.
His pulse no stronger than the pulse of air.

Dying, he grows more tender, learns to teach
Himself the mysteries I am left to trace.
As I bend to say "Till next time", I search
For signs of resurrection in his face.

Two Funerals

I

For once, they're gathered as a clan:
Faces exchanging words of smoke,
Bodies in out-of-date dark suits
Moving in guarded unison;
Debaters all, yet no one disputes
The facts, and no one points the joke:
It's death that straightens out a man.

I think, we have all donned the mask
Of his dead face; it seems an age,
Under the few birdless trees.
That, like a chorus at its task,
We tread the graveyard as our stage,
Half-sharers in those litanies
Which promise what we dare not ask.

II

It's one of those funerals where the relatives
Rather pointedly decline to mourn.
At times like this the staring will can turn
Flesh to stone. The chief mourners
Move with gallantry, not grief: the brother
Managing his feelings like the family business,
The mother grey with whisky and
Late hours of savoir-faire.
In the pinched field the gravestones look
Modelled in clay. The firing party,
Pimply before a brisk W.O.,
Adjust their eyes, thinking about their rifles.
Half captive, I allow myself to share
My neighbour's sotto voce confidence:
"As if he'd been an Irishman he managed
To prang in the flattest landscape in England.
He made a hole in his motherland
Thirty feet deep.

They say there's not an ounce of him in that box,
Just clods, pebbles, God knows what,
Scraped together. They couldn't find a scrap
Except, you'd never credit this, his great
Pukka moustache."
The Union Jack with its stretched colours
Guards the brave deception;
Over clods the flyting of the bugles,
Barely competing with such knowledge.

Hunger-strike

Warrior: I. One whose occupation is warfare; a fighting man; in eulogistic sense, a valiant or an experienced man of war. Now chiefly *poet.* and *rhet.*, exc. as applied to the fighting men and heroes of past ages and of uncivilized peoples. *Shorter O.E.D.*

To Redefine "Warrior

Through this season
of hot clouds, you have needed
to redefine "Warrior": One
who makes war, with no weapons
but the sticks of his forearms,
the electric pain of his body
in his cell, away from the air
his family breathes, drenched with sweat
of armed men, with machines,
robots, automatics, clockbombs,
hijacked milk-lorries,
sprayguns and knapsacks of gas,
plastic bullets, shields, visors:
For the armed man is known by his tools,
but a warrior by the death of his terrors

and of their monstrous dream prototypes:
tortured heads, with holes large as faces
opened in them; a corpse hung at the ford;
a serf enduring the thousand lashes;
statues fighting; a masked man
beckoning between the armies;
a comrade lasting into his sixtieth day;
a lark, as he said to himself, at the window
but caught, crying, by the foot, in black wire.

Bobby Sands: One

Now he is laid on the sheepskin rug
so that his bones will not burn him,
pads are put on his heels
against the bedsores. He is blind
and deaf. The pain they told him of
jolts its thin current
into every movement. His teeth
protrude like the bones of a dead man.
He is dying for his word. *Geronimo.*

They would not let him alone.
Day and night they came and went
stirring his pallid shadow,
interpreters of his dying.
Day and night he hung on the wire,
his curled body outlasting them
till they fell silent; "he was the piper
walking in the front of battle".

Then, he died in a clean place,
crooked, on the waterbed, the Pope's
crucifix proudly beside him, his mind
open as a galaxy.
Le dur desir de durer
saw him buried as Geronimo.

Sands: Two

But, before that, he was lowered
into the deep trough
of others' wills, his wire thin bones
buzzing with speeches, lights
thick on his shrinking face,
died badgered with help,
not hearing
the faraway words his mother
spoke to the microphone.

For her the hard thing
must have been keeping her eyes down,
her lips steady, while blurting out
what they had said to each other: "We talked
about old times … when he was at school
… and in the youth club …"

This was the time when
everyone came to talk at him
and to come out and tell the world
what he wanted, and why
he should/should not want it
                    [But he wanted not to give up,
                    and not to die either. Geronimo.]

The sky was full of mouths: except the father,
who said nothing, the brother,
who was an arm to lean on
for the sister, who could not hide her eyes,
and the mother, all large
unweeping features, and going in,
and coming out, and going
only to come back next day
to the reporters husking like bees:
"How is he today?" "He's dyun."

Francis Hughes

Colonel, press your cap down hard
or keep your fingers in your belt,
searchlights and men in every yard,
the tree beside you red with haws,
Saracens in the windgreen lanes,
the day they bury Francis Hughes.

Is this the corpse you hate so much,
that awesome boy, going to Mass
on a weekday morning in Bellaghy,
loitering so the late dews pass
along his footstep to the door,
thinking the land's his own, perhaps?

Go to your tea, sergeant, trooper,
his shadow follows you with scorn
now that you've lowered his starved face
deep in the ground where he was born:
the long-eyed kinsman drumming on it
tunes you will never learn or bear.

Raymond McCreesh

Weeks later, it was his face
that loomed on the hourly news,

tilted back, fragile, laughing.
To whom someone said, on the 58th day,
do you want a drink of milk?
He was blind now. He said, I don't know.
Batlike his brain in and out
of his body-shape, the mind's landscape
entering and leaving sun and shade.
For days, on the wire services,
in press statements, they took his name:
Do you want a drink of milk? I don't know.

And they talked of his family
as if he were straining
to leave some mad priesthood,
or to break some taboo of the townland,
and the people he loved would not let him.
Eloquent assassins,
Oxbridge men, Sandhurst men,
I am almost too ashamed
to mention your shame.

Interlude for Exploration

Standing at the microphone,
he shot his cuffs and said, earnestly,
"Good God, we're not barbarians,"
while the other railed against all violence
booming, "kill the killers."
None of them is a barbarian
they are all against violence
which (let us be quite clear)
they totally and unequivocally reject.
What they *do* support
is the police and the army
and Saladins in the closed streets
and plastic bullets at walking schoolgirls
and blackened faces waiting in the darkness
after the local dance; and the spacemen
on each corner, with their guns cradled,
and the knowledge that the Opposition is with them

and that the Bishops, who hate violence,
will ask no hard questions, and the columnists
will be as full of similes as the poets,

lightheaded (this way, that way)
and Oxford will debate measure and process,
and the *Tablet* moral or some other theology
(all against, utterly against violence)
and the sun will rise in the West
if we want it, for we are dying
as much, but not as fast, as
their unarmed prisoners.

Interlude for Execution

On the waste ground where they shot him
two or three birds fly up
flapping, as if the air's too heavy.
The ground is drifting with lead.
Nothing grows. Vanished even
the permanent knuckles of the plane-trees,
and the people who heard him screaming
can grow nothing inside,
and can say or think nothing
while they wait for the suicide hour
flashing with law and order.

Patsy O'Hara

Fourth, Patsy O'Hara. We had seen his sister
moving from door to door,
from taoiseach to taoiseach,
with her unanswered face.
while all the time he sat, with hunched beard,
in his bugged, photographed cell,
waiting till they would make him
carry his body down the Creggan
moving in procession
slow and quiet as a milkman
while the young boys in their staring thousands
drummed their heels on Derry's walls.

Joe McDonnell

who said, and became famous for it,
"I've got too much to live for,"
and said later (or it may have been Kiernan Doherty),
"I don't want to die over a food parcel,"
died on my birthday. It was almost exact mid-summer.

The black flags at Walkinstown roundabout
were held up for hours by the waiting faces
and the midges at Phoenix Park
stung even the feckless Spanish students
in hot moist green that seemed to grow warmer
in the encroaching shadows

And Martin Hurson on Grania's birthday.
And Kevin Lynch and Kiernan Doherty
died shortly after the Commission
had failed to solve the English.
        (That question of the ages:
        How do you solve the English?)

And Thomas McElwee, the shy-looking cousin
countryman, a proper devil for cars;
whose eight sisters carried his coffin
into the silent crowded roadway,
then on, with other bearers, into
the roaring graveyard, where
the whole countryside swayed in late summer.

And another long-eyed northerner
enrolled in their love compact.

Louisa Stewart is Foaling

Winter has coloured the straw dark as sweat.
Louisa Stewart is foaling. Nothing keeps clean;
but the stable rats, if they're watching, do it quietly
at the sight of the mare named for the gentry foaling.

Lord Waterford is dead, so the rebels sang
in '98, and most of the Beresfords
have gone, to hell or London. But they've come back
as magistrates, bosses, titular studmasters.

The corners of our house look cold as iron;
the cobbles of the yard shine hard as an axle
between the midwinter stars. She is grunting. Strange
vanity, to name your racemares after yourselves.

And the devil makes his bed, the song went on.
Sweat-oiled, named for the grandee's family,
Louisa Stewart, stifflegged on her side,

lies foaling; her head wags; the great damp arse

heaves up and down on straw. Noise grinds the yard
where the blind mare, who's not in foal this year,
stretches her neck, twists out her head like rope
for what is listening with her. A thread of wireless

harpmusic out the window, warm as twined fingers.
In the one acre we have the bard's triad,
music, fertility, blindness,
the whole of life: and Louisa voiding her colt

with the ropes tied to his forelegs, and three of us
haul on the rope, heavy as bellringing,
our legs braced, clutching each other's waists,
to force out blazed forehead and marble eyeball.

O she did it well without fuss. Cool as the gentry.
I think if I go out into the forest I'll hear
in the long paddock the whole coven running,
mares and foals together, in startled bursts

set off by her unheard breathing in the darkness;
and now they are streaming down over the ditch
in a delighted joke of unity. Louisa Stewart,
who did her job in style, will need clean straw.

J. R. ROWLAND 1925–1996

John Russell Rowland grew up on a farming property near Armidale, New South Wales, and was educated at Cranbrook School in Sydney and at the University of Sydney and joined the diplomatic corps in 1945. He had many overseas postings and was Australian ambassador to France from 1978 to 1982. He published seven volumes of poetry and translated a number of 20th-century Russian poets. Many of his poems reflect his experience of the countries where he was posted, but the national capital, Canberra, was where he returned at the end of his postings.

Canberra in April

Vast mild melancholy splendid
Day succeeds day in august chairmanship
Presiding over autumn. Poplars in valleys
Unwavering candleflames, balance over candid
Rough-linen fields, against a screen of hills

Sending invisible smokes from far below
To those majestic nostrils. A Tuscan landscape

On a larger scale; for olives eucalypts
In drifts and dots on hillheads, magpie and crow
For field-birds, light less intimate, long slopes stripped

Bare of vine or village, the human imprint
Scarcely apparent; distances immense
And glowing at the rim, as if the land
Were floating, like the round leaf of a water-plant
In a bright meniscus. Opposite, near at hand,

Outcrops of red brick houses, northern trees
In costume, office-buildings
Like quartz-blocks flashing many-crystalled windows
Across the air. Oblivious, on their knees,
Of time and setting, admirals pick tomatoes

In their back gardens, hearty
Bankers exchange golf-scores, civil servants
Their after-office beers; the colony
Of diplomats prepares its cocktail parties
And politicians their escape to Melbourne.

This clean suburbia, house-proud but servantless
Is host to a multitude of children
Nightly conceived, born daily, riding bikes,
Requiring play-centres, schools and Progress
Associations: in cardigans and slacks

Their mothers polish kitchens, or in silk
White gloves and tight hats pour each other tea
In their best china, canvassing the merits
Of rival plumbers, grocers, Bega milk
And the cost of oil-fired heating or briquettes.

To every man his car, his wife's on Thursday
Plus one half-day she drops him at the office
(Air murmurous with typewriters) at eight-forty
To pick him up for lunch at home; one-thirty
Sees the streets gorged with his return to duty

And so the year revolves; files swell, are closed
And stored in basements, Parliaments adjourn
And reassemble, speeches are made and hooted.
Within the circle of the enfranchised
These invite those and are themselves invited,

At formal dinners, misprints of the *Times*
Compete with anecdotes of Rome or Paris
For after all, the capital is here.
The general populace sprays its roses, limes
Its vegetable patch and drinks its beer:

Golf at the weekend, gardening after five,
Indoor bowling, TV day and night
Lunchtime softball, shopping late on Friday
As under glass the pattern of the hive
Swarms in its channels, purposeful and tidy,

Tempting romantics to dismay and spite,
Planners to satisfaction, both to heresy.
For everywhere, beyond the decent lawn
A visionary landscape wings the sight
And every child is rebel and unknown.

So long as daylight moon, night laced with stars
And luminous distance feed imagination
There's hope of strangeness to transcend, redeem
Purblind provincial comfort: summer fires
Under prodigious smokes, imperious storms,

A sense of the pale curving continent
That, though a cliché, may still work unseen
And, with its script of white-limbed trees, impart
A cure for habit, some beneficent
Simplicity or steadiness of heart.

FRANCIS WEBB 1925–1973

Francis Webb was born in Adelaide, and, following the death of his mother when he was two years old, grew up with his paternal grandparents in North Sydney. His father, Claude Webb-Wagg, a professional musician, went into depression after the death of Webb's mother and had himself admitted to Callan Park Mental Hospital in Sydney, where he died in 1945. This was a hospital where Webb was later to be confined under distressing and inhumane conditions. Webb was educated by the Christian Brothers, became a devout Catholic, and learned from his grandfather a love of classical music and sailing. He came second in the State in the Leaving Certificate for English, and aged seventeen had a poem published in the *Bulletin*. In 1943 he joined the Royal Australian Air Force, training in Canada, but was not involved in combat. He was a flight sergeant when demobilised in 1946.

On his return to Australia he enrolled in an Arts course at the University of Sydney, but did not complete the first year. His first book of poetry, *A Drum for Ben Boyd* (1948), a sequence about a 19th-century whaling entrepreneur, with illustrations by Norman Lindsay, was published to acclaim. This was an immature work, criticised twenty years later by Sir Herbert Read as having a prosody that was "rather slack and slapdash" and "rhetoric" that was "forced". By the time it was published however, Webb had gone back to Canada, working as a farm labourer and in publishing. He wrote a poem "For Ethel" and had girl-friends, it would seem, for the only time in his life.

In 1949 he suffered his first breakdown. His schizophrenia, as it was diagnosed, gradually worsened and he was to spend almost the entire second half of his life in mental asylums, at first in England, and later in Australia. There were periods when he led an itinerant life outside institutions, but he was always then re-institutionalized. He was given electro-shock treatment in Canada in 1953, and later in England, after he broke a shop window and was committed to the hospital at Winson Green, Birmingham. He received a Commonwealth Literary Fund grant and came back to Australia, late in 1960, to be admitted to Parramatta Psychiatric Hospital. In the early 1960s he lived for a few months in Sydney, in lodgings that a priest arranged for him. He would go to confession twice a day, and to Mass every day and several times on Sunday. At his own request he was returned to institutional care. At first this was in Melbourne, near his married sister, then later in Sydney. Sir Herbert Read, the English poet and critic, visited him, and wrote that he was one of the major poets of the century, to be ranked with Eliot, Rilke and Pasternak.

Webb's standing as a poet (he published five books of poetry) contrasted savagely with his personal circumstances. For a period when institutionalised at Sydney's Callan Park, he was disfigured by eczema and so heavily sedated he could not maintain a coherent conversation, with probable bromide poisoning. Piety and fear of communism obsessed him, but his personal dignity and courtesy survived this ordeal. He carried his small stock of possessions in a string bag. Admirers bought a transistor radio for him so that he could listen to classical music, but it was stolen. Sometimes there was a scuffle between patients which he would mediate. His medication was later reduced; his coherence returned, his eczema went and he was allowed to go on walks with visitors through the grounds. He died in 1973, aged 48.

Critical opinion is divided on Webb's poetry. Some have inclined towards Read's assessment. Others have found his work turbid. Webb's poetry shows the influence of the heavily metred and rhymed early style of Robert Lowell, and an attraction to a similar vehemence and strain in R. D. FitzGerald. "Morgan's Country" refers to a bushranger, and Webb here intentionally conveys the feeling of madness, with a real frisson.

Morgan's Country

This is Morgan's country: now steady, Bill.
(Stunted and grey, hunted and murderous.)
Squeeze for the first pressure. Shoot to kill.

Five: a star dozing in its cold cavern.
Six: first shuffle of boards in the cold house.
And the sun lagging on seven.

The grey wolf at his breakfast. He cannot think
Why he must make haste, unless because their eyes
Are poison at every well where he might drink.

Unless because their gabbling voices force
The doors of his grandeur – first terror, then only hate.
Now terror again. Dust swarms under the doors.

Ashes drift on the dead-sea shadow of his plate.
Why should he heed them? What to do but kill
When his angel howls, when the sounds reverberate

In the last grey pipe of his brain? At the window sill
A blowfly strums on two strings of air:
Ambush and slaughter tingle against the lull.

But the Cave, his mother, is close beside his chair,
Her sunless face scribbled with cobwebs, bones
Rattling in her throat when she speaks. And there

The stone Look-out, his towering father, leans
Like a splinter from the seamed palm of the plain.
Their counsel of thunder arms him. A threat of rain.

Seven: and a blaze fiercer than the sun.
The wind struggles in the arms of the starved tree,
The temple breaks on a threadbare mat of glass.

Eight: even under the sun's trajectory
This country looks grey, hunted and murderous.

The Gunner

When the gunner spoke in his sleep the hut was still,
Uneasily strapped to the reckless wheel of his will;
Silence, humble, directionless as fog,
Lifted, and minutes were rhythmical on the log;

While slipstream plucked at a wafer of glass and steel,
Engines sliced and scooped at the air's thin wall,
And those dim spars dislodged from the moon became
Red thongs of tracer whipping boards aflame.

Listening, you crouched in the turret, watchful and taut
– *Bogey two thousand, skipper, corkscrew to port* –
Marvellous, the voice: driving electric fires
Through the panel of sleep, the black plugs, trailing wires.

The world spoke through its dream, being deaf and blind,
Its words were those of the dream, yet you might find
Forgotten genius, control, alive in this deep
Instinctive resistance to the perils of sleep.

Five Days Old

for Christopher John

Christmas is in the air.
You are given into my hands
Out of quietest, loneliest lands.
My trembling is all my prayer.
To blown straw was given
All the fullness of Heaven.

The tiny, not the immense,
Will teach our groping eyes.
So the absorbed skies
Bleed stars of innocence.
So cloud-voice in war and trouble
Is at last Christ in the stable.

Now wonderingly engrossed
In your fearless delicacies,
I am launched upon sacred seas,
Humbly and utterly lost
In the mystery of creation,
Bells, bells of ocean.

Too pure for my tongue to praise,
That sober, exquisite yawn
Or the gradual, generous dawn
At an eyelid, maker of days:
To shrive my thought for perfection
I must breathe old tempests of action

For the snowflake and face of love,
Windfall and word of truth,
Honour close to death.
O eternal truthfulness, Dove,
Tell me what I hold –
Myrrh? Frankincense? Gold?

If this is man, then the danger
And fear are as lights of the inn,

Faint and remote as sin
Out here by the manger.
In the sleeping, weeping weather
We shall all kneel down together.

A Death at Winson Green

There is a green spell stolen from Birmingham;
Your peering omnibus overlooks the fence,
Or the grey, bobbing lifelines of a tram.
Here, through the small hours, sings our innocence.
Joists, apathetic pillars plot this ward,
Tired timbers wheeze and settle into dust,
We labour, labour: for the treacherous lord
Of time, the dazed historic sunlight, must
Be wheeled in a seizure towards one gaping bed,
Quake like foam on the lip, or lie still as the dead.

Visitors' Day: the graven perpetual smile,
String-bags agape, and pity's laundered glove.
The last of the heathens shuffles down the aisle,
Dark glass to a beauty which we hate and love.
Our empires rouse against this ancient fear,
Longsufferings, anecdotes, levelled at our doom;
Mine-tracks of old allegiance, prying here,
Perplex the sick man raving in his room.
Outside, a shunting engine hales from bed
The reminiscent feast-day, long since dead.

Noon reddens, trader birds deal cannily
With Winson Green, and the slouch-hatted sun
Gapes at windows netted in wire, and we
Like early kings with book and word cast down
Realities from our squared electric shore.
Two orderlies are whistling-in the spring;
Doors slam; and a man is dying at the core
Of triumph won. As a tattered, powerful wing
The screen bears out his face against the bed,
Silver, derelict, rapt, and almost dead.

Evening gropes out of colour; yet we work
To cleanse our shore from limpet histories;
Traffic and factory-whistle turn berserk;
Inviolate, faithful as a saint he lies.
Twilight itself breaks up, the venal ship,

Upon the silver integrity of his face.
No bread shall tempt that fine, tormented lip.
Let shadow switch to light – he holds his place.
Unmarked, unmoving, from the gaping bed
Towards birth he labours, honour, almost dead.

The wiry cricket moiling at his loom
Debates a themeless project with dour night,
The sick man raves beside me in his room;
I sleep as a child, rouse up as a child might.
I cannot pray; that fine lip prays for me
With every gasp at breath; his burden grows
Heavier as all earth lightens, and all sea.
Time crouches, watching, near his face of snows.
He is all life, thrown on the gaping bed,
Blind, silent, in a trance, and shortly, dead.

Hospital Night

The side-room has sweated years and patience, rolls its one eye
Skyward, nightward; hours beyond sleep I lie;
And the fists of some ardent Plimsoll have laboured this wall
Clear of its plaster beside my chosen head.
Someone murmurs a little, dithers in bed.
Against that frail call
Are imminent the siege-works of a huge nightfall.

Trees, drawn up, rustle forward in the steep time of gloaming;
Crude green labours, gathers itself to a darkness, dreaming
Of perished ice-world summers, birds few, unwieldy, tame.
Darkness is astir, pondering, touching
Kinship with the first Dark in a trunk's crouching.
Darkness lays claim
To that vague breath-labour of a century, my name.

Someone calls again in his sleep, and my thought is pain,
Pain, till chanticleer will carol truce again
To the faceless joustings of green and green by an old cell,
With time roundabout, and labouring shapes of sin;
To the knotted fists of lightning, or tilting rain;
To the wind's lapse and swell
– Old die-hards of whom the birds shiver to tell.

Sleep is a labour amid the dilatory elder light;
But now a star is uttered in the long night,

Pitched beyond altercations of tree and storm;
For these, isled upon time, are murmuring, murmuring ever
Of good or evil becoming a darkness; but never
Darkens that star,
Housed in a glory, yet always a wanderer.

It is pain, truth, it is you, my father, beloved friend,
Come to me in the guile and darkness of a day's end,
As a frail intense blue burning, near nor far.
Old hands were stripped from the keyboard of time, they favour
White notes nor black, but they glitter and glitter of a lover,
As out of war
I labour, breathing deeply, and tremble towards your star.

Legionary Ants

The world, the tranquil punctual gyroscope,
Is more or less at peace after her fashion,
Broad bowels work, creatures rejoice or mope,
There is clash of interests in all dogged creation,
When silence comes as at noiseless thwack of a drum,
And look! the warriors come.

First shudder away the birds, all flaking, wheeling
Out of range and all forgetful of their young,
Crying at the ominous shadowy floor stealing
Over their earth; and then not giving tongue.
Now all things hold silent, and the surf
Breaks on beleaguered turf.

They come. And whose ear can divine the awful waves,
Signals of command suspired by what demagogue?
They tumble in orgies of commitment, these black slaves,
All activity, but insensible as rotted log.
Their mad absorbed unity of hunger and mirth
Is the belly-heave of earth.

The wounded mammal whimpers and butts and runs,
Glazing, eaten alive. The three-days' chick
Shrills fear, and like a paradigm of guns
Anarchy gorges itself and life is sick.
Look close for a second, stranger, you will find
Blear paradigm also of our mind.

For this is our mind for today – never creation
But all nakedness. Odours and colours blent

And sounds and shapes, swivel throughout that ration
Of basic nerves, like darkness imminent;
But sometimes in moments of withdrawal one sees, feels
Certain subterranean wheels.

As their cloud progresses it may assume strange shapes:
Of devouring lover and organ, it may weep
Like mandibles of rain and whatever rapes
The fruit and flesh of life in very sleep.
Sleep is ever the enemy, it seems,
To all who dream these dreams.

But punctilious night now sweeps away all lust
On wheels, and another, a blessed, silence broods
Over many bones left twinkling in the dust.
Earth debates bitterly in these solitudes
Whether she dare replace, below, above,
The singings, ramblings of love.

Pneumo-encephalograph *(from* Ward Two*)*

Tight scrimmage of blankets in the dark;
Nerve-fluxions, flints coupling for the spark;
Today's guilt and tomorrow's blent;
Passion and peace trussed together, impotent;
Dilute potage of light
Dripping through glass to the desk where you sit and write;
Hour stalking lame hour ...
May my every bone and vessel confess the power
To loathe suffering in you
As in myself, that arcane simmering brew.

Only come to this cabin of art:
Crack hardy, take off clothes, and play your part.
Contraband enters your brain;
Puckered guerilla faces patrol the vein;
The spore of oxygen passes
Skidding over old inclines and crevasses,
Hunting an ancient sore,
Foxhole of impulse in a minute cosmic war.
Concordat of nature and desire
Was revoked in you; but fire clashes with fire.

Let me ask, while you are still,
What in you marshalled this improbable will:

Instruments supple as the flute,
Vigilant eyes, mouths that are almost mute,
X-rays scintillant as a flower,
Tossed in a corner the plumes of falsehood, power?
Only your suffering.
Of pain's amalgam with gold let some man sing
While, pale and fluent and rare
As the Holy Spirit, travels the bubble of air.

Harry *(from* Ward Two*)*

It's the day for writing that letter, if one is able,
And so the striped institutional shirt is wedged
Between this holy holy chair and table.
He has purloined paper, he has begged and cadged
The bent institutional pen,
The ink. And our droll old men
Are darting constantly where he weaves his sacrament.

Sacrifice? Propitiation? All are blent
In the moron's painstaking fingers – so painstaking.
His vestments our giddy yarns of the firmament,
Women, gods, electric trains, and our remaking
Of all known worlds – but not yet
Has our giddy alphabet
Perplexed his priestcraft and spilled the cruet of innocence.

We have been plucked from the world of commonsense,
Fondling between our hands some shining loot,
Wife, mother, beach, fisticuffs, eloquence,
As the lank tree cherishes every distorted shoot.
What queer shards we could steal
Shaped him, realer than the Real:
But it is no goddess of ours guiding the fingers and the thumb.

She cries: *Ab aeterno ordinata sum.*
He writes to the woman, this lad who will never marry.
One vowel and the thousand laborious serifs will come
To this pudgy Christ, and the old shape of Mary.
Before seasonal pelts and the thin
Soft tactile underskin
Of air were stretched across earth, they have sported and are one.

Was it then at this altar-stone the mind was begun?
The image besieges our Troy. Consider the sick

Convulsions of movement, and the featureless baldy sun
Insensible – sparing that compulsive nervous tic.
Before life, the fantastic succession,
An imbecile makes his confession,
Is filled with the Word unwritten, has almost genuflected.

Because the wise world has for ever and ever rejected
Him and because your children would scream at the sight
Of his mongol mouth stained with food, he has resurrected
The spontaneous though retarded and infantile Light.
Transfigured with him we stand
Among walls of the no-man's-land
While he licks the soiled envelope with lover's caress

Directing it to the House of no known address.

ALAN RIDDELL 1927–1977

Alan Riddell (which he pronounced "Riddle"), an international leader in the second wave of concrete poetry that began after World War II, was born in Townsville, Queensland, of Scottish parents and was educated in Scotland, graduating with an M.A. from the University of Edinburgh. He also lived in Greece, Spain and France. While working as a journalist in Edinburgh he founded the poetry magazine *Lines* in 1952. Its early issues published some of the greatest names in Scottish poetry at that time, including Hugh MacDiarmid and Norman MacCaig. While living in Australia in the late 1960s Riddell worked for a number of newspapers. Although he is best known for his concrete poetry, he published in 1968 a book of poems using conventional typography, *The Stopped Landscape*. The concrete poems here come from his 1972 volume, *Eclipse*. He edited and introduced an anthology *Typewriter Art* (c. 1975).

Australian journalists and writers Sandra Jobson and Robert Darroch recall: "We met Alan Riddell in the late 1960s when he was a subeditor on a Sydney newspaper. We later moved to London where Alan had preceded us, and we went to parties in his small flat in Moscow Mews, Queensway. There was not much food at the parties, but a great deal of alcohol and some celebrities, including the actress Susan George and the Shell heiress, Olga Deterding. Alan had a 'literary look'. He was like an Anthony Powell character, with his turtleneck sweaters or tweed sport coat, and sandals which he wore with socks. He identified with Scotland and regarded MacDiarmid as the greatest living poet, but did not speak with a Scottish accent. When he fell ill, Sandra [Jobson] visited him in Hammersmith Hospital. Alan said: 'They don't know what's wrong with me.' Sandra had an awful presentiment and burst into tears by his bedside. The following day he died of a brain aneurysm. Rob [Darroch] wrote an orbituary and sent it to Betty Riddell, then literary editor of *The Australian*. She refused to publish it.

"When we knew him in London, Alan gave us a series of typewriter artworks which celebrate the seasons. They were typed onto sheets of paper, using red, violet, green and yellow typewriter ribbon that he would splice together. He planned the length of a colour to fit the number of letters, which he calculated in advance. He would then use a manual typewriter to type strips of colour, creating different geometric shapes – a bit like a rainbow. Each season had its own colour. The execution of each work required planning and precision. This was before the development of computer graphics. Alan told us he had been in signals in the navy and he'd had to be extremely precise sending coded messages. Although he had a lot of friends, he was almost constitutionally lonely. He'd felt unappreciated in Australia, but had some tincture of respect in the United Kingdom. He had a strong belief that his concrete poetry expressed the Zeitgeist."

Goldfish at an Angle

Fish in the bowl have no depth at all
to my eye at this angle.

And even head-on
curiously they flatten

themselves against glass against eyes against
– the world. Fenced

round they are, yet not
round but flat

they are
there.

At the Hammersmith Palais ...

the woman is using a handkerchief
to wipe the sweat from under her armpits.
She has just finished dancing a medley
of Latin-American numbers, and is as well known
in the home
for her
intolerance towards children
as
on the floor
for
the sustained violence of her terpsichorean expertise.

Recessional

HOMMAGEHESIT
HOMMAGEHESI
HOMMAGEHESITA
HOMMAGEHESIT
HOMMAGEHESITAN
HOMMAGEHESITA
HOMMAGEHESITANT
HOMMAGEHESITAN
HOMMAGEHESITANTA
HOMMAGEHESITANT
HOMMAGEHESITANTAG
HOMMAGEHESITANTA
HOMMAGEHESITANTAGU
HOMMAGEHESITANTAG
HOMMAGEHESITANTAGUI
HOMMAGEHESITANTAGU
HOMMAGEHESITANTAGUIL
HOMMAGEHESITANTAGUI
HOMMAGEHESITANTAGUILL
HOMMAGEHESITANTAGUIL
HOMMAGEHESITANTAGUILLA
HOMMAGEHESITANTAGUILL
HOMMAGEHESITANTAGUILLAU
HOMMAGEHESITANTAGUILLA
HOMMAGEHESITANTAGUILLAUM
HOMMAGEHESITANTAGUILLAU
HOMMAGEHESITANTAGUILLAUME
HOMMAGEHESITANTAGUILLAUM
HOMMAGEHESITANTAGUILLAUMEA
HOMMAGEHESITANTAGUILLAUME
HOMMAGEHESITANTAGUILLAUMEAP
HOMMAGEHESITANTAGUILLAUMEA
HOMMAGEHESITANTAGUILLAUMEAPO
HOMMAGEHESITANTAGUILLAUMEAP
HOMMAGEHESITANTAGUILLAUMEAPOL
HOMMAGEHESITANTAGUILLAUMEAPO
HOMMAGEHESITANTAGUILLAUMEAPOLL
HOMMAGEHESITANTAGUILLAUMEAPOL
HOMMAGEHESITANTAGUILLAUMEAPOLLI
HOMMAGEHESITANTAGUILLAUMEAPOLL
HOMMAGEHESITANTAGUILLAUMEAPOLLIN
HOMMAGEHESITANTAGUILLAUMEAPOLLI
HOMMAGEHESITANTAGUILLAUMEAPOLLINA
HOMMAGEHESITANTAGUILLAUMEAPOLLIN
HOMMAGEHESITANTAGUILLAUMEAPOLLINAI
HOMMAGEHESITANTAGUILLAUMEAPOLLINA
HOMMAGEHESITANTAGUILLAUMEAPOLLINAIR
HOMMAGEHESITANTAGUILLAUMEAPOLLINAI
HOMMAGEHESITANTAGUILLAUMEAPOLLINAIRE

H

HO
H
HOM
HO
HOMM
HOM
HOMMA
HOMM
HOMMAG
HOMMA
HOMMAGE
HOMMAG
HOMMAGEH
HOMMAGE
HOMMAGEHE
HOMMAGEH
HOMMAGEHES
HOMMAGEHE
HOMMAGEHESI
HOMMAGEHES
HOMMAGEHESIT
HOMMAGEHESI
HOMMAGEHESITA
HOMMAGEHESIT
HOMMAGEHESITAN
HOMMAGEHESITA
HOMMAGEHESITANT
HOMMAGEHESITAN
HOMMAGEHESITANTA
HOMMAGEHESITANT
HOMMAGEHESITANTAG
HOMMAGEHESITANTA
HOMMAGEHESITANTAGU
HOMMAGEHESITANTAG
HOMMAGEHESITANTAGUI
HOMMAGEHESITANTAGU
HOMMAGEHESITANTAGUIL
HOMMAGEHESITANTAGUI
HOMMAGEHESITANTAGUILL
HOMMAGEHESITANTAGUIL
HOMMAGEHESITANTAGUILLA
HOMMAGEHESITANTAGUILL
HOMMAGEHESITANTAGUILLAU
HOMMAGEHESITANTAGUILLA
HOMMAGEHESITANTAGUILLAUM
HOMMAGEHESITANTAGUILLAU
HOMMAGEHESITANTAGUILLAUME
HOMMAGEHESITANTAGUILLAUM
HOMMAGEHESITANTAGUILLAUMEA
HOMMAGEHESITANTAGUILLAUME
HOMMAGEHESITANTAGUILLAUMEAP
HOMMAGEHESITANTAGUILLAUMEA
HOMMAGEHESITANTAGUILLAUMEAPO
HOMMAGEHESITANTAGUILLAUMEAP
HOMMAGEHESITANTAGUILLAUMEAPOL
HOMMAGEHESITANTAGUILLAUMEAPO
HOMMAGEHESITANTAGUILLAUMEAPOLL
HOMMAGEHESITANTAGUILLAUMEAPOL
HOMMAGEHESITANTAGUILLAUMEAPOLLI
HOMMAGEHESITANTAGUILLAUMEAPOLL
HOMMAGEHESITANTAGUILLAUMEAPOLLIN
HOMMAGEHESITANTAGUILLAUMEAPOLLI
HOMMAGEHESITANTAGUILLAUMEAPOLLINA
HOMMAGEHESITANTAGUILLAUMEAPOLLIN
HOMMAGEHESITANTAGUILLAUMEAPOLLINAI
HOMMAGEHESITANTAGUILLAUMEAPOLLINA
HOMMAGEHESITANTAGUILLAUMEAPOLLINAIR
HOMMAGEHESITANTAGUILLAUMEAPOLLINAI
HOMMAGEHESITANTAGUILLAUMEAPOLLINAIRE

H

HO
H
HOM
HO
HOMM
HOM
HOMMA
HOMM
HOMMAG
HOMMA
HOMMAGE
HOMMAG
HOMMAGEH
HOMMAGE
HOMMAGEHE
HOMMAGEH
HOMMAGEHES
HOMMAGEHE
HOMMAGEHESI
HOMMAGEHES
HOMMAGEHESIT
HOMMAGEHESI
HOMMAGEHESITA
HOMMAGEHESIT
HOMMAGEHESITAN
HOMMAGEHESITA
HOMMAGEHESITANT
HOMMAGEHESITAN
HOMMAGEHESITANTA
HOMMAGEHESITANT
HOMMAGEHESITANTAG
HOMMAGEHESITANTA
HOMMAGEHESITANTAGU
HOMMAGEHESITANTAG
HOMMAGEHESITANTAGUI
HOMMAGEHESITANTAGU
HOMMAGEHESITANTAGUIL
HOMMAGEHESITANTAGUI
HOMMAGEHESITANTAGUILL
HOMMAGEHESITANTAGUIL
HOMMAGEHESITANTAGUILLA
HOMMAGEHESITANTAGUILL
HOMMAGEHESITANTAGUILLAU
HOMMAGEHESITANTAGUILLA
HOMMAGEHESITANTAGUILLAUM
HOMMAGEHESITANTAGUILLAU
HOMMAGEHESITANTAGUILLAUME
HOMMAGEHESITANTAGUILLAUM
HOMMAGEHESITANTAGUILLAUMEA
HOMMAGEHESITANTAGUILLAUME
HOMMAGEHESITANTAGUILLAUMEAP
HOMMAGEHESITANTAGUILLAUMEA
HOMMAGEHESITANTAGUILLAUMEAPO
HOMMAGEHESITANTAGUILLAUMEAP
HOMMAGEHESITANTAGUILLAUMEAPOL
HOMMAGEHESITANTAGUILLAUMEAPO
HOMMAGEHESITANTAGUILLAUMEAPOLL
HOMMAGEHESITANTAGUILLAUMEAPOL
HOMMAGEHESITANTAGUILLAUMEAPOLLI
HOMMAGEHESITANTAGUILLAUMEAPOLL
HOMMAGEHESITANTAGUILLAUMEAPOLLIN
HOMMAGEHESITANTAGUILLAUMEAPOLLI
HOMMAGEHESITANTAGUILLAUMEAPOLLINA
HOMMAGEHESITANTAGUILLAUMEAPOLLIN
HOMMAGEHESITANTAGUILLAUMEAPOLLINAI
HOMMAGEHESITANTAGUILLAUMEAPOLLINA
HOMMAGEHESITANTAGUILLAUMEAPOLLINAIR
HOMMAGEHESITANTAGUILLAUMEAPOLLINAI
HOMMAGEHESITANTAGUILLAUMEAPOLLINAIRE

Revolver II

BRUCE BEAVER 1928–2004

Bruce Beaver was born and educated in Manly, an ocean-front suburb of Sydney. In 1945, aged 17, on the evening when the bombing of Hiroshima was reported, he responded by writing his first poem. In the same year he had his first manic-depressive (or bipolar) attack, a condition that would stay with him for the rest of his life. He believed the medication for this illness was responsible for the dialysis which was a bane of his final decade. Aged 19, he worked on his uncle's dairy farm for a year, which is recalled in "Pea Picking", "Silage" and "The Hunting Girl" (all from *As it Was* (1984)). He laboured for six years in the Hunter Valley as a chainman in a team surveying the route for a new railway line. Aged 30, he visited Norfolk Island and New Zealand, working as a proof reader for the *New Zealand Herald* (1960–62) and at other jobs, such as fruit picking.

It was in New Zealand that he met his future wife, Brenda. She was married and had a child. She divorced, and they married and settled in Australia. Soon after their arrival in Australia, Beaver was hospitalised in a mental asylum. The marriage survived this shock and Brenda Beaver provided their income in ensuing years by working as a stenographer, while her husband became a full-time poet and writer. They lived with Beaver's mother in her cottage in Manly, his childhood home, located a couple of blocks back from the surfing beach. Beaver entertained other writers in the small garden at the back of the house. His friend, the poet, John Millett, who was a solicitor and property developer, arranged for an apartment block to be built on the site of the house and Beaver, his wife and mother lived in an upstairs apartment in the block.

Another of his close friends, the poet and medico Grace Perry, who was the founder and editor of the journal *Poetry Australia*, published Beaver's *Letters to Live Poets* (1969), the collection that established his reputation and in which he showed a truly distinctive voice, even though influenced by the American Confessional and New York schools. *Letters* is a long poem-cycle, written on a day-to-day basis, with the parts occasionally linking up, but with no overall schemata. The coherence of the sequence derives from the poet's own personality, appreciating, responding, joking, pestered by sinusitis, praising his wife or condemning involvement in the Vietnam War. Beaver presented himself with candour and lack of pretension, involved in the dull round of shopping, wandering along the beach, but always concerned with the life of the imagination.

Beaver published fifteen volumes of poetry, ten novels and an autobiography. The sheer volume of his poetry, and its relaxed, unpretentious approach mean his output is uneven and it is easy to underrate his achievement. He is often at his strongest when expansive; we have represented him mainly by middle-distance poems.

from Letters to Live Poets

V

Three images of dying stick in my mind like morbid transfers
of the other side of life. First, a cow on my uncle's farm
had broken a leg calving. My uncle held a shot gun to its poll
and fired both barrels. The dogs ran in to lick the blood welling from
the nostrils. We hauled the carcase behind a wooden sled to the burial
ground,
a small island of dark trees centring a wide field.
On the way the top of the cow's head came loose and left a trail.
Heifers followed us and shrieked with eyes rolling at the blood.
We piled the heavy carcase high with old tyres and lit the pyre.
Sleeping and waking I saw the shattered head for many years to come.

The second incident occurred years later in a goods' yard.
Near to a storage shed I came across a group of cats surrounding
such a scrawny bag of fur and bone it wasn't a bit funny.
This cat had eaten poisoned corn or a rat poisoned.
At first I'd thought it starving and had brought bacon from the galley.
The other cats moved back from me while I offered it the bacon.

It stretched out a claw at the meat, hooking it towards its mouth
then died before it bit. I watched the twitch of life pass up its spine,
centre, then go out like a light snuffed. Its eyes had closed before
its life. Blinded. Starved with poison. The other cats began to move
away. I stood and looked and knew mortality like an old wound.

The third time clawed me in a room filled with smoke and proof readers.
The air clanged with advertisements read aloud like crazy psalms.
A man was dying at his desk. His heart was broken and the kiss
of life rejected. As he died his fellow workers chanted on
and he was left with a handkerchief over his face where he lay dead
in his chair in a room full of the loud chanting of the living.
No one pleaded for silence while he remained or when he was gone stayed
their tongue. I read on then, knowing not a minute's silence will
the rest of us get. When they rang his ninety year old mother all she asked
for
were his keys. Tomorrow we'll talk of life and sundry other things.

XIX

I welcome the anonymity of the middle years, years of the spreading
girth and conversational prolixity, when the whole being loosens
the stays of the thirties and lengthens out into paragraphs of perceptiveness
where once had bristled the pointed phrase. And the other aspect, the
merely boring
raconteur, the redundant conversationalist; the not young
not old, twice told tale teller; the paunched, bejowelled double-chinned
bumbler. These I welcome, also the watcher unperceived on corners
from verandahs of youth, voyeuristic, grateful beyond the tang of sour
grapes to be no longer privy to the ingrowing secret, the deathly
held breaths of years, the cold and burning self-trials. The quaintly
acquainted with the antique masques of childhood, the mummies and
daddies,
the nurses and doctors, the pantomimic routines of getting the hang of
living and dying young. No, childhood's well and truly categorised
and pigeon-holed somewhere within that depot of lapsed tenders, the
unconscious. It's the witnessing
of the adolescent saga that sometimes chills me to my still vulnerable
marrow, burns me down to the fire of being and sifts me into a vacuum
of loveless nine to five nightmares on wretched wages, the between grown
and ungrown, the lonely braggart loping like werewolf past the
unattainable beauties on the peeling posters, past the burning
girls that, plain as sisters, would, and onto the illimitable
utmost, absolute and factual plateau of the self's serfdom

to solitude, the sad king in the bone castle, the bitter end
of beginnings and the beginning of fiddling appetites and the myriad
arbitrations of early manhood (in my case, alas, a prolongation
of mad simulated adolescence). Only now with hypertensive
head and lazy bowels, with a heart as whole as a tin of dog's meat
may I pause between poems of letters to you, my alter egos, and pronounce
peace be occasionally with you all and, at no matter what cost, with me
here,
no longer (I pray) completely at odds with self and world, accommodating
room by room like a shabby genteel boarding house, age.

from Lauds and Plaints

XXIV

even while pausing beside the lattice-framed sweet peas
smelling them with the flexible nostrils of an animal

it was the human ache returned   the inevitable
sad happy old sense of belonging somewhere

called home   passing shrub-enfolded
lazing-in-shade gardens and creeper-hung

side entrances to houses from a time called then
from those other years when the harbour frontages

offset in a possibly workable democracy
the raffish and the elegant   shacks of parched

timber white painted once with open
hot and cool breeze-haunted verandahs

cotton lacecurtained windows opening onto
a tiled pathway to plank steps

or bungalows of dark brick
not quite liver-coloured not quite purple

the generous walled-in verandahs
leaded circular small windows

above porches   the clipped redolent
square yard of shaded lawn

overhung by revelations
of loose-petalled taut-budded roses

holding their perfume in like girls
at an important interview   beside them

duennas of lavender a buzz
of early bees and save for a baby's

faint hiccuping wail an unbroken
ambience of gentle welcoming elders

how overheard the landscape was
of an exiled folk   even the wide open

yards of the little wooden cottages
the shacks of weekend sailors echoed chanties

some of the sparrows had cockney accents still
so to feel nostalgia now for espaliered flowers

to hear the quaint leaf unfolding wing whir
pod vibration herbal earth exhaling

sigh of a Delian tune from Grez-sur-Loing
though having much to do with selective memory

seemed as innate to those streets
as another harsher sound belonged

to the wild reserve adjoining them
a truer background to the sunbleached sky

it had not changed in near two hundred
years of English speaking occupancy

whatever sound was left in hollowed
rock or trunk's convexities was purged

each summer by the hymning tides
of the bull-roaring cicada hordes

but seen from the little cove where an
abandoned gas works darkens still

the punky air across the harbour hovers
the ephemeral superstructure of a city

noted in passing from years of yesterdays
back to one yesterday in the Thirties

when a disgruntled child wandering
abandoned in wastes of daylight saving

by every guardian angel benevolent deity
comic strip hero and companionable

contemporary fronted the harbour's
always alien stretch of severance

then turned and paused by a strange front gate
nearby and without entering partook

of what seemed to be homeliness
emanating from a streetful of the simple

and the complex shells of families
their lean-tos   their caves   their fragrant gardens

Pea Picking

To realise the futility of pea-picking,
its broken-backed and bruised-kneed endurance
tested up and down the crowded rows
of squat, green, sparsely bearing bushes;
the side-of-the-finger-splitting ritual,
left and right forefingers and thumbs
cut and bruised bloody, the neck breaking
under the bludgeoning sun, the eyes, ears, nose
and lips crawling with stickybeaking flies;
the stink or perfume (sometimes vaguely both)
of your fellow pickers beside and ahead of you;
to understand why you are doing this at all
day after blistering day for four shillings
a bushel or two kerosene tins full you had to be
either seventeen and desperately
in need of more than two pounds to buy the Collected
Letters of John Keats (that is ten bushels
when you were averaging four bushels a day
for the several days allotted to the picking).
Or perhaps you had to be Aboriginal
and aged from fifteen to sixty-five (male or female)
and be able to knock off ten bushels a day,
bushes and all, when you were supposed to pick
selectively, that is to leave the younger,
smaller pods for a second picking. Or you
might have even needed to be the farmer
himself. Too busy to supervise; keeping up
with most of the Aboriginals, only picking
selectively. Up five chains of bushes
and down five chains of bushes for about
five or six aching hours a day. I say
"futility" for I was too tired each day
to read the book when I had it; the Aboriginals

spent most of their pay on headache engendering wine;
and the farmer, my uncle, always seemed to time
his pickings to coincide with a glutted market.
The whole thing was an exercise in futility.
The old hands had pads of cloth or soft leather tied
to their knees and kept their backs fairly straight.
But if you were seventeen as I was then
and uninstructed you simply agonised
on sore knees shuffling forward boustrophedon
in a more or less literal way. Knee-nudging
over soft and lumpy strips of bare earth
getting to feel a tiny twig or pebble,
even the compressed soil's own modifications
and innate consistencies of texture. The bushes
themselves becoming flayers of raw thumb
and finger-pad, splitters and groovers of nails,
the plump pods' contents edible but eventually
uninviting. Something like a vestigial
competitive spirit drove one to try and at least
keep up. The dust of earth and leaf-dust crimping
the nostrils, the heat of days turning the tongue
into a strap of hide cleaving to white paste.
The crazy fantasies: would Toulouse-Lautrec
have walked on his half-length legs and have merely plucked
the bushes' burdens without even looking down?
Would the Aboriginal girl in front have underwear
beneath her sack-like skirt, or a brassiere under
the off-white shirt? No, you saw small breasts
and purple-brown nipples once, and when she saw
you looking she smiled but not invitingly.
The black folk smelt of wood smoke and leaf mould.
I had been told I would smell to them of sour milk
and rancid butter. There were several deodorants
on sale even then but none of us thought to use them.
The girls had thin legs, thin thighs, and almost all
were waistless. But their faces were like a friendly
fruit, large, dark, with rounded features full
and ripe until the faces of my own kind
soured and flattened out to thin diminished
creases, cracks and bumps. At day's end I
would go to wash and eat and sleep at the farmhouse.
The Aboriginal pickers lolled or squatted

in the big barn's earth floored musty gloom, gathering
beside the several loaned hurricane lanterns
and about the central fire of sticks on which
a frying pan sputtered blessings on eggs and bacon
and later the communal billy black
as the brew it smokily and sweetly boiled.
Aperitifs of muscat and sweet sherry
were passed from hand to hand in the habitual
surreptitious manner, and the pouches
or battered tins lay open between crossed legs,
rice paper stuck to bottom lips as coarse
tobacco was reduced to fragrant shreds
in hands still acrid with the bushes' juices.
Then soft guitar accompanied song and softer
talk and sudden swallowed shouts as someone
gulped who should have sipped. And I awake
upon a sheeted bed two hundred feet
away, aware would lie and wonder if
the younger ones would go into the night
and love, as I would have given Keats's Letters
so to do. And out across the back
verandah of the farm I'd peer into
the starlit dark – so large the distant stars –
while through the barn's gapped timber walls the lanterns
and the dull glow of the compact cooking fire
showed, even the spark-sized crimson points
of hand-rolled cigarettes would wink and almost
beckon. Now I think the only ones
to leave the barn a while went to excrete.
More privacy was needed than a darkened
cow-bail or a tree's wide bole to lure
those shyest lovers out. They slept together
in a tribal dream of tiresome work and welcome
food and memoried rest. No taboos but
commonsense and something like distaste
to elevate a white farm to the stature
of home-ground. The elder ones, perhaps, while partly
drunk may have partly scored, but when the last
birds had quietened and the only sound
was cattle foraging about the dry lawn's
dew-soaked chaff, both barn and farmhouse turned
lights down and out. And then across the cooling

fields came mistily and fragrantly
sleep to all and Alchera's dreams to some.

Silo Treading

At silo filling time the air was similarly wet
between the dense-packed, leaf-clustered corn rows, in the little
shed that housed the howling, belting, stalk-chopping silage-
making machine and in the empty silo, treading under
a rain of moist fragments the corn leaves, corn stalks, stray cobs
into a green pudding that would cook itself, beginning
the thermic process even while we trod that upright vintage.
But the whole process depended on corn. And corn is a truly magic
thing. As much a gift from the gods as the grape. It shares with the grape
religious rites and its history is linked with the dismembering
and rebirth of a god. I was nearly partially dismembered myself
one season, hacking at heavy stalks and zipping swiftly upwards
with a saw-bladed reaping hook. It slipped from my grasp in my sweat-
slippery hand
and I mechanically hauled at it stuck in the base of a stalk and tore
a half inch gash in my second finger, nearly lifting off
the top of it, only the bone and the nail held things together until
about forty-eight hours had passed and my relatives said they needed more
help.
But sometimes there was the picking of the fruit of the corn. I dimly
remember as a child it must have been picked in its husk because
there would be at the appropriate time get-togethers of neighbouring
families
after tea and late into the night for little boys and girls.
After the fiendish games of pursuing the nesting mice to their deaths
from the barn's cornerfuls of unhusked corn we would at first
with enthusiasm gradually turned into lethargy run the finger
taloned with leatherheld three inch nail down the harsh cocoon
of the husk to disclose the gold, the betel-red, the milk-white grains,
until someone would carry us snoozing into a shadowy corner on top of
more corn (and mice) and fulsome sacks of sweet and foul smelling mixtures
of things that only adults understood the use of. But in
the later years my uncle husked the cobs on the standing stalk
and fed them to the cattle as an additive or prelude
to the plum-pudding silage that the cows went crazy over, screaming
like overweight adolescent girls to get at it as though
it were some edible pop-performer, another dismembered god
and would roll their eyes and bony hips and bump the stalls and belch

and shit while gorging. Cows are unmentionably crass and canny
at the same time. Bulls are bulls – that is, you keep out of their way
in and out of serving times. Sometimes they sing in Brahmsian
monotones, sometimes they shriek and kick up clods, sometimes
they even rupture their pizzles masturbating into a grassy
mound. But only cows really care for them. And only
they really care for cows as cows despite the farmer's habitual
endearments and namings. But corn – or the stalks thereof – and the
sandpaper raspy
leaves. And the thick, wet air between the neverending rows.
One humid day after several hours of hacking, humping and dumping
those full green six feet and more stalks I fell down dead asleep
in a chocolate furrow and did not dream of anything for the first
and last time in my life. When I awoke an hour later
my disgusted cousin was half a dozen rows on having left mine
like gapped teeth in between. However, my uncle even stopped letting
the cobs grow on the green stalks and soon it was cut and hack
and stack on the sled and chop and stamp down, and that was it.
The neighbour's son upheld the Attis myth in the form of adding
three severed fingers to the silage pudding. Those machines
were gluttonous for everything choppable. But while there was
the neighbour's mutilated son, there were also the neighbour's
daughters to help stamp down the silage and in between loads there were
sessions of mutual inspection. Then, one sad afternoon
the good share-farmer's better daughter, sweet Laura of the warm,
wide face and narrow hips and feet like pizza plates came shyly
up to me as I stamped on and on under shower of fragrant,
tickling chips and looked at me from the ladder top and spoke
with eyes as large as curiosity, and I nodded, thinking
she was offering maximum assistance with her remarkably functional
feet, not knowing both of us may have been blessedly released
from virginity's yoke. So we glumly trod. And I kept wondering why
she looked and looked with sadder and sadder, if not wiser, blue eyes
towards me. And as I'd shrug heaps of the wet green chips from my shoulders
she'd briefly
smile, and then there was a welcome pause and as I rolled
a cigarette with far from trembling hands she slowly crossed
without a word to the ladder, leaving as silently as she came.
And that no doubt is why her eldest child is one or two years
younger than it might have been. Then the roar and green rush
of relentless ensilage in the making all but drowned my donkey-
at-the-water-wheel treading, till I prayed like some mad catherine-wheeling

anchorite those masochistic prayers of pious-randy
youth, and trod and trod the green wheel of the neverending
hours, stained green and yellow, smelling like a sweaty stalk,
talking and singing songs of food and drink and love to myself
in the most innocuous words ever disassembled, the cowboy tunes
of the Thirties and Forties: "San Antonio Rose",
"You Are My Sunshine", "Be Honest With Me",
"I'm Walkin the FloorOverYou", "Goodbye Little Darlin",
"Old Shep", "Cool Water" – delirious with weariness and love
unsatisfied while the Niagara of shredded stalks descended
upon my cropped head, down my neck, inside my khaki shirt,
even into my underpants. Deluged with god, the blood
and semen on the cornstalk deity, I trod and chanted,
always ascending like an apprentice shaman towards that last
hole in the concrete roof from whence I'd issue on leaf-green wings
and tread upon the air up to the glazed galactophil-
ideal heaven of Khamaduk, the celestial bovine with ever-
flowing teats and other accommodations – for bulls. Back to
the heavy-footed, the Frankensteinian monster's tread. Boris's
bandy, soulful plod. In several months we'd shovel off
the top muck and the chooks would gobble it, a solid cross
between Drambuie and mud, and lurch and flap drunkenly for
a few days. Then the silage would be ready. And ploughing begin.

The Hunting Girl

Once at bright mid-morning on an easy weekend day
coming down from the hill paddock I saw the girl Laura,
daughter of the neighbouring farmer's assistant, a brown skinned girl
with yellow hair, limbs long and stick-thin as a young Aboriginal's,
overlarge bare feet planted firmly at the creek's edge,
all of her poised and balanced to propel a home-made spear
longer than herself and tipped with a wire-fastened knife-blade
into the seemingly empty and shallow waterflow, I assumed
she was playing at her brothers' games and stopped chasing heifers
down the hill, making them dance about, and watched as she poised,
flexed and threw the spear into the quietly moving water.
Then, tucking her cotton dress into her plain white underwear,
she waded in after the upright spear. She did not seem so thin
then, her thighs exposed seemed fuller, rounder, and her legs
slim rather than thin. I sat on the grass a little way off
and concentratedly watched her natural balletic movements.

Back on the bank Laura re-arranged her dress and I thought
she must have seen me but, no, after another lunging throw
into the centre of the creek she tucked her dress in again,
high up on her thighs, the white underwear clung and now I noticed
the widening hips and shapely small buttocks. But Laura and I
had trodden down the silage in friendly silence many a time.
I knew the way her yellow hair tufted at the back
and how she would suddenly brush the front strands from her freckled forehead,
and the pale blue eyes would lower with the very slightest rising
of the wide mouth's corners. Her nose was not small yet attractively upturned
and stamped with freckles. She was not the kind of girl I'd begun to dream of
at about her age, but neither was any other that I'd seen.
I wondered then what kind of boy she dreamed of, or if any,
as she poised and lunged and waded to retrieve the unwieldy spear.
She seemed intent on hunting and to have no other thought
or feeling save to aim and throw as best she could, and to spear
an eel. Then the spear fell sideways in the water and she leapt,
untucked dress and all, in after the waving wood, for the blade
had transfixed something that moved. I nearly ran to help, but knew
she needed none, she was the mistress of the situation.
She emerged with a medium sized eel wriggling at the end of the spear.
Driving it into earth to pinion it, she placed one large bare foot
behind the eel's head, and drew a hunting knife from the grassy bank
and hacked the live eel's head off. Then she stood aside to wring out
her dampened dress and briefly smile – or it seemed a smile – towards me.
I summoned up a gesture, half salute, half wave. She appeared
to nod, then took her spear, her knife, her catch, both severed head
and the still slightly writhing body, back along the creek's
edge towards the other farm. She never looked back once.
I came down to her hunting – I cannot call it fishing – place
and saw the blood upon the wettened grass and stood there musing
how I so full of Endymion should come upon a true
Diana and not say a word but merely witness her prowess,
and the beauty of her brown and rounding thighs, the summer moonlight
of her hair, the pallid summer dawning of her woken eyes.
Would she have rounded breasts beneath her dress? I had thought her earlier
a living marionette, a girl Pinocchio; had liked her
but not engaged her interest. I realised then the man

she would consider was so unlike me that I had been to her
but one of the other farm boys, an elder brother, a part companion,
touchable even in the silo's privacy. How I longed
for such another opportunity, but the silage was packed
and cooking itself. I watched for her then and saw her often enough,
even spoke a kind of half-speech, words about the farm and its peoples,
never about ourselves. I did not dream about Laura but she
had become a kind of muse to me. Poised between girl and woman,
she bled at times and was unafraid, and silent. Now her silences,
the faint smile and the unreadable pale blue eyes, the thin
yet rounding body, stayed with me – not obsessing, but making me
want the company of such women, calm yet inwardly passionate,
capable of the sudden precipitate plunge, the unstudied action.
Though I feared to think of the eel's beheading, my own sex shrivelling at
the thought of such an obvious symbol. No, not then so consciously
apprehended, more a shocked distaste at the callous necessity.
I was appalled at the killing yet it was natural and swift.
I realise I might have dreamt of meeting her naked, of rising to
the brown thighs' darker centre, of receiving a kiss that pinned
and then emasculated me – but I didn't, then or afterwards.
The truth of what I had seen remained sufficient in itself.
Laura must have come again to the creek at the foot of the slope,
but I never witnessed her more than once, so perfectly attuned
to who she was and what she was doing; a truly intuitive huntress
food gathering for herself and her father's hungry family.
In a short while I had left the farm forever and never forgot.

A Pair

Mother and daughter. Note the familiarities
and then the differences. First the bodily
similarities, the generously rounded shaping
throughout, the classically full faces
with otherwise unremarkable features,
the models' legs. Else unalike. The elder
easygoing almost to a fault, Cockneyish,
adventurous, sexually free as a terrier.
The younger cooperative yet inhibited,
not without charm yet judgmental, expecting
too much or the worst from life and the living, quietly raped
at seventeen, impregnated at twenty. The two women
were constantly critical of each other and complemented
one another's lives in every possible way.

And yet they differed as much as two women could
and still be familial. The mother dressed
with the rakish nonchalance of a Hollywood film star,
the daughter dutifully translated stenographese
into the language of fashion. The mother kept
a bachelor establishment. The daughter
appended herself in the manner of the day.
The apartment never looked like becoming a salon,
neither intellect nor orgies eventuated.
But there was an "aura of femininity"
and this attracted varieties of males.
Other women hardly ever attended,
the mother not caring for their company.
The daughter philosophically went along.
When a lover made the mother's life absurd,
wrecking her economy and self-respect,
her otherwise critical child would forgive all,
lead her to an invalid's bed and brew
tisanes as soothing as the softest words
in the bruised ear. When the best of girls
was three months gone and afflicted with eructations
of a nervous nature the usually unsympathetic
parent arranged the procedure that put things to rights
in that particular family. The pair were never
really far apart in the process of living.
Seeing them together on a beach
posing like odalisques in their one-piece costumes
of cerulean or jade-coloured cloth
their marbled limbs more rounded than the visions
of amorous geometers, their breasts
small and emphatic, shoulders and throats beseeching
caress of lips – To watch their shining faces
watching the lovely bodies surrounding them
so long ago in that last year of war
was to forget in strange bewilderment
the world and its inevitable turning
and celebrate the ambience of art.

PETER PORTER 1929–2010

Peter Porter was born in Brisbane; his mother died suddenly when he was nine years old, and this catastrophe was followed by exile to boarding school. His father, a warehouseman in the manchester trade, was withdrawn and had little rapport with his only child. Boarding school was "near murder, at times. There were rituals where they stripped people naked and beat them with sticks, immersed them in horse troughs full of piss, that sort of thing. But the education wasn't bad." He was able to read endlessly at school, poets such as Donne, Shakespeare, the Victorians and Browning in particular. There had been no books in his parents' house.

After leaving high school, Porter tried cadet journalism, but felt out of place with Australians – a cave-dweller among the beach-goers – and in 1951 left by ship for England. He lived in London on a clerk's wage in unheated bedsitters, read from public libraries, learned about classical music with Australian friends, and continued, as he had done since high school, to write hundreds of poems. In 1954 on the disintegration of his relationship with the Australian novelist, Jill Neville, he returned to Australia, but ten months later was back in England, this time to live there permanently. He was introduced into "The Group", a circle of poets, including Philip Hobsbaum, Peter Redgrove, Martin Bell, Alan Brownjohn and occasionally Ted Hughes, who met regularly in London during the early '60s to analyse and discuss each other's work. Porter feels his poetry did not greatly benefit from this contact, but he enjoyed the sense of community and began to publish prolifically and win acceptance for his work.

He married Jannice Henry in 1961 and they had two daughters. For some years he worked in advertising, without ambition. In his 40s he became a full-time freelance reviewer. In 1974 his wife Jannice, who had been an alcoholic, committed suicide. Porter's seventh book, *The Cost of Seriousness*, is preoccupied with her death, and is uncharacteristically emotive and direct. After a visit in 1974, Porter regularly returned to Australia. In 1991 he married Christine Berg, a psychologist.

A prolific poet, who published seventeen collections of poems, Porter's poetry is known for its intellectuality: in his work every experience is mediated through the intellect, copious allusions attaching to it in the process. "Ode to Afternoon" is typical, sprinkled with esoterica, deliberately dubious assertions and quotations from Tennyson and T. S. Eliot – yet this hyperactive detail is absorbed into the plangent nostalgia of the poem. Despite its displays of intellectuality, his poetry is about a sceptical and satirical denial of all intellectual systems – political, literary, philosophical – on behalf of rationality and critical thinking. But while rejecting monistic solutions and seeing only "a jumble of contrivances .../the dirt-caked misery of the way the world survives", he is not a facile sceptic but a defender of liberal humanist attitudes. A great admirer of Auden and Wallace Stevens, his earlier work has an expressionistic fervour, which is quite unlike anything in his examplars. After the *Collected Poems* (1983) he became more than ever cerebral, aphoristic, and disjunctive – "philosophising" in fleeting "captions".

A Consumer's Report

The name of the product I tested is *Life*,
I have completed the form you sent me
and understand that my answers are confidential.

I had it as a gift,
I didn't feel much while using it,
in fact I think I'd have liked to be more excited.
It seemed gentle on the hands
but left an embarrassing deposit behind.
It was not economical
and I have used much more than I thought
(I suppose I have about half left
but it's difficult to tell) –
although the instructions are fairly large
there are so many of them
I don't know which to follow, especially
as they seem to contradict each other.
I'm not sure such a thing
should be put in the way of children –
It's difficult to think of a purpose
for it. One of my friends says
it's just to keep its maker in a job.
Also the price is much too high.
Things are piling up so fast,
after all, the world got by
for a thousand million years
without this, do we need it now?
(Incidentally, please ask your man
to stop calling me "the respondent",
I don't like the sound of it.)
There seems to be a lot of different labels,
sizes and colours should be uniform,
the shape is awkward, it's waterproof
but not heat resistant, it doesn't keep
yet it's very difficult to get rid of:
whenever they make it cheaper
they seem to put less in – if you say you don't
want it, then it's delivered anyway.
I'd agree it's a popular product,
it's got into the language; people
even say they're on the side of it.

Personally I think it's overdone,
a small thing people are ready
to behave badly about. I think
we should take it for granted. If its
experts are called philosophers or market
researchers or historians, we shouldn't
care. We are the consumers and the last
law makers. So finally, I'd buy it.
But the question of a "best buy"
I'd like to leave until I get
the competitive product you said you'd send.

The Sadness of the Creatures

We live in a third-floor flat
among gentle predators
and our food comes often
frozen but in its own shape
(for we hate euphemisms
as you would expect) and our cat's
food comes in tins, other than
scraps of the real thing and she
like a clever cat makes milk
of it for her kittens: we shout
of course but it's electric
like those phantom storms
in the tropics and we think of
the neighbours – I'm not writing
this to say how guilty
we are like some well-paid
theologian at an American
College on a lake
or even to congratulate
the greedy kittens who have
found their mittens and are up
to their eyes in pie. – I know
lots of ways of upsetting
God's syllogisms, real
seminar-shakers some of them,
but I'm an historical cat
and I run on rails and so
I don't frame those little poems

which take three lines to
get under your feet –
you know the kind of thing –
The water I boiled the lobster in
is cool enough to top
up the chrysanthemums.
No, I'm acquisitive and have
one hundred and seven Bach
Cantatas at the last count,
but these are things of the spirit
and my wife and our children
and I are animals (biologically
speaking) which is how the world
talks to us, moving on the billiard
table of green London, the sun's
red eye and the cat's green eye
focusing for an end. I know
and you know and we all know
that the certain end of each of us
could be the end of all of us,
but if you asked me what
frightened me most, I wouldn't
say the total bang or even
the circling clot in the red drains
but the picture of a lit room
where two people not disposed
to quarrel have met so
oblique a slant of the dark
they can find no words for
their appalled hurt but only
ride the rearing greyness:
there is convalescence from this,
jokes and love and reassurance,
but never enough and never
convincing and when the cats
come brushing for food their soft
aggression is hateful;
the trees rob the earth and the earth
sucks the rain and the children
burgeon in a time of invalids –
it seems a trio sonata

is playing from a bullock's
skull and the God of Man
is born in a tub of entrails;
all man's regret is no more
than Attila with a cold
and no Saviour here or
in Science Fiction will come
without a Massacre of the Innocents
and a Rape of El Dorado.

Ode to Afternoon

A command to the middle-aged,
you shall write disguised love poems
so that the young may respect you
when the truth is known

They will ensex your abstracts
wink knowingly at all
the stale erudition
which so enrages your critics

You must make capital out of despair:
real pain is never art,
turn instead to quotidian tasks,
Grub Street at the obsessional!

In your review of *The Romance of Linear B*,
notice that all the texts are Official Art,
the numbers of the king's combs and cattle –
their songs you must imagine for yourself

Of *The Eighteen Chorales*, there is much love of God –
you alone have cracked the cypher
and know what he meant when he told
the soul to bedeck itself for its bridegroom

In the middle of *The Children's Crusade*
you may put two adolescents under a tree
poking bits of bark down each other's front,
music by Puccini, the sun declining

Having set the scene, you are in the Land
of Afternoon. Sex, if it comes, will be late,
up some stairs following a nervous lunch,
her eyes like a Florentine postcard

In the afternoon they came unto a land
in which it seemed always afternoon:
The fathers were at the races
and the lawnmowers ran all over the hills

Afternoon men in the morning of the world,
we donate our three score and ten
to a beleaguered maturity –
province of afghan hounds and honeydew

Mother, the girls you warned me of
are waiting behind the rector's hedge,
I can hear their voices: they are content
with the usual menagerie

Home of averages where human kind
cannot bear very much reality
but the sun is always over the yard-arm
and we are for the dark

Der Untergang des Abendlandes
is still a best seller though it sounds
better with a stierhorn's blast
than a song at twilight

These quotations will keep nobody warm,
so put away the deck chairs
and the half-finished poem
and return to your research

Which was into the lineaments
of great fiction, and began
with the motherless boy
circuiting his grown-up garden:

Huge tears are in the pond,
every hurt has a face like a flower –
that will be music across the road
from the long-dead birthday party

O sprays of scent and my blue aunts,
I am coming with my excuses ready:
I was reading down in the boatshed,
how shall we get through the afternoon?

The Easiest Room in Hell

At the top of the stairs is a room
one may speak of only in parables.

It is the childhood attic,
the place to go when love has worn away,
the origin of the smell of self.

We came here on a clandestine visit
and in the full fire of indifference.

We sorted our books and let the children
sleep here away from creatures.

From its windows, ruled by willows,
the flatlands of childhood
stretched to the watermeadows.

It was the site of a massacre,
of the running down of the body
to less even than the soul,
the tribe's revenge on everything.

It was the heart of England
where the ballerinas were on points
and locums laughed through every evening.

Once it held all the games,
Inconsequences, Misalliance, Frustration,
even *Mendacity, Adultery* and *Manic Depression.*

But that was just its alibi,
all along it was home,
a home away from home.

Having such a sanctuary
we who parted here
will be reunited here.

You asked in an uncharacteristic note,
"Dwell I but in the suburbs
of your good pleasure?"

I replied, "To us has been allowed
the easiest room in hell."

Once it belonged to you,
now it is only mine.

An Angel in Blythburgh Church

Shot down from its enskied formation,
This stern-faced plummet rests against the wall;
Cromwell's soldiers peppered it and now the death-
    watch beetle has it in thrall.

If you make fortunes from wool, along
The weeping winter foreshores of the tide,
You build big churches with clerestories
    And place angels high inside.

Their painted faces guard and guide. Now or
Tomorrow or whenever is the promise –
The resurrection comes: fix your eyes halfway
    Between Heaven and Diss.

The face is crudely carved, simplified by wind;
It looks straight at God and waits for orders,
Buffeted by the organ militant, and blasted
    By choristers and recorders.

Faith would have our eyes as wooden and as certain.
It might be worth it, to start the New Year's hymn
Allowing for death as a mere calculation,
    A depreciation, entered in.

Or so I fancy looking at the roof beams
Where the dangerous beetle sails. What is it
Turns an atheist's mind to prayer in almost
    Any church on a country visit?

Greed for love or certainty or forgiveness?
High security rising with the sea birds?
A theology of self looking for precedents?
    A chance to speak old words?

Rather, I think of a woman lying on her bed
Staring for hours up to the ceiling where
Nothing is projected – death the only angel
    To shield her from despair.

An Exequy

In wet May, in the months of change,
In a country you wouldn't visit, strange
Dreams pursue me in my sleep,
Black creatures of the upper deep –

Though you are five months dead, I see
You in guilt's iconography,
Dear Wife, lost beast, beleaguered child,
The stranded monster with the mild
Appearance, whom small waves tease,
(Andromeda upon her knees
In orthodox deliverance)
And you alone of pure substance,
The unformed form of life, the earth
Which Piero's brushes brought to birth
For all to greet as myth, a thing
Out of the box of imagining.

This introduction serves to sing
Your mortal death as Bishop King
Once hymned in tetrametric rhyme
His young wife, lost before her time;
Though he lived on for many years
His poem each day fed new tears
To that unreaching spot, her grave,
His lines a baroque architrave
The Sunday poor with bottled flowers
Would by-pass in their mourning hours,
Esteeming ragged natural life
("Most dearly loved, most gentle wife"),
Yet, looking back when at the gate
And seeing grief in formal state
Upon a sculpted angel group,
Were glad that men of god could stoop
To give the dead a public stance
And freeze them in their mortal dance.

The words and faces proper to
My misery are private – you
Would never share your heart with those
Whose only talent's to suppose,
Nor from your final childish bed
Raise a remote confessing head –
The channels of our lives are blocked,
The hand is stopped upon the clock,
No-one can say why hearts will break
And marriages are all opaque:
A map of loss, some posted cards,

The living house reduced to shards,
The abstract hell of memory,
The pointlessness of poetry –
These are the instances which tell
Of something which I know full well,
I owe a death to you – one day
The time will come for me to pay
When your slim shape from photographs
Stands at my door and gently asks
If I have any work to do
Or will I come to bed with you.
O scala enigmatica,
I'll climb up to that attic where
The curtain of your life was drawn
Some time between despair and dawn –
I'll never know with what halt steps
You mounted to this plain eclipse
But each stair now will station me
A black responsibility
And point me to that shut-down room,
"This be your due appointed tomb."

I think of us in Italy:
Gin-and-chianti-fuelled, we
Move in a trance through Paradise,
Feeding at last our starving eyes,
Two people of the English blindness
Doing each masterpiece the kindness
Of discovering it – from Baldovinetti
To Venice's most obscure jetty.
A true unfortunate traveller, I
Depend upon your nurse's eye
To pick the altars where no Grinner
Puts us off our tourists' dinner
And in hotels to bandy words
With Genevan girls and talking birds,
To wear your feet out following me
To night's end and true amity,
And call my rational fear of flying
A paradigm of Holy Dying –
And, oh my love, I wish you were
Once more with me, at night somewhere

In narrow streets applauding wines,
The moon above the Apennines
As large as logic and the stars,
Most middle-aged of avatars,
As bright as when they shone for truth
Upon untried and avid youth.

The rooms and days we wandered through
Shrink in my mind to one – there you
Lie quite absorbed by peace – the calm
Which life could not provide is balm
In death. Unseen by me, you look
Past bed and stairs and half-read book
Eternally upon your home,
The end of pain, the left alone.
I have no friend, or intercessor,
No psychopomp or true confessor
But only you who know my heart
In every cramped and devious part –
Then take my hand and lead me out,
The sky is overcast by doubt,
The time has come, I listen for
Your words of comfort at the door,
O guide me through the shoals of fear
"Fürchte dich nicht, ich bin bei dir."

Non Piangere, Liù

A card comes to tell you
you should report
to have your eyes tested.

But your eyes melted in the fire
and the only tears, which soon dried,
fell in the chapel.

Other things still come –
invoices, subscription renewals,
shiny plastic cards promising credit –
not much for a life spent
in the service of reality.

You need answer none of them.
Nor my asking you for one drop
of succour in my own hell.

Do not cry, I tell myself,
the whole thing is a comedy
and comedies end happily.

The fire will come out of the sun
and I shall look in the heart of it.

What I Have Written I Have Written

It is the little stone of unhappiness
which I keep with me. I had it as a child
and put it in a drawer. There came
a heap of paper to put beside it,
letters, poems, a brittle dust
of affection, sallowed by memory.
Aphorisms came. Not evil, but
the competition of two goods
brings you to the darkened room.
I gave the stone to a woman
and it glowed. I set my mind
to hydraulic work, lifting words
from their swamp. In the light from the stone
her face was bloated. When she died
the stone returned to me, a present
from reality. The two goods
were still contending. From wading pools
the children grew to darken
gardens with their shadows. Duty
is better than love, it suffers no betrayal.

Beginning again, I notice
I have less breath but the joining
is more golden. There is a long way to go,
among gardens and alarms,
after-dinner sleeps peopled by toads
and all the cries of childhood.
Someone comes to say my name
has been removed from the Honourable
Company of Scribes. Books in the room
turn their backs on me.

Old age will be the stone and me together.
I have become used to its weight
in my pocket and my brain.
To move it from lining to lining

like Beckett's tramp,
to modulate it to the major
or throw it at the public –
all is of no avail. But I'll add
to the songs of the stone. These words
I take from my religious instruction,
complete responsibility –
let them be entered in the record,
What I have written I have written.

Bad Dreams in Venice

Again I found you in my sleep
And you were sturdily intact,
The counsel you would always keep
Became my dream's accusing tract.

Still I dared not think your force
Might even slightly slack my guilt
This wasn't judgement but a course
Which self not knowing itself built.

It scarcely mattered where I dreamed,
The dead can choose a rendezvous:
You knew that nothing is redeemed
By blame, yet let me conjure you.

And this was Venice where we'd walked
Full tourist fig, first man and wife
On earth, and where we'd looked and talked
Your presence could outlive your life.

But now Venetian vapours clung
To every cold and wounding word
The spectres which we moved among
Came from the phrases I had stirred.

They could not harm you but they bit
Into whatever had not died;
However we might reason it,
Your face and mine marched side by side.

And those old harshnesses which you
Muttered to me unrestrained,
Like Venice, loved but hated too,
Were all the closeness which remained.

BRUCE DAWE 1930–

Bruce Dawe was born in Geelong, Victoria, the last of four children, during the Great Depression. His father was a farm labourer, often unemployed or absent from home. He attended seven schools before leaving high school, an educational "drop-out" at the age of sixteen. Encouraged by his mother, who often recited poems she had learned in her childhood, he was the only one of his family to attend secondary school. A sister published some poems in a newspaper. He held a variety of menial jobs, and tells of how one day, while working on a building site at a university, he watched the students arrive and remarked to a fellow worker, "What lucky bastards, I wish I was one of them." He decided to complete his matriculation, went to night school, and then in 1954 began an arts degree at Melbourne University.

While there, his interest in writing poetry was stimulated by a group of poets on the academic staff: Vincent Buckley, Chris Wallace-Crabbe and Philip Martin. He also became a Catholic and the influence of a humanist Catholicism remains fundamental to his work. Dawe dropped out of university and worked as a factory labourer, postman, and self-employed gardener. In 1959 he joined the Royal Australian Air Force, initially as a trainee telegraphist, and remained there until 1969, becoming an education assistant. While in the RAAF he married, published two books of poetry, and completed a degree from the University of Queensland. After working as a teacher in Toowoomba, Queensland, he became a lecturer at the Darling Downs Institute of Advanced Education.

Dawe is a public poet who takes up social causes in his work: homelessness, unemployment, opposition to capital punishment and to the Vietnam War. He is not a propagandist for a political program; his stance is a more basically humane one. A watchful critic of totalitarianism he has rejected sweeping social prescriptions. Nor does he try to idealise the victims, the "lost people" he speaks for in his work. Their weaknesses are portrayed with affectionate irony, or exasperation at the seemingly intractable condition of their lives. A widely felt change of heart throughout society would seem to be what he prescribes.

Dawe's use of colloquial speech, and his feeling for the details of suburban life, are unsurpassed by any Australian poet. He is a compelling reader of his own poems and has become Australia's largest-selling poet. By 2005, when his collected poems *Sometimes Gladness* was republished, more than 100,000 copies had been sold.

Katrina

Katrina, now you are suspended between earth and sky.
Tubes feed you glucose intravenously. Naked you lie
In your special room in Ward Fifteen. Is your life
Opening again or closing finally? We do not know, but fear
The telephone call from a nurse whose distant sympathy
Will be the measure of our helplessness. Your twin brother's
Two-month-old vigour hurts us, remembering
Thin straws of sunlight on your bowed legs kicking

In defiance of your sickness, your body's wasting.
Against the black velvet of death threatening
Your life shines like a jewel, each relapse a flash of light
The more endearing. Your mother grieves already, so do I.
Miracles do not tempt us. We are getting in early,
Although we know there is no conditioning process which can counter
The karate-blow when it comes,
No way we can arrange the date-pad to conceal
The page torn-off, crumpled, thrown away.
Katrina, I had in mind a prayer, but only this came,
And you are still naked between earth and sky.
Transfusion-wounds in your heels, your dummy taped in your mouth.

Drifters

One day soon he'll tell her it's time to start packing,
and the kids will yell "Truly?" and get wildly excited for no reason,
and the brown kelpie pup will start dashing about, tripping everyone up,
and she'll go out to the vegetable-patch and pick all the green tomatoes
from the vines,
and notice how the oldest girl is close to tears because she was happy here,
and how the youngest girl is beaming because she wasn't.
And the first thing she'll put on the trailer will be the bottling-set she never
unpacked from Grovedale,
and when the loaded ute bumps down the drive past the blackberry-canes
with their last shrivelled fruit,
she won't even ask why they're leaving this time, or where they're heading
for
– she'll only remember how, when they came here,
she held out her hands bright with berries,
the first of the season, and said:
"Make a wish, Tom, make a wish."

Homecoming

All day, day after day, they're bringing them home,
they're picking them up, those they can find, and bringing them home,
they're bringing them in, piled on the hulls of tanks, in trucks, in convoys,
they're zipping them up in green plastic bags,
they're tagging them now in Saigon, in the mortuary coolness
they're giving them names, they're rolling them out of
the deep-freeze lockers – on the tarmac at Tan Son Nhut
the noble jets are whining like hounds,
they are bringing them home

– curly-heads, kinky-hairs, crew-cuts, balding non-coms
– they're high, now, high and higher, over the land, the steaming *chow mein*,
their shadows are tracing the blue curve of the Pacific
with sorrowful quick fingers, heading south, heading east,
home, home, *home* – and the coasts swing upward, the old ridiculous curvatures
of earth, the knuckled hills, the mangrove-swamps, the desert emptiness ...
in their sterile housing they tilt towards these like skiers
– taxiing in, on the long runways, the howl of their homecoming rises
surrounding them like their last moments (the mash, the splendour)
then fading at length as they move
on to small towns where dogs in the frozen sunset
raise muzzles in mute salute,
and on to cities in whose wide web of suburbs
telegrams tremble like leaves from a wintering tree
and the spider grief swings in his bitter geometry
– they're bringing them home, now, too late, too early.

Phantasms of Evening

Light fails. From here
it's hard to see
whether those young men ghost-dancing into their graves
are Viet Cong or Sioux.

Listen. Over the traffic
guns sound as though it were midday.
Rorke's Drift, Adobe Wells, Pinjarra
– the magic of kraal and gunyah
is nothing beside the magic of factories.
Dust swirls through sonless camps.

Look. The moon's ancient blade
falls flat across the shoulders of women.
Fools! Will you never learn?
All causes falter and go down
in this valley or the next.

Say, are those plumed shadows
Flying Horsemen of the First Air Cavalry Division,
or Hittites bringing the gospel of iron
to confound the Egyptians!
What war are we up to now?
Whose mourning is it?

The Rock-thrower

Out in the suburbs I hear
trains rocketing to impossible destinations
cry out against the intolerable waste,
at 3.40 in the morning hear the dog-frost
bark over the dark back-yards with their young trees
and tubular-steel swings where tomorrow's children
laughingly dangle their stockinged feet already
and the moon coats with white primer
the youthful lawns, the thirtyish expectations.

Midway between the hills and the sea
our house rocks quietly in the flow of time, each morning
we descend to sandy loam, the birds
pipe us ashore, on the rimed grass
someone has left four sets of footprints
as a sign to us that we are not alone
but likely to be visited
at some unearthly hour by a dear friend
who bears a love for us, wax-wrapped and sealed,
sliced, white, starch-reduced …

Sometimes I wake at night, thinking:
Even now he may be at work,
the rock-thrower in the neighbouring suburb, turning
the particular street of his choice
back to an earlier settlement – the men armed,
mounting guard, eyeing the mysterious skies,
tasting the salt of siege, the cleansing sacrament
of bombardment, talking in whispers, breaking humbly
the bread of their small fame,
as the planes going north and south
wink conspiratorially overhead
and the stones rain down …

And sometimes, too, dieselling homewards
when the bruised blue look of evening
prompts speculations upon the reasons for existence
and sets the apprehensive traveller to fingering thoughtfully
his weekly ticket, when the sun draws its bloody
knuckles back from the teeth of roof-tops
and the wounded commuter limps finally up the cement path
– I think of the rock-thrower, the glazier's benefactor,

raining down meaning from beyond the subdivisions,
proclaiming the everlasting evangel of vulnerability
– and the suburbs of men shrink to one short street
where voices are calling now from point to point:
"Is that you, Frank?"
"Is that you, Les?"
"Is that you, Harry?"
"See anything?"
"Nup ..."
"Nup ..."
"Nup ..."

At Shagger's Funeral

At Shagger's funeral there wasn't much to say
That could be said
In front of his old mum – she frightened us, the way
She shook when the Reverend read
About the resurrection and the life, as if
The words meant something to her, shook, recoiled.
And sat there, stony, stiff
As Shagger, while the rest of us, well-oiled,
Tried hard to knuckle down to solemn facts,
Like the polished box in the chapel aisle
And the clasped professional sorrow, but the acts
Were locked inside us like a guilty smile
That caught up with us later, especially when
We went round to pick up his reclaimed Ford,
The old shag-wagon, and beat out the dust
From tetron cushions, poured
Oil in the hungry sump, flicked the forsaken
Kewpie doll on the dash-board,
Kicked hub-caps tubercular with rust.

The service closed with a prayer, and silence beat
Like a tongue in a closed mouth.
Of all the girls he'd loved or knocked or both,
Only Bev Whiteside showed – out in the street
She gripped her hand-bag, said, "This is as far
As I'm going, boys, or any girl will go,
From now on."

Later, standing about
The windy grave, hearing the currawongs shout

In the camphor-laurels, and his old lady cry
As if he'd really been a son and a half,
What could any of us say that wasn't a lie
Or that didn't end up in a laugh
At his expense – caught with his britches down
By death, whom he'd imagined out of town?

Wood-eye

No nursing-sister ever walked
into our ward but Wood-eye cocked an eye
(the good one, still unbandaged)
in our direction, lay there like a lamb
thinking his lion's thoughts. Calm fingers took
like a professional sneak-thief his stirred pulse.
I've never seen a man whose libido's red-light
as steadily burned in that last street
whose name nobody knows. In Wood-eye's world
all roads led to Gomorrah where he practised
as a sort of resident specialist on call
24 hours a day. No instrument
but had its phallic relevance: thermometer,
spatula, syringe were sign-posts on the way
to a consummation devoutly to be wished.
"Would I?" he murmured, writhing on the rack
of unrealizable possibilities as some cool
sister exited: "Oh Jesus, would I, what!"

So we called him "Wood-eye". Something in his look
suggested that that eye-ball swivelling
in its carven socket, and that unseen eye
under the gauze-pad were like wooden things
intent on meaning more than just themselves
– totems, you might say, to which we looked
for meaning while we hunched around the ward
or lay like anchorites on sheets that smelled
as clean as baker's aprons. Wood-eye's wit
flapped like a pennon on a distant hill. He was the ravaged,
he was mystery, the figure slouching off into the night,
into the gun-fire crackling like leaves,
coming back at dawn and saying nothing
or nothing with his lips that could drown out
the heavy music of his silences.

And if now I could know
his cancer cured, the bandages dispersed,
the hospital a fleering memory,
the knives not feared, the sexy sisters gone
from his mind's racing rink,
the need to grin upon a leaden fate,
all passed away, all passed,
                                        would I rejoice
until this sober skin
burst open like a grape from which might be stamped out
the final wine of love, would I rejoice, then,
would I, *would* I what!

Provincial City

Climbing the range
your ears pop like champagne
and your heart distends
with something other than relief.

You can smell the peace up here.
The proportion, the narrowness.
Traitor, traitor, whines that piano-wire voice
as you swing past the Welcome sign

To find nothing is changed.
Overhead the clouds boil past,
low, friendly, meaning no harm.
The thunder moving into position

Shortly after five o'clock is stolid
as a furniture removalist.
The lightning jerks its thumb:
Over here, Fred.

When it rains
the gutters run red
but it's innocent. Dogs and magpies
the red soil stains.

In season the currawongs in the camphor-laurels
cry like tin-shears.
(The jacarandas hang their sheets
of blue water in mid-air.)

Down James Street the semis hurtle
nightly, brutalising through the quiet

civilized dark like the Eumenides,
or conscience, or history.

Here the elderly come to convalesce
after life's anxious illness; the young
leave daily for the Cities of the Plain
where there is work (or the hope of it.)

On the hillside at Drayton
the cemetery glitters like a dream;
asterisks of light
on the wind-screens of mourners' cars

Glint remotely as stars
in a heaven-deep well.
We will never get there.
This is a city which is all *present*:

It moves, but oh so slowly
you would have to sleep years,
waking suddenly once in a decade
to surprise it in the act of change.

Saturday night, in the main street kerb,
the angle-parked cars are full of watchers,
their feet on invisible accelerators,
going nowhere, *fast*.

EVAN JONES 1931–

Evan Jones was born in Melbourne and educated at Melbourne High School and the University of Melbourne, where he then taught history. In the 1950s he began publishing poetry that was formal and clear, and with a classical bent. He was part of the group of Melbourne poets that included Vincent Buckley, Chris Wallace-Crabbe, and R. A. Simpson. In 1958 he went to Stanford University, California, on a Creative Writing Scholarship. On his return he became an English academic, first at the Australian National University in Canberra and then the University of Melbourne. The influence of the poet and critic Yvor Winters at Stanford, who was a charismatic teacher, and strongly rationalist and anti-romantic, appears to have strengthened a tendency already present in Jones's poetry to use a plain, stripped-back language. In his later poems he largely jettisoned classical or biblical references, relying on the here-and-now for his subject matter: the pain of divorce, his experiences as a separated parent. He is particularly accomplished in his wry and bitter aphorisms. Wallace-Crabbe wrote of Jones: "… he wants to assert the value of a stoical approach to life and to criticize acutely the limits of stoicism." (*Meanjin Quarterly*, vol. 20, no. 2, 1961).

Honeymoon, South Coast

Sometime shortly after the rain began
A quarrel began also:
Fish, chess, magazines and toothpaste
Fed into an argument that ran,
Alto and basso,
Through stave on stave of waste.

All night the water shambled on sand,
The wind complained poorly:
Insomniac, snoring, they lay back to back;
Next morning they walked hand in hand,
But insecurely,
Through mile on mile of wrack.

Molly-hawks, ocean gulls, mostly silver gulls
Welcomed the brighter weather
That lay along a hundred miles of coastline:
But in the shadow of the hills
They set out together
Through years and years of rain.

Study in Blue

In his blue suit, an Oxford Standard Authors
Caught in his hand, I watch him passing by:
Nothing could be more sober, more discreet.
It's me O Lord – or rather, it is I.

VIVIAN SMITH 1933–

Vivian Smith grew up in Hobart, Tasmania, during the Depression and the years of World War II. He was educated at the Hobart High School and the University of Tasmania, where he lectured in French. He moved to Sydney in 1967, obtained his doctorate from the University of Sydney, and became Reader in English. He was the literary editor of *Quadrant* for many years. His wife, Sybille, who lectured in languages at the University of Tasmania, was born in Vienna.

Smith's literary affinities include Rilke, of the *Neue Gedichte*, James McAuley, Shaw Neilson and Philip Larkin. His poetry has a lyrical purity. Although the metrics are strict, and the meaning and imagery lucid, the overall mood is one of uncertainty, with an underlying sense of mortality. The earlier poems about Tasmania, evoke a chill, bony, almost empty and sometimes punishing landscape. Later poems, after his move to Sydney, celebrate subtropical light and colour, but psychological ease still remains elusive. Smith has published eight books of poetry including selected editions. He is not prolific, and each poem is economical. He has also published some critical studies, and translations from the German, particularly of Paul Celan.

At an Exhibition of Historical Paintings, Hobart

The sadness in the human visage stares
out of these frames, out of these distant eyes;
the static bodies painted without love
that only lack of talent could disguise.

Those bland receding hills are too remote
where the quaint natives squat with awkward calm.
One carries a kangaroo like a worn toy.
his axe alert with emphasised alarm.

Those nearer woollen hills are now all streets;
even the water in the harbour's changed.
Much is alike and yet a slight precise
disparity seems intended and arranged –

as in that late pink terrace's facade.
How neat the houses look. How clean each brick.
One cannot say they look much older now,
but somehow more themselves, less accurate.

And see the pride in this expansive view:
churches, houses, farms, a prison tower:
a grand gesture like wide-open arms
showing the artist's trust, his clumsy power.

And this much later vision, grander still:
the main street sedate carriages unroll
towards the tentative, uncertain mountain:
a flow of lines the artist can't control –

the foreground nearly breaks out of its frame
the streets end so abruptly in the water …
But how some themes return. A whaling ship.
The last natives. Here that silent slaughter

is really not prefigured or avoided.
One merely sees a profile, a full face,
a body sitting stiffly in a chair:
the soon forgotten absence of a race …

Album pieces: bowls of brown glazed fruit …
I'm drawn back yet again to those few studies
of native women whose long floral dresses
made them first aware of their own bodies.

History has made artists of all these
painters who lack energy and feature.

But how some gazes cling. Around the hall
the pathos of the past, the human creature.

Early Arrival Sydney

Red cockatoo crests caught on coral trees:
my Sydney emblems. Dragging the land in view
our ship hauls glass and concrete to its side
as gulls fly up and snatch and scream and glide
away on a sea smeared with a trace of blue.

The neons flicker and the skyline wakes.
The orange suburbs float through miles of calm;
a pastel-coloured terrace shades its slope.
While five gulls fight for nothing on a rope,
the breeze picks out a single listless palm.

The city's like a room far undersea
with locked arcades where shadow-waves subside.
Grey windows bend great cloud-shapes as they pass.
Beyond these tiles, tunnels, iron, glass,
the flat waters of green inlets ride
where all the folded yachts are chained away.

But here the huge hotels still sway in space
with the exactness of a foreign place.

Warmth in July: Hobart

Sybille's

Warmth in July like first clear days of spring,
and sunlight glints in mirrors. windows, pools;
the heat hangs in the garden like a stare.
The light is still abrupt with winter's sting
but change is upon us; change is everywhere.

The sun shows nothing but a strict repose:
a net of trees, each twig a wired nail.
I look as through a cage into the sky
and see beyond the blue this season chose
the strident blue within a peacock's tail.

Why should this warmth remind me of my death,
and could I bear such clarity while dying?
Such hard precision suggests nothing more.
The sharpness of the light has caught my breath
with so much stillness. Not one insect flying.

The light is caught: no shadow overflows.
And nothing's yet begun. No season's ended.
All buds are merely knowledge in the mind.
Implicit in the twig are hip and rose:
but waiting, waiting too is still intended.

We seek too soon the end, the final things:
we try to grasp the whole where meanings start
in detail that may never reach design.
But feel the light and how it soaks and stings
and taste the blue where branches fall apart

till all your knowledge is mere warmth and glow,
all apprehension – as of sensual ease:
a sense of sure precision deep in things.
The year has still its separate months to go
but change is promised, and awakenings.

Tasmania

Water colour country. Here the hills
rot like rugs beneath enormous skies
and all day long the shadows of the clouds
stain the paddocks with their running dyes.

In the small valleys and along the coast,
the land untamed between the scattered farms,
deconsecrated churches lose their paint
and failing pubs their fading coats of arms.

Beyond the beach the pine trees creak and moan,
in the long valley poplars in a row,
the hills breathing like a horse's flank
with grasses combed and clean of the last snow.

Gabrielle

My daughter runs a hospital for moths
and seems to be on duty at all hours.
Her mantelpiece has cotton wool for beds,
a cup of water, frangipani flowers.

She brings them home, the fallen and the torn –
a blunt moth with one bedraggled wing
a Christmas beetle looking beyond help
a dragonfly past flying.

She never talks of pain or mere survival
or any of the meanings in her reach.
saving bees from drowning, moths from cold
and butterflies wind harries on the beach.

Mother Teresa of the butterflies
I tease her and she smiles too.
She knows their lives have hardly any hours,
she knows exactly what she has to do.

BARRY HUMPHRIES 1934–

Barry Humphries, Australia's best-known satirist, was born in Melbourne in 1934 and educated at the University of Melbourne. He began his lifelong involvement with the theatre in university revues. There are many stories of his Dada activities during his student years: of his secreting sliced ham amongst lingerie displays in department stores; of being served an elaborate breakfast on a suburban train, each course brought on at a different station; and of holding an art exhibition featuring such objects as "Pus in Boots", which made use of custard. After graduating, Humphries worked as an actor and as a revue performer, and in 1959 moved to London to work in theatre and television. In 1962 he toured Australia with *A Nice Night's Entertainment*, his first full-scale, one-man show, in which he played various *kitsch* characters. Since then he has become famous in English-speaking countries for satirising the philistinism of the Australian middle class. His most famous creation is Edna Everage, who has evolved from a tasteless, pretentious housewife and mum into Dame Edna, international mega-star. A celebration of vitality underlies Dame Edna's vulgarisms. Offstage Humphries has artistically flopping hair, wears bow ties and large hats, collects art, and has a reticent, charming manner. He has been married four times and has two daughters and two sons. A selection of his light verse and some serious poems, *Neglected Verse*, was published in 1991.

"The Pavlova Stamp" is written as if by Edna Everage. "Ode to the Nine-By-Five", one of his more serious works, was presented at the inauguration of a new exhibition commemorating the first Australian Impressionist Exhibition in August 1889, where most of the pictures were painted on cigar box lids measuring nine by five inches. The envoi of the poem, which was relevant for the purposes of inaugurating the commemorative exhibition, has been deleted.

Humphries has notes on the following poems:

"Ode to the Nine-By-Five": Mallee: "Ethnic fuel deracinated from the mallee region"; Jennings and Craig Davis: "Builders of popular suburban villas"; Smike and Bulldog and K: "Nicknames for Streeton, Roberts and Conder, Australian impressionists, later much sought after by *Noveau Riche* collectors"; Henry Bolte: "comparatively distinguished Premier of Victoria (1955 to 1972), and a keen advocate of laissez faire excavation."

"Wattle Park Blues": "Mercurochrome, a bright yellow and antiseptic palliative for grazed knees"; "Dixies were cylindrical ice cream receptacles of wax paper"; "to shout *Colloq.* to treat, to buy for, to pick up the tab for".

"Threnody For Patrick White": "Bea Lillie, celebrated review artiste"; "Douglas Byng (1893–1987) cabaret performer and female impersonator".

Ode to the Nine-by-Five

G & S on the pianoforte,
The babble of laughter and wine,
Melbourne Bohemia nicely naughty
In 1889.
Stock, Japonica, daffodil,
Cigar lids and cigarette fumes,
Liberty silks from Cullis and Hill
On the walls of Buxton's Rooms.
McCubbin smiling, Streeton merry,
Conder paralytic;
A nice cheroot and a glass of sherry
For Smith, the *Argus* critic.
Smith took a cab through the August vapour,
Sat at his roll-top desk,
Roberts was first to see the paper,
"A pain to the eye ... grotesque."

. . .

Of the artists who painted on cedar board
Not one remains alive,
And only a used-car man can afford
An original "nine-by-five".

But a spinster in nineteen fifty-four
Who dwelt in the Yarra Valley
Found some funny old lids at the back of a drawer
Ideal for kindling a "mallee".
Cold grey ash in an Ivanhoe grate
Are those poems the artists gave us,
And the hills that enraptured them groan with the weight
Of Jennings and Craig Davis.
Boxes at Box Hill, poor Bulleen,
Bulldozed and desecrated;
Templestowe plundered and obscene,
And Doncaster castrated.
The riverbank Roberts used to roam
Makes a beautiful Shopping Mall,
And why not erect a Prestige Home

With a sling to your Council pal?
Gone are the rooms they held their club in,
Smike and Bulldog and K,
Richardson and Prof McCubbin,
Long ago – far away.
Lopped are those Heidelberg orchard twigs
Where the spring of our art unfurled,
While Sir Henry Bolte proudly digs
A quarry for the world.

The Pavlova Stamp

Marie Antoinette of France was a very selfish queen,
It's not surprising that she ended on the guillotine;
She ate rich gateaux all day long as though she'd never seen them,
Though her starving subjects barely had a vanilla slice between them.
"Let them eat cake!" she cruelly spake, forgetful of their misery,
But the hungry horde could not afford to shop at her pat-isserie.
So the proud queen was defeated, despite her fine regalia,
But we have our cake and eat it, in heaven-blest Australia!
Pavlovas are a national treat, and lest we grow too greedy
Let's spare a prayer (as we eat) for all the poor and needy.

There's a moral to the pavlova
With its luscious creamy clots –
It's like mankind all over:
The Pavs, and the Pav-nots!

The Wattle Park Blues

Back in the wattled thirties
Before the world went dark,
They built a noble chalet
On the crest of Wattle Park.
The trammies on their days off
Came for Devonshire teas,
And outside the kiddies seesawed
With mercurochromy knees.
A graveyard for old cable trams
Lay below us in the valley,
Where we played till creamy soda time
And dixies in the chalet.
How we envied the conductor
On the tram on which we'd come.

With his cubes of coloured tickets,
Nippled rubber on his thumb.
Loved his uniform of navy serge,
Scarlet piping on lapel;
Wished we could say, *Move down the car*,
And tug that leather bell.
Above us in the giant gums
Were bird houses built on high,
Little chalets for the maggies,
Tudor suburbs in the sky.

. . .

We grew older, came less often,
To watch the wattles burst here,
Though Geoff, Jeanette and Alison
Each had their twenty-first here;
But we'd outgrown creamy sodas,
Were spottier – and thirstier.
We drank Pimms and puffed on Garricks,
Hugged gardenia'd girlfriends hard,
As we parked our mothers' cars by night
Along the Boulevard,
And Wattle Park was quite forgotten
And the trams' metallic rumble.
Dear to the heart of childhood,
Like the taste of Violet Crumble.
And so good friends and strangers
I presume to be your guide
To the terminus of memory
I have shouted you a ride.
To the place where me and Colin
And a thousand kiddies more
Picnicked underneath the pollen
In the days before the War.
Today the trees seem sparser
The old cable trams have gone,
But they still serve in the chalet
Melbourne's finest buttered scone.

Threnody for Patrick White

For Geoffrey Dutton

In a Federation bungalow beside Centennial Park,
With its joggers in the daytime, perves and muggers after dark,
Lived a famous author hostesses pretend that they have read;
A querulous curmudgeon with a tea-cosy on his head.

He had a vulnerable hauteur, he was arrogant and shy
He had the visage of a dowager with a beady light blue eye,
He wrote at least two masterpieces, his correspondence flowed in torrents
With Firbank in one pocket, in the other D. H. Lawrence.

He was generous to young artists; often petty, never mean,
He was a typical high-minded, interbellum, stage-struck queen.
Before the War he would have queued to hear Bea Lillie sing,
One imagined him in private dragging up like Douggie Byng.

He had a few friends (mostly female), whom he wrote to all their lives,
And he loved his male friends too until they traded in their wives.
Then he cut them and he dropped them and defamed them on the page
You felt he'd once been dropped so cruelly he had to share the pain and
rage.

He dropped Sid and Geoff and Lawrence, he dropped Bruce and Brett and
me
He preferred those lisping toadies who wouldn't dare to disagree.
With lickspittles round his table he was the Venerated Crank
But the malady was in his bones and he shrank and shrank and shrank ...

Now his writing light is switched off, though his wall-eyed dogs still bark
In that Federation garden beside Centennial Park,
Home of the family picnic and the jogger and the mugger;
Oh I pray God doesn't drop *you*, you miserable old bugger.

DAVID MALOUF 1934–

David Malouf was born in Brisbane. His mother was of English-Jewish and Portuguese descent. His father was of Lebanese Christian extraction and owned a department store. Malouf attended Brisbane Grammar School and the University of Queensland. In the 1960s he was a school teacher in England, and from 1968 to 1978 was an English academic at the University of Sydney. He became a full-time writer and in the 1980s and 1990s spent part of the year in Campagnatico, a small village in Southern Tuscany. He now lives in Sydney.

Malouf is one of Australia's most acclaimed writers of fiction – "among the front rank of world writers" (J. M. Coetzee) – his fiction having won numerous Australian and international awards, including the first International IMPAC Dublin Literary Award, the largest and most international prize of its kind. He has published ten novels, three books of short stories and an outstanding *The Complete Stories* (2007). He has also published three opera libretti and seven collections of poetry. One of Malouf's strengths is his sympathy with a wide range of people – something that is reflected in the tone of his writing voice. His poem "Typewriter Music" brilliantly mimics the action of an old-fashioned manual typewriter. When manual typewriters exist only in museums, will readers be able to understand the uncanny accuracy of this poem?

The Year of the Foxes

For Don Anderson

When I was ten my mother, having sold
her old fox-fur (a ginger red bone-jawed
Magda Lupescu
of a fox that on her arm played
dead, cunningly dangled
a lean and tufted paw)

decided there was money to be made
from foxes, and bought via
the columns of the *Courier-Mail* a whole
pack of them; they hung from penny hooks
in our panelled sitting-room, trailed from the backs
of chairs; and Brisbane ladies, rather
the worse for war, drove up in taxis wearing
a G.I. on their arm
and rang at our front door.

I slept across the hall, at night hearing
their thin cold cry. I dreamed the dangerous spark
of their eyes, brushes aflame
in our fur-hung, nomadic
tent in the suburbs, the dark fox-stink of them
cornered in their holes
and turning.

                    Among my mother's show pieces –
Noritake teacups, tall hock glasses
with stems like barley-sugar,
goldleaf *demitasses* –
the foxes, row upon row, thin-nosed, prick-eared,
dead.

            The cry of hounds

was lost behind mirror glass,
where ladies with silken snoods and fingernails
of chinese lacquer red
fastened a limp paw;
went down in their high heels
to the warm soft bitumen, wearing at throat
and elbow the rare spoils
of '44; old foxes, rusty red like dried-up wounds,
and a G.I. escort.

Typewriter Music

Hinged grasshopper legs kick
back. So
quick off the mark, so
spritely. They set
the mood, the mode, the call
to light-fingered highjinks.

A meadow dance
on the keyboard,
in breathless, our-of-bounds
take-offs into
flight and giddy joyflight without
stint. The fingerpads

have it. Brailling through
études of alphabets, their chirp and clatter
grass-choppers
the morning to soundbites,
each rifleshot hammersrroke another notch
in the silence.

Seven Last Words of the Emperor Hadrian

Animula vagula blandula
hospes comesque corporis,
quae nunc abibis in loca,
pallidula, rigida, nudula,
nec, ut soles, dabis iocos?

1
Dear soul mate, little guest
and companion, what
shift will you make

now, out there
in the cold?
If this is a joke,
it is old, old.

2
Soul, small wandering one,
my lifelong companion,
where will you go
– numb, pale, undefended –
now the joke we shared is ended?

3
Little lightfoot
spirit, house
mate, bedfellow, where are you off
to now? Cat got
your tongue? Lost your shirt, caught
your death? Well, the last laugh
is on you. Is on us.

4
Sweet urchin, fly-
by-night, heart's guest, my
better half and solace,
you've really done it
this time. You've played one trick
too many. Fool, you've laughed us
both out of breath.

5
If this is one of your jokes,
my jack, my jack-in-the-box,
layoff. Where
have you got to?
It's cold out there.
And what will you do
without me, you sweet idiot? Go naked?
Homeless? Come back to bed.

6
What's this, old mouse, my secret
sharer? Gone

where? Did you think I'd let
you slip away without me after
a lifetime of happy scrapes? Who
warmed you, clothed you, fed you, paid with laughter
for your tricks, your japes? Is this the one
joke, poor jackanapes, dear bugaboo,
your emperor does not get?

7
So you're playing fast
and loose, are you? You've cut
the love knot. Well, let's see how you get
on out there without me. Who's kidding
who? Without my body, its royal
breath and blood to warm you, my hands, my tongue
to prove to you what's real,
what's not, poor fool, you're nothing.
But O, without you, my sweet nothing,
I'm dust.

CHRIS WALLACE-CRABBE 1934–

Chris Wallace-Crabbe was born in Melbourne and grew up there, becoming a cadet metallurgist. He then went to the University of Melbourne and graduated in English, where he was to become Lockie Fellow in Australian Literature (1961–1963) and ultimately to hold a personal chair. He has occupied a number of overseas posts, including Professor of Australian Studies at Harvard (1987–1988). On his retirement he became Professor Emeritus in the Australian Centre at the University of Melbourne. He has published more than twenty volumes of poetry, including selections from his work, and also collections of critical essays and a novel. In the 1950s and 1960s Wallace-Crabbe was associated with the Melbourne school of academic poets, which included Vincent Buckley, Evan Jones, R. A. Simpson and later Peter Steele. More explicitly than any of them, and with a balanced grace in poems such as "Wintry Manifesto", he was an exponent of the restrained tone of the British Movement poets of the 1950s, as exemplified in Donald Davie's poem "Remembering the 'Thirties". In his essay "The Habit of Irony? Australian Poets of the Fifties" (*Meanjin Quarterly*, vol. 20, no. 2, 1961) Wallace-Crabbe wrote: "If poetry is to represent our age and our condition in any positive sense, it must, in some measure at least be ironic". Wallace-Crabbe's poetry is optimistic, urbane, and concerned to demarcate limits and draw intellectual conclusions. Over the last thirty or so years his poetry has opened out and become freer, more direct and colloquial. "The Domestic Sublime" exemplifies this later style. "In Light and Darkness" refers to an "Eton crop" which is a short, slicked-down hairstyle.

In Summer

As the long afternoon went drifting on
Words took their pattern in an ordered dance
Until, at last, the low red sun had gone
And all things by some quiet ordinance
Shared the one shade.
                                        A flood of indigo
From peak to plain set off the western glow
While dusk obscured the pine-trees standing near
And fell between the talkers and their beer.

In Light and Darkness

To the noonday eye, light seems an ethical agent,
Straight from the shoulder, predictable, terribly quick, though
It climbs in a curve to space's unlikely limit,
    Thus posing a problem for mathematicians and God,
Whatever He turns out to be and wherever His dwelling.
Rich is the clotting of gold in the late afternoon or
Turning to twilight, one last blaze of watery colour
    Where man can project his false dreams in figures of light,
Pretending that all his environment loyally loves him,
Seas of ice and burning plains.
                                                            Too easy
Bending nature before us, but light is defiant
    Coming by night from dead stars with terrible speed.
So is our planet rebuked, and we meet in mirrors
Desperate masks, eyes of imprisoned strangers
And lips that open to say, "We are only mirages",
    While the lawns outside are green and the roses real.

You dub the sun a realist? Then it will plague you,
Wading with stork-legs into the green water,
Lending the oak-bole moss its leopard shadows
    Or streaking paddocks darkly with sunset sheep
Fifty feet long.
                                                Nothing is quite so rococo
As dawnlight caught on a fishscale formation of cirrus,
Nor quite so romantic as one gilded westering biplane.
    We just don't live in a hard intellectual glare.

No one, of course, endures darkness or daylight entirely:
Cyclic change betrays our terrestrial journey
And what looked like trees at dawn turn out to be crosses,

Suddenly black as the florid sun goes down,
And maybe at midnight resemble gallows or statues
As we slip past, childlike, alone.
No wonder
Sly poets admiringly use, but will not warm to
The subtle machines that teach our world to spin.
These are too steady for reverence: gods must be changeable
Since worship is saved for what we cannot govern;
Gods push up grass, channel the dense sap through pine-boughs
And amass the pewter cloudbanks of summer storm.

Once I awoke, a child in a chill mountain morning,
To see the small town – undreamed transfiguration –
Mantled in white, its slate and stone and timber
Bright with that foreign cloak of innocence.
And I walked into old-world beauty; the gilt sun rising
Fell in a garden where time itself was congealing
As we shaped wonderful igloos under the stringybarks
And took no account of thaw. But noon came on.
Something was lost in the brown receding slush there
Which has not returned, something other than childhood:
A notion, rather, of clear crystalline standards
Freezing life to one shape, like a photograph.

Yet this is the point:
a photograph leaves out living
For Eton crops, old blazers, baptismal lace or
Some late-Victorian smile turned stiff and waxy,
All arabesques, but never the heart of the thing,
Which is neither good nor bad, but one maze of motion
Through which we dance, into and out of the darkness
To tireless music: motes in the curled winds' breathing
And more than motes, faced with the corners of choice.
And so at night below all the brilliant clusters
Of lamps in the sky, the living, dead and dying
Poised in their dance, I cling to the crust here stolidly
And pray for a perfect day.
Out in the cold
Of hoarfrost and starlight, we fear for tomorrow's choosing
And cherish dreams made in meticulous patterns;
But come tomorrow, we will neither be Christ nor Gandhi
But will breathe this common air and rejoice with the birds.

All that I ask is that myriad lights, ever changing,

Continue to play on this great rind of ranges and gullies,
Flooding the vision of dreaming dwellers in cities
    Who walk out in summer pursuing something to praise:
    We will neither be simple nor clear till the end of our days.

Wintry Manifesto

It was the death of Satan first of all,
The knowledge that earth holds though kingdoms fall,
    Inured us to a stoic resignation,
    To making the most of a shrunken neighbourhood;

And what we drew on was not gold or fire,
No cross, not cloven hoof about the pyre,
    But painful, plain, contracted observations:
    The gesture of a hand, dip of a bough

Or seven stubborn words drawn close together
As a hewn charm against the shifting weather.
    Our singing was intolerably sober
    Mistrusting every trill of artifice.

Whatever danced on needle-points, we knew
That we had forged the world we stumbled through
    And, if a stripped wind howled through sighing alleys,
    Built our own refuge in a flush of pride

Knowing that all our gifts were for construction –
Timber to timber groined in every section –
    And knowing, too, purged of the sense of evil,
    These were the walls our folly would destroy.

We dreamed, woke, doubted, wept for fading stars
And then projected brave new avatars,
    Triumphs of reason. Yet a whole dimension
    Had vanished from the chambers of the mind,

And paramount among the victims fled,
Shrunken and pale, the grim king of the dead;
    Withdrawn to caverns safely beyond our sounding
    He waits as a Pretender for his call,

Which those who crave him can no longer give.
Men are the arbiters of how they live,
    And, stooped by millstones of authority,
    They welcome tyrants in with open arms.

Now in the shadows of unfriendly trees
We number leaves, discern faint similes
    And learn to praise whatever is imperfect
    As the true breeding-ground for honesty,

Finding our heroism in rejection
Of bland Utopias and of thieves' affection:
    Our greatest joy to mark an outline truly
    And know the piece of earth on which we stand.

The Secular

However you look at it,
The abundant secular,
How splendid it all appears
Shifting and coruscating
All over and everywhere,
All at once, repeatedly,
In little waves of motion
And stubbornly tangible.

Look, I grant all that you say:
Whoever the creator
He brutally botched the job,
But how tough his furniture
Really is made, piece by piece!
I jump on his solid stones
Or dance on these rustling fields
And hear the sap leap in trees
Already marked out for death.

The Domestic Sublime

"My dears, my dears, I say to the plates and the spoons."

Iris Murdoch

The Surface of Things

Pleasantly rolling deodorant into an oxter
  He thought of the shave ahead,
Whether to start in the upper left-hand comer
  Or the slant of his jaw instead.

From the loose aggregate of these choices
  A common life is made,
Fate no more than a thicket of brand-names
  And the moment when you delayed.

Saucer
who first spotted the lack
not that is the slip
in between the cup and lip
but down under a hot mug
                                        or cup?
yet if it comes to that
a plate would merely be over the top

something then to stop the drips
or keep the pea soup off your lap
complicate the washing up
stop a simple splash
                                        or slop
and sit here for the waiter's tip

sad without a cup

Indoor Yachting
Has any mere scribbler
ever spotted or caught

that fine dramatic gesture
by which a homebody

standing down at the bed-end
flourishes a wide clean sheet and

blows it out like a spinnaker
so that the far end

will flutter down in place
where a pillow will be,

once again
getting it right?

Coat Hangers Galore
Clubbable and promiscuous,
                                                they hang around
getting under your feet
while always intending to be helpful;

wiry and would-be athletic
they just keep falling into a tangle
putting a foot
                              in somebody else's mouth.

Garlic

Adhesive, papery,
the wan delicate skin
sticks for just a smidgen
too long, until

a naked clove
comes out successfully
shining
virginal as the dawn

yet leaving
its ripe sex on your fingers
for quite some time.

At the Clothesline

What I'd thought a fallen shirt
Under the line, flat on the grass
Was nothing but my shadow there,
Hinting that all things pass:

That many we loved or used to know
Are dragged already out of sight,
Vanished fast, though stepping slow,
Folded into remorseless night.

My dark trace now has quit the lawn.
Everything slips away too soon,
Yet something leaves its mark here like
A rainbow ring around the moon.

RANDOLPH STOW 1935–2010

Randolph Stow was born in Geraldton, a coastal town of Western Australia. His father was a lawyer and his mother came from a long-established pastoralist family, among the earliest pioneers of the state. Stow grew up on the dynastic property with the workmen – the Kevs and Harrys and Jabulmaras of one of his poems – and throughout his life has found an affinity with working and tribal people. By the time he graduated from the University of Western Australia in arts, he had already published a volume of poetry and two novels.

Stow went to work as a storeman on an isolated mission station in the Kimberley Ranges, before being invited to the University of Adelaide as a tutor. Missing the outback, he decided the way to return was to train as an anthropologist, a course he took at the University of Sydney. Short of money after two years there, he became in 1959 a cadet patrol officer and assistant to the Government Anthropologist in New Guinea. However, while leading his first patrol, in the Trobriand Islands, he contracted a severe form of malaria and was invalided home with suicidal depression. From 1960 he spent three years in London as an outpatient of a hospital for tropical diseases. He then lived in a number of countries before returning to England to settle in East Anglia, from where his forebears had emigrated in 1830.

In 1969 he began *Visitants*, which is widely regarded as the best of his novels and is set in the Trobriand Islands, but he was unable to finish it until ten years later. This writing block he attributes to an addiction to the drug mandrax, prescribed after a car accident. During his years of creative inactivity Stow lived in obscurity in a rented farm cottage, on a trickle of royalties. For much of this period he worked as a barman in a village pub, unpaid except for his drinks. His writing of the novel *The Girl Green as Elder-flower*, long researched but actually produced in one month in 1979, helped him complete *Visitants* in the same year. Stow then settled in Suffolk in a small terrace house in Old Harwich, by the docks, "within walking distance of seventeen pubs and crawling distance of four."

The main influences on his poetry, he said, were Whitman, Rimbaud and St John Perse, who loosened the line of his extremely precocious juvenilia and gave his work the associative daring of its imagery. "The Language of Flowers" and "For One Dying" – which seems to be about his childhood nurse – were written between 1954 and 1956, when he could at most have been 21. Stow's verse has a characteristic high-pitched emotionality. He is unusual in that his novels and poetry are equally outstanding. A theme of his work in both forms is isolation: a sense of "otherness" within nature and society. Despite the subjectivity of the imagery in his poems, what he says of his novels is also true of his verse: "I always was a quite fanatical realist, always attempting to be more exact about things ..." Stow's output of poetry was small, even though it was his preferred medium: he published three slim volumes, including a selected edition, *A Counterfeit Silence*, and nine new poems in an anthology of his work, *Randolph Stow* (1990).

"The Language of Flowers"

A Handbook for Victorian Lovers

I sent my love clematis. She, walking white
in her garden, reading Rossetti, veiled her sight
under blue eyelids, blushingly comprehended
her *mental beauty* was thereby commended.

My love sent me the bud of a white rose
to say *her heart knew naught of love*. Repose
fled from my days, to tell her of my *flame*
I sent an iris. Swift her answer came.

She had gathered mouse-eared chickweed, flowers which swear
ingenuous simplicity. Despair
seized me, I sent gum cistus, saying: "*Tomorrow
I die*." She sent me yew, expressing *sorrow*.

True to my word, I died; and to my tomb
she mourning came. Her hat was all abloom
with rosemary, which vows *not to forget*,
and rue, to tell the world of her *regret*.

But when upon my grave, my life, my dove,
stooped to plant myrtle, signifying *love*,
then garden daisies in my dust were bred,
and "Sweet, *I share your sentiments*," they said.

For One Dying

Miss Sutherland MacDonald, 1873–1956

Now, in that place where all birds cease to sing,
and paths grow faint and melt into the hills,
you pause, tasting the wind; for it is spring,
and down on Ellendale's wide water spills
a dust of petals. In this last September,
opening your hands to seize the golden light
(your hands, which flowers and animals remember,
and trees, and children) you will enter night.

I am no more the child whom you made cry
so readily with your sad ballad-tales,
not skilled to soothe the life that prays to die,
not skilled to pray. But must, since all else fails,
trust that your Lord, who owes you some amend,
grant you a quiet night, and a perfect end.

The Ghost at Anlaby

For Geoffrey and Ninette Dutton

Now sulkies come haunting softwheeled down the
leaves; on the cool veranda, over
whisky, wistaria, gentlemen admire
antwaisted, hamsleeved, bellskirted ladies
crossing the lawns with fishtailed racquets
intent on tennis. Heart, unlearn your fire.

Forget now, forget. Below the willows
Tom Roberts squatters, George Lambert ladies,
whose boats and fancy made this dam a lake,
speak of, remember, no visitant stranger.
Once time was a sportsman, and I the quarry,
who now would sleep with death, for sleep's kind sake.

But O whose fingers, soft as wistaria,
played with my watch-chain, under the crabapples;
under the lilacs in October flower
whose fingers like lingering tendrils twined in
my hair, my beard? What phantom remembers
that wicked, warm, Edwardian midday hour?

Rosella-plumed sun, go quickly down on
my afternoon ghosts. Let purple night that
brings all lovers to their billiard-rooms descend.
Click of the balls. Among wraiths of cigar-smoke,
with rib-nudging stories I died before telling,
I shall go haunting in search of a friend, a friend.

Ruins of the City of Hay

The wind has scattered my city to the sheep.
Capeweed and lovely lupins choke the street
where the wind wanders in great gaunt chimneys of hay
and straws cry out like keyholes.

Our yellow Petra of the fields: alas!
I walk the ruins of forum and capitol,
through quiet squares, by the temples of tranquillity.
Wisps of the metropolis brush my hair.
I become invisible in tears.

This was no ratbags' Eden: these were true haystacks.
Golden, but functional, our mansions sprang from dreams
of architects in love (*O my meadow queen!*).
No need for fires to be lit on the yellow hearthstones;
our walls were warmer than flesh, more sure than igloos.
On winter nights we squatted naked as Esquimaux,
chanting our sagas of innocent chauvinism.

In the street no vehicle passed. No telephone,
doorbell or till was heard in the canyons of hay.
No stir, no sound, but the sickle and the loom,
and the comments of emus begging by kitchen doors
in the moonlike silence of morning.

Though the neighbour states (said Lao Tse) lie in sight of the city
and their cocks wake and their watchdogs warn the inhabitants
the men of the city of hay will never go there
all the days of their lives.

But the wind of the world descended on lovely Petra
and the spires of the towers and the statues and belfries fell.
The bones of my brothers broke in the breaking columns.
The bones of my sisters, clasping their broken children,
cracked on the hearthstones, under the rooftrees of hay.
I alone mourn in the temples, by broken altars
bowered in black nightshade and mauve salvation-jane.

And the cocks of the neighbour nations scratch in the straw.
And their dogs rejoice in the bones of all my brethren.

The Land's Meaning

For Sidney Nolan

The love of man is a weed of the waste places.
One may think of it as the spinifex of dry souls.

I have not it is true, made the trek to the difficult country
where it is said to grow; but signs come back,
reports come back, of continuing exploration
in that terrain. And certain of our young men,
who turned in despair from the bar, upsetting a glass,
and swore: "No more" (for the tin rooms stank of flyspray)
are sending word that the mastery of silence
alone is empire. What is God, they say,
but a man unwounded in his loneliness?

And the question (applauded, derided) falls like dust
on veranda and bar; and in pauses, when thinking ceases,
the footprints of the recently departed
march to the mind's horizons, and endure.

And often enough as we turn again, and laugh,
cloud, hide away the tracks with an acid word,
there is one or more gone past the door to stand
(wondering, debating) in the iron street,
and toss a coin, and pass, to the township's end,
where one-eyed 'Mat, eternal dealer in camels,
grins in his dusty yard like a split fruit.

But one who has returned, his eyes blurred maps
of landscapes still unmapped, gives this account:

"The third day, cockatoos dropped dead in the air.
Then the crows turned back, the camels knelt down and stayed there,
and a skin-coloured surf of sandhills jumped the horizon
and swamped me. I was bushed for forty years.

"And I came to a bloke all alone like a kurrajong tree.
And I said to him: 'Mate – I don't need to know your name –
Let me camp in your shade, let me sleep, till the sun goes down.' "

Endymion

My love, you are no goddess: the bards were mistaken;
no lily maiden, no huntress in silver glades.

You are lovelier still by far, for you are an island;
a continent of the sky, and all virgin, sleeping.

And I, who plant my shack in your mould-grey gullies,
am come to claim you: my orchard, my garden, of ash.

To annex your still mountains with patriotic ballads,
to establish between your breasts my colonial hearth.

And forgetting all trees, winds, oceans and open grasslands,
and forgetting the day for as long as the night shall last,

to slumber becalmed and lulled in your hollowed hands,
to wither within to your likeness, and lie still.

Let your small dust fall, let it tick on my roof like crickets.
I shall open my heart, knowing nothing can come in.

The Singing Bones

"Out where the dead men lie."

Barcroft Boake

Out there, beyond the boundary fence, beyond
the scrub-dark flat horizon that the crows
returned from, evenings, days of rusty wind
raised from the bones a stiff lament, whose sound
netted my childhood round, and even here still blows.

My country's heart is ash in the market-place,
is aftermath of martyrdom. Out there
its sand-enshrined lay saints lie piece by piece,
Leichhardt by Gibson, stealing the wind's voice,
and Lawson's tramps, by choice made mummia and air.

No pilgrims leave, no holy-days are kept
for these who died of landscape. Who can find,
even, the camp-sites where the saints last slept?
Out there their place is, where the charts are gapped,
unreachable, unmapped, and mainly in the mind.

They were all poets, so the poets said,
who kept their end in mind in all they wrote
and hymned their bones, and joined them. Gordon died
happy, one surf-loud dawn, shot through the head,
and Boake astonished, dead, his stockwhip round his throat.

Time, time and time again, when the inland wind
beats over myall from the dunes, I hear
the singing bones, their glum Victorian strain.
A ritual manliness, embracing pain
to know; to taste terrain their heirs need not draw near.

Frost-parrots

Hunted south-east, the Cape unglimpsed, from Tristan,
we met a coast not known till then, a stone
unwieldy country, fringed with trees in flower,
which flowers all at once blew towards us, crying.

Parrots – but vast; and death-chill, lovely things.
For in their glinting feathers was the blue
of broken glaciers and the talc of rime
and all the shades of ice: as lilac, rose,
the greens of clefts and flame of midday sunsets.
As for their trees, without them those were bare
and black as frosted charcoal, branched like coral.

Their cry was like the creak of snow you ache through
or chink of ice-spikes in a bough long martyred
or locked streams breaking up. And colder things;
jangling bedsprings in contemptuous attics,
and bottles rolled down alleys we forgot.

Their eyes were frost-stars! In their look was death.
To something. Something needed, till that day.

KATE LLEWELLYN 1936–

Kate Llewellyn (née Brinkworth) grew up at Tumby Bay on Eyre Peninsula in South Australia, and became a registered nurse at the Royal Adelaide Hospital. She owned and directed two art galleries in Adelaide, before graduating in history and classics in 1977 from the University of Adelaide. She later moved to New South Wales and became a full-time writer. She is the author of nineteen books, including the bestselling *The Waterlily: A Blue Mountains Journal*, has published six books of poetry and co-edited *The Penguin Book of Australian Women Poets* (1986). She has written a number of travel books and an autobiography, *The Dressmaker's*

Daughter. Llewellyn's poetry is consistently open, enjoyable and explicit. She is a confessional poet who has a natural, lyrical gift with an occasional sharp edge.

Breasts

As I lean over to write
one breast warm as a breast from the sun
hangs over as if to read what I'm writing
these breasts always want to know everything
sometimes exploring the inside curve of my elbow
sometimes measuring a man's hand
lying still as a pond
until he cannot feel he is holding anything
but water
then he dreams he is floating

in the morning my breast is refreshed
and wants to know something new
although it is soft it is also ambitious
we never speak
but I know my breast knows me more than I do
prying hanging over fences
observant as a neighbour
or eager as a woman wanting to gossip
they tell me nothing
but they say quite a lot about me

there is a dark blue river vein here
straggling down taking its time
to the little pale strawberry
picked too soon and left too long
in the punnet in a warm shop

when I lie
these breasts spread like spilt milk
and standing naked in the sea
float like figs
as you will realise
these are my body's curious fruit
wanting to know everything
always getting there first
strange as white beetroot
exotic as unicorns
useless as an out of order dishwasher
more of a nuisance than anything else

some men seem to think highly of them
peering and staring
what they don't know is
the breast stares straight back
interested as a reporter

some love them
and invest them with glamour
but like life they are not glamorous
merely dangerous

JUDITH RODRIGUEZ 1936–

Judith Rodriguez (née Green) was born in Perth and educated in Brisbane and Cambridge. In 1964 she married a Colombian, Fabio Rodriguez. From 1969 to 1985 she was an academic in the English Department of La Trobe University, Victoria; was poetry editor of *Meanjin* from 1979 to 1982; and edited the Penguin Australian Poetry Series from 1988 to 1997. She wrote the libretto for the opera *Lindy* performed in the Sydney Opera House in 2003 and there have been several exhibitions of her linocuts. She is now married to the poet Tom Shapcott. Rodriguez presents herself as an imposing, no-nonsense, good-humoured woman – her poetry is strongly imbued with her personality. You feel her behind the poem, giving it a shake as you read it, as in "Eskimo Occasion", one of her best-known pieces.

In-flight Note

Kitten, writes the mousy boy in his neat
fawn casuals sitting beside me on the flight,
neatly, *I can't give up everything just like that.*
Everything, how much was it? and just like what?
Did she cool it or walk out? loosen her hand from his tight
white-knuckled hand, or not meet him, just as he thought
You mean far too much to me. I can't forget
the four months we've known each other. No, he won't eat,
finally he pays – pale, careful, distraught –
for a beer, turns over the pad on the page he wrote
and sleeps a bit. Or dreams of his Sydney cat.
The pad cost one dollar twenty. He wakes to write
It's naive to think we could be just good friends.
Pages and pages. And so the whole world ends.

Mudcrab at Gambaro's
For Tom Shapcott

At Gambaro's, we are fearfully pleased
to light on land-agents in threes
and fours for lunch.
They check us for affluence
and return to their talk.
Well, and so the Big Boy's coming back –
did he tie it up?

Conducted, placed,
we toast the midday feast.
Morning's boom holds up,
zooms into the order of mudcrab.
You pour, you tumble
ice, you burrow the bottle. I tipple and wonder
how light's wine-colour.

The pallid easy oysters
pass, precursors
to here it comes! the roseate big'un!
platefuls of plated pincers,
shanks, joints,
every one neatly smashed, our own Big Boy,
heaped up high.

We eat, ingenious and attentive.
The land-agents breathe heavily.
Among tables, through the room
grave women come
gathering greaves,
flanges, splinters we forced with hands bleeding –
devotees

of smooth encapsulated
flesh, the tingling white
of beachsand at daybreak.
Staggering, the land boys push back
their dogged chairs.
Mere steak. They diminish sweating in the late-lunch glare.
We are mudcrab, and air.

How Come the Truck-loads?

Somehow the tutorial takes an unplanned direction:
anti-Semitism.
A scholastic devil advances the suggestion
that two sides can be found to every question:

Right.
Now, who's an anti-Semite?
One hand.
Late thirties, in the 1960s. Bland.
Let's see now; tell us, on what texts or Jews
do you base your views?
There was a landlord, from Poland, that I had.
Bad?
A shrug. Well, what did he do?
Pretty mean chasing up rent. Ah. Tough.
And who
else? No-one else. One's enough.

Eskimo Occasion

I am in my eskimo-hunting-song mood,
Aha!
The lawn is tundra   the car will not start
the sunlight is an avalanche   we are avalanche-struck at our breakfast
struck with sunlight through glass   me and my spoonfed daughters
out of this world in our kitchen.

I will sing the song of my daughter-hunting,
Oho!
The waves lay down   the ice grew strong
I sang the song   of dark water under ice
the song of winter fishing   the magic for seal rising
among the ancestor-masks.

I waited by water to dream new spirits,
Hoo!
The water spoke   the ice shouted
the sea opened   the sun made young shadows
they breathed my breathing   I took them from deep water
I brought them fur-warmed home.

I am dancing the years of the two great hunts,
Ya-hay!
It was I who waited   cold in the wind-break

I stamp like the bear   I call like the wind of the thaw
I leap like the sea spring-running.   My sunstruck daughters splutter
and chuckle and bang their spoons:

Mummy is singing at breakfast and dancing!
So big!

LES MURRAY 1938–

Les Murray, who has the biggest international reputation of any Australian poet, comes from Bunyah, a farming district long settled by the Murray clan, near Taree on the north coast of New South Wales. He grew up on the dairy farm that his father rented from his father. Murray's mother died suddenly when he was thirteen, which seems to have been the crucial experience in his life. Murray was an only child, and father and son were both emotionally devastated. He remained at high school through these comfortless, depressed years, and then went to the University of Sydney. Having dropped out of university, he was taken on as a translator of technical and scholarly works by the Australian National University in Canberra. He married Valerie Morelli, a Swiss-Hungarian whom he met at university, converting to Catholicism.

His first book, *The Ilex Tree* (shared with Geoffrey Lehmann), was published in 1965. In 1967 and 1968 Murray and his wife (now with two small children) lived, precariously, in England and on the continent. Returning to Australia, he resumed his university course and received in 1969 "the least distinguished BA ever awarded by Sydney University" (his words).

After graduating, Murray found it hard to get work and was unemployed for more than a year, perhaps because he insisted on describing himself as a poet in his job applications. He was rescued by a government grant from the newly formed Australia Council, which was established by the Whitlam Labor government in 1970. Murray was for some years consistently supported by the Literature Board of the Australia Council, but the relationship soured.

He has published more than 25 books of poetry, including two verse novels, and selected and collected editions of his poems. He has also produced several books of essays and edited a number of anthologies, including *The New Oxford Book of Australian Verse* (1986). He edited *Poetry Australia* magazine for some years, was poetry adviser for the publisher Angus & Robertson and more recently the literary editor of *Quadrant*. He is an adviser to the *Macquarie Australian Dictionary*. Murray's agrarian, populist politics, and his anti-feminist and anti-abortion stance have made him controversial. He has five children, one of whom is autistic.

The most significant early influence on Murray's work was that of Kenneth Slessor. Slessor's physicality, his richly packed detail, his mimetic use of sound and rhythm, his hobbyist's enthusiasm for arcana were all formative values for Murray. His earlier poetry has a lyrical freshness that is missing from his later work. Many later poems are dense and riddling. The main line of development has come about through reactiveness, a sense of embattlement, reflected in the title of one of his volumes, *Subhuman Redneck Poems* (1996), which has led to a combative, brilliantly baroque, often witty, polemic. The ideal of community is a central preoccupation of Murray's writing, and the main body of his work can be seen as a defence of the values of his local farming community at Bunyah, and of other Bunyahs across Australia. This loyalty may be an outcome of his early loss of family life, and was embodied in his return to live in Bunyah with his elderly father, who has since died.

"The Away-bound Train" is one of Murray's quintessential early poems. It appeared in his first book, was not included in his *Selected Poems: The Vernacular Republic* (1976) and then reappeared in *The Vernacular Republic: Poems 1961–1981* (1982) with a significantly shorter and improved text. It illustrates poignantly the tension the young poet experienced as a farm boy who was in the process of becoming an urbanised man of letters. Murray's resolution of this dilemma was to return to live in Bunyah with his father and continue writing poetry of increasing complexity and sophistication, while affirming his loyalty to Bunyah, encapsulated in the title of one of his volumes, *Subhuman Redneck Poems* (1996).

The importance of Murray's father, whom he greatly loved and is the subject of many of his poems, may have been critical in allowing this resolution. Cecil Murray's role is epitomised by a story Murray told friends in the late 1950s. The young poet, during one of his absences from the university, was sitting alone in a paddock, when he saw his father advancing across the grass with an impish grin and playing a fiddle. Cecil stopped and said, "Cheer up, Leslie, my boy."

Murray has been regarded as a nature poet, but what matters to him is always people in the landscape, working the land. He is not an environmentalist, and one of the contradictions in his ideological position is that between praise of technology and a defence of local, rural values. Murray's great interest, outside his own work, is factual information. Technical, natural, linguistic, culinary or social oddities, obscene or grisly stories, and popular inventions of speech – all feed into the wordplay of his work. He displays, among poets writing in English at present, a unique gift for language. He has earned his living through reading tours of Europe and the United States. In recent years he has suffered from depression which he has written about in his poetry and prose.

"The Buladelah-Taree Holiday Song Cycle", in some ways his greatest achievement, very broadly takes its structure and rhythms from "The Song Cycle of the Moon Bone", an Aboriginal song cycle translated by R. M. Berndt. (See page 406.) Murray's poem intends to assert through this allusion, against Aboriginal land-rights activists like Judith Wright, that white Australians, too, have developed their own deep attachments to this country, and have also mythologised it for themselves – something that is not to be devalued and overlooked. At the same time, Murray's imitating an "Aboriginal" form, or transliteration of an Aboriginal manner, indicates a respect for that culture, which indeed he has spoken for and has long supported. As always, it is a sense of harmony, of community, free of sophisticated antagonisms, that is his ideal.

Murray has been a target for detractors in Australia, but he has won the Queen's Medal for poetry, the T. S. Eliot Prize, the Petrarch Prize, was interviewed in *The Paris Review*'s series, and has been the subject of lengthy critical appreciation in the *Times Literary Supplement*, *The New York Review of Books* and *The New Yorker.*

The Away-bound Train

For Con Kiriloff

I stand in a house of trees, and it is evening:
at the foot of the stairs, a creek runs grey with sand.

A rocking, unending dim sound,
a racket as if of a train,
wears through my sleep, and I wake
to find it late afternoon

at which I sit up, rub my eyes –
beneath us, the carriage-wheels moan
on their winter-wet, wind-polished rails,
but the train hurries on, hurries on.

The loco horn beams out its admonition
at a weatherboard village standing on the fields.

The near hills rise steeply and fall,
the hills farther off settle down:
I light up a cigarette, wipe
my breath from the cold window-pane.

The upland farms are all bare,
except where dark, storm-matted fern
has found its way down from the heights,
or landslides have brought down raw stone

for, outside, it's silent July,
when wet rocks stare from the hills
and thistles grow, and the rain
walks with the wind through the fields –

and this is my country, passing by me forever:
beyond these hills and paddocks lies the world.

Outside, it is timeless July,
when horses' hoofs puncture the chill
green ground, mud dogging their steps,
and summer's plough sleeps in the barn,

when rabbits camp up in the mouths
of flooded burrows, and dogs
under creekbanks wince at the thump
of a gun fired close to the earth.

The cold time, the season of clouds
beyond the end of the year,

when boxwood chunks glare in the stove –
but that is the past. I am here.

I look across the clear, receding landscape:
from a distant ridge, a horseman eyes the train.

The train never slackens its speed:
an iron bridge echoes, is gone,
on the far bank, twilit and tall,
the green timber gathers us in.

And we dash through the forest, my face,
reflected, wanders and sways
on the glass of the windowpane, and
I press my nose to my nose ...

the loco horn sounds far across the uplands:
a man with no past has all too many futures.

I take out a book, read a phrase
five times – and put the book down.
The window-sash chatters. My mind
trails far in the wake of the train

where, away in the left-behind hills,
through paddock and cattlecamp I
go drifting down valleys towards
the peopled country of sleep ...

I wait in the house. It is raining in the forest.
If I move or speak, the house will not be there.

Driving Through Sawmill Towns

1.
In the high cool country,
Having come from the clouds,
Down a tilting road
Into a distant valley,
You drive without haste. Your windscreen parts the forest,
Swaying and glancing, and jammed midday brilliance
Crouches in clearings ...
Then you come across them,
The sawmill towns, bare hamlets built of boards
With perhaps a store,
Perhaps a bridge beyond
And a little sidelong creek alive with pebbles.

2.

The mills are roofed with iron, have no walls:
You look straight in as you pass, see lithe men working,
The swerve of a winch,
Dim dazzling blades advancing
Through a trolley-borne baulk
Till it sags apart
In a manifold sprawl of weatherboards and battens.

The men watch you pass:
When you stop your car and ask them for directions,
Tall youths look away –
It is the older men who
Come out in blue singlets and talk softly to you.

Beside each mill, smoke trickles out of mounds
Of ash and sawdust.

3.

You glide on through town,
Your mudguards damp with cloud.
The houses there wear verandahs out of shyness,
All day in calendared kitchens, women listen
For cars on the road,
Lost children in the bush,
A cry from the mill, a footstep –
Nothing happens.

The half-heard radio sings
Its song of sidewalks.

Sometimes a woman, sweeping her front step,
Or a plain young wife at a tankstand fetching water
In a metal bucket will turn round and gaze
At the mountains in wonderment,
Looking for a city.

4.

Evenings are very quiet. All around
The forest is there.
As night comes down, the houses watch each other:
A light going out in a window here has meaning.

You speed away through the upland,
Glare through towns

And are gone in the forest, glowing on far hills.

On summer nights
Ground-crickets sing and pause.
In the dark of winter, tin roofs sough with rain,
Downpipes chafe in the wind, agog with water.
Men sit after tea
By the stove while their wives talk, rolling a dead match
Between their fingers,
Thinking of the future.

The Ballad Trap

In the hanging gorges
the daring compact wears thin,
picking meat from small skeletons,
counting damp notes in a tin,

the rifle birds ringing at noon
in the steep woods,
hard-riding boys dazed at the brink
of their attitudes,

the youngest wheedling for songs,
his back to the night,
dark mountains the very English
for souring delight:

Remember the Escort? Remember
lamps long ago
and manhood filched from the horse police
and a name from Cobb and Co.

Their metre hobbled, the horses
hump their dark life,
longing for marriage, the tall man
sharpens his knife –

Yes, let us sing! cries the Captain
while we have breath.
Better, God knows, than this thinking.
The ballad ends with their death.

The Broadbean Sermon

Beanstalks, in any breeze, are a slack church parade
without belief, saying *trespass against us* in unison,
recruits in mint Air Force dacron, with unbuttoned leaves.

Upright with water like men, square in stem-section
they grow to great lengths, drink rain, keel over all ways,
kink down and grow up afresh, with proffered new greenstuff.

Above the cat-and-mouse floor of a thin bean forest
snails hang rapt in their food, ants hurry through several dimensions:
spiders tense and sag like little black flags in their cordage.

Going out to pick beans with the sun high as fence-tops, you find
plenty, and fetch them. An hour or a cloud later
you find shirtfulls more. At every hour of daylight

appear more that you missed: ripe, knobbly ones, fleshy-sided,
thin-straight, thin-crescent, frown-shaped, bird-shouldered, boat-keeled
 ones,
beans knuckled and single-bulged, minute green dolphins at suck,

beans upright like lecturing, outstretched like blessing fingers
in the incident light, and more still, oblique to your notice
that the noon glare or cloud-light or afternoon slants will uncover

till you ask yourself Could I have overlooked so many, or
do they form in an hour? unfolding into reality
like templates for subtly broad grins, like unique caught expressions,

like edible meanings, each sealed around with a string
and affixed to its moment, an unceasing colloquial assembly,
the portly, the stiff, and those lolling in pointed green slippers ...

Wondering who'll take the spare bagfulls, you grin with happiness
– it is your health – you vow to pick them all
even the last few, weeks off yet, misshapen as toes.

The Buladelah-Taree Song Cycle

1

The people are eating dinner in that country north of Legge's Lake;
behind flywire and venetians, in the dimmed cool, town people eat Lunch.
Plying knives and forks with a peek-in sound, with a tuck-in sound
they are thinking about relatives and inventory, they are talking about
 customers and visitors.
In the country of memorial iron, on the creek-facing hills there,
they are thinking about bean plants, and rings of tank water, of growing a

pumpkin by Christmas;
rolling a cigarette, they say thoughtfully Yes, and their companion nods, considering.
Fresh sheets have been spread and tucked tight, childhood rooms have been seen to,

for this is the season when children return with their children
to the place of Bingham's Ghost, of the Old Timber Wharf, of the Big Flood That Time,
the country of the rationalized farms, of the day-and-night farms, and of the Pitt Street farms,
of the Shire Engineer and many other rumours, of the tractor crankcase furred with chaff,
the places of sitting down near ferns, the snake-fear places, the cattle-crossing-long-ago places.

2

It is the season of the Long Narrow City; it has crossed the Myall, it has entered the North Coast,
that big stunning snake; it is looped through the hills, burning all night there.
Hitching and flying on the downgrades, processionally balancing on the climbs,
it echoes in O'Sullivan's Gap, in the tight coats of the flooded-gum trees;
the tops of palms exclaim at it unmoved, there near Wootton.
Glowing all night behind the hills, with a north-shifting glare, burning behind the hills;
through Coolongolook, through Wang Wauk, across the Wallamba,
the booming tarred pipe of the holiday slows and spurts again; Nabiac chokes in glassy wind,
the forests on Kiwarrak dwindle in cheap light; Tuncurry and Forster swell like cooking oil.
The waiting is buffed, in timber village off the highway, the waiting is buffeted:
the fumes of fun hanging above ferns; crime flashes in strange windscreens, in the time of the Holiday.
Parasites weave quickly through the long gut that paddocks shine into;
powerful makes surging and pouncing: the police, collecting Revenue.
The heavy gut winds over the Manning, filling northward, digesting the towns, feeding the towns;
they all become the narrow city, they join it;
girls walking close to murder discard, with excitement, their names.
Crossing Australia of the sports, the narrow city, bringing home the children.

3

It is good to come out after driving and walk on bare grass;
walking out, looking all around, relearning that country.
Looking out for snakes, and looking out for rabbits as well;
going into the shade of myrtles to try their cupped climate, swinging by one hand around them,
in that country of the Holiday …
stepping behind trees to the dam, as if you had a gun,
to that place of the Wood Duck,
to that place of the Wood Duck's Nest,
proving you can still do it; looking at the duck who hasn't seen you,
the mother duck who'd run Catch Me (broken wing) I'm Fatter (broken wing), having hissed to her children.

4

The birds saw us wandering along.
Rosellas swept up crying out *we think we think*; they settled farther along;
knapping seeds off the grass, under dead trees where their eggs were, walking around on their fingers,
flying on into the grass.
The heron lifted up his head and elbows; the magpie stepped aside a bit,
angling his chopsticks into pasture, turning things over in his head.
At the place of the Plough Handles, of the Apple Trees Bending Over, and of the Cattlecamp,
there the vealers are feeding; they are loosely at work, facing everywhere.
They are always out there, and the forest is always on the hills;
around the sun are turning the wedgetail eagle and her mate, that dour brushhook-faced family:
they settled on Deer's Hill away back when the sky was opened,
in the bull-oak trees way up there, the place of fur tufted in the grass, the place of bone-turds.

5

The Fathers and the Great-Grandfathers, they are out in the paddocks all the time, they live out there,
at the place of the Rail Fence, of the Furrows Under Grass, at the place of the Slab Chimney.
We tell them that clearing is complete, an outdated attitude, all over;
we preach without a sacrifice, and are ignored; flowering bushes grow dull to our eyes.
We begin to go up on the ridge, talking together, looking at the kino-coloured ants,

at the yard-wide sore of their nest, that kibbled peak, and the workers
heaving vast stalks up there,
the brisk compact workers; jointed soldiers pour out then, tense with acid;
several probe the mouth of a lost gin bottle;
Innuendo, we exclaim, *literal minds!* and go on up the ridge, announced
by finches;
passing the place of the Dingo Trap, and that farm hand it caught, and the
place of the Cowbails,
we come to the road and watch heifers,
little unjoined Devons, their teats hidden in fur, and the cousin with his
loose-slung stockwhip driving them.
We talk with him about rivers and the lakes; his polished horse is stepping
nervously,
printing neat omegas in the gravel, flexing its skin to shake off flies;
his big sidestepping horse that has kept its stones; it recedes gradually,
bearing him;
we murmur *stone-horse* and *devilry* to the grinners under grass.

6

Barbecue smoke is rising at Legge's Camp; it is steaming into the midday air,
all around the lake shore, at the Broadwater, it is going up among the
paperbark trees,
a heat-shimmer of sauces, rising from tripods and flat steel, at that place of
the cone shells,
at that place of the Seagrass, and the tiny segmented things swarming in it,
and of the Pelican.
Dogs are running around disjointedly; water escapes from their mouths,
confused emotions from their eyes; humans snarl at them Gwanout and
Hereboy, not varying their tone much;
the impoverished dog people, suddenly sitting down to nuzzle themselves;
toddlers side with them:
toddlers, running away purposefully at random, among cars, into big
drownie water (come back, Cheryl-Ann!).
They rise up as charioteers, leaning back on the tow-bar; all their attributes
bulge at once;
swapping swash shoulder-wings for the white-sheeted shoes that bear them,
they are skidding over the flat glitter, stiff with grace, for once not travelling
to arrive.
From the high dunes over there, the rough blue distance, at length they
come back behind the boats,
and behind the boats' noise, cartwheeling, or sitting down, into the lake's
warm chair;

they wade ashore and eat with the families, putting off that uprightness, that assertion,
eating with the families who love equipment, and the freedom from equipment,
with the fathers who love driving, and lighting a fire between stones.

7

Shapes of children were moving in the standing corn, in the child-labour districts;
coloured flashes of children, between the green and parching stalks, appearing and disappearing.
Some places, they are working, racking off each cob like a lever, tossing it on the heaps;
other places, they are children of child-age, there playing jungle:
in the tiger-striped shade, they are firing hoehandle machine guns, taking cover behind fat pumpkins;
in other cases, it is Sunday and they are lovers.
They rise and walk together in the sibilance, finding single rows irksome, hating speech now,
or, full of speech, they swap files and follow defiles, disappearing and appearing;
near the rain-grey barns, and the children building cattleyards beside them;
the standing corn, gnawed by pouched and rodent mice; generations are moving among it,
the parrot-hacked, medicine-tassled corn, ascending all the creek flats, the wire-fenced alluvials,
going up in patches through the hills, towards the Steep Country.

8

Forests and State Forests, all down off the steeper country; mosquitoes are always living in there:
they float about like dust motes and sink down, at the places of the Stinging Tree,
and of the Staghorn Fern; the males feed on plant-stem fluid, absorbing that watery ichor;
the females meter the air, feeling for the warm-blooded smell, needing blood for their eggs.
They find the dingo in his sleeping-place, they find his underbelly and his anus;
they find the possum's face, they drift up the ponderous pleats of the fig tree, way up into its rigging,
the high camp of the fruit bats; they feed on the membranes and ears of

bats; tired wings cuff air at them;
their eggs burning inside them, they alight on the muzzles of cattle,
the half-wild bush cattle, there at the place of the Sleeper Dump, at the place of the Tallow woods.
The males move about among growth tips; ingesting solutions, they crouch intently;
the females sing, needing blood to breed their young; their singing is in the scrub country;
their tune comes to the name-bearing humans, who dance to it and irritably grin at it.

9

The warriors are cutting timber with brash chainsaws; they are trimming hardwood pit-props and loading them;
Is that at an order? they hoot at the peremptory lorry driver, who laughs; he is also a warrior.
They are driving long-nosed tractors, slashing pasture in the dinnertime sun;
they are fitting tappets and valves, the warriors, or giving finish to a surfboard.
Addressed on the beach by a pale man, they watch waves break and are reserved, refusing pleasantry;
they joke only with fellow warriors, chaffing about try-ons and the police, not slighting women.
Making Timber a word of power, Con-rod a word of power, Sense a word of power, the Regs. a word of power,
they know belt-fed from spring-fed; they speak of being *stiff*, and being *history*;
the warriors who have killed, and the warriors who eschewed killing,
the solemn, the drily spoken, the life peerage of endurance; drinking water from a tap,
they watch boys who think hard work a test, and boys who think it is not a test.

10

Now the ibis are flying in, hovering down on the wetlands,
on those swampy paddocks around Darawank, curving down in ragged dozens,
on the riverside flats along the Wang Wauk, on the Boolambayte pasture flats,
and away towards the sea, on the sand moors, at the place of the Jabiru Crane,

leaning out of their wings, they step down; they take out their implement at once,
out of its straw wrapping, and start work; they dab grasshopper and ground-cricket
with nonexistence ... spiking the ground and puncturing it ... they swallow down the outcry of a frog;
they discover titbits kept for them under cowmanure lids, small slow things.
Pronging the earth, they make little socket noises, their thoughtfulness jolting down and up suddenly;
there at Bunyah, along Firefly Creek, and up through Germany,
the ibis are all at work again, thin-necked ageing men towards evening; they are solemnly all back
at Minimbah, and on the Manning, in the rye-and-clover irrigation fields;
city storemen and accounts clerks point them out to their wives,
remembering things about themselves, and about the ibis.

11

Abandoned fruit trees, moss-tufted, spotted with dim lichen paints; the fruit trees of the Grandmothers,
they stand along the creekbanks, in the old home paddocks, where the houses were;
they are reached through bramble-grown front gates, they creak at dawn behind burnt skillions,
at Belbora, at Bucca Wauka, away in at Burrell Creek, at Telararee of the gold-sluices.
The trees are split and rotten-elbowed; they bear the old-fashioned summer fruits,
the annual bygones: china pear, quince, persimmon;
the fruit has the taste of former lives, of sawdust and parlour song, the tang of Manners;
children bite it, recklessly,
at what will become for them the place of the Slab Wall, and of the Coal Oil Lamp,
the place of moss-grit and swallows' nests, the place of the Crockery.

12

Now the sun is an applegreen blindness through the swells, a white blast on the sea-face, flaking and shoaling;
now it is burning off the mist, it is emptying the density of trees, it is spreading upriver,
hovering above the casuarina needles, there at Old Bar and Manning Point;
flooding the island farms, it abolishes the milkers' munching breath
as they walk towards the cowyards; it stings a bucket here, a teatcup there.

Morning steps into the world by ever more southerly gates; shadows weaken their north skew
on Middle Brother, on Cape Hawke, on the dune scrub toward Seal Rocks;
steadily the heat is coming on, the butter-water time, the clothes-sticking time;
grass covers itself with straw; abandoned things are thronged with spirits;
everywhere wood is still with strain; birds hiding down the creek galleries, and in the cockspur canes;
the cicada is hanging up her sheets; she takes wing off her music-sheets.
Cars pass with a rational zoom, panning quickly towards Wingham,
through the thronged and glittering, the shale-topped ridges, and the cattlecamps,
towards Wingham for the cricket, the ball knocked hard in front of smoked-glass ranges, and for the drinking.
In the time of heat, the time of flies around the mouth, the time of the west verandah;
looking at that umbrage along the ranges, on the New England side;
clouds begin assembling vaguely, a hot soiled heaviness on the sky, away there towards Gloucester;
a swelling up of clouds, growing there above Mount George, and above Tipperary;
far away and hot with light; sometimes a storm takes root there, and fills the heavens rapidly;
darkening, boiling up and swaying on its stalks, pulling this way and that, blowing round by Krambach;
coming white on Bulby, it drenches down on the paddocks, and on the wire fences;
the paddocks are full of ghosts, and people in cornbag hoods approaching;
lights are lit in the house; the storm veers mightily on its stem, above the roof; the hills uphold it;
the stony hills guide its dissolution; gullies opening and crumbling down, wrenching tussocks and rolling them;
the storm carries a greenish-grey bag; perhaps it will find hail and send it down, starring cars, flattening tomatoes,
in the time of the Washaways, of the dead trunks braiding water, and of the Hailstone Yarns.

13

The stars of the holiday step out all over the sky.
People look up at them, out of their caravan doors and their campsites;
people look up from the farms, before going back; they gaze at their year's worth of stars.

The Cross hangs head-downward, out there over Markwell;
it turns upon the Still Place, the pivot of the Seasons, with one shoulder rising:
"Now I'm beginning to rise, with my Pointers and my Load ..."
hanging eastwards, it shines on the sawmills and the lakes, on the glasses of the Old People.
Looking at the Cross, the galaxy is over our left shoulder, slung up highest in the east;
there the Dog is following the Hunter; the Dog Star pulsing there above Forster; it shines down on the Bikies,
and on the boat-hire sheds, there at the place of the Oyster; the place of the Shark's Eggs and her Hide;
the Pleiades are pinned up high on the darkness, away back above the Manning;
they are shining on the Two Blackbutt Trees, on the rotted river wharves, and on the towns;
standing there, above the water and the lucerne flats, at the place of the Families;
their light sprinkles down on Taree of the Lebanese shops, it mingles with the streetlights and their glare.
People recover the starlight, hitching north,
travelling north beyond the seasons, into that country of the Communes, and of the banana:
the Flying Horse, the Rescued Girl, and the Bull, burning steadily above that country.
Now the New Moon is low down in the west, that remote direction of the Cattlemen,
and of the Saleyards, the place of steep clouds, and of the Rodeo;
the New Moon who has poured out her rain, the moon of the Planting-times.
People go outside and look at the stars, and at the melon-rind moon,
the Scorpion going down into the mountains, over there towards Waukivory, sinking into the tree-line,
in the time of the Rockmelons, and of the Holiday ...
the Cross is rising on his elbow, above the glow of the horizon;
carrying a small star in his pocket, he reclines there brilliantly,
above the Alum Mountain, and the lakes threaded on the Myall River, and above the Holiday.

Bent Water in the Tasmanian Highlands

Flashy wrists out of buttoned grass cuffs, feral whisky burning gravels,
jazzy knuckles ajitter on soakages, peaty cupfuls, soft pots overflowing,

setting out along the great curve, migrating mouse-quivering water,
mountain-driven winter water, in the high tweed, stripping off its mountains
to run faster in its skin, it swallows the above, it feeds where it is fed on,
it forms at many points and creases outwards, pleated water
shaking out its bedding soil, increasing its scale, beginning the headlong
– Bent Water, you could call this level
between droplet and planetary, not as steered by twisting beds laterally
but as upped and swayed on its swelling and outstanding own curvatures,
its floating top that sweeps impacts sidelong, its event-horizon,
a harelip round a pebble, mouthless cheeks globed over a boulder, a
finger's far-stretched holograph, skinned flow athwart a snag
– these flexures are all reflections, motion-glyphs, pitches of impediment,
say a log commemorated in a log-long hump of wave,
a buried rock continually noted, a squeeze-play
through a cracked basalt bar, maintaining a foam-roofed two-sided
overhang of breakneck riesling; uplifted hoseless hosings, fully circular
water,
flattened water off rock sills, sandwiched between an upper
and a lower whizzing surface, trapped in there with airy scatter
and mingled high-speed mirrorings; water groined, produced and spiralled
– Crowded scrollwork from events, at steepening white velocities
as if the whole outline of the high country were being pulled out
along these joining channels, and proving infinite, anchored deeply as it
is in the groundwater scale, in the silence around racy breccia
yet it is spooling out; the great curve, drawing and driving,
of which these are the animal-sized swells and embodiments
won't always describe this upland; and after the jut falls, the inverse
towering on gorges, these peaks will be hidden beneath
rivers and tree-bark, in electricity, in cattle, on the ocean
– Meditation is a standing wave, though, on the black-green inclines
of pouring and cascading, slate-dark rush and timber-worker's tea
bullying the pebble-fans; if we were sketched first at this speed,
sheaths, buttocks, wings, it is mother and history and swank here
till our wave is drained of water. And as such it includes the writhing
down in a trench, knees, bellies, the struggling, the slack bleeding
remote enough perhaps, within its close clean film
to make the observer a god; do we come here to be gods?
or to watch an alien pouring down the slants of our anomaly
and be hypnotized to rest by it? So much detail's unlikely, for hypnosis;
it looks like brotherhood sought at a dreamer's remove
and, in either view, laws of falling and persistence:
the continuous ocean round a planetary stone, braiding uptilts

after swoops, echo-forms, arches built from above and standing
on flourish, clear storeys, translucent honey-glazed clerestories –

Equanimity

Nests of golden porridge shattered in the silky-oak trees,
cobs and crusts of it, their glory-box;
the jacarandas' open violet immensities
mirrored flat on the lawns,
weighted by sprinklers; birds, singly and in flocks
hopping over the suburb, eating, as birds do, in detail
and paying their peppercorns;
talk of "the good life" tangles love with will

however; if we mention it, there is more to say:
the droughty light, for example, at telephone-wire
height above the carports, not the middle-ground
distilling news-photograph light of a smoggy Wednesday,
but that light of the north-west wind, hung on the sky
like the haze above cattleyards;
hungry mountain birds, too, drifting in for food, with the sound
of moist gullies about them, and the sound of the pinch-bar;
we must hear the profoundly unwished
garble of a neighbours' quarrel, and see repeatedly
the face we saw near the sportswear shop today
in which mouth-watering and tears couldn't be distinguished.

Fire-prone place-names apart
there is only love; there are no Arcadias.
Whatever its variants of meat-cuisine, worship, divorce,
human order has at heart
an equanimity. Quite different from inertia, it's a place
where the churchman's not defensive, the indignant aren't on the qui vive,
the loser has lost interest, the accountant is truant to remorse,
where the farmer has done enough struggling-to-survive
for one day, and the artist rests from theory –
where all are, in short, off the high comparative horse
of their identity.
Almost beneath notice, as attainable as gravity, it is
a continuous recovering moment. Pity the high madness
that misses it continually, ranging without rest between
assertion and unconsciousness,
the sort that makes Hell seem a height of evolution.
Through the peace beneath effort

(even within effort: quiet air between the bars of our attention)
comes unpurchased lifelong plenishment;
Christ spoke to people most often on this level
especially when they chattered about kingship and the Romans;
all holiness speaks from it.

From the otherworld of action and media, this
interleaved continuing plane is hard to focus:
we are looking into the light –
it makes some smile, some grimace.
More natural to look at the birds about the street, their life
that is greedy, pinched, courageous and prudential
as any on these bricked tree-mingled miles of settlement,
to watch the unceasing on-off
grace that attends their nearly every movement,
the same grace moveless in the shapes of trees
and complex in our selves and fellow walkers: we see it's indivisible
and scarcely willed. That it lights us from the incommensurable
that we sometimes glimpse, from being trapped in the point
(bird minds and ours are so pointedly visual):
a field all foreground, and equally all background,
like a painting of equality. Of infinite detailed extent
like God's attention. Where nothing is diminished by perspective.

The Quality of Sprawl

Sprawl is the quality
of the man who cut down his Rolls Royce
into a farm utility truck, and sprawl
is what the company lacked when it made repeated efforts
to buy the vehicle back and repair its image.

Sprawl is doing your farming by aeroplane, roughly,
or driving a hitchhiker that extra hundred miles home.
It is the rococo of being your own still centre.
It is never lighting cigars with ten-dollar notes:
that's idiot ostentation and murder of starving people.
Nor can it be bought with the ash of million-dollar deeds.

Sprawl lengthens the legs; it trains greyhounds on liver and beer.
Sprawl almost never says Why not? with palms comically raised
nor can it be dressed for, not even in running shoes worn
with mink and a nose ring. That is Society. That's Style.
Sprawl is more like the thirteenth banana in a dozen
or anyway the fourteenth.

Sprawl is Hank Stamper in *Never Give an Inch*
bisecting an obstructive official's desk with a chainsaw.
Not harming the official. Sprawl is never brutal
though it's often intransigent. Sprawl is never Simon de Montfort
at a town-storming: Kill them all! God will know his own.
Knowing the man's name this was said to might be sprawl.

Sprawl occurs in art. The fifteenth to twenty-first
lines in a sonnet, for example. And in certain paintings;
I have sprawl enough to have forgotten which paintings.
Turner's glorious *Burning of the Houses of Parliament*
comes to mind, a doubling bannered triumph of sprawl –
except, he didn't fire them.

Sprawl gets up the nose of many kinds of people
(every kind that comes in kinds) whose futures don't include it.
Some decry it as criminal presumption, silken-robed Pope Alexander
dividing the new world between Spain and Portugal.
If he smiled *in petto* afterwards, perhaps the thing did have sprawl.

Sprawl is really classless, though. It's John Christopher Frederick Murray
asleep in his neighbours' best bed in spurs and oilskins
but not having thrown up:
sprawl is never Calum who, drunk, along the hallways of our house,
reinvented the Festoon. Rather
it's Beatrice Miles going twelve hundred ditto in a taxi,
No Lewd Advances, No Hitting Animals, No Speeding,
on the proceeds of her two-bob-a-sonnet Shakespeare readings.
An image of my country. And would that it were more so.

No, sprawl is full-gloss murals on a council-house wall.
Sprawl leans on things. It is loose-limbed in its mind.
Reprimanded and dismissed
it listens with a grin and one boot up on the rail
of possibility. It may have to leave the Earth.
Being roughly Christian, it scratches the other cheek
and thinks it unlikely. Though people have been shot for sprawl.

Midsummer Ice
(*from* Three Poems in Memory of My Mother)

Remember how I used
to carry ice in from the road
for the ice chest, half running,
the white rectangle clamped in bare hands

the utter cold
in all those summer paddocks?

How, swaying, I'd hurry it inside
en bloc and watering, with the butter
and the wrapped bread precarious on top of it?
"Poor Leslie," you would say,
"your hands are cold as charity –"
You made me take the barrow
but uphill it was heavy.

We'd no tongs, and a bag
would have soaked and bumped, off balance.
I loved to eat the ice,
chip it out with the butcher knife's grey steel.
It stopped good things rotting
and it had a strange comb at its heart,
a splintered horizon rife with zero pearls.

But you don't remember.
A doorstep of numbed creek water the colour of tears
but you don't remember.
I will have to die before you remember.

The Dream of Wearing Shorts For Ever (*from* The Idyll Wheel)

To go home and wear shorts forever,
in the enormous paddocks, in that warm climate,
adding a sweater when winter soaks the grass,

to camp out along the river bends
for good, wearing shorts, with a pocketknife,
a fishing line and matches,

or there where the hills are all down, below the plain,
to sit around in shorts at evening
on the plank verandah –

If the cardinal points of costume
are Robes, Tat, Rig and Scunge,
where are shorts in this compass?

They are never Robes
as other bareleg outfits have been:
the toga, the kilt, the lava-lava
the Mahatma's cotton dhoti;

archbishops and field marshals
at their ceremonies never wear shorts.
The very word
means underpants in North America.

Shorts can be Tat,
Land-Rovering bush-environmental tat,
socio-political ripped-and-metal-stapled tat,
solidarity-with-the-Third World tat tvam asi,

likewise track-and-field shorts worn to parties
and the further humid, modelling negligée
of the Kingdom of Flaunt,
that unchallenged aristocracy.

More plainly climatic, shorts
are farmers' rig, leathery with salt and bonemeal,
are sailors' and branch bankers' rig,
the crisp golfing style
of our youngest male National Costume.

Most loosely, they are Scunge,
ancient Bengal bloomers or moth-eaten hot pants
worn with a former shirt,
feet, beach sand, hair
and a paucity of signals.

Scunge, which is real negligée
housework in a swimsuit, pyjamas worn all day,
is holiday, is freedom from ambition.
Scunge makes you invisible
to the world and yourself.

The entropy of costume,
scunge can get you conquered by more vigorous cultures
and help you to notice it less.

Satisfied ambition, defeat, true unconcern,
the wish and the knack for self-forgetfulness
all fall within the scunge ambit
wearing board shorts or similar;
it is a kind of weightlessness.

Unlike public nakedness, which in Westerners
is deeply circumstantial, relaxed as exam time,
artless and equal as the corsetry of a hussar regiment,

shorts and their plain like
are an angelic nudity, spirituality with pockets!
A double updraft as you drop from branch to pool!

Ideal for getting served last
in shops of the temperate zone
they are also ideal for going home, into space,
into time, to farm the mind's Sabine acres
for product or subsistence.

Now that everyone who yearned to wear long pants
has essentially achieved them,
long pants, which have themselves been underwear
repeatedly, and underground more than once,
it is time perhaps to cherish the culture of shorts,

to moderate grim vigour
with the knobble of bare knees,
to cool bareknuckle feet in inland water,
slapping flies with a book on solar wind
or a patient bare hand, beneath the cadjiput trees,

to be walking meditatively
among green timber, through the grassy forest
towards a calm sea
and looking across to more of that great island
and the further topics.

When Bounty is Down to Persimmons and Lemons

In May, Mary's month
when snakes go to sleep,
sunlight and shade lengthen,
forest grows deep,

wood coughs at the axe
and splinters hurt worse,
barbed wire pulls through
every post in reverse,

old horses grow shaggy
and flies hunker down
on curtains, like sequins
on a dead girl's ball gown.

Grey soldier-birds arrive

in flickers of speed
to hang upside down
from a quivering weed

or tremble trees' foliage
that they trickle down through.
Women's Weekly summer fashions
in the compost turn blue.

The sun slants in under things
and stares right through houses;
soon pyjamas will peep, though,
from the bottoms of trousers.

Night-barking dogs quieten
as overcast forms
and it rains, with far thunder
in queer predawn storms;

then the school bus tops ridges
with clay marks for effort,
picking up drowsy schoolkids,
none of them now barefoot,

and farmers take spanners
to the balers, gang ploughs
and towering diesel tractors
they prefer to their cows.

On Removing Spiderweb

Like summer silk its denier
but stickily, o ickilier,
miffed bunny-blinder, silver tar,
gesticuli-gesticular,
crepe when cobbed, crap when rubbed,
stretchily adhere-and-there
and everyway, nap-snarled or sleek,
glibly hubbed with grots to tweak:
ehh weakly bobbined tae yer neb,
spit it Phuoc Tuy! filthy web!

It Allows a Portrait in Line Scan at Fifteen

He retains a slight "Martian" accent, from the years of single phrases.
He no longer hugs to disarm. It is gradually allowing him affection.
It does not allow proportion. Distress is absolute, shrieking, and runs him at

frantic speed through crashing doors.
He likes cyborgs. Their taciturn power, with his intonation.
It still runs him around the house, alone in the dark, cooing and laughing.
He can read about soils, populations and New Zealand. On neutral topics he's illiterate.
Arnie Schwarzenegger is an actor. He isn't a cyborg really, is he, Dad?
He lives on forty acres, with animals and trees, and used to draw it continually.
He knows the map of Earth's fertile soils, and can draw it freehand.
He can only lie in a panicked shout *SorrySorryIdidn'tdoit!* warding off conflict with others and himself.
When he ran away constantly it was to the greengrocers to worship stacked fruit.
His favourite country was the Ukraine: it is nearly all deep fertile soil.
Giggling, he climbed all over the dim Freudian psychiatrist who told us how autism resulted from "refrigerator" parents.
When asked to smile, he photographs a rictus-smile on his face.
It long forbade all naturalistic films. They were Adult movies.
If they (that is, he) *are bad the police will put them in hospital.*
He sometimes drew the farm amid Chinese or Balinese rice terraces.
When a runaway, he made uproar in the police station, playing at three times adult speed.
Only animated films were proper. *Who Framed Roger Rabbit* then authorised the rest.
Phrases spoken to him he would take as teaching, and repeat.
When he worshipped fruit, he screamed as if poisoned when it was fed to him.
A one-word first conversation: *Blane. – Yes! Plane, that's right, baby! – Blane.*
He has forgotten nothing, and remembers the precise quality of experiences.
It requires rulings: Is *stealing very playing up, as bad as murder?*
He counts at a glance, not looking. And he has never been lost.
When he ate only nuts and dried fruit, words were for dire emergencies.
He knows all the breeds of fowls, and the counties of Ireland.
He'd begun to talk, then resumed to babble, then silence. It withdrew speech for years.
When he took your hand, it was to work it, as a multi-purpose tool.
He is anger's mirror, and magnifies any near him, raging it down.
It still won't allow him fresh fruit, or orange juice with bits in it.
He swam in the midwinter dam at night. It had no rules about cold.
He was terrified of thunder and finally cried as if in explanation It – *angry!*
He grilled an egg he'd broken into bread. Exchanges of soil-knowledge are

called landtalking.
He lives in objectivity. I was sure Bell's palsy would leave my face only when he said it had begun to.
Don't say word! when he was eight forbade the word "autistic" in his presence.
Bantering questions about girlfriends cause a terrified look and blocked ears.
He sometimes centred the farm in a furrowed American Midwest.
Eye contact, Mum! means he truly wants attention. It dislikes I-contact.
He is equitable and kind, and only ever a little jealous. It was a relief when that little arrived.
He surfs, bowls, walks for miles. For many years he hasn't trailed his left arm while running.
I gotta get smart! looking terrified into the years. *I gotta get smart!*

The Conversations

A full moon always rises at sunset
and a person is taller at night.
Many fear their phobias more than death.
The glass King of France feared he'd shatter.
Chinese eunuchs kept their testes in spirit.

Your brain can bleed from a sneeze-breath.
A full moon always rises at sunset
and a person is taller when prone.
Donald Duck was once banned in Finland
because he didn't wear trousers,

his loins were feather-girt like Daisy's
but no ostrich hides its head in sand.
The cure for scurvy was found
then long lost through medical theory.
The Beginning is a steady white sound.

The full moon rises at sunset
and lemurs and capuchin monkeys
pass a millipede round to get off on
its powerful secretions. Mouthing it
they wriggle in bliss on the ground.

The heart of a groomed horse slows down.
A fact is a small compact faith,
a sense-datum to beasts, a power to man
even if true, even while true –
we read these laws in Isaac Neurone.

One woman had sixty-nine children.

Some lions mate fifty times a day.
Napoleon had a victory addiction.
A full moon always rises at sunset.
Soldiers now can get in the family way.

JAS H. DUKE 1939–1992

The anarchist and Dadaist poet, James Heriot Duke, was born in Ballarat, the son of parents who were both teachers. He wrote that all of his immigrant ancestors arrived in Australia before 1850. "The Real Hero of Eureka 2", from a series that appears not to have been completed, celebrates two of those ancestors, who observed from a distance what has come to be known as the "Eureka Stockade", a rebellion of miners against the authorities that took place at Ballarat in 1854 and has been mythologised.

Duke, as he described himself, "changed gradually from a shy diffident and rather beautiful young man to an ugly self-assertive and loud-mouthed one". He became obsessed with chess, but decided he was better at postal chess than face to face over a board. As explained by the anarchist poet Π O in his introduction to Duke's posthumous *Poems of Life & Death* (2003), Duke became increasingly isolated from "normalcy", including sex, which Duke said he found "hard to keep away from ... having worked my way through the sexual spectrum from blonde drag queen to Australia's answer to King Farouk, and this despite heavy natural handicaps like premature baldness, missing front teeth, a bad stammer and a basic feeling of inferiority, not to mention a very respectable set of parents". As a member of the Communist Youth League he was ordered to paint "Pig Iron Bob" (the nickname of the then Prime Minister, Robert Menzies) on an overhead bridge. Duke started painting the name, leaning over the railing, noticed the letters were upside down, but decided to continue, rather than spoil the effect. He was expelled from the league after this incident.

He lived in England in the second half of the 1960s, associating with anarchists. At a poetry reading in Brighton he stood up and began dancing and counting, screaming louder and louder. This epiphany and the enthusiastic response of the audience were a transforming experience and he realised his vocation was poetry, not politics. He later went to Germany with his then partner, Anne Kavanagh, and they had a child in 1972, but he encountered visa problems and returned to Australia "with my psyche in ruins". In 1973 he graduated as an aeronautical engineer from Royal Melbourne Institute of Technology and worked for many years as a public servant for "the sewerage department". In Melbourne he associated with a group of anarchist poets and artists, and was active as a performance and concrete poet, reciting "sound poems". Π O records that he first met and heard Duke in winter 1973 at a sparsely attended poetry reading. Π O saw this man with "a Kaiser Bill moustache, Cossack-overcoat [+ hat]" who looked as though he was from the Russian Front. Π O asked him if he would like to read. Duke took off his hat, revealing a startlingly bald head. When he recited, he began screaming "Dada" repeatedly with "a kind of symphonic verve to it". Until then Π O had regarded Dada as something light and funny, associated with the Goon Show or Barry Humphries, but as Duke did it, "it wasn't a JOKE! ... it was somehow *'primal'*, and dangerous ..."

Duke's health began deteriorating in the last few years of his life. In June 1992, while collecting mail from the post office box of the Collective Effort Press at Melbourne's GPO, he slipped on the steps and shattered a bone in his leg. Tests showed he was diabetic. A few days later he died of a massive heart attack at St Vincent's Hospital. Half an hour before he died a doctor and nurse were told by his friend Thalia (the concrete poet), as she relates, that:

> they had on that bed "Australia's best poet". Jas laughed. The nurse asked him to read her a poem and Jas sat up and recited "Solidarity Explained".
>
> > When the axe first came into the forest
> > the trees said to each other "the handle is one of us".

"Solidarity Explained" is not a poem of Duke's, but is a Turkish proverb. It does typefy his aesthetic approach. After his death, Π O found many scraps of poems on the floor of Duke's flat, which he included in *Poems of Life & Death*. Π O points out that the first three lines of "When I was young" are by the Australian anarchist poet Harry Hooton, and he found Duke's lines, which tried to expand on Hooton's original lines, on 6 different scraps of paper, with the view perhaps to making a poem. Π O took "the liberty of stitching those fragments together". As Duke did not have the opportunity to edit his poems in book form, we have minimally edited "Sherlock Holmes" by eliminating "and greatest", from the start of the second last line, which we feel sure he would have fixed, as he was an exacting stylist.

There is nothing invented about Duke. He was original and strange, with a driven personality, but the man who emerges from the poems is likeable, modest and self-aware, with a critical intelligence – a sceptical Dadaist with a streak of puritanism.

Sherlock Holmes

I'm a student of Sherlock Holmes
I'd read every story before I was 12
one of the more pompous friends of the family
who believed in such things as
THE MUSES, SPIRITUAL UPLIFT
and ART, THE DIVINE PURSUIT
cautioned me about reading such low brow drivel.
at the time
I couldn't think of a defence but I can now.
"Sherlock Holmes" I should have said
was the apotheosis
of a great tradition
What is he after-all?
this solitary ascetic?
this pure intellect?
this grappler with the human mysteries?

dynamic and static simultaneously
foiling crime, upholding morality
and good government
mainlining on cocaine
dressing in funny clothes
being a bit too friendly
with honestly manly, handsome Doctor Watson
what is our Sherlock after all?
but a thin Rossetti
a Walter Pater in sleuth clothes
an individualist William Morris
(keeping Socialists in their place)
a Burne-Jones with a brain
a Holman Hunt with talent
a Millais who never sold out
a sane Ruskin
the last
and finest
the greatest Pre-Raphaelite of them all

Alekhine and Junge at Prague

In the year 1942
there was a chess tournament in Prague
nominally to honour the veteran Czech master Oldrich Duras (born 1882)
In 1942 Prague was in the Protectorate Bohemia-Moravia
ruled by Reich-Protector Reinhard Heydrich
second in command of the *SS*
Hitler wished to spread the message
that "*normal conditions*" prevailed throughout his Empire
so sporting events were encouraged
provided the right people competed
and the right people won

It was an all-play-all event with 12 players
there were the Czechs Foltys, Opocensky, Zita, Kottenauer, Rejfir, and Hromadka
there were two Germans, the veteran Sämisch and the youngster Junge
and the World Champion, Alexander Alekhine
a Russian emigre who had settled in France
where he deserted his Russian wife and married a wealthy American
a chess player of tremendous ability
famed for the depth of his thought and his commitment to the game

Alekhine the player evoked universal admiration
but Alekhine the man often aroused hostility

The outbreak of war found Alekhine in Argentina
competing in the Chess Olympiad
this was a team event
Germany narrowly won from Poland
as Poland was eliminated from the map
the German and Polish masters stayed in South America
Alekhine did not
he returned to France and joined the French Army
on the French capitulation he was demobilized
he went to Portugal for a time
then returned to France
he mingled with the Nazi conquerors
played in their tournaments
wrote articles for their newspapers
where he stated that only *"Aryans"*
could *"play chess artistically"*
(to prove this point
the *SS* murdered the Jewish masters
Landau of Holland, Wolf of Austria, and Przepiorka of Poland)
Alekhine was brusque and rude and often drunk
but he was still Champion of the World

Klaus Junge was the Champion of Germany
he was 19 years old
the greatest German player since Lasker and Tarrasch
born in Chile of German parents
blond, blue-eyed, handsome and sensitive
liked by all who knew him
for years German chess had floundered
despite lavish state assistance
the victorious team in Argentina had included two Austrians
(Eliskases and Becker)
made German by the march of conquest
but now Germany had a genuine grandmaster
and he was not a Jew

Junge started brilliantly
he won game after game
Alekhine had no losses
but he drew with Foltys, Zita and Rejfir

Junge surged ahead
there were murmurings among the Czech spectators
they did not see Alekhine as a drunken lout
in favour with Hitler
but instead
"a Slav like us"
during the tournament
the Russians began the offensive
designed to cut off the German Army besieging Stalingrad
rumours of this had reached Prague
Slavs advanced and Germans retreated
and the Czech Resistance
killed Reinhard Heydrich in a bombing attack
which in turn led to the murder of about 10,000 Czechs
all *"Slavs like us"*
Junge drew some games
Alekhine could still catch up

The last round was reached
neither Junge nor Alekhine had lost
but Junge had less draws and more wins
he led by a whole point
they still had to play each other
if Alekhine won they would be level

Alekhine had White
he played the Catalan System
a tense position was reached
Junge had a slight advantage
Alekhine dipped into his bottomless bag of tricks
found something
sacrificed the exchange (Rook for Bishop)
great complications ensued
Junge lost his way
made a less than the best move
and Alekhine overwhelmed him

So they finished level
but Alekhine had won their individual game
so the spectators
and the world
regarded it as another Alekhine triumph
he won thought the Czechs

he won
and he is a Slav like us

The German fronts gave way at Stalingrad and Tunis
there were mass surrenders
Hamburg collapsed under a hail of bombs
the U-Boats in the Atlantic were mastered
there was less interest in Hitler-sponsored chess tournaments
Hitler was going to lose the war

Junge was inducted into the German Army
there were no soft options for him
he was killed in battle in April 1945
still fighting for Hitler
Alekhine went to Spain in 1943
he remained on the Iberian peninsula for 3 years
living in cheap hotels, giving chess lessons, playing exhibition matches
there was intense feeling in France about *"collaborators"*
he thought it dangerous to return

But he was still World Champion
the USSR sent in a formal challenge for its leading player
Mikhail Botvinnik
the match was to be played in London
Alekhine accepted
he needed money to stay alive
but before the match could start
he died

Eventually a Championship Tournament was arranged
and this was won by Botvinnik
in the years after Alekhine's death
master chess was dominated
by citizens of the USSR

In the circumstances at Prague
Alekhine and Junge could no longer be individuals and chess players
(the pleasant boy and the wily veteran)
the insanity of the Hitler regime
turned them both into soldiers
the Czech spectators thought the right man won
do you think that they were right?

Dark Night at Ballarat Railway Station 1942

A little green light and a little red light. Smoke under the roof.

Tall woman with white hair. Coal dust up my nose.
Smell of oil. Heavy things turning round.
Dark. No lights. Just a little green light. And a little red light.
On the boiler barrel. Beneath the handrail.
Under the roof. Coal burning. Engine breathing like a person.
Silent people. Deep breathing.
A little green light. And a little red light.
And Da said, isn't it gloomy. And I said
Da I like the gloom.

When I was young ...

When I was young
I thought I knew everything
now I know everything.
When I was young
I thought there was an explanation for everything
Now I know there is an explanation for every explanation.
When I was young
I thought there was a battle between
style and content.
Now I know that the content
of every style depends on the style
of every content.
Once I thought that life was a mystery
Now I know that the only
mystery was why I thought it was a mystery.
Once I thought
I was destined to do great things
Now I know that
the great things I was destined
to do failed to wait for me to do them.

The Real Hero of Eureka 2

The real heroes of Eureka
were my great grandparents
Mary Carroll and Arthur Duke
potato farmers
both aged 22 years
of Brown Hill, near Ballarat
but formerly of County Cork
in Ireland.

On the day of Eureka
they loaded their Enfield rifle
and their Adams revolver
and stood on the boundary of their Farm
waiting to shoot anyone
soldier or miner
rebel or tyrant
pauper or moneygrubber
who came too close
they heard the firing at the stockade
they heard the shouting and the death
they waited all day
but no one came.
When it was dark
they went inside
unloaded their guns
and went to bed.
In their district they were known as "hard people"
Protestants among Catholics
self-sufficient and unsociable
honest people
but intolerant
ruthless, relentless and unforgiving
they hated miners and mining
riches and poverty
wealth without work
those who had too much
and those who had too little
governments of all sorts
empires and republics
they believed in no power but their own bodies
perhaps they were right

Presentations

I surprised you
when your lover
was giving you
a beautiful diamond
however it was not a diamond
it was a book
despite this
it wasn't your lover

it was me
and I gave you
a concrete mixer
a concrete mixer filled with all the colours of the rainbow

Isn't ...

Isn't this music great!
It makes you want to get up and
invade Poland.

J. S. HARRY 1939–

Jan Harry was born in South Australia and grew up in Adelaide, but has lived most of her life in Sydney. She has had a variety of jobs, including educational bookselling. She edited the ABC Radio National poetry programme "A First Hearing" and has been a writer-in-residence at the Australian National University. Harry has published eight volumes of poetry. Tom Shapcott in *The Oxford Companion to Twentieth Century Poetry* described her as a "reclusive and unpredictable poet" and wrote of her "ability to range from experimental modishness to formal tautness, from scintillation to savagery."

In a rare statement in Brooks and Walker's *Poetry and Gender*, Harry explained that she has been distant from contemporary Australian poetic factions, and has employed her initials rather than her given name for publishing, because as a person she is not significant to a reading of her poems. Ludwig Wittgenstein has been a continuing influence in her work – an influence which Colin Dray has discussed in *Australian Literary Studies* (October 2005).

An important character in her more recent poetry is a British-born rabbit, Peter Henry Lepus. Her poems about him and his travels and relationships with actual and imaginary human beings are collected in *Not Finding Wittgenstein* (2007). This is a collection of narratives, some sharp and some deliberately and charmingly fey. We have included two poems from that volume: "Circles" and "They". In "Circles" Peter Henry seems to have travelled to Japan. His acquaintance "Russell" is the British philosopher and mathematician Bertrand Russell.

Reading Harry can be disconcerting, with coarse, savagely satirical poems interspersed among minimalist lyrics of great delicacy. Her poetry, particularly before she discovered Peter Henry Lepus, has an abrupt, idiosyncratic voice, that treats each poem as a new experiment. Having found this character, the tone of voice – a sort of jerky shorthand – has become more predictable, although his travels and travelling companions are not.

The What O'Clock

A puffball
on a slim green stem
is more attached
to earth than I.

The wind will tear
its seed away –
perhaps they'll root –
Words root. My words? Mine?

Living all in your head
is a kind of thistle-madness,
anyway, but, close, grass is,
birds are –; the people
outside
    seldom sing

People in pain
I brush against;
I rip. And they hold me.
But, when I roll away,
in my mind I am a puff-ball
about to leave earth;
again,
    the wind isn't far away.

How?
Grown from a thin green shoot
with a root in earth
to this airy death?

Even as a child
I could feel   for days on end
the isolating air, cool and strange,
around my head.

The Gulf of Bothnia

in the gulf of bothnia near the top the
salinity's between
four to six parts   per thousand
flounder & pike   live
in the same "sea"
also seaweed & freshwater plants sit
side by side

as grandmother & grandfather
on the veranda
in their rockers might have done
could they've lived
in the gulf of bothnia
near the top
the land is rising at one hundred millimetres
per metre per hundred year – out of the sea –
boat houses sit in cow paddocks
falling green on their knees into grass
waiting for the sea to come back
& the boats to visit –
much as grandfather & grandmother
might have waited   for "life" to come back
to visit them
on the old-age farm – had they lived
by the gulf of bothnia near the top –
& reindeer step down the bogs
delicately
lowering   one after the other
soft
reindeer's mouths
into the rich bog plants –

cows drink the sea   in the gulf of bothnia
                                    near the top
fresher   water on the surface
salt-er   lower down

we are unable   to breathe
in the gulf of bothnia

though have often dreamed

of visiting   our imaginary relatives
the seaweeds & the freshwater plants

besides those ancient farms

Hand-Me-Downs

Clunk! Clunk!   What's that?
Only a bulbul
rapping his hard bread –
a sun-cemented slab
of ant-enlivened white –

on the corrugated, dull,
elephant-grey hills of the roof
that are flecked with rust plants,
to work it? to soften it up? –
smashing the slab's
apparent, white setness
into rigid roughcast knobs
slightly less
than the dimensions
of his beak-opening.

The rocklike
dingy pebbles
go down his bird-gullet fast.

Words
break down into their syllables; stone bread
breaks differently, into its parts.
What's left, the grits
minute
as letters of pin-head type, thin brown ants
will find & carry off.

Doves, often, on an old worn roof,
'll pick up antique flakes of paint,
bark boats, rusty twists
of roofing-nail –
or fallen
slivers of slate –
test
& discard them,
as a person might, differently,
pick up – & hold, on the tongue,
for the ears to savour – consider –
an ancient withered, weathered word –
17th-century lexical item,
product
of a chance encounter,
that proves,
after a mind's
mute, dumb probe-&-test, & a
consultation with some fat-gut
arbitration-commissioner

dictionary,
to be
          unsound
                              for current
nutriment.

This bulbul
needs no tests. His selection
of found-food is flawless.

A Page for a Lorikeet

If
you are lucky enough
to have, as good friend,
a female   rainbow
lorikeet, she
will have two toes forward
& two toes backward
on each of her feet, i.e.
she will be of the older
form of bird, non-passerine.
Her toe-nails, minute, the
cloudy, tawny-brown
of combs sometimes made
from turtles hauled from the sea,
turn firmly, sharply in,
on whatever they grip.
Lorikeet toe-nails leave thin
scratchmarks   like delicate
birds' writing – nib
of a metal pen dipped in pink –
on the pale
skin of a human
leg, arm, hand, or wrist. Your
bark is skin;
they walk you as their tree …
it is here … i climb … it is here …
i cling

If she lands
on the front of your face,
she will have to sink
her beak & toes

into the flesh of your nose
& dig in, aiming for bone
to get a firmer grip.

If she climbs
the next
more dicey bit,
sometimes unnerved,
with one foot
resting lightly on
one of your awkward,
open, oddly-spongy eyes,
she'll stop –
unable to move
for panic.

You
at this distress
may choose

to offer her
an arm as a branch of escape

& she
may choose
to take it.

If she has made it
up the vertical   to the
tussocky, grippable hair
she too   is very pleased
& from her vantage point
tries to steer you eagerly
in the most suitable
north-south-east-or-west-erly
kitchen direction
which she will indicate
by rapid vehement nods.

You will be unable to see these
because of where she is.
Anyone else
will be able to read
& re-lay them too slowly for her.

Frustrated as a quick wit

trying to train a clot,
over & over, she will point you,
with her beak, to
a cupboard-caged,
crinkly, Savoy cabbage – for it –
instantly – to be lifted out; she wants
to play "tough", quick! quick! jumping,
                              landing on top of it,
& ripping it up,

with her lorikeet beak
which is so good
at gouging
& at picking up
saucers, cups, dishes, flinging or pushing
them off shelves
for the floor to shatter,
at the sound of which she utters
gleeful, crowing screams.
                                        These
will go on,
as shards bounce & scatter, becoming chortles,
if you're crawling innocently beneath her,
with your unsuspecting head down,
cleaning broken –
glassy mess – prime target –
with your
back *unguarded* –
to be landed on
for a rowdy play
or king-hit
by some prized missile
from her arsenal
of lids.

A rainbow lorikeet
that has grown up
around humans
will expect
that whatever she sees
you put in your mouth
will be good
for a rainbow lorikeet.

She will also expect
that you share it.

If you try to write when she
is out of her cage,
she will strut up to the pencil
& try to take it away from you.

If you put the pencil down
& play, she will not want
her game to include it
& will persistently entreat,
with inviting forward-nods
& intent, beseeching sideways-looks,
that *you*
should follow *her*
away from it.

Alternately,
if you have a sheet of paper out
when she arrives,
she will try – by lifting up a corner –
to get under it.

It is hard   to write
on a piece of paper
that has the energetic back
of a rainbow lorikeet   under it
pushing up at you.

Finding a Destiny that Fits

Few
choose to suicide
by leaping into the pit
of the Manchurian tiger

as a young Chinese man
did
at Shanghai zoo 4/1/85

Clasping
its jaws
over the young man's head
blocking
his view
of a banished world

the tiger
accepted
the offered life

Tiger, I will
be flesh of thy flesh

Afterwards
it was said
the young man
was of unsound mind

No one
doubted the sanity
of the tiger

From HIV to Full-blown …

Moths blown away
from their deaths in the high country
die on the coast

He will go, with his tears & his
typewriter, down below,
& type one more poem out
that he doesn't want to write.
His lover cannot hear it.
He is writing for those of his friends still alive.

To them, he types, very slowly –
because his arms are shaking
& his skin
has the night sweat fever:
All the faces you love
will become ash or dust
if only
you can wait long enough …

He has waited enough.

Circles *(from* Not Finding Wittgenstein*)*

When he wakes, Russell is standing over him.
W. & I have argued for three days, he says.
His new work is important, & original –
but I am not at all sure
that it is true. Peter sees the tide has come in –
underneath all the buildings. The shrine

seems to be floating. Russell says it looks
like a mother-duck building, surrounded –
at discrete intervals – by the smaller
wooden ducklings of the lesser shrines.
Peter does not know about that.
He hasn't seen many ducks …
        Once he caught a glimpse
of the Waddle-Splat girls – but they
were upside down in a pond & had
wispy bottoms where their heads should be.
They did, perhaps, look a bit like shrines.
What were their names? Becky? … Jemmy? …
It has got dark. There is no moon.
Wittgenstein has paid   for the priests
to light the stone lanterns in the pine trees
& has taken his shoes off. Peter wonders why
because the ground is   so cold …
Perhaps it is Wittgenstein's bedtime?
W. does not tell him & goes off to look at holes
in the ground in the dark
under trees that are farthest
from the priests' holy glow.
Peter thinks if his mother were out at night,
& so sick she got lost, & their burrow were under
those pines, she would know where to come.
Russell looks out at the lights:
Each one is shut in on itself   like a human being,
he notes. *None of the light circles touch one another.*
At the edges the light   gets gradually darker – ;
it's not clear   where light begins & darkness stops.
Wittgenstein   will write about this.

They *(from* Not Finding Wittgenstein*)*

They use a pronoun called I
all the time. It seems to hop around
with them.
But you can't see it properly
not all of it. Not like you can see
ears or whiskers,
or paw or a sun shadow.

This is what Peter tells the flowerbed rabbit
who lives deep in dark leaves

that grow straight to a sky of apple-red flowers.
She can't read.
He shows her   the straight line
her paw scraped
on the rained-on damp
green-growing ground: *that's "I"*; he puts
two short, stiff twigs – one each – same length –
at the line's
head & foot: *that's their*
Capital I.   *But it doesn't MOOOVE,*
she objects: *those twigs, that scrape*
will NEVER hop.
Peter's ears twitch – but he has to agree. Goes on.
Struggles – how   to explain: "I's written representation"?

It's a picture,
he says at last, *it's a stand-for*
what lives in each of them, it's common
to all of THEM – as the earth beneath our paws
is common to all of us (including them)
who run, hop, walk,
fall, lie, or die on it.
She doesn't know what die is. *It's a word,*
he says, *like I is: nobody knows what it's like*
inside it.
    I die, you singular die, he dies, she dies, it dies,
    You plural die, we die, they die –

He's given her a lecture
when all he wanted to do
was follow the white
bobs of her tail
disappearing
into the scarlet flowers.

CLIVE JAMES 1939–

Clive James was born in the Sydney suburb of Kogarah. When he was six, his father died in a plane crash on his way back to Australia, having survived a Japanese prisoner of war camp. He says: "I am trying to lead the life [my parents] might have had." An only child, brought up by his mother, who did not remarry, he studied arts at Sydney University – all well-known facts because of the immense success of *Unreliable Memoirs,* the first volume of his autobiography. At university he was preoccupied with theatrical revues, and was a prolific writer of skits. James went on to complete a second degree at Cambridge, and worked as a freelance literary and TV critic in London, also establishing a reputation as a writer of accomplished light verse. He became a television personality and humorist, hosting his own programs. He has written pop lyrics, and published fifteen books of essays, four novels, five volumes of autobiography, mock-heroic epics, and selections of his light and serious verse. He married Prudence Shaw, an Australian, who has had a distinguished career in Italian studies at Oxford. They have two daughters.

Like Barry Humphries, James is able to move with naturalness and ease between popular and high culture. He is an admirer of A. D. Hope's poetry, and this has influenced certain of his own poems. Another influence may be John Betjeman, particularly in poems of family reminiscence such as "Occupation: Housewife". Jamie Grant, writing in *The Oxford Companion to Twentieth-Century Poetry*, has pointed out that James would not have been able to accomplish all he has if he had remained in Australia, adding: "To those readers who did not feel obliged to sneer at his public persona, a customary treatment for Australia's successful expatriates, it was apparent that his poetic skill extended beyond light verse. He is a considerable poet with a voice all of his own".

Like his friend Peter Porter, he has not returned to Australia to live, but his subject matter and voice have remained more distinctively Australian than Porter's. Comparing his 1986 selected poems, *Other Passports*, with his selected of 2008, *Opal Sunset*, there has been a gravity shift from vers d'occasion to poems of personal history. In "What Happened to Auden", "salonfähig" means "socially acceptable".

Johnny Weismuller Dead in Acapulco

Apart possibly from waving hello to the cliff-divers
Would the real Tarzan have ever touched Acapulco?
Not with a one-hundred-foot vine.
Jungle Jim maybe, but the Ape Man never.
They played a tape at his funeral
In the Valley of Light cemetery of how he had sounded
Almost fifty years back giving the pristine ape-call,
Which could only remind all present that in decline
He would wander distractedly in the garden
With his hands to his mouth and the unforgettable cry
Coming out like a croak –
This when he wasn't sitting in his swim-trunks
Beside the pool he couldn't enter without nurses.

Things had not been so bad before Mexico
But they were not great.
He was a greeter in Caesar's Palace like Joe Louis.
Sal, I want you should meet Johnny Weissmuller.
Johnny, Mr Sal Volatile is a friend of ours from Chicago.
With eighteen Tarzan movies behind him

Along with the five Olympic gold medals,
He had nothing in front except that irrepressible paunch
Which brought him down out of the tree house
To earth as Jungle Jim
So a safari suit could cover it up.
As Jungle Jim he wasn't just on salary,
He had a piece of the action,
But coming so late in the day it was not enough
And in Vegas only the smile was still intact.

As once it had all been intact, the Greek classic body
Unleashing the new-style front-up crawl like a baby
Lifting itself for the first time,
Going over the water almost as much as through it,
Curing itself of childhood polio,
By making an aquaplane of its deep chest,
Each arm relaxing out of the water and stiffening into it,
The long legs kicking a trench that did not fill up
Until he came back on the next lap,
Invincible, easily breathing
The air in the spit-smooth, headlong, creek-around-a-rock trough
Carved by his features.

He had six wives like Henry VIII but don't laugh,
Because Henry VIII couldn't swim a stroke
And if you ever want to see a true king you should watch Weissmuller
In *Tarzan Escapes* cavorting underwater with Boy
In the clear river with networks of light on the shelving sand
Over which they fly weightless to hide from each other behind the log
While Jane wonders where they are.
You will wonder where you are too and be shy of the answer
Because it is Paradise.

When the crocodile made its inevitable entry into the clear river
Tarzan could always settle its hash with his bare hands
Or a knife at most,
But Jungle Jim usually had to shoot it
And later on he just never got to meet it face to face –
It was working for the Internal Revenue Service.

There was a chimpanzee at his funeral,
Which must have been someone's idea of a smart promotion,
And you might say dignity had fled,
Bur when Tarzan dropped from the tall tree and swam out of the splash

Like an otter with an outboard to save Boy from the waterfall
It looked like poetry to me,
And at home in the bath I would surface giving the ape-call.

Egon Friedell's Heroic Death

Egon Friedell committed suicide
By jumping from his window when he saw
Approaching Brownshirts eager to preside
At rites the recent *Anschluss* had made law.

Vienna's coffee-house habitués
By that time were in Paris, Amsterdam,
London, New York. Friedell just couldn't raise
The energy to take it on the lam.

Leaving aside the question of their looks,
The Jews the Nazis liked to see in Hell
Were good at writing and owned lots of books –
Which all spelled certain curtains for Friedell.

Friedell was cultivated in a way
That now in Europe we don't often see.
For every volume he'd have had to pay
In pain what those thugs thought the fitting fee.

Forestalling them was simply common sense,
An act only a Pharisee would blame,
Yet hard to do when fear is so intense.
Would *you* have had the nerve to do the same?

The normal move would be to just lie still
And tell yourself you somehow might survive,
But this great man of letters had the will
To meet his death while he was still alive.

So out into the air above the street
He sailed with all his learning left behind,
And by one further gesture turned defeat
Into a triumph for the human mind.

The civilised are most so as they die.
He called a warning even as he fell
In case his body hit a passer-by
As innocent as was Egon Friedell.

What Happened to Auden

His stunning first lines burst out of the page
Like a man thrown through a windscreen. His flat drawl
Was acrid with the spirit of the age –
The spy's last cigarette, the hungry sprawl
Of Hornby clockwork train sets in "O" gauge,
Huge whitewashed slogans on a factory wall –
It was as if a spotlight when he spoke
Brilliantly pierced the histrionic smoke.

Unsentimental as the secret police,
Contemporary as a Dinky Toy,
On holiday in Iceland with MacNeice,
A flop-haired Cecil Beaton golden boy,
Auden pronounced like Pericles to Greece
The short time Europe had left to enjoy,
Yet made it sound as if impending doom
Could only ventilate the drawing room.

Splendidly poised above the ashtray's rim,
The silver record-breaking aeroplane
For streamlined utterance could not match him.
Oblique but no more often than the rain,
Impenetrable only to the dim,
Neurotic merely not to be insane,
He seemed to make so much sense all at once
Anyone puzzled called himself a dunce.

Cricket pavilion lust looked a touch twee
Even to devotees, but on the whole,
Apart from harsh reviews in *Scrutiny*,
All hailed his triumph in Cassandra's role,
Liking the *chic* he gave her, as if she
Wore ankle-strap high heels and a mink stole –
His ambiguity just further proof
Here was a man too proud to stand aloof.

By now, of course, we know he was in fact
As queer as a square grape, a roaring queen
Himself believing the forbidden act
Of love he made a meal of was obscene.
He could be crass and generally lacked tact.
He had no truck with personal hygiene.
The roughest trade would seldom stay to sleep.
In soiled sheets he was left alone to weep.

From the Kurfürstendamm to far Shanghai
He cruised in every sense with Isherwood.
Sadly he gave the talent the glad eye
And got out while the going was still good.
New York is where his genius went to die
Say those who disapproved, but though they could
Be right that he lost much of his allure,
Whether this meant decline is not so sure.

Compatriots who stuck it out have said
Guilt for his getaway left him unmanned,
Whereat his taproot shrivelled and went dead,
Having lost contact with its native land.
Some say it was the sharing of his bed
With the one man nobody else could stand
That did him in, since poets can't afford
The deadly risk of conjugal concord.

But Chester made bliss hard enough to take,
And Wystan, far from pining for his roots,
Gaily tucked into the unrationed steak.
An international figure put out shoots.
Stravinsky helped the progress of the rake:
Two cultural nabobs were in cahoots.
No, Auden ageing was as much at home
On the world stage as Virgil was in Rome,

If less than *salonfähig* still. Regret
By all accounts he sparingly displayed
When kind acquaintances appeared upset,
Their guest rooms wrecked as if by an air raid.
He would forgive himself and soon forget.
Pig-like he revelled in the mess he made,
Indecorous the more his work lost force,
Devoid of shame. Devoured, though, by remorse,

For had he not gazed into the abyss
And found, as Nietzsche warned, that it gazed back?
His wizardry was puerile next to this.
No spark of glamour touched the railway track
That took whole populations to the hiss
Of cyanide and stoked the chimney stack
Scattering ash above a vast expanse
Of industry bereft of all romance,

The pit cooled down but still he stood aghast
At how far he had failed to state the case
With all those tricks that now seemed so half-arsed,
The inconceivable had taken place,
Waking to find his wildest dreams outclassed
He felt his tongue must share in the disgrace,
And henceforth be confined, in recompense,
To no fine phrase devoid of plain prose sense.

The bard unstrung his lyre to change his tune,
Constrained his inspiration to repent.
Dry as the wind abrading a sand dune,
A tightly drafted letter of intent,
Each rubric grew incisive like a rune,
Merest suggestions became fully meant.
The ring of truth was in the level tone
He forged to fit hard facts and praise limestone.

His later manner leaves your neck-hair flat,
Not standing up as Housman said it should
When poetry has been achieved. For that,
In old age Auden simply grew too good.
A mortal fear of talking through his hat,
A moral mission to be understood
Precisely, made him extirpate the thrill
Which, being in his gift, was his to kill.

He wound up as a poor old fag at bay,
Beleaguered in the end as at the start
By dons appalled that he could talk all day
And not draw breath although pissed as a fart,
But deep down he had grown great, in a way
Seen seldom in the history of his art –
Whose earthly limits Auden helped define
By realising he was not divine.

Bring Me the Sweat of Gabriela Sabatini

Bring me the sweat of Gabriela Sabatini
For I know it tastes as pure as Malvern water,
Though laced with bright bubbles like the *aqua minerale*
That melted the kidney stones of Michelangelo
As sunlight the snow in spring.

Bring me the sweat of Gabriela Sabatini
In a green Lycergus cup with a sprig of mint,
But add no sugar –
The bitterness is what I want.
If I craved sweetness I would be asking you to bring me
The tears of Annabel Croft.

I never asked for the wrist-bands of Maria Bueno,
Though their periodic transit of her glowing forehead
Was like watching a bear's tongue lap nectar.
I never asked for the blouse of Françoise Durr,
Who refused point-blank to improve her soufflé serve
For fear of overdeveloping her upper arm –
Which indeed remained delicate as a fawn's femur,
As a fern's frond under which cool shadows gather
So that the dew lingers.

Bring me the sweat of Gabriela Sabatini
And give me credit for having never before now
Cried out with longing.
Though for all the years since TV acquired colour
To watch Wimbledon for even a single day
Has left me shaking with grief like an ex-smoker
Locked overnight in a cigar factory,
Not once have I let loose as now I do
The parched howl of deprivation,
The croak of need.

Did I ever demand, as I might well have done,
The socks of Tracy Austin?
Did you ever hear me call for the cast-off Pumas
Of Hana Mandlikova?
Think what might have been distilled from these things,
And what a small request it would have seemed –
It would not, after all, have been like asking
For something so intimate as to arouse suspicion
Of mental derangement.
I would not have been calling for Carling Bassett's knickers
Or the tingling, Teddy Tinling B-cup brassière
Of Andrea Temesvari.

Yet I denied myself.
I have denied myself too long.
If I had been Pat Cash at that great moment

Of triumph, I would have handed back the trophy
Saying take that thing away
And don't let me see it again until
It spills what makes this lawn burst into flower:
Bring me the sweat of Gabriela Sabatini.

In the beginning there was Gorgeous Gussie Moran
And even when there was just her it was tough enough
But by now the top hundred boasts at least a dozen knock-outs
Who make it difficult to keep one's tongue
From lolling like a broken roller blind.
Out of deference to Billie-Jean I did my best
To control my male chauvinist urges –
An objectivity made easier to achieve
When Betty Stove came clumping out to play
On a pair of what appeared to be bionic legs
Borrowed from Six Million Dollar Man.

I won't go so far as to say I harbour
Similar reservations about Steffi Graf –
I merely note that her thigh muscles when tense
Look interchangeable with those of Boris Becker –
Yet all are agreed that there can be no doubt
About Martina Navratilova:
Since she lent her body to Charles Atlas
The definition of the veins on her right forearm
Looks like the Mississippi river system
Photographed from a satellite,
And though she may unleash a charming smile
When crouching to dance at the ball with Ivan Lendl,
I have always found to admire her yet remain detached
Has been no problem.

But when the rain stops long enough for the true beauties
To come out swinging under the outshone sun
The spectacle is hard for a man to take,
And in the case of this supernally graceful dish –
Likened to a panther by slavering sports reporters
Who pitiably fail to realise that any panther
With a top-spin forehand line drive like hers
Would be managed personally by Mark McCormack –
I'm obliged to admit defeat.

So let me drink deep from the bitter cup.
Take it to her between any two points of a tie-break

That she may shake above it her thick black hair
A nocturne from which the droplets as they fall
Flash like shooting stars –
And as their lustre becomes liqueur
Let the full calyx be repeatedly carried to me.
Until I tell you to stop
Bring me the sweat of Gabriela Sabatini.

Occupation: Housewife

Advertisements asked "Which twin has the Toni?"
Our mothers were supposed to be non-plussed.
Dense paragraphs of technical baloney
Explained the close resemblance of the phoney
To the Expensive Perm. It worked on trust.

The barber tried to tell me the same sheila
With the same Expensive Perm was pictured twice.
He said the Toni treatment was paint-sealer
Re-bottled by a second-hand car dealer
And did to hair what strychnine did to mice.

Our mothers all survived, but not the perms.
Two hours at most the Toni bobbed and dazzled
Before the waves were back on level terms,
Limp as the spear-points of the household germs
An avalanche of Vim left looking frazzled.

Another false economy, home brew
Seethed after nightfall in the laundry copper.
Bought on the sly, the hops were left to stew
Into a mulch that grunted as it grew.
You had to sample it with an eye-dropper,

Not stir it with a stick as one mum did.
She piled house bricks on top, thinking the gas
Would have nowhere to go. Lucky she hid
Inside the house. The copper blew its lid
Like Krakatoa to emit a mass

Of foam. The laundry window bulged and broke.
The prodigy invaded the back yard.
Spreading across the lawn like evil smoke
It murdered her hydrangeas at a stroke
And long before the dawn it had set hard.

On a world scale, one hardly needs to note,
Those Aussie battlers barely had a taste
Of deprivation. Reeling from the boat
Came reffo women who had eaten goat
Only on feast days. Still, it is the waste

I think of, the long years without our men,
And only the Yanks to offer luxuries
At a price no decent woman thought of then
As one she could afford, waiting for when
The Man Himself came back from Overseas.

And then I think of those whose men did not:
My mother one of them. She who had kept
Herself for him for so long, and for what?
To creep, when I had splinters, to my cot
With tweezers and a needle while I slept?

Now comes the time I fly to sit with her
Where she lies waiting, to what end we know.
We trade our stories of the way things were,
The home brew and the perm like rabbit fur.
How sad, she says, the heart is last to go.

The heart, the heart. I still can hear it break.
She asked for nothing except his return.
To pay so great a debt, what does it take?
My books, degrees, the money that I make?
Proud of a son who never seems to learn,

She can't forget I lost my good pen-knife.
Those memories of waste do not grow dim
When you, for Occupation, write: Housewife.
Out of this world, God grant them both the life
She gave me and I had instead of him.

The Place of Reeds

Kogarah (suppress the first "a" and it scans)
Named by the locals for the creek's tall reeds
That look like an exotic dancer's fans
When dead, was where I lived. Born to great deeds

I stripped the fronds and was a warrior
Whose arrows were the long thin brittle stem
With a stiff piece of copper wire or
A headless nail to make a point for them.

The point went in where once the pith had been
Before it crumbled. The capillary
Was open at the other end. Some keen
Constructors mastered the technology

For fitting in a feathery tail-piece,
But they made model aeroplanes that flew.
Mine didn't, and my shafts, upon release
Wobbled and drifted as all missiles do

With nothing at the back to guide their flight.
Still, I was dangerous. My willow bow
Armed an Odysseus equipped to smite
Penelope and let her suitors go.

The creek led through a swamp where each weekend
Among the tangled trees we waged mock war.
At short range I could sometimes miss a friend
And hit the foe. Imagine Agincourt

Plus spiders, snakes and hydroponic plants.
I can't forget one boy, caught up a tree
By twenty others, peeing his short pants
As the arrows came up sizzling. It was me.

Just so the tribesmen, when our ship came in
Bringing the puffs of smoke that threw a spear
Too quick to see, realised they couldn't win.
It was our weaponry and not their fear

Defeated them. As we who couldn't lose
Fought with our toys, their young men dived for coins
From the wharf across the bay at La Perouse,
Far from us. Now, in age, my memory joins

Easy supremacy to black despair
In those enchanted gardens that they left
Because they knew they didn't have a prayer:
Lately I too begin to feel bereft.

Led by the head, my arrow proves to be
My life. I took my life into my hands.
I loosed it to its wandering apogee,
And now it falls. I wonder where it lands.

Whitman and the Moth

Van Wyck Brooks tells us Whitman in old age
Sat by a pond in nothing but his hat,
Crowding his final notebooks page by page
With names of trees, birds, bugs, and things like that.

The war could never break him, though he'd seen
Horrors in hospitals to chill the soul.
But now, preserved, the Union had turned mean:
Evangelising greed was in control.

Good reason to despair, yet grief was purged
By tracing how creation reigned supreme.
A pupa cracked, a butterfly emerged:
America, still unfolding from its dream.

Sometimes he rose and waded in the pond,
Soothing his aching feet in the sweet mud.
A moth he knew, of which he had grown fond,
Perched on his hand as if to draw his blood.

But they were joined by what each couldn't do,
The meeting point where great art comes to pass –
Whitman, who danced and sang but never flew,
The moth, which had not written "Leaves of Grass,"

Composed a picture of the interchange
Between the mind and all that it transcends
Yet must stay near. No, there was nothing strange
In how he put his hand out to make friends

With such a fragile creature, soft as dust.
Feeling the pond cool as the light grew dim,
He blessed new life, though it had only just
Arrived in time to see the end of him.

PETER STEELE 1939–

Peter Steele was born and grew up in Perth, and moved to Melbourne in 1957 to join the Jesuits. At the University of Melbourne he wrote a doctoral thesis on Jonathan Swift, which became a book. His other prose works include: *Expatriates: Reflections on Modern Poetry* (1985); *The Autobiographical Passion: Studies in the Self on Show* (1989); and *Peter Porter: Oxford Australian Writers* (1992). Steele has published five volumes of poetry. Except for six years as Provincial of the Jesuit Order in Australia, he has since 1966 been a member of the English Department of the University of Melbourne. He held a Personal Chair and is now a Professor Emeritus. He has been Visiting Professor at American universities, including Georgetown, and delivered the Martin D'Arcy Lectures in Arts and Sciences at the University of Oxford.

Steele's unique voice is detectable in his earlier volumes, but only in his later work does he display the elegant, calibrated syntax which allows him to express nuanced content freshly and vividly and with warmth. Our selection is from among his later poems. His work is influenced by Peter Porter, but the voice is mellower, less anxious. In "Pomegranate" he deftly juxtaposes the golden orb of the warlord, Bolingbroke, who usurped the English throne to become Henry IV, with the pomegranate which the Christ child reaches out for with astonishment in Sandro Botticelli's painting "Madonna of the Pomegranate". Typically in a touching elegy for his brother, there is a play of language in the last line, with Steele in effect punning on his Christian name, Peter, which means rock. The subject of Steele's "Praying with Christopher Smart" was overcome by religious mania and had to be confined to inhumane lunatic asylums, "the foetid warren of Bedlam" described in Steele's poem. Samuel Johnson remarked: "My poor friend Smart showed the disturbance of his mind by falling upon his knees, and saying his prayers in the street, or in any other unusual place."

Confluences

Whether or not the man was Shakespeare's hog,
    I can't forget standing beside
the plate let into the soil where he fell: "Here
    died Richard, last of the
Plantagenets". The brook's still there, just
    too broad for leaping if you're armoured,
tired with fighting, unhorsed and out of heart.
    Perhaps it's because his deathday is
my birthday that the spot stays marked for me:
    perhaps because, later that day,
we drove to Coventry, marked still by the traces
    of efforts to terminate many lines.
Epstein's wing-borne Michael thrusts a spear
    at a cringing, snarling Satan on
the wall of the post-war cathedral. Nails
    forged in the middle ages, found
in the rubble of the fallen house, are welded
    crosswise in lieu of crucifixion;
and metal sheared from a smashed car is wrought
    into a head of Christ in passion.
Afterwards we ate whitebait, I remember,
    putting the small dead things
to good use, and drove home in the rain.
    The stream was too much for Richard, slighter

even than Rubicon though it is. If ever
the trumpets sounded for him, it wasn't
on the other side at Bosworth. Conceivably,
the real man's well placed
to explain the matter to Shakespeare, who managed to die
on his birthday, feast of St George,
that honorary Englishman, and who
went wherever they go on the same
day as that master-forger of knights, Cervantes.

Ape

Watching the mind go out when a friend or brother
is dying, it's as if a great
ape were given his freedom at last. No more
need for the taking of clues from those
so like and so completely other; an end
to being thought a harbinger
of ill for those who happen to dream about you;
and silence, in place of the loud taxing
with lust, with sloth, with all the cavalcade
of things resented because feared.

Instead, there's the immitigable forest,
greening itself in vindication
of hope's archaic shoots. The deeper you move,
the more your solitude is licensed,
displayed at last as a kind of radiant darkness
where stalk, bewildered, memory,
adumbration, doubt, incomprehension,
hatred's net and trident, and,
recalcitrant to saddles but receptive
to innocence, the unicorn of love.

San Sepolcro

after Piero della Francesca, Resurrection, 1463: mural in fresco and tempera

Back from the keep of iron hearts, the magma
of hatred still shocking his eyes,
he puts one foot on the lip of the world and waits
to see which way things will turn,
given his drastic insurrection. Someone,
perhaps the spearsman locked in sleep,

took the measure of his heart. It shows,
as does the chiselling invasion
of nails driven in with a will. Now,
the light folding him like a second
banner, his garb the rose of dawn, he
warms again to middle-earth.

Imperial crocus may be thrusting skyward
out of the pummelled earth behind him,
and the filing trees borrow green from the gear
of the troop dead to the world at his coming,
but consummation waits. If he says, "Even
the smallest of creatures carries a sun
in its eyes", the hulled body proclaims, "At the roots
of Eden, there is an abyss".
What will they do, those four, our fellows, when
they too are back in time to mount
alone the sinuous or the cypress way,
on this the first and the last day?

Invisible Riders

Some days, it's a gaucho in command,
Hickory-tough, illiterate, stinking of sweat
And violence, plunging into the sea
Of grass, unbiddable, stoic. On others, it's
Elisabeth of Austria, the habit
Sewn onto her each morning, spurring away
From the forty tons of luggage and special train,
Imperial in alien Ireland. Or it's
One of those wizened children, painted like
Willie Shoemaker onto the horse, a half
Ton of upheaving flesh and bone beneath him.

Whichever of these it is, the invisible riders
Who, said Emerson, whip us through the world,
The brunt of the problem is timing. Yes, there's occasion
For the will's brandish, caparison of decorum,
Or a flogged-out ramp of intellect – the whole
Capriole and cadenza of the heart –
But why me, and why now? They hear us,
The ones who have their knees about our flanks,
And are unmoved. It is as if their heads
Have all been turned by a report of centaurs,

Two in one flesh, the commander never in question.

Praying with Christopher Smart

I'd as lief pray with Kit Smart as anyone else. Samuel Johnson

Your knees hitting the cobbles the way a goldsmith
        pounced his metal, you still alarm us,
for all that your yard-and-a-bit of bones are buried.

I remember a student calling your "Song to David"
        a berserk thing, and though he was wrong
the fling of a raw, unkenneled heart had caught him,

as it could many. You found the trace of its music
        when stashed and barred for exhibition
in your century's nightmare, the foetid warren of Bedlam,

and rejoiced, though God knows how, at seeing the Lamb,
        all radiant victim and focal creature,
where knave and fool and we the bewildered are welcomed.

So I too would be glad to pray, if you came
        to this other world, where the mettlesome stars
patch the darkness after a different fashion

of the thing we call the cosmos, meaning always
        something beautiful, something entire:
glad to be taught by someone unguarded, the lilt

of jubilation practised at every hour,
        and the coarse roads conceived as channels
of grace, that naked investment of love. So come,

for a season at least, to a country of goshawk and ibis,
        where the diamondbird flickers in tilted leaves
and the needletail swift feeds and drinks on the wing,

where reindeer moss, and sea tassel, and fireweed
        come out with archaic flair, and leopard
and tiger and waxlip are so many orchids, and heal-all

and hound's-tongue and bulrush and running postman
        are out for show with the black swans,
the crimson rosellas, the wedge-tailed eagles, and the swallows:

come down, little man, in your dirty linen, and your need
        for help back from the alehouse, and your love
of the one whose beauty sent you to sea for pearls.

Brother

No day goes by without your haunting me,
You, whose tongue was always heavy with silence.

Watching myself taped, a mouth pouring
Word on crested word, I am ashamed

To have outlived you, whom first I saw huddled
Behind glass some wars and loves ago.

There is, as your brooding gaze always implied,
Nothing to say. But as I back towards

Your veiled country, let me say only
That you were never slight, nor I the rock.

Pomegranate

for Adrienne Clarke

Given the puckered crown and the sleek orb,
        a warlord's reach makes all the sense
those courtiers of doom can manage. "Sour,
        yet sweet" was Bolingbroke's device,
the yellow nob brought home from Moorish kings,
        England astringent in his grasp.

Still, while our feckless breed pays out its danegeld
        year by year to the Prince of Darkness –
so many bodies drained of their dearest blood –
        a fresher image buds to rebuke
that yield of heartlessness, the bright grenade:
        to the cupped palm of Sandro's Madonna

the child's astonished hand goes out, and fingers
        a little globe of lavishness.
The company about have not so much
        as a smile between them: yet all sweetens,
gravity blossoming into joy, the mind
        cheered as by juice blended with snow.

Rehearsal

Upright again, fritters of mint in my fingers,
        I'm given pause in the kitchen patch
by the cars' whine, the loud harrumph of lorries
        that round the stand on Two-Tree Hill
                and hustle past the boneyard.

I've taken leave of the Cliffs of Moher, the unsmiling
campus guard at Georgetown, the fall
of Richelieu's scarlet enclosed by the London gloom:
I've watched my last candle gutter
for dear ones, back in Paris,

sung, as with Francis, the spill of an Umbrian morning,
each breath a gift, each glance a blessing:
have said farewell to Bhutan of the high passes
and the ragged hillmen, to the Basque dancers
praising their limping fellow,

to the Square of Blood in Beijing, to the virid islands
that speckle the Pacific acres,
to moseying sheep in Judaean scrub, to leopard
and bison, a zoo for quartering, and
to the airy stone of Chartres.

But here's the mint still on my hands. A wreath,
so Pliny thought, was "good for students,
to exhilarate their minds." Late in the course,
I'll settle for a sprig or two –
the savour gracious, the leaves brimmingly green –
as if never to say die.

GEOFFREY LEHMANN 1940–

Geoffrey Lehmann grew up at McMahons Point on Sydney Harbour and in the Sydney suburb of Gordon. He was educated at Anglican schools and studied Arts and Law at the University of Sydney. He practised as a solicitor, then taught law in the Faculty of Commerce at the University of New South Wales, and from 1988 to 2008 was with the international accounting firm PricewaterhouseCoopers as tax partner, then tax counsel. He has been chairman of the Australian Tax Research Foundation, and has been involved in the development of tax law, as a consultant and member of government bodies. He has five children. Lehmann's first book of poetry *The Ilex Tree* (1965) was shared with Les Murray. He has since published five other collections of poems as well as a selected and a collected poems. He edited two anthologies of Australian comic verse, and co edited with Robert Gray two anthologies of Australian poetry prior to this one. "The Animals", written in 2007, is an addition to his sequence *Spring Forest* (1994), spoken through the voice of an actual farmer, Ross McInerney, who lived in Cowra until his death in 2010 and whose anecdotes were the departure point for many of the poems.

Summer Night

Gardenias scent the blue-black sky which glows
Over grey lawns – blurred glimmering lakes of space.
Leaves patter with the fine spray of a hose.
A woman with a watchful, downturned face
Shining a pocket torch walks through the night,
And on the ground a circle of weak light
Hovers, dancing before her as she goes.

Fall of a Greek City

From a theme of E.M. Root

Running and running through the dust and heat,
The city waits in silence for this man,
A speck of light moving on silent feet.

The lines began to crumble and retreat,
Swords flashed. He watched and noted and began
Running and running through the dust and heat.

Through granite passes where harsh sunlight beat
And water dripped in shade with pain he ran,
A speck of light moving on silent feet.

How long he trained to make his limbs complete
These bitter honours never in the plan,
Running and running through the dust and heat.

The city waits for what he will repeat,
Mothers will mourn tonight in every clan
A speck of light moving on silent feet.

To fall down on his knees and gasp defeat,
He knows that he must do this, and he can,
Running and running through the dust and heat,
A speck of light moving on silent feet.

Pear Days in Queensland

Based on comments of Judith Wright and an article of James Wansfell

Days of pear-murder, nights of pear-madness we spent
Digging and burning the prickly pear,
Poisoning, crushing with rollers drawn by bullocks,
Standing in pubs and swapping pear yarns,
Scraping the spines off with knives,
Sponging our thorn wounds with mustard,

Scratched brown and purple with Condy's and gentian violet,
While beyond the pressure lamp's wavering circle
The pear massed its nightmare armies by moonlight
And peered with balloon green faces over pub railings.

We hacked, we poisoned, we crushed, but the pads
Just split and sprouted again.
A tree grew from a burned green ear.
Eating the yellow flowers and soft red fruit
A wandering cow scattered the seeds in her stools.
The pear flew in the stomachs of birds,
Breathed on the fur of bees,
A pad lived for three years hung in a room.

How could we fight what stuck to our boots and travelled
The red volcanic soil on our clothes and horses?
We sweated, were smeared with pear.
Pear cities covered millions and millions of acres,
Our horses galloped,
Pear leaves flying in all directions,
The roads just narrow green tunnels.
We climbed up trees to spot the heads
Of cattle amongst the plazas of cactus.
Our horses jumped and crashed in the pear,
As we tried to muster
A strange new race of small, dodging beasts
With horny palates and nimble gait.

We bred and we hacked in the great pear-loneliness,
Close neighbours cut off by the walls of thorns
That buried wire fences and boundaries,
Creeks and even hills lost,
No one quite knew where.
We walked the moonlit track to the privy
Striking with sticks at slits in the moonlight,
The small death-adders who swarmed among the cactus.
We cut and we slept,
Afraid of losing our one track out,
And stared at night from our verandas
Looking for neighbours' lights.

But we learned to live with these miles
Of green intestine digesting the world into pear.
We mashed the pads for feed,

Fermented them into alcohol
And extracted second grade dyes and oils.
We used the big yellow thorns for gramophone needles
And heard Enrico Caruso husky and faint
Sing from a thorn as we boiled in hot pear nights.

Then a moth came and Troy fell overnight.
The cactoblastis chewed through green cities,
And the arcades of pear collapsed.
We blinked at the sky
And a hemisphere of grassland tilting to the sea.
Our houses stood unpainted and rusty
In acres of pear-slime and melting branches.
And we waded through the slush
To shake the hands of forgotten neighbours.

Now the hillside is a honeycomb crumbling with fire
As in winter we burn the sugarcane
In blue indigo twilights blowing with orange smoke.
Our rivers and country daze us with largeness.
But at night we doze in mosquito nets
And smell ghost armies of cactus
In the heart of the rain forest,
New resistant strains sending out clouds of pollen.

from Roses

For Charles and Barbara Blackman

I

We left our bodies and we dreamed of roses,
But woke to shrapnel whining over the tundra,
Faces drained in the time of great bombardments,
Staggering through gas and mud, eating from tins.

Clutching a crumbling edge, our deafened minds
Reached for the tiny bursts and pops of space.
Then the guns fell silent, men climbed from their holes,
We laboured back along exhausted roads

To find the house and village of our birth,
Veterans of all denominations, ranks
Erased, the convoys thundering back at sunset
To a place of weeds, cattle munching wild peaches.

The lily pond and garden beds were gone,
And gates were chained and windows boarded up.

The simple climbing roses, the shy cousins,
With trunks like trees were thick with flowers and insects.

In rooms of fading brick on dusty floorboards
We dreamed of children's voices in a treehouse
And girls in silk shawls and their mothers' clothes,
Who hated boys and played with coloured drinks.

An old sun-weathered ghost stood by our heads,
An earth-stained mattock glittering in his hands.
"The windlass by the well needs a new rope.
This is the childhood house you never left."

VI

A man is coming back along the roads
Of crumbling bitumen, thistles in potholes,
Wading a river where a bridge has fallen,
Dossing at night by trees, in empty barns,

A man whose papers have been burned is coming,
Mud-stained, baked to the colour of the country,
Coming through passes, crossing plains and borders –
But all the guards are gone, the gates collapsed.

He briefly smiles at strangers as they pass.
Walking past blackened villages, his eyes
Look straight ahead, and still with bandaged feet
He seeks a hearth he knows, a weatherboard house

Amongst the medlar apples, airy verandas
With currants hanging from a trellis, insects
Drifting like dust, air bitter with roses.
At night on the ground beside him, stirring faintly

A woman sleeps in a silk camisole,
Cattle stare from the orchards of his seeking,
Eggs nestle in the seat of a rusting truck.
He wakes alone, walks on month after month.

VII

The briar rose with its apple smell means somewhere
Their families meet, where two old roads join up,
As plants and beasts meet at an earlier place.
The hand with its five petals holds a rose,

The body with its head and hands and feet,
Five pointed star, five petalled rose, the fives

Are spinning from the darkness, flowers and bodies
Flung from the die in their allotted shapes.

VIII

The harvest moon above the thistle forests,
The cattle snuffling follow at a distance,
Dust rising from their hocks, browsing in briars.
Boots that have marched and now must learn to walk

Are hesitant to leave the road and find
Mint under foot, fresh roses in a glass,
A lantern flickering on a pine veranda,
And fingers darning clothes torn on a journey.

IX

At winter sundown following warmth up slopes,
The tracks of cattle are a thermal map
Of an abandoned mountain valley.
Through raspberries and wild chillies brown sheep skelter.

Children have taken to the roads, the children
From ruined cities and bombed tenements,
Living on fruit and game, sleeping on earth,
Finding again the land their parents lost,

Finding among the green of bunya pines
A roofless house with feather mattresses
And frugal oranges in waist-high grass.
They fill old kettles from a gravel creek.

Who left a ladder weathering against a tree,
A rusting bath which cattle sleep beside?
The children call the animals by name
And come in from the dark to share our fires.

X

At night an old man on an island waits,
His lamp reflected in the window pane,
For the brown girl, last of his mistresses,
Who stole the boy he cherished as his son,

His coffee drained, the polished chronicler
Of love and hate, the aquiline nose, pale eyes
Asleep across a page on which he finds
All pain redeemed, all lovers reconciled.

XI

The characters, their history, who remembers?
The plots and scripts are interchangeable.
Who knows who threw what spear or fired which rifle?
The earliest cottages are under clay.

What matters is a rose grew in wild places
And that all space is immanent with roses,
And strangers, who had little, cared to bring
The grafts and cuttings to a southern climate,

Who suffered, cared for roses as a notion
Of excellence in rugged, lonely places,
Damask and hybrid tea, rambler and moss,
The precious amber hips wrapped in brown paper.

There was no comfort in the heath and sandstone,
But still they built their huts and brought their plants
To scatter fragrance by cold bays and mountains
Growing roots from the centre of the world.

XII

Girls check themselves in mirrors, mothers fuss.
Welcoming fires are burning in the hills.
Tonight your sons will come back from the war,
Crowded in trucks, lights filing through the dust.

Women are reading letters from the dead,
Will dim their lights and lie in bed alone,
But there's a band of welcome, couples embracing,
The soldiers see their wives reflect the light

Of wheat-fields, faces given shape by hardship.
They find each other quickly in the dark.
The voices of the dead touch sleeping foreheads,
And when they wake they will not be consoled.

Old earth, moss-rose, rambler rose in space,
Pinching between your polar caps this garden,
These fleecy blues and greens, this fist of life,
This whorl of petals where we meet and part.

Parenthood

I have held what I hoped would become the best minds of a generation
Over the gutter outside an Italian coffee shop watching the small
Warm urine splatter on the asphalt – impatient to rejoin

An almond torta and a cappuccino at a formica table.
I have been a single parent with three children at a Chinese restaurant
The eldest five years old and each in turn demanding
My company as they fussed in toilets and my pork sate went cold.
They rarely went all at once; each child required an individual
Moment of inspiration – and when their toilet pilgrimage was ended
I have tried to eat the remnants of my meal with twisting children
Beneath the table, screaming and grabbing in a scrimmage.
I have been wiping clean the fold between young buttocks as a pizza
I hoped to finish was cleared from a red and white checked table cloth.
I have been pouring wine for women I was hoping to impress
When a daughter ran for help through guests urgently holding out
Her gift, a potty, which I took with the same courtesy
As she gave it, grateful to dispose of its contents so simply
In a flurry of water released by the pushing of a button.
I have been butted by heads which have told me to go away and I have done so,
My mouth has been wrenched by small hands wanting to reach down to my tonsils
As I lay in bed on Sunday mornings and the sun shone through the slats
Of dusty blinds. I have helpfully carried dilly-dalliers up steps
Who indignantly ran straight down and walked up by themselves.
My arms have become exhausted, bouncing young animals until they fell asleep
In my lap listening to Buxtehude. "Too cold," I have been told,
As I handed a piece of fruit from the refrigerator, and for weeks had to warm
Refrigerated apples in the microwave so milk teeth cutting green
Carbohydrate did not chill. I have pleasurably smacked small bottoms
Which have climbed up and arched themselves on my lap wanting the report
And tingle of my palm. I have known large round heads that bumped
And rubbed themselves against my forehead, and affectionate noses
That loved to displace inconvenient snot from themselves onto me.
The demands of their bodies have taken me to unfamiliar geographies.
I have explored the white tiles and stainless steel benches of restaurant kitchens
And guided short legs across rinsed floors smelling of detergent
Past men in white with heads lowered and cleavers dissecting and assembling
Mounds of sparkling pink flesh – and located the remote dark shrine
Of a toilet behind boxes of coarse green vegetables and long white radishes.
I have badgered half-asleep children along backstreets at night, carrying
Whom I could to my van. I have stumbled with them sleeping in my arms

Up concrete steps on winter nights after eating in Greek restaurants,
Counting each body, then slamming the door of my van and taking
My own body, the last of my tasks, to a cold bed free of arguments.
I have lived in the extreme latitudes of child rearing, the blizzard
Of the temper tantrum and my own not always wise or honourable response,
The midnight sun of the child calling for attention late at night,
And have longed for the white courtyards and mediterranean calm of
    middle age.
Now these small bodies are becoming civilised people claiming they are not
Ashamed of a parent's overgrown garden and unpainted ceilings
Which a new arrival, with an infant's forthrightness, complains are "old".
And the father of this tribe sleeps in a bed which is warm with arguments.
Their bones elongate and put on weight and they draw away into space.
Their faces lengthen with responsibility and their own concerns.
I could clutch as they recede and fret for the push of miniature persons.
And claim them as children of my flesh – but my own body is where I must
    live.

The Golden Wall *(from* Spring Forest*)*

Don't ask Uncle Pat why the night sky is dark –
in hot weather
taking his mattress out on the grass
inside his dog-proof fence to sleep.
When Pat lifts his face up to the night –
propped on a pillow
of kapok stuffed in mattress ticking –
he'd fix you with sheep drench if you told him
that his line of sight
should intersect at every point
with a near or distant star
glimmering in the transparency of space
so the whole sky
should be ablaze from end to end like "a golden wall".
Pat's golden wall was his orange tree.
Like Uncle Pat it had never borne fruit
until I dumped five tons of chicken manure on its roots.
His line of sight
from the cane lounge where he sprawled
intersected at every point with oranges
twenty feet up in the sky,
a Utopia of fruit
which the district came to visit and eat,

oranges with no ending
like the return veranda
around the four sides of his house
where nephews and nieces ran forever
and their children after them.

Pat forgot his promise to pay for the manure
and the oranges didn't come back.
But he didn't miss them,
so don't ask Pat why the night sky is dark.

Olbers' riddle has hung around
for centuries.
You can't explain it by absorption.
Gas and dust heat up and glow.
Nor by absences or voids.
Every square inch has its galaxies.

Ask the cells inside your head
the same riddle,
why don't they all blaze at once
a golden wall of noise,
each neuron singing its own note
deafening your mind with light.
Political and religious visionaries
promise us this,
every cell singing in unison,
a mass of indistinguishable stars.

But something in the universe denies
the golden wall,
some structure which became Uncle Pat
calling to his nephews from his cane lounge,
"Now don't trample them tomahawk plants!"
(meaning hollyhock plants).

Pat prefers his own company on hot nights
leaving Auntie Bridge inside
with pictures of saints on the bedroom wall.
He takes his bedding
and lies in a darkness
where each star can broadcast as a soloist.

The universe
is a composition of unique bodies
on display,

and the night sky of the mind
allows a single file of thoughts
to light up as a sentence.

The Animals *(from* Spring Forest*)*

A "domesticated bearded dragon $400"
is not my idea of an animal companion.
A calf asleep on a double bed, perhaps,
or a hare with long ears
crouched under a mahogany sideboard,
thumping the floor.
Or a koala that climbed up a four-poster bed
surprising a seventeen-year-old in her nightie.

They were here before us – the animals –
and we were once them.
Without understanding we watched the sunrise
and the coming of night,
registered the changing of seasons
and dew on leaves that brushed our flanks.
We, the animals,
knew feelings, had a memory,
exchanged sounds and visual cues,
but did not know
what came before
or ask what was to come.

A neighbour sleeps with a wombat in her bed,
and her husband sleeps on the veranda.
Kangaroos watch TV through her sitting room window.

Bottle-fed joeys get osteoporosis
if the composition of the milk isn't right.
The females make better companions.
With shy brown eyes
they hop along beside you
as you collect mail from the gate at dusk.

We were once them,
and now are their custodians.
They know we are different
and their eyes tell us to keep our promise.

Bill came home after a fortnight away.
Pot plants had been kicked off the veranda,

there was an awful smell,
and the front door was ajar.
Inside the house
chairs were overturned,
papers and cushions trampled on floors,
and in the bathroom,
wedged against the washbasin,
her putrid flesh held together by hide,
Twinkle, a pony.
A tractor winched the body out.

Father and Sons

I

He's been away for a week,
so I telephone.
"Dad, your voice is too loud."

II

Two weeks with my sister-in-law
and her ordered parenting:
my boys are like polished silver.

III

As I wash his dirty feet in the bath
his toes curl coquettishly.

IV

The cap still on the lens
he points his new red telescope.
"I can see the craters on the moon!"

V

Between courses my two boys
leave the Peking Inn
for a yoyo break.

VI

Hiding in a distant room
crying under a bed
sobbing to himself in gasps
I can't see him in the twilight.
"I was cleaning the car as he said,
but he kept on at me, finding fault.

It's always like this.
He doesn't want to pay me the money."

VII
Your flight aims toward Delhi at midnight.
Brown eyes gaze up, his arms reach up
and draw me down, planting a chaste kiss on my lips.
Then he says: "And good night mum, wherever you are."

Next morning
taking his school bags from my car
face blank as a wall, he doesn't say goodbye.

VIII
"There are eighty seven different vegetables in this shop
and you'll eat only three.
How boring to be your father."

IX
Looking for a poem to read
at school assembly,
my ten year old packs in his school bag
Frank O'Hara's "Lunch Poems".

X
"Good night, Mr Bubby," I say.
"Bubby," he says
testing the word doubtfully – a pet name or an insult.
Years later, aged 14, he still wants to be tucked up
and a good night kiss.
He smiles: "Good night, Mr Lovely One."
"That's what I was just about to say," I say.

XI
The teenager's unblinking gaze: "Dad,
you're too kind to be any good as a lawyer."

XII
I pick up a beetle struggling in illuminated water
and launch it at some bushes.
Both taller than me now, we swim at night
in the blue glass mosaic pool
(affordable only at the end of their childhood –

inhabited by childish shouts and screams
for just two or three summers).
The heater's on and steam rises from the surface.
As we swim lengths
the underwater pool light refracts through wobbling liquid
and a ghost light bobs in distant eucalypts.
I stand at the shallow end
watching a large aircraft fly over, red lights blinking,
as young baritone voices
call out my given name.

Self Portrait at 62

Aged 62, I like what I do.
Minus a prostate, I have erectile dysfunction,
but we make love in our way, and still with fervour
within my altered body map.

I lunch outdoors at a Buddhist restaurant
with three of my children
between the white pendulous flowers of a datura
and a giant ginger plant.
Lucy, to show she's in recovery,
closes her eyes and touches the tip of her nose
with her index finger.
Her elder brother does the same.
They laugh and explain –
if you have MS, you're OK
if your finger can locate your nose.

It changes your consciousness,
he says at another lunch,
eating gado gado with chopsticks,
and sometimes you remember a time before MS.

Aged 62, I like what I do
and remember an earlier body map.

A young person has left a message on my voice mail.
"I have an insoluble problem," she says,
"with untaxed profits in a unit trust,
and if you could call me, I'd be oh so grateful."

A young person has donated the body I inhabit.
Its shins tend to flake,
so I rub in a white medicinal cream.

It makes the skin supple and smooth
and pleasantly fragrant.

My body sits in an office tower (one of a pair).
The twin towers overlook a geometrical garden
with a family of three bronze wombats
through which I walk
to lunch at the Buddhist restaurant.

The eyes of my body peer at a screen,
a diagram of forty or so companies,
connected by coloured arrows and dotted lines.
My fountain pen leaves red ticks on a sheet
where the companies are sorted by class
then stops at a name
I can't classify.

I am married to beautiful, argumentative you.
You say, "When I'm talking about me,
how do you always change the subject to you?"

I'm completing a survey for prostate cancer survivors.
"Do you have feelings of worthlessness?" I circle "Never".
"Do you feel positive?" I circle "Always".

My son Harry, six foot one,
has a gentle manner.
We drive in each morning,
have coffee in the travertine foyer of the twin towers
and he walks to school.
He dismisses the applied sciences
at some traffic lights.
I brace myself, unsure where this leads.
"Electron clouds interest me. Air pollution doesn't."

Now we come to the day of this self portrait,
an ordinary day when no one dies or falls in love,
aged 62, a few days south of 63.
I forget to say good-bye to the dog.
(Your job is to make his breakfast,
my job is to play –
sometimes I lie on the grass
my hands shielding my face from his tongue.)
After squeezing orange juices for three
my sixteen year old and I
are strapping ourselves in.

The garage door rolls up.

We drive through refrigerated stillness,
early, to beat the traffic,
not for the poetry of empty streets,
blue mornings and a white winter sun.
He abstains from catching the train with friends.
Perhaps because he's my youngest
"estremo unico fior" – but for my child
I hope the cold earth is a distant prospect.

I order two cappuccinos in the travertine foyer.
"He's your son?" they ask.
"My fifth and last child."
"He must be spoilt."
Not so, I say inwardly.
He's the last of siblings
who've grown up and left,
ignoring his hey wait for me.

I unlock the glass door of my office
and am hemmed in by pale wood and papers.
My window doesn't look out on the geometrical garden.
Switching on my computer
I look down at three freeways, some hotels,
a construction site for a cross-city tunnel
as mechanical shovels empty earth
into waiting trucks.
The cars are army ants that do not stop
until one detaches from the flow
and hesitates
where a freeway splits in two.
Indicator flashing,
it creeps across a white hatched dividing strip,
locates the missed route and speeds up.

I answer phone calls and emails.
Eight levels above the construction site I hear
a jackhammer faintly tapping,
almost inaudible through plate glass.

Mid-morning there's a panic. By tonight
I am to write a fifteen page opinion
on a fictional gain
that would stop a large transaction.

I assemble my thoughts.
I look across at a slowly moving cloudscape,
university towers on the rim of our planet,
aircraft tilted upwards, gaining height.
I search my hard drive for text that I can paste.
After two hours
I've little to show, a few unimpressive sentences.

So I lunch by myself in a deli –
antipasto and salad leaves.

Mid-afternoon my edifice of words
is taking shape on screen.
My opinion balances hope and risk,
and with a flip of logic
eliminates doubt.
Below my window
a screw drill suspended from a crane
withdraws from the hole it has bored,
swings free with a reverse twist,
cascading dirt.

I hardly notice, as the day declines,
the flashing orange lights of mechanical shovels
moving about in compacted mud,
the cold earth, an approaching prospect.
I'm absorbed in formatting
the analysis of facts,
the cadences of reassurance.
The pages compose themselves on my screen,
the cursor lifts and re-arranges text.

At twilight, land and sky
are a pool of luminous indigo-violet,
my office and image, brightly lit,
suspended on the glass.
The red tail lights of the army ants head west.
I speak to you on the phone.
After 23 years your voice still thrills me –
Aphrodite or Pallas Athene or both?

Outside it's gone black, there's no construction site,
just a void,
as my two fingers tap into the night.
The people who were waiting for my opinion
have gone home.

Finally I type
yours sincerely, my name, Tax Counsel.
It's marked draft, more refinements are needed,
and I push the send button.

There's a distant alarm.
I consider the fire stair while I wait.
The lift arrives.
Crossing the deserted travertine foyer,
I pass abandoned coffee machines.
The alarm is ringing loudly, intensely.
Some one must have breached a security door.
In the car park my ignition key starts the motor
and sound system – Pandolfi Mealli's "La Stella".

There's a fire engine outside the building,
its lights blinking lazily red, white and blue.
I swing across oncoming headlights,
head up a lane, turn left for home.
Poetry is incidental.
I am my poem.

JAN OWEN 1940–

Jan Owen (née Sincock) went to school in Adelaide and Melbourne, and first worked as a laboratory assistant. She studied Arts part-time at the University of Adelaide, obtaining her master's degree in 1974. While a librarian, she began writing poetry, in her thirties, and since 1985 has been a creative writing teacher and editor, basing herself in Adelaide. "The Visitation" has been significantly revised since it was first anthologised. Her poetry shows an ability to compress disparate experiences and thoughts into a convincing formal arrangement.

The Visitation

No angel has descended here;
only the woman's shining hair
shows feather-soft beneath the wings
of a white starched cap whose ribbon clings,
looped in a Moebius strip of faith,
transparently against black cloth.

She's leaning right so we centre on
the outstretched arms of her first-born –
the solid hands of the two-year-old
are flat on hers in the pat-a-cake hold.

It's a medical photograph without
the faces of the mother and child blocked out.
We guess from her bewildered eyes
before we read and realise –
Six-fingered dwarfism: Amish boy
with Ellis-van Creveld syndrome. Why

this should be, his mother's ceased to ask;
but takes this witness as her task,
shuts the Book, fastens her cap,
lifts the baby onto her lap.

A certain beauty lights them both –
this trust unveiling all the truth
hallows them brightly as any Raphael
Madonna and Child. Sad and still,

her look pierces the quick of now;
his searches stolidly past as though
half sizing-up all that's to come.

So steadily they stare down time.

Blue Bowl

This pedestal bowl against the light
shows a leftward tilt,
a yen toward some philosophy
other than fruit.
The obtuse angle makes me think
of a certain man:
what that cocked head had on its mind
was Kierkegaard not Zen.
I admire asymmetry luckily
but balance too.
So did my doctor when we were young,
lowering his stethoscope
with a little frown
then deftly tilting my left nipple back
to match its mate.
A purely aesthetic gesture
like my picking lint off his coat.
I remember we used to laugh a lot
at next to nothing.
Later I heard his marriage fell apart

and thought of that year
when we both felt
regular check-ups advisable.
Was it training or natural bent
that helped him keep things straight?

Left

Maybe coming late from the womb
I stayed out of sync
between is and was,
watching the ants or the clouds too long,
seeing things from behind,
tender and strange.
Days like provincial towns
with every gallery just on closing time
and the crowd streaming by
the other way.
Or the only open one
is an archaeology museum
and very quiet.
I stare alone at spearheads
and stone axes marching back
to the twenty-fifth millennium BC
with a firm declaration of war.
Four rooms ahead
the guided tour has sighted Ur.
Back here, some bungling guard
has bolted the intervening door.
I'm left in the Palaeolithic,
trying to dream up fire.

Our Lady, Notre Dame, Paris

She was sitting one row in front, to my right,
oddly angular in a bright red dress.

In that ornate half-dark, stained shards
of lucent rose, azure, emerald, and gold,

melted down through the air
and over the heads and tiles like angels' blood.

She was weeping silently, eyes fixed on the altar:
not crying, weeping, that slower, fuller grief

as river is to rain. And rivulets were coursing down
through her thick and careful make-up

so the close-shaved stubble showed
like tiny wounds. Or splinters of wood.

One way to bear your cross. If the soul descends
from truth, it is male and female, turn and turn about,

with all its disguises and dishevelments
so lightly worn it is the world you had

before your face was born.
She blew her nose and stood with us and sang:

the organ notes and colours streaming down
were throw-backs to the muted light,

paths diverging to rejoin. I followed him out
thinking to say *Très chic, Madame*,

(while meaning brave) but lost her in the crowd
and sat down on the low brick wall

fifteen metres from the portico
by a crisp little hedge just in front

of a cobble-stone carved MARGUERITTE.
I've no idea why or who. For whom.

GEOFF PAGE 1940–

Geoff Page was born in Grafton, New South Wales, and grew up in that district at a cattle station on the Clarence River. The family has a long rural and political tradition. His grandfather, Sir Earle Page, was the leader of the Country Party (renamed the National Party) and was briefly Prime Minister. Page, unlike his three brothers, did not remain on the land, and has been an active Labor Party supporter. He has published eighteen collections of poetry, two novels, four verse novels, anthologies, translations and a biography of the jazz musician Bernie McGann. From 1974 until his retirement at the end of 2001, he was in charge of the English Department at Narrabundah College in the Australian Capital Territory. He has lived in Canberra since the 1960s, organising poetry readings there and writing occasional articles for the national capital's newspaper.

Although sometimes rising to vehemence, as in "Grand Remonstrance", the voice in Page's poetry is generally dry and low-key. There is a great cumulative sense of his own world. He is principally concerned with wastage: lost potential, lost opportunity are the basic themes of his work. There is a consistent decency and understatement and an imaginative range of sympathies in his work, which is most impressive in its totality. Having mastered the stringencies of William Carlos Williams's language, his poetry has gone on to become more discursive, and recently he has written rhymed and metred poetry, usually light in nature. Rather than present a bare image, as in his early poem "Bondi Afternoon 1915", many of his later poems explain and comment, and in some he has become a social critic. In "Comparisons" the barbaric practice of sending six-year-olds to boarding school is compared, but not equated, with the barbarism of taking Aboriginal two-year-olds from their mothers.("Globites" in this poem refers to a fibreboard suitcase for school children.)

His cast of observed characters is wide: women and the old, soldiers, Aborigines, suburbanites, small farmers. In poems such as "Cassandra Paddocks", "Grit" and "My Mother's God" Page evokes a traditional Australia, which he has rejected personally, but regards with an ambivalent fondness, a critical nostalgia. "The Sky" affirms his acceptance of the world he has chosen.

Bondi Afternoon 1915

Elioth Gruner

The wind plays through
the painted weather.

No cloud. The sea
and air, one blue.

A hemisphere
away from gunfire

an artist finds
his image for the year:

a girl in white
blown muslin, walking

in the last
clear afternoon.

Inscription at Villers-Bretonneux

The dead at Villers-Bretonneux
rise gently on a slope towards
the sky. The land is trim – skylines

of ploughed earth and steeples; unfallen
rain still hanging in the air;
confusion smoothed away

and everything put back – the village
too (red brick/white sills) in nineteen
twenty, unchanged since. Headstones

speak a dry consensus. Just one
breaks free: "Lives Lost, Hearts Broken –

And For What?". I think of the woman

and those she saddened by insisting –
the Melbourne clerk
who must have let it through.

Cassandra Paddocks

He was a reader, the great-niece says
waving a hand over tea and scones
cancelling a dozen outer paddocks
and bringing out like heirloom silver
components of a life between the lines:
the delicate mother who insisted
on Oxford for the eldest – and lost
the rest before the age of two;
the classical Tripos – the governess
began it … a smattering of myth,
nothing much else on these upper reaches,
curly haired gods the only suitors
and a classical slant to the gums.
After the young sea voyage, quiet towers,
leather shelves and well-honed conversation
he rode the paddocks differently
and left things to a string of overseers.
Stockmen held back from the distance
in his eyes, different, even deeper, than their own.
Named the paddocks Cassandra, Agamemnon,
the great-niece recalls with a laugh;
made all the wrong decisions –
instead of cattle, sheep (which went
to tallow and would not wait for wool).
But books were different.
Had them sent by the crate-load,
clipper, coastal steamer, a final
team of bullocks; the ritual
delving from straw; then open to the nose,
inhaling – a draught of laudanum.
As cedar shelves filled tight
a rim of paddocks fell to neighbours;
the perimeter tightened on the homestead
where slewing gutters and flaky paint
waited a better season.

Wresting himself from leathered air
he'd sometimes take a horse, ruminate
sales, inspect diminishing outposts,
peopling as he rode, fern gullies
with dryads and bacchantes, hearing
in a sudden rush of hooves the flight
of centaurs and in the whipbird's call
the opening note of Pan.
Ambling beside a swayback fence
he'd dream instead down his agent's list –
one book implied at least another two.
Odd trips down to Sydney to the Club
brought in the usual disappointments –
the climate, it seemed, engendered only
saleyard talk and backroom manoeuvre in railways.
Could've lost the lot, you know,
only he died first. His descendant takes
more from the uncle, riding up
after the telegram to set things straight
and hold the borders, the man who stalks
through an absence of maids
to the only real room in the house
and stops, unsettled by something
he'd never wish words to,
a wavering – in the lotus scent of leather,
before the old imperatives
could break in again to save him.

Grit

A doxology

I praise the country women
of my mother's generation
who bred, brought up and boasted
six Australians each –
the nearest doctor fifty miles
on a road cut off by flood;
the women who by wordless men
were courted away from typewriters
and taught themselves to drive –
I praise their style
in the gravel corners.

I praise the snakes they broke in two
and the switch of wire they kept in a cupboard.
I praise what they keep and what they lose –
the long road in to the abattoirs,
the stare which cures
a stockman of shooting swans.
I praise the prints, the wide straw brims
they wore out to the clothes line;
I praise each oily crow that watched them.
I praise the tilting weather –
the dry creeks and the steady floods
and the few good weeks between.
I praise each column in the ledger
they kept up late by mosquito and lamp-light;
the temerity of the banker
reining them in at last – or trying;
the machinations for chequered paddocks
swung on the children's names;
the companies just one step ahead;
the tax clerk, in his way, also.
I praise each one of their six children
discovering in turn
the river in its tempers
the rapids and the river trees;
the children who grew up to horse sweat
and those who made it to the city.
I praise the stringy maxims
that served instead of prayers;
also the day that each child found
a slogan not enough,
surprising themselves in a camera flash
and bringing no extra paddocks.
I praise the boast of country women:
they could have been a wife
to any of a dozen men
and damn well made it work.
I praise what I have seen
to be much more than this.
I praise their politics of leather;
the ideologies in a line of cattle;
the minds that would not
stoop to whisky.

I praise their scorn
for the city of options, the scholars
in their turning chairs and air-conditioned theories.
I praise also that moment
when they headed off in tears –
the car in a tool shed failing to start,
a bootful of fencing wire.
I praise the forty years
when they did not. I praise
each day and evening of their lives –
that hard abundance year by year
mapped in a single word.

Grand Remonstrance

So much she never
could abide

so much always
to resent

the sulkiness
of mother's teats

the boy next door
astride her scooter

a teacher's random
sudden justice

the tardy flowering
of her breasts

the unfair cycles
of the moon

the owlish eye
of Mr Sims

over her shoulder
as she typed

the gossip that stopped
as she drew near it

the vague delays
of a fiancé

leaning on
the town's opinion

the wedding with relatives
thrice-removed

the uninvited
winsome babies

the hardwon 13-
carat ring

the three-day honey-
moon and then

suddenly
her own two children

the martyrdom
of 3 a.m.

the thoughtless toys
and dirty curtains

smears across
the morning light

the silences
that each child kept

seeking to
outlast her own

the son who sideslipped
out of school

the daughter year
by year resuming

her mother's skin
the husband too

his daily leavepass
to the world

the false compliance
of his slippers

and then the last
two years in bed

unvisited
and fingering

the soiled card-index
in her head

of grievance going
decades back

to taunts and snubs
in corridors

snideness in
the vivid playground

and so to a slab
of immaculate granite

the lengthening rancour
of the grave

six feet down
and now at last

the stunning
equity of death.

My Mother's God

My mother's God
has written the best
of the protestant proverbs:

you make the bed
you lie in it;
God helps him

who helps himself.
He tends to shy away from churches,
is more to be found in

phone calls to daughters
or rain clouds over rusty grass.
The Catholics

have got him wrong entirely:
too much waving the arms about,
the incense and caftan, that rainbow light.

He's leaner than that,
lean as a pair of
grocer's scales,

hard as a hammer at cattle sales
the third and final
time of asking.

His face is most clear
in a scrubbed wooden table
or deep in the shine of a

laminex bench.
He's also observed at weddings and funerals
by strict invitation, not knowing quite

which side to sit on.
His second book, my mother says,
is often now too well received;

the first is where the centre is,
tooth for claw and eye for tooth
whoever tried the other cheek?

Well, Christ maybe,
but that's another story.
God, like her, by dint of coursework

has a further degree in predestination.
Immortal, omniscient, no doubt of that,
he nevertheless keeps regular hours

and wipes his feet clean on the mat,
is not to be seen at three in the morning.
His portrait done in a vigorous charcoal

is fixed on the inner
curve of her forehead.
Omnipotent there

in broad black strokes
he does not move.
It is not easy, she'd confess,

to be my mother's God.

The Sky

"All poetry," says Ashbery,
"is basically about the weather."
And paying for a view at last

I find that I agree.
I like to watch it blowing in,
the stateliness of clouds through glass.

I like to see the shift of showers
sideways through the postcodes,

the way they bump against the hills.

Connoisseur of mountain haze,
I watch the blues of smoke or mist
out there on the ranges.

Also the indigos of dusk,
the violets dropping off the spectrum,
the streetlights coming on.

Some people like to feel the soil
dissolve between their fingers,
the flowers it might,

with care, supply.
My balcony's low maintenance.
I cultivate the sky.

Comparisons

Six-year-olds at boarding school
will be a ready measure,
children of the western gentry
too far out to go –
or mother *done a bunk.*
Three times each year
they'd be bussed home
and then come back in tears.
At sixteen I had charge of three:
Wake them at eleven;
get them up to pee,
Point them at the toilet bowl
their height had just achieved.
How did one get used to it,
that dazedness in their faces?
Today you'd think it medication
but this was separation only,
whisked away from all they knew:
pony or a kelpie dog,
a mother too much sloshed to care,
a creek that spooled its way through trees,
some special rocks beyond the hill,
worlds that we had left as well,
our Globites on the tops of buses
and pockets full of reasons.

But we were ten years further on
which somehow made the difference.
At six they had no sense of time
except that each day smelled the same –
lino in the corridors,
concrete in the changeroom.
The bus back home in sixteen weeks
could hardly be imagined.
But this was white and middle class.
If things got really bad sometimes
they'd let you use the phone.
Later on I'd learn of others
trucked off at the age of two
from shacks of hammered
tin and cornbags,
the howling of their mothers,
hauled away to what would prove
a school with no bus home.

ANDREW TAYLOR 1940–

Andrew Taylor was born in Warrnambool, Victoria, and educated at the University of Melbourne, from which he holds the degree of Doctor of Letters. He has taught literature and creative writing at universities in Melbourne, Adelaide, Perth, Shanghai and Tübingen (Germany). In 1992 he was appointed Foundation Professor of English at Edith Cowan University in Perth, Western Australia, where he is now Professor Emeritus. In 1999 he was a By-Fellow of Churchill College, Cambridge (UK), and in 2006 Visiting Professor at the Shanghai University for Science and Technology. He was co-founder, with Ian Reid and Richard Tipping, of Friendly Street Poets in Adelaide in 1975 and has chaired the Writers' Week of the Adelaide Festival of the Arts, and in 1985 became the inaugural chair of Australia's first Writers' Centre. He is a keen kayaker, and divides his time between Perth and Wiesbaden in Germany. Taylor has published more than sixteen books of poetry, and a bilingual collection of poems by four German and Austrian women writers, translated in collaboration with Beate Josephi, his wife. He has also written two opera libretti and the critical study *Reading Australian Poetry*. His output is various, ranging from poems in a confessional mode to a minimalist surrealism. Travel in foreign countries is a recurring theme. The poems selected here were written early in his career and show playfulness and imaginative wit.

The Nocturne in the Corner Phonebox

Someone is playing a trombone
in the telephone box outside my room.
It's 1 a.m.,

and he's removed the globe.
He's playing a melancholy cadenza
probably over the S.T.D.
to his girl in Sydney.

I can imagine ...
she's curled to the telephone
listening to that impossible music
a smile curving her face.
I wonder if he has enough change
for all those extensions.
Could he reverse the charge?

Somebody called Hugh Adamson
blares out a nocturne in a phone box.
His father's old and dying,
his mother's dead, his girl's away,
he's very sad, his nocturne's very sad,
his trombone blares and flares and says
"He's very sad, yair yair, he's very sad".

Maybe he's only playing to a friend
in East St Kilda.
Maybe he hasn't any change.
Someone is playing a trombone – impossible –
in the phone box with the door shut.
I've no idea who he is. I'm waiting
for my phone to ring. I like this music.

Developing a Wife

In the one cool room in the house
he held her face two inches under the water
rocking it ever so gently
ever so gently. Her smile
of two hours earlier came back to him
dimly at first through the water, then with more
boldness and more clarity.
The world is too much with us
on a hot day (he thought); better
this kind of drowning into a new degree,
a fraction of a second infinitely
protracted into purity. Her smile
free now of chemical and the perverse
alchemy of heat dust and destroying wind

free from the irritation, the tears
and the anger that had finally driven him
down to this moment,
was perfect, was
irreversible, a new reality.
Is it, he thought, that there is truth
here which she imperfectly embodies?
Or is it I that I'm developing here –
my dream, my vision of her,
my sleight of hand?
Perhaps, he thought, our marriage is like this? –
flimsy, unreal, but in its own way real:
a moment, a perfection glimpsed, then gone, gone utterly,
yet caught all the same, our axis, stationary,
the other side of drowning?
He bore
her smile out in the heat to her, as a gift.

Slide Night

I

Examine my window carefully:
it is covered with grass – thrown up
by the mower and stuck because it was
even at 3.30 yesterday
still wet with dew. It's going brown.
Some insect has laid twelve rows
of eggs, fragment of a giant
thumbprint – nature's – in a corner.
It's dirty, and paint spatters it
from a bad paint job. Moths crawling.

II

Put it under the microscope.
Do you see the man, head full
of grass, moth eggs, paint,
sitting at a desk? See insects
clamber through his eyes, ferret his ears
for light, twaddle his page?
Stamped in one corner, Certified
Fit To Rage? A host of caterpillars
populate and perish out of that script?

III
Or flash it on a screen (memories
of the Uffizzi and/or was it Utrecht?)
a meadow scholar, flowery page be-sprent,
or a firm burgher, pastoralised.
In one corner the museum stamp,
inscrutable as a postmark from Taiwan.

IV
From here, inside, it's largely black
– because it's night – and that's where you are,
all of you: in the dark! Moths,
heads ablaze, patrol my image
my giant ghost on the glass,
merino bodies quiver at my eye.
Larger than the huntsman I am the sky.
My galloping fingers sweep the universe. No stars.
Moths instead, heads flaming as Betelgeuse.

V
Switch out the show. It's time to sleep. To sleep.
My head expands to the brilliance of a quasar,
space swallows my wavelength, hour after hour.

NIGEL ROBERTS 1941–

Originally a New Zealander, Nigel Roberts came in his early twenties to Australia where he has now lived for most of his life. He has been a teacher of art in high school, was the main instigator of the annual Balmain Poetry and Prose Readings, and has edited a roneo-ed underground magazine *free poetry*. Roberts commented in a note to his third volume of poetry, *Déjà vu tours* (1995): "I began writing 30 years ago because I needed a tool to examine my life & while I was at it the lives of others". In his books he interpolates graphics, photographs and collages of advertisements (typically for psychic and New Age products) among his poems. Roberts has a small output. Much of his poetry is satirical, but in his best poems satire is not an end in itself. His popular recitation piece "The Quote from Auden" can be seen as commenting on the politics of sexual relationships and bohemian group dynamics, but its revised ending makes clear (as reprinted in *Déjà vu tours*), this is a love poem. Michael Sharkey has described him as "a superb ventriloquist and mimic, and something else: Roberts conveys a melancholy, that many attempt but rarely achieve with such deftness."

The Quote from Auden

At the conclusion of breakfast –
in that space   moment   question
of the first cigarette
or the washing up
she relayed
the quote from Auden.

I faked
message received & understood
thinking it
offering
or, her inductive incidental
to the day and its work
– I knew only that
it was a quote from Auden.

Later
I found the *Norton Anthology*
open
where a hand
had underlined & annotated with
too true
the quote from Auden.

And again
later
in a brief drink at the pub
she, enthusiastically
told M & C
one of whom, I forget which
looked sharply at me
the quote from Auden.

Another round?
– my shout
and the bar had taken it up
Something,
was going down –
I knew its key, in
the quote from Auden.

2.

I talked of everything but
at the Bon Gout
to affirm Fuck
and deny
after-dinner screw –
unsuccessfully!
How could I
in a dozen words or a score
be briefed
to hold the floor, with
the quote from Auden?

As she showered –
the water slapped
a dactylic cadence
on her skin
the cadence of
the quote from Auden.

& somehow –
her, do this
do that
kiss me
bite
you're the best
on top
don't move
kept me there
waiting, for
the quote from Auden.

3.

From then
all speech   action   written word
in part or principle
deferred to
the quote from Auden.

On T-shirts –
the Quote from Auden.
From, one in The Doug Walters Stand
formerly known as "The Hill" –

to Michael Holding
after bowling three consecutive bumpers
at Redpath –
the Quote from Auden.
Joni Mitchell's next album
the Quote from Auden –
on Radio National, the News & Weather
followed by the Quote from Auden.

a most quotable quote
the Quote from Auden
every future kiss tainted with
the Quote from Auden
get the boot in first
the same applies with the Quote from Auden.

So, I was introduced
to her intent: –
to quit.
Sock it to me:
The Quote from Auden.

I have not
been true to love
or it true to me
goes hand
in glove with
The Quote from Auden

Come live with me
and be my love
and we shall
all the pleasures prove
is not
the Quote from Auden.

You played it for her
you can play it for me
play it Sam
play, The Quote from Auden.

Reward / For a Missing Deity

maybe / yr on sabbatical
maybe yr in the dunny / reading yr reviews
maybe yr in the Pacific/ on a Women's Weekly Cruise
& maybe
yr preparing a statement for the six o'clock news
that perhaps
you were trapped in a ski hut / by an avalanche
of Betty Hutton

maybe / yr a war criminal / farming in Chile
maybe yr tapping phones / of subscribers to Dial a Prayer
maybe yr breaking that record / buried alive
12 ft underground
maybe yr weeping / in Farmer's Lost & Found
or perhaps
yr taking an angel out to lunch

maybe / yr in conference
or hitting off from the Club House tee
maybe yr demanding / a fat personal appearance fee
maybe yr on strike / & wont accept / arbitration
maybe yr being impeached / for yr crook administration
or perhaps
yr competing / in a Twist Marathon / on Taiwan

maybe / yr doing / In Service Training
maybe yr delivering newspapers
to pay yr way through Uni
maybe yr doing / Pestilence & Famine / I
& Destruction II

maybe yr on safari / collecting / for a private zoo
or perhaps
you farted / & very quickly / left the room
maybe / yr a casualty / of future shock
maybe yr in the mountains / plotting revolution
& a second coming
maybe yr the phantom of the opera / alone in the box
maybe yr wanking over Japanese woodcuts
of geishas sucking cocks
or perhaps
yr being interviewed by Frost / Fantastic / or Hef.

maybe / yr establishing an alibi
maybe yr being / held / incommunicado
maybe yr holed up / in Chicago
with a contract on yr head
maybe yr loning it in Denver
in boxcars / boxcars boxcars

maybe you've been transferred to another branch
maybe yr in Paekakariki
maybe yr in Nimbin
maybe yr walking / nicotine desperate / up the road
& perhaps
yr going to be back in five minutes

But
& most probably i would think –
you were horribly scarred
in a laboratory accident / &
yr too sensitive / to
show yr face.

Art History

She & I
are briefly modest –
that is
we undress as if reserved, or
compliant to
some local protocol
of disinterest
by one, in one, that
one will bed.

I had come
yes, at invitation
to unwrap her
as a neat trim package
to accord & escalate
the response
to response

& ready
I turn
to see form explained
by Art History

by Caravaggio
by a light from a single source, that
rakes down her right
& the suspected attitude of her
tits, confirm.

&, I am left
hard, by this.
Renascent
a boy again
perving
a boy again
to the majas & madonnas
of the Prado & the Louvre
a boy again, to confuse
the sacred with the profane.

& so, by her now I affirm
& make this poem
believing
life & art
should frame
the genital response

more sex in art / more art in sex.

The Gulls' Flight

The gulls' flight
is low

flat
& hard

they go
to sea

to the edge / where
the day's fire
is lit

they go
as shiftworkers
to the dawn.

A Nigger & Some Poofters

The support act
at "The Club"
is a drag show –
Their silicone & outrageous
razzle dazzle of Tallulah
Judy, Marlene, Bette
& Mae
plays to the indifference
of the poker machines
& to
the dull & predictable wit
of the schools
thick & safe
at the bar.

The main act
is a circuit black
of such clubs
& talk shows –
He works & excites
the passing interest
of an obituary –
&, at the bar provokes
a renewed assault
of whose shout, until
the m.c. suggests
"Fair go for the nigger, or
we'll bring the poofters back"

& so it is,
they hold it down
at the bar
& give the nigger
a fair go;
until a handful begins
to bark a preference
for bringing
the poofters back.

The House Special

Bellino, of Dynek International
has ordered a Whisky Sour
so, I punt on a Banana Daiquiri,
The House Special.

That's a fag's drink, declares
Bellino, as he moves
to check out a chick, with whom
he's established some eye contact

A Gin & Tonic, Chuck
& I follow.

This is Nigel, from Australia;
Hello / Hi
but I don't catch her name, as Bellino
is hustling the conversation on
from the who are you
to the who she wants to be.

&, she is telling him of
her spotlight ambition
to be a singer, a variant of Roberta Flack
& in time, a piano bar, or
a small club, somewhere.

The sometime & somewhere schedule
sets Bellino's index pecking
at her left tit –
as he believes in Target Setting
Assertiveness & Self Maximization
to which, he puts his wallet
on the bar and asks her price on
ten Carnegie Hall tickets in a year's time
because, if she wants to
that's where she could be.

Well, the singer demurs, as
I fetch new drinks, & obviously
I miss something, for when I return
Bellino is stabbing at that breast again

I told you, I don't eat
garbage, & you
are feeding me garbage,
crap & garbage.

The way it goes
she says
Thanks, for the advice & drinks, but
I've got a vocal coach in the morning

Crap & garbage, says Bellino
who then pays his tab
& goes.

So.
I'm cut loose
in the Valley Bar & Grill, just
on closing.
One on the house? asks Chuck
what will it be?
& without hesitation, I say
a Banana Daiquiri.

One Banana Daiquiri
coming up, says
Chuck.

ROBERT ADAMSON 1943–

Robert Adamson grew up in Neutral Bay in Sydney and on the Hawkesbury River. He was educated at Crows Nest Technical College. His grandfather was a fisherman who introduced him to life on the Hawkesbury River where he now lives with his partner, the photographer, Juno Gemes. In his autobiography *Inside Out* (2004), Adamson relates that while still at school he read about birds and kept notebooks on them. He became obsessed with the rare *Ptilorus magnificus*, (the "magnificent riflebird") and decided to steal the live specimen in Taronga Park Zoo. He researched the bird's requirements, bought snakeskins to line a nest, stole three electric frypans that had thermostats to provide humidity, and after trial and error created a humid, subtropical atmosphere for the riflebird's cage in his pigeon coop. The finishing touches were white mice and mangoes for the bird's demanding diet. After midnight he climbed a fence into the zoo. His first attempt to steal the bird failed, but a second attempt a few days later succeeded and he was able to install the bird in its elaborately prepared home. A couple of weeks later, he retrieved an escaped kookaburra called "Jack" from a neighbour's yard. She reported him to the RSPCA and his theft of the riflebird was discovered. He spent two weeks in the Yasmar centre for boys under twelve, before being given a suspended sentence. This was the prelude to spending much of his adolescence in and out of boys' homes and prison, working as a pastrycook when free. Prison introduced Adamson to debating and literature, and he began writing poetry.

Adamson has published more than twenty books, including fifteen volumes of poetry. He was editor of the Poetry Society of Australia's magazine *New Poetry* from 1968 until 1982. With Juno Gemes and Michael Wilding, he founded Paperbark Press in 1986. He was a key figure in the "New Australian Poetry" movement, which looked towards contemporary American exemplars. He organised Australian reading tours for the American poets Robert Creeley and Robert Duncan. But, unlike some of his contemporaries, he was not overwhelmed by the exposure to American poetry and in his poems has continued to write from his personal experience and preoccupations, employing a unique, localised imagery. He eclectically sees the French Symbolists, C. J. Brennan, Hart Crane, Francis Webb and the late poems of James McAuley as part of his poetic inheritance.

Adamson is a regular contributor to the magazine *Fishing World*. While he is a full-time poet, Adamson's poetry is fed by a rich life he has outside his writing: this includes his interest in birds and fishing. He says: "I am lucky to have the actual Hawkesbury; I love it, it's beautiful, it is the world flowing through my life, full of birds, fish, mangroves, mud and stars. I'm fortunate enough to be able to live here because my grandfather gave me the river. And yet it's not the river I try to write, my poetry's landscape is darker. I am writing about the internalised landscape."

Adamson's work has become increasingly rigorous. Some of the poems selected here have small but significant revisions that occurred between his 2004 selected poems *Reading the River* and his 2008 selection *The Golden Bird*. In "The Goldfinches of Baghdad" the language has tightened and the reference to Saddam Hussein, identifying the poem with the Second Iraq War has been deleted, making the poem timeless, but without any loss of immediacy. The captured mulloway in "The Gathering Light", that was fifty years old for his 2004 selected, became twenty years old in 2008: the decision to make this revision must have been painful, as some of the power of the earlier version was the great age of the fish. But accuracy was more important. Much of the strength and eloquence of Adamson's work is its authorial sincerity.

5 (*from* Sonnets to be Written from Prison)

I brood in solitary, it's a way to flagellation: thinking
of my "day of release" – I shuffle friends like dates
on my calendar, marking them off at random.
Here's the world – the stewed tea I'm drinking
cold – how I suffer. When I walk through the front gates
into the country, what will I become?
I'll throw away the sufferer's comforting mask
and turn against my memories, leaving a trail of perdition
behind me. Children and women will fall to my simple
intuitive reactions – not even the New Journalists will ask
questions, nothing will be able to feed on
my actions and survive. My prison sonnets will be drugs
relieving pain: I have remembered helpless men
knocking their bars for hours with aluminium mugs –

My House

My mother lives in a house
where nobody has ever died

she surrounds herself and
her family with light

each time I go
home I feel she is
washing
and ironing the clothes of death

these clothes for work
and for going out
to the Club on Sunday
and for Jenny to take her baby
to the doctor in

death comes on the television
and mum laughs

saying there's death again
I must get those jeans taken up

My First Proper Girlfriend

The first girl I wanted to marry
was Joan Hunter
her father owned more oyster leases
than anyone else on the river

she had buck teeth
but she looked okay really

we'd sit on her father's wharf
and watch the mullet together for hours

they will take over the world one day

we loved each other alright

my parents hated us being together
and called her Bugs Bunny

One night my father cut Joan's dad
with a fishing knife
right down his left cheek

that little protestant bludger
with his stuck-up bitch of a daughter

The Gathering Light

Morning shines on the cowling of the Yamaha
locked onto the stern of the boat

spears of light shoot away
from the gun-metal grey enamel.
Now I wait for God to show
instead of calling him a liar.

I've just killed a mulloway –
it's eighty-five pounds, twenty years old –
the huge mauve-silver body trembles in the hull.

Time whistles round us, an invisible
flood tide that I let go
while I take in what I have done.
It wasn't a fight, I was drawn to this moment.
The physical world drains away
into a golden calm.

The sun is a hole in the sky, a porthole –
you can see turbulence out there,
the old wheeling colours and their dark forces –
but here on the surface of the river
where I cradle the great fish in my arms
and smell its pungent death, a peace
I've never known before – a luminous absence
of time, pain, sex, thought, of everything
but the light.

Father's Day

I cart home sugarbags of coke from the gasworks.
My hands smudge the cream-painted icebox. My father
throws spuds on the fire, sending sparks up the flue.

On the hill outside, trucks growl and strip their gears.
I imagine the peach-faced finches of Madagascar.
After tea, Dad slumps in his chair, tall brown bottles

standing empty on the table. At school each day I fail
my tests. My mother's face hardens when I try to speak.
She irons starch into my sister, from her straight black

hair to her school uniform's box-pleats. In the backyard
cuckoo chicks squawk from a magpie's nest. The hedge
man's finished clipping the hedges along our street.

My brothers bob down to do their homework, into
the learning stream, heading for their lives,
biting the heads off words.

Cornflowers

In memoriam Robert Harris

In a skiff, anchored
on the edge of a mangrove
swamp, he gave me

a version,
an unpolished song,
something that might have

gone unspoken
in our bright lives;
there is no dark side

he told me: things
will glow, sing or die though
if we want them to,

it's all alive,
I just want to know
who owns the conversation

we may have some day, who
owns the dialogue
he repeated as

a flathead slapped
and shuddered
in the belly of the boat,

its pale speckles
flaring, the blue
barred tail fanning air,

who owns the words
as they hovered
with plump mosquitos

and collided with
a whiting in flight
down a cadence of dancing

particles, our
hearts locked in their
cages of singing muscle;

it was concerning
this theme, he continued,

that I composed a tune

for the cornflowers
to sing, cut, sitting
on my table in an indigo jar.

The Goldfinches of Baghdad

These finches are kept in gold cages
or boxes covered with wire mesh,
they are used by the falcon trainers as lures,
and rich patriarchs choose these living ornaments
to sing to them on their death beds. Their song is pure
and melodious. A goldfinch with a slashed throat
was the subject of masterpiece painted in the
sixteenth century on the back of a highly
polished mother-of-pearl shell – it burns
tonight in Baghdad, along with the living
caged birds. Flesh and feathers, hands
and wings. Sirens wail, but the tongues
of poets and the beaks of goldfinches burn.
Those who cannot speak burn along with the
articulate – creatures oblivious to prayer burn,
along with those who lament to their god.
Falcons on the silver chains, the children
of the falcon trainer smother in the smoke
of burning feathers and human flesh.
We must sing or die, singing death
as our songs feed the flame.

A Visitation

All night, wildfire burned in the tree-tops
on the other side of the river. Now it's morning.
Smoking embers from the angophoras
are landing on the near shore
as a yellow-footed rock wallaby limps, dazed,
from the scrub, its fur matted,
its tail barely able to support its weight.
Although wounded, it seems miraculous:
the soft yellow of its feet, the hard, sharp black
of its claws. It's the first yellow-footer
I've seen for more than forty years. It takes
me back immediately to the time I was a kid,

rowing my grandfather's tallow-wood skiff across
Big Bay: I spotted a mob of four rock wallabies
that stood there as I sat silently in the boat
and let the tide carry me right by them.
One, I noticed, seemed to have mange –
it had mottled fur on its back – like the river foxes
in those days. Then a panic ran through
them: the largest buck bounded, almost flew,
straight up an enormous rock; the sheer wildness
and ferocity of it shocked me. Afterwards,
the atmosphere was thick with an odour unlike
anything I recognised. This morning, it's in the air
again. I turn to take another look, but the
rock wallaby's gone.

My Grandfather's Ice Pigeons

My grandfather would walk into the house,
on a summer evening after his work, then empty
his catch of mudcrabs into the bath-tub;
they'd flow out in a stream of ice-flurry from
his four-gallon drums, then settle in a heap of
black and olive speckled claws, spikey legs
and back flappers waving frantically. One night
my mother caught me holding a broom-stick
with an angry muddie's claw clamped around it.
She ordered me to stay away from the crabs
reminding me why Uncle Eric lost his finger,
besides they could snap a clothes prop in two.
My mother went back to the city. I stayed
a week and my grandmother showed me
what to do, first throw one into a bucket of ice
to slow it down, then bind the claws together
with kingfisher-blue twine in a slipknot.
Old Dutch would come to take them
to the Co-Op in his truck, packed in fish boxes
covered with ice. My grandfather would leave
again for his next catch, he'd take some pigeons
with him in a cage on his trawler. If he
had a good haul, he'd let one of the birds go,
when it came home it was my job to ride my bike
into town to order the ice. When I reached
the Co-Op, Dutch would ask how many pigeons?

If more than one, it was a box of ice a bird.
He'd send the ice to my grandfather next morning
on the mail boat. They talk about the time
Fa Fa got drunk up the river at Spencer,
the river postman saw him through the mist
one morning, balancing on net-boards at the stern
of his boat, singing aloud, throwing pigeons at the sky.

JOHN TRANTER 1943–

John Tranter lived his early years on a farm on the south coast of New South Wales. He studied at an agricultural college and the University of Sydney, and has worked in printing, publishing and as a radio producer. In the early 1970s, he edited a number of underground poetry magazines, and later an anthology, devoted to younger Australian poets whose work reflected American *avant-gardism*. Since then he has edited three further anthologies. He has published twenty volumes of poetry, and founded and edited the electronic magazine *Jacket*.

Important influences on Tranter's poetry have been the early T. S. Eliot, for the fragmentation and impersonality of style, and John Ashbery, recognisable in the *non sequiturs*, the self-deconstruction and the allusions to pop culture. Tranter has an alternative plain style, reminiscent of translations from Chinese poetry and the modern Greek poet Cavafy, in which he writes about disaffected middle-class urban lives or artists, well-known or imagined. Much of Tranter's subject matter is mediated through imagery from films. His poetry often has a polished, metallic surface, with references to electronics and high-tech. The last two poems we have used are a response to 19th century poets, including Charles Baudelaire. By adopting a Baudelairean tone, Tranter is able to achieve directness and simplicity.

Tranter is the most prominent of a group of "internationalist" Australian poets who emerged in the late 1960s and are oriented to the New York School. There has always been a tendency to narrative in his poetry, which has become more pronounced in his later work. Andrew Riemer described Tranter's volume of four long narrative poems *The Floor of Heaven* (1992) as: "a tour de force, a devious and profoundly subversive conjuring trick ... the book pulses with a curious resonance ... [and] reminded me irresistibly of the best moments in *Twin Peaks* ... a strange lyricism."

Sonnet 55: A Hard Art *(from* Crying in Early Infancy*)*

Waiting and waiting, there's an end to it.
Eating bad food, sleeping on the floor,
there's an end to that too. One day
your enemies reach out of your head quickly
and take you to the cold and dirty places,
and you're too old for that sort of thing.
The bad music keeps you there, and makes you cruel,
and you are the loved one you are least kind to.

Waiting and waiting for the good weather,
there's a hard art in that, and a sour man –
too old for that sort of punishment – does it badly.
But one day you wake up and go back home and if you're
tough and lucky you leave most of it behind.
Eating good food, accepting kindness – there's an art in that.

Glow-boys

Four a.m. At the reactor an alarm begins
howling. The core's full of shit: get out
the gloves, the phosphorescent rakes.

A burnt-out star hangs low on the horizon.
The Harrisburg glow-boys knuckle down
to work, poking around in the ashes.

They gaze out through glitter: behind the visor
putty imitates a human face, the lips
gritty, frayed, as they reach for speech

across the static field. Now a bell rings
and they wade thigh-deep into the muck,
their eyes the colour of lightning.

Five years of that and they're
too hot to touch; they wake screaming
before dawn, the pillow soaked.

What have they seen: their children's future
flare and crackle, a vast Christmas tree
flashing up from the skyline?

Rake it up, Ratshit! In a month
vacation in the Rockies, drinking rye and
blowing rattlesnakes away with a shotgun.

Now, like any cleaners, they go to work
deft and grumbling, their wives awake
in nylon nighties staring at the ceiling

and the glow of the luminous clock.
The pot of coffee popping on the stove.
The kids asleep, dreaming fitfully.

Lufthansa

Flying up a valley in the Alps where the rock
rushes past like a broken diorama

I'm struck by an acute feeling of precision –
the way the wing-tips flex, just a little
as the German crew adjust the tilt of the sky and
bank us all into a minor course correction
while the turbo-props gulp at the mist
with their old-fashioned thirsty thunder – or
you notice how the hostess, perfecting a smile
as she offers you a dozen drinks, enacts what is
almost a craft: Technical Drawing, for example,
a subject where desire and function, in the hands
of a Dürer, can force a thousand fine ink lines
to bite into the doubts of an epoch, spelling
Humanism. Those ice reefs repeat the motto
whispered by the snow-drifts on the north side
of the woods and model villages: the sun
has a favourite leaning, and the Nordic gloom
is a glow alcohol can fan into a flame.
And what is this truth that holds the grey
shaking metal whole while we believe in it?
The radar keeps its sweeping intermittent promises
speaking metaphysics on the phosphor screen;
our faith is sad and practical, and leads back
to our bodies, to the smile behind the drink
trolley and her white knuckles as the plane drops
a hundred feet. The sun slanting through a porthole
blitzes the ice-blocks in my glass of lemonade
and splinters light across the cabin ceiling.
No, two drinks – one for me, one for Katharina
sleeping somewhere – suddenly the Captain
lifts us up and over the final wall
explaining roads, a town, a distant lake
as a dictionary of shelter – sleeping
elsewhere, under a night sky growing bright with stars.

Crosstalk

The way you lie there, it's an opinion, those
bronze medal limbs, the sheets crumpled,
your body the site and centre of conspicuous
waste. It's a vote against the mob,
the way you flick the lamp out, thoughts
akimbo, and stare at the visual display.
Sleep, says the computer.

It sounds brilliant in the dark, at 2 a.m., that
breathing in stereo, so crisp, or rain
in the mesh grille of a microphone.
Is it recording a storm, or sound effects?
The machine listens to its own astrology. Who
left the screen on? That red, that luminescent
green, I must be sleepwalking. Toast,

ham and eggs for two, all on the video.
Does a wish flicker, like that?
Then you disappear leaving a faint ghost
and go to black, as the program dumps
a bracelet of digits in the outboard memory.
The printout spelling doom, do you carry it
with you through sleep, a gift, a poison?

And when you wake at sunrise, heavy breather,
golden in the light, will you be content?
Hush – the shower's whispering, breakfast is ready,
and two expensive German microphones wait for
breath, for movement, for the trace of your desire.

After Hölderlin

When I was a young man, a drink
often rescued me from the factory floor
or the office routine. I dreamed
in the mottled shade in many a beer garden
among a kindness of bees and breezes,
my lunch hour lengthening.

As the flowers plucked and set in the little bottle
on the table still seem to hanker for the sun,
nodding in the slightest draft, so I
longed for a library loose with rare volumes
or a movie theatre's satisfying gloom
where a little moon followed the usherette
up and down the blue carpeted stairs.

You characters caught up in your emotions
on the screen, how I wish you could know
how much I loved you; how I longed
to comfort the distraught heroine
or share a beer with the lonely hero.

I knew your anxieties, trapped
in a story that wouldn't let you live;
I felt for you when you were thrown from the car
again and again; when the pilot
thought he was lost and alone,
I was speaking the language of the stars
above his tiny plane,

murmuring in the sleepy garden, growing up
among the complicated stories.
These dreams were my teachers
and I learned the language of love
among the light and shadow
in the arms of the gods.

Under Tuscan Skies

In the calm of a Lyons' Tea Shop near Piccadilly
punctuated with rustling noises and clinkings,
Edward found himself looking back
on his time in Tuscany. He had seen it then
as "the life so short, the craft so long to learn",
in fact venomous to endure, those
horrible neighbours, but useful fodder
for his writing project, at the time, but now
in the British gloom it seemed fleeting and fruitless,
like the life of a white foam flake
amid a clashing of steel knives and hot looks –
why had he written it up in the form of little
poems, clotted with factitious insights? –
tissue-paper in a threshing machine – in fact,
he now prefers the incomplete circle of his drafts
to the blunt certainty of the finished book, as
the months of hope spent plotting his little holiday
were better than the awful actuality.
What had he written? Watery flashback –

The ancient Roman sun preserves the sky,
reserving his warmth to faithfulness,
shining upon the undismayed towers,
whose images enscrolled the situation.
Lucy, recently rebuffed, sat speaking her mind
to her frequent and attentive male companion,
to hew a passage to his understanding.

"He, the God of Love and Shopping
may not have been hurt by your bruising snub,
to Him it's just water off a cold shoulder,"
she murmured, nudging closer. Would
clutch come to seize? And seize
to feed a passion? Eager boys, she knew,
would be prostrate at her feet, if they could.

A conversation in the forest, the grove
that borders the municipal zoo:
Her sex makes a brief longing.
– Thank you, more of the same.
I went straight to the heart of the matter.
– My dear, gentlemen are different.
But these two ladies are as bright as possible.
– Then what are you made of?
The same stuff as parsons are, but
with a warmer blood in my body.

They were walking about like restless animals,
ursine, almost blasphemous in their excessive exercise.

In a deft aside Edward explained the meaning
of the landscape, I mean the Mediterranean.
It was satisfying to imagine those huge
geological forces striving for a million years
to provide a vista that perfectly illustrated
certain Romantic imaginings that gushed out of
the tail-pipe of the Industrial Revolution.

The scene: The arrival. *The action:* She knew.
Lucy rehearsed her emotions under Parnassus,
till the late hour caught in her throat.
I was a young fool! That fight with the driver!
Blunder, irretrievable, and so forth.
The clumsy dolt. Social gaffe. Red face.
Lucy, wincing, understanding everything.
Ow! He will never forgive me! Fuck it!

But why should she be upset? She's just a girl,
and one day as a lady she will sweep away
the wraiths that cloud the view, just as
a Viennese mind doctor with a gesture
calms a dog. But now, at muggy midnight,
she found herself alone on the road,

engraving her love malignantly upon a stone,
as a seething of hyacinths breathed
upon the hushed evening. So be it!
In the snows of recognition there is little warmth
and less life; better to guess and hesitate.
Now a storm yells and clambers over the horizon,
battering rain herds them into a shelter,
among the shadows comes forgiveness,
a prison of green centuries gladly huddled into.
Shuddering they reach out for
one another's mortifying spasms ...

I had read, Edward murmured to himself,
that the floods of love in their urgent spate
magnify a horoscope, and that the god of fate,
leaning on the sky, counts our chances
on enormous fingers – so let the storm cease:
now the world is soaked and glittering,
and the young lovers creep back to find
their place in it, among the clattering traffic
and the rattle of cups.

Columbo's Kangaroo

Detective Columbo is questioning a clever murderer
who is a magician in his day job, with his own
television show. Here we are in the back lot,
sun beating down, between the villain's
trailer and the waiting studio, a script in his hand. "Oh,
just one more thing, sir," says Columbo, preparing
a subtle query to slip in between the man's ribs
and drain the blood from his heart – 1976 –

and we notice, a hundred yards away, between
two hangar-like studio buildings, an actor
in a Roman Centurion costume, smoking
and talking to a friend, and beside him
a kangaroo on a lead looking around
then tentatively sniffing the ground.

Little Dog

There you are, your paws on my knees,
your head tilted to one side. You gaze at me
with that puzzled look, your eyes full of

loyalty and complicated queries.
That cat I chased yesterday, where is it?
Who is that stranger? What's that scent?
Can we go for a walk now, and explore
the paths that wind through the park by the bay?

Wise creature, you know where that bone
is buried, where the rats hide in their burrow
by the water, why the cat fears you.
You know many subtle facts, old friend,
except for one sad particular: how
brief a time we have left together.

CAROLINE CADDY 1944–

Caroline Caddy was born in Western Australia, where she has lived for most of her life, but she spent significant parts of her childhood in the USA and Japan. She has worked as a nurse in Road Dental Units throughout Western Australia and has lived on small properties on the south coast of Western Australia raising two children. She has published seven volumes of poetry and a selection with new poems *Esperance* (2007). Caddy is at her best when she can revel in complex detail. Geoff Page in his *A Reader's Guide to Contemporary Australian Poetry* (1995) warned that "the reader will find many poems deterringly dense and their meanings elusive, despite her capacity to bring things neatly back into focus at the end with a sharp and summary image". Page did not find her occasional opacity "wilful" but "an inevitable aspect of her angle to her subject matter". The exuberance of Caddy's often rococo imagery is matched by a sharp intelligence, as exemplified in the sober and surprising ending of "The Great Whales". Caddy's China poems, of which "Bamboo" is an example, are remarkable: a jumble of exquisite and outlandish images, flung on the page with a raw vitality, forcing the reader to experience them as Caddy herself did.

Study of a Squid

There is a point in the ganglia of a squid
where it might be said
                                        to approach a brain –
right between the eyes!
And it would take something more
                                                        to coordinate
the view from those guillotined planets
              ringed with the flash of lagoons.
Dead innocent/evil eye.
        The pure concentration of universe
at you.

Squid just looks its prey to death.
Centurion spear-helm –
octopus could be its innards.
On my kitchen sink now –
bled dragon's tail.
Stretch its mesenteric camouflage
and tiny freckles spread pale or bunch
into flames and cinders.
Scraped clean
it's the skull of a god of wisdom –
computer pod with a crotch of tentacles
that stick like miniscule new-borns.
Cut the sculpted tofu –
dollops of ink on stainless steel.
Pull a finger through and I'm writing
kana
with no effort at all
or understanding.
Sometimes they are found
stranded in shallows
by their fondness for moon-gazing.
I remember one summer night
a white glow out to sea ...
can there be a mirage at night –
antarctic inversion?
it was
a sea-market!
Boats of strung incandescence that lure
squads of them into the nets
finishing as vellum rockets
or this unusual pasta.
Thumb and finger grip
slides out the welded quill.
What organ queasy inside me
recognises this celluloid goose feather?
Every thing anticipates every thing.
I make a meal of soft compendiums.

The Great Whales

They open the bays of their mouths engulf
lagoons –

balloon like tidal bores to sieve
fiords through frayed trees
of baleen
or prowl suctioned depths
and let their food embrace them
long cobra-headed hoses
reeling back to leave
scars like moons.
We whistle tins into space
but they are the gravity kings
punching the coal face
reaming its tonnage.
We squeak into the vacuum
they muezzin whole oceans
life on the grand scale
engendering progeny the size of ships
with organs that could grace
a cathedral –
cylinders of sperm
that would not be lost
at a fuel depot.
Washed up or revealed under dunes
after winter storms
their bones are like the white gears
of unthinkable engines
or petrified logs
nosing out of a desert
of vanished redwoods.
Once we found their earwax priceless
as we now find
the idea of them –
revelling in our new relationship
closer than we imagine –
the entropy of the organic
favouring insects.

Bamboo

I watch labourers climb bamboo scaffolding
wearing bamboo
safety helmets
and hear bamboo cables going down

thousands of feet for brine
and natural gas flowing
through bamboo pipes
in another millennium.
Everything has seeded here
inherent evil   inherent good
reform by education
reform by the rod
cut down as fast as it grows
a generation so vigorous
you could believe
there is no such thing as death
only migration
and every soul that ever lived on earth
decamped   tenaciously alive
for China.
A scale that dissolves
our mightiest wars and greeds
leaves me feeling I am visiting
a trial planet and
end-product
like thinking you are unique
and headed somewhere
then discovering
that Jupiter
is heavily populated.

ROBERT GRAY 1945–

Robert Gray grew up on the north coast of New South Wales, where his father had been exiled from Sydney onto a banana plantation by his family, for drunkenness. Gray's mother brought him up as a fundamentalist Christian. He left school early to become a journalist and moved to Sydney when he was nineteen. Along with Robert Adamson, he is one of the few poets of his generation not to have attended university. After working in magazine publication and as an advertising copywriter, he was for many years a buyer for a bookshop. He has published eight individual volumes of poetry and an always revised series of *Selected Poems*. He has written a memoir, *The Land I Came Through Last* (2008), and edited the journals of the painter John Olsen, selections of the poetry of Shaw Neilson and Roland Robinson, and co-edited several anthologies of Australian poetry. He is an amateur painter who has travelled widely, "to see all the great paintings of the world", and has written reviews for Australian and overseas publications.

Flame and Dangling Wire

On a highway over the marshland.
Off to one side, the smoke of different fires in a row,
like fingers spread and dragged to smudge.
It is a rubbish dump, always burning.

Behind us, the city
driven like stakes into the earth.
A waterbird lifts above this swamp
as a turtle moves on the Galapagos shore.

We turn off down a gravel road,
approaching the dump. All the air wobbles
in a cheap mirror.
There is fog over the hot sun.

Now the distant buildings are stencilled in the smoke.
And we come to a landscape of tin cans,
of cars like skulls,
that is rolling in its sand dune shapes.

Amongst these vast grey plastic sheets of heat,
shadowy figures
who seem engaged in identifying the dead –
they are the attendants, in overalls and goggles,

forking over rubbish on the dampened fires.
A sour smoke
is hauled out everywhere,
thin, like rope. And there are others moving – scavengers.

As in hell the devils
might poke about through our souls, after scraps
of appetite
with which to stimulate themselves,

so these figures
seem to come wandering, in despondence, with an eternity
where they can find
some peculiar sensation.

We get out and move about also.
The smell is huge,
blasting the mouth dry:
the tons of rotten newspaper, and great cuds of cloth …

And standing where I see the mirage of the city
I realise I am in the future.

This is how it shall be after men have gone.
It will be made of things that worked.

A labourer hoists an unidentifiable mulch
on his fork, throws it in the flame:
something flaps
like the rag held up in "The Raft of the Medusa".

We approach another, through the smoke,
and for a moment he seems that demon with the long barge pole.
– It is a man, wiping his eyes.
Someone who worked here would have to weep,

and so we speak. The rims beneath his eyes are wet
as an oyster, and red.
Knowing all that he does about us,
how can he avoid a hatred of men?

Going on, I notice an old radio, that spills
its dangling wire –
and I realize that somewhere the voices it received
are still travelling,

skidding away, riddled, around the arc of the universe;
and with them, the horse-laughs, and the Chopin
which was the sound of the curtains lifting,
one time, to a coast of light.

Diptych

My mother told me she had often stayed awake
in those years, and of a certain night
at a rented farm,
on the end of the dark leaf-mulch of a drive,
where she sat in the doorway with mosquito-smoke,
listening for my father, after the pubs had closed, knowing he would have
    to walk
"miles, in his state", or sleep in weeds by the road,
if no one dropped him at our gate
(since long before this he had driven his own car off a mountain-side
and becoming legend had ridden
on the easily-felled banana palms
of a steep plantation, right to the foot and a kitchen door,
the car reared high, and slipping fast, on a vast
raft of sap-oozing fibre,
from which he'd climbed down, unharmed, his most soberly polite,

had doffed his hat
to the terrified
young woman, with a child in arms – who must have appeared
slowly as a photograph
developing in a dish – and had never driven again).
This other night my mother was reluctant to go out, poking with a stick
under the lantana, down every slope,
and leave us kids in the house asleep, a cough
trundled among us,
and fell asleep herself, clothed, on the unopened bed,
but leapt upright, sometime later, with the foulest taste – glimpsed
he was still not home – and rushed outside, gagging,
to find that, asleep, she'd bitten off the tail
of a small lizard, dragged through her lips. That bitterness (I used to imagine);
she running onto the verandah to spit,
and standing there, spat dry, seeing across the silent, frosty bush
the lights of town had died.

And yet my mother never ceased from what philosophers invoke,
from extending "care",
although she only read the *Women's Weekly*,
and although she could be "damned impossible" through a few meal-times, of course.
That care for things, I see, was her one real companion in those years.
It was as though there were two of her,
a harassed person, and a calm, who saw what needed to be done, and
stepped through her, again.
Her care you could watch reappear like the edge of tidal water
in salt flats, about everything.
It was this made her drive out the neighbour's bull from our garden with a broom,
when she saw it trample her seedlings –
back, step by step, she forced it, through the broken fence,
it bellowing and hooking either side sharply at her all the way, and I
six years old on the back steps calling
"Let it have a few old bloody flowers, Mum."
No. She locked the broom handle straight-armed across its nose
and was pushed right back herself
quickly across the yard. She
ducked behind the tomato stakes,
and beat with the handle, all over that deep hollowness of the muzzle,

poked with the straw at its eyes,
and had her way, drove it out bellowing;
and me, slapping into the steps, the rail, with an ironing cord,
or rushing down there, quelled also,
repelled to the bottom step, barracking. And all,
I saw, for those little flimsy leaves
she fell to at once, small as mouse prints, among the chopped-up loam.

2

Whereas, my father only seemed to care that he would never appear a drunkard
while ever his shoes were clean.
A drunkard he defined as someone who had forgotten the mannerisms
of a gentleman. The gentleman, after all, is only known,
only exists, through manner. He himself had the most perfect manners,
of a kind. I can imagine no one
with a style more easily and coolly precise. With him,
manner had subsumed all of feeling. To brush and dent the hat
which one would raise, or to look about over each of us
and then unfold a napkin
to allow the meal, in that town where probably all of the men
sat to eat of a hot evening without a shirt,
was his dry passion. After all, he was a university man
(although ungraduated), something more rare then. My father, I see, was hopelessly melancholic –
the position of those wary
small eyes, and thin lips, on the long-boned face
proclaimed the bitterness of every pleasure, except those of form.
He often drank alone
at the RSL club, and had been known to wear a carefully-considered tie
to get drunk in the sandhills, watching the sea.
When he was ill and was at home at night, I would look into his bedroom,
at the end of a gauzed veranda,
from around the door and a little behind him,
and see his frighteningly high-domed skull under the lamp-light, as he read
in a curdle of cigarette smoke.
Light shone through wire mesh onto the packed hydrangea-heads,
and on the great ragged mass of insects, like bees over a comb, that crawled tethered
and ignored right beside him. He seemed content, at these times,
as though he'd done all that he need
to make a case against himself, and had been forced, objectively, to give up.

He liked his bland ulcer-patient food
and the heap of library books I brought. (My instructions always were:
"Nothing whingeing. Nothing by New York Jews;
nothing by women, especially the French; nothing
translated from the Russian.")
And yet, the only time I heard him say that he'd enjoyed anything
was when he spoke of the bush, once. "Up in those hills,"
he advised me, pointing around, "when the sun is coming out of the sea,
standing among
that lifting timber, you can feel at peace."
I was impressed. He asked me, another time, that when he died
I should take his ashes somewhere, and not put him with the locals, in the
cemetery.
I went up to one of the places he had named
years earlier, at the time of day he had spoken of, when the half-risen sun
was as strongly-spiked as the one
on his Infantry badge,
and I scattered him there, utterly reduced at last, among the wet, breeze-
woven grass.
For all his callousness to my mother, I had long accepted him,
who had shown me the best advice,
and left me to myself. And I had come by then to see that we all inhabit
pathos.
Opening his plastic, brick-sized box, that morning,
my pocket-knife slid
sideways and pierced my hand – and so I dug with that one
into his ashes, which I found were like a mauvish-grey marble dust,
and felt I needn't think of anything more to say.

16 Short Poems

Soaking in a bath.
On a radio somewhere
time-pips. Three o'clock.

Mountain-side dusk;
white flowers through the bush
the milking-shed lights.

4 a.m.; the Milky Way
blowing high over the forest.
A truck changes down.

Daytime movie;
and coming outside, it's dark.

I turn another way.

I get up. Bright moonlight.
The sea is a glass brimming
under the tap.

Drying her eyes,
outside on the hilltop street;
hiding in the wind.

Across the level
eucalypt forest, the sunlit
afternoon sea.

The torch beam
I feel with, through the pouring night,
is smoke.

A milky-grey twilight.
Raindrops on the window,
gulls on the grass.

A cathedral –
long tapers of rain light
candles on the twilit river.

Two magpies stepping
on the veranda. Ploughed hillside,
smoke and cumulus.

I sit and watch
the way rain is falling,
its eyes closed.

In the room at dusk
a piano-lid propped. Urgent
sail, far from home.

Open the door on
the gunshot of the morning –
work all day wounded.

The sky, thick with stars,
is the floor of a saucepan
that's about to boil.

On the bus, white neck,
black hair. Light has paused
in its endless journey.

The Life of a Chinese Poet

In his youth, as he recalled, the Great Causeway of the Heavens and Earth trembled
and the stars were spilled like dust, at the overthrow of a dynasty.
It would seem that he was old from birth, who was always saying goodbye.
During ninety years he wrote five thousand poems, in a rhyming prose or as songs for the lute.
Otherwise, his life was uneventful, except for the always-remembered love that he had for a certain courtesan.
His mother refused to let him marry this girl, who was called Scented Jade,
and soon afterwards he was ordered as a minor clerk to the far province of Fukien.
There he discovered, at times, the consolation of nature – its vividness, and its unthinkable reality.
He writes of the wild mountains, that were as sharp and glittering as dog's teeth,
and that could be seen from among the hanging flowers of the white lanes.
The river there he also admired, which he says was like the great dragon of Ch'i
that turned upon itself in all the twelve directions, while subduing the five elements.
It was his dream from youth to take arms against the Golden Tartars,
but the northern frontiers had been made safe; there was no fighting, but only an endless boredom there.
At fifty-four, he went home to his native village, having never gained a preferment,
distressed by what he heard of the luxury and incontinence of the court.
He dreamed in his work of the "vast smoke" of chariots, as they raced upon the plains;
he described his travels to far outposts, by night on a river that was held in the moon's white stare.
Though he styled himself the Hermit of the Mossy Grove, and said that he was wild, irascible and drunken, it seems he longed for the company of other poets.
He had married a local girl, when she was fifteen, and spent most of his time quietly lost in his books.
Pondering both the Taoist and Ch'an Buddhist teachings, he grew more and more enamoured of nature,
and found his companionship in mountains, flowers, and trees.
In rainy weather he would put aside his studies and trudge to the inn, to drink with the farming hands.
"Daily the town inn sells a thousand gallons of wine. The people are happy:

why should I alone be sad?"

He was utterly sincere in his love of beauty. The thing he has seen appears on the white paper. There is a sense of overbrimming life.

A Chinese critic has said, "His poetry has the simplicity of daily speech; in its simplicity there is depth, and in its poignance there is tranquillity."

When he was seventy-one, the Mongols arose once more, and began to attack the Celestial Horde;

the armies of the Sung were continually defeated, and were even driven out of Szechuan.

Again, he applied for enlistment, but amidst the turmoil in the corridors at the provincial capital he was pushed aside and ignored.

Giving up all hope that before he died he would see himself in battle, he returned to his village in disgust.

His songs were now being sung by the muleteers in far mountain passes, by girls bringing silk to be washed in the streams.

In the capital, they were exclaimed over at wine parties, and were murmured beside the Imperial Lake.

He was revered, if rarely seen, in his village, but finally one morning the word went around that he had fallen hopelessly ill.

Everything was made ready – the thin coffin, the two thick quilts, and the payment for the monks;

the earth was thrown out of his grave onto the hillside, and the incense was bought that would smoulder among the graveposts there.

But then, the next day, he rose on his couch, and called for wine to be brought him from the marketplace;

he had the blind rolled up on his view to the south, and he wrote some impeccable verses, in the tonally-regular, seven-syllable form.

In Departing Light

My mother all of ninety has to be tied up
on her wheelchair, but still she leans far out of it sideways;
she juts there brokenly,
able to cut
with the sight of her someone who is close. She is hung
like her hanging mouth
in the dignity
of her bleariness, and says that she is
perfectly all right. It is impossible to get her to complain
or to register anything
for longer than a moment. She has made Stephen Hawking look healthy.
It's as though
she is being sucked out of existence sideways through a porthole

and we've got hold of her feet.
She's very calm.
If you live long enough it isn't death you fear
but what life can still do. And she appears to know this
somewhere,
even if there's no hope she could speak of it.
Yet she is so calm you think of an immortal – a Tithonus withering
forever on the edge
of life,
though never a moment's grievance. Taken out to air
my mother seems in a motorcycle race, she
the sidecar passenger
who keeps the machine on the road, trying to lie far over
beyond the wheel.
Seriously, concentrated, she gazes ahead
towards the line,
as we go creeping around and around, through the thick syrups
of a garden, behind the nursing home.

Her mouth is full of chaos.
My mother revolves her loose dentures like marbles ground upon each
    other,
or idly clatters them,
broken and chipped. Since they won't stay on her gums
she spits them free
with a sudden blurting cough, which seems to have stamped out of her
an ultimate breath.
Her teeth fly into her lap or onto the grass,
breaking the hawsers of spittle.
What we see in such age is for us the premature dissolution of a body,
as it slips off the bones
and back to protoplasm
before it can be decently hidden away.
And it's as though the synapses were almost all of them broken
between her brain cells
and now they waver about feebly on the draught of my voice
and connect
at random and wrongly
and she has become a surrealist poet.
"How is the sun
on your back?" I ask. "The sun
is mechanical," she tells me, matter of fact. Wait
a moment, I think, is she

becoming profound? From nowhere she says, "The lake gets dusty." There
is no lake
here, or in her past. "You'll have to dust the lake."
It could be
she has grown deep, but then she says, "The little boy in the star is food,"
or perhaps "The little boy is the star in food,"
and you think, More likely
this appeals to my kind of superstition – the sleepless, inspiring homunculus.
It is all a tangle, and interpretations,
and hearing amiss,
all just the slipperiness
of her descent.

We sit and listen to the bird-song, which is like wandering lines
of wet paint –
it is like an abstract expressionist at work, his flourishes and
then
the touches
barely there,
and is going on all over the stretched sky.
If I read aloud skimmingly from the newspaper, she immediately falls asleep.
I stroke her face and she wakes
and looking at me intently she says something like, "That was
a nice stick." In our sitting about
she has also said, relevant of nothing, "The desert is a tongue."
"A red tongue?"
"That's right, it's a
it's a sort of
you know – it's a – it's a long
motor car."
When I told her I might go to Cambridge for a time, she said to me,
"Cambridge
is a very old seat of learning. Be sure – "
but it became too much –
"be sure
of the short Christmas flowers." I get dizzy,
nauseous,
when I try to think about what is happening inside her head. I keep her
out there for hours, propping her
straight, as
she dozes, and drifts into waking; away from the stench and
the screams of the ward. The worst
of all this, for me, is that despite such talk, now is the most peace

I've known her to have. She reminisces,
momentarily, thinking that I am one of her long-dead
brothers. "Didn't we have some fun
on those horses, when we were kids?" she'll say, giving
her thigh a little slap. Alzheimer's
is nirvana, in her case. She never mentions
anything of what troubled her adult years – God, the evil passages
of the Bible, her own mother's
long, hard dying, my father. Nothing
at all of my father,
and nothing
of her obsession with the religion that he drove her to. She says the magpie's
song,
which goes on and on, like an Irishman
wheedling to himself,
and which I have turned her chair towards,
reminds her of
a cup. A broken cup. I think that the chaos in her mind
is bearable to her because it is revolving
so slowly – slowly
as dust motes in an empty room.
The soul? The soul has long been defeated, and is all but gone.
She's only productive now
of bristles on the chin, of an odour
like old newspapers on a damp concrete floor, of garbled mutterings, of
some crackling memories, and of a warmth
(it was always there,
the marsupial devotion), of a warmth that is just in the eyes now, particularly
when I hold her and rock her for a while, as I lift her
back to bed – a folded
package, such as,
I have seen from photographs, was made of the Ice Man. She says, "I like it
when you – when
when
you ..."
I say to her, "My brown-eyed girl." Although she doesn't remember
the record, or me come home
that time, I sing it
to her: "Sha lala
la la lala ... And
it's you, it's you," – she smiles up, into my face – "it's you, my brown-eyed
girl."

My mother will get lost on the roads after death.
Too lonely a figure
to bear thinking of. As she did once,
one time at least, in the new department store
in our town; discovered
hesitant among the aisles; turning around and around, becoming
a still place.
Looking too kind
to reject even a wrong direction,
outrightly. And she caught my eye, watching her,
and knew I'd laugh
and grinned. Or else, since many another spirit will be arriving over there, whatever
those are – and all of them clamorous
as seabirds, along the walls of death – she will be pushed aside
easily, again. There are hierarchies in Heaven, we remember; and we know of its bungled schemes.
Even if the last shall be first, as we have been told, she
could not be first. It would not be her.
But why become so fearful?
This is all
of your mother, in your arms. She who now, a moment after your game, has gone;
who is confused
and would like to ask
why she is hanging here. No – she will be safe. She will be safe
in the dry mouth
of this red earth, in the place
she has always been. She
who hasn't survived living, how can we dream that she will survive her death?

A Bowl of Pears

Swarthy as oilcloth and as squat
as Sancho Panza
wearing a beret's little stalk
the pear

itself suggests the application of some rigour
the finest blade
from the knife drawer
here

to freshen it is one slice and then another
the north fall south fall
facets of glacier
the snow-clean juice with a slight crunch that is sweet

I find lintels and plinths of white marble
clean angled
where there slides
the perfume globule

a freshness
like the breeze that is felt upon
the opening
of day's fan

Enku
sculptor of pine stumps
revealed the ten thousand Buddhas with his attacks
the calligraphic axe

Rationalised shape shaped with vertical strokes
I have made of your jowled
buttocks
a squareness neatly pelvic

A Sunday of rain
and like a drain
a pipe that was agog and is chock-a-block the limber thunder
    rebounds
and bounds

it comes pouring down
a funnel the wrong way around
broadcasts
its buffoon militance over the houses all afternoon

Undone
the laces of rain
dangle on the windows
now slicing iron

a butcher is sharpening
the light
of his favourite knife
its shimmers carving stripes into the garden

And I have carved the pear-shaped head
with eyes

close set
as pips that Picasso saw his poor

friend who had gone
to war
a cubist
snowman the fragrant and fatal Apollinaire

The School of Venice

for Michael and Kathrin Hulse

I

The Grand Canal can seem a swan,
with its throat stretched out, when it is drawn
on the map. A creature that makes such opulent enquiry
could be the emblem of this city
and of its art.
The canal is a light green jade upon the chart
as so often
it is in life. Or it's found among the finely-crazed porcelain
of an old, snapped-off medallion –
lanes and alleys
and equally profuse the waterways.
This swan, with neck unfurled,
has shown the enterprise of Zeus, in its seduction
of all the world.

Abundance through ardent compensation
for natural lack is what
the city means. Although some have thought
locale is all we're taught,
I am inclined for once to be more Nietzschean.
Venice created Bellini
out of a particular paucity –
you'll find
finely limned
behind his Madonnas' resignation
the perspectives of deprivation
in those blue earliest landscapes, which open out of smallness so spaciously.
In the same way,
the few, secretive Venetian gardens
provoked a memory of woods and mountains
for the young Titian – "perhaps the first painter to show a love

of particular mountains", in his case of
those types
which can be seen from his birthplace in the Dolomites;
and similarly with the perfect groves,
amid all their stroked leaves,
in his rhythmic idylls
and satin bacchanals.
This tight city
produced out of insubordinance the immensities of Veronese;
while insouciant Tiepolo,
whom we rightly view from below,
gawping, made escape
upwards from restriction – we levitate
among the soles
of feet, calves, elbows, palms rested on air, the elbows of pinions,
blown hemlines, plump chins,
clouds like flung-off ermine stoles,
somersaulting *putti*
above a trampoline, and a view of a charger's hooves and belly.
His solution
was the one they would take up in Manhattan.

Turner's response to Venice, though, is too insubstantial,
too formless and "spiritual";
he painted the city romantically,
isolating one attribute, what we see
making it a vision. Venice isn't a dream,
or something made out of "tinctured steam".
Whatever might
its atmosphere has, the place is of stone as much as light.
(For bees, it's been found, only that is seen which has the brightness of
jewels,
yet a swarm reels
from the reality of walls.
One's narrowed attention, out of incapacity, or thought,
cannot negate
the world, whose nature remains inviolate.)

Still, the light of Venice is the essence of light,
a seething, powdery,
sifted light, especially
of a late afternoon. Then, it can seem that pink and white rose petals are
strewn

over the city, that a whole mountain
of petals, blown on,
has whirled down
into the lagoon; and the petal-soaked water slaps
at St Mark's steps
and keeps on with its feathery
short movements, as it is becoming a greenish honey.
(We were waiting with petals at our feet
for a motor boat
to take us to the cemetery,
to an island of blackly-wrapped cypresses, like Böcklin's "Isle of the Dead",
but walled and elongated, where they have buried
E.P.)

This city was great when the Antipodes
were still undiscovered
by Europe. It has sung before it dies;
it is retired.
Nothing is being painted there or said
of merit now, as James Morris decades since claimed, and one soon believes.
Venice is a diet of pastries.
Ruskin's stones
resound to schoolgirl excursions, on their mobile phones.
Two umbrellas wide, most *calle*
are lined with small shops, like bright cabinets – it is sideshow alley,
a fairground without ferris wheel,
a place of knick-knack and bauble,
a sticky light
to catch the world's shoppers, its overloaded freight.
Only very late
of an evening can we guess at the animus of other times:
along passageways,
unfolded emptily before us, there are footfalls like Harry Lime's
or the Doge's
agents, but no one's in sight,
just a shadow, sucked about
a corner. And in the furthest reaches, where a lane becomes almost a tunnel,
beneath a slippery stone lip, the water's sinister as petrol.

The *palazzi* are dying on their feet, seen to be gangrenous at low tides,
although grandeur subsides
grandly. Their facades have minaret-shaped windows, lattice-work in stone,

small fenestrations in a four-leafed clover design,
great plinths for steps and sills,
columns, and decorative metal grilles.
They are always veiled by shutters
and in subdued colours:
terracotta, bone,
rust, or tan; occasionally a borsch, a blue-grey,
a lightest green.
Too eccentric a place to want to stay:
it was spring but the only bloom
was in buckets, or arranged in one's room.
Nowhere here
were there mountains in the end of a street, at the end of the day.
Yet, something not found elsewhere,
nor hoped for – that one could be ravished by decay.

II

Forgive this tourist's impression,
but Venice ought not to be an abstraction,
a word only; rather, it is water and stone, and a time, and a person.
I was in Venice for your wedding, with to follow
lunch at Torcello,
another island, where you had us go
by speedboat. It was quiet and dry there, mainly in ruins,
the trees like brambles. We were led to a garden's
fine gravel, of an amber afternoon. The restaurant formerly
a wooden farmhouse. But what we first must see,
you told us, was the Byzantine interior
of Santa Maria dell' Assunta,
from about 600, its marvellous
mosaics, a short way off. I became at once preoccupied with the fear
and obsequiousness
that had gathered there
for so long; it was probably because of the Virgin's stare,
remote and superior,
within freezing stone.
The place was as cold as God's love. I tried to imagine their religion:
icy Hell on one cheek, on the other
the effervescent thin light of a steamy Heaven …
Whereas, the love
of feeling oneself alive,
a confident, sure

grasp of the world, and the triumph of pleasure,
are, according to Berenson,
in his book, what we owe the Venetian
school of art. Employees of the Church, he praises in them their happy treason.
That day, sun shone
and the cold that could take your face off the bone
was left behind. Flowers, for which men work
for their own sake,
had appeared, once more, in the garden
where we were seated, for the best of cuisines, the Italian.

III

Here in Rome, resident
for a while, I make this wedding present,
and remember unexpectedly a Chekhov story,
called rather daringly
"A Boring Story."
You most likely will know it – a young woman
visits an aged professor,
her guardian, whose illness means that he can't survive much longer,
and asks him in desperation,
and in the Russian way, to give
her advice, how she's to live.
"Help me!" she sobs. "You are my father,
the only one in whom I have faith, you are clever,
educated, you
have lived so long. What am I to do
with myself?" (She has wanted to be an actress
but in her distress
tells him she's a failure
at that: no talent.) "Which way do I go?"
He has to say, "Upon my word, Katya,
I do not know."
But he implores her,
all the same, "Let us have lunch, Katya, dear"; which provokes her disdain
and she leaves. And he is sure
there won't be time to see her again.
"Farewell, my treasure ... "
How wise a man
Chekhov was. Perhaps unknown
to his character,

"Let us have lunch" is a serious rejoinder.
This is a toast I ought to have made,
at your table, for us, and for everyone
(I am anxious that it be taken
in its wide
implication) –
I don't mean we should do so intemperately,
except perhaps occasionally,
and of course it is not enough of an answer
(thinking of Venice, and of Italy,
with their culture
diminuendo), as Chekhov knew. Through any book
of his, there is another
piece of advice, repeatedly (it's in his letters, and his life) – that we should
work
for what is human.
Some complain
of such talk, that the air of the Enlightenment is too thin.
This is hardly our choice, or of our doing. Still, here where we finally belong,
the lungs grow strong;
and Enlightenment means that something is done
about certain of God's more intricate design
(You will have guessed that I am feeling deluged by religion
in this city. Too many churches visited;
high camp, practically
all, though I've admired
Santa Cecilia, and Santa Maria in Trastevere …)
Chekhov came to Rome
not long before he was to die of TB, on returning home,
at forty-four. In the Vatican
he watched a procession with a friend, and that man
said, "What splendour …
How would you describe this?" Chekhov's answer:
"A long line of silly monks dragged tediously by."
What I wanted to say
is, Don't you think the Enlightenment could have had an origin,
or have found a way-station
on its way from Greece,
in the real light
of Venice,
and of Tuscany,
which is evoked and dwelt on in those places' art?

It descended through Claude, and many another,
who kindled their brushes in its fire,
and took it hence,
first of all to France.
Anyway, I can see,
as clearly as on their panels, a wooden trestle, with leaf-shadow and wine
before each one
of our small party, met again,
from the world, in Europe.
Our glasses are raised another time, as though each of us held a peony or
tulip.

MARK O'CONNOR 1945–

The son of a Melbourne judge, Mark O'Connor was born in Ararat, Victoria, and grew up there and in Melbourne. He began a degree in engineering, but switched courses and graduated from the University of Melbourne in English and classics. While in Canberra as a post-graduate student, he began a friendship with A. D. Hope, with whom he shared an interest in scientific discoveries as subjects for poetry. O'Connor is a knowledgeable amateur biologist. However, Les Murray, rather than Hope, is his strongest stylistic influence. In the early 1970s he worked as a diver on the Great Barrier Reef and then as a gardener on Dunk Island. In 1976 O'Connor received a travelling fellowship and spent the next four years in Europe, surviving "by minding houses and winning literary competitions". Back in Australia he has made a living as a poet, particularly as writer-in-residence at many tertiary institutions across the country, and more recently as a marriage celebrant. He was the H. C. Coombs Fellow at the Australian National University in 1999 and subsequently a Visiting Scholar in Archaeology and Natural History.

O'Connor has published sixteen books of poetry and two books on environment and population, the most recent being *Overloading Australia* (co-authored with William Lines, 2008) and has edited *Two Centuries of Australian Poetry* (OUP, 2nd edition 1996). O'Connor's poetry covers a wide range: the culture of the classical world, problems of population and ecology, and religion (from a critical standpoint). His main subject, however, is the natural environment of Australia. He believes it is his duty as a poet to draw our attention in this country to "places ... we have scarcely begun to notice, much less revere". He has been a particular critic, in his book *Modern Australian Styles* (1982) and in reviews, of those poets who have ignored Australia for the sake of an abstracted internationalist *avant-gardism*. His work might be seen to prove the continuing vitality of the Jindyworobaks' ideals. He draws on a classical tradition in regarding poetry as a means of communicating important information, but seems at times to be impatient with style and form. At his best, he is able to present his strong subjects in language that is fully alive.

Reef

High by the long island's side
the rubble banks swim in the evening light
death-grey and bleached white, speckled together.

The Wind sings over the coelenterate dead
the hollow-gutted stone-sheath-dwellers
the lace-masons, the spicule shapers

the island-makers.

The Beginning

God himself
having that day planted a garden
walked through it at evening and knew
that Eden was not nearly complex enough.
And he said:
"Let species swarm like solutes in a colloid.
Let there be ten thousand species of plankton
and to eat them a thousand zooplankton.
Let there be ten phyla of siphoning animals,
one phylum of finned vertebrates, from
white-tipped reef shark to long-beaked coralfish,
and to each his proper niche,
and – no Raphael, I'm not quite finished yet –
you can add seals and sea-turtles & cone-shells & penguins
(if they care) and all the good seabirds your team can devise –
oh yes, and I nearly forgot it, I want a special place
for the crabs! And now for parasites to keep
the whole system in balance, let ...

"... In conclusion, I want," he said
"ten thousand mixed chains of predation –
none of your simple rabbit and coyote stuff!
This ocean shall have many mouths, many palates,
many means of ingestion. I want
say, a hundred ways of death, three thousand of regeneration –
all in technicolor naturally. And oh yes, I nearly forgot,
we can use Eden again for the small coral cay in the center.

"So now Raphael, if you please,
just draw out and marshall these species,
and we'll plant them all out in a twelve-hectare patch."

For five and a half days God labored
and on the seventh he donned mask and snorkel
and a pair of bright yellow flippers.
And, later, the host all peered wistfully down
through the high safety fence around Heaven
and saw God with his favorites finning slowly over the coral
in the eternal shape of a grey nurse shark,
and they saw that it was very good indeed.

Turtles Hatching

Waiting for weeks till the last one is ready to run

they break through to twilight: the life-race is on.
Winds and oceans that call give no order but one:
"Downhill, fast; when you hit water, swim." Last

will be picked; so will first. One in a hundred survives.
So they break sand & run, downhill as if cursed. (Seagulls
halloo joy, ghost-crabs skitter out.) They are high-revving toys

each wound for his chance. The course is uncertain,
ten sandy yards to cool foam, or half of a low-tide mile
over pits and castles of rock-crab, every hole an abyss,

every cross-ridge a death-lane; unable to stop,
indifferent whether scrambling in sand, scrabbling in slime,
or sculling deluded through sand-pools to beaches of death.

Caught in cracks they push hard down the crab's throat,
still punting on while life lasts, in search of the dark
and lovely reef water, the splash in the in-walled ear.

Their limbs have no setting but go. Friendly and clean,
with their leathery touch in the palm, likeable
as a dry handshake, a childish pleasure to handle, determined

as cats; this driving downhill force that will reach,
tourist, twice the mass of your coffin, yet weigh,
till it comes ashore, not a gram.

Tweaks the heart, though, to see them seek fate in a crab-hole.
I pulled one out once, wedged and still struggling
down, dropped it with a jerk – a great horny claw

like a parrot's beak had crushed the midsection, sheared
off the head, and behind moved the armoured tarantula legs
of a hairy scuttler with lobe-stalked eyes.

In pity I gathered a living brother, hiked it over the rock-flats,
(fighting on in my hand) while its brethren, obedient,
filed along moonless crevices, sating ambuscades of queued-up crabs,

laid it down on a rock slope, a foot from the water. It flopped
on straight for its freedom, tripped over a two-inch ledge –
fell and rocked on its back. (A crab darted out, saw my shadow, back-

sidled to shadow.) It squirmed and righted itself, hurried
on (since Nature has taught them to fear no predator
but time, no approach will deflect them), found the slight wash of

a ripple and lost half its weight; then, re-stranded, pressed on, met
the incoming surf of a wavelet, capsized, scrambled up, then
plugged on, hit new surf and breasted it well; turned its

flippers to sculling, still floating, too light to submerge;
spiralled a clumsy provocative line, spinnering out
to the moon, lucky with absent sharks and gentle water.

Slipping in, as it left, the shadow, a thousand times larger,
of a parent come shoreward to lay; two ends of the earthbound process
linked in the uncomprehending meeting of kin.

As the small shadow pedalled and bobbed, the great one wavered and slid;
for a second the greater obscured the lesser, then as surely
slid on; and the lesser was gone.

A Cuttlefish Bone

She picks it up, knowing it floats,
expecting white styrofoam strength,
tough but fluffy-light.
She finds it dense as a white stone-axe
– a live foundation-stone
that a flesh-house was built around
by the nervous colour-changing
ink-squirting ten-tentacled swimmer.

Its delicate gristle edges
are not yet ground away.
She scrapes them with enamelled nail.
The airfoil top
has a sharp nose and duck-billed tail;
the underside is a boat,
hollow, with streamlined hull.
She feels its two curves,

each perfect but different
like a high-heeled shoe,
then discards it to him:
"The smartest fish in the sea."

"Why does it wear its shell inside?"
– he senses the weak mollusc-thing
shrinking round its inner base of rock,
sphincters squeezing,
juicy flesh wanting to go inside
when the barracouta swirled.
In his hand it tapers, smooth
as a mannequin's back.
But air-cells and muscle-hooks
prove it was engineered;
a precise object for tendons to work on.
Strange!
so perfect a shape inside another.
She says "It's what we mammals use"
thin skin, large brains,
and something hard within.

The Olive Tree

Nobody knows how long it takes to kill an olive.
Drought, axe, fire, are admitted failures. Hack one down,
grub out a ton of mainroot for fuel, and next spring
every side-root sends up shoots. A great frost
can leave the trees leafless for years; they revive.
Invading armies will fell them. They return
through the burnt-out ribs of siege machines.

Only the patient goat, nibbling his way down the ages,
has malice to master the olive. Sometimes, they say,
a man finds a dead orchard, fired and goat-
cropped centuries back. He settles and fences;
the stumps revive. His grandchildren's family prosper
by the arduous oil-pressing trade. Then wars
and disease wash over. Goats return. The olives
go under, waiting another age.

Their shade still lies where Socrates disputed.
Gethsemane's withered groves are bearing yet.

SANDY FITTS 1946–

Sandy Fitts was born in England, grew up on the coast of Yorkshire, and arrived in Australia in 1962. She has published one book of poetry, *View from the Lucky Hotel* (2008). Her poems have a strong sense of place and about half of them are located in Hanoi. As well as containing a note thanking her children for "supportive noises", her book states: "Fitts has worked on trains and boats, in factories, cafes, schools, and in many offices as community activist, policy analyst, management consultant, research director, and senior executive. Her various university studies include an M.B.A." The voice in her poems is friendly, and not afraid to generalise.

Waiting for Goya

(Alte Nationalgalerie Berlin)

And so, as you see, quite a journey, and now
here I am, doodling postcards and zapping text
in the crush of the blockbuster queue snaking
slowly over that antique bridge and past those
colonnades, past the iron Kaiser riding high
on his horse, to arrive at the neo-Roman temple,
those massive steps, with still time – we hope –
to see the show before the doors are closed.
What a circus! What ever for? I hear you, mate,
even from this distance. And yes, the books,
catalogues, probably tell me all I need to know;
and yet, call me romantic if you like (you will!
you will!), I'm still curious to find out what –
if anything – the originals might have to say.
Yes, I know, a fine copy often does the job
(and your latest on the simulacra just blew
me right away), with no need for the fetish
of the great artist's mark. And, what today
could be gained from viewing an old etching –
itself a print? Though just writing this flares
a Goya work long-branded in my brain:
those men, mutilated, and that body hacked
to bits, stuck on branches of the dead tree.
So why look at the original? To admire the artistry?
Obscene! Yes, point taken. And yet. And yet
the paintings … and the rest … it's not only
me (look at the queue!) who thinks they might
find something vital in the presence of the thing
itself. More than pure aesthetics. (*Or is it?*)
All I know is – for me this looking comes close

to word of mouth, the personal voice, direct.
In the age of copies, this still touches, speaks:
here is this piece of paper bearing the human
imprint, its moving signs, its imperfections.
Old ground, you say, and yes, mate, I'll now pause
to shuffle with the queue past this classic building
to our next stop. We're in a battleground here,
of course. The bullet holes are real. Odd to stand
in a quiet line for art where men have screamed
and died. Years of rain have washed the blood
away but, I ask you, what form of art could touch
as the pocks on these stone walls? (And if I frame
the silent hollows and call it art – what loss?)
Small pits with no plaques, they hold more power
for the lack of naming and yet – without words –
seem overlooked. In this busy queue from every
elsewhere, most pass by unknowing, though we
all admire the sensational artistry of that statue –
the giant commander, his beautiful war horse.
It was ever thus. Fool. What the hell do you expect?
OK. You're right. And I'm not against heroics,
large or small; nor against the just war. But
today I'm thinking simply – why not some
thanks – why not plant statues thick as traffic
lights on all corners, witness to those who tried
to bring light into the world – not through war
but thought: altruists, thinkers, doers who go
beyond the self. *You're off your head! It'll never fly.*
Maybe. But since I'm here, I'll start with those
near to Goya. For, as they tell it, until mid-life
Goya was more or less court lackey. Interior
decorator with ambition. Tapestries to please.
Dazzling portraits for the rich and famous.
Yet his private work moved on. Fired by new
ideas. Ill health. War. And men, like Jovellanos,
whose thoughtful painted face looks out – alive –
to us: reformer, writer, doer. (The Inquisition
banned his book on economics.) Man of his time,
he's history now. Will words like his ever turn up
in art – or are their unlovely syllables too heavy,
too Latinate for our tastes? CRIMINAL LAW REFORM?
INSTITUTE OF AGRICULTURE? TECHNICAL EDUCATION?

POLITICAL ECONOMICS? *Stop! It's sinking! Keep to*
the poetic diction! Not yet. MINISTER OF GRACE AND
JUSTICE. Poet too. Prison. Exile. What do we,
in our comfort, know of that? Easy to take
pot-shots from the safe remove. So, friend, I
will insist on this: our great legacy – reason,
(*crazy! against the tide!*) joined with compassion,
ethics. Yes, today I'm leaving the carping pomo
to their pottage. (The DO NOWT species, I mean,
of course.) I'm moving on. Taking a small step
along with this marvel of civilised patience,
the queue, toward the first age of, shall we say,
enlightenment (*goodbye career and publication!*). Or
at least a higher aim and a bit more common
sense. Yes, I know, tracking truth through reason
is hard work along muddy trails – and dangerous
in a mad age of faith and war. Jovellanos knew.
Goya too. And in our time, the brave souls you
speak of – Shaima Raazi, Safia Amajan, Zakia Zaki,
Shakiba Sanga Amaj, public servants, journalists,
educators, gunned down by the zealots for being
women. I keep their names close by. Humanity
slaughtered by those raging forces that forever
fight to destroy all questions. It sits on my desk,
a copy of that famous etching, *the sleep of reason*
brings forth monsters, the writer slumped asleep,
darkness exploding its creatures across the page.

ALEX SELENITSCH 1946–

Alex Selenitsch is a Melbourne poet and architect and a senior lecturer in the Faculty of Architecture, Building and Planning at the University of Melbourne. He writes reviews of art, craft and design for various journals; works collaboratively on artists books and in the theatre; and was the Gordon Darling Fellow, National Gallery of Australia, Canberra, in 2001. Initially inspired by Kurt Schwitters, his first concrete poem was published in *OZ* in 1968. He produces poems as prints and objects. He is represented by grahame galleries+editions, Brisbane, Queensland, and Place Gallery Melbourne, Victoria. Most good painting "does what it says", to some degree with its non-semantic elements. Concrete poetry does so purely visually. Alex Selenitsch is an outstanding presence in the international concrete poetry movement.

Delta

delta
delta a
delta a
delta a
delta t a
delta e t
delta e e a a
delta l e l t e t a
delta e l et t t a t a
delta d l l d t t l t t
delta e d l d l e d l t a d
delta d d d l e l d t l t l d a
delt d e e e d l l e d a t d
delta d d e e d t l l d t
delta d d e l d t l t a
delta e d e a a
delta e e l t t a d a
delta e l l a a a
delta e e l t
delta e t l a a
delta t
delta a a
delta a
delta a
delta

ddddddddddddddddddddddddddd ddddd dd ddd dddd dddddd dd
d d d dd d ddde de deed ee
d d d ddd ded dde
d e e d ddd dd dd
e e e ee e deede ee
e e e ee eed eee dee
eeeeeeeeeeeeeee eeeeeeeee eeeeee eee eee ee ee eeeee ee
e e e e e e leelell eel
e e e e l e ee lelel elel
l l ll l ll leeell llel
l l ll l l e lele llllel lle
l l l ll lll l l lll lllellll lllll
llllllllllllllllllllllllllllllllllllllllllllllll lllllllllll lll lllllll llllll lllll lllllll lllllll lll ll
l l l l l tllllt ll llllll
l l l l l lllll ll tlll ttl lt
tt t l t l llt ll ll llt
t t t t t t t t l ttt ltt t
t t t t tt t t t tttt ttt tlttt
tttttttttttttttttttttttttttttttttttttttttt tttttt tttt tttttt ttttttttt ttttt ttt tt
t t t t ttttt att tttat
t t t a a tt ttta ttta
a t a a a t a tt at a
a a a t a a t aat aat
a a aa a a a a aa taaaa aaa
aaaaaaaaaaaaaaaaaaaa aaaaa aaaaaa aaaa aaaa aaa aaaa aa

d e l t a
d e l t a
d e l t a
d e l t a
d e l t a
d e l t a
d e l t a
d e l t a
d e l t a
d e l t a
d e l t a
d e l t a
d e l t a
d e l t a
d e l t a
d e l t a
d e l t a
d e l t a
d e l t a
d e l t a
d e l t a
d e l t a
d e l t a
d e l t a
d e l t a
d e l t a

d e l t a
d e l t a
d e l t a
d e l t a
d e l t a
d e l t a
d e l t a
d e l t a
d e l t a
d e l t a
ddddddd dddddddddd dddddddd ddddd dddddddddddd dddddddd
eeeeee e eeeeeeeeee eeeeeeee eeeee eeeeeeeeeeee eeeeeeee
lllllllllll llll llllllllllllllll ll llllllllllll lllllllllll llllllllllllllllllllll lllllllllllllll
tttttttt tttt tttttttttttt tt ttttttttt t ttttttt t ttttttttttttttt ttttttttttttttt
aaaaa aaa aaaaaaa a aaaaaa a aaaa aaa aaaaaaaa a aaaaaaaaa
d d e e l l t t a a
d d e e l l t t a a
d d e e l l t t a a
d d e e l l t t a a
d d e e l l t t t a a
d d e e ll l t t t aa a
dd d e e e ll l t t t a a a
d d d e e e l l l t t t a a a
d d d e e e l l l t t t a a a
d d d e e e l l l t t t a a a

ddddddddddddd dddddddddddd dddddddddd ddddddddddddddd
a a a a a
eeeeeeeeeeeee eeeeeeeeeeeeeeeee eeeeeeeeeeeee eeeeeeeeeeeeee
t t t t t t t
t t t t t t t t t t
tttttttt ttttttt tttttttt tttttttt ttttttttt tttttttt tttttttt tttttttt tttttttttt
e e e e e e e e e e e e e e e e
e e e e e e e e e e e e e e e e e e e e e e e e
e e e e e e e e e e e e e e e e e e e e e e e e e e e e e e e e e
e e e eee ee e ee e ee ee e e eee eee eeee e e e e eee e e e e e
aaa aaa aaaa aaa aaaa aaa aaa aaaa aaaa aaa aaa aaa aaaa aaa
d d d d d d d d d d d d d d d d d d d d d d d d d d d
d d dd d d ddd ddd d d d d d d d ddd d d d d d ddd d d d dd d d d d
dddddddddddddddddddddddddd dddddddddddddddddddddddddd
d d d d d d d d d d d d d
d d d d d d d d d d d d d d d d d d
d d d d d d d d d d d d d d d d d
d d d d d d d d d d d d d d d d d d d
ddddddddd
ddddddddd
ddddddddd
ddddddddd
ddddddddd
ddddddddd
ddddddddd

from Lightning

from Weeds

w w ∫ ≥ §
w Ω å
∂ ß µ
e w ∞ w π
w w ¢ w ¡ · °
∫ Δ ∂ ´ ß
w w µ ¥ ¢
•w w ∂ ° ∫ ≈
• w´ † å œ ≤ ÷
··
w ∞
• w π w
w• ™ ° – ≠
w• ¡ w w ¬
• w• ˆ w ≈
£ ü √
· ˆ o ´ ¶ w
w• ≤ ∞ π æ
ç ww œ ¢ w £
• ∑ ¥ “
w• © ø
•w• ÷ § w Δ
• w• • ° ≠
∂ w ° ¬
w•• ∫ £ ß µ
° w · © å
™ • ° ‘
• √ w ≈ Ω œ §
[w•w w ∞ ¡ ≠ ∂
w• w · Δ †
••• w• ß ™
˜ ∫ w ∂
w ∂ ˆ ®
w † ww π ˆ ¥
w ∞ ∂
§ w £ –
• ÷ ≤ · ß

GARY CATALANO 1947–2002

Gary Catalano was born in Brisbane of Italian and Anglo-Australian parentage. He was brought up by his Sicilian grandparents, market gardeners, when his parents separated, and was educated at the Anglican boys' school, Trinity Grammar, Sydney. He worked in a number of jobs until he became an art critic for *Art and Australia* magazine from 1973, and he was art critic for *The Age* newspaper, Melbourne, from 1985–1990. He published five studies of Australian art and many essays and reviews on art that have not been collected. Eight volumes of his poetry appeared during his lifetime. A collection, *New and Selected Poems 1973–2002*, was prepared by Les Murray and Jamie Grant and published posthumously in 2007. In the last decade of his life he largely withdrew from the world of art criticism, except for a study of the Melbourne painter Rick Amor, and instead concentrated on literary essays about older Australian poets, such as Shaw Neilson, James Devaney, William Hart-Smith and Mary Gilmore. When he died of lung cancer, he was working on a proposed book-length study of David Campbell.

Catalano's poems tend to be either pared-back imagism in short free-verse lines, or prose poems in which images emerge with a softer focus. An essay on Catalano (*Quadrant*, June 2003) by Vivian Smith commented: "There is a tension in Catalano's work between the factual and immediate and the numinous and symbolic, which I think accounts for the enduring power and resonance of these otherwise quite fragile pieces."

Signs

As you stood at the rain-washed window you saw that the lights in the valley below were just like slivers of ice. They were working themselves into the dark body of the night. And then you heard the thin, needle-sharp bark of a dog as it threaded its way through the dark. It had come, you thought, from somewhere far in the distance. Unable to save the world, you quietly went on with your business, which was placing the cutlery back in its drawer and stacking away the clean plates. Yes. And on the latter you happened to notice that the knife tracks resembled the fine-grain lines on your undamaged palm.

The Bone

I have brought you a bone. Like the most precious of objects, it must be kept in a dark and secret place, a place from which it should only be removed when you wish to escape from the world and contemplate a thing which has passed beyond use. Only then may you run your fingers along its polished barrel and gaze at that spot in which its blood-red bullets once lodged. Who would have thought that murder or suicide lurked in this bone, this bone which has borne without complaint the burden of its fate and thereby entered the white and glittering world of pure form? Here, I have brought you a bone.

A River and Some Hills

We are driving south. The road winds down through the trimly-muscled flanks of the hills, then skirts the western edge of the river flat. Were we to stop the car and step into the roadside grass our ears would soon detect a dry papery sound, for that large paddock on our left is crowded with dead thistles. The river flows at the far end of the paddock, where it is half-hidden behind a bank of tall casuarinas. Every now and again we catch a glimpse of its cool waters, the glint of tinfoil in the sun. If water and earth are indeed part of each other, this river is flashing a signal to these hills and schooling them in the movement of water, for their flanks are so criss-crossed by sheep tracks that they have broken into waves. Driving here with a river on one side and watery hills on the other, we can almost imagine what the Israelites must have felt at the parting of the Red Sea.

Australia

I breathe the air of another country
when I walk among these people.
How terrible it is!

Generations have yearned for the new life
and it comes to this!
What will hold them upright

when their dreams are repossessed
and sold again at a discount?
But give me the smell of used nails

rusting in tins, and the dreams
that were swaddled in hessian.
I want the scene before it changed –

the blackberry-choked creeks,
the roads going nowhere, the shyness
of youth. Let me see again

the glitter of galvanised iron,
the scatter of farms and chicken sheds,
and pictures like this:

in an afternoon of its own
a tortoise makes its slow way
across a road of blue metal and tar.

It pulls in its head at the sound
of an approaching car, whose driver stops,
gets out, then moves it into the tall grass

at the edge of the road,
where a creek has begun to unthread itself
from a soak, and etch its straggly line

across the adjoining paddock,
whose wall of trees closes off the scene
from all the other countries in the world.

Workmen

Workmen are fixing the road.
Each day they come
and move piles of dirt

from one of its sides
to the other. Some
have red flags and

hold up signs which say
"Stop" or "Slow"
while others lean

on their shovels
as though posing for Millet.
With luck, in a month or so

the road will look
as if it were new;
its glistening ribbon

will guide us to
yet another tableau
in which the same workmen

will flourish a red flag
– or imitate the pose
of people at prayer.

Gallery Days

1

I could never get over
how casual Matisse looked
when I first came across him
in the flesh: being
a poor antipodean,
my thin, starvation diet
of glossy reproductions

had led me to the belief
that he was a real aesthete,
but when I got to Europe
I was made to realise

that he was just a workman
who scrubbed his pigment on
as though engaged in cleaning
a dirt-encrusted window.
But for shock value, that guy
Picasso was far better.
Right up close, it seemed as though
he'd never quite forgotten
his pinched, bohemian days
for painting after painting
looked painted with toothpaste.

2
I was slow to cotton on
to the whole point about
conceptual art, and insisted
on finding it in such things
as a tombstone engraved with
"Heavy Aesthetic Content"
and an ordinary light bulb
attached to an equally ordinary

block of wood; that a truly
conceptual work should have no
physical form was an idea
I found difficult to grasp
until a really bright spark
made the observation that all
such art was trying to do
was rival telepathy.

3
Something about the idea
of earthworks was appealing
but they were clearly old hat
if you'd had the fortune to come
from a farm: how could you
possibly get off on a pair

of parallel lines in the desert
when you'd seen how the
cucumbers used to draw
their scraggy and far
more expressive lines
along their beds?

4
Now that I look back on it
I realise that art must have
begun to lose me when it stopped
being made of things like
paint and canvas: until then,
one could always take refuge
in the fact that, however
horrifying a work may be,
it was still only imaginary,
but once art began to encroach

on the real and thereby enhanced
its capacity to offend
it lost both its *raison d être*
and its power to please. I
guess this is why my tastes
are now quite simple: given
a choice from all the genres,
I'll take a good conventional
portrait, honest decoration,
and landscapes painted *en plein air.*

"The best Corots ..."

The best Corots are invariably found outside the museums. My favourite is the one you see each night when the vedettes cruising up and down the river momentarily imprint the shadows of trees on the nearby buildings. When I first witnessed this phenomenon I thought I was looking at a kind of magic lantern show, yet now I know the thing is a Corot, for the tonality of that ephemeral shadow is as delicate as those in one of his wistful *Souvenirs*. Which, in one sense, puts it exactly, for wasn't he born almost on the river, just around the corner in the rue du Bac? Every night I come out here to watch the show, and every night I know I have seen the best Corot.

Translation

There's absolutely no one to be seen. Yet you're certain there's someone directly behind that line of trees, for when you hear the sound that comes from that direction – the sound, to be precise, of a thirsty dog drinking from a bowl of water – you know that you can safely translate: horse on blue metal road, walking slowly.

MARTIN JOHNSTON 1947–1990

Martin Johnston was born in Sydney. At the age of four he moved with his parents, both writers, to London when his father, George Johnston, who had been a distinguished war correspondent, was appointed Bureau Chief for an Australian newspaper chain. The family later moved to Greece so that the parents could concentrate full time on their writing. They remained for twelve years on the island of Hydra where Johnston and his sister were educated in Ancient and Modern Greek. Conversing in Greek with each other they only spoke English to their parents.

The family was often strapped for funds in Greece until Johnston's father had success with his award-winning novel *My Brother Jack* (1964). The family returned to Australia that year. His mother, Charmian Clift, already a published author, became a popular columnist with the *Sydney Morning Herald*, and Johnston began working there as a journalist, after dropping out of university. His first serious book review for the newspaper impugned the knowledge of Greek history of "an old Greek-hand". This resulted in a defamation suit against the paper. However, Johnston's assessment was supported by the Professor of Greek at the University of Sydney and the court dismissed the action.

Both his parents and his sister died when he was in his middle 20s. After having lived again in Greece for three years, he came back to Australia in 1978 and soon after joined the fledgling multicultural television channel SBS (Special Broadcasting Service) as a Greek sub-titler and subsequently Senior Editor. He went to live in Italy in 1988 where his last collection of poetry was written and the first draft of a novel about General Makrionnis: his boyhood hero from the Greek War of Independence. Apart from 1988, he remained with SBS and "his polyglot colleagues" until shortly before his early death in 1990.

He published three books of poetry in his lifetime, and a novel, *Cicada Gambit* (described by Chris Wallace-Crabbe as a "minor masterpiece"). A posthumous collection of his prose and poetry was published in 1993. Johnston had an encyclopaedic knowledge of European and South American literature. He greatly admired the South American writer J. L. Borges. He was, however, mainly influenced by Greek literature, especially poets like Cavafy, and this is reflected in his exact but elusive style. This exactness is best represented in his shorter poems. He has written longer, more discursive poems that are well regarded, but we feel he had difficulty maintaining in a larger format the deliberately inconsequential precision that makes his shorter poems so memorable. The space allotted to him here does not adequately represent the worth of his poetry vis-à-vis his contemporaries.

Vernal Equinox *(from* Uncertain Sonnets*)*

for Julie

Polychromatic springtime's gay cadenza
fades, and the colour harpsichord is still,
then tinkles in the dark a chord of chill
deep green of Marvell, brittle green of Spenser.
The trees are green and silver in the rain,
in trees' bright traceries emerald peacocks roost,
in mirror-silver mail knights prance and joust
and motleys sing the summer in again.
This is the no-man's-land of time. The fingers
rustle across the keys. The scudding face
of the moon fades ... but the tourney lingers
under long tides, in coral where jewelfish race
among lutes and visors, and the dumb sharks sail.
The surface flashes like a coat of mail.

The typewriter considered as a bee-trap

is no doubt less than perfectly adapted
to its function, just as a bee-trap,
if there are such things, would hardly be the ideal contrivance
for the writing of semi-aleatory poems about
bee-traps and typewriters. Why, in any case,
you are entitled to ask, should I
want to trap bees at all? What do with them
if caught? But there are times, like today,
when bees hover about the typewriter
more frequently than poems, surely knowing best
what best attracts them. And certainly at such times,
considered in terms of function and structure,
the contraption could be argued to be
anything but a typewriter,
the term "anything" being considered
as including, among all else, bee-traps,
softly multiplying in an ideal world.

6 The Café of Situations *(from* In Transit: A Sonnet Square*)*

for Grace Edwards

In this café they have solved the problem of names.
Orders go to the bar: "Coffee for Calendar,

two cognacs for Backgammon Board and Football Poster."
You are where you are. They know names must be revealed
most cautiously and that numbers only serve numbers.
In the café of situations they have found the golden mean:
sit there often enough and you'll win a table and name,
Clock, say, or Air Vent, which feeds not on you but you,
drop in occasionally and you're still gifted
while you're here with just that identity-in-place
you've been so long in quest of. Wherever I go
I wear the café walls around me, and the shuffling step
of the invisible waiters brings subtly misconstrued orders
to Broke or Loving or Drunk or wherever I happen to be.

The Scattering Layer

Rain walks all night across the greenhouse roof
on awkward spike-footed stilts, and in the yard, where weeds
and furtive clothespegs interweave, it smears
bluegreen on appleblue leafmould frottage, snaps open
galls where grubs gleam and wrinkle, silverfoil
uncurling waterfalls among the twigs, and cats stare up at the stickman.
The stock-car races slide across the compass,
lurch with a crunch and glass breaking up against the end of the street
burglars are picked out in light on the doorsteps, even primroses
glow, and the wingcases of dazed beetles. There are chalk diagrams but what
goes on
up beyond the Van Allen belt, the scattering layer,
we're not sure: pick up glittering striations, unreadable patterns of dots
in the strepitant blueblack undersea rivers, krill or seedspill
raining on us, down here where we swirl in our own light.

PETER KOCAN 1947–

Peter Kocan was born Peter Raymond Douglas in Newcastle. His father, an engineer, was killed in a road accident three months before his birth, and his mother remarried. The marriage failed, but only after Kocan had endured a childhood of loneliness, disadvantage and domestic violence. He left school at fourteen and worked as a laborer and station-hand. While he was a factory-hand in a dye factory, aged nineteen, under the influence of political zealots who had befriended him, he attempted to assassinate the Labor politician and Federal Opposition Leader, Arthur Calwell, during an election campaign. He was sentenced to life imprisonment for attempted murder. After imprisonment in the notorious Long Bay gaol, he was transferred to Morisset Psychiatric Hospital, near Lake Macquarie, north of Sydney. Calwell visited him at Morisset to forgive him.

His first two books of poetry were published while he was confined there. Kocan was released in 1976, ten years after his sentencing. Following this he published two short and powerful autobiographical novels about his confinement, and lived on the Central Coast of New South Wales, teaching, acting, and writing. In 2003, Kocan moved to Brisbane, Queensland. *Fresh Fields* (2007), another fictionalised account of his youth, was named a Book of the Year by *The Times Literary Supplement*.

Kocan has published six volumes of poetry, including a book he shared with Andrew Lansdown and Hal Colebatch. The extreme experience of ten years internment in a mental hospital has given Kocan's poems from that period a particular intensity and sympathy for outcasts. Since his release his poetry has become preoccupied with a critique of modernity and an unfashionable defence of traditional values.

Cricket

Thud of leather on willow – and the ball
Streaks by the incompetent outfielders
To hit the wall for 2. A bright Sunday.
My discontent squirms at the guffawing

Good humour of my fellows. A Sunday
To consign to the past like a package
Mailed to an unknown address; the waste
Will be an agony to remember.

Thud of leather on willow – the batsmen
Blunder back and forth. Flocks of birds drift high
Over the lake. The trees glisten with light
Like a Monet painting, still as canvas.

Frankie sits cross-legged in the long grass;
George heaves rocks at the wall; Tom rolls a smoke;
And I hang about waiting for a catch,
Full of the sap … my twenty-first summer.

Wheelchair Cases

Come to Ward 7 and see them,
Wheelchair cases, parked on a scrap
Of lawn, in the sun; enduring
The minute, the hour, the year.

The flies crawl over their faces,
Drawn by the spittle and vomit,
And epileptic froth shining
On their raw-veal coloured lips.

You see them being moved about
Like furniture by the newest
Of generations of nurses
Who have fed, washed and ignored them.

From bed to bath, chair to toilet,
A massive tedium pressing
On them, like the grip of concrete
Around the roots of dying trees.

In the snail-pace of their lives
Little happens – a change of ward
Once in a decade, a visit
From a relative presumed dead

Once within memory. Far, far
From the deep world's kaleidoscope
Of birth, marriage, ripenings,
They are hidden like their own sores;

Though granted, sometimes, a forced
Institutional largesse;
As at Christmas, dribbling plum cake,
Mocked by streamers and party hats.

And oh, how eagerly they respond
To the least show of interest!
With their guffaws and lolling grins!
Mirth to freeze your mirth for ever.

Here is a depth of injustice,
– Ordained, hopeless of repeal –
As the zoo-animal knows it,
As the cripple knows it. You watch,

Then you turn finally away
With no emotion, just a hope
That their hearts might hurt as little
As their shrivelled and nerveless legs.

Retards

They, more than we, know the real world
Still fresh with the first footprint,
The animals unnamed, the heavens
Innocent of God or Galileo.

For them no inkling of Time,
Just a simple moment of truth
Without end; punctuated, perhaps
By a dreamless blink of sleep.

Like the boy clad in singlet
And one shoe who sits for hours
On the lawn, charmed by the grass
Which reappears each time he looks.

Or like the sallow mongoloid
Solemnly tasting the concrete,
Or the one who stares past you
With the whole sky in his eyes.

One could say that this is Man unruined,
Sharing the stone's theology,
The vegetable's science,
The meditations of the mouse.

Cows

Cows graze across the hill,
Measuring the day
As their shadows tell
Irrelevant time. Their gait is half-way
Between moving and standing still.

The sun is gentle on the green
Of their meadow, their mouths deep
In its heavy warmth.
A watcher could fall asleep
Into the depth
Of that untroubled scene.

From each dewdrop morning
To every day's end
They follow the cycle
Of the rhythm of the world turning
In its season. A miracle
Of normalcy is a cow's mind.

Beyond thought's prickling fever
They dwell in the grace
Of their own true concerns
And in that place

Know they will live for ever
With butterflies around their horns.

Johnson and Garrick Leave Lichfield

I imagine the townsfolk hardly knew
Or noticed the departure of the two:
It was just Sam, ungainly and uncouth,
With Davey, that flibbertigibbet youth.

And even as the morning vista showed
Their figures disappearing down the road,
The business of the day was carried on
For all the world as if they hadn't gone.

The ordinary happened just the same.
Normal hours passed and evening came.
There were the usual effects of light
To colour the cathedral dark or bright.

And doubtless as it faded to a close
There was no earthly reason to suppose
That date would be remembered any more
Than thousands which had faded out before –

And certainly no evidence to say
The town had been immortalised that day
Because an odd, unprepossessing pair
Rose early and departed for elsewhere.

Cathedral Service

I'm only here because I wandered in
Not knowing that a service would begin,
And had to slide into the nearest pew,
Pretending it was what I'd meant to do.

The tall candles cast their frail light
Upon the priest, the choir clad in white,
The carved and polished and embroidered scene,
The congregation numbers seventeen.

And awkwardly I follow as I'm led
To kneel or stand or sing or bow my head.
Though these specific rites are strange to me,
I know their larger meaning perfectly –

The heritage of twenty centuries
Is symbolised in rituals like these,

In special modes of beauty and of grace
Enacted in a certain kind of place.

This faith, although I lack it, is my own,
Inherent to the marrow of the bone.
To this even the unbelieving mind
Submits its unbelief to be defined.

Perhaps the meagre congregation shows
How all of that is drawing to a close,
And remnants only come here to entreat
These dying flickers of the obsolete.

Yet when did this religion ever rest
On weight of numbers as the final test?
Its founder said that it was all the same
When two or three were gathered in his name.

Tyburn

On one side is a bustling city street
And over on the other side the park.
You loiter on the corner and you watch
The afternoon beginning to go dark.

This unassuming spot was the abyss,
The gaping terror of so many hearts,
And here for generations they were brought
On a never-ending convoy of carts.

How grimly in the mind's eye they pass
As here and there you recollect a name,
A few who have a mention in the books,
The tiny consolation of their fame.

But mostly you are dimly picturing
The sadder multitudes of the unknown,
Whose anguishes were never History
But just a little matter of their own –

Who swung for a petty misadventure,
Some desperate, impulsive little theft,
Some error now too utterly obscure
For any knowledge of it to be left –

Or even were entirely innocent
And who died by some malice or mistake:

The juvenile, the imbecile, the scared,
Who didn't know the right reply to make.

Remember that there wasn't any drop.
The dangling figure had to choke to death,
Would go for several minutes treading air
In the mad frenzy of that fight for breath.

Apparently the smallest suffered most
For the lack of sufficient body-weight.
The lucky had a friend who'd cling to them,
To help them throttle at a faster rate.

Eternities before the mind went blank,
Of attempting to scream or plead or curse.
Eternities they had in which to know
The howling horror of the universe ...

Think of it happening here for centuries!
And think of all the minutes that were spent!
Imagination quails and pulls away,
Refusing to consider what it meant.

You hurry to rejoin the commuters
Who never want to meditate on that,
Who keep their sanity by going home
To tend the garden and to feed the cat.

RHYLL McMASTER 1947–

Rhyll McMaster was born and brought up in Queensland. Brisbane is a subtropical presence in the poems about her childhood and parents. She has worked as a secretary, a burns unit nurse and a sheep farmer and has three daughters. She has been poetry editor of *The Canberra Times*, a reviewer for the *Sydney Morning Herald* and *The Australian*, a manuscripts assessor for the National Book Council, and a film scripts assessor for the Film Finance Corporation. She is now a full-time writer, living in Sydney, and has published five collections of her poetry. Her first novel, *Feather Man* (2007), was set in Brisbane and London.

McMaster's poetry is due for critical appraisal. From the start it was clear she was a brilliant and exact imagist, with a flair for quirky and inventive language. Her earlier poems also made room for whimsy and affectionate reminiscence. In her second book, *Washing the Money* (1986), she included remarkable portraits of eccentric family members recalled from childhood. Her output is relatively small with more than ten years intervening between her first and second books. *On My Empty Feet* (1993) contained her outstanding nine-part sequence "My Mother and I Become Victims of a Stroke" (from which we have selected six parts). From that time on there is an increasing disillusion and unrepentant bleakness in her work, verging on savagery, particularly apparent in the last three poems selected here (which are as yet uncollected).

Judith Wright has commented on the importance of historical context when understanding and appreciating a poem. The context of the poet's own work is equally important. In McMaster's early poem "Within Creation" both the title and the last three lines "at our clean and/ meaningless/ design" have an increased resonance when read in the context of her later poetry. As her work has revealed itself over a lifetime, the early poems may be seen as characters speaking happy lines in a tragic play.

Within Creation

What are moons
on fingernails
that they grow so ovally
like half-cut custard pies or
backing out shelled snails
in line?
Where do you come from
and what is your purpose in my life?
We make you wonder,
they softly scream in milky voices,
at our clean and
meaningless
design.

The Acquaintance

We came across each other
in the garden.
Beg pardon, he said, as he bit my hand.
With such good manners
and clean-green looks I let it stand.
Presently, with a long-feelered sweep
he gravitated to my knee
where he speck-of-lime-grasshopper-squatted politely
gnawing casually;
I was consoled for a time
by the small pain
of his friendliness to me.

Crab Meat

We would go down along the creek
which tainted its way, drain-choked, to the beach,

over a sandstung bridge
to where stain-red tins and drums rusted in a bend.
That was where we bought our crab meat.

A not young
woman owned the place –
lived among discarded claws and legs,
rotting carapaces
and a dead sea stench.
Death-clenched or mangled-open claws grew on the drive
along with a forest of dried-up
crabs' eyes.

Opening the finger-marked door
we would pause as the breath
from the pots grabbed at our teeth
then reach in, for the crab woman
to say "More?"

Yes – more sweet, red tipped, white string meat
wrapped, paper-clean, small-packaged by her stalk-eyed
sullen children.

They would scuttle
sideways, gazing at our feet
while we discreetly
ignored the whistling screams
and steam-dim, hot water struggles
of the tossed in victims.

Then, out again,
into the stiff air,
away from the scraped-out-armour carapaces
and the papier-mâché faces of the crab woman and her brood;

and just think of it as sea food
to be delicately eaten.

Shaking the Flame

I saw a black man through a green
wire screen
and caught his silver eye;
I spread my fingers red with light
to call him in – but a wind came
shaking the flame.

A door slams shut –
the flame bends and gutters.
What refrain does the flame sing within its purple sheath?
Again and again I reach in through the screen
but wind breath cuts like a clean and molten
magpie's song after rain.

The song the flame utters is sometimes
glimpsed in an eye
or that knowing, solid eye, out of time,
is seen in the flame,
if you stare and burn
without looking away.

Tile Table

That tile table (paddock size)
would be remarked on now.
Then, it was just "the table" where cups went "clunk"
and the enamel pot rang.
So big we all had afternoon tea
along one yellow and green perimeter without disturbing
a central heap of peas (erratic bull-ants in old newspaper).

The linoleum was darker
mossier green,
gloom on gloom tartan to rub a toe along
to trace a pattern of good luck;
(move on darker bars past the scullery hole that smelt
of Sunlight Soap and steel wool in decay,
hop to a lighter edge
past the one-step-down bathroom).

That bathroom housed a bath with white claw-legs.
The cement floor was painted red.
The whole house smelt of ferns, rusted mesh and seeping gas.
The water heater poked its tongue and lit the match.
What child would not be terrified?
"I'm not dirty today," I lied brightly
covered in fern spores like instant-coffee dust.

One morning (was it just dawn?)
I braved the milk-grey wash of still-night-things,
cattle cupboards, steel uncertainties,
to find my grandma in the kitchen wrapping mounds

of sandwiches.
A woollen ravelled comforter that charged on one battery
she said, "It's just your Uncle Arthur off to work."
She put a cosy on an egg, placed toast in a rack.
"Early off is early back."

Profiles of My Father

I

The night we went to see the Brisbane River
break its banks
my mother from her kitchen corner
stood on one foot and wailed, "Oh Bill,
it's *dangerous.*"
"Darl," my father reasoned,
"don't be Uncle Willy,"

And took me right down to the edge
at South Brisbane, near the Gasworks,
the Austin's small insignia winking
in the rain.

A policeman helped a man load
a mattress on his truck.
At a white railing we saw the brown water
boil off into the dark.
It rolled midstream higher than its banks
and people cheered when a cat on a crate,
and a white fridge whizzed past.

II

Every summer morning at five-thirty in the dark
I rummaged for my swimming bag
among musty gym shoes and Mum's hats from 1940
in the brown hall cupboard.

And Dad and I purred down through the sweet, fresh morning
still cool, but getting rosy
at Paul's Ice Cream factory,
and turned left at the Gasworks for South Brisbane Baths.

The day I was knocked off my kickboard
by an aspiring Olympian aged ten
it was cool and quiet and green down on the bottom.
Above in the swaying ceiling limbs like pink logs,

and knifing arms churned past.
I looked at a crack in the cream wall
as I descended and thought of nothing.

When all of a sudden
Dad's legs, covered in silver bubbles,
his khaki shorts and feet in thongs
plunged into view like a new aquatic animal.

I was happy driving home;
Dad in a borrowed shirt with red poinsettias
and the Coach's light blue, shot-silk togs.

Woman Crossing the Road

It's cold, wind gusty,
I can smell rain.
She crosses toward me
her mouth asking something.

At a certain point
our eyes are forced to meet.
Do I smile?
Wave?
You could take away everything
except the feet
self conscious, steady
edging the pavement.
She moves and looks with care to right and left
("She was run over coming to say hullo").

You could slide all the pieces
out of the picture
except her arms
and her eyes and mouth smiling –
her arms hug her tight,
are posed.

She wants to come over just for a minute.
Halfway across now
assured, determined.
(Overhead two crows are fighting with a blue jay)
She says, "I meant to ..."
But the backwash from a car fades her words away.

from My Mother and I Become Victims of a Stroke

Lost

"For once in my life,"
she says, "on my empty feet."
"For once in my life
give me something"
and looks at me with yearning,
bland old eyes.
"I've never had
not once, not once!" she shouts
but the sentence scoots away
before she can struggle with it.

"I just need a vimsin tripe,"
she says, putting tea bags in the toilet
quite surprised
to find cheese sweating in the biscuit tin
the Nescafe jar full of water.

"You need a rest
you're my daughter,"
she smiles and tells an inside joke
that ends instead in tears.
She shuts all doors and windows.
She'd lose the keys if she was given them.
Her hard-held territory
full of unidentified badmen
who jeer, nod and disappear.

She stares in the mirror
adjusts her glasses
a drawer full of oddments at her feet.
She needs a decade
to sort through all she has collected.
"I can't with my fat head," she cries.
"Disgusting."

"It's no good.
It's folded up – a damn shame.
Look at me!
I used to be a young girl."
Her voice fades. She leans one elbow
on her bed, quite conversational.

She peers at me over a pinnacle of handbags.
"I've lost everything now," she says.

Residues

Her brain is stripped
to its inessentials.
She's disposed of the gears.
Her mind is full of old shoes
that don't fit.
Clothes. Which? Which?
She twitches a pair of slacks
over her shoulders.
"I used to have such lovely … lovely …"

"What do you think?"
She empties drawers full of soft bras and nighties
onto the floor.
Surrounded by debris.
Life at full tide
was just a big shopping trip.
"I've got nothing to wear," she states
calmly surveying
a cupboard full of clothes.

Junk

Get rid of it all.
Make archaeologists accountable
for digging more of it up.
Old stuff.
Skeins and strands and tentacles,
browning indoor plants.
Bits and broken pieces.
Watches with inscriptions
that don't tock.
Knick-knacks.

Shoes full of smells.
Old hats, grim faces
old hates, odd glances.
Cracked handbags.
Bad dreams, forgotten pledges
mirrors with no frames,
might-have-beens.
Four potato peelers, rusty, from Taiwan.

Don't even give it away for a song.
Burn the St Vincent de Paul's.
Stand on a headland and fling it over the edge.
The ocean glitters
with family-crested silverplate.
Nests of occasional tables go in at a cant.
Bakelite radios that still play
surge in the waves.
"Thor" washing machines agitate, churning sand.
Bagfuls of family photos subside silently.

Just the Frame
Once so beautiful, wilful, mild.
Happy at the trot
from one cup of tea to the next.
A guileless discontent.
It's all still there
but under a grey coat of paint.
Her brain's in despair.
Her hate has caught her up.

Stubborn.
At thirty had her teeth ripped out,
though Dad said "Not."
Killing herself
and why shouldn't she?
Her eyes flash murder.
My life to maim if I like.
Under the grapefruit tree she stops suddenly,
one hand on her clothes basket
on its rusty iron frame.

Washed Up
She goes to bed
with two pairs of glasses
neatly on her nose.
Next morning she can't see a thing.
She stares out her hutch door, devoid of happiness.
"Isn't it lovely?" She speaks quickly.
"I don't know what."
She recedes into the gloom.
The poinciana trees, arching and touching

their light liquorice green,
red flowers blaring, pulse on.

My Brother Died

Well, then my brother died.
My only surviving ...
And I said, "I'll take the thing."
And he said, "Put it in the pergalum."
And then he died.

But before he died –
I wanted it –
it had been in the for years and years –
long before I ...
They were marvellous to him.
Then he died.

He told me, "If you want it take it."
And I said, "Well" – so I did.

It was the most beautiful –
I'd had my eye on it.
So he was still breathing.
Then he died.

The Shell

After that rasping second when the woman died
she was bleached pale on the surface like a sponge.
Slightly yellow slightly grey.
When the nurse-aide touched her skin it was leached fibrous.
Her blood had drained from the periphery
to pool centrally a rusting lake.
Her platelets desiccated and curled like dropped contact lenses.
This much that was invisible I knew like a fairy-tale.
But where was her mere self
the intrinsic insubstantial that life ventures?
It went – no longer atomically spinning.
It went – proteins unfolding their brotherly three-dimensional grasp.
She was airy impervious unpledged.
A hardening shell a celluloid doll.
When we tried to slip in her dentures they didn't fit.
On edge we laughed.
There was no disrespect – no one there.
The formality of death is due to emptiness.

When molecules cease their high humming
dark space appears.
It radiates in waves and disperses in continuous air.

Arrogant Animals

The sheep is an arrogant animal.
Like us it is sure of its place
in a myopic world.
It sees what it sees
grass leaf wire
knows that it knows
it's the top twig
of life's arborescence.

It has a name
for what it feels – *BAA* and *BAA*.
That's why it's certain.
That's why its eyes
are a blatant challenging yellow
why it stamps its foot
ushers its lamb away
from human contamination.

When a sheep dies
racist star-gazing
it totters aside
across an unbridgeable creek
trailing wisps of dignity.
It will die adamant.
It will think react
be contained in the superior
essence of sheep.

A sheep's skull is a sculpted housing
fine and hard for a sheep's brain
built to retain
its idea of itself.

Arachnophobia

At one stage I was dying.
Then I lived on.
Life sticks to you
a cobweb more involved with design
than concerned with your form.

Ephemeral signs of grief
huge helplessness
pain's needling bites
it discounts.

Life holds you in its sights.
It wraps you
a mummified meal.
Life squeezes and molds you
a spider detailing a fly.

Life looks through its faceted eyes
warmly mechanical.
Avoiding emotion
busy all night
your meaning is *food-to-go*
its ticket to tomorrow.

HOMER RIETH 1947–

Homer Rieth was born in Stuttgart, Germany, in 1947 of German and Georgian parents and came to Australia in 1952. He went to school in Catholic colleges and after a short period in the Jesuit novitiate at Loyola, Watsonia, attended the University of Melbourne. He has taught Greek and Roman literature and philosophy, English literature and medieval and modern history. He lectured in Classical Studies at RMIT University, Melbourne. Since 1999 he has lived in the township of Minyip in the Wimmera, in western Victoria. Rieth has published two books of poetry, *The Dining Car Scene* (2001), from which the two poems here have been chosen, and *Wimmera* (2009), a 359-page epic about the geography and history of the Wimmera landscape. Rieth's poems often read like overheard private rhapsodies, in which the arcane and everyday mingle. He employs an ebullient, rococo language in long breathless sentences. There are only two full stops in "Dining Car Scene", and one in his Duns Scotus poem.

The Dining Car Scene in *North By Northwest*

Everything about Eve is captured in that gesture;
the sun blinking through the window, is going down
on a ridge of distant mountains,
the river, drawn to something more mysterious
than microfilm and secret agents
is following the train;
it has the curve of the Twentieth Century Limited
in its sights, the sleek silver Pullman
kicking over the rails at a speed to match

the gale force winds gathering off Lake Michigan;
it catches first his eye, then hers;

suddenly, the oboe begins the love theme;
it comes into their presence
unnoticed, but for the quiver in her voice;
each keeps up a cool *patois*,
they are old hands at this;
the steward arrives, takes down the order;
she suggests "brook trout";
he sips on a Gibson, worrying about honesty
in women, but not about his own;
and then, seeing her reach into her clutch bag
for a cigarette,

Thornhill strikes a customised match
suavely, from a matchbook;
she leans forward, into the flame,
takes his hand, with the match in it,
doesn't let go,
but draws the smoke in slowly,
pulls him towards her, by the fingertips,
with no apparent pressure,
until his hand is in the magnetic field
of her face, where the matchlight
plays on the groomed perfection
of her platinum blonde hair;
and then, in a glance that becomes a look,
there is an electric pause,
and she blows the match out;

across their table, through the dining car window
you can see the soft dissolves
of sunset, river and mountain scenery,
the milestones of another journey.
Later, after betrayal has left its wound,
you will remember all this;
you will see it set in the resolute faces
on Mount Rushmore; you will see it as it was
that evening in Drawing Room E, Car 3901,
as she leaned towards him,
revealing an ambiguous smile;
only later, will he understand how much
it meant to her; how for the first time, like him,

she had a chance of doing something,
finally worthwhile.

A Day in the Backyard Thinking About Duns Scotus

And when the light falls
like this, under the guard of the shade,
ripe as juniper berries,
it's difficult not to be a bit prone to being
filled with a sense of is-ness,
joining the tesserae of patches, of hedge and shrub,
the dogs lying about on the lawn,
pavers, roan and piebald,
a rickety back fence, about to fall,
and the parched grass, waiting all day
for the sprinkler's
"Shhh ..."

and when the shade spreads
like this, under the guard of the light,
the geraniums nozzle the kink in the hose,
trains toot, Frankston-bound,
over igneous crumble and bolted sleepers;
our apple tree buds without me lifting
a finger, or catching a breath;
Jackson, the pomeranian, barks at swooping magpies,
Buster, his *bête noire* from the bush,
follows suit;

and when the light falls
like this, in an ambience of astonishment,
that's as it should be;
you consider how much a figment of the mind
the ordinary day is,
how little it salvages, yet how much it purloins
from the real;

and when the shade spreads
like this, mothy, spidery,
hidden worlds comes into their own,
they make us conscious at last
of Duns Scotus, his living presence,
the sheer amazingness of animals,
of birds, the philharmonics of their wings
above a patch of pulses, or a row of cruciforms;

other scraps of existence are rendered as insect,
or mineral quiddity, each with its own
template and atomic weight;

and when the light falls
like this, the wind is a coat of paint
on peeling weatherboard,
daisies dance with shrinking weeds;
they catch the sunlight out on a rusty latch,
or in the toolshed where the sky-
light dazzles;
it gets under the guard of the axe, the pick and shovel,
a mattock or an orbital sander,
as if to say to the camellias, to the trumpet tree,
"give the dog a bone,
I am you   you   and you
forever
                    "Shhh ..."

JOHN ANDERSON 1948–1997

John Anderson grew up on an orchard in the Goulburn Valley, near Kyabaram, Victoria. He began living in Melbourne in 1966. He travelled extensively in Australia and also in Europe, South East Asia and New Guinea. He died suddenly of leukemia in October 1997, in Melbourne, soon after a three-month tour of the Hamersley Ranges in Western Australia.

Anderson published three poetry collections and often participated in Melbourne poetry readings. He wrote some cryptic, aphoristic and surrealistic pieces, many contained in his last book *The Shadow's Keep* (1997) which are not entirely successful, being lines that he said "represent a variety of dream phenomena ..." In general, his shorter pieces are unsatisfying. Anderson is strong however where he has a keen interest in his subject matter and where he wants to convey information – something unusual for a poet in the last hundred years, with perhaps only Mark O'Connor in this book using poetry to inform readers. Anderson's originality emerges in his remarkable meditations on landscape, two of which are represented here. Stylistically they can be seen as a frontal assault on the well-made poem, often beginning with a deliberately prosaic statement that reads like the start of a technical article. But as Anderson warms to the subject, the language picks up and there is an intensity and momentum that many well-made poems cannot match. Alex Miller has commented regarding Anderson's song cycle *the forest set out like the night* (1995): "Accurate observation of exact detail underpins and grounds the larger metaphysical structures, rendering the tone both accessible and sublime."

Ned Johnson has these recollections of Anderson: "'Stop the car,' he would call, then clamber out onto an unremarkable roadside to find the thing he was looking for – a wildflower, an insect, a fungus, or, down a slope in a hidden gully, a particularly fine specimen of gum tree. Sometimes it required an effort of imagination to see what he saw, sometimes the revelation was powerful and immediate … He had no interest in money or possessions – apart from books, small artworks and found objects that he collected. He loved to travel, and knew most of Australia. He walked, he slept on the ground in the open, he knew places intimately …".

from the forest set out like the night

. . .

The idea that the Australian bush is drab and monotonous is well established in our literature. It has some truth, but even the greyest bush is sometimes relieved by a certain fragile glittery sub-theme, on the drier inland slopes more crystalline and unsoftened by climate.

The theme is picked up on the tips of things: gumleaf glitter, red gumtips, twigs white sheened or enamelled in Chinese Oxblood; and in the crevices: exposed quartz, an ant dragging its shiny abdomen over leaf litter, knobs of hardened gum sap (kino) fastened like rubies to trunks.

Movement is part of its quality and its keenest edge is animate. Insects and birds are its untrapped – its most unstable cells.

It seems the spectrum poured itself in an almost pure prismatic form on the parrots, finches and wrens, which act as its agents, flitting through a leached backdrop distributing colours.

In the dry sclerophyll iridescence is almost a general principle for beetles, wasps and flies, even occurring in some moths.

The theme is elusive, sometimes little more than a jewelled crinkle moving before the wind or heat, yet at other times it seems one need only upend any piece of curling bark to have the hand fill with precious stones.

In some respects I think Balinese music provides a successful metaphor. Despite its origins Balinese music catches something in the Australian setting, and I think because it provides the same tinkling contrast to the bush as is suggested by its own metallic glints and shining surfaces.

It seems to pick its way in a series of disconnected points. It gives just the right amount of form without imposing too much. Its rhythms are hidden and natural. Subtle enough to catch and lend fluency to the songs of crickets, frogs, cicadas and bellbirds, sometimes disappearing like an invisible songbird behind a static screen of notes. And capable of exuberance too. Gumleaf glitter in wind is the visual equivalent of a torrent of gamelan.

If it is conceded that life evolved from the sea maybe in Australia it drew something too from the stars, fire, mineral springs, frosts, lightning, blue distances and waterfalls.

Or is even some process of refraction from the glass of the Simpson gibber involved?

. . .

Like so many of Australia's distinctive rock formations the Grampians are surrounded by plains.

They can be encircled, encompassed, easily known as a coherent geological entity.

They are dwelt upon by the plains

They are magnified by the lens of the plains

They are islands of the plains, engaged in meditative retreat

Set apart.   Like Ulum, Kata Tjuta, the Warrumbungles, The Rock, Hanging Rock, Mt. Arapiles, Pyramid Hill, Mt. Buffalo, the Stirlings

They rise like a great earth monastery
Within each rock and plant seems sanctified, part of a design more exactly wrought. They have a focused beauty.

> It is in such places that one might expect to find clues to the continent.

The Grampians were known to the aboriginal people as the "jump up" mountains.

The Grampians jump up from the Western District plains. It is a source of surprise even to those who know them well how small a range they are. They intrigue from afar. From within they are so consistently and everchangingly engaging, from heathland, swamp to manna forest; gorge, waterfall to mountain rockface; from panorama to panorama, that the suggestion that such invention is endless is happily and naturally surrendered to.

Their wandering advance and dramatic easterly escarpments give an illusion of great depth and monumental size.

They are too a laboratory of Australia's essential forms which are here tried out in combination after combination.

The rich variety of plant life seems like a further expression of the inherent imagination of the place.

The plants in these heaths are related to those of South Africa and South America. They corroborated before the continents split and drifted apart.

In Australia the development of the heaths was favoured by changes in climate and isolation. The descendants of the heaths spilled out and colonized most of the available niches in the continent. Gave Australia its characteristically heathish appearance.

Here they are in many of their primal forms, wiry and tenacious, tying knots and juggling seeds.

Telling stories: How the eucalypt began as an unruly shrub.

Perfecting the spring. Slaves to their art.

Some of the plants that occur here in the Grampians are only found again hundreds or thousands of miles further on, over plains and seas and deserts, in Tasmania, Western Australia and the Blue Mountains.

Here they sit still upon an ancient throne that preserves a record of their past community, their primacy, more completely than any other point in Australia.

On an island within an island continent.

Poised for conquest.

These mountains
In their southernmost reaches grey green and woolly textured, clustered rocky formations, the complement of a more coastal climate and grey bellied clouds. A horse shoe fortress protecting a well watered valley from cutting winter westerlies. The winds are carried up and over the long backs of the mountains, which seem themselves set to the winds and to maintain a wave like profile.

Here the aborigines came.

To the North increasingly arcane, drier, gaunt and orange. A patina of the desert borne above grassy flats marking the former bed of an ancient sea.

The escarpments snake in more complex patterns

What are these mountains?

Are they the accumulations of the fantastic that have rolled in from thousands of square miles of open country? The inmost thoughts of the plains

are they the nomadic encampments of the dreaming spirits still engaged in their trek over the original flat earth?

Plains wanderers.

Or part of some largely subterranean animal whose backbone will wriggle before you when you climb Mt. Sturgeon or Mt. Abrupt and shake it by the tail.

Some beast on which the rarest plants mark the most sensitive whiskers and the succession of blooms its moods, the pattern of its thoughts

are they an integral part of an organic Australia and globe, whose powers augment those of Uluru and Kata Tjuta?

In aboriginal times many parts of the range were seldom entered.

But perhaps the reverent steps and soft breath of the aborigines drew blessings nonetheless from each untouched stand of wildflowers high on its rocky stage

Perhaps for us too such places are that part of the earth brain, that part of our own brain, of so temperamental and delicate an ecology and of such a vital nourishing force that it must be entrusted to the currawongs and cockatoos.

I imagine in the deep shade of Bullace's Glen the ferneries and soft feathery tangles of undergrowth protect an avenue of the brain that can be flown into in dreams

as it was when the mountain sawtooth silhouette marked the border of a dream set down on earth

---

DENNIS HASKELL 1948–

Dennis Haskell grew up in Sydney, worked as an accountant and then became an English academic at the University of Sydney. He moved to Perth with his family in 1984 and is Professor of English and Cultural Studies at the University of Western Australia. He is co-editor of the literary magazine *Westerly*, is the author or editor of 17 books, including five collections of poetry, literary and social criticism and literary scholarship. He co-edited the *Collected Poems* of Kenneth Slessor. In 2009 he became Chairman of the Literature Board of the Australia Council. Haskell's poetry is one of understatement, a quietist search for meaning – the emotional logic of his work is often reflected in its syntactical movement. Although not a confessional poet, he typically writes about personal experiences with a real intimacy.

For Thomas Hardy

Start with simple things:
Grass, the earth, the roots of grass.

Perhaps meaning is found

Only in the minute perception
Of old and familiar objects.

What more do you have?
If you wish to discover
The Gods you must look
To things, not into
Your own mind.

And be specific: kikuyu, the dark soil.
Our discordinate minds
Shake at the roots:
Larkin, to construct a religion,
would choose nothing more solid than water.

Because this can be counted on
To move, and to capture
Every angle contained in colour.

Because everything breaks down
Into perception, the onrush of light
Running toward and across our eyes.

Because this is opposed to
The assumption that perfection exists
Whatever perfection might mean to us: hands
Untouched by wrinkles, grass
That spreads untiring shoots like green fingers
Whose knuckles never coarsen,
A life of no conceivable pain.

But the mind holds colour
Spreading from somewhere outside the mind;
Light breaks onto our eyes
And leaves us simple things: earth and water,
Suffering, joy, the roots
Of a coarse religion.

One Clear Call

Holidays, the bush, dusty Coonabarabran
and out of the blue your friend has rung
you, caught on the hop; an engineer
who never looks at a book, whose father's died;

the service is soon; and he wants to read
something – not scriptural – literature perhaps:

the skilled academic that you are,
you suggest – a good choice – "Crossing the Bar".

"Where can I buy it?" he asks, "and quickly?"
"I know it," you say, down the glistening, impersonal wires,
"I'll repeat it, slowly." He waits, still, fingers
at the ready, for the first poem he's heard since school.

So you start, inexpressively, enunciating each syllable,
"'Sunset and evening star, / And one clear call for me'",
into a vast tide of silence at the end of the line,
the unmoving pen you cannot see, foaming at the words

until his wife picks up the mouthpiece, and the pen,
and you are Tennyson's mouthpiece, shaken a little
and wondering now, as you begin again
before a face you cannot see: "'Sunset and evening star …'"

until she is choking too, and her wrist falters
across the lines, registering the scatter of words
as they lift from Tennyson's dead mouth and your own voice
where they have lain like subject matter of no-one's choice,

that past sensation of syllables sweeping you and your friends
across the bar of technique, of grieving, of consolation.

The Raising of the Cross

after Rembrandt

His strangely y-shaped body
is angled to the earth
as he is lifted up out of it
like a tree whose only fruit is flesh,

like death on a candlestick,
and all our hopes
that there is a body beyond this body,
more clear, more pure, more insubstantial,

is locked on this tattered figure,
even his beard looking ragged
as a surrounding thief's
in a B-grade movie. Oh the relief

if this were not art but truth
soaring above us, firm and whole,
the scratchings of paint merely symbols
substantial, insubstantial as the soul.

KATE JENNINGS 1948–

Kate Jennings was raised on a farm near Griffith, New South Wales, and graduated in Arts from the University of Sydney. She was active in left-wing and feminist politics, editing a controversial anthology of women's poetry, *Mother I'm Rooted* (1975). She is the author of two partly-autobiographical novels which have had critical acclaim. She has also published a memoir, books of essays and short stories and two books of poetry. For many years she has lived in New York City, where she has been a Wall Street speechwriter, and an outspoken and independent journalist. Geoff Page in *A Reader's Guide to Contemporary Australian Poetry* (1995) described her first book of poetry *Come to Me My Melancholy Baby* (1975) as "like a freeze-frame of the seventies ... the days when four-letter words were first finding their way into Australian poems ... [and] when 'second-wave' feminism was in its more rowdy and explicit beginnings". Her brief second book of poetry, *Cats, Dogs and Pitchforks* (1993) in Page's view was "of a very different order", and is composed of disciplined, incisive, mainly autobiographical poems. The centrepiece is the twelve-page "Without Preamble: Martin Johnston 1947–1990", an elegy for the Australian poet. The poems selected here are from this second book.

Kathleen Marie Flynn

She was eleven, the girl strangled in the woods,
a scrappy patch of ailanthus and poison ivy

through which I have often taken shortcuts
and thought, in derelict and unprepossessing places

such as this, women are murdered, and dared
myself to see a grub-white limb. My neighbour Bea

recollects seeing her doing homework in the kitchen
of her father's restaurant. I saw her once, too.

She was walking home from school. It was raining
hard and straight. Her hair was slicked to her skull,

and her skirt and blouse stuck to her skin. She wiped
the rain from her mouth with the back of her hand

and stared straight at the window where I stood.
My name is Kathleen, she said. *I am going to die.*

Assassin

A baby squalling. A rodent squealing.
The phone. We capsize into consciousness.

A woman, neither young nor old,
Southern accent, panicked, pleading.

She wants to speak to my husband,
"Yes?" he asks, into the receiver.

As always on waking, his face has
the creased innocence of a newborn.

"Nobody there." I try. "Hello. Hello."
No intake of breath, no echo.

A still silence. A back road
on a cloudless winter's night.

Click. Dial tone. I wait, fully
expecting my emotions to bolt,

but feel only sisterhood
with a woman whom need

has made a bottom dweller:
headlight eyes, bag-needle teeth.

Her belly! It distends to three times
her size to accommodate her prey.

She is an assassin of assumptions
and peace of mind. I have been her.

The next morning, my husband says
he has no idea who the caller was.

We speculate as to her identity,
and then, because it is laundry day,

strip the bed. A minor argument
erupts: he likes patterned sheets,

I have a preference for plain.
We fold and tuck. Fluff and plump.

TONY LINTERMANS 1948–

Tony Lintermans was born and grew up on a farm in Victoria. He has written children's books, television scripts and short stories and two books of poetry. His work has verve and assurance. "A Bone from the Misty Days" is from his second book *The Shed Manifesto* (1989).

A Bone from the Misty Days

For there is much to be learned from dogs.
For the dog is focused upon the immediate, as in the startled rabbit chased,
    or the scent reciprocated.

For the dog goes crabwise through the day, sidewise he goes with prancing joy.
For the dog is aimlessness creatively tuned, exact opposite to a briefcase.
For my first dog was Whisky, a blue heeler who worked with cattle and was well trained.
For he was a way-back dog, a down-boy, sit-fella skitch-it dog who always did.
For he was my friend in the days of mist, those early school days.
For he was there the day that raincoated Freddy Hayes rode up to the front door demanding to know where his cows were.
For Freddy's fences meant well.
For my mother this was the last straw.
For the hearts of snapdragons had been bitten out, and the stocks trampled by these same cows on earlier visits.
For she answered, "If I see 'em, I'll shoot 'em!"
For my father was a flower farmer with finicky customers.
For Freddy Hayes turned his horse and rode away, drawling over his shoulder "Well shoot 'em!"
For he was nonchalant like his fences, slack tempered.
For three days nothing happened.
For the bees in their box on the old wooden dray it was buzzing as usual.
For the kookaburra flying across the dam with a black snake dangling from its mouth it was one more long lunch.
For Whisky and me lying in long grass it was Saturday, and cloud-watching time.
For we were friends in the misty days, those early school days.
For the cows would come back, and they did.
For they were skinny and ridiculous in their wooden head-frames to stop them jumping fences.
For they jumped anyway.
For they landed in our newly planted lawn, and went four-stepping all through the pouring night.
For the rain called their tune as they waltzed and slithered and squelched in the new-raked soil in their ruinous moo-less ignorance.
For morning came, and with it my father's wrath.
For he was shouting, "The pound! This time it's the bloody pound for Hayes' cows!"
For it was five miles to the Ferntree Gully pound, with six cows accused.
For I was to help with the droving, and Whisky too on this suddenly blazing no-school morning.
For now it was holler time, pick up stick and hurl it time, hoo those cows along!

For the cows it was incomprehensible hoo-ha, humans going ga-ga time.
For what are we but cows? their sad eyes asked, for what are we but cows?
For their flanks were heaving and soaked with sweat.
For they would stop to eat, or enter someone's driveway before they were hit again, or nipped, or barked at.
For it was "Get along there!" or "Move you mongrels!" or "Gorn!" all the way along.
For righteous anger ruled, like a stirred-up snake it whipped those cows along.
For I was nine years old and innocent, but helping anyway.
For they were Freddy Hayes' cows, the errant ones, the high jumping ones with moons in their eyes who'd moseyed neighborwards once too often.
For the day was sunny and the gravel road glinted in the morning's dappled shuffle.
For mushrooms were pushing up by the bucketful in Thompson's paddocks there as we crashed past, but I could not stop.
For the creeks were running, three of them in that five mile walk, snug in their ti-treed banks winding like dull green ribbons through the passing farms.
For the Gully pound was near now, and half the morning gone.
For the bridge where the swaggie slept was passed.
For the acre of pumpkins gone wild was passed.
For Alberni's and Sharp's and the mad lady with the black horses were all watching, and were all passed.
For the pound was reached at last.
For one father, one son, one old dog and four cows it was "Phew" time, and one exhausted "Moo".
For two of the beasts had bolted, got clear away to the paddocks.
For the pound keeper penned the cows while telling my father the rules of redemption, the money that was needed to get them back.
For my father nodded.
For he nodded again and said he would tell the owner *immediately* where his cows were, but did he?
For not on your Nellie, sport.
For let him sweat, thought he, let him sweat like the flanks of his cows.
For I was late for school, too late for "Show and Tell" but I told them anyway.
For the subject was "How We Drove The Cows To The Pound" and it was good.
For Whisky died soon after, just lay down in the long grass near the dray and became disinterested.
For he was buried in the re-raked, re-sown lawn, and a plum tree planted

to mark the spot.
For the days of mist were finally over.
For I consider there is much to be learned from dogs.
For they nuzzle and nip only what is wholly present.
For they zig-zag everywhere, never going direct on their tail-wagging
business.
For the world is always teasingly new, and they know it.
For memories of the misty days are buried like bones, and sometimes when
I dig them up, I know it too.

JOHN A. SCOTT 1948–

John Scott was born in Sussex, England, and came to Australia when a child. In the 1970s, living in Melbourne, he wrote TV comedy for the *Auntie Jack Show* (1974), *It's Magic* (1974) and the *Gary MacDonald Show* (1977). He became a lecturer in media in Canberra and later at Wollongong University. He is now a full-time writer, who has published eight volumes of poetry, the last being *Selected Poems* (1995). Many of Scott's poems are complex narratives, and he has turned his attention to the novel, publishing five novels between 1988 and 2003. Scott's poetry is often bleak and sexually explicit, with undertones of violence and ennui. His language is formidably elegant, seductively dark, with a droll, understated wit.

Man in Petersham

He's dropped his heart!
His heart has fallen to the footpath.
But no-one seems surprised and least of all
the office girl whose stockings violin
across this empty road. He's dropped his heart!
It surely must be this and not his cigarettes.
The way he stares so long and makes no effort
to redeem it. And his suit is an immaculate grey,
and his shoes a duco white. And his feet are
frozen in the tiny refrigerators of his shoes.
With all the colours running out, he stares
upon his fallen heart. His mild-blue heart
shattered in its twenty filtered pieces.

Samba *(from* After the Dance*)*

He showers. He pulls back
the foreskin. Remembers curtains opening.
Feels his penis might have been vaudeville
or a theatre of luxury. He wonders at
the mild abrasives that surround him:

ash of cigarettes, dust or soap; finer grains
of attachment that might be seen to determine
an inevitability or disappearance. Closes
his eyes. Remembers his body as it appeared
in the mirror. That what mirrors tell us deceives.
They out-wait us; reverse the balances.
And that what can be seen of the body without
the aid of mirrors is another deception.
  The tree, and not the forest.
  The branch, and not the foliage.
  The vein, and not the leaf.
We miss it every time. And so he wears down.
He erodes. Examines the head of the penis;
the glans, as doctors call it, without desire;
the corona; the shaft of the penis. Stands
in the recess, above two floors of showers,
and below seven. Ponders how many men
stand with him in this great vertical line.
The habits of washing; preparing for work.
Living with the weight of themselves.
"Missing it", as it were. Somewhere.
  The frame, and not the framing.

Plato's Dog

Thirty years ago, Marseille lay burning in the sun, one day. That's Dickens. Tonight when I go home, everything's going to be exactly where I left it, this time. That's me. I'm good with words. For example, this bar reminds me of someone eating with their mouth open.

Tonight's a bad night. Tonight I'm on milky drinks because I've seen people drink them and the barmaid told me how some older blokes order "koala and milk" – and not joking either – because they've just heard it wrong. When you swirl them round the glass they settle into these curves. Like the rings of Saturn. I'm good with words. Though someone once told me I "possessed a humour incompatible with sexuality". That is, I entertain, but at the end of the night they go home with someone else.

Tonight's not a good night. At the table behind me there's an argument about Human Nature. Someone brings up Plato's dog. And someone else says "who?" and the first bloke explains, except I know it's not *Plato's* dog, and be blowed if I can think whose dog it should be. I stare at the ashtrays, all an equal distance above sea-level. Like lane-markers in the pool of the bar.

The barmaid's reaching for bottles; lost in her unrequited dance. I swirl the last of my milky drink and engage this couple across from me in conversation.

– Excuse me, I say. Remember when you were a kid and listening to the radio, and there'd be songs you'd sing all the way through, and years later you'd hear the song again and realise you'd been singing the wrong words.

They look up and wait a bit.

– You know *She Loves You,* she says. There's a line in that that says "Pride can hurt you too" and for years I thought it was "Invite her to your room".

– And sometimes you never *knew* the words, I add. But you could imitate the sounds. And you'd be singing along with all these nonsense words. That's how I figure life. You're either misunderstanding or not understanding at all.

We fall silent. The way you do after laughing a lot.

– I never knew if it was "inside a zoo" or "in Xanadu" in *Baby You're a Rich Man,* the man offers. But the moment's passed.

Maria would've been fixing me something to eat right now, so I'd have something to sit down to when I got in. A bowl of soup, say. And the idea of the soup almost makes me cry – the way I almost cried when I caught a glimpse of her standing on the front porch in that dreadful pink wrapper as I drove off. And the slippers she wore that looked like she was treading on two poodles.

You see, I can cope with the people, and the arguments. But the objects defeat me every time.

Outside it's drizzling again. But tonight's been OK. No-one asked me to leave. They just watched me – maybe listened to me. I was probably the centre of a dozen conversations back then, while I sat there, and while I walked out, one day.

A Visit from the Doctors

When Dr Skrimshire, who certified him in 1841, was asked to state whether [the English poet John] Clare's insanity had been "preceded by any severe or long-continued mental emotion or exertion", he answered, with decisive brevity: "After years addicted to Poetical prosing."

John Press, *The Chequer'd Shade*

Returning from the death of Sally Mason's
first-born, Page and Skrimshire – vanity
of vanities – from Peterborough, persons
come to declare escape's insanity.

The patient is familiar: stout and florid –
whereas Page, asleep-by-fireplace,
has let the pencil drop upon his namesake's
pale and singularly vacant face.

"Now if you were a Shakespeare or a Byron,
John, what substance to my disquisition!"
Thus, the author of The Village Pastor's
Guide in Letters from an old Physician.

Awakening, Page mistakes the pencil-mark
for hair; attempts to brush it free, perforce.
The poet shifts tobacco in his mouth;
thinks contrary; at times says something coarse.

Detained by them above an hour, they offer
little-detailed judgment, thus, in closing:
madness – stemming from the family – after
years addicted to Poetical prosing.

They drag him, struggling, screaming, from the door;
return him to a madhouse in the dene;
condemn him to that Sodom, or that Hell,
whose wooded grounds slope gently to the Nene.

The houses emptied of their demons, fall.
The houses, exorcised, grow dark too soon.
Relieved of blessed rantings, walls grow cold,
draw dampness from the seeping afternoon.

ALEX SKOVRON 1948–

Alex Skovron was born in Poland, lived in Israel for fifteen months, and at the age of nine emigrated with his family to Australia, settling in Sydney. His parents were Holocaust survivors. After high school, he obtained degrees in Political Science and Government. From the early 1970s he worked as a book editor for publishers in Sydney and Melbourne, and was general editor of *The Concise Encyclopaedia of Australia* (1977–79). He now lives in Melbourne. Skovron began writing poetry in 1968, but did not publish until 1982. He has produced a novella and five books of poetry; one of these is a book of prose poems, *Autographs* (2008).

Skovron's poetry is Central European in its sensibility, reflecting his parents' experience. His poetry also shows his training in the political sciences and work as an editor, particularly his involvement with encyclopaedias. There is a search for an organising principle, a concern for correctness and precision, a fascination with atlases and maps. But at the heart of his poetry is the unsettling realisation that there is no pattern. There will perhaps always be burnt books and smoking cathedrals. The 19th and 21st centuries are simultaneously present ("The Centuries"). Skovron is able to invent potent Borgesian allegories, impossible Escher-like constructions – "The Guilt Factory" and "The Colours" are examples. The narrowness of his vision is its strength. His best poems are claustrophobic and strangely beautiful.

On the Theology of Ants

Picture an insect
circling a lifetime
in a covered jar. Secure the jar
inside a canvas bag stuffed with
faded clothing, rags and torn stockings.
Enclose this in a suitcase full of books
and old journals, sealed, strapped and slotted
in the back of a rusting station wagon
locked in a cluttered shed. Now imagine
that the garage is appended to a cottage
strung to a tree within a sprawling suburb
whose proximity to the city is ambiguous.
Elevate your vantage to locate the black towers
puncturing clouds that suspend them in space. Go
higher, higher, to incorporate the spill
of a massed metropolis, and then its edges
fringing the urban dusk and blending fast
with fields and pastures, plains and rolling earth.
A moment, and you stack
the crisscrossed chiaroscuro geometric grid
slanting, sliding north – and to the south, and west,
and east into the sea. Then the horizon and the end
of earth: receding, fading, darkening,
unreal – perspectives vanish, and
the thud of black.

The imprisoned ant,
still circling, nearly dead,
has spent his life devising metaphysics.
He has thought out the nature of the universe,
the origins of matter, the designs of time.

Serene and certain, he loves the calm of knowledge,
prepares glowingly to confront his Maker:

Whom most of his kind believe to be six-legged
but his own rarer perception, its divining spirit,
already can sense more correctly …

The Guilt Factory

From far away it is a constellation
of cubes and cylinders, pyramids and spheres
that interrupt the night-infested sky.
From closer up the shapes take substance,
and immensity, shadows expose texture,
structures reveal their form. But barely a sound
escapes the network of imposing designs:
platforms, barracks, engine-halls and towers,
and the myriad smaller annexes and links
that cluster the system – no sound, except
a faint monotonous hum, sometimes transmuted
to a rhythmic pulse as if from aeons away,
inferred only from the expectant air,
the haze shivering over certain canopies,
or the expression on a wall or brickline.
Nobody knows how far below the ground
the construction flows, how far into the sky
its elements incline – nobody has circled
the factory from without, it is too vast.
And no-one has ever returned from the bowels
of the enclosure. Those who have even touched
the walls or looked into the outer corridors
report familiar images: lanterns, picture-rails,
a complex of washrooms, dormitories, a huge
curved auditorium where curtains hang,
and many signs warning of great danger.
The engine-rooms and the assembly-lines
are only seldom glimpsed, and those who try
to look more closely come back with memories
so confounded, or in such forgetful calm,
that nothing can be gleaned. There is a point,
it seems, beyond which none can go –
those that defy it are never heard of again.
But on one aspect all are unanimous:

inside the plant, inside its very soul,
resides a silence, shrill and impassable,
a silence that accuses, and annihilates
with its ferocious gaze. And from within,
moving in a procession ghostly as life,
the manufactured shapes slide endlessly
along their endless tunnels, to emerge
nobody knows where. Sometimes a filmy smoke
is registered above a funnel or a tower.
Nobody has ever dared to capture it,
let alone to inhale its dark perfume.
They say it is the very smoke of death
and that the factory must disseminate it
through every inch of the metropolis;
and yet the substances burning underneath
remain obscure. There are those who say
that time is non-existent in the factory,
that space is an illusion, that no light
penetrates from below. This may be true.
But in the night, if one dares to approach
and enter the compound, and place a hand
upon a wall and stare into the stone –
at night the factory glows.

The Centuries

It is necessary to remind oneself
that the nineteenth century never really left us:
it has been here all along, biding its time –
like the fussy old colonel exhumed one graveyard night
who, barely have the encrusted nails been wrenched free,
pushes the lid up and bellows,
"About bloody time – thought you'd *never* get here!"

It's there, back of the musty wardrobe,
concealed behind a loose brick, in a mouldy pouch;
between the bones of a wall, on yellow newsprint
lining the floorboards to preserve the names of the dead
in the South African War; under the house
in a blackened strongbox packed with Victorian cards;
next to the ruby cufflinks in a crevice behind the chimney;
or in the attic – the mahogany dresser, the doll's house
decades empty, the chest of drawers with the huge metal key
misplaced since memory, jammed with maps and titles.

It is necessary to remember, too,
that the twenty-first century has been amongst us forever:
it squats alone, or winks from the electric arcade,
yells at the top of its voice from the wall of a tram,
gazes all night into its binary navel,
and of course (remembrance being what it is)
continues to mutter to itself
from railway cars, burnt books, smoky cathedrals,
gutters with stains ancient and black as blood.

The Colours

The conveyor belt oozes
at the speed of time
trailing only itself

Nobody attends
nobody is watching
the great hall is deserted

An enormous clock
guards the black aperture
where the belt begins

The opposite wall
sucks the infinite tongue
into itself a mile away

In between only the din
of pulleys and gantries
mechanical arms

Wheels and cylinders
the frenzy of pistons
the dance of steel

*

Exactly above the heart
of the advancing causeway
endless and empty

A skylight
high among the crossbeams
and girder vaults

High above
the planetary floor
and its clockwork geography

A many-faceted canopy
of stained-glass lozenges
in fabulous colours

Colours rich and unthinkable
in the perfumed depth
of their beauty

*

Every day at noon
the conveyor belt stops
for sixty seconds

Stops to take stock
of the luminous kaleidoscope
to admire and to praise it

Kandukur

She travels across her atlas every day,
loves all the shades and shapes, the way they often
uncannily echo each other. New Zealand, for instance,
is Italy upside-down, but flopped and chopped.
Or Madagascar, sliced with a surgeon's panache
from Mozambique. Such thoughts sometimes remind her
of Kezelco, a map she could never quite follow.

The experts come, but nothing seems to change.
The monitor winks like an understanding uncle, the drip
a laconic sentinel over the bed. He used to say her voice
was a fobwatch swinging, it soothed and hypnotized;
she never really believed it. A world ago her classmates
would tease at her stutter, a childish thing she ditched
along with Ludo, but the damage was done.

She'd never told Kezelco, and never mentioned the reason
behind her "shyness" (his awkward euphemism
that only made things worse). Three or four months, they say,
six at the most. She folds her shoulder into the too-soft pillow,
she'd like to sleep but the memories won't let her.

The channel up above flicks and flickers, the anchorwoman
brushes the wind away, some urchins crowd around her,
some helmets grin. Zoë resists the urge to listen in,
picks up the atlas again, screws up her eyes, opens a page
at random, taps a spot. Where has she landed this time?

Kandukur! *He* would have known – or galloped at once
for Google to look it up. It sounds exotic.
She must remember to ask her Indian oncologist.

ALAN WEARNE 1948–

Alan Wearne was born and grew up in Melbourne. He became friendly with Laurie Duggan and John Scott at Monash University, where he studied history, which he describes as his only intellectual love. He hosted "Conversations with a Dead Poet" (1999) a television documentary about his friend, John Forbes. A supporter of Essendon, the Australian Rules football club, since 1954 he helped found the Nunawading District Junior Football League and has published a prose satire about Melbourne's Australian Rules culture. He now teaches creative writing at the University of Wollongong, living part of the year in Wollongong and part in Fremantle, Western Australia, and regards himself as an exile from Melbourne.

Wearne has published three poetry collections and two verse novels, including the 757-page *The Lovemakers* which appeared in two parts. He established his distinctive voice in his first poetry collection, *Public Relations* (1972), with its matter-of-fact tone, short narratives about invented characters, abbreviated and disjointed style, replete with contemporary allusions (not all of which might be familiar to readers), and with sparse use of conventional poetic props such as scenery and imagery. His verse novels are similarly "unpoetic", but over time he has increasingly employed rhyme and verse forms to carry his narratives forward.

All of the poems selected here are from *The Australian Popular Songbook* (2008). They are self-contained and more readily anthologised than excerpts from his verse novels. Also the later Wearne, although he has not lost all of his early aggression, has an added dimension, the perspective of time, and at times glows with an attractive mellowness. "On the Road to Gundagai", a Forsyte Saga compressed into fourteen lines, is a technical tour-de-force. In "Knox City: A Ballad" the narrator refers to Target (a shopping chain), the "Red Rooster" (a restaurant chain), and to Bob Hawke crying, an incident when the Australian Prime Minister cried on television following the Tiananmen Square massacre. Wearne has provided the following note for "The Argonaut's Theme": "From the early 40s to the late 60s the Argonaut's Club was the intellectual heart of the *ABC Children's Hour.* Through entertainment and instruction the arts, sciences and benign moral precepts for living were passed on to the coming generations."

On the Road to Gundagai

" ... heading straight for home"

– Jack O'Hagen

After church the drive, the singsong: Dad in tenor mode
winds the Vauxhall down Mount Dandenong Road;

lulled, Mum's glad, these patterns still keep:

Janet reading, Carol pulling faces, Margie asleep.

Till, beyond such certainties, each arrives
(stride-, stroll- or stumbling through their lives)

out of those soul-on-sleeve
days, with what was/ is/ might be something to believe.

So Dad dies, Mum re-marries and shifts,
Janet lectures, Carol designs, Margie drifts.

Oh millstone/ loadstar
(that time of faiths/ a Sunday in the car)

behold your future, its, by extension, splendour:
welcome, ladies to The Age of Gender!

The Argonaut's Theme

for Miriam Jamieson

Wireless days, *Good Rowing!* days, and days when the spaceship lands,
the beings look almost like us and come in peace;
popular science days of lab-coated boffins with their utilitarian facts;
and the acme days of what just had to be high art:
painters in smudged smocks and clear, warm sopranos
who could be Auntie Pat or Auntie Iris in their crisp, floral frocks;
of course we were snobs and knew things couldn't be otherwise
(you'd only to hear the laconic wing commander's
Roger, over and out to realise how hawk-nosed trim
he must be, though ever the wag under pressure);
oh yes those really-mean-it days when smart kids had to *know* things:
weren't we the last generation to rote-learn *Recessional* let alone sing it?
being prepared for the 21st century when we'd hardly arrived in the 20th,
such muddleheaded days *Adventure Ho! Argonauts row … row … row!*

Knox City: a Ballad

She kept me waiting out the front of Target.
After an hour it seemed the surest sign
this love was like all others: set to cark it,
yet I trawled my brain for ways to make her mine;

knowing how all that high octane, madly
This one's the best and it is going to last
lava'd passion of Beverley and Bradley
seemed but a puddle, evaporating fast.

*

We'd met when I got hired to clear her guttering.
Given a week, falling pretty bad,
she sighed (although you sensed some neighbours muttering)
"We kinda love sortov each other ... Brad?"

Wide hips, great tits (doubt if they'll see saggage!),
a heavy moaning gurgle, then she'd come;
followed by that introductory baggage
to the juggling, stop-start life of a single mum:

"My ex? A deadshit!" (No need to blurt out *Really?)*
"He reckons remand's like waiting to be paged."
Sibling rivals? And Bev shrugged up *We're nearly*
just this low key side of disengaged.

(Her older sister sniffs aromatherapy.
The brother's backing Richmond, for his sins.
The younger one lives heading towards Werribee.)
Tuesdays I rolled out the wheelie bins.

Wednesday nights it always seemed Red Rooster.
In the backyard grew sand pit, swing and slide.
Who, you ask, took Kai to get his booster?
And like Bob Hawke I was the one that cried.

Then add a man's tears to all the local data,
and though it may seem a minority report,
camomile, wind-chimes, crystals, Desiderata,
aura'd every third house in the court.

And a decade on from dropping out of uni
this lumpenproletariat ding-a-ling
finds he's the very newest New Age loony
shuffling tarot, tossing the I Ching.

*

For what? For what? Answer *that* Knox City!
This bunny-with-women always gets the gong!
And options arrived, propped by my best self-pity
which goes with your finest easy-listening song.

Should I work out until my pecs turn granite?
Or reinvent that more basic bloke?
(There's girls-a-plenty down at The Daily Planet
for cuddles, sex and, sometimes, share-a-joke.)

When suddenly my eyes are being covered!
By some Wantirna scrubber on the make?

Not so! It's Bev guess-whoing her beloved
as head-in-hands he prays for this circuit break.

So time to repent, time to quit my fuming.
a junkyard dog can turn to the meekest hound.
She'd been for tests. Our future started looming.
Within a month we view the ultra-sound.

*

Yet, with a howl shoppers mistook for heinous,
"Before," I cried, "it's home to a queen-size tryst,
just this once let a man come Venus,
you sit here, give me the shopping list!

And ahh Knox City view your poor petitioner:
fatherhood-charged, rushing into Coles
he grabs shampoo (mistakes it for conditioner!).
Then we resumed our mainstream gender roles …

Poem for Cathy Coleborne

(Fitzroy the early to mid 1990s)

Bohemia gone mad!

– John Tranter Sonnet 95, "At the Pool"

Put aside your essays, theses
kids in black, it's Friday night.
Time to seek out from our species
Ms or Mr Maybe Right.
Clear the decks and clear the sinus,
what has gone will come around,
whilst we peek at Melbourne's finest
happy het'ro hunting ground.

Early twenties to mid thirties
see them primp, preen, proffer, prowl.
From assertors to assertees
one almighty mating growl.
Take a brace of Bruegel peasants,
add hormones from an on-heat hound:
behold our own post adolescence
happy het'ro hunting ground!

Every urge deserves depiction
(pluralists behold, rejoice!)

even (yes) young adult fiction
offers no invalid choice,
whilst, so faintly s-and-m-ey
micro whipped and lightly bound,
Fitzroy remains at least a semi-
het'ro happy hunting ground.

There was once this swingin' couple,
likeminded duos made 'em click.
His tolerance seemed mighty supple
till she dumped him ... for a chick.
"How'd," he mused "that option get her?"
Beer by beer his sorrows drowned.
The ex meanwhile composed this letter
from her former hunting ground:

Please dad didn't want to scare you,
girl-love though seems quite the rage ...
our word is 'choice' so mum don't dare you
think I'm going through a 'stage'.
Been eyed off by heaps of ladies,
some were jeaned and some were gowned
and some would sooner head to Hades
than any het'ro hunting ground.

Young, gay, proud and inner-metro
sense the limits, know the load:
"When Fridays get so hyper-het'ro
here we come Commercial Road!
Party's over, must say byebyes,
feel embarrassed hanging round
XY chromosomes and YYs
in *your* happy hunting ground!"

Then one winter, doped on Codral,
some poor loser simply sooked:
"Madame, may I dance this quadrille?"
"Sorry sport my card is booked."
Whither happy? Whither hunting?
Uppers upped and downers downed,
his psyche through its manic shunting
would fill a Melbourne Cricket Ground.

Like martyrs frying o'er a griddle
or madman in some film noir

("Gentleman with ancient riddle
seeks lady to replace his ma …")
this hero's role might suit a canto
(though they went out with Ezra Pound!).
O tragi-comic/ soapie-panto/
unhappy-happy hunting ground!

One evening, blatant as the mulga
two kids locked their eyes and gaped.
I might say more but aren't that vulgar
(it's as if I had them taped).
Itemise each short 'n' curly?
Labia and pubic mound?
Let's just say they went home early
from the het'ro hunting ground.

Whatever then they did they did right,
age-old normal, on the square.
Imagine though an hour past midnight
eavesdrop on this lucky pair:
"We've been happy-hunting-grounded!"
"Now are verbed who once were nouned!"
And their carnal joy resounded
through you-damn-well-know-what ground:

"All praise for this thing between us!"
Some nights it seems The Builder's Arms
worships nothing short of Venus,
whose excursions and alarms
for postgrad, activist, backpacker
(careful, don't swoon in a swound!)
brings forth that pleasantest of yacker
whilst Planet Earth turns hunting ground:

L.A. blondes (perhaps their mommies)
(soft) dealers at their hallowed task,
darkest koories, palest pommies,
Sydney "wits" who smirking ask
"Can't this town get colder? Moister?"
Kiwis straight from Milford Sound …
Fuck the world, *you* were our oyster
happy het'ro hunting ground!

KEVIN BROPHY 1949–

Kevin Brophy grew up in the Melbourne suburb of Coburg, was educated by the Jesuits, and studied literature and psychology at the University of Melbourne. He has been a seminarian, ballet stagehand, disability worker, teacher's aid, concrete labourer, and for one day was a roof tiler. He edited the magazine *Going Down Swinging* from 1980 to 1994. He teaches creative writing at the University of Melbourne, has published four books of poetry, three novels, two collections of essays and a collection of short fiction. He now lives in Brunswick, close to where he grew up. His diverse early work experiences may have contributed to an empathy with a wide range of human beings and human experience, that is somehow able to co-exist with a psychologist's detachment and alert observation. When the British poet Carol Rumens chose Brophy's "Painters" in January 2009 as poem of the week for *The Guardian*, she commented: "The detached clarity of the description somehow suggests that the painters are being seen by the speaker for the first time, or even that he is reporting back on an interesting new species." Regarding his poetry generally she said: "Family life is a frequent topic, quizzed wryly and affectionately, de-familiarised and not quite put back together again. There is a compelling mix of the local and the strange, the scientific and fantastical, the philosophical and the domestic, all adding up to a homely surrealism which may owe something to Lewis Carroll as well as the great prose-poet Russell Edson."

Forty-five Years on a Bicycle

The bicycle-keel counterweights him as he takes the corner
more smoothly than a delivery van that rattles up the gutter
and blasphemes against his cyclist's devotion to a curving idea.

The bike beneath him is his insect-double
humming plagues on cars and trucks.
It is all spokes and handlebars, subtle brakes,
an exoskeleton with silver guards and leather saddle;
this insect takes the man above it through unlikely gaps
sliding buoyant on the rim of death.

Under him the bike is in another element
translating wildly as it goes his legs and arms and torso
to the chirring speech of wheels and gears
that slice down waves of air,
a sciagraphy of shadows on stunned sunlight.

Its pencil lines barely needing three dimensions –
the bike is an idea that found us dazed, unwheeled.
It chained our legs to its ease, made speed
a fizzing ear-filled water-eyed human thing.

The bike is a dream of low flying,
deep diving in air against the bluff of wind,

it teaches us hills and timing, slides us into curves
like a poem that fits this world.
Even the map of our country is the outline of a rider
crouched over a machine of wind and motion,
a dragon shadowed by its jockey
whose shape strains to hold in the spin
and dip of this planet of waves, sand and ice.

A bird flew beside me keeping pace
waiting for the lift from my handlebar-wings
touching time with time, feather with frame,
until it was satisfied I was no fish of air
but a flightless bird or hapless insect overgrown,
or a hallucinated memory of the nineteenth century
and left me with this truth.

Walking Towards Sunset

I could have kept going past my front door
all the way to the end of the street and across
the tops of the shops, on over Moonee Ponds Creek
and beyond the hills of Essendon to a stony ledge
where the sky drops to the floor of the galaxy
and bends back up, an infinite dome, over my head.
I would have stood there, toes over the rocky edge,
knowing my eyes were made for looking at this:

the last slant-wise flash of careless brilliance
from that unimaginable bomb in the daily sky,
as silent as a distant war, filling doubt with light;
and from that ledge it would have seemed an answer
to last night's dream. I would have stayed
until the day abandoned me as each one does.

Difficult

It is difficult to choose the reader for this poem.
I have left its windows open
so you might as well climb inside
where you can be safe for now from weather,
and though your sudden presence feels intrusive
think of yourself as a museum visitor
to a reconstruction of a life now silenced.
The bed, I know, has not been made
but the silver cutlery on the formal dining table is meticulous.

You will not be roped out of any room
and you can be confident
the writer left before you and your party arrived.
The place is left as realistic as anything you might write yourself.
Dirty clothes (for instance) are piled into a predictable straw basket,
their odour not quite human,
though the stiffening socks were plainly meant for feet.
It is difficult to choose a visitor
who must arrive by chance.
Parents too are difficult to choose
though they're chosen all the same.
The plain truth is the bricks outside are wet with rain
and now you find yourself inside
the couch is sprinkled with the drops that just blew in with you
through the curtains of the open window.
Sounds of possums in the poem's ceiling must distract you,
a blackbird in the yard outside is startlingly alive,
the cat in here will stay asleep despite your tread,
and a green bin steaming with the evidence of wasteful life
in a corner of the kitchen is what you've come to expect from art.
The lived-in emptiness of every room
makes it difficult to choose a reader for this poem.
No meal has been prepared and no money has been left
in an envelope with your name on it.
The vases are all empty.
A man has written this you must suspect.
Blue sky outside presses down on us its single thought.
A green and oily ocean's creeping closer every century
and an ochre desert lies less than three thousand kilometres away.
It is difficult to know what is the greatest threat to this poem:
reader, silence, landscape, weather or its absent occupant.

Painters

It is as if each one had been sent to colour in the world,
and to do it between the showers of rain
so that colours will have time to fix themselves
on walls and pipes and window ledges.
When it rains the painters in their speckled overalls and spotty shoes
sit quietly in vans
with ladders like folded wings above them.
They drink white coffee with two sugars
and treat themselves to doughnuts from the local bakery,

sugared cinnamon.
At night they dream of edges of immaculate neatness.
They admire leaves and what autumn does to them.
Their lives are short, for each painted colour releases
a poisonous fume like a sigh
as it spreads and dries and makes our lives feel
deeply real.
The painters speak less and less
as the fumes take hold.
Their wives and children watch the painters going
like elves to another kind of existence.
You ask them what to do with leftover cans of paint
and they tell you it's not easy,
for paint would stain the sea and kill the fish if you let it go.
There are places, deep and foul, where paint must go
when its colour is no longer favoured, they will say,
and you will feel they are the enemies
of the paint they love. Their elf hearts move inside them
at each slap of colour on a wall or fence or seedy chair.

After Rain

There are six thousand languages still spoken on the planet
and within each one the word for rain makes people look at the sky.
As it rains outside the radio talks low in the kitchen,
those small dry voices going on, reassuring me.
When the rain is here the sound of it is better than thinking.
My son asks me if a baby could be taught to speak
every language on the earth and we agree it might be possible
if the rain keeps up to teach a baby anything we wish.
The rain makes pairs of us, it muffles wars and panics ants;
the rain gives all its knowledge to the earth;
and after rain the birds around here have much to say.
They're out there now like children let out of a classroom,
shaking themselves on Anna's roof and in the bottlebrush
where there must be mouthfuls of insects like lollies in the air.

A Dictionary of Sentences

After being away from my son for a day his size frightens me.
Always I am surprised at the bitterness of coffee.
As she speaks I become aware of her breathing, and want to listen to this.
"Even in prison", he said, "I gave myself four weeks' annual leave."
He shows me a photo of his father, gassed.

I pedal for an hour and a half convinced I am going nowhere.
In his grey shirt my colleague speaks of ethics as a thing of doubt and compromise.
My Christian friend says it is all right to be without faith, for this is the most authentic condition for any Christian.
"Suddenly" my daughter's French sounds French *(tout à coup).*
The barking of the dog next door is always expressed as a question.
The motor mower has one thing to say and like knowledge it fills the head briefly.
The nearest I can come to conversion is to begin each day immersed in water.
The visit: pointing to a chair he closes the door.
This novel, she says, is too wordy (and I want to tell her it is the words that I love).
We speak of the weather because in truth it tells what is within us.
When a man's beard is that luxurious it becomes impossible to listen to what he says.

JENNIFER COMPTON 1949–

Jennifer Compton was born in Wellington, New Zealand. Her father was a director of a company making wooden boxes, and he and his brother worked in the factory alongside the men. She remembers that when she was a child, "New Zealand was like a paradise. It was God's Own Country. We called it Godzone. Doctors were free. Schools and universities were free. Milk and butter were heavily subsidised and cost next to nothing. The world wanted to buy all the wool, meat, butter and cheese that we could produce." Then her father became seriously ill and died at the age of 50. She dropped out of university after six weeks. When she was twenty she met her husband, who was an actor. "He was bored. I was bored. We set sail for Australia in 1972 and we never looked back." She has had a number of plays produced and published, and at least three books of poetry and a chapbook. Her poetry is romantic and abrasive, and although she has written long poems, her work is distinctive for its abrupt, economical style.

The Woman of Rome

La Romana. By Alberto Moravia.
I read it at 13 snugged up in bed
in my aunt's house in Kilbirnie –
having rejected my own home in
Rongotai. For the usual reasons.

One hand on my mons veneris
eyebrows approaching hairline
at the spendthrift and amoral

atmosphere, the recklessness,
Europe! Not knowing yet that

I am reading in translation –
there are other languages.
But panting towards the source.
And my father arrives. Like a prince.
Offering me a packet of scorched almonds.

I accept them – like a princess –
like one who will one day be a queen
turn back towards the appalling book.
Scorched almonds are marvellous but
La Romana has my complete attention.

Brick

Mum sluiced us up and down in the Red Indian water
sent us running up the hall to the fire and Dad
the warm towel crouched by the fire at exactly my height.
Soon you won't be able to run about like that.

My grandmother's mammoth sideboard looming – *Why not?*
bought when she was married to last until she died which it did.
Why not! Tossing my little hips and skinny legs prancing about
my mother's face above and my mother's face on the wall above.

The night of the earthquake Dad ran us into a doorway
with a sudden anxious look at the ceiling – all of us littlies
in the doorjamb under his outstretched arms leaning towards us
the chimney could come through the roof – well a brick fell on my head.

A thought flew in my head with a why not with his sad answering look
the way he took the look of me with him forever wherever that may be
my father loved my child's body and held me in his two hands.
All men are my father – they are beautiful and good and sad.

Octopus Speaking

In the underwater tunnel of the civic aquarium
the octopus leaned his wretched head

against the glass of his turbid pool
sucking on his breathing tube, like

a severed vein
so he could live.

He asked for his ocean. He asked me,
the daughter of the powerful race.

I was standing alone like a child stands
with her entry ticket in her hand.

Electric Fan *(from* Rome*)*

The obedient fan
turns his blind face
to me – with interest.
The obedient fan
turns his blind face
to me – with interest.

Cut Your Cloth

Take up the scissors, the fingers of your right hand know
where to find them, how to work them. Like that! And that!
Cut the air in two. Crunch the blades with your expertise.
Like a little song of emptiness, find the snip snip that makes
a snarl. Now what was it you were about to do, my friend?

The cloth is streaming off the loom with a shudder and thud
and I know the way the women stand back, I have seen them,
watching, deftly, their big soft hands unflexed on their bellies.
They shift from foot to foot on the long shift, and hum under
the roaring thunder of machines making material and stuff.

I have seen a brisk woman seize a bolt of cloth in a shop
and hurl it on the counter so it unfurls like an omen exact
to the lip, put out one sharp hand to stop the flutter and
measure with both arms what you might want. A yard.
Or more. Sometimes she rips it for you and it screams.

Sometimes she cuts it with a slick kerplunk, kerplunk.
I have seen a woman, dreamy and dismayed by plenty,
listen to the crackle of the taffeta, the purr of velveteen,
hat awry, unable to begin, picking at a cuticle inchoately
as if her hands, and her scissors, are useless things.

LAURIE DUGGAN 1949–

Laurie Duggan was born in South Melbourne and now lives in London. He became a friend of John Scott and Alan Wearne while studying at Monash University, and organised several of the Monash University poetry readings in the late 1960s. He later studied at the University of Sydney and has a Ph.D. in Fine Arts from the University of Melbourne. He has taught media at Swinburne College and at Canberra College of Advanced Education and worked as an editor, scriptwriter and art critic. Duggan has published thirteen volumes of poetry, including translations, one of these books being shared with other writers. Much of his poetry has from the start been bricolage, found poems sandwiched between brief comments or images, sharp cultural aperçus, quips about his own or friends' incongruities. His poetry generally avoids personal commitment, except to a sense of contemporary style. "The New Australian Poetry Now!" is a series of parodies Duggan wrote on his contemporaries, many of them friends, basing the title on John Tranter's anthology *The New Australian Poetry* (1979). All of the parodies reproduced here are of poets we have represented. Duggan has written over many years a discontinuous series under the title "Blue Hills" label, named after an Australian radio serial that ran for 27 years. Outstanding amongst his work are Duggan's translations from the poems of the Italian Futurist Ardengo Soffici (1879–1964), who writes about the quotidian, the contingent, the strangeness of life with a flamboyant irony and Mediterranean theatre that would not be available to Duggan if he were writing in his own voice.

from The New Australian Poetry, Now!

"During the first half of the nineteenth century, a vast change began to make itself felt through every aspect of European Society ..."

– John Tranter

"The now scene, baby"

– Thomas W. Shapcott

DIRTY WEEKEND
The old drunk
standing

out front
of the Queanbeyan

C.W.A.
said, "I

never heard
of William

Carlos
Williams.

I never
heard of

William Carlos
Williams."

FIVE POEMS
looking at a sunset

mango stains on my shirt!

*

waking in the middle of the night
– the digital clock radio!

*

the washbasin in my bathroom
it's like soap held in a big pink hand!

*

my disco suit
falls off the chair
like an advertising executive!

*

a paper butterfly
sails over the windowsill
– my Australia Council cheque!

FROM THE PAPERWEIGHT

Eric "Gonzo" Smythe, a young chemist from Burwood (an outer suburb of Melbourne), makes a long-distance phone call from Auckland, New Zealand, where he is holidaying, to his parents' place to see how his ill father is holding up. He is surprised by the voice of Bunny Madigan, his old high-school fiancée with whom he used to sit until dawn watching the British football on television with the volume down and a pile of 45s from the early 1960s on the turntable. He remembers to ask her how Labor is doing in the elections held the day before …

"Oh Bunny … it's you … You wait up late for Wembley?"
And, "How's my li'l ol' goodtime gal today?
and what – dear me – 's the results in the L.A.?
(that's not Light Ale, it's Legislative Assembly)."
"I thought," she joked, "you meant the, er, Light Album
… you know … a recent (bad) Beach Boys L.P.,
but of course – you smartypants – you meant L.C."
"The *Assembly*, not the *Council* (!), funnybum …
Anyway, how was Christmas … and how's Dad?"
"Oh the usual: bubbly, apple sauce, a chook,
pulling of bonbons – he's not half as crook
as was before you O.S.'d, you'll be glad
to know … How'd the Bay of Islands be?"
"Sounds like a brand of sauce – a burning chili

– that funny brand name – Lingham's." "Don't be silly
I yoni asked (she laughed)." "And Mum, how's she?"

WHAT I CAME ONTO
My aunt is ironing the socks of death
I think it is strange that
death wears odd socks

I examine my sister's clitoris
& try to imagine someone
from the A.B.C. reading my poems

their voice full of pain
Then my uncle comes into the room
eating a tripe sandwich

he kick-starts the television
& a talking head appears
"It's death," my aunt says,

"And he's reading your poems."

South Coast Haiku

Rain drips through
the tin roof
missing the stereo

Blue Hills 23

In this town a dance is
the dance.
                    The chill
of shoulder straps, Friday night
outside the Main Hotel,
a sacrifice for style.
                                        Sunday, the glint
of a flute in the trees up the Mitchell's bank;
snatches of Mozart: skewed notes running off the scales.

The path goes on endlessly, crackling with twigs.
Auxiliary generators whine over the agistments.

Across the river,
white branches lean in the wind
that blows down from the Divide.

Blue Hills 44

So much of a city
is light on stonework, woodwork,
demolition turns us into archaeologists
using the maps;
                    memory,
a particular daub of colour
there, to the right,
of that mountain down the street.

Blue Hills 52

night lights
            the 191 bus
down Vernon Terrace
                        half-lit books
in the hall
                a rattle of venetians
as the change moves in.

Blue Hills 53

powder blue, then

cerise over magenta

trucks on the Gateway bridge

a glittering airliner

Blue Hills 55

already

September

the air

dank

lying on my back

under the vent

Blue Hills 64

stretch of the building, torsion,
heard night after night,
storm   hard and distant
over Stradbroke and Moreton islands

the little lights across the river
damped, as if
shut inside a grand piano

Boredom (after Ardengo Soffici)

Between 8.45 and 10.10
I have watched the bloodstained world
through a rectangle of red glass
with white lettering:
"Bisleri – sparkling digestive mineral water:
gout cure and uric diet".

What else should I hope for?
Our fate is death by retail,
our calendar scheduled by economists.

The modernist dream is as dead as Rameses II.
The big cities don't even notice spring
returning each year like an usherette with a tray of cigars,
though the moon's electric crescent promotes itself:
"founded anno one – still going strong";
and the stars always find some muddy pool to wink at
like the smacked-out eyes of streetwalkers.

Trams, yellow housemartins, dip into the streets and are gone
buses scatter for the suburbs like magnetised filings;
car headlights whirl in primitive blizzards
(the pigeons are mass-produced like pigeons everywhere else)
The sky – full of sign writers –
looks like a lunatic has been loosed with an icing gun,
but the banknotes smell like almond blossoms.

The Town Hall clock is several minutes slow
(what a symbol to live under!).
Everything else repeats itself:
each house, shuttered, as though the apocalypse were forecast;
each room holds secrets too dull to mention:
bidets, mauve shirts, sweaty skin, suggestive notes, dirty postcards.
The heart closes its hatches, like a bank teller
on the dot of 3.30 p.m.

Our lives bump together in a gossip-column
assembled by cadet-journalists on the Great Daily.
Imagination belongs only to window-dressers.

The universe, all that tiresome cosmology, disappears with a stroke.
A new alchemy welds daylight to dusk;
a seasonless glow of artificial fire and mellow acetylene.

"Gentleman wanted:
must have clown-suit, powder and paint,
scarlet quiff, scarlet heart.
Green eyebrows essential.
Should be able to dance,
laugh,
sing;
be a masked god on a high wire
stretched from alpha to omega
over this fleapit, waiting for encores".

Rainbow (after Ardengo Soffici)

April 1915. Seven colours
arch across the sky. Seven brushes
(hidden behind my back)
drip from a 36-year inscription.
I'm straight-faced as a mermaid on a merry-go-round
back from other cities, their strange geographies and crazy citizens.
There's no church, cinema, editors office, tavern en route
I haven't visited; no bed I haven't slept in
(a stale carnival of emotions, misplaced
with my umbrella in the cafés of Europe;
remembered briefly as I left, handkerchief flapping,
on sleeping-cars heading north,
heading south).

Time and place are a duet, like dog and moon.
Sirens wail in a blurry dawn; half-forgotten dreams
arise from night's choking armpit.
These cold jonquils on my desk
were painted once, on the walls of room 19, Hôtel des Anglais, Rouen:
a train passed nightly under our window
splitting the reflections of a streetlamp into component hues;
the Seine was a garden of burning flags.

A decade shrinks like a worm in phosphorus
and everything is present:
it's 1902, I'm in Paris, in an attic, under glass
(a 35 centimetre skylight);
each morning the city offers fresh flowers from the Place de Cluny;

trams and buses burst from the Boulevard Saint-Germain,
overnight news hits the stands on the Rue de l'Harpe:
Paris Gazette, Hard Copy, The Truth.
Raoul's Shoe Shop competes with the stars.
Smashed on the liqueurs of sunset
like a potential suicide
I shake hands with total strangers
near the house of Rigoletto.

So much of this is best forgotten.
I'd be happier if witless ...
(look at this passing gent lighting his cigar,
pacified by a page three girl;
or that cavalry soldier, galloping towards the barracks,
strands of pubic hair between his teeth ...)
Eternity? See it in a blowfly's wings.
Our eyes knit colour into sense,
the bow is drawn: let history slip away
like a platform of sobbing cousins,
let the sun's shafts dumbly break their own records.
Remember kissing in the dark?,
the glass case of a German bookseller, Avenue de l'Opéra?,
a goat that ate brooms on the ruined staircase of the Temple of Darius, Persepolis?

Forget it!

Remember instead the geography of our touching bodies:
snow,
yellow seas,
temple gongs,
caravans;
carmine from Bombay,
hieroglyphs from Iran.

Blood circulates: a seasonal dance
more beautiful than its sense.
The rainbow, the poem, marry this day to all others.

I sit at my table, smoking and watching:
a young leaf shakes in a garden opposite;
white pigeons flutter in the air like love letters thrown from a window:
New theory: tell me about it!
(the structure of language, circuit diagrams, the discourse of love)
as this bright wreath stretches over Easter,

leaving untouched the fruit, light and multitudes below.
Day sinks in the scarlet basin of summer;
there are no more words
for a fiery bridge.

Youth, you pass like the end of a movie I walk out on,
lit up by the rolling credits
in a fabulous suit of old manifestoes.

ALAN GOULD 1949–

Of English and Icelandic background, Alan Gould came to Australia aged seventeen after living at garrisons in Northern Ireland, Germany and Singapore; his father was in the British Army. Since graduating he has published 20 books – twelve poetry, seven fiction, and one collection of essays. His poetry, often using a maritime or historical setting, has meditated a range of concerns such as the interplay of fate and free will, how occupation colours character, and the manner by which human consciousness and imagination grow. For all that their formative influences come from Old World sources – Conrad, the Icelandic Sagas, Browning, Hughes and Auden – the poems in Gould's *The Past Completes Me – Selected Poems 1973–2003*, show an affinity with Slessor's preoccupation with time and aspects of David Campbell.

Galaxies

Hamburg: the clockhands move upon their star.
A liner glides along the Elbe, its lights
move through the city's lights, a galaxy
passing in silence through a galaxy.

My girl's behind me on the bed. She smokes
and minutes tick. Her time is waiting for
a time to end, a time to start. As mine is.
We are the flowers of our lineage,

were sinuous, bluff-mannered in the wine room
with all our company at like pursuits,
transactions that the liquor tantalised,
that led into this silence and this calm.

Yes, here I took myself, yes here was taken.
And here she chose to lie and here was laid.
Our choices and our fates, we house them both
like galaxies that pass through one another.

The liner disappears behind the docklands:
my girl is getting dressed again behind me.

I'll close the curtain on this night sky's map,
step out into the dark I know knows me.

Tightrope Walker

He climbs the vertical on all four hands,
discards the third dimension, dances off

as though he were a stick-man drawn on paper.
His mystery? It's simple. Dream a floor,

then walk or climb on it, for space is strung
with rafters of theory. Hah, what might he prove

for physics, this hare-brained fellow with his pole,
this baggy-trousered monocycling spirit.

Perhaps one night he'll amble to the moon
along his wire, umbrella on his shoulder,

or stretch a line between the now and then
to cycle there and back, his silver girl

astride his narrow shoulders. His family
includes all sparrows perched on telegraph wires,

all pirouettists, and the earth that walks
on its invisible rail around the sun.

But now, perhaps because the plains of mind
cause him to yawn, he lies on his one-strand bed

and goes to sleep with one foot dangling in space,
space-shuttler, hung above the slow continents,

the sapphire oceans rolling under his rest,
while from below come cheers which, ah, he should

with one limp hand-wave presently acknowledge.

Rain Governs the Small Hours

It starts as it might end,
a one-finger typist
composing on my roof.
Then cause and effect, the long
ovation of a vast convention.

Really the downpour is
an efficient administration.
A directive zones the world

along an apartheid of surfaces;
the Wet, the Dry, let there be

no infringements for all that
mine is the zone beleaguered
as sleep beleaguers life.
Like the unborn I repose
content to curl in the midst

of active waters. Nearby
the red digits of the clock
flicker like a blood-vessel,
and remotely a five a.m.
kitchen neon wavers,

a world at a tunnel's end.
The rain ends, not quite
as it began – one finger
tap-tapping a single key.

The First Real Frost

Now you can go out, now the gardens are
markets of such fancy crystalware,
and all that your footsteps do not bid for
the sun will nod for. It is the tycoon
that has already scooped the northeast lawn,
and by the afternoon
will have put its seal upon this trade
but for the odd soiled tray in the fence's shade.

Now you can go out, for now the windscreen
grows an old man's beard. The dawn shift
of cakemakers has iced the compost bin,
confectioners have re-leafed
the apple trees with sugar, and all night, unseen,
a team of twenty glass-sculptors has cut and roughed
a white simulacrum of the lawn.

First time, every time, the thing is like
a brilliant undergraduate hoax.
Whenever the star withdraws and the tree contracts,
when traffic dwindles to a traffic light's click
when mallard and water-rat must endure their thickets
and the cold must talk and talk
to your tightly folded bones,

a *Geist* with a genius for detail will have been
behind the scene,
and turned the world's array into some casual other,
stylish, throwaway, and a whole world further.

Demolisher

By six he's started. I wake to the wince and arrh,
the animal protests of my neighbour's iron roof.
Behind a cypress-dark, the February sky

is blue as gin. The house is nineteen twenties;
he moves along its apex removing it,
and at this hour he's higher than the sun,

flexing a torso of cinnamon brown, his singlet
dangling whitely from his belt. Slav
or Italian, perhaps, he applies that rigid serpent,

the pinch-bar, to open unconsidered caches
of darkness. His work is wholly restoration –
he is recovering horizons, and

with the long arm of Archimedes, brings
sunlight to gulf the spiders' vertical suburbs,
dense as hairballs in their sudden light.

So ridge cap, gutter, sheet iron are grimaced free
from battens; sheets of fibro drop-shatter,
nails, clenched in the pinch-bar's one knuckle

come out with a sigh. By lunchtime the house
is a birdcage of timbers; by evening it's gone,
and the man sits, gleaming like resin,

rolling cigarettes, drinking water,
looking through a gap at new hills,
peering down the shaft he's made in sixty years.

Lacemaker

She works in such a flush of windowlight,
by loop and twist is reassembling sea-spray
          or the mantilla of after-spray
          that falls from a wave's shoulder.

Such bobbin-work with threads of Flemish linen;
she leans to her slow progress, scallops and spangles
          white instantaneities,

knots them, nets them, and will

remember nothing of this time. The clock
above her head is ticking beyond her earshot.
If the white walls of her room are hung
with maps or pictures, they

cannot represent her present world.
She's in a time that's utterly her own,
inaudible to her as her breathing
now is. And her eyes,

which through this patience may well suffer ruin,
are now enclosed within her whitening field,
within this ground of patient frost,
this snow that will not melt.

Pliers

Fist to grip the slippery, twist-easing
the recalcitrant, little mastiff nosing
into crannies of blind manipulations.
The clench we reach for in tight situations.
As once, did Miss Tarbuck, a hard-nosed, roughly
middle-aged science teacher who took us briefly.

It was the period before lunch: *muscle forms*
in earthworms. Earthworms led to tapeworms,
and one of Miss T's field trips, bottling species
in a jungle hut (Dahomey or one of the Guineas).
Times were late colonial when tapeworms could
grow long as garden hoses. She had one, she said.

It grew, and grew snug in her intestinal miles,
shared her meals. *Uncompanionably,* she smiled.
Prospect of starving. *No medicines. But pliers,*
I had pliers. Also meat, a pair of mirrors,
and I like to think, my nerves. For a week I fasted,
let the meat grow foul. O very foul indeed,

then, on a day, arranged my mirrors, the view
not, ahem! flattering (a snigger or two
though most of us were too agog). *I squatted,*
cheeks distended, pliers in hand, waited,
O, not long, for whatever might come out.
Sure enough. A head! No, more a puckered snout!

Unpretty! I chose my moment. Then . . . snap! I bagged it
(unsqueamish fellows jumped in their seats) *I tugged it.*
Quite a tussle. (Blokes who played in the scrum
were turning green as they imagined this grim
alimentary pull-through. Tarbuck, unphased,
stuck with the facts, if anything surprised

by our pallor). *Useful gadgets, pliers. Of course*
I bottled it. Ha ha, no, not the pliers, Macinnes.
And here (rummaging under her trestle)
. . . it is. She flourished briefly a large vessel
above her head, placed it with a bang.
Inspect it as you leave. Then the school bell rang

for a lunch now suddenly more complex. We filed
past the pale, well-nourished horror, coiled
in its urinous solution, this worm, flattened
like white pantyhose loosely filled with sand;
it crammed the entire jar. And in the pocket
of her white coat we noted the pliers. Useful gadget,

we agreed, an opposable thumb with uncommon nip
for the use of anyone not wishing to lose their grip.

JAMIE GRANT 1949–

Jamie Grant was born in Melbourne, his father a company director, and boarded from the age of eleven at Geelong Grammar. It was an experience he did not enjoy, until his last year when he became serious about cricket. He has since played the game at grade level. He graduated from La Trobe University with a B.A., had a brief career in advertising, and then worked for ten years with Cambridge University Press in Melbourne. In 1984 Grant moved to Sydney and has worked as a freelance editor. He co-edited a book of literary writings on Australian cricket and another on golf and edited *100 Australian Poems You Need to Know* (2008). Grant has been actively involved in bringing up his children as the husband of the literary agent Margaret Connolly. He is known as an acerbic reviewer. The seven collections of his own poetry met with retaliation from some quarters. Initially his poetry was influenced by the "Martian" style of English poets like Craig Raine, his imagery precise and cool. He has increasingly come to employ rhyme and syllabic metre and to incorporate in his poetry, in a surprising way, material that might usually appear in prose. The mood has also changed from one of "Martian" distance to greater intimacy. Close relatives are often his subjects. He remains a fastidious writer with measured wit, who when writing about family members, observes them with an almost nonchalant detachment.

Digging Machine

The Water Board was digging up our street,
so that for weeks it looked as though
one of those rocket-powered missiles, heat-
seeking, computer-controlled, had flown

here to gouge a man-deep trench, in an act
of senseless war. The destruction
wrought on kerbs and flowerbeds was, in fact,
achieved by a few construction

workers, most of whom stood about to watch
while the youngest of them wielded
a truck-sized digging machine with the touch
of a billiards player. Shielded

by our cherry tree, I joined the audience.
The machine had the yawning jaw
of a hippopotamus, the presence
of a yellow-scaled dinosaur,

and, folded on its back, a scorpion's
tail. Or so it seemed. In practice
that trailing limb could be both a weapon
and a tool used with the finesse

of surgical tongs. The wide mouth had scraped
up rubble from the road surface,
browsing a silt-choked riverbed, and gaped
with appetite, before the service

of the sting was called for. It then attacked.
The layer of bedrock concealed
beneath the concrete was easily hacked
away – a hot blade through congealed

grease – exposing pipes deep in the ground, rust-
caked like sunken treasure-casks.
The machine raised up these iron hulks just
as primly as somebody asked

to sip tea from expensive porcelain:
the terrible blade which could cut
through stone might also take hold of a grain
if required. The young man who sat

on its leather office chair held levers

taut in both hands as if playing
a video game, his lips pressed together
in a focus that could be saying

This is an art form. All that had been built
in this scene, with the destruction,
was the product of pure human skill.
Crows watched, hoping for carrion.

Social Behaviour of Minted Peas

Contradicting a proverb, the pot
I am watching boils, and resembles
the pool beneath a waterfall.
Then I pour in the frozen peas,
an avalanche of green stones, and at
that the pan no longer trembles.
For a while the peas lie as still
as the stony floor of the sea,
or else like a mountain of skulls
in South East Asia; they wait as
rigidly as an audience
with numbered seats, afraid to move.
Then one pea, on an odd impulse,
breaks away, and, with a skater's
motion from side to side, ascends
to ride the surface far above
the others, a non-conformist
with a notion all its own.
Another, hesitant at first, glides
up to join it, and others still,
one at a time, cannot resist
the temptation to follow on,
behind the first one who derides
the common and conventional.
And then it is clear there's a trend,
and all those peas who had hung back
now clamour to be allowed in.
Anxiously they jostle and sprint,
needing to belong in the end
among the upward-mobile pack,
elbowing each other, crowding
up to the air which smells of mint.

Mon Père est Mort

For an oral exam, when aged thirteen,
my father was asked questions in French
by a visiting professor in trench-
coat and gold-rimmed spectacles, who was lean

with the thin, pursed lips of an enemy
interrogator. He pressed my father
to say what his father's *métier*
was – an awkward question, for how many

schoolboys know the French for "Real Estate
Agent"? Adopting a tragic expression,
my father just replied *Mon père est mort.*

The professor blushed to commiserate;
when the results of the examination
were known, my father had the highest score.

The Rime of the Ancient Cricketer

The first two balls he swung and missed;
the third ball struck his knee:
he is an ancient cricketer
and he stoppeth one of three.

Getting a Girl into Bed

Did any Lothario
struggling to undress a girl
with her contrivance
(disguised as coy resistance)
confront such an obstacle
as that posed by a four-year-old

who won't undress for the bath?
It was easier for Don Juan
to get a girl into bed
putting false ideas in her head
than to cross the bear-strewn,
doll-and-toy-cluttered path

to lure a child to sleep; yet had he guessed
the routines which would fill his life
if the sheep's membrane failed
him – voices which wailed

all night, a surly wife –
would he be impressed?

Such a fate is what Casanova fears,
of course, and takes pain
to avoid. Yet who is to measure
a fleeting pleasure
against what there is to gain,
having it in one's power to end those tears?

Hands

"You have the most beautiful little hands,"
the mathematics teacher would exclaim,
reaching tenderly toward my fingertips,
which he would brush with his own gnarled spin-bowler's
claws. Despite appearances, no blame
attached to his actions. He spoke with a lisp
and had gnome-like mannerisms, and molars
  which had grown without bands

to fix his jaw in a permanent grin.
For each class he took, he would bring a box
of chocolate-coated icecreams, and give
one to all his pupils, not just as a treat
once or twice, but every time he taught; his stocks,
it seemed, were inexhaustible. Did he have
wealth to subsidise his teaching? We would eat,
  unquestioning, then begin

our sums. Some students may have developed
a trained attraction to mathematics
like one of Pavlov's dogs, but I only
acquired an interest in chocolate-
coated icecream, and the complex topics
we were meant to absorb remained a mystery;
in algebra, I became illiterate,
  which could not be what was hoped

for by that kindly man who loved to hold
my hands. He returned to a place in mind
when I covered my youngest daughter's little
knuckles with my own, and saw how their perfect
form and unblemished skin compared with the lined
and mottled surface on the hands that futile

teacher once admired. Vein-ridged and scar-flecked,
  they now belonged to one of the old.

DFC

On printed envelopes and lists which came
  through in the mail, our father's name
was followed by the letters DFC.
  We knew what they stood for, but he
would never talk to us about the feat
  which it warranted. On the street
where we lived, he implied, such a medal
  was common, so that to retail
heroics out of a forgotten past
  would serve no purpose. In the last
months of his life, however, the younger
  of my brothers, filled with hunger
for truth – or else with mere curiosity
  about the rest of his family –
persisted until our father would tell
  his story. He was far from well
as he spoke, and needed to interrupt
  himself from time to time, hands cupped
over the mouthpiece of an inhaler,
  but he became the narrator
of a tale in which the drama was enhanced
  by these pauses for breath. Entranced,
my brother attended. A flying boat
  high over the submarine route
in the Indian Ocean was the setting.
  Our father, the pilot, getting
the aircraft close enough to a U-Boat
  for the bombardier to float
a depth charge in its direction, watching
  the explosions swell like hatching
underwater creatures, was at the controls
  when the opposing combatants' roles
were exchanged, and the U-Boat surfaced, guns
  blazing. There were detonations
in the air, blinding lights and oily smoke,
  and when at last the pilot spoke
into the intercom he heard that two
  men on the Catalina's crew

had been injured, while one of its engines
was on fire. Above the ocean's
cold expanse, hours away from land, he turned
the plane around while the fire burned
and wind was pouring through a jagged hole
in the cockpit. The wings would roll
to one side unless the pilot grappled
with the joystick, and the crippled
co-pilot beside him was unable
to help keep the aircraft stable.
Alone, in the dark and the biting cold,
the pilot was fighting to hold
on to the controls with all his strength,
and he did so the entire length
of the flight back to land. The squadron's base,
located in an awkward place
on the crater-lake of a long-extinct
volcano, had lanterns which winked
to guide the flying boats when they landed
at night; but hope was abandoned
for a plane which was limping home hours late:
the pilot had to calculate
his approach in utter dark, the lighting
long extinguished. He was fighting
exhaustion, without modern instruments:
one mistake, and the consequence
would be deadly, as jagged mountains rose
on every side to enclose
the base. Moonlight flickered between racing
clouds, so that by quickly tracing
a route he made his descent almost by
instinct. When he first learned to fly,
in Canada, on runways slick with snows,
he landed a plane on its nose,
and ever afterward kept a photo
of the machine tilted down to
the ground, tail high in the air: such mishaps
amused him. Now, in the dark, flaps
down, he wrestled the damaged flying boat
to force its wings to level out,
and somehow it touched the unseen water,
skimming to a halt, no thought or

possibility of error coming
  into his mind. He was humming,
as the great plane turned and motored along
  the lake to its mooring, the song
Lloyd George knew my father, Father knew Lloyd George.
  And at last, with an inward surge
of gratitude, he stood on solid ground
  beside the lake. A snorting sound
came from the inhaler. He had not moved
  from the chair while memory roved
back over an incident which had passed
  almost sixty years before. Vast
ocean swells were breaking over black reefs
  while all of his unclear beliefs
gazed down at the engulfing dark which could,
  my brother suddenly understood,
prevent his own existence. Gusts of wind
  snored outside. The old pilot grinned.

SUSAN HAMPTON 1949–

Susan Hampton was born in Inverell and grew up in suburban Newcastle in New South Wales. After graduating from Newcastle Teacher's College in 1967, she has worked as a writer, teacher and editor. Her books include four volumes of poetry, a co-authored teaching text *About Literature* (1984), and a collection of short stories and performance pieces, *Surly Girls* (1989), which examines personal relationships from a feminist lesbian perspective. She compiled with Kate Llewellyn *The Penguin Book of Australian Women Poets* (1986). Hampton has two approaches in her poetry: a style which plays language games, and a realistic and detailed often explicitly autobiographical style. Hampton's output is small but incisive. She is able to express emotion with a lightness of touch. "Vegemite" is a yeast extract paste and "Sao" is a brand of dry biscuit.

The Kitchen of Aunty Mi and Aunty Pearl

I am fourteen, and I've run away from home. On purpose.
Aunty Mi is eating grapes in the sunroom; her comment
is to nod her whole body when she nods her head, and to go on
eating, spitting the pips into her apron. Her hair
is creamy white and neat with natural butterfly-clip curls.
In her eighty-six years she has always loved Jesus,
she knows all the words to "When Mothers of Salem"
which I learn to play on a dusty zither. Aunty Pearl
is only sixty-two, but short of breath and can't sing

for fear of an attack. She keeps her asthma powder in a tin
beside the vegemite in the kitchen dresser. We three virgins
get on well: we make satiric comments about wedding pictures
in the Inverell Times, we feed the chooks, we eat meat
and three veg every night dead on six. When I buy the bread
from Cohen's corner shop, I steal licorice for them.
The kitchen fire has to be lit at six every morning –
they've done this job week about for forty years, taking
a cup of tea and two buttered saos to the one in bed.
On Sunday mornings, the radio, and then the bus to church.
Passing my house, I wave to my five sisters on the lawn,
dressed up and waiting to go to a different church.

Stockton

So I moved in with Nana, learning to cook
Irish stews in a long narrow kitchen with a smelly
gas stove and cupboards full of dinner sets
brought home by the boys full of grog. Or Pappy,
even fuller ... but now dead, and so I inherit
a bamboo fishing rod. The breakwater, the breakwater.
I beachcomb or light fires and wait for the tide;
Nana is a pirate with her eyepatch from the cataract op.
We joke like sisters, scoffing brown muscat
with her pensioner pals and talking about who's died.
About arthritis and rheumatism and bad eyes and swollen
legs from falls on footpaths bumped up by tree roots.
I fit in remarkably well, here. I like her friends:
I trim their horny toenails with my pocketknife,
and cut their soft white hair which floats down
between the planks in the back verandah. One day
we empty the kitchen cupboards and wash everything:
a gravy boat, a vegetable dish that belonged to Pappy's
mother; glass soup bowls from the war. A cheese dish,
cut-glass water jugs. I wash the glass on a photo of
Nana at twenty with waist-length thick black hair, and I
say to her, Violet Lillian Gertrude Murphy.
"That's me," she says. I decide to grow my hair.

Yugoslav Story

Joze was born in the village of Loski Potok,
in a high-cheek-boned family. I remarked

that he had no freckles, he liked to play cards,
& the women he knew were called Maria, Malcka, Mimi;
& because he was a "handsome stranger"
I took him for a ride on my Yamaha
along the Great Western Highway
& we ate apples; I had never met someone
who ate apples by the case, whose father
had been shot at by Partisans in World War II,
who'd eaten frogs & turnips in the night,
& knew how to make pastry so thin
it covered the table like a soft cloth.
He knew how to kill & cut up a pig,
& how to quickstep & polka. He lifted me up in the air.
He taught me to say *"Jaz te ljubim, ugasni luc"*
("I love you, turn off the light")
& how to cook *filana paprika, palacinka,*
& *prazena jetra.* One night in winter
Joze & two friends ate 53 of these *palacinke*
(pancakes) & went straight to the factory
from the last rummy game. Then he was my husband,
he called me *"moja zena"* & sang a dirty song
about Terezinka, a girl who sat on the chimney
waiting for her lover, & got a black bum.
He had four brothers & four sisters,
I had five sisters.
His father was a policeman under King Peter,
my father was a builder in bush towns.
Joze grew vegetables and he smoked Marlboros
and he loved me. This was in 1968.

The Fire Station's Delight

The fire station's delight
is the energy of sudden arrival
this red love that burns through cities
and sets whole buildings awash.
There are no fires today: in the station
near the deli, the men concentrate on the
Jarlsberg, brie, blue castello, roll-mops,
cottage cheese, Latvian black bread, olives,
the dry white wine. One of the men
has hung a bird cage at the window
of the lunch room.

Now one fireman, leaning back and
patting his flannel shirt, looks out at
The Alternative Grass Centre, the new shop
across the road. The owner's cat
is walking across the display of
All Purpose Super-grass Carpet Turf.
The cat has the appearance of a tiger
because the display is a miniature
garden scene. There is an oblong
swimming pool, as long as the cat
which stretches out on the synthetic turf
beside it. Reclining on a banana chair
is a doll dressed in a bikini and
sunglasses. On the grass beside her is a
miniature bottle of Bio-therm.
Behind the firemen, coming down
from the upstairs room, is one
of their wives, carrying a tray of
just baked strudel. She accuses them
of not making the coffee, and they laugh,
pointing to the display in the window
across the road. She waits for the traffic
to pass, and looks intently at the cat
and the doll. "The cat looks like a tiger,"
she says, "doesn't it."

Just then the phone rings, the bell goes wild,
there is a rush for serge and brass buttons,
huge boots are pulled on and the men leap away,
the town is burning somewhere.

Stranded in Paradise

Your fuselage, your entourage,
your wingtip. now your eyes.
your feet which touch the ground.
stranded in Paradise
I'm climbing over your body
the hill of your breast
stranded. what god put me here.
my time with you. will you
kiss me again. like this. here.
now here. hold my head.

hold my feet down, I'm levitating.
it's so easy. when you roll over
onto me, I hold your fuselage.
I pat your wingtip. I touch your teeth
and your shoulders. you are sinking
into me. I balloon under your hand.
                                                            The night sky
is humming with crickets. and humming birds,
which only live in Paradise. which only exist
here. soon they will stop. the noises will stop
and we'll lie still. only the sound of the cars
and the clicking inside the metal boxes
for the traffic lights. someone slowing up
for a hitchhiker. and off again.
another person who'll be stranded.
will it be in Paradise, at the corner shop,
the fruit stall. will she hover over
the apples, delicious or jonathan.
she can't decide. it's because she's stranded,
and thinks it's only the fruit stall, or the corner shop.
it's only Paradise, I want to say. it's only here.
the planes going over. the traffic passing by.

Cunningly Downwards

where quite brightly
most wisely
further out earlier
very overseas
more sweetly
ever before

had been lonely
had been attentive
more frequently, then
where, often
suddenly, here, there
why, more quickly

laughed
did come
soon
would pardon

more seldom

now
how
so soon
not graciously
merrily now

but folded up
or in, up into
after
taken off
turned out
and

down, nimbly
when, there
never, again

MARTIN HARRISON 1949–

Martin Harrison is a graduate of Cambridge University and began publishing poetry in London in the mid 1970s. After living in New Zealand for three years, he settled in Sydney in 1978. He has been a producer and broadcaster on radio of literary programs, poetry in particular, and is a well-known critic. He teaches writing, poetry and sound studies at the University of Technology, Sydney and was a visiting writer at San Diego State University and at Yaddo. He has published five collections of poetry in the last twenty years. His collection of essays *Who Wants to Create Australia* (2004), mainly about contemporary poetry, was selected as one of the *Times Literary Supplement*'s "International Books of the Year" for 2004. The subject matter of his poems is wide, including letters to friends, family reminiscences, and observations about art, literature, music, and of people. But his most distinctive poems are those about the Australian landscape, where his highly original approach is to describe and analyse his own reactions, and critique the landscape as though it were a work of art or piece of music. Some memorable and beautiful poems, in which layers of images and feelings accrete, are the result.

Stopping for a Walk in Reserved Land near Murra Murra

It's a stop-over on a Spring day
when, walking through the bush, I see them.
Bees. Wild bees, already clustered,

already swarmed. A galaxy of living honey,
they hang on a branch –
in a swollen, brown gourd, a primitive shape

caught on the move. All gouache, clay, and bubble,

it's hard to fix it for what it is,
frightening to imagine stumbling into its pelting dust,

having just landed from the horizon's blue planes
of Spring light, dwarf ti-tree, red earth.
Pummeled soil, hanging, between sky and ground,

it takes on a flickering, gold-dyed sheen,
gold as in a strand of hair
that's threaded, quartz-like, in that ochre mass: bodies, heads, legs,

writhing on each other, pinioned there.
It's as if each is already a future cell.
Or as if the air has opened up a hasty, war-time grave

where corpses, tossed into the pit, drown each other
with their awkward, rotting limbs.
This swarm is that exposed. That stark.

A wattle-and-daub affair, compacted
in a furious swerve
to a taller tree's white branch, the swarm hangs there

sandstorm-brown,
a haze of movement
and molecules. It's as sharp and deafening

as if all the body's sensations arrive
at one go, or as if a life-time's
thoughts are suddenly, spontaneously, recalled

by someone moving, at the very edge of life,
when the mind's
sky-white with memories, swelling with

the fruit of experience, swarming
at death,
yet holding all feelings together;

or as if, veil-like, it's summed up later (generations later,
after the earth
has soaked up spilt blood and honey-streams)

by the philosopher who says:
Things are not things,
but groups, sets, swarms, flux –

playing their music of ant
and bird. The swarm
is light. It's energy. Fruit of the desert's edge.

Fruit, indeed, is fruit. Yet, whether
in grief or orgy,
these bodies pile on top of each other:

they're a huge brown pear,
they're an outsize bobbin of unwashed flax,
hanging from a yellow-gum.

It takes for ever to focus on. It swirls.
It implodes in the branches,
hanging like a wind-harp

of silk-glitters and half-dried mud
with outriders taking off and returning,
like flies to a carcase. Not beautiful,

dark, full of anger, full of sting,
it changes shape
like a pot spun between invisible hands,

slowly growing bulbous, then tapering to a narrow neck,
in danger of falling apart
or attacking like a Mongol horde

yet still clustering, still forming itself
from Spring's exile
and the struggle of poisoned virgin grubs –

till it steadies its larval magic
into an Earth-Mother drone
of particles, dynamos, ancestral flight.

Remembering Floodwater

Back of the mind, it's the white sliver which is
neither misty trace nor meaningless: it probably
isn't snow, nor that glare effect of a white line
which the sea's horizon can sometimes have
on days when the air's clear as untouched cellophane.
It's a particular white sliver, or smear of white,
like a patch of sand bursting through leaf-cover,
held forever, remembered, from some walk years back.
It's the stripe of light on sandhills towards dusk,
caught just once, recalled, seen again somewhere else.
Or it's untouchable shadow on the white metal of the roof
of the house next door, a shadow that's also a silhouette
of a bougainvillea, cascading red flowers

down the walls, overgrown round the drain pipes –
and, above the roof, three pelicans hanging in the sky
as if they're boats moored in wind-slopped water.

This is the brightness I usually wake up to, or
which wakes me, after a night of dreamless sleep.
I slept like that last night. After weeks away,
I wake up once again in a house tranquil as summer,
a house full of things (lamps, sinks, chairs, doors)
which do not need to sleep. Just for those first
few moments, after I've come into the kitchen,
everything's as calm and cool as the fridge.
Then it hums, quietly, and the lazy, gliding pelicans
flap their wings. It could be once or for ever,
like a particular sensation which arrives and goes,
before it's anchored, then felt again. Getting back,
I've that feeling that somehow things
have changed, when really they haven't:
perhaps they should have changed. They haven't.
You're still asleep. The neighbour's roof offers
back a little ultraviolet to the unsmudged blue,
while I'm thinking of the time away, the journeys,
the days and days on arid, high-speed roads.
It could be you're dreaming of it right this moment, curled over
like a slope of land. Nothing changes. Or perhaps it's country light
that's burned itself behind my eyes. Now the trace
becomes that sliver. Like a shadow getting through
the lids, I remember spilt-out glaze on flooded wetlands
with their dead, grey trees still standing there
and ibis cruising down to land. A string of fence posts
wades into the water's middle, before it drowns. Up close,
two swallows, scissoring, vanish across the sun.

JOHN JENKINS 1949–

John Jenkins was born in Melbourne and has published eight books of poetry, including a verse novel, and non-fiction, including travel-writing and books on music and music theatre. He works as a writer, journalist, editor and teacher and lives on the rural outskirts of Melbourne. His poems often deal with densely technical subjects, in which striking imagery and scientific or expert information are fused, as in "Cold Press" – a tour de force where the poet's love and knowledge of his subject generate athletic and elegant language.

Cold Press

Noir skies above the Yarra Valley, thick rain
curtains and cold seams, then sun-shot.
A neat stud slides out to free steel jaws at gelid
dawn-start. This is how we put the wine
back into winter. A day (another day) upon the ridge
with the patch-work itinerants. More sheer
and smoky light is poking through the weave than
yesterday, when you wounded a riot of sleeping

cane and repaired its latency with structure.
The long mounded tillage is punctuated by posts
and the dumb dormancy of vines. The sap is falling
to a root mass below these chocolate acres,
curled roots, stiff hands, dull fingers in the earth.
Curt work to toss the curly cuttings anywhere,
rain weeping down our backs, in this mud-splattered
surgery, where vintage is asleep beneath the happy

splash and patter of weeds against your boots.
Elegance cannot be cultivated without us.
We strip excess from aisles of skeletons, leave
bone-arms in our wake. Main canes thrown wide,
twisted over wires, then end-tied with a clip.
Start to see the shape of things to come, when the
scribbly disarray of waste is deftly edited. Each plant
becomes a trunk, with two arms lashed to the fruiting wire

upholding ten short stubs, of three buds each,
poking up from the old wound-wood like blunt thumbs.
A tractor rolls down these rows, its whirring blades
held high to rubbish, the canes confetti in its wake,
followed by gun pruners, the grim gangs, with jobs
still to do, only just holding onto their edge.
Machine pruning is too crude for premium wine,
and the old hands sculpt endless hills of skinny

Christs from the vine mass, pull out moons-and-back
of tangled canes to make a topiary of daylight.
Crab slowly down these rows with me – tense against
your own bent back, in a sullen muscle-trance,
worming down the automatic aisles of day,
a slow stagger to the dark fugue of fatigue.
A simplifying landscape stands out like Granny's

tooth between the cold, cross-hatched cordons.

Each vinous trunk a fist pushed up from dirt,
grasping at the light with new leaf and tendrils,
its story told in scars, lopped arms and leathery
layers: the new wood seals fresh tissue spilling up.
A reek of sweat and dull ache to your feet:
two scarves with a silly floppy hat and creeping
bone-chill. You are a cold and concentrating cipher.
The spring compresses with each cut, the beak

springing back for more, and metal slides on
metal as it bites, hinging on an easy pressure bolt:
snap-happy with a thin grin, closing on vine fingers.
Remove dead wood, nip unwanteds in the bud.
The canopy is divided into "Grecian lyre", or "Scott Henry"
style, or "Ballerina", so leaf faces are offered
to full light, air circulates and vines stay free
of spoil, the new shoots promised perfect fruit.

The day ends with a beer. We have opened
a thousand stark wire windows onto winter hills.
Thirty buds are left to rise, vertical as an ideal,
to light green fuses from each living candelabrum.

JENNIFER MAIDEN 1949–

Jennifer Maiden was born in Penrith, New South Wales. She left school at thirteen, then in the early 1970s undertook an Arts degree at Macquarie University. She has published sixteen collections of poetry and two novels and been writer in residence at a number of tertiary and secondary teaching institutions and at The New South Wales Torture and Trauma Rehabilitation Service. Her earlier poems are often densely written. Recently her language has opened out and become discursive and she has begun to write what she calls "cluster poems"– in these she employs a lively stream of consciousness technique to encompass a great range of material within the envelope of her "cluster". By way of contrast, her "parallel poems", as David McCooey states (*Macquarie PEN Anthology of Australian Literature* 2008) "illustrate hidden connections between apparently divergent topics". Her poetry often has an overtly political intent, as in "Positional Asphyxia". The reference in this poem to Thredbo is to a 1997 landslide at that winter resort in which 18 people were killed.

The Winter Baby

For my daughter Katharine Margot Toohey

So, babies are primal: Moore-sculpted rock
– rock from a flood as sleek as stone –
that has no more, no less than body warmth,
the warmth of the dusk sun.
                                        Her strength
is absent-minded and wordlessly good,
a sleepsong sung in the key
of a satisfied short groan.
                                    Her laugh
is as wide and wise as winter.
There is nothing filmy
nor flimsy about her.
She feeds as firmly
as the heart mills blood,
her needs as fair as Milton's God
and her eyes like night on water.

Menopause as a Bee Freed from a Fairy Floss Machine

Menopause
feels good, like being eight and sturdy
unencumbered by internal taps and dams
and looking forward to the wind and sunlight
hoisting oneself up taller and taller
on solid things which like to be climbed
by children, including people. I am
forty-eight and will ride on the shoulders
of the world, I think, as I walk through Australia's
Wonderland themepark, behind Katharine and
her friend Gemma. The Fairy Floss
is the luscious wild sort swirling from
a machine onto sticks in impossible colours,
but in its dome near the rotor
is a bee flapping desperate, beyond screaming
in a heaven-into-hell of sugar. David says,
"There's a bee in your Fairy Floss machine." The boy
already knew, but, since so does a customer, thinks
and at last lifts the lid. The motor lists
sideways awkwardly, the bee sits on the counter,
stunned. Katharine, almost 11, cries, "Its wing is gone."

I say "Poor little bastard", but then
it flies up like a swallow, over trees, is
visible longer than I had hoped, black clear. I think:
I hope it got some sugar, but not
enough to clog its limbs. I'd like with real reason
to hold Katharine on my back and fly
up like that in an arc of freedom, two
children oblivious to blood, any stickily
sweet biological season.

Reflected Hearth at Bowen Mountain

This is not a cluster poem. This
is a parallel poem.
Katherine, beautiful as a firelit window
is reflected with her violin, as is
her beautiful violin teacher's fine
kind quirky face. The sky is like
a snow sky, smooth as the crystal hub
in a flame. Breeze tears the treetops.
The primary colours
of someone's neighbouring TV
dance in an upstairs pane, vast glass
where worlds juxtapose unmoved.
If I lean forward
I am in the window, but the fireplace
with its stove and chimney dominates
as if the outside bush were made to frame it,
not just its reflection. The tree boles
lean on the wind fully-charactered
like those by a river, like firewood
in this fire. The sky is not grey but
colourless-cold and vibrant-cold with power.
The fire
in the glass is clearly somehow beyond
the glass. The twin violin bows move
in the glass so there are four, the two
songs, one a jig, become four, yet the black
reflective chamber, the chamber of reflection
in the night glass has silence, even
the woodsmoke smell has a dark
freezing mountain silence in it. Then, too,
even the wind makes no noise, not even in

its real, rough, tuneless thump which is
happening and is one of life's most sudden
noises, like an earthquake's quick door slam.
            The bush world, nevertheless, beyond
the stove-starred window is nothing like a door.
It allows no entrance and no exit, reflects
all but is not deflective. Reflects all?
But now the big window pane
            is surprisingly selective: reflects
only some objects from the room. The fireplace
like all fire in glass seems ungrounded
and hovers in air.   Looking at
the fireplace itself I realise that all
fireplace fires follow laws like mountains
in their natural arrangement. The little
flickering fire mountains have the rhythm
of the mountain winds outside and, too,
there are redgold landforms, yellow
caves in which one's childhood tried
to see small fire-spirits, the land
in the grate so intricate in flux that
the trees in the window flicker like
the hearth. The light on the violins, however,
is the colour of ironbark honey, not
yellow, not fire. There is no merger.
There is the glass, the room, the woodsmoke
in and out, the falling night, which
doesn't fall because night as always
clambers up from the earth with a
flickering, smoky smell that has a glassy,
glacial clarity, a silent sound.   And I believe no sounds
but two distinct violins, one new and deep,
the other practised, lively.
This poem is a parallel poem.

Positional Asphyxia

For Katharine Margot

Watching the second but not last massacre
by the Israelis in Qana, my daughter
hopes that the scores of dead children
died in their sleep, and I reassure her

hollowly, "Perhaps", but I remember
Thredbo, where the Coroner said some victims
were alive at first, died later
of "Positional Asphyxia". Families cradling
limp, lovely, livid Qana children say after
the bombing at first they heard them
crying under the concrete. Their asphyxia
in a tight compartment there perhaps is over,
while need to breathe safe air in a sealed nation
traps their enemy, trauma-rigid and forever.

PHILIP NEILSEN 1949–

Philip Neilsen was born in Brisbane and studied English at the University of Queensland where he taught for nine years. He founded the creative writing program at the Queensland University of Technology in 1997, and is a professor of English and creative writing there. He has published five books of poetry, a number of books for children and young adults and has edited two collections of Australian satirical verse. Much of his own poetry has a satirical edge, but in "Roy Orbison in Germany" and "Metamorphosis" the feeling transcends satire. "Les A. Murray versus John Tranter at the Sydney Cricket Ground" satirises the "poetry wars" of the 1970s and 1980s, where major protagonists were John Tranter, for the American-influenced internationalists or "generation of '68", and Les Murray for the Australian traditionalists.

Roy Orbison in Germany

A life-sized Roy Orbison statue in Houston
distils a single drop of water from the left eye
on each anniversary of his birth. A tiny bead
trickles from behind the wax sunglasses.
My Munich taxi driver has read this somewhere.
Only the Americans could be so gullible
and show also such little respect he says.

He asks me my favourite Orbison song.
He has a PhD in Norse sagas and his wife
has just left him. My girlfriend has phoned
asking for time out from our relationship
to see someone else. It's a lot of new information
to process. At midnight we are headed
for a castle an hour away in the country,
because all the hotels are full for a convention.
The castle will be expensive and festooned

with the small heads of horned creatures.

I decide it is not "Pretty Woman" but "Only the Lonely".
Ah, says the driver, *but – Nur die Einsamer –*
in German you lose both the rhythm and rhyme.
The Autobahn sucks us into black night,
We sing in English, the driver a third above.
It feels very good, so we sing "Blue Bayou"
and a couple more. He turns off the meter.
Such a plain, shy man, he says – *but that voice.*
When I was young *I thought Mozart's requiem*
said it all. I did too. We drive on in silence,
sure that Roy knows the way we feel tonight,
though probably not if she's coming back to me.

Les A. Murray versus John Tranter at the Sydney Cricket Ground

It's a capacity crowd for today's Poetry Cup Final
and a colourful sight they make.
At the centre of the oval the poets shake hands
and the umpires take up their positions.

Les won the toss, so he occupies the crease
and Tranter runs in with some nasty non-referential similes:
"She has a smile like Sydney Harbour. Her new boyfriend
is like a swimming pool with a headache, or adultery in Borneo".

Murray forward defends with a country afternoon:
there's a fete on, brown-armed mothers in white aprons
smooth their hair back from honest foreheads
and hum quietly to themselves
as they lay out strawberry jam and cream.

Tranter sneers, and tosses up
five hundred cheerleaders and a New York rock band.
Their wicked smiles and soaring riffs
have the crowd clapping in unison.
The young women blow kisses like Doris Day.

Murray twirls his bat, strokes through the covers
and it's a family barbeque. Then he cuts savagely past point
for the big one: it's five hundred milk cows,
their eyelashes catching the golden twilight
that trickles down gullies. They call softly to each other
with the simple wisdom of their race.

Their flanks are like velvet. As night falls
in the distance, a lone harmonica plays.

The crowd begins to feel ashamed –
they look at one another in confusion.
But from a longer run up, Tranter bangs in a bouncer
and the crowd holds its breath:
a crazy squadron of Sabre jets circles the Ground:
the pilots are karate experts with broken hearts –
their engines run on perfume and neurotic dreams.
"A second chance," they moan, "I want to grow young!"
Their intentions growl like the monster from a 50s movie,
then the monster is you, and it's 2.00 a.m.
with the kids in bed, a police siren in the distance,
and the au pair asleep with her head in your lap …

Murray staggers backwards and the crowd gasps –
can Les be weakening? He closes his eyes
and extends his arms, Christ-like.
Suddenly there is the smell of wattle and Sunday baking –
Mum's starched apron and the promise of ponies,
dew on the paddock,
children laughing under the peppermint trees.
They hear Dad's voice calling from the veranda –
and Mum's singing now,
in the time of holiday, and stories by the fire.

The crowd all start to cry. They're crying in public,
and within themselves. Big pie-stained tears.
They're embracing one another
when Tranter shouts "Foul! Image tampering!"
The umpires confer and fidget with their counters.
Tranter strides down the pitch – but Murray pivots,
tackles him head-on and they crash to the ground.
Murray goes for the North Coast head-lock, but Tranter
does a Singapore twist and rolls free.

The crowd looks up and the sky is filled with angels.
There are golden ones in singlets and shorts, swinging axes,
and scarlet ones packing Lugers and French dictionaries.
They hurl themselves at one another time and again,
delicate pieces break from wings and flutter to the grass.
The crowd is silent.
A small dog faints.

Play is abandoned due to bad light.

Metamorphosis

A beetle woke up one morning
to find it had become Franz Kafka.
There were many challenging issues.
It had no literary background,
so its books came slowly.
It was stuck with a tedious
public service job.
An angry fiancée turned up
and demanded it marry her
without further delay.
The beetle felt no attraction to her
but could not explain why.
How it yearned for its
former life, free amongst
the silky flowers
and fragrant leaves.
The beetle's journals
in their scratchy scrawl
were dark with pessimism
and thoughts of suicide.
What is the point of books
it kept asking. What is the point.
In the end they will
only be consumed
by insects.

VICKI RAYMOND 1949–

Born in Victoria, Vicki Raymond grew up at Geeveston in the isolated south-west of Tasmania, where her parents ran a small, almost self-sufficient property. She studied English at the University of Tasmania in Hobart when James McAuley was there, and her poetry, although more witty than his, suggests his influence – also Peter Porter's. On graduating, she edited the staff newspaper of the university's English department. Her first poems were published at this time in *Quadrant*, the magazine of which McAuley was the founding editor. She moved to London in 1981, worked at Australia House, and married. Raymond has published three books of poetry, the last being her *Selected Poems* (1993). Her poetry, often witty, is always tough-minded in its content and its formal severity. This is apparent in "Roaring Beach", a self-aware comment on her determination not to play the poetess. Her small output is distinguished by a classical restraint.

Don't Talk About Your Childhood

Don't talk about your childhood.
Anyone can do that.
We were all sensitive once,
and most of us hated school.

That man who made his millions
from guns: even he
can recall the smell of his mother's dress,
rain on leaves.

And as for the dark cupboard
and what you did to the cat,
confession of childish guilt
is a form of boasting.

You risk nothing, singing
your song of a small ghost.
Don't talk about your childhood:
say what you are now.

The People, No

You never hear "the People" now:
that thundering, slightly frightening sea
has been oiled flat.
But "people" you hear everywhere,
a baby chirrup sensuously drawn out.

The People used to be a little
too fond of crowds for their own good.
Like movie extras, they
were sent from place to place, kept standing
long hours in the sun and, finally,
given their fortnight's pay.

People, on the other hand,
were sensitive, and cared;
and they agreed they needed
to keep their weight down,
running around the park each morning.
No wonder that they superseded

that poor old dinosaur, the People,
who smoked, and never understood

that to survive you have to be quite small,
and sometimes seem not to be there at all.

Let's hear it, then, for people,
their sensitivity and taste,
their sets of values
like sets of willow pattern,
so delicate, so easily replaced.

On Seeing the First Flasher

Grey-coated, solitary stranger, hail!
Thou harbinger of summer's lusty days,
tracing through country parks thy mazy trail,
or lingering by some brook to catch the gaze
of passing schoolgirl, who, with scornful eye,
remarks upon thy manhood's lack of length,
then vanishing, before her angry cry
shall summon to her aid the studded strength
of forty skinheads, or, with deadly aim,
her dainty foot shall plunge into thy crotch –
when shalt thou find a partner to thy game,
a maid whose pleasure is to stand and watch?
As soon, alas, as poets shall enthrall
commuter crowds, or fill the Albert Hall.

King Pineapple

Of all minor deities, remember
fat Pineapple, swinging complacently
in string bags along the Harrow Road.

You know he's male by his sudden
rude spiking of ladies' buttocks
in crowds. His crown is a jester's cap.

Guest of the rich, he sometimes presides
over linen antarcticas, shoals of silver;
but he is Poverty's true friend-in-need,

and will feed you from his sugary paunch
for seven midnights, in dripping communion
with sunlight, over the frosty sink.

Roaring Beach

for Edith Speers

The sea was cold enough to burn you,
in spite of sun. We plunged
under the waves, and came up cursing,
lungs crushed. That was at first.

Later, we could relax neck-deep.
Our heads bobbed like apples on the surface,
as we talked – about what? Not poetry,
I think. There was, as well,

a smell of smoke from illicit fires
somewhere on shore. We could see,
looking down, clear to the wrinkled floor.
One of us, surely, must have mentioned that.

TRANSLATIONS OF TWENTIETH-CENTURY ABORIGINAL SONGS

As with other translations of Aboriginal poetry in this volume, the words translated and reproduced here are only part of "an artistic whole, made up of song, music, and often dance, with its accompanying body paint icon" (Lee Cataldi, *Journal of Australian Studies*, 1998). Despite being torn from their cultural and artistic context, it is surprising how effective and moving these translations can be. The notes which follow paraphrase comments in the books from which the songs are taken.

"Combing Her Hair" and "The Red Gown" come from R. M. W. Dixon's and Grace Koch's *Dyirbal: Song Poetry, the Oral Literature of an Australian Rainforest People* (1996). Dixon notes: "The sight of a white woman combing her hair early in the morning, appearing to lift up the hair with her comb, so impressed the Girramaygan people that they composed this song ['Combing Her Hair']; the accompanying dance mimed the woman's movements. [And regarding 'The Red Gown'] In the early days of contact, Girramaygan people saw a white girl wearing a red dress with white spots. As she danced with happiness, it seemed to wave, like a flag or the leaves on a palm tree, the dancers mimed the movement of the girl."

"The Spirit Song about Lake Eyre" is from *The Honey-Ant Men's Love Song and Other Aboriginal Song Poems* (1990) edited by R. M. W. Dixon and Martin Duwell. An old Wangkangurru man who went from the desert to the Killalpaninna Mission in the late 19th century claimed that a spirit led him over the Lake Eyre country and gave him songs which he handed on to young relatives, Jimmy and Leslie Russell. "Only Eyebrows" refers to a mythical being who travels over Lake Eyre as a whirlwind, with only his eyebrows showing. The *piyatja* goblins live on the slopes of Mt Margaret on the west side of the lake.

"Into the Waves" is from the same book. Dixon explains: "A love-struck man lies on the beach, watching nubile young girls play in the foam, jumping into waves and making them 'burst'. By social convention, he could not go in too."

"Little Eva at Moonlight Creek" is from *Little Eva at Moonlight Creek and other Aboriginal song poems* (1994) edited by Martin Duwell and R. M. W. Dixon. This song and dance, transcribed by John J. Bradley, which became known in several languages and was performed as late as 1988, deals with the crash of a United States Air Force B-24 bomber, *Little Eva*, at Moonlight Creek (Dulijarrba) in the Gulf of Carpentaria on 1 December 1942. The plane crashed in a tropical storm, after a bombing raid. The pilot of *Little Eva* is referred to in the song as the engineer. Yanyuwa and Garrawa people from nearby cattle stations participated in the search for missing aircrew, only one of whom survived. Dancers represent biplanes, which were also used in the search and were sighted by the search parties on the ground. The throbbing sound of a biplane engine was mistaken for the noise of guns. A young member of the search party is frightened when he is seen by airmen in the biplanes. The searchers respond to a flag being waved from a biplane by waving their hats. The pilot of the biplane (referred to as "the publican", being a figure of authority) indicates the scene of the crash is far away to the north.

The remaining song poems are all from *Little Eva at Moonlight Creek and other Aboriginal song poems.*

The following six songs were transcribed by John J. Bradley. Suzanne Jujana and Darby Mulwamara, the composers of "Arriving at the Jetty", admire the skill of the pilot, Harry Marrkulkardu, bringing a lugger alongside the jetty. The composer of "Deaf to the Conch Shell's Call" had harpooned a dugong, and blew a conch shell to alert those at the camp to prepare a ground oven, but his call was not heard. "The Wind and the Turtle" is about a hunter sitting in his canoe, waiting for a dugong or turtle. "The Trepang Gatherers" dates back to the 1920s when the Yanyuwa people worked, diving for trepang or bêche-de-mer. The "Morning Glories" is a cloud formation that appears in the late dry season and which the Yanyuwa believe carries flying foxes and species of birds that arrive to eat the blossoms of flowering plants. The composer of "Oh! To Be a Bird!" is sitting on an island, pining for her boyfriend and sees a fire burning on the mainland and wonders if he may be there.

"The First Rabbit" is a transcription by Luise A. Hercus. Charlie Karnapiti, who composed this song, was a Birdsville tracker, and was one of only three survivors of the massacre, in about 1878, of hundreds of people performing the Mindiri ceremony at the Koonchera waterhole. He survived by smearing himself with his grandmother's blood and feigning death. This song was sung by Frank Crombie in August 1987, shortly before his death on a trip into the Simpson Desert, and transcribed by Hercus with help from Linda Crombie.

Unlike the other songs listed above, which are not traditional and mostly have an identifiable author, "Sulphur-crested Cockatoo" is traditional, being a song of the Wora clan, and is among a group of songs about birds sung at a funeral in 1975 by Peter Mondjingu and Runggurr and transcribed by Ian Keen with help from Mondjingu and Bariya. Keen suggests that many of the connotations, including complex religious symbolism inherent in the songs, have no equivalent in other cultures and strictly speaking the songs are untranslatable. The dots indicate where the text of the song became unclear, because the words of the two singers were different or inaudible. A dash indicates where the singers have added an extemporised coda at the end of a formal verse. Keen pointed out that the songs can be seen at one level as descriptive of natural phenomena – the birds – but other meanings can be read into them. For example by mentioning place names, the singer may construct a journey to guide the deceased's spirit to its homeland.

Keen commented on how with the Wora clan song, the "text" of a song "gradually transforms from song-item to song-item; bringing in new phrases, and putting words and phrases already used in a different order and combining them in new ways." A number of the commentators also refer to the fact that Aboriginal song poems often use obscure grammatical forms and "poetic" language that is not commonly used or may be incomprehensible to some members of the audience. What is striking about all of the Aboriginal song poems grouped together here, from the short imagist pieces such as "Combing Her Hair" and "The Red Gown" to the longer, elaborate songs of the Wora clan, is their aesthetic sense and strong sense of form.

Combing Her Hair

Pick it up with a comb, early in the morning
Pick it up with a comb that which is hanging down
Pick up your long tresses, with a comb
(Sung by Jimmy Murray in Girramay language, Gama song style recorded, transcribed and translated by R. M. W. Dixon)

The Red Gown

The red gown we see is like a butterfly
A red gown that catches the eye
Red gown that will dance in joy
(Sung by Jimmy Murray in Girramay language, Gama song style recorded, transcribed and translated by R. M. W. Dixon)

The Spirit Song about Lake Eyre

"Only Eyebrows" he is called,
He is only eyebrows.
"Only Eyebrows" he is called.

"Only Eyebrows",
"Only Eyebrows"
He travels crossway, across the lake,
Crossways indeed
"Only …

"Only Eyebrows",
"Only Eyebrows",
He travels crossways across the lake.

The *piyatja* goblins, the *piyatja* goblins are painted up
Like banded snakes they look,
Yes, like banded snakes.

They are dancing now, painted up

You see them sleeping by the creek.

They are painted, all painted,
Like banded snakes they are painted.

They resemble dark flowers
Flowers in the distance by the lake
Flowers in the distance by the lake
Dark flowers
In the distance the huge flock
Of crows.

In the distance the huge flock
The flock of crows
Flowers in the distance by the lake
Dark flowers.
(Jimmy and Leslie Russell, 1968)

Into the Waves

Jumping up into the water
The teenage girls
Jumping up into the water
Into the waves
Foam and spray bursting
Into the waves
Jumping up into the water
The teenage girls
Foam and spray bursting
Into the waves
Jumping up into the water
The teenage girls
Jumping up into the water
The teenage girls
Foam and spray bursting
(Sung by George Watson in Mamu language, Burran song style recorded, transcribed and translated by R. M. W. Dixon)

Little Eva at Moonlight Creek

GOING HOME (1)
Continuously the propellor turned,
At night,
The pilot he searched,
For his home,

So as to land the plane,
At the place with many lights.

STORM WINDS
Leaning to the side,
The plane was travelling,
Heading eastwards,
The winds struck it,
Twisting it off course.

"LITTLE EVA" CRASHES
The plane was falling,
Nose to the east,
Falling with outstretched wings,
At that place,
Dulijarrba.
The engineer,
Hits the ground,
The plane's nose to the west,
With wings outstretched,
He put it on the ground.

TWO OF US WILL GO
By foot,
Walking,
We too are about to go.
In this relation country of mine.
In this country,
We two are walking.

SPINIFEX COUNTRY
Here we all are,
We are all walking,
In this spinifex country.

AT BURRULHUWARRA
Here it is,
Burrulhuwarra,
Here it is,
This country,
Your country,
It is for the Rrumburriya people.

FIGHTING PLANES

You two listen!
To the north,
the throbbing sound,
He is fighting.

SO HIGH UP

You two look!
High, high up,
Coming from the east,
So far up,
It is faint,
Why is the pilot
Not afraid?

BIPLANES SEARCHING

With wings placed,
One on top of the other,
The biplanes travel northwards,
One in front of the other.
The propellors are turning,
On the camouflaged planes,
The planes have wings,
That have armpits.

TWO PLANES TOGETHER

Two planes,
Running together,
From the north,
They are seeing him,
My younger companion,
Closer together they are coming,
The two of them together,
"Look!"

WAVING A FLAG

Downwards
He pulled the flag,
Upwards,
He dragged the flag,
The engineer,
Looked over,

The tipping side,
Of the plane.

WAVE YOUR HAT
He waved his hat,
He shouted,
"Wave your hats upwards,
For those two pilots!"

THE PUBLICAN
He showed himself,
The Publican,
He indicated the location,
As the plane tipped,
Far to the north,
Far to the north.

GOING HOME (2)
They saw
The two planes,
Their backs,
Going eastwards,
They were returning home.

MAYBE BORROLOOLA
You two look!
The resounding noise,
Of the plane,
It comes from the east.
Where will it land?
Here?
Maybe Borroloola,
Or maybe,
In another place.
(Frank Karrijiji)

Arriving at the Jetty

To the south side of the jetty,
To the north side of the jetty,
To the centre.
He will measure it.
Behind the prow
A bow wave silently flows.
(Suzanna Jujana and Darby Muluwamara)

Deaf to the Conch Shell's Call

The conch shell called out
From Marani.
It was not heard.
(Peter Jangurringurri)

The Wind and the Turtle

Silence,
A stirring of wind,
Bringing,
The Flat Back Turtle.
(Jack Baju)

The Trepang Gatherers

Covered with mud,
Are the genitals
Of the working boys,
They bring up the trepang,
To tip into the boat.
(Jack Baju)

His First Trousers

You two!
Look at him,
His trousers
Are slipping down,
He's too skinny.
(Jack Baju)

Morning Glories

You two!
Look to the north,
The Morning Glories
Carry with them
The migratory flying animals.
(Jack Baju)

Oh! To Be a Bird

I wish that I were a bird,
I would fly,
And maybe see you
At the fire,
Burning in the south.
(Harriet Johnson Mambalwarrka)

The First Rabbit

They were frightened of a rabbit
Frightened of a rabbit!
A stretched-out, elongated creature
A stretched-out elongated creature
Frightened of a rabbit!
A stretched-out, elongated creature
Frightened of a rabbit!
(Charlie Karnapiti)

Sulphur-crested Cockatoo

White cockatoos fly calling
"noopil noopil".
"jikidjng jikiding"
calling as they fly,
enjoying the breeze,
alighting in the tall paperbark
trees at Balthawun.

"noopil noopil noopil",
"noopil noopil".
they called, "jikiding",
calling as they fly,
happy in the breeze,
calling as they fly,
the wind ruffles their crests,
happily they cried, "jikiding!"

"noopil noopil noopil",
"noopil noopil noopil",
"jikiding jikiding"
calling as they fly.
...
endless chatter of cockatoos
unceasingly they call
Garpirra wind, Yawukul wind
blowing towards Balthawun

Gurnbuma cockatoos,
Sulphur-crested cockatoos,
feathers ruffled in the wind
blowing towards Balthawun
...

talking there.
at Barlawatji, Murruwana,
Djikarnmurru,
the wind ruffles their crests
Crests ruffled in the breeze,
they called "jikiding",
Gurnbuma cockatoos,
wind blowing their feathers,
at Balthawun;
– South wind blew their crests,
the breeze from the north
  makes them croak.

"noopil noopil",
"noopil noopil",
Gurnbuma cockatoos,
Gurnbuma cockatoos,
feathers ruffled in the breeze,
Galumaluma cockatoos.
– Over there they called
at Barlawatji, Murruwarna.

Marrparrama cockatoos,
Galumaluma cockatoos at Yawukuyala,
...
Gurnbuma cockatoos,
wind ruffling their crests,
At Balthawun;
– South wind catches their feathers,
the light breeze from the north
  makes them croak

"noopil noopil noopil",
"noopil noopil noopil",
Gurnbuma cockatoos,
Gurnbuma cockatoos;
– wind in their feathers,
in the Balthawun paperbark trees,
talking happily away,
towards Yawuku.

"noopil noopil noopil",
Galumaluma cockatoos,
Marrparrama cockatoos,
towards Yawuku;
– Gurnbuma cockatoos,

powerful south wind after the rains,
wind from the north-east,
happily they talk.
(Song of the Wora Clan, sung by Peter Mondjingu and Runggurr, 1975)

JOHN FORBES 1950–1998

John Forbes was born in Melbourne. He studied English Literature, Latin and Philosophy at the University of Sydney, before dropping Latin. He loved the Latin poets and later felt that he should have dropped English instead, as he had never found it useful for his writing. His undergraduate thesis was on John Ashbery. After graduating, he travelled in Europe, began a Master's thesis on Frank O'Hara, and abandoned it. He worked in labouring and similar jobs, eventually becoming a removalist. In 1989 he moved from Sydney to Melbourne, teaching poetry and writing literary reviews. He travelled overseas again, teaching at Loughborough University. He died of a heart attack in Melbourne, aged 47, in the company of friends. Gig Ryan delivered the eulogy at St Brigid's Church, Fitzroy North.

Forbes published six collections of poetry during his lifetime and a seventh, *Damaged Glamour* (1998) posthumously. Alan Wearne relates that Forbes "was probably the most democratic reader I've known. He loved Ken Slessor (whom he regarded as Australia's finest) and a lot of Les Murray and Bruce Beaver, whose work he defended as if it were his own … He often spoke with awe about Gig Ryan's sombre lyrics and was anxious for the continuing reputations of Martin Johnston, Robert Harris, Jas H. Duke and John Anderson, four of his contemporaries who predeceased him."

Gig Ryan, in her foreword described his *Collected Poems*, as: "comparatively slim, yet there are few, if any, poems that fail to interest." She sees as a reason for this that his poems "brim with argument and ideas and out of the seeming chaos of often complicated Latinate sentences come lucidity and humour".

Four Heads & How To Do Them

The Classical Head

Nature in her wisdom has formed the human head
so it stands at the very top of the body.

The head – or let us say the face – divides into 3,
the seats of wisdom, beauty & goodness respectively.

The eyebrows form a circle around the eyes, as
the semicircles of the ears are the size of the

open mouth & the mouth is one eye length from
the nose, itself the length of the lip & at the top

the nose is as wide as one eye. From the nose
to the ear is the length of the middle finger

and the chin is 2½ times as thick as the finger.
The open hand in turn is as large as the face.

A man is ten faces tall & assuming one leaves out
the head the genitals mark his centre exactly.

The Romantic Head
The Romantic head begins with the hands cupped
under the chin the little fingers resting on the nose
& the thumbs curling up the jaw line towards the ears.

The lips are ripe but pressed together as the eyes
are closed or narrowed, gazing in the direction of
the little fingers. The face as a whole exists to gesture.

The nose while beautiful is like the neck, ignored,
being merely a prop for the brow that is usually
well developed & creased in thought – consider the lines

"the wrinkled sea beneath him crawls" locating the centre
of the Romantic head above the hairline & between the ears;
so the artist must see shapes the normal eye is blind to.

This is achieved at the top of the cranium where the skull
opens to the air, zooms & merges with its own aura.
Here the whole diurnal round passes through. In this way

the dissolution the quivering chin & supported jaw seemed
to fear, as the head longed for, takes place. The head, at
last one with the world, dissolves. The artist changes genre.

The Symbolist Head
No longer begins with even a mention of anatomy,
the approach in fact leaves one with the whole glittering
universe from which only the head has been removed.
One attempts, in the teeth of an obvious fallacy, to find
the shape, colour, smell, to know the "feel" of the head
without knowing the head at all. And the quarry is elusive!
If the stomach disappears, butterflies are liberated & while
the head teems with ideas who has ever seen one? Equally,
the sound of a head stroked with sponge rubber or the sound
of a head kicked along the street on Anzac Day could be
the sound of a million other things kicked or stroked.
The head leaves no prints in the air & the shape of an
absence baffles even metaphysics. But the body connects
to the head like a visible idea & so has its uses, for

what feeling is aroused by *The Winged Victory of Samothrace*
but piercing regret for the lost head? And beyond the body,
a landscape is not just our yearning to be a pane of glass
but a web of clues to its centre, the head. And here, like one day
finding a lone wig in the vast rubbish dump devoted to shoes,
the Symbolist head appears, a painting filled with love
for itself, an emotion useless as mirrors without a head.
This art verges on the sentimental. It's called "Pillow Talk"

The Conceptual Head

1) The breeze moves
the branches as sleep moves the old man's head:
neither move the poem.

2) The opening image becomes
"poetic" only if visualised

3) but even so
the head can't really be
seen,
heard,
touched
or smelt –
the Objective Head would be raving nostalgia.

4) Yet the head is not a word
& the word means "head"
only inside the head or its gesture,
the mouth.
So the poem can't escape,
trapped inside its subject
& longing to be a piece of flesh and blood
as
Ten Pounds of Ugly Fat
versus
The Immortal Taperecorder
forever.

5) While anatomy is only a map, sketched
from an engaging rumour,
metaphor is the dream
of its shape –
from 'head in the stars'
to 'head of lettuce'

Between the two
the poem of the head is endless.

6) Now the world of the head opens
like the journals of old travellers
                                        & all your past emotions
seem tiny, crude simulacra of its beauty.
& you are totally free

7)   Greater than all Magellans
you commence an adventure more huge and intricate
than the complete idea of Mt Everest.
And this academy can teach you no more.
                                        The voyage will branch out,
seem boring & faraway from the head,
but nothing can delay you
for nothing is lost to the head.

8) Goodbye,
                     send me postcards
                     and colourful native stamps,
                                                  Good luck!

Breakfast

for Ranald & Julie Allen

to wake up & throw
two bowls of muesli
at the wall miss &
crack a louvre is no
way to start married
life in Coffs Harbour
which makes you laugh
& that's better than
not, helping to clean
the marvellous organs
of the lungs & muscle
which are more than
our names / air & blood
flowing inside us
like currents that
travel up & down the
coast. The beaches
shift around & we go

after them as though
swimming & golf are
what we're "made for"
at least they keep us
on the go so that
love arrives like
dawn in hot climates
– neither arse nor
class – just there
as the beach fills up
with light & you
swim out together
for the morning's first
wave before breakfast

To the Bobbydazzlers

American poets!
you have saved
America from
its reputation
if not its fate
& you saved me
too, in 1970
when I first
breathed freely
in Ted Berrigan's
Sonnets, escaping
the talented earache of Modern
Poetry.
                    Sitting
on the beach I
look towards you
but the curve
of the Pacific
gets in the way
& I see stars
instead knocked
out by your poems
American poets,
the Great Dead
are smiling
in your faces.

I salute their
luminous hum!

Rrose Selavy

for Julie Rose

"A transistor & a large sum of money to spend"
Steely Dan

Julie the beauty of a tooth
& from the red & white checked tablecloth's back garden
                when we're quietly avoiding lunch
                        Julie begins to somersault
O facelift sing of Julie!
O mascara croon!
And Ireland green as hair let every crystal drop of whisky
                                                flow to me
          as a fish knife's clatter falling sounds the name of Julie –
                                    the blue day collects her
                                    & disappears
Julie breathing like a T-shirt after a swim
                        in Crete, Julie
                  in Rangoon a Chevrolet Impala
          & in it Julie. She watches osmosis on television combing
                  her hair
                  & FLASH!
appears like an ice cream to Fragonard, aeroplane bliss Julie
                        helping the air of London get cleaner
                  Julie, her watch stopped exact
                  sneeze balloon happy griefs
                  of the portmanteau
Julie, passing exams
Julie the hand-made spine of rare first editions sunburns
                                              under the Eiffel Tower
                  O golfball of insomnia!
Julie the wedding dress cries like an Italian face
& when the aftershave factory explodes the Spirit of Alcohol
                                                      beams on Julie.

Imagine an iceberg's ideal form
or an escaped embrace (!) Avoid such horrors with Julie
                  and on a weekend hike with Julie
        the snapshot of a bear!

Julie invites a drop of foam to eternity as a blood bank
bursts pulpily,
every corpuscle
dying in love
with Julie,
more luminous than a burning patio /
more tasteful
than a day at the zoo.
Julie, surfing the night away
and in the dark beauties of drugs on the pension, Julie,
a crazed spanner in the intricate works of death!
O bored cigarette Julie!
Julie the myth of beauty where sex is "concerned"
and Julie the myth of ugliness where helicopters are learning,
slowly,
to dance (their feet are clumsy but tender
tender!)
Even the windscreen wipers on their electric stage swivel
for Julie, even the Enos bubbling in its glass.

More precise than a stocking,
Julie lounges at the pool
she moves like a heatwave in December. It's the year slipping by
it's the strange coast of Mozambique I've never seen –
no it's Julie
buying a blazer.
O abhorrent sunglasses!
I peel an orange listening to the fridge erupt in the night
& in the morning I go to the movies
with Julie.

Drugs

for Jenni Baker and in memory of Simon Bronski

Marijuana lets you know
what you really feel about
this, that, these & those

but cigarettes are just
something to breathe against

while speed wraps itself around you
the way a speeding car
wraps itself around a telegraph pole

and all cough medicine can do
is make it a pure delight

to read the *Times Literary Supplement*

But a wallet full of money
is a different thing entirely

– you know about amyl nitrite,
the Heart Attack Machine?

it's far cheaper than cocaine
& the cat's whisker you can afford

won't give you much of a flash
as opposed to the massive rush
of amyl nitrite's darker hit

So why bother with coke? Rock stars
I don't mean you! But the best

of all is heroin. One day.
One day you'll own a big house.

Then by way of light relief
there's my own favourite, alcohol

which is not really a drug
at all, just as the motto
"lips that touch liquor will never

touch mine" doesn't mean
the girl of your dreams won't be

a problem drinker. Even hippies
will, reluctantly, get pissed

& talk about tripping I won't
because real acid is a thing
of the past & besides I could

be busy, like you are, drinking
which means we both have
a Reason to be Cheerful. Another

is when you're on mandies
you don't need drugs

the body is so calm it could be
a bag of soft expensive stuff

& the brain is as pure
as foam on central ocean tossed
or the driven snow

a girl from Sydney
is hoping she'll find in America

along with the drugs I've left out here
because I can't remember

a thing about them except
they felt like I was swallowing a pill

washed down with a lot of vodka
so that the pill & I both forgot

that we've been mingled
happily ever after. & I've forgotten too

about drugs & music –
how they meet inside you

in pubs & rooms & dances –
blind chemicals to make you freak

or sparkle / rock'n'roll music
to bounce you around.

Europe: a guide for Ken Searle

Greece is like a glittering city
though only in a political speech

but Italians believe in *bella figura*
& mis-use the beach. In Germany there's

Kraftwerk & acres of expressionist kitsch.
Oil-rich Norwegians don't need to ski

they just like it & Iceland is famous
for its past. Doing their physical jerks,

a quiet pride permeates the Swedes.
Denmark is neither vivid nor abrupt

& Belgians have a ringside seat
to observe the behaviour of the Dutch.

The French invented finesse but it's
their self-regard that intrigues us.

We pity the English, though they get on
our wick, pretending to understand us

& Scotland is old-fashioned like a dowry
but unusual, like nice police. Mention

Ireland & you've already said enough
The Spaniards are not relaxed about sex

& tourists are attracted to this. Some
Portuguese exist entirely on a diet of fish

but rich cakes, finance & guest workers
sustain the Swiss. Consult my *By Trailbike*

& Hot-Air Ballon Through Middle Europe
for details of the Austrians & Czechs

but don't forget Bavaria's Octoberfest
or that Rococo architecture was designed

to be passed out under, pissed, & it's
aesthetically edifying to do this.

For the rest; give Russia a miss,
the Poles will appreciate hard currency

but only as a gift & the fleshpots of
Split will leave you a physical wreck.

This guide stops short at the Balkans
as it omits the Finns. I won't apologise

– many guides to Australia include
New Zealand or leave out Tasmania.

No doubt some thorough American manual
can give you the lowdown on Europe's margins

but mine, designed for only one traveller,
is better written & much shorter.

Besides, if you remove the art, Europe's
like the US, more or less a dead loss

& while convenient for walking
& picturesque, like the top of a *Caran*

D'Ache pencil case or a chocolate box
what do you make of a landscape

that reminds you of itself? Is this why
the people are sure they're typical

not standard? I can't advise you on this
but I know how I enjoyed myself; though

knocked out by what convinced me
"Great Art" without inverted commas is

(but not because of this) I hung around
with other Australians & hit the piss.

Death: an Ode

Death, you're more successful than America,
even if we don't choose to join you, we do.

I've just become aware of this conscription
where no one's marble doesn't come up;
no use carving your name on a tree, exchanging vows
or not treading on the cracks for luck
where there's no statistical anomalies at all
& you know not the day nor the hour, or even if you do
timor mortis conturbat me. No doubt we'd
think this in a plunging jet & the black box recorder
would note each individual, unavailing scream
but what gets me is how compulsory it is –
"he never was a joiner" they wrote on his tomb.
At least bingeing becomes heroic & I can see
why the Victorians
so loved drawn out death-bed scenes:
huddled before our beautiful century, they knew
what first night nerves were all about.

Love Poem

Spent tracer flecks Baghdad's
bright video game sky

as I curl up with the war
in lieu of you, whose letter

lets me know my poems show
how unhappy I can be. Perhaps.

But what they don't show, until
now, is how at ease I can be

with military technology: e.g.
matching their *feu d'esprit* I classify

the sounds of the Iraqi AA – the
thump of the 85 mil, the throaty

chatter of the quad ZSU 23.
Our precision guided weapons

make the horizon flash & glow
but nothing I can do makes you

want me. Instead I watch the west
do what the west does best

& know, obscurely, as I go to bed
all this is being staged for me.

Ode to Karl Marx

Old father of the horrible bride whose
wedding cake has finally collapsed, you

spoke the truth that doesn't set us free –
it's like a lever made of words no one's

learnt to operate. So the machine it once
connected to just accelerates & each new

rap dance video's a perfect image of this,
bodies going faster and faster, still dancing

on the spot. At the moment tho' this set up
works for me, being paid to sit and write &

smoke, thumbing through Adorno like *New Idea*
on a cold working day in Ballarat, where

adult unemployment is 22% & all your grand
schemata of intricate cause and effect

work out like this: take a muscle car &
wire its accelerator to the floor, take out

the brakes, the gears the steering wheel
& let it rip. The dumbest tattooed hoon

– mortal diamond hanging round the Mall –
knows what happens next. It's fun unless

you're strapped inside the car. I'm not,
but the dummies they use for testing are.

Warm Snipers

Under mid-winter light in an antique hall
"the fall of because" scrawled on a wall

suggests why Europe's just a highbrow joke –
they invented causation in place of hope

but all their culture is really worth
is its potential for embittered mirth;

what else can it do but amuse them when
the radio plays the following gem:

a Sarajevo professor of Comparative Lit
knits trigger-fingered mittens
                    & they're a hit!

– 20 deutschmarks each – so she'll survive

The Four Horsemen & the freezing skies

while like the rest of Europe she ignores,
because she must, the fall of because.

Lassu in Cielo

i.m. Martin Johnston

my first dream of home
from Loughborough U

involves two poets arguing
over a lunch time stew

remember those post-binge
mid-seventies Glebe mornings –

lantana & sandstone,
bits of Harbour out the window

& the light, intense & blue?
I crawl downstairs & there's

Martin chopping garlic to
vague, patrician interjections –

"mate, isn't garlic something
one can overdo?"

Martin pauses, mock pedantic –
"Aristotle, Galen, Hippocrates

& all the authorities agree,
                    garlic, *de natura*
is not subject to degree!"

then, as if it's worried him
for years, David Campbell DSO, DFC,

takes another swig of whisky
looks up & says "I see. I see."

Anzac Day

A certain cast to their features marked
the English going into battle, & then, that

glint in the Frenchman's eye meant "Folks,
clear the room!" The Turks knew death

would take them to a paradise of sex

Islam reserves for its warrior dead

& the Scots had their music. The Germans
worshipped the State & Death, so for them

the Maximschlacht was almost a sacrament.
Recruiting posters made the Irish soldier

look like a saint on a holy card, soppy & pious,
the way the Yanks go on about their dead.

Not so the Australians, unamused, unimpressed
they went over the top like men clocking on,

in this first full-scale industrial war.
Which is why Anzac Day continues to move us,

& grow, despite attempts to make it
a media event (left to them we'd attend

"The Foxtel Dawn Service"). But The March
is proof we got at least one thing right, informal,

straggling & more cheerful than not,
it's like a huge works or 8 Hour Day picnic –

if we still had works, or unions, that is.

PHILIP SALOM 1950–

Philip Salom grew up on a dairy farm at Brunswick Junction in Western Australia. He attended Muresk Agricultural College and after graduation he spent two years on a cattle research station. He began writing poetry while he was a student at the Western Australian Institute of Technology and graduated a Bachelor of Arts (English) in 1976. He has published nine collections of poetry and two novels. He now teaches creative writing at the University of Melbourne.

The Song of Hair

In four houses now I've seen her
taking her hair for its long swim like freestyle

through basins and towels, through conditioners
and wraps, tuning the waters, solving the combinations

of taps. I have seen her, from washing
and combing out, take in her strong hands

and lift to the right like playing a flute
her long hair, her long blonded dream of the scalp.

Nothing rushes her. Nothing is left out.
The drying machines, the hand-held wind

tunnels: and she, her sleek hair and face
like aerodynamics, so keen is her beauty

with this fullness of work. In her house,
and mine, in London once, in Rome, I've

seen her, as this known world repeats
each combing and hair-touch and rightful place

as if the world would not be worth living
if this were not so, made so and found so

in her fabulous patience, her beautiful hair.

The Family Fig Trees

Seeing them through the mist, on the downslope
from the house, into the wing-lift of swallows,
the fig tree branches rose up like crow's-nests,

the ships underground. Or like quattrocento paintings
of the New Testament, each fig tree quite separate
and solid enough to sit on, like a wooden cloud.

When the mist shone flat and silver in the sunlight,
like a thin swamp suspended above the ground,
the fig trees floated in it looking for land.

Each fig split open is the night sky in starburst
down small, ovum and sap, the far-off itching sky,
words I moisten with my mouth like mist.

As a child I sat in the wizened tree, its branches
flattened by my weight, and thought of flat figs
by Cezanne, old varnished figs by the Masters,

these same figs, the pagan, the Biblical mouthfuls,
the erotica of swollen fig, entering the opened fig,
these metaphors which took me past the itch

metaphors stand in for: elsewheres, and sometimes
the lost. I was young, I had not lived, I imagined
the dove returning from dry land, with no branch.

I'd look over to the swamp from my seat in the trees,
the lost banks of the river, wind rafting the surface,
the sky scoured into this water like a metal plate.

The fence posts luxurious with generations of lichen,
and each fence wire rolling mezzotint of stormy skies.
Endless versions. Days passing like drafts of poems.

The fig trees are gone now, dismantled by my brothers.
Too old and too much in the way, old characters
left over from a dream. But I am hurt by what is lost.

Now I sit above another tree, my family, the figurative,
on the table: proof, but only recent, of flattened branches
where the old Sephardic blood-line stops

two layers back: my Jewish grandfather who married out.
When people asked about our name, I might have thought
of figs, opened, like Palestine. But the family denied it.

One tree they took down quietly before we knew of it.
Said we were English, and Spanish married into Welsh.
But close-up, these names are like watermarks.

There's no-one to engulf them, or embrace them
now. And now because I cannot claim them right
I call up their music, and if I cannot hear it quite

there's a sweetness I can taste above the branches
in my chest, in this tree, this wooden cloud of names:
Mordecai and Sarah. Noah and Ruth. Shalom.

ANDREW SANT 1950–

Andrew Sant was born in London, came with his parents to Melbourne as a child, and graduated from La Trobe University in Arts. He co-founded the literary magazine *Island*, based in Tasmania, and was its editor for ten years. He has been a writer-in-residence at Peking University and a Writing Fellow at the University of Leicester. He has taught in secondary and tertiary education institutions and been a copywriter and editor. Sant has published eleven collections of poetry and edited two anthologies. His poetry seems English in its reticence and use of the middle tone of voice. His early poem, "Homage to the Canal People", derives from his working on narrow boats in the north of England.

Homage to the Canal People

Steered straight into this century I see narrowboats
loaded with coal, cheese, vats of vinegar trailing
a hard century behind them along
the polluted Grand Union, yet their cabins are bright
as their paintings of roses and castles

entering Oxford or Chester, a vivid variation
on a theme bleak and slow
as three-miles-an-hour journeys for boatmen
with more rain than sun
working into their faces.
It's pride that brightened them, and acceptance
that heaven's easy chair was far off as the dandies
composing themselves to ignore their progress through towns
like the arrival of gypsies,
cloth caps pulled down against
complacency. So they denied them a privilege –
their cabin doors closed tight
on china, brasswork and lace
fine as webs slung
across the just-after-dawn hedges, yet
those cabins were smaller than a gentleman's pantry.

Long damp days scattering moorhens
from the pounds, then a staircase of locks,
instinctive manoeuvrings through gushes of water,
hard hands straining on ropes
to steady a full seventy-foot boat –
I imagine eyes also twisted
like knots between man and wife
till a good pint could loose them,
could knock over incidents like skittles
and with a brutal laugh set them up again;
that's canal pub community –
a sharing of feelings, an abandonment
with gossip flying so fast it was prophetic
the boats outside moored with the children
like all relevant history, in the shadow
of the Swan or the Bird in Hand.

Pencils

1

I celebrate and sharpen
that masterstroke,
the pencil. Its touch

is firm but not final,
subtle foreplay
across the page

towards liberties
of print; and gentler
than a pen. Poised.

Blunt, near a rubber,
on my desk. Unless
it gets lost, another

one in a billion
with all its retractable
words yet to come.

2

Brilliance, mostly,
of length and width
at 45° pressure

of habit connects it.
I write "such keen
engineering

receives scarce heed"
with this newly bought
shiny Staedtler HB.

3

My Spirax notebooks
agree – these descendants
from the original

Borrowdale graphite
models (cedar-cased)
are all the stationery

I need to keep
up to date. Line
breathing into line

down the page,
champion the heart
minute by minute;

chart regions
familiar and remote.
Ah, it's great

the way pencils brave
gales, or emotion,
and remain unbroken.

Nightfall

The leaves release their light.
Bees, the fuchsia's guzzlers,
quit their day routine as
somewhere a voice calls,
"Come inside." No need,
sitting here, to tame
the inside table's
fresh disorder. Or, going
further, mind whether
amid our silhouetted hills
you need elect blind chance
as the designer which offered up
the adapted fish
for dinner. Everything's
complete and steady
as rooftops beneath the stars:
the past and future
fold in the breadth
of all the air. Till wait –
now of a sudden, later,
it's all so lidded, silent
for no waking reason;
it seems a brink.
Unless it's a crater
one plummets into speaking
the town's two urgent
syllables. Then try repeating:
"Dark clouds over Siberia"
and "I write with Russian ink".

STEPHEN EDGAR 1951–

Stephen Edgar was born in Sydney where he grew up and went to school. After working in London for three years he moved to Hobart in 1974. He studied Classics and English at the University of Tasmania. For many years he worked in libraries and in 2005 returned to Sydney. He now works editing and proofreading. He is married to the poet Judith Beveridge. Seven collections of his poetry have appeared, and he regularly publishes in *Poetry* (Chicago) which has said of him "he achieves, overall, a supple classicism that earns him a place next to the best twentieth-century American formalists." A note to "Oswald Spengler Watches the Sunset" states it is drawn from the opening paragraphs of the first chapter of volume II of The *Decline of the West* by Oswald Spengler, translated by Charles Francis Atkinson.

Destiny

It was a simple melody on two flutes,
Brief, meagre, somewhar plodding,
Unembellished,
A slight piece, as I thought, concluding
A side of *La Flûte Indienne*. What the notes
Said of it I forget, except its title,
Destino – Destiny. Destiny?
How did that name get itself attached
To a tune with so thin a
Resonance, that offered so little?

Yet, later, those narrow notes, that solemn fluting,
Playing on, played on the mind,
Thin and cold
As Andean air and its barren ground
That offers so little. And an image was competing,
Now recalled and Indian too, a hall
Of mummies, ancestors,
Trussed and rigid, upright underground, marshalled
There, bearing a bleak justice
That could prove perpetual,

Their dead mouths singing, singing, round and stretched,
Two opposite dry lines of O's,
Two hollow ranks
Of flutelike ceaseless crying that rose
Above hearing, and brought to mind the things you've wished
Never to know, what you hear
In lulls, behind all sounds,
Or when the first bird sings and its little chinks
Gather from the morning air
The whole weight of silence.

The Secret Life of Books

They have their stratagems too, though they can't move.
They know their parts.
Like invalids long reconciled
To stillness, they do their work through others.

They have turned the world
To their own account by the twisting of hearts.

What do they have to say and how do they say it?
In the library
At night, or the sun room with its one
Curled thriller by the window, something
Is going on,
You may suspect, that you don't know of. Yet they

Need you. The time comes when you pick one up,
You who scoff
At determinism, the selfish gene.
Why this one? Look, already the blurb
Is drawing in
Some further text. The second paragraph

Calls for an atlas or a gazetteer;
That poem, spare
As a dead leaf's skeleton, coaxes
Your lexicon. Through you they speak
As through the sexes
A script is passed that lovers never hear.

They have you. In the end they have written you,
By the intrusion
Of their account of the world, so when
You come to think, to tell, to do,
You're caught between
Quotation marks, your heart's beat an allusion.

Sun Pictorial

How formal and polite,
How grave they look, burdened with earnest thoughts,
In all these set-up sepia stills,
Almost as if embarrassed and contrite
To be caught practising their fatal skills,
They'd stepped aside from slaughter for these other shots.

The American Civil War,
The first war captured by the photograph
In real time. Even the dead
Seem somehow decorous, less to deplore
The sump of blood to which their duty bled
Than to apologize, humbly, in our behalf.

We know how otherwise
It was. They knew it then. The gauche onset
Of murderously clumsy troops,
Dismemberment by cannon, the blown cries
Through powder smoke, mayhem of scattered groups
In close engagement's pointblank aim and bayonet.

How far from then we've come.
The beauties of the Baghdad night still stun
Me: a blue screen where guns and jets
Unloose the lightnings of imperium –
Intense enough to challenge a minaret's
Aquamarine mosaic in the blinded sun

At noon – and smart bombs fall
Through walls to wipe the city street by street.
Morning, and in the camera's light
The formal corpses ripen. Who can recall
By day precisely what they watched last night?
Or find the unknown soldier in a field of wheat?

Being surplus, like the killed,
Millions of those old plates were simply dumped.
And in a modern version of "swords
To ploughshares", many were reused to build
Greenhouses, ranged and set in place as wards
Above the rife tomatoes as they blushed and plumped,

While through the daily sun's
Pictorial walls and roofs, the long, desired,
Leaf-fattening light fell down, to pore
Upon the portraits of these veterans
Until their ordered histories of the war
Were wiped to just clear glass and what the crops transpired.

Another Country

She said she loved being a woman.
Her skin pressed mine, my face her hair.
And I a man? Just being human
Can sometimes seem too much to bear:

The hands remember what they held,
The tongue recalls the salt-sweet skin.
Who was it said that "her hair smelled
Like a country I could be happy in"?

It's not in human form that I
Have leave to stray in that domain
But only now as the swept sky
Or a thin fall of cold sweet rain.

English as a Foreign Language

One day in bed I read Cavafy
In Greek – her favourite: "Ithaca" –
And in return I won the trophy
Of her admiring Ah!

And I was flattered to astonish
That way. It wasn't much to do.
She put in a request for Spanish
Bedtime recitals too,

Hoping that she might thereby sharpen
Her skills in the language she loved best.
In the event it didn't happen,
Like most things she'd suggest.

And Pushkin too, a modest portion,
But that was pushing it too far,
Though I taught her "I love you" in Russian:
That's *ya lytublyú tebyá*,

A lover's commonplace avowal,
But rather difficult to sound
In Russian; it can be a trial
To get your tongue around.

But she repeated those words over
And over till she had them pat.
In English, though – well, she could never
Quite manage to say that.

Nocturnal

It's midnight now and sounds like midnight then,
The words like distant stars that faintly grace
    The all-pervading dark of space,
    But not meant for the world of men.
        It's not what we forget
But what was never known we most regret
Discovery of. Checking one last cassette

Among my old unlabelled discards, few
Of which reward the playing, I find you.

Some years after her death, but years ago,
Hearing Gwen's voice recite "Suburban Sonnet",
    At first we could not focus on it,
    So jolted that the radio
        Should casually exhume
From our shared memory the woman whom
We knew and make her present in the room,
As though in flesh, surprised to find that she
Had earned this further immortality.

Who ever thought they would not hear the dead?
Who ever thought that they could quarantine
    Those who are not, who once had been?
    At that old station on North Head
        Inmates still tread the boards,
Or something does; equipment there records
The voices in the dormitories and wards,
Although it's years abandoned. Undeleted,
What happened is embedded and repeated,

Or so they say. And that would not faze you
Who always claimed events could not escape
    Their scenes, recorded as on tape
    In matter and played back anew
        To anyone attuned
To that stored energy, that psychic wound.
You said you heard the presence which oppugned
Your trespass on its lasting sole occasion
In your lost house. I scarcely need persuasion,

So simple is this case. Here in the dark
I listen, tensing in distress, to each
    Uncertain fragment of your speech,
    Each desolate, half-drunk remark
        You uttered unaware
That this cassette was running and would share
Far in the useless future your despair
With one who can do nothing but avow
You spoke from midnight, and it's midnight now.

How Long Have You Been Having These Feelings?

So I made it to the portal
And stopped to rub my eyes.
Here was the guy who would immortalize

The cure for mumps with bracken.
I checked him off my list:
Astral adviser and tobacconist.

His name plate was the rebus
Of an untranslated quote
In neon from the end of the Liebestod,

Flanked and borne up by hated
And handbagged parodies
Of Kath and Kim as caryatides.

"Remind me to forget it,"
I thought. "My mind's a sieve.
This game's becoming too competitive."

I had to grope the doorman
Before he'd let me past
And stepped from Mother's Day to Gormenghast.

He was acting like a madman
Doing salsa with a desk.
His stance was Wildean, wit Bradmanesque.

"Is this the place?" "Who's asking?"
"It's me. Consult my nape."
He scribbled something down on masking tape

And, reaching for me slowly
(Could he really move so slow?),
He stuck it on my blue portfolio

And said, "Now wait a minute.
Pick a number between three
And the left-hand square root of infinity."

I bluffed, "How about a googol?"
"Pass, crow. When you're reborn
I'll play it for you on the flugelhorn."

As I stumbled down the hallway
I heard the doorman shout,
"He makes appointments but he's always out.

But if you're very very

Lucky – lucky as sin –
You just might find his secretary in."

She was. The chair she sat in
Swung round. "Well, I am vexed.
I can't make head or tail of this Latin text.

Do you have the tongue?" "I'd rather
You didn't ask," I lied.
"It brings me out in hives since my father died."

"I'm sorry to embarrass
A man of pure intent,
Subjecting him to textual harassment."

I was hot under the collar
And my cuffs began to drip.
"How do you rate on pluvial scholarship?"

She reached for the weather index:
"Hmm. Inventory of rains
With references that the wind explains.

Ah: 'Hung from its isohyets
Like curtains, rain as yet
Is silent on the question why it's wet.'"

"That so? You're quite a wonder –
So much at your command."
I hoped she'd think that I could understand.

"I'll set you one more challenge,"
She said, "you may prefer,
Unless you're shy as J D Salinger."

She had some mole – or freckle –
That she asked me to inspect.
It took some finding, as I recollect,

And a good deal of laughter
From her – buttons and cords –
And a long time in the bathroom afterwards.

"Is this," I asked, "all licit?"
And she replied, "Why, sure.
My pulse was checked by the solicitor."

Then she rubbed me with her flannel
And grabbed me by the wrist
And said, "Report me to your analyst."

Oswald Spengler Watches the Sunset

The air is drenched with day, but one by one
The flowers close on cue,
Obedient to the declining sun.
Forest and grasses, bush and leaf and stem,
They cannot move (and nor, you dream, can you);
It is the wind that plays with them.
Only the little midges dancing still
Against the evening move at will.

This tiny swarm still dancing on and on
Like something in a net
Expanding and contracting, that late swan
Towing its wake, a solitary crow
Crossing the twilight in its silhouette,
The fox proceeding sly and slow:
They are small worlds of purpose which infuse
The world around with will to choose.

An animalcule in a drop of dew –
And so diminutive
That if the human eye should look clear through
That globe there would be nothing there to see –
Although it only has a blink to live,
Yet in the face of this is free;
The oak, in whose vast foliage this dot
Hangs from a single leaf, is not.

PETER GOLDSWORTHY 1951–

Born at Minlaton in South Australia, Peter Goldsworthy grew up in country towns of that state and in Darwin in the Northern Territory. Both his parents were schoolteachers. He qualified as a medical doctor at the University of Adelaide in 1974. As well as publishing five collections of poems, Goldsworthy is an acclaimed writer of fiction and has written the libretti of two operas. He has continued in medicine as a general practitioner on a part-time basis, since he regards it as important for his writing. In his poetry Goldsworthy combines wit with the minimalist form and moral concerns of 20th-century Polish poetry (he particularly admires Tadeusz Rosewicz). His output of poetry is comparatively small, but all of it is honed and concentrated. In an interview, "beautiful" was a word that Goldsworthy favoured. His own poetry is cleanly and beautifully articulated. "Roy G. Biv" is a mnemonic for the colours of the spectrum.

To Poetry

Poetry, you seedy
House of Reps:
your absurd electorates
named Tyger and Greek Urn,
your constituencies
of Lovely Scenery!
Don't try to convince me
with nuances,
all those wheel-barrows,
rain-varnished,
those pairs of cycle-clips,
fine-detailed, inset.
As for Love –
what word is that?
Keep your feelings
to yourself, Poetry,
squashed in ever slimmer
volumes like centrefolds.
My designs for you are these:
if the word is quicker than the eye,
then your little line-drawings,
your funny stick-shapes
might come flickeringly alive
read fast enough,
as if words are really thoughts,
as if poetry is the way we think:
the cartoon, fully animated,
of the book,
of the life.

My Last Rabbit

My first rabbit was the hardest.
Unscrewing the neck,
flipping gut-things between my legs.
Later I developed forehand,
and the traps set themselves.

And then my first two-legged corpse,
my first day in dissection.
There was cold pork for dinner, inevitably –

but coming up hot later.
I never ate meat again – till the next week.

I should mention also a slaughterhouse
downwind from memory.
A place I might have visited,
or might have not. It was all long ago.

Because always this forgetting.
This bringing kill home in butcher's paper,
picked like fruit off a shelf,
smothered with herbs and euphemisms
till it could be anything.

At times I seem almost to remember
the sealed trucks arriving,
the sheep hurrying to be meat.
At times I count them at night,
trying to stay awake.

The Blue Room

I sit on a warm stone step in a doorway
to the Blue Room, the Morning Room.

There is much bee-noise and the noise
of birds: the acoustics are fine in the Blue Room.

Usually it may have rained overnight
in the Blue Room: this clear aquarium air.

In the Blue Room there is always one dove
– *hidden here, hidden here* –

and many honeyeaters,
up for hours, loony as tunes.

Today the Blue Room is available.
I sit among ants, between bees,

amid designer vegetation:
fine-detailed, non-repeating,

in the Blue Room, the Morning Room,
the wide Waiting Room.

Nocturne

Rain in the large
small hours, bulging
gutters and bladders.

We stand at an opened window:
woken, emptied, listening
to the textures of darkness,

the ear-braille,
the nose-braille,
the rain sprinkling down,

the perfumes of the earth
folded back on themselves,
and multiplied …

Remember that childhood trick?
The single leaf of paper
folded, and re-folded,

a sudden book,
very small very thick,
unable to be torn.

We sniff the wet
of the garden.
Such strength in things!

The press of rain
on the earth, unseen.
The million-ply, tough layers.

A Statistician to His Love

Men kill women in bedrooms, usually
by hand, or gun. Women kill men,
less often, in kitchens, with knives.
Don't be alarmed, there is understanding
to be sucked from all such hard
and bony facts, or at least a sense
of symmetry. Drowned men – an
instance – float face down, women up.
But women, ignited, burn more fiercely.
The death camp pyres were therefore,
sensibly, women and children first,
an oily kind of kindling. The men
were stacked in rows on top. Yes,
there is always logic in this world.
And neatness. And the comfort
of fact. Did I mention that suicides

outnumber homicides? Recent figures
are reliable. So stay awhile yet
with me: the person to avoid, alone,
is mostly you yourself.

Suicide on Christmas Eve

After the doctor, the steam-cleaners,
more usefully. I drive home to bed
through intersections sequined with glass:
it's Christmas Eve, season of donor organs.

What is the meaning of life? I shake you
gently awake. What answer would satisfy?
you mumble, yawning, from Your Side.
To understand is to be bored, you say,
practising, perhaps, for Speech Night.
Knowledge is a kind of exhaustion, you say.

A child enters our room: is it morning yet?
Not Yet. In another room the lights of the Tree
wink colourfully, and when the telephone rings
again, it is almost, but not quite, in time.

Roy G. Biv

1 Red

Two colours are enough
to map the world
for frugal tribes,
red or not, hot or cold,
colour-deaf to all the shades
between, because unnamed
they can't be seen,
and names would be
a waste of useful breath.
Which makes me think
what I must miss
without the words to look:
what bloody riot lies between
the bars of salmon-pink and puce,
or herring-red and rouge?

2 Orange

Orange is also things, hazard-lamps
that hang in citrus trees, still glowing
when the world's gone grey. They guide
our pale moth-hands through dusk:
the torch of a valencia, a smaller-wattage
tangerine, a navel like a big bed-lamp
that hoards the light, and gives it back
all night, or till we've peeled the last
thick scab of orange hide, and sucked
our juicy luminescent fingertips,
and cleaned the whiter rind
that's wedged beneath the nails.

3 Yellow

High in the blue is a big Yellow Page
advertising summer, a yolk-yellow
sun, hotter than the moon but also
made of cheese, or melted butter.
It stings our upturned faces, rubs
our skins with sulphur mustard till
those tender body-bags hurt like hell.

4 Green

Greens make me want to eat.
Even when those greens are grass
they still look good enough
to graze. I like them vined
in little balls, or bunched
in brittle clumps I rip apart
and toss. They come in shapes
and sizes, all part of greater
green, a crazy-pave mosaic
pea-, leaf- and olive-,
gooseberry- and lime-
(Wherever green is worn
I write it out in rhyme).

5 Blue

Blue-light in dairies gives better milk
which may be why Whomsoever chooses
chose blue for His or Her ceiling-theme,

a colour-scheme that makes us all
feel good, or not so blue.
I remember my first set of Derwents
and the sky and sea I coloured-in.
The blues in their flat tin box
were a rainbow of blue themselves,
smalt- and sky-, cobalt- and Prussian-.
There were even more if you could trust
British Paints, or even Roget's
where I found two separate words
whose pigments seemed to run together,
cyanotic hyacinth, my favourite colour.

6 Indigo
Indigo is another sound
that's justice to its sight,
a noise that looks like inky dusks
silting up the air with dark.
Each night the other colours leave us
first, sucked down the western plug
in order of appearance. Indigo
remains, inking in its xerox silhouettes
and knife-edge lunar cut-out shapes:
the last to leave, its job to turn
the light out, shut the door, and leave
no chink of colour in the night.

7 Violet
More cello-coloured than viola,
more iodine than violin, violet
is the bloom of the double-bass
wavelength; light at largo pace,
eyes set at widest-aperture,
so wide that they are really ears.
Beyond here, everything is ultra.

ROBERT HARRIS 1951–1993

Robert Harris was born in Victoria. "Six Years Old" records his mother's death when he was that age and the disrupted childhood that followed. He enlisted in the Australian Navy in 1968, during the Vietnam War, and in the 1970s spent time in a commune. He worked in occupations such as labourer and security guard. In

Melbourne he was involved with *Overland* magazine and the La Mama poetry readings and published his first collection of poetry, *Localities*, at the age of 22. He later described his poetry written during those years as "a lax, Frenchified English/ derived from reading the Symbolists/in translation." He married but separated from his wife in the 1980s with no children. An event which transformed his life and his poetry was his conversion to charismatic Christianity; he became "intensely involved in lay ministry" and was confirmed as an Anglican. In the later part of his life he lived in Sydney. Harris published five collections of poetry. Aged 41 he died of a heart attack or influenza in an almost empty single room, where his body was belatedly discovered. His friend Barry Dickins wrote: "Robert Harris had only known two things in his short life: poverty and poetry."

"Riding Over Belmore Park" refers to a Sydney park, overlooked by Central Railway, where alcoholics congregated. "Tobacco" comes from his second book *Translations from the Albatross* (1976), before his religious conversion. This early poem has a feeling strangely similar to his later poetry, in that tobacco is a provider of solace and calm to the working people with whom Harris felt kinship. There is a similar feeling of quiet transcendence in his post-conversion poem "High and Low". Harris's later poetry has a purity of feeling and diction that has been admired by non-religious poets as diverse as John Forbes and David Malouf.

Tobacco

Flavour the days, tobacco.
Bind together a cluster of months
With the other aromas of places
Where they're spent. Become the clean
White odour of the woodchips, place
Of the melting ice cream on the street
And parting veil through which an eye
Alters a life as its prisms shift;

One more branch line out to the upcountry
Where fossickers have to find rivers fit
To squat beside, to endlessly sift.
What will it be?

It will be light and dark ready rubbed
In a gaudy box,
Shared with the mud on a hop farm at planting time.
Rice papers tearing your lips, the stale
Tobacco no more than a nominal pause
In what later will come to be felt as years
Of grinding, repetitive, ceaseless noise.

It will be in the morning,
That first one had on the way to work
Among the dumb files

That are forever hinting
Something about the facts they record
Which slips from sheet to shuffled sheet
Evasively, a grey
Taste to match the midwinter.

And it will be fine to sit at noon
On a broken drum in the loading bay
Smoking and nodding the universe by
For fully half an hour in thc sun.

Thin housewives will light up another one
In the chain securing hope and harangue,
The lubricating cups of tarry tea ...

Immaculate cooks will step outside
For a smoke. Step briefly away
From the kitchen routine
They could follow by rote wearing blindfold.
They will reflect
On the boring adventure that does not admit
The slowly hunting, ever following
Processes of the dark. Maybe they'll note
The cherry tree's thousand new blossoms
Heaved about on an August wind
Fly and return like tethered snow.

It will be whatever the penniless hands
Can lay a hold on, whatever butts
Come wallowing by
On the water hands hold that have to reach
Out to each slim possibility.
Hands that would upend the sky!

And present, too, at a junction of roads,
Thick and silent when only taxis cruise
Across and across the overpass like sharks
And each choice leads only to one avenue –
The curdling smoke recreates and revolves
The scene below it absently, abandons direction
Becoming a daybreak of hair
Strewn on a pillow, a flock of wings
Beating above an imagined bay –
Gull's wings, a gull's beak
Opened to large blue areas in a cry.

Then steadies, gathers, exactly rolls
The pillow's curve and the beat of blood
The tiger springing along the nerve.

Made for ignition and burning
What will it be? The packets of days
Curling up in long fingers to rest on a shelf in the air

That are left there
To dissolve

The Call

Still, I lay awake in the dark ...
I thought pretty lusts had some ugly results
and that the world's bright trash was occult.

And carnage steals us from the eye of summer,
we cannot explain; but sometimes
the cockatoos are upset,
the flock miss one of their number.

And still I lay awake in the dark,
that was where I would have to fall –
out there somewhere in consequences,

in a desert become too hostile for survival;
if by weapons, disease, or auto design,
a cipher subjected to die for enormous grudges.

A cigarette answered that I was alive
though it seemed I had waited for centuries
becoming sure that the dark itself was active.

I was counting too a propensity to misfortune
back to great-grandfather's funny ways.
He worshipped a spurious architect of nothing

and walked on his hands on ordinary Sundays.
But He who drained the cup once for all
and did so under hell's lowest stair,

Christ, called me through from the other side of lightning.
Now I would seek out a comelier praise;
then I felt like one in a room of crimes

as the blind rattles up, and the light crashes in.

The Wish

My father wanted to travel in Soviet Russia
on the Trans-Siberian Railway. I heard him express
the wish a few times, at long intervals. It was truer
for being seldom, so that when he said
I'd like to travel in Russia
the more it seemed a genuine wish had escaped him,
that the actual person had briefly, even fragmentarily, spoken.

Shostakovitch's Symphony No.7
causes me to remember it and I spot him
pushing a steel cart along the aisles
when men who shop alone are rare.
It must be a Thursday evening one September
because a new lettuce has skipped the keys
where he waits looking tired after work, in a queue, and displeased.

A little dust is at large in the mechanism,
a ball of dust shadows the lightly-greased tabulation
hands render intelligent, plunging
from forearms, retracting, like swans –
and the types suspended before a roll
to strike a violet character:
impress and calculated stamp
discharge a recognised price from whirr and fidget
into durable, functional Arabic.

Then, going outside, I sight him again.
he is carrying his shopping across the car park,
attracting names that vary from Daddy to Rommel,
    it is a Thursday evening and must be early in one September,
sometime round Indonesian Confrontation and Ryan's hanging,
he looks more relaxed at having left the large building,

as a breeze distributes salt from the Bay
he is walking these years when silence is probably
    wisest concerning a pleasure,
when you do not for example say that you might like
    to travel in Russia.
There the moon has gone down at last behind a forest
    in physical earth, having all night
raked every compartment; looking, looking.

High & Low
(Eph. 1:3)

Do I reach too high,
                will the judgment which I come under
be therefore greater?
                Between the world and my brothers – it's
there to puzzle for cleaners, for African busmen,
                as in this present where I work:
a tavern useful pillaging tables for glasses,
                while I reach through close packed drinkers
it seems that I reach as far as a past
                that God has remembered, and which He
keeps, motionless motion,
                to draw those whom He chooses
into Mercy. And there
                I delve, my arm slipped between
their shoulders, for an ashtray.
                Perhaps I reach too high, too far?
There, it's a pile of butts I withdraw,
                and tip from a glass dish
into a bucket I carry. Then I wipe it off
                until it beams. When I find a gap
it goes back
                from the future.

Riding Over Belmore Park

Riding across the town in a dirty carriage
to read at the library Modern Jewish Poets
I thought of last war's troops in rain at Central,
then the junkies of a decade ago. Men younger

than I am have died for allowing moonlight
to rest on a button. A few have followed
by serum hep., some went ga-ga tripping
& stayed that way, but none of this happened often.

Enough to sense empty chairs on rare occasion,
enough to long for McAuley's baroque sarcasm
to flay alike counsel to rebel, and the nuclear lobby.

What do the Jewish Moderns say
to someone as well dressed as I am?
The vile rooms are not far. I survived them.

Six Years Old

Others were still kept in their sleep
by four angels
guarding the bed's each corner,
but mine it seemed had flown away.
They had flown away with a tempered regret,
right through the ceiling
and out, away into purpose.
I didn't hear their wings depart
but a dressing gown on a door revealed terror.

My work on the earth was to stare it down and say nothing.
Orphans taste wan distinction,
my work in life was to negotiate
each new regime with its wisdoms about
manners, teeth, education.
Cleanliness in every house smells different,
the kindnesses and cookery taste foreign.

I was used to my mother's ways
my talisman that one day I would re-interpret
every chance word of hers I would remember.
And it is possible to do
if one keeps to the evidence,
a couple of dozen sentences,
so that, on the whole, I have not suffered as once I thought.
Memory and fair inferences
have helped me to know her character
and to read no more than is evident
in her needlework or her Hemingway.

I also remember a woman who was childless
who got me alone, a sullen child,
and tickled me on an enormous bed.
How hilarious we were for twenty minutes.

Bush Cemetery

To dig a grave in snow
                              you light a fire
using wet sticks, to
                              warm yourself,
to warm the handles
                              of shovels,

pick and mattock,
to warm the crowbar.
As it goes down
by turns between two
grave diggers,
the hole and the fire
keep you from winds,
odd rain, sleet,
and you joke there,
straightening up,
"It's not a bad life at all out here".

Deeper
and
deeper,
the hole becomes
colder and
colder. First level the floor
then chip out
a new depth to start from,
taking turns
to get out and go to the fire.
And it takes
three days, your legs
grow weak your
arms ache. The hole
has become more
and more
a grave.

Tools, warm breath,
the rhythmic conversation
keep you from staring
too long at the earth,
the tiny grass-roots
in grey soil at eye level.
The snow wets your shoulders
arrives
in audible
muffled
plops
the crowbar
chips clay
the shovel scrapes.

When you get out and walk around
                                        reading inscriptions
I am the resurrection and the life ...
            then
My Grace is sufficient for thee ...

you still have to go back
                                          and finish it off,
not sadly, relieved because
                                              it isn't a child's
          grave
                an adolescent's or
      like one of those
                                        young women's, nothing
      by accidents,
                                  typhus,
                                              influenza.

When the undertakers
                                        show up to fuss
you greet them as men
                                        wait at the fence
through the service
                                  when everyone's gone
go and fill it in

while the snow whirls down
                                              on the cemetery
and looks for a moment like phlox.

Π. O. 1951–

Π. O. was born at Katerini in Greece and arrived in 1954 in Australia, where he went with his family to the Bonegilla migrant reception camp near Albury/ Wodonga. He describes himself as "raised in sly-grog gambling shops in fitzroy + thornbury. * reason for living: Stupidity! occupation: draughtsman*". He has worked for many years in the Titles Office in Melbourne and enjoys the mathematical element of surveys and documents, and the freedom working gives him from "writing applications for grants and for pats on the back and that kind of stuff." He edited *Off the Record* (1985), an anthology of performance poetry and he co-edited with Alex Selenitsch and Peter Murphy an anthology of visual poetry. From 1978 to 1983 he co-edited 925, a magazine of workers' poetry, as well as *Fitzrot* magazine. He was a founding member of the Poets Union and Collective Effort Press, and has been involved in the Anarchist movement in Australia since 1970. He edited Jas H. Duke's *Poems of War + Peace* and *Poems of Life + Death*.

Π. O. has published more than half-a-dozen collections of his poetry, including the 740-page *24 Hours* (1996). He is well known as a performance poet, has performed at festivals, prisons, universities, schools, offices and factories in Australia, and has toured in the USA. He is also an accomplished visual (concrete) poet. The unique appearance of his poems reflects both influences: he uses typography and spelling to mimic on the page the delivery of his poems as performed. Π. O.'s poetry has a depth and richness that go beyond playing up to audiences for an instant response. As well as challenging and entertaining the reader, there is a humanity and sympathy for the people who inhabit his world.

Billy Marshall Stoneking relates: "Π. O. took me on a midnight tour of Fitzroy . . . We ended up outside the flats in Gertrude Street where his dad had owned a café in the 'fifties and 'sixties; where Π. O., himself, had worked and listened to the voices of the city that came in for coffee and cards. The way he talked about it, it was like he was still there, and it was all still happening. It was the voices, the yabba-yabba: the men in the back playing cards, the waitress on the phone talking to her lover and then to her kid; the boss yelling at the kids on the street. The language with a swagger of Elvis would provide the basis for much of the poetry Π. O. would later write and perform – a poetry that for some of us would transform that whole stretch of inner-city Melbourne real estate between the M6 freeway and Punt Road into sacred ground."

The title of his poem "Mo" McCackie' refers to one of Australia's greatest comedians, Roy Rene (1891–1954), also known as "Mo" McCackie, who was characterised by his black-and-white makeup and stock phrases such as "Strike me lucky!"

The Paper Round

when my father lost his job at FORDS
i was dangling upsidedown on the monkey-bar;

he walked along the lane (thru the back) SLAMMING
the frontdoor on his way out; dressed
in a suit & tie), heading up YOUNG ST.
on his way to the Clubs
to earn money, in a language
he could understand:
♦♥♠♣

we were living in Fitz., abutting
the "kinda & swings"; crammed into one room
of a two storey house.

my mother cooked our meals
on the small kerosene heater (in the middle
of the room), around which she
told stories, stirred the pot
& cried.

my father bragged (in the Clubs)
that *even* at FORDS (where he worked as a mechanic)
he always clocked on, in a white shirt,

(which my mother ironed
sitting on the side of the bed, while we played *on*
or *under* the table).

if he won: he'd go
to the VIC MARKET (as the interstate
& country trucks came in
loaded with fruit) & buy crates
of ORANGES, APPLES, and GRAPES (which we'd find
stacked-up next to the chair
on which he hung
his shirt & coat).

but that wasn't often,

so i got a job selling HERALDs (after school)
for the paper shop (which was also
a POST OFFICE) in
Gertrude;

i walked upndown Gertrude St
screaming . "h'E-rol!" . "Pay-per!" . "Ex-tra!" .
& a hand came out of the crowd
& ... slapped me!
& ... slapped me!

there was a huge row (at home)
about MONEY, & DIGNITY, & ... a hand came
out of the crowd, & ... SLAPPED her
& ... slapped me!

but he was always out

so my mother
got a job (behind his back)
at the back of COLES (on the afternoon shift);
coming home (at night) still panting
her handbag full of knitting
as tho, as tho ... , she was just down the street
visiting

he never found out

... or, if he did
he never came HOME to find out
tho her hands had
little cuts on them, and got harder
from the textiles.

him

him punch him
him punch him too

him hit him
him hit him 2, 3, 4, ...

him not hit him
him hit

"Yoo no hit him!"
him hit

"Liv him alon wil-yum!"
him hit him mor

"Eye punch yoo on noz!"
him punch him in stomaak

him kik him in lek
him skrech him in fayc

"Gon to Hospitaal!"
"Gon to Hospitaal!"

him en him
gon to Hospitaal

Anna

Anna
talking
to her daughter
over the
phone:
Hul'o Hunn-ee.
Woch yoo do-in'? Dij yoo?!
Eye kumming soon.
Yoo "Good gel"?
Yoo woch Tivi?
How itz yoo doggie?

Anna
pissed-Of
with one of the blokes
at work: Don
shitz mi!
Don shitz mi!
Yoo think eye dint sor. Veri funni.

Verrrri funni.

Anna
pissed-Off
with one of the blokes
at work: Lenni.
Lenni!
Yoo *pig!*
Yoo tel mi eye hhhhhhoribool.
Ey'm thinking
yoo mai
fren.

Anna ringing-Up the
creche
about
her daughter:
Hul'o?
Hul'o!?
Wot taym ey'm kumming pik hair up?
Ey'm
keching bus 6 a'
klok.
Tenk yoo.
Tenk yoo.
(Bai!)

Anna pissed-Off
with one of the blokes
at work: Don bi started!
Kwai'!
Ey'm
neva saw may layf
drrugz!
If she be do sum thing schoopet
eye
send hair bek to
P'olaan.   [Egzsaakli!]
Hiz a Nnnutz!
Ey'm
say to yoo
Shoosh!

Inuf!

Anna pissed-Off

with one of the blokes
at work:
Hooz
tok to yoo
Missta?!
Eye be tok to yoo fren: N-o yoo!
Den eye woz undisten good!
Oh yer.
Oh y-----------er!
Oh shoor.
Ey'm
jus' evridai
evridai
tha
saym
for yoo: Waa-
Wa!

Anna
first thing in the
morning: Hoo n-o sumthing abewt mous?

Anna
eating a
Hamburger: Ey'm n-o bi FET don worriz!

Anna
talking to
a bloke [at
work] after lunch:
Whair yoo bin?
Did yoo . bot?!
Mai dotta, she got chek-Up.
Wood
yoo layket to
mi gon?!

Anna
talking to
her daughter [over the
phone]:
Eye n-----o.
Eye no yoo waant.
But. But yoo "sik", daarli.
Kummun daarli, b-i "Good gel".

Bi “Good gel” for Mummi.
Eye n-o bi long.
Lisen. Ey’m going to shop
en if ey’m
got
left munni
ey’m
bai yoo wun horrse. Promis.
Promis. Lis-en ....
Eye
wunt to tok to Graaan-
maatha.

Anna
talking
to a bloke [at
work] about
doing over-
time:

        Yoo war-kking tonayt?

Ey’mm war-kking.

                Fil war-kking.

                        Richart.
Wot abewt yoo Mista?

        Yoo
            war-kking
                    tonayt?

Balcha

Eye finish wit
da Hhorses --- tha gamboling
ROO-in mi!, Balcha sez.
When he dies
he wants them to put the “†” in the middle
of the grave
so that when a bloke, he owes money to
comes over to SHIT on him, he won’t do it
in his mouth!: Wen eye woz yung
eye woz playing for buttonz on trewwsez (robbing
mai frenz, ... en eniTHING!). Eye woz
betting en betting, en loozing en loozing

en eye set "NO MOR!" . "NO MOR!" en eye
bekum a MAN!
He looks down at the bloke in front of him (reading from
the Form Guide): Eye don plai
enimor DEEZ "Donkiz", he sez.
Nuthing! Kros-mai-haar!
The bloke turns around, and sez: Wai yoo kros-yoo-Haar'?!
Yoo n-o KRISCHUN!
Balcha tries to ignore him: *Wot yoo tel him*
hee tel da Boocha, en yoo kun gon
to Boocha (aafta).
He reckons the definition
of "patience", is when yoo giv to tha Donki "lemon"
en yoo ar wayting for tha Donki
to giv yoo "Lemonayd"!
Don't listen to him!, a bloke sez. It's all BULLSHIT!
He'll be back at the T.A.B. tomorrow
backing the favourite
Hoo WIN lus' wik?!, the bloke sez
and Balcha LOSES it! --- He gets up
paces up'n'down the table (infront of the bloke)
and sez: Koorva! Koorva! Proppa koorva!
Mayk mi ssss-ik! ---- 2 inchez ov LIPZ
en NOZ Fuk-awl!

Balcha isn't a man
to be trifled with; he isn't STUPID either.
Eye studi ... awl dis Histori! Whenever the Boss
wants to know something
he doesn't go to Vlaadich, or Darko, or David
he goes to "Balcha"!
Wot Vlaadich no? --- Fuk awl! ----
En Aapostol? --- Nuthing! --
But does he get any *kudos* for it???? ---No ----
No-wun sai mi "Tenkyoo very much *Baalcha*, today
eye LEN sumthing!
Dai awl tha taym poot "Shit" on mi
but wen eye poot littil-bit on dem ::::::::::::::: Oh-mai-Got
dai sssssssssssssss-krimmmming!
They're not generous of Spirit.
They've got a saying in his country: Hee hoo giv mi EGG
eye giv him CHIKEN!
Not that Balcha (himself) is

some kind of Saint (or
something), cos he loves *needling* 'em.
I saw him once, he was watching
2 blokes playing cards. Everytime the Turk won (he
couldn't help it) he went over
an' shook the bloke's hand ... (Not cos
he liked the Turk, but just so he could
stick-it-Up the Greek).
The Greek bloke :::::::: looked at him, the 1st couple of times
and then told him to Get Fucked. (Not cos he
couldn't take a joke, but cos
he was losing his NUTS
to the bloke). So Balcha ran-out of the shop
stuck his face up-against the window
and signaled to the Turk
to stick-it-Up the Greek with a HOT pepper!!!
Eye hev to fayn-ouwt
wot kayn ov *FOXEZ dai ar!*
Bloo 'o *'Silva?!*

I got to know Balcha
quite well, over the years;
I knew him, an' he knew my Father.
I remember him waiting for me, one night.
He'd just gotten a postcard
off an "Old" Australian family, he'd met
26 years ago, when he was sent to Queensland
from Bonegilla, to cut sugar.
He wanted me to write to them, for him.
He wanted me to tell Judy
he'd just spent 10 days in Pentridge
for trying to *smuggle* rare-birds (and parrots)
out of the country (including
a *rare* lizard destined
for Japan), but
got caught at Station/Pier instead.
He wanted her to know, he said
true to his word that he was still trying to
raise the money to take her to Paris
like he'd promised. (Only,) he still couldn't work out
why she'd want to give up Jerry (after
all these years), for a speaking Dummy
like HIM (on account of their

vast Age-difference, and
his weak-heart).
He wanted me to tell them (cos he
wanted them to know) that he wouldn't be able
to make it Up this year like he'd promised.
Maybe the next one.
He said, he didn't have
all that many friends (left)
in this World ---- Noone remembers him! ----
Not even his children!
But each year (without
fail) Judy (an' the kids)
send him a Postcard (and a little bit of money)
to keep him going.
Then he told me, he wanted me to tell them
that he was writing all this
from an Expresso bar, in Gertrude Street
and that his health, and blood-pressure
were improving, like
his "Sex-life" *That'll make them laugh!*
and that he was sworn off gambling FOREVER now
and that he just made
a "new" friend, with the little mouse
at the bottom of his bed.
He said, he set 2 traps for it.
1 with cheese, and the other with bacon
(only,) it wouldn't bite *He loves his guts too much!*
He thinks it might be Vegetarian.
So he just lays there of a night
watching it eat-Up all the crumbs
off the floor.

All of which
sounds rather attractive (I'm
sure), but he had another aspect to him
which I only saw once; The old Yugoslav woman
who used to walk around Fitzroy with a walking stick
and who all the men hated, cos *Iz bich!*
Look for men ... etc
came into the cafe (as usual) on Pension day
looking for someone to
fill-out a WITHDRAWAL SLIP (so she could
get her money out of the Bank)

only, nobody wanted to do it that day
except Balcha. ---- He never knocked her back! ---
He always filled it out for her (except for
the signature, which she
kept to herself). I don't really understand
all the politics that goes on there
but on this occasion, Balcha said something to her (in
Yugoslav) and she ½ raised
her walking-stick, to HIT him over the head
and he kind of ½ cringed (with
a smile on his face). She wanted
to *SLAM down* the walking-stick over his head
Her mouth tightened, and
I saw her leave the Café
with everybody inside *laughing.*

*

There was a moon out (that night).

Moonlight

11111111111111111111111111
11111111111111101111111111
11111111111110000011111111
11111000000000111111111111
11111111100000000000011111
10100000000001110000000001
11111111111110000001111111
11111100000000011111111111
11111111100011111111111111
11111111111111101111111111
11111111111111111111111111

*

She leaned her body up against me

Wool

33^{3}333333333^{3}333333333333
33^{3}333333333^{3}333333333333
333^{3}3333333333^{3}3333333333
33333^{3}3333333333^{3}33333333
3333333^{3}3333333333^{3}333333
333333333^{3}3333333333^{3}3333
33333333333^{3}33333333333^{3}3
3333333333333 3^{3}333333333
3^{3}333333333333333^{3}3333333
333^{3}33333333333333333^{3}333
3333333^{3}3333333333333333^{3}3

"Mo" McCackie

A Proboscis monkey has got a nose
that hangs down 7 inches below its mouth.
The word *facetious* has got all its vowels in the right place.
A dugong is a cross between an elephant and a pig.
Chyacking: a corruption of the word *Cheek.*
"How True. How very very True"; bouncing around
in the back of a ute (a deserted track)
apostrophizing an oath: *"You filthy*
( ) Beast! I'm a wake up to you" . *"Cop that*
young Harry!" (Kelp is brown).
The greatest number of plates that can be
spun simultaneously is 89. People who chew (a) lot (of ice)
have got a very very very high sex drive.
In Bulgaria a nod means No, and the shaking of
the head Yes; (i'm using the crimsonest
of adjectives here) (Shooting gorillas, and dressing them up
as Clowns). *"Strike me lucky!"*
A crow's nest made up of barbwire.
"What's əəəəəəəə- that?". "A drongo!" (Cocks
are the ensigns of the Goths) (Talk about, talking about
talking (behind somebody's back)). To accost someone
is to barge straight up to 'em. Polar bear!
A Polar bear is left-handed; Clear the air!
A *@! *fart's* a combination of gasses: *Nitrogen,*
Nitrogen (Oxygen) Hydrogen (Sulphide)
A leer can get you a laugh on the screen. A rising
eye-brow, a Puckapunyal cocktail, a *liquid*
spit*ing-splu#tter (from the Palestinian parrot
on a Jerusalem jeep); *"I got the bastards*
didn't i, Pal?"

It's been estimated that 80% of the animals (on
this planet) have got 6 legs. *"Other mug*
jus' haven't got it, Aye?"
Freud identified 4 types of Humour: Hostile,
Cynical, Sophisticated, and Obscene.
A *Nip:* a ¼ of a bottle (here). (A *Baby:* an l/8th or so).
Toilet paper's got a one hundred (and 40) (7) year old history.
White face . Battered hat . Black beard .
The inner ear))) vibrates, to let the brain know that
the head has stopped moving. (To bite
one's thumb at one!): *"That'll do young Harry!"*

Proso 'p-o-agghnosia is the complete inability
to recognize a familiar face. *"Turn up your radios, Possums!"*
The Mona Lisa's only got One eyebrow.
I don't know whether to ki*ss him, or √ ! kick him"
)))))) *Where are ya Dad?!"*
"Gor-blimey!" You've been listening to
another episode of McCackie's Mansion [applause]
staring Roy Rene [applause] as "Mo" McCackie [more]
from the sound studios of 2GB
            13 Coffin Street
                        Fawlty ⚡ Towers
              "Oh, you dirty Mug!"

ANIA WALWICZ 1951–

Ania Walwicz was born in Poland and came to Australia in 1963. She graduated from the Victorian College of the Arts, Melbourne. She has published several collections of prose poems and theatrical pieces, performed experimental prose-poetry and exhibited visual art works. As well as acknowledging the tradition of Joyce, Stein and surrealism as an influence in her work, Walwicz stated in a 1996 interview that she sees it as "coming from a tradition of electronic music, John Cage, language and sound composition ... Surrealist technique has formed my work ... Nevertheless, the sort of Surrealism that was produced by the original Surrealists is definitely not the kind of Surrealism that I'm engaged with because I'm not discovering any new forms there, I'm re-using different forms that have been used by other authors from a sort of postmodernist stance." Much of Walwicz's poetry has a socio-political intent. This is largely absent from "travelling", a piece which has affinities with the repetitions and gradual transformations of American minimalist music, in particular that of John Cage's disciple, Morton Feldman.

travelling

the train goes and the station moves away what time is it we're going to a jungle hot palms i fall asleep drunk talked to himself i know what i have to do did you see the house on fire out of the window did you see the house on fire out of the window did you see the house on fire out of the window where are we now in my map i don't know too scared to ask am i on the right train are we going the right way where are we now voices in the train soldiers coming loud louder then soft softer then they go away i was asleep then i woke up voices come back then loud then softer then they very soft now softer whisper it is dawn first little pink line in the moving sky gets lighter can i roll the blind now put your blanket little lights of waking towns pass us at night houses sleep in the field dawn drunk gone i didn't see him my ticket and coffee my cup jumps they play cards and laugh little reading light i can't sleep the ship in my port they opened the porthole the ship moves to sea huge wave curls near my fingers shining on edges surges wave rises curls slowly near me i can touch it i can touch it sun on water green deep bending a wave right near me crashes i am wet i woke up at the middle of the night they lit a fire in a field they stood around and warmed their hands near the border when the plane lifts there is music and lift we fly in a soft cloud the train flew over the lake i couldn't see the rails the bridge flashed by with girders with girders with girders the boat leaves the pier swims away the lake was so still you couldn't see horizon oars dip are we moving it is quiet now the dusk is the same as dawn over india red soil i flew above the alps they were below me sharp peaks model mountains the train goes into a tunnel it is dark and dark i'm scared it was hot my feet got too big for my shoes we were going back there is going to be a war he told us the train is slow we were standing in the middle of dark there was an accident at the railway crossing we have to wait when is the train coming the station had big black numbers on each platform my sister told me funny stories we were cold put your arms in your trousers put your legs in your jumper on my feet i wear my hat i put my pants on my head i was laughing and laughing and laughing i lost three hours on the plane it gets earlier all the time people stand in my lit up window did i pack everything did i leave the window open it's too late we are far away now i left my jacket i ride backwards we eat red lolly berries he was talking africa and tigers she was with her son she gave him an apple she eats sausage greasy fingers talk how to use a camera i can't listen greasy fingers and the sausage a book of lists and murders fall asleep it's faster how the lens goodbye at the station she waves her arms and disappears i am flying little cars he went away plane a dot in the sky at night houses have lights on and look warm the city below sparkles diamonds the last tram at night travels home

IAN McBRYDE 1953–

Born in Toronto, Canada, Ian McBryde has lived in Australia since 1972. He travelled extensively before settling in Melbourne. McBryde's poetry has been widely published internationally. There are several collections of poems and he has released CDs of his readings. Dorothy Porter described his poetic voice as "darkly insidious". His live readings have been described as "deep and engaging". On the page his poems have a cinematic quality.

Stalingrad Briefing, 1943

The patrols are told to eat snow as they go.
If they do this the enemy marksmen cannot see
the give-away plume of their breath. Smoke

closes over the Volga, awash with bodies entwined
with detritus, riding the dead river, bumping up
against its broken shores. Even colour has been

bombed and shot away; everything has taken on
greyness. The men are grey, their rations are
grey. The light is black and white. The only true

colour left is red. Explosions, blood, a bit
of ribbon. Replacements are told only to carry
their rifles at the ready and step in the footprints

of the men before them. Don't bunch up. Expect
worse than you can imagine. Do not speak.
Stay low and in shadow. Eat snow as you go.

Beyond Omerta

"You can feel the cold metal of the gun against your skin. You can almost hear your heartbeat. You're alive, really alive."
– Sam Giancana, Chicago, 1938

1. Awkward gloves. A stiff fit, but no time. Past
one. The docks. Six of us. The distant rumble
and hum as their vehicles come off the bridge.

2. My wife's eyes full of the certain knowledge
of everything I can never mention. Her ragged,
troubled sighs as I hold her while she sleeps.

3. His startled look as the pick goes in, his
backward lurch and collapse and the noise
in his throat that the others mimic, laughing
in the Cadillac on the way back.

4. Stacked hand. A bad roulette, a black
abacus. Too late to imagine having gone
back, or ahead, or right instead of left.

5. How their eyes roll up, how bonelessly
they crumple. How I shook the first time.

6. The splash of handguns thrown into
the middle of the river. Expensive suits
burned in Brooklyn wastelands because
the blood just won't wash out.

7. My wife's back as she stands at the window.
Coat on. House keys in her hand. The last
of her notes on the hall table.

8. Late calls. Hidden drawers, closed cars,
smoke in the rain. The shadow that moves,
and the shadow that moves away.

KEVIN HART 1954–

Kevin Hart was born near London, and came to live in Brisbane at eleven years of age. His father was a factory employee and a union representative; his mother was a dressmaker. Hart became Christian in his youth, and converted to Catholicism in his early twenties. He graduated in philosophy from the Australian National University, winning a Fulbright Fellowship scholarship to Stanford University. His doctoral degree in Philosophy is from the University of Melbourne. After holding a Personal Chair in English and Comparative Literature at Monash University, in 2002 he took a Chair in Philosophy and Literature at the University of Notre Dame; since 2007 he has been Edwin B. Kyle Professor of Christian Studies in the Department of Religious Studies at the University of Virginia, where he also holds professorships in English and in French. His early book *The Trespass of the Sign* explored philosophical framings of mystical theology. Hart is the author of seven individual collections of poetry, and two editions of selected poems. His poetry is known for its sense of mystery.

The Horizon

Whenever you take a step
I am with you leading you meeting your eyes
I am here at dawn watching
The old priest hurrying to Mass
Ready to greet him with my gift of blood.

How easily I shed the clothing
You try to give me
You who cannot bear to see me as I truly am
Your trees mountains buildings I have no time for them.

I was here
Before the stone received its hardness,
This entire world could not be conceived
Before the thought of me.

You comfort yourselves:
You say I am only a line never reached
That I do not exist as you do
But none of this is true:
You see only the top line of my head
Beneath that I have the world
With all its fields sun moonlight and rain.

You who hate departures,
You who forever try to shut me out
Listen to me:
Whenever you think of death,
Whenever you enter the room of someone gone from you,
I will be peering through the window.
I will catch you
Even though my net has just one string.
You have no need for mirrors
Who lie to you until it is too late,
Look at me and see the only truth
Your past what you are now
All your future sorrows and your only blessing.

A History of the Future

There will be cities and mountains
as there are now,

and steeled armies
marching through abandoned Squares
as they have always done.

There will be fields to plough,
the wind will shake the trees, acorns
will fall,

and plates will still crack
for no apparent reason.

And that is all we can truly know.

The future is over the horizon, we cannot hear
a word its people say,

and even if they shout to us
to make us cease
bombing their lands, destroying their cities,

a shout from there would sound like an acorn
dropped on cement,

or a plate on the shelf
beginning to crack.

The Members of the Orchestra

Walk onto the dark stage dressed for a funeral
Or a wedding and we, the anxious ones, quieten
As we wait to discover which it will be tonight:

They sit or stand before thin books written
In a foreign script, more alien than Chinese,
But its secret contents will be revealed now

As at the reading of a dead relation's will,
For the last member has entered, slightly late
As befits his honour, like a famous lecturer

With a new theory and a pointer to make it clear.
Alas, he too cannot talk except in the language
Of the deaf and dumb, but as he waves his hands

The members of the orchestra commence their act
Of complicated ventriloquism, each making
His instrument speak our long-forgotten native tongue.

Now one violin speaks above the rest, rehearsing
The articulate sorrow of things in this world
Where we have suddenly woken to find a music

As curious as the relation between an object
And its name. We are taken by the hand and led
Through the old darkness that separates us

From things in themselves, through the soft fold
Of evening that keeps two days apart. And now
Each instrument tells its story in details

That become the whole, the entire forest contained
Within a leaf: the orchestra is quickly building
A city of living air about us where we can live

And know ourselves at last, for we have given up
Our selves, as at our wedding or our funeral,
To take on something new, something that was always there.

The Stone's Prayer

Father, I praise you
For the wideness of this your earth, and for the sky
Arched forever over me,
For the sharp rain and the scraping wind
That have carved me from the mountain
And made me smooth as a child's face.

Accept my praise
For my colour, a starless night,
That my width is that between the first two stars of evening
Reflected in the water,
That my quartz flashes like lightning
And reflects the glory of your creation,

That you have seen fit
To place me near a stream and thus to contemplate
The passing of time;

For all that is around me I sing your praise,
For the fierce concentration of ants, their laws,
For all that they tell me about you.

Keep me, I pray, whole,
Unlike the terrible dust and pieces of bone
Cast about in the wind's great breath, unlike men
Who must suffer change,
Their endless footprints deep as graves;

Keep me in truth, in solitude,
Until the day when you will burst into my heavy soul
And I will shout your name.

The Last Day

When the last day comes
A ploughman in Europe will look over his shoulder
And see the hard furrows of earth
Finally behind him, he will watch his shadow
Run back into his spine.

It will be morning
For the first time, and the long night
Will be seen for what it is,
A black flag trembling in the sunlight.
On the last day

Our stories will be rewritten
Each from the end,
And each will end the same;
You will hear the fields and rivers clap
And under the trees

Old bones
Will cover themselves with flesh;
Spears, bullets, will pluck themselves

From wounds already healed,
Women will clasp their sons as men

And men will look
Into their palms and find them empty;
There will be time
For us to say the right things at last,
To look into our enemy's face

And see ourselves,
Forgiven now, before the books flower in flames,
The mirrors return our faces,
And everything is stripped from us,
Even our names.

The Past

I used to see her in a sandwich shop
On Brunswick Road. She made me toasted cheese.
I liked her ponytail and gypsy scarf,

I liked her running shoes and sawn off jeans,
I liked a little bruise beneath her knee,
And so my sandwiches got high with ham:

They dripped with mayonnaise and frayed with sprouts
While I just gazed at her and murmured, "Swiss;
Tomatoes; onion; lettuce; pepper; salt."

I had to ask her out: my sandwiches
Had got too big to eat! We lived off Smith,
I did Philosophy, and wrote all day –

"Is Death Impossible?" – and jumped on her
The moment she was home from work at five.
Our neighbour was a Physicist, and yarned

Of flavoured quarks and tachions, those things
That speed into the past, and wrote SF
About a "Tachion Machine": a burst

Would put you with the apes or dinosaurs
While very few would nudge you back a week.
"What would you like on that?" Susanna asked

When kissing me in bed. "The lot," I'd say.
Some nights I'd wake up scared to hell by time.
Susanna was still there, in white whipped sheets,

And sleepily I'd hold her tight, and hold
Our evening tight, and whisper to the dark,
"Release a tachion – just one, just one."

ANDREW LANSDOWN 1954–

Andrew Landsdown was born in Pingelly, a small town in Western Australia. He has arts degrees from the Western Australian Institute of Technology and Murdoch University (now Curtin University) He has worked as a tutor in creative writing at tertiary institutions and TAFE colleges, as an education officer in Western Australian prisons, as a journalist on a country newspaper, as the editor of a magazine, and as a Baptist pastor. He is married with five children. Lansdown is the author of fifteen books of poetry and fiction. Geoff Page commented in *A Reader's Guide to Contemporary Australian Poetry* (1995) that Lansdown is "a poet who is working consciously in a tradition … that of the imagists such as the early Pound, William Carlos Williams and the Wallace Stevens of 'Thirteen Ways of Looking at a Blackbird' … At his best Lansdown is able to suggest very deftly and concisely the so-called 'thisness' of things, especially things in nature … at his worst he runs the risk of … whimsy or of trying a little too hard for his images … It is strange then that Lansdown is often at his most memorable when he abandons his imagistic method for (or perhaps develops it into) something more extended and more imbued with moral force – not the force of his apparently fundamentalist Christian conviction … but the force seen for example in the poem 'Four Men'". In *The Oxford Companion to Twentieth Century Poetry* (1994) Jamie Grant points out: "Unusually for a poet of the late twentieth century, the mood in his poems is generally one of contentment or joy, causing fashion-conscious readers to overlook his consistent technical excellence." A decade and a half later, Lansdown's self-evident strengths as a poet are still overlooked.

Four Men

The contraption is like a small
merry-go-round at a country fair:
five cradles at the end of five arms
which meet at a hub and turn

on an upright axle. Inverted
stirrups are welded to the sides
of each cradle. A man stands at,
and a lamb lies in, four of the cradles.

Four lambs on the merry-go-round.
The fourth man tosses one off. Spin
round. The first man lifts one up
and lays it on its back.

Much as a gynaecologist might
hook a woman's legs out and back,

he hooks the lambs hocks
in the stirrups. Spin round.

The second man injects a poison
for parasites, stabbing a needle
in the sternum, and clips a piece
from an ear. No sound. Spin

round. The third man holds
a pair of sharp shears. He pinches
the fleece beside the tail
and snips. A crisp fibrous sound,

like cutting cloth. It is an art
to cut no deeper than the depth
of the skin. Blood spurts out,
a thin jet, as from a water-pistol

or, thinner yet, like a spray of juice
from an orange as it is peeled.
From the root of the tail, he cuts
along the side of the anus,

the vulva, skinning the lamb
alive. The exposed meat films
with blood. Barely a struggle.
Only a single, bleating scream

with the first cut. Mulesing,
they call it, and do it to safeguard
the flock from fly-strike.
Between the third man's boots,

shaped like a cow-pat, a pool-pile
of coagulating blood wobbles
like a jelly. Snip. Snip round.
the fourth man slips a rubber ring

on the tail. (With a ram lamb,
he clamps another ring around
the scrotum – that little purse
from which no ewe will ever receive

conception's shining currency.)
Then he unhooks the legs
and dumps the lamb in the dirt.
Spin round. Begin again. It takes

barely one minute. Mulesing.

I jot a few notes. The four men
are uneasy. What will the townie
write. "Y'aren't an animal libber,

are ya?" Banter among the blood
and bleating. I concede there is
no mercy in a death by maggots.
The last lamb hobbles, bellowing,

to its mother, a red glare
at its rear. The pasture is splotched
with crimson. "They've got their
tail-lights on," the third man grins,

wiping the blood from his hands.

The Grasshopper Heart

That man with the cowboy hat and tan and tattoos
is holding his little white-skinned daughter
very gently in the shallow water. Now he is
zooming her along, but not too quickly
for fear of her fear. He tosses her up,
catches and hugs her, holds in check
the fierce tenderness that craves to crush her.
Her father. His wholly holy love. He is smiling
and I know his heart is like a grasshopper –
leaping and landing spring-loaded to leap again.

A Good Night

The mulies are in the harbour,
shoals of them, teeming unseen
in the opaque sea. On the wharf,

in rubber boots and yellow raincoats,
a team of professional fishermen
lure the fish with food and light.

They have hung a lantern, hissing
incessant warning, just above
the quilted surface of the quiet water;

and they have strewn pollard –
the pollen grains, the yeasty smell –
on the water, below the lamp,

above the submerged net – an iron hoop
looped with mesh, long and tapering

like a wind-sock. Near the net,

a ship shifts uneasily. Its rope,
a catenary from prow to bollard,
strains and straightens. Bilge-water

spouts from the hull. On the wharf,
an enormous, enclosed conveyor-belt
rolls on its gantry. Grain

cascades into the hold. Behind
the ship, winnowed by the wind
and stretching as far as the shining

of the harbour lights, barley husks
form a yellow slick on the black
water. Between the lamp and the net

the mulies, the bait-fish, swirl
like long-bodied moths. At a command,
the men hoist the net. It is a crucible

bubbling with molten silver.
Poured out, the fish separate
into small, oblong ingots. A young man

smooths them into shallow crates,
ready for freezing. But the fish
are not ready. Frenzied,

they flick and twist, scales flying off
like sequins from a silver purse.
Their gills gape, the red frills

clogged by air. Their mouths gasp,
transparent lips extended
like trumpets, blaring, "O! O!"

The conveyor-belt and the bilge-pump
drone a duet to drown Death's reveille.
The ship's rope heaves and relaxes.

In a child's hand, a line twitches
like a caught nerve. In the crates,
the fish have gone off the boil

and lie eternally still. The men
lower the net again. "Gonna be a good
night," smiles one man, his hair

spangled with scales, like confetti.

The Muff Bees

My daughter called them "muff bees",
mistaking them for moths that sting.
But apart from the beauty of her name,
I had thought they were merely ugly,
the March flies, with their blowfly
bodies and cicada wings, their
bulging eyes and long proboscises.
They look like homunculi in gas masks
or bug-eyed children with straws
in their mouths. With those inflexible
trunks, they are tiny winged elephants,
the Dumbos of the insect world.

In the shade of a karri one autumn
I swatted dozens of the suckers
as they came for the blood
that happened to be in my legs. It was
a slaughter. It was a satisfaction.
Inspecting their bodies, I found the pests
guilty of ugliness, their iridescent-
green eyes compounding their crime.

But this afternoon I saw one
hovering in a shaft of sunlight,
its body buoyant, its wings burring,
its proboscis protruding in exact
proportion to its other parts
and angled exquisitely
according to the tilt of the head.
It was like a humming bird.
It was, without a murmur, a muff bee.

Warrior-Monk

i

A warrior-monk,
the heron stands at the brink
of the floating world.

ii

Spear at the ready
the heron warrior-monk
meditates on death.

iii
Meditation, step
the heron warrior-monk
resignation, stab.

iv
The grey heron's koan:
the monk and the warrior,
how can they combine?

Lighting a Match

She has learned at last to strike
the red end on the rough edge.
But still they break mid-stroke
or burn her fingers when they burst
to flame. Each match seems to provoke
a failure, invoke from her a cursed
performance. She has begun to learn
what some Professors profess to spurn:
from literacy to love to lighting a match,
excellence is the objective ledge
onto which each labour must latch.
No charge of "elitism" can hedge
this reality from our sight.
For even small things exact a pledge
that we shall do as they like.

DOROTHY PORTER 1954–2008

Dorothy Porter was born in Sydney, her father a well-known barrister, and her mother a high school chemistry teacher. She graduated from the University of Sydney, majoring in English and History. She worked on an Israeli kibbutz, as a conductress on Sydney buses and for a number of years supported her writing by part-time teaching. She became a lecturer in Poetry and Writing at the University of Technology, Sydney. In 1993 she moved to Melbourne to be with her partner, the writer Andrea Goldsmith. When she died of breast cancer at the age of 54, her death was reported on the front page of Australian newspapers – a rare event when a poet dies. She had become known to, and loved by, a wide Australian public, principally for her verse novels of which she wrote five. Porter was the author of eight other books of poetry, libretti, song lyrics and young adult fiction. *The Monkey's Mask* (1994), a "whodunit" in verse form, has been reprinted many times, became a film and was dramatised.

From the start there was an energy in her poetry, which Robert Adamson recognised, as publisher of her first book *Little Hoodlum* (1975): "Her poetry is totally different to any of her contemporaries. the language she employs … is direct and riddled with every imaginable poetic cliche; but the language is a mere surface, the force behind it is that of a Proteus. She is the *Ice Queen* singing a phillipic to Bob Dylan …" Porter later became critical of the obscurity of some of her earlier poetry. In her 2001 Judith Wright Memorial Lecture "Lucidity: The Poetry of Making Sense" she said: "To be taken really seriously, to be truly shocking, a poem has to be understood." Porter began writing verse novels because she "was sick of not being read. I was sick of my books not being on display in bookshops – either hidden away so successfully that not even I, their vain and insecure author, could find them or simply not there at all." Porter's stand-alone lyrics have admirers, but she is represented here by extracts from her last crime novel in verse *El Dorado*, as it is in her verse novels that her strengths are fully realised.

from El Dorado

The hand
The little girl's
dead hand
is sticking stiffly
up
as if reaching
to grab an angel's
foot.

Detective Inspector Bill Buchanan
puts out his gloved
hand
in the dead foul air
and touches the tiny
heaven-stretched fingers.

The gold blessing
"Just like the others, boss,"
Detective Sergeant Rodney Mason
shifts his great big slow arse
out of my view

and the little girl's face
is revealed
grubby from the grave
but without trauma
just dead

just dead
and *just like the others*

with a gold thumb print
on her forehead
as if she'd been laid to rest
cherished, gilded and blessed.

Making them gold
Six months before
after the second child
was found

just like the first
smothered, unmolested,
ritually, even gently, buried
in a shallow grave
meant to be found

a letter appeared in the *Age* –
My hands make them gold.
My hands make them neverold.
I am where they want to go.
I am El Dorado.

Why did a bragging child killer
identify himself
with a South American myth
– Bill did his homework –
of lost kingdoms, gold lust and delusion?

Emma
The killer had buried her
  with her purple octopus
    backpack

Bill fixes on it

someone, her mother perhaps,
  had written her name
    in black texta
along one of the octopus'
  sucker padded arms –
EMMA.

Not tears,
rather a dehydrating
  bleakness
blasts Bill's eyes

as if some great deadening
  evil
is draining
  his own ocean
and all its resilient purple life
  away.

Eastern rosellas

Eastern rosellas!

That flashing bee-line
of red. blue. green.

Then
the music
of their only slightly muffled
bell notes
from their palm leaves
roost.

Why am I birdwatching?

My grandfather's chattering
ghost
pointing them out.

Look, Billy! Eastern rosellas!
Should be a good day, son.
They're very lucky birds.

Lucky?
Oh Pop.
Even dead
you're a lovely old optimist.

Lucky? Today?
How lucky is it
to be spending such a beautiful morning
with Detective Sergeant Rodney Mason –
"ya know they used
fucking psychics
on the Beaumont case, boss
don't ya reckon
it's about time
we hauled
one of those ratbags
in?" –

as we interview
not clairvoyants
but
a sad and sorry line-up
of rock spiders.

Maybe I should be thinking
lucky. eastern rosellas.
and pretend I'm in
your happy company, Pop,
and hope
one of these – what on earth
would you make of them? –
cringing, or worse,
pathetically cunning perverts
is somehow. unlikely.
my man, El Dorado.

The albino guinea pig
And suddenly Bill remembers
from searing nowhere
his old friend Cath's
pouchy albino guinea pig.

Bill grins
with an exhausted stupid
nostalgia,
christ almighty, Cath and all
her bloody pets!
Didn't her dad
once give her a tortoise?

And those secret adventures
in her canoe ...
his spine prickles
christ, is he going mad?

Didn't Cath tell him
one hot blue summer holiday
that she knew
where a golden city
was hiding in the mangroves?
And one late golden
afternoon
they both nearly saw it.

He doesn't need one of DS Mason's
"fucking psychics",
he needs Cath,
he needs the hypnotic imagination
of his old best mate,
he needs the woman
who's making a fucking fortune
in Hollywood,
he needs –
his head read!

Is he this desperate?

Four dead kids
in twelve months.
El Dorado still at large.
The police effort
being pissed on.
The greedy media giving the bastard
oxygen,
despite injunctions, pleas
and threats.

You bet.
He's desperate.
But could Cath help?

Cath has always seen things
no one else can see.
Could Cath see in to
this El Dorado fucker's mind?

What would the super say?

Fuck the super.

All will be forgiven
when El Dorado is pinched.

Howzat!
But perhaps
I can do it on my own.

Uncanny
how in every investigation
one thing leads to another
just like in a nail-biting Test match

when the big wicket falls
to a lazy shot
and then
the rest tumble like lemming
dominoes.

Last night
I'm having an exhausting old
fight with my daughter
about what she's wearing –
and not wearing
to meet some disgusting
heavy metal bad-boy band
backstage
and then *Howzat!*
staring at her flushed sullen
grotesquely made-up
ludicrously young
face
I see
she's glaring at me
from under *gold* tinted
eyelids.

"What are you wearing
on your eyelids?"
I ask hoarsely.

"None of your fucking business."

She waits a little
anxiously
for me to say my usual
Righto, Caitlin.
You've done your dash.
You're staying home.

But instead
I stand under the ball
and take the catch!

"What's that muck
on your eyes *called?*"

"I dunno," Caitlin mumbles
too confused to dispute

the umpire's decision
"something weird like ...
El Dorado."

His Cath

He hasn't seen Cath
for two years

so Bill watches
with bemused surprise
the slight tremor
in his fingers
holding his lite beer

he's known Cath
all his life
and knows
she'll be late
as she knows
he'll be early

but he's content
to sit in the cool
gloomy bar
and wait

even enjoying
the faintly nervous
adolescent knot
in his gut.

He wonders
if Hollywood
will have changed
his Cath much.

His Cath?

Christ almighty.
Where did that come from?

The besotted fourteen-year-old
locked up in his heart
still howling for her?

OK. He'd give himself
a break.

It was a clean wound.
And a long time ago.

His Cath.

And what would
she be like?
Did she have someone?

She was a crap
correspondent
her infrequent emails
were confused and confusing
as they scattered
the odd, but always changing,
girlfriend's name

but she was making
a real name
for herself
converting that
reckless and adventurous
imagination
Bill remembered so well
into real money.

What did she now call
herself?

Something New Age
wanky.

Imaginary Worlds Specialist Director –
it said after her name
on the credits
of so many big budget
fantasy worlds movies –
that disgorged everything
from knights in not so shining
armour
to insect sex predators
on impossible planets.

Did that translate
into grown woman
curled up
sucking her thumb

still in her old treehouse
cubby
waiting for Santa's reindeer
to park their rumps
on the next branch?

Bill didn't care.

Wherever Cath's
creative immaturity
had taken her
she was an expert.

And this terrible case,
with the super
with every politician playing
the paedophile card
breathing down his neck
needed someone
a wild card –

even if it were
a raving childhood sweetheart
ratbag.

Needed perhaps
the lateral thinking
of an intelligent child
spliced with
an intuitive adult's experience.

Needed an imagination
with guts enough
to climb the beanstalk
right into El Dorado's
evil head.

Among friends
Cath had forgotten
the comfort
of sleeping in the arms
of Bill's things.

Even his lovingly framed
fading photos
of long-dead dogs
all tongue-lolling

ill-assorted mongrels
and, surprisingly,
his father's beautiful old yacht
snuggled up to Cath
and held Bill's so comfortable
warm oil smell.

The very bed
Bill had made up for her
of worn soft sheets
and his daughter's discarded
doona
covered with romping
hippos
enclosed Cath
like a sacred chrysalis.

Among Bill's things
it was always so easy
to just let
all pain, fret and fever
go.

Even his old rusty toaster
leaking a century's worth
of crumbs
Cath loved
with a serene passion.

Funeral
Cath and Bill sit themselves
discreetly at the back

but within minutes
Cath feels as if she's been bled
white

there is nothing in the world
more viscerally draining
than a murdered child's
funeral.

Appalled at herself
Cath can't resist
checking out
how the parents, grandparents,

siblings and friends
are holding up –
mostly, to her surprise,
with an eerie mesmerising
dignity.

Emma. Emma. Emma.

The murdered girl's name
floating as gently as a cobweb
while the threads of grief
hold them all down
with an unfightable net of steel mesh.

Something scratches the back
of Cath's throat –
is El Dorado here
in the quietly snuffling crowd?

Are his eyes
welling
as Emma's best friend
reads out
her fresh raw poem
in a choking monotone?

Emma, I know you're here
and I know you're listening.
I don't believe
you could be nowhere.
You've just gone somewhere
really awesome –
maybe the Disneyland
in the clouds with blue angels
and the most cool rides.

Ride the sky, Emma,
you'll always be my friend
you'll always be awesome
I will always miss you.

Cath wipes her eyes
and sneaks a look
at dry-eyed stony-faced Bill
and wonders if he could have penned
such a beautiful poem for her

if she'd been murdered
when they were nine.

Bill would have been distraught –
she knows that –
but that flight of feeling and imagery
would have been totally beyond him.

Does El Dorado
(and Cath insists they call him that
rather than "the offender" or "perp"
or "kiddie killer")
still have that fervent childhood faith
in the Special Place
where childhood is perfect
where childhood is permanent?

Meanwhile
the Uniting Church minister
a pleasant youngish blonde woman
as unremarkable as any of the mothers
in the church
leads the singing
of "The Lord's My Shepherd"

whose ancient lonely brave words
build a massive golf ball
in Cath's tight throat
that simply won't be swallowed.

His kids

All the autopsies
of the murdered children
indicate a gentle death.

Some kind of suffocation,
possibly a hand over the victim's
mouth and nose
at worst El Dorado lying on their chest
to compress their lungs.

Bill won't buy
Cath's floated theory
of a female offender.

Were the kids drugged first?
Part of Bill hopes so,

if it made their deaths
less terrifying.

But there was no trace left
of any likely drug
by the time the bodies
were found.

Bill mulls
over Emma's autopsy report.

Clearly El Dorado
doesn't want to be cruel.
Just lethal.

What is he doing?
How does he see himself?

The Vampire Monster
of the tabloids?

Cath says,
"El Dorado doesn't see him
or herself, Bill,
as a monster at all.
These gentle
even respectful
deaths
seem expressive
of a kind of –
love."

Bill shudders –
and thinks of Caitlin
lying sweet
and quiet
in a shallow grave
with a gold thumb print
pressed tenderly
on her dead face.

Does El Dorado dote
on his cherished
victims
so they become
not murdered children –
but his kids?

JENNIFER HARRISON 1955–

Jennifer Harrison was born in a motorcycle shop in Liverpool, Sydney, and completed a degree in medicine in 1979; she began practice as a psychiatrist in 1990. Her first poems were written in Boston. She runs the Developmental Assessment Program for children and adolescents at the Alfred Hospital, Melbourne. She rows with the Dragons Abreast dragon boat racing team and lives with her husband and two adult children. Harrison has published four collections of poetry and co-edited *Motherlode* (2009), an anthology of Australian women's poetry. She is a poet who tackles big and difficult subjects and brings a scientific objectivity to strongly felt, often autobiographical, experiences. "Arriving", from a series of "Boston Poems", refers to Newbury Street in Boston's CBD, and the 60-story Pei building, known for its "glass skin" with 10,000 windows.

Chemotherapy

This man I see daily
in the hospital gym, is nobody's father.
He strains beneath the barbell
but doesn't forget the small observation
sheltering between his thighs.
He drags his body back and forth
pumping sero-positive blood
out from his heart into his muscle
and back to his heart
in a silent daily circuit
a smooth oiling of sweat
a machine fear won't quit with.
He throws caution aside
and looks in the mirror, seeing thinness.
He wipes away chalk from his hands
while I continue laps in the 25-metre pool
pushing my arms through water
the temperature of warm blood.
His bald head is a twin moon to mine.
I feel for him, as for a brother
the intimacy of the sick.
We need not speak to know the task.
We exercise away our particular knowledge
mine of motherless children
and his of a death
sewn into quilts the size of football fields.

Outrider

Deviants cluster to the mean.
Even eccentricity has its own
parabola.
You might expect
epidemiology to pinpoint
a unique axial path
but the non-significant statistic
melts into the human sample
the way a comma of sun disappears
into a crystal ball covered with dust.

The null-hypothesis is tested
and in the final non-parametric analysis
five-year survival
knocks at the doorstep chosen at random
from the telephone book.
Ten toes balance
on a slender beam – the odd probability.

Maturana says everything is illusion
even the facts.
That you might as well call in at the Ocean View Motel
knock at number 13
and finding a traveller by chance at home
enquire of him: how could it be
because I fell at the perimeter
a skewed outrider messing up the data sheet
how could it be

because I fell before my prescribed time
my fault the plank was rotten?
And he might tell you the story
of the silver ring he lost in the Gulf of Thailand
and dived for like a native pearling man
but could not find the jewellery in the coral.

Arriving

It was always arriving, although we didn't realise
until it had arrived, how far
it had travelled, how weary the cancer must have been
to sleep so tenderly, not bothering anyone

and how quickly the word
fitted our lives, easily, as the Charles river

or Thanksgiving or the story of Martin Luther King

how it crept along the soul
like a shadow on Newbury St

and drank Paul Revere's painted vine of blood
so that the Freedom Trail
would be remembered by the children who followed after.

It must have been arriving, always,
for your hand to know most surely
when and where it would declare its thirst

(a traveller like us making excursions
into cultures we trust will
accommodate our oddities)

now I read my children the happiest stories
and not the ones I didn't believe at the time
about the disappointed woman

who, when she thought ahead,
swore that her numbers cried blood.

I disembark at Copley
and push through the turnstile
behind a boy with a map and backpack
who turns to me for directions.

I confuse his arriving eyes with mine
and point him towards the Pei building
where the city reflects liquidly
in the largest mirror known.

Changzhou's Bees

Here is a photograph of Changzhuo, the Chinese apiarist
who sculpts with bees, who tucks the queen under his chin

calling the swarm to his face, the workers settling into the shape
of his mouth, nose, brow, until he has a mask of bees

and the stillness of marble or ice. Imagine the vibrato
of his chest; how he must delve into his breath, until

it is the breeze of the flower tipped over by dew.
Pollen and hive – the dizziness.

Pieta of bees – he is motionless as a pixilated mother
looking down at the first tug on her breast –

does she, too, exhale? Yet Changzhuo looks up

so as not to trap the bees between his chin and chest –

the gesture armours him as the word mother can.
Summer's sublime lavender store? A shell finding form?

Here is a son's school project on Virudunagar
and here a daughter's violin, its dusty case full

of her scratchy wings. Here are kindergarten art works
locks of floss-soft hair in a grandfather's collar-box.

Here are beloved masks, gathered as discarded.
Breath of the bee, what needs have shaped me?

The swarm must have lifted from Changzhuo's face but I haven't
yet seen a picture of that. Was he unscathed, always?

Hand, Chainsaw and Head

Mortlake Buskers' Festival

He juggles a chainsaw, a rubber hand and plastic head
the ghoulish toys of Quake's dark alphabet – Widow Maker,
Skull Splitter, Brain Biter – old Nordic weapons – their names

too, might find a place in his Mortlake armoury. The day
is sodden, and grey – even the fine patinating rain
feels like sprayed blood on my face and lips. The children

are bored and wish they hadn't come, but when he kick-starts
the chainsaw, they sense the danger of an R-rated thrill.
We're afraid he'll slip and fall on the wet road

but he juggles his macabre salad well, measuring
the saw's jittering arc between eye and wrist, and I admire
the steadiness of his touch as the children become bored even by this.

Returning to Melbourne, they sleep in the back of the car.
The sky falls thick as silk across the windscreen, and over the sound
of wipers and tyres I hear the wind's faint carousing polyphony.

A star drags the ceiling of a cloud. Now and then
houses eulogise the emptiness. The radio crackles and fades
as laden lorries sweep past like mescaline thunder.

The gossip of a child asleep is beautiful, I think,
but where to place ghosts, ghouls and opiate séances –
corpses and the whiskey games of death?

I juggle a machine, the mist and the night – the road thinner
darker than before – danger ahead, out of sight.
Wanting to be entertained, the landscape leans in – watching.

PETER ROSE 1955–

Peter Rose grew up in rural Victoria, an exception in a prominent sporting family. He studied at Monash University and worked as a bookseller. During the 1990s he was a publisher at Oxford University Press, Australia. Since 2001 he has been the editor of *Australian Book Review*. He has edited two poetry anthologies, published four collections of poetry, a family memoir, *Rose Boys*, and a novel, *A Case of Knives*, set against a backdrop of opera, publishing and politics. In his introduction to *The Best Australian Poems 2007*, Rose wrote: "I have looked for poetry that is ... highly expressive and resonant and open-hearted". These qualities are present in Rose's best poems, which are those where he is most personal and the natural elegance of his style is incidental to the poem. "Morbid Transfers" has brief quotations from the fifth of Bruce Beaver's *Letters to Live Poets*, which is also in this anthology.

Ladybird

For my brother

One year ago almost to the hour
we got the news about our father
and it was downhill all the way,
six weeks of crisp mordacity.
No quarter-century lessening for him:
just a curt sentence and eclipse.

Yes, one year ago, almost to the hour.
Except you weren't there,
dead yourself these five years –
on your daughter's birthday.
You never understood my lexical craze
but I could spend eternity hunting for a
long beautiful word for addicts of anniversaries.
There must be a name for it, a need.

Five years. No time, but all time:
lustrum of encyclopedic loss.
You were twenty-two when it happened;
forty-seven at your death, younger than I am.
Why is it that only now do I feel
the full burden of its grotesquerie,
the callous moral heft of it –
not those bulky limbs we lifted
and straightened a thousand times,
but the early loss of you, the spasmic curse?

And still I go on reading:
for distraction or enlightenment.

Today I'm deep in Gosse's *Father and Son*,
so numb at the horrors of the Brethren
I put myself to sleep quite deliberately –
for thirteen minutes, my watch tells me
when I stir. Well, my father's watch.
Our mother slipped it off his wrist as he lay dying
and handed it to me, consolation in time.
"Not that it's worth much," she said,
reminiscing about the notorious clip
that always failed him at critical moments.
Collingwood veterans still laugh about it,
how it was always coming undone
during halftime speeches. They'd wait
for Dad to punch his fist for emphasis.
Now it brings me undone too,
during meetings or writing this poem.
Often it dangles down or pinches me,
like a warning, a reminder.

Suddenly I'm dreaming on my bed.
It is a cursory dream, a digest from the dark,
sharp as the flick that wrenched your neck,
your birthright, your physicality.

Thirteen minutes. It feels longer –
curdling a long life into an hour.
That's how long our tennis matches took.
We'd set off on Sunday afternoons,
always fretting about the weather.
You weren't playing, of course.
Patient in your wheelchair, you'd umpire
by the net, laughing at our squabbles,
our limp trademark backhands.

Today, though, in my dream,
it's you I'm competing against –
though the court resembles my bedroom
with its monographs and cityscape.
The game is tense and visceral.
Neither of us bothers to remark
that you're nimble again, competitive.

Tense as compasses we hunt down balls
and eye each line like jealous colonizers.
When your deft backhand hits a corner

I'm about to call it out until I notice
a damp mark on the en tout cas – rather,
my pallid carpet, which shows every stain.
With queasy sportsmanship I call it in
and we play on. I lose the point.
Next game, I watch my nervous backhand
miss by an inch and am surprised when
you hunt it down. But your cross-court shot
misses by feet and seconds later you call "Out" –
meaning mine. "A bit late!" I pout,
trudging back and sinking into clay
which oozes now and swallows me,
this high bedroom become a mire.
So the tubercular diva splutters on her deathbed,
impatient for a word. *E tardi.*
I await your response but wake too soon.
The contest is over, always unfinished.
I cannot will it back, resume the game.
Too late, indeed. We leave it much too late.

Yet when I take up my Gosse –
one anniversary over, another to come –
what do I find but a ladybird
creeping over the yellowing Penguin
and settling on my father's watch.
I haven't seen one since Wangaratta.
Straight as an arrow it takes me back
to the bridge we played beneath as boys,
dumping our bikes by the road.
Teasing each other, we'd compete
to find the most ladybirds,
rapt, jostling each other, ecstatic.

Morbid Transfers

i. m. Bruce Beaver

Yes, stalwart, you were right, intoning it
in that honest old-fashioned undemonstrative voice
recorded back in the Seventies. Round death
there is an eerie unremitting babble,
as with the third of your "morbid transfers".
No quiet is granted the lost proof reader
nestling on his page beyond typo or felicity

or "death-dealing comma" – a handkerchief
his only shroud and a last pungent cigarette
burning down in the ashtray. Burning down.
His sole requiem is the chatter of the living,
their grim polyphony and purposing.
Not to mention the poet's sudden rapt knowledge:
"not a minute's silence will the rest of us get."
Even seeking it, beseeching it, would be a farce.
They will babble on till the siren lures them
to their bars or chapels, their Masses or beats –
while the proof reader's mother, in her nineties,
rung up in the middle of the night, only thinks
to ask for his keys back. It comes down to this,
the domestic returns.
                                        I watched it once;
death that is. *My* victim was a stranger,
a volley of raps in a void. One night
several of us were playing table tennis
in the old Olympic stadium by the lake,
puffing in our corporate T-shirts,
sweat forming new industrious logos.
The gym was packed with duos and foursomes,
all graded as in life or commerce,
the waspish ones capable of spin
infinitely closer to the door and glory –
a kinetic conference like a dream of Bosch.
Low fences separated the courts,
low fences to stop balls and sequester
the gods from the inglorious,
the spinners from those of us incapable of slant.
Looking round mid-point, disturbed by something
(instinct or a second's spastic silence),
I saw the brilliant boy already prostrate where he served,
so quick no one had registered the fall,
not even his opponents, eyes only on the ball.
Soon they gathered round him, incredulous,
almost jovial at first, thinking it a prank,
then urgent and clamorous and shrilly capable,
ripping at the shirt with its own bleached logo,
then standing back to marvel at the scar
stitching down his chest,
though he was only eighteen or twenty

or whatever they are when it happens –
whatever it is. Then someone, surer,
with a certificate, was pumping the boy,
rhythmic as a metronome, pausing now and then
to measure the effect as if with dough.
Nil, the minutes told us. Nil effect.
                                        Others came,
rows of them: a punctilious chemist,
an off-duty policeman who was playing nearby,
then authorities and paramedics
and the weary manager of the stadium,
almost querulous at this cessation
so late in the night, just ten minutes to go.

By now so many things were obvious
the four of us put away our silly bats and balls,
half ashamed – half ashamed to be leaving alive.
Elsewhere the games, those few interrupted,
began to resume, tentative at first then louder,
with a new kind of wilfulness and artistry,
as if making up for lost time –
so that despite the blatant cardiac affront
all we could hear was the gossip of balls
and the futility of widening scores
and the sibilance of rubber soles
as they slid and slid and slid –
until it was a kind of mutiny,
"the loud chanting of the living",
their way of saying to the irresponsive boy
this was their angle, their tactic, their victory,
a kind of spin that none of us enjoyed.
Finally, a bouncing ball invaded the mortuary
and the server, too spirited for niceties
or condolences, stepped over the low excluding fence,
negotiated the crumpled mystery at his feet
and retrieved his urgent ball without a word.

JUDITH BEVERIDGE 1956–

Judith Beveridge was born in London, came to Australia at the age of three and has since lived in Sydney. She completed an Arts degree at the University of Technology, Sydney and has worked in offices, libraries, schools, adult education and as a bush regenerator, and since 2002, as a teacher of poetry at postgraduate level at the University of Sydney. She is the poetry editor of *Meanjin*. Beveridge has published four collections of her poetry. The meticulousness of her style and the care with which she writes is indicated by her comparatively small output. Beveridge often writes poems through the voice of another person – one sequence is written in the voice of Siddhattha Gotama (the Buddha) – and rather than write about herself, she writes about people she has observed (particularly in India) and animals and birds. She is able to express emotion by combining an almost Buddhist self-effacement with synaesthetic imagery of great delicacy. Beveridge has the following note: "'Dog Divinations' contains lines culled from the *Sarngadhara Paddhati* which I have edited, rewritten and reassembled. *Sarngadhara Paddhati* (Sarngadhara's Guidebook), is a medieval encyclopaedic anthology written by Brahmin priests. The relevant section is chapter 83, the 'science of omens' from which Verses 1–120 have been reproduced. See 'Predicting the Future with Dogs', by David Gordon White, in *Religions of India in Practice*, ed. Donald S. Lopez, Jr. (Princeton University Press, 1995)."

The Domesticity of Giraffes

She languorously swings her tongue
like a black leather strap as she chews
and endlessly licks the wire for salt
blown in from the harbour.
Bruised-apple eyed she ruminates
towards the tall buildings
she mistakes for a herd:
her gaze has the loneliness of smoke.

I think of her graceful on her plain –
one long-legged mile after another.
I see her head framed in a leafy bonnet
or balloon-bobbing in trees.
Her hide's a paved garden of orange
against wild bush. In the distance, running
she could be a big slim bird just before flight.

Here, a wire-cripple –
legs stark as telegraph poles
miles from anywhere.
She circles the pen, licks the wire,
mimics a gum-chewing audience
in the stained underwear of her hide.

This shy Miss Marigold rolls out her tongue

like the neck of a dying bird.
I offer her the fresh salt of my hand
and her tongue rolls over it
in sensual agony, as it must
over the wire, hour after bitter hour.
Now, the bull indolently
lets down his penis like a pink gladiolus
drenching the concrete.

She thrusts her tongue under his rich stream
to get moisture for her thousandth chew.

Making Perfume

So, that summer I picked everything:
the hibiscus that shut at six o'clock,
the white-pollened flower
I called The Baker's Daughter,
the yellow rose that lasted weeks beyond its season
and the great pale flower with a cold look –
Queen in the Tower.

Then I took some bottles from their cupboards
and their lids twirled off and their perfume
came three voices high in my head.
I lined them like wineglasses on the sill
and filled each with petals and water
and gave them keyboard names like
Chandelier and Tier on Golden Tier.

I remember how I lived that summer
in a room with a thousand windows in blue and green.
I'd stay out late to pick and soak the petals
and pour them into bottles and bury them in the earth
with a made-up name for a simple flower plus water.
Later, I'd wash and line the bottles on the sill
and read their labels until each one rang

a terrace of bells in my head.
I mourned the bottles I named for my heroines of hopeless love
and stood them in kitchentapwater
and stored them out of the light.
I dreamt of Balls, dinner roses,
a woman gently naming herself to herself.

Now I wonder whatever happened to Lavinia,
the Fourteen Nights, Ballet Blanc,
the fragrance in the blue twirled bottle
I named Pirouette.
Months later I probably poured them down the sink.
But no-one suspected that summer
why my eyes were suddenly circled with a dark pencil,
why my cheeks had the faint glow of day,
why I swished my skirts as I moved.

I kept the bottles with me, moved them about the room
vowed not to open them for seven years,
and named them after the girl kept at home
who never stopped saying as she stirred her pots:
"O, I wish, I wish, I wish ..."

Orb Spider

I saw her, pegging out her web
thin as a pressed flower in the bleaching light.
From the bushes a few small insects
clicked like opening seed-pods. I knew some
would be trussed up by her and gone next morning.
She was so beautiful spinning her web
above the marigolds the sun had made
more apricot, more amber; any bee
lost from its solar flight could be gathered
back to the anther, and threaded onto the flower
like a jewel.
    She hung in the shadows
as the sun burnt low on the horizon
mirrored by the round garden bed. Small petals
moved as one flame, as one perfectly-lit hoop.
I watched her work, produce her known world,
a pattern, her way to traverse
a little portion of the sky;
a simple cosmography, a web drawn
by the smallest nib. And out of my own world
mapped from smallness, the source
of sorrow pricked, I could see
immovable stars.
    Each night
I saw the same dance in the sky,

the pattern like a match-box puzzle,
tiny balls stuck in a grid until shaken
so much, all the orbits were in place.
Above the bright marigolds
of that quick year, the hour-long day,
she taught me to love the smallest transit,
that the coldest star has a planetesimal beauty.
I watched her above the low flowers
tracing her world, making it one perfect drawing.

The Dung Collector

Tarn Taran Rd, Amritsar

Each morning she wipes the sweat that runs
from under the red dupatta veiled across
her face and lifts another load with a gasp.
Soon, she'll sit with her stupas of dung
and hallow the flies. Soon, she'll pray
each stack into the day's chapatis;
each new vat of dung into a tureen of dahl
to stir above the evening smoke. And she'll
work another hour or two raking the unbaked
yet steaming dung from the mud.
                                        I have seen heifers
given more freedom to wander the earth
than this woman who carries another load
to her wall then chants with the traffic.
                                        She could almost be any
woman humming at a task – moving a ladle
through vichyssoise in a perfumed apartment
off a sunny boulevard; watching light
slip into a room like a spoon into ingredients
for hollandaise sauce while she contemplates
the arrival of guests, the early yellowing
of the alder leaves.
                                        Clearly, though, this is not
about workmanship; not about having a thankful
heart in a beautiful place; not about
being a speck in the slurry of a rushing
Punjabi street, or about a woman who must
save herself by labour and prayers.
                                        It's about a woman who

must live under the anus of a cow as if
it were her star, who must slap dozens of
discoloured moons onto the side of her house
for an orange sun to bake; who hears
the sighs of the world as her bracelets
slip up and down her arms like the songs
of insects in overflowing grass; about
a woman who bends to scoop dung into a dish
each morning with her arms and hands
and looks straight into my eyes.

Bahadour

The sun stamps his shadow on the wall
and he's left one wheel of his bicycle
spinning. It is dusk, there are a few minutes

before he must pedal his wares through
the streets again. But now, nothing
is more important than his kite working

its way into the wobbly winter sky.
For the time he can live at the summit
of his head without a ticket, he is following

the kite through pastures of snow where
his father calls into the mountains for him,
where his mother weeps his farewell into

the carriages of a five-day train. You can
see so many boys out on the rooftops this
time of day, surrendering diamonds to

the thin blue air, putting their arms up, neither
in answer nor apprehension, but because
the day tenders them a coupon of release.

He does not think about the failing light,
nor of how his legs must mint so many steel
suns from a bicycle's wheels each day,

nor of how his life must drop like a token
into its appropriate slot; not even
of constructing whatever angles would break

the deal that transacted away his childhood –
nor of taking some fairness back to Nepal,
but only of how he can find purchase

with whatever minutes of dusk are left
to raise a diamond, to claim some share
of hope, some acre of sky within a hard-fisted

budget; and of how happy he is, yielding,
his arms up, equivalent now only to himself,
a last spoke in the denominations of light.

Dog Divinations

(an adaptation)

A dog that barks while facing the sun at the end of the day
portends danger for the ploughman, axeman, and soldier.

A dog that barks while facing south in the middle of the night,
portends injury to peasants and forecasts the death of cows.

When several mad dogs howl by night during the autumn,
then nothing evil will come of it, but if they do so at some

other time, then nothing good will occur. If a dog, after
howling in a village, then howls on a cremation ground,

then this is the end of the head honcho. A dog heralds death
when it runs away, whimpers for no reason, or else descends

into a river while it carries in its mouth fragments of bloody
bone. A dog laying hold of a piece of cow dung portends

the rustling of cows, but a dog rubbing its hindquarters
against a doorway means the occupants will become rich.

A man whose well-fed dogs fight at dawn to the east of
his house will himself fight with felons and murderous thieves.

When a scraggly dog rubs its right eye, licks its navel, climbs
up on a bed located on the roof of a house and urinates,

then a war will erupt in which all will be consumed by fire.
A she-dog who attempts sexual intercourse at a crossroad

with the King's Road, portends danger from royal enemies
in the course of that same day. A dog scratching its brow

with its right paw augurs that a young prince, whose chariot
has humbled the mighty, will be crowned with a royal tiara

and his subjects enjoy fortune and a great supply of food.
If a dog licks his penis during a marriage ceremony,

then the bride, even if she be equal to a goddess, will bring disease and disgrace upon her family. If a dog defecates

after digging on the upper side of a house, then the mistress's
paramour is on his way. If it defecates on the lower side,

it means her husband is coming. If a dog remains constantly
curled up on a cotton pillow, then a paramour will enter

the bedchamber at nightfall. When a dog carries a mortar,
a pestle, a winnowing basket, an arrow, or a sword to a pillow,

the dog's master can be sure the paramour is in his house.
If during the dry season, a dog howls with an upturned nose,

then a stream of water will fall from the sky in eight days' time
and bring hope to all outcasts. If a dog standing on the shore

of a sacred bathing place, causes its body to tremble, then
clouds will amass, and heavy rain bring a cessation to grief.

During a game of dice, if a dog makes left-sided movements
while breathing, hiccupping, lying down, panting, or yawning,

then these dice will become prophetic. A dog that scratches
the region of its right ear with its right paw and makes sounds

of pleasure during the playing of sitars, tablas and sarods
knows that merciful kings will have dominion over the earth.

All movements of the dog's nose toward the right are known
to portend happiness; all movement and motion toward the left

misfortune – as when a dog yawns, vomits, runs away, stretches,
trembles while asleep, agitates its forehead, chews on some

body part, hiccups, coughs, covers itself with ashes, digs,
wags its head, cries, hides its food, shuts its eyes, seizes on

a bone, or looks into the sun – then the omen-master should
offer incense and honey, place a hand on the dog's forehead,

and say: O blessed one, you of the deep voice, O knower
of acts, O swift one, you who are awake by night, O curled one,

O lord of creatures *Om, Hum, Phat, Svāhā,* and perform
the proper rites at the solstices and at the end of each day,

and pray to all subliminal Hellhounds, that these, his blessed
omen-creatures, always be given protection in this world.

ELIZABETH HODGSON 1956–

Born in Wellington, New South Wales, Elizabeth Hodgson is of the Wiradjuri people and one of the "stolen generation". She spent her childhood in a home for fair-skinned Aboriginal children in a Sydney suburb. After many years travelling, Hodgson decided to settle in Wollongong, New South Wales, and has been officially welcomed into Wadi Wadi country. She has explored her Aboriginality and spirituality in depth since moving there over a decade ago. She has been a member of the New South Wales government Arts panels and is the facilitator, mentor and writer for the South Coast Writers' Centre Aboriginal Oral History Project. Hodgson has fashioned for herself a unique, present tense, deceptively simple style, that is able to express irony and deep emotion, often with great bitterness. Unlike some contemporary Aboriginal poets she has not moved towards a creole for her poetry. She has published only one collection of poems *Skin Painting* (2008). "Mr Cage can you imagine" appears to be addressed to the American composer, John Cage, one of whose pieces "Living Room Music" specifies the use of any household object as a musical instrument.

from Skin Paintings

This is my memory of my life
no-one else can own this memory. I can tell you anything
I can manipulate the truth to my advantage –
        how would you know?

When I speak my memory,
its force makes people forget
I can make them doubt their own past
my words can insinuate themselves into their reality
I stand my ground and wait; *yes,* they tell me, *you are right.*

My memory is long and dangerous
I can frighten people with my memory.

If you had my memory how would you hold it?
Could you touch its heart,
feel it beating in the palm of your hand?
Could you breathe in its scent,
hold it in your nostrils; carry it with you
to be recalled anytime?
What if it scratched you, bit into your flesh
jabbed roughly into your tender places?
Would you drop it; try to push it away?

There are too many things I want to forget
but I have a memory that never stops turning.

This room where I sit and remember

is not large,
my life is painted on these walls
my head is a canvas of memories –
            painted with splatters, dots
some framed, others are loose, hung askew
I could carry this room in my head.

Mr Cage, can you imagine
a world where the only music
was the music of life; the percussion of the everyday?
clanging of plates, the jangle of cutlery, utensils,
swishing of the straw broom across the wooden floor
empty beer bottles ringing
impatient drumming on an old table
heavy boots pacing the floor.
This was the world into which I was born –
            my four years and thirty-three days of life music.

Then the music changed;
            the crescendo
a big, black car, a new home.

A life without the sound of my mother.

I know many places well – some I can still smell
the coke burning in the huge combustion stove
the bread – day-old – toasting on the top
under the weight of the lid,
slice after slice of warm brown toast
tumbling from the wire racks. Toast enough
for ten children at one time
the steam captured under the cotton cloth trapping the heat
but always cold by the time
we sit down for breakfast.

On a high stool in the kitchen,
writing my first words,
while she works across the table from me;
I with my pencil
she with her fat fingers working flour and lard
milk and sugar to a sweet pastry dough
rolling and shaping, cutting and trimming
I write two words for every dozen pies
her deft fingers could turn out

quick floured hands – scooping
sprinkling – pie after pie
lined along the table ready for baking.

Whenever I write she leans across the table
takes the paper; she reads and frowns.
In silence she raises the lid
on the combustion stove
drops my words inside.
I watch as the fire leaps up
then dies away from my sight,
write something nice, she says.
She teaches me to write
and teaches me to destroy.

My best friend Vicky and I were invited to the minister's place for tea
he said we would be eating fish fingers
we puzzled the whole afternoon
about fish with fingers
swimming around picking up food
from the bottom of the ocean

after tea we were more puzzled
to learn that some fish somewhere
had rectangular fingers

My mother knitted herself a yellow jumper
and wears it when she visits
she said she had some wool left over
and had knitted another jumper
small enough for a little girl
small enough for her little daughter.

She pulls the jumper over my head
and kisses my face.

That Saturday afternoon
we sit together on the low garden fence
in our matching jumpers.

The tree-lined street where my guardian's lover lived
is close to the water on Sydney harbour
polite old houses of the upper-middle classes
not identical but all the same.
She had a hedge and a neat path to the front door.

I remember the scent of the flowers in her garden
I remember the scent of her, I do not remember her face.
(when I think I see her in my mind
it is not her face I am remembering
but the face of my mother).

Each Wednesday when we visit
I step into another place
small, compact, tidy.

In her house, I know my place.
She brings me milk and biscuits.
My guardian barks her last orders at me
to stay and be quiet,
then she slips through the door with her lover
closing it quietly behind them.
I hear the creaking of footsteps on stairs,
another door closing
while I wait in the lounge-room
with a ticking clock for company.

The street was silent,
the clock ticked.
I could wait forever while her clock ticked.

Later, my guardian sat on a chair
her long legs spread,
hair hanging loosely down her back
buttoning her shirtwaist dress,
while her lover serves her tea and biscuits.

Sometimes we would knock and knock but the door was still shut
my guardian's strong fist
pounding louder and louder
I stare at the ground
willing the door to open; to let us in,
to relieve the sexual ache in my guardian's body.

Her lover didn't open the door
she had gone out.
She was married and had obligations
to her man.
My guardian hated men
I would see it in her eyes as she clutched
the girls to her side.

I caught her signals, and kept them.

The door remains closed.
For the next week, my life
will be hell.
My guardian impotent and stupid with lust,
rounds on me *It's your fault*
you were naughty last time,
she yells as she pulls me roughly into the van
slamming doors.

We don't go far, down to the jetty
to sit and stare at the water
she – cross and brooding
me – impatient to return to the house
to knock one more time.

She never cried
my tough guardian;
she sat sullen and silent
in her rejection; they had an arrangement
every Wednesday afternoon.
She needed her sweet-sex fix.

Father gained custody of me and my siblings
We had lived at Lutanda for nine years
Lutanda accepted us –
          we could be changed, moulded
made into better human beings
they were doing god's will.

For nine years –
          I had watched the children come and go
saw the fear grow in their eyes
the nervous looks
the marks of abuse clearly showing on their bodies –
          the way it was on mine.

For nine years –
          I had watched the makeover attempts
the dull dirty dormitory walls painted,
torn brown blinds and faded curtains thrown away
for cream blinds, white gauze curtains
carpet replaced the once ripped linoleum.

I saw the changes as they toned down, opened up
I left with fear in my eyes
a nervous look
the marks of abuse etched in my mind.

My father is waltzing me around the lounge room
teaching me to dance for the school formal
he complains that I keep treading on his feet
the way my mother used to.

We go through the dance, step by step –
        but slowly and always
he loses interest in being a tutor
and becomes entranced by the music.
Its rhythm takes him away from me.

He pulls me to him.
I am frightened by the firmness of his body
too close to mine.
As I dance with him,
he is dancing with my mother
many years ago.

I tread on his feet
and break the spell.

GIG RYAN 1956–

Gig Ryan was born in England, but her parents returned to Australia in 1957. She is the fourth of ten children and was educated in the Catholic school system. She has performed and recorded with the groups Disband and Driving Past, writing songs for them, singing and playing the guitar. She is a freelance reviewer and poetry editor for *The Age* newspaper, Melbourne. Six collections of poetry have been published. Alan Wearne wrote in 1990:"Gig Ryan commenced her poetry career as an out-and-out original ... Her language refuses to behave like anyone else's – it fractures with anger, it reassembles the pieces with astringent love." In early poems of Ryan's, such as "If I Had a Gun", there is an unstoppable *joie de vivre* although the voice is angry. Since then Ryan's poetry has become increasingly reflective and fragmented, less accessible and sometimes elegiac, but the reader senses an undiminished, cauterizing power.

If I Had a Gun

I'd shoot the man who pulled up slowly in his hot car this morning
I'd shoot the man who whistled from his balcony
I'd shoot the man with things dangling over his creepy chest

in the park when I was contemplating the universe
I'd shoot the man who can't look me in the eye
who stares at my boobs when we're talking
who rips me off in the milk-bar and smiles his wet purple smile
who comments on my clothes. I'm not a fucking painting
that needs to be told what it looks like.
who tells me where to put my hands, who wrenches me into position
like a meccano-set, who drags you round like a war
I'd shoot the man who couldn't live without me
I'd shoot the man who thinks it's his turn to be pretty
flashing his skin passively like something I've got
to step into, the man who says *John's a chemistry PhD*
and an ace cricketer, Jane's got rotten legs
who thinks I'm wearing perfume for him
who says *Baby you can really drive* like it's so complicated,
male, his fucking highway, who says *ah but you're like that*
and pats you on the head, who kisses you at the party because
everybody does it, who shoves it up like a nail
I'd shoot the man who can't look after himself
who comes to me for wisdom
who's witty with his mates about heavy things
that wouldn't interest you, who keeps a little time
to be human and tells me, female, his ridiculous
private thoughts. Who sits up in his moderate bed
and says *Was that good* like a menu
who hangs onto you sloppy and thick as a carpet
I'd shoot the man last night who said *Smile honey*
don't look so glum with money swearing from his jacket
and a 3-course meal he prods lazily
who tells me his problems: his girlfriend, his mother,
his wife, his daughter, his sister, his lover
because women will listen to that sort of rubbish
Women are full of compassion and have soft soggy hearts
you can throw up in and no-one'll notice
and they won't complain. I'd shoot the man
who thinks he can look like an excavation-site
but you can't, who thinks what you look like's for him
to appraise, to sit back, to talk his intelligent way.
I've got eyes in my fucking head. who thinks if he's smart
he'll get it in. I'd shoot the man who said
Andrew's dedicated and works hard, Julia's ruthlessly ambitious
who says *I'll introduce you to the ones who know*

with their inert alcoholic eyes
that'll get by, sad, savage, and civilized
who say *you can* like there's a law against it
I'd shoot the man who goes stupid
in his puny abstract how-could-I-refuse-she-needed-me
taking her tatty head in his neutral arms like a pope
I'd shoot the man who pulled up at the lights
who rolled his face articulate as an asylum
and revved the engine, who says *you're paranoid*
with his educated born-to-it calm
who's standing there wasted as a rifle
and explains the world to me. I'd shoot the man who says
Relax honey come and kiss my valium-mouth blue.

When I consider

When I consider what my life has been
the tightening streets that stuck me to their side
the turning penitential globe inscribed
with gold and thorn, I picket what I've seen
as if the will were new, the heart were keen
before despair became where you abide
alone with cold ideals and clinging pride
acts and dreams spread out across the screen
I pause at the silky prolonged sunset
that death or god should taper off and shrink
as all the city's woe and all the skies
say not to remember but to forget
and chafing through the cars I fall to think
how sorrows lift and pleasures cauterize

Heroic Money

I throw in my lot with them
showing me the crashed lights they drove into
cold isolate Bohemians
My mind is filled with condiments
pompous and self-pitying, which they escape
"I am unworthy". You bow and leave
and rationalise it by saying it was wrong
Maybe in another world I feast on the detritus
like a business like a hospital
the Star Trek editors watch Australiana on TV

the personalities philosophising
Tell the Central Committee we feel bad
lancing the streets
past the brideshops' dulled marbled gleam
It was weather like this when we buried him
drugs and sex cancelling nausea
like it's going out of style
Now the train rides over green palaces of trees
and dribbling oracles

She righteously tails the issue of the week
Here curtained bricks shimmer
Coats of politeness drop each sopping word
I contemplate Autumn behind the rust
sponged red trees flat against mist
like a bandage
Pragmatism makes its corporate entrance
It was good you discovered a galaxy
Goodbye, palindrome.
taxes are close to my heart
Drive behind the Big Events numberplate
where cars jam to the crash or street demonstration
and we wave from our democracy

ANTHONY LAWRENCE 1957–

Anthony Lawrence was born in Tamworth, New South Wales, and left school at sixteen to become a jackaroo. He then travelled for several years. While working as a fisherman in Western Australia he was awarded a literary fellowship. He returned to New South Wales, then moved to Tasmania to be with his son, where he lived for some years, and is now back in New South Wales, living in Newcastle. Lawrence persevered for fourteen years writing poetry, before his first book was published. He has now published twelve poetry collections and a novel. He comments: "For years I've been called a narrative poet. This might be so. I like telling stories within the boundaries of a poem, be it over two or thirty pages. I also like to refine and burnish. Lyrical poetry has a different breath and afterglow. When I've successfully combined a narrative and lyrical vein, I'm amazed." In a 2001 interview he said: "Ten years ago I was probably satisfied with the well-crafted poem. I still am, of course I am, but now I want there to be a little more light and air between the lines". One of Lawrence's strengths is his energy. In his 2001 interview he said: "Writing poetry is a very physical act. I write with my whole body. I break bread with myself." Another strength is his ability to handle painful facts about his own life – as in "The Drive", "The Law of Bleak Averages" and "Hammering at Clouds" – in a matter-of-fact way, and with irony. He writes about subject matter that many would find too confronting. He is illusionless, yet not lacking in sympathy, and the result is often exhilarating.

The Drive

My father could not look at me
as we sat in the back of a white sedan
on our way to the police station.
But I looked at him. He was staring
straight ahead through all the years
his son had disappointed him.

News had come through of the boy
who'd fire-bombed the car outside
the Methodist Church. When the detectives
arrived, I was having a family
portrait taken. I saw the suits and ties
in the window, then the doorbell rang.

I smiled into the flash, ran to the bathroom
and vomited my head off. I wanted to make
the Australian team as a fast bowler.
I wanted Frances Clarke to love me.
But instead I'd struck a match and immolated
the minister's new Valiant, my breath

punched out of my lungs by the boom.
I ran behind the Sunday-school buildings
and confessed to the lawn-raking currawongs.
I watched black smoke like useless prayer
gutter into the Sydney sky.
The sirens were a long time coming.

As we pulled into the station carpark,
dead leaves and the two-way static
sounded like years of thrashings: blue
welts across the backs of my legs like
indelible neon, and my mother's weeping
for the times I nailed her with insults

to the wall. But now, after breakdowns,
divorce and a distance of eighteen years,
we can talk about the sound a belt makes
as it flies in the bathroom; about
the violent spirit of a teenage son.
My mother kisses my eyes to stop

the sadness we've known from breaking
through. My father tells me about his life
instead of brief reports from the office.
I love them, these parents and strangers,
these friends who appear from time to time,
sharing their names, their blood.

Whistling Fox

My father could whistle up a fox
with the bent lid of a jam tin.
Pursing his lips, he would blow the cries
of a wounded hare into cold Glen Innes hills.
Into a giant's marble game of balancing granite;
the wind-peeled stones on the tablelands
of New England; a sound like a child
crying called the fox from its nest of skin and bones.

I was there the day my father blew
the eyes from a small red fox.
He fired, opened the shotgun over his knee,
and handed me two smoking shells.
It had come to us like any whistled dog,
leaving its padmarks in frosty grass.
That day it left its winter coat behind
with blood like rubies sown into the dripping hem.

from Two Poems

At the Sydney observatory, the roof cracks open
slowly, like the distended eyeball
of a giant with a hyperactive thyroid.

Outside, on the grass below the bandstand,
a bridal party lights
the underside of a Moreton Bay fig.

You are ten years old the night you climb
to put your eye to the glass. You are too young
for extensive knowledge of astronomy

but old enough to see, in the flame
of a star, a white dress
being lifted by the wind, from behind.

The Language of Bleak Averages

1

After a four hour workout under my father's skull,
the young neurosurgeon's hands are white.

His eyes are Concentration Red. Caffeine-numb,
on a grid of hospital floors, I walk, seeing

the shaved scalp cut, peeled back and clamped, stagehands
in a spotlight trimming a blood-curtain's advancing folds,

then a plate of fretworked bone, lifted clear to expose
the source of my father's unbalanced body and moods –

a tumour, like the dark, cystitic head of a swamp flower
grafted to a host of nerveless coils.

After *Recovery*, that post-operative word for half an hour
of being watched and questioned back into the world,

a man I barely recognise sits up, stares through me,
and tries to claw the bindings from his head.

His corner of Intensive Care is lit with a gleaming life-
support machine and metal stand. A slow drip feeds

the line that feeds his vein. Beside his bed, flower-prints
on linoleum fast become a swirl of congealing blood.

A frozen splinter of tumour is with Pathology.
The test results are two days off, though the surgeon

tells me, in the language of bleak averages, that even
weeks of radiation will simply stall

the way this kind of cancer blooms again. I think
of a mangrove tree's air-drinking tapers, like a cluster

of slime-nourished, black asparagus. I think of how
the unfiltered shadows of grief return for years

beyond a life or love. As I rise to go, moonlight flares
into the ward, turning hospital gowns into folds

of alabaster, wired to fluids and electricity.
Somewhere near, a woman laughs from the depths

of sleep or delirium. As if in response, my father raises
his upturned palms and says *She's right, it's a joke,*

giving voice to uncertainty and pain – the stable currencies
of his faith. Then he coughs – a wet, bright sound –

nothing like *a trickle of small change being poured*
from hand to hand, which is what I thought

before poetry fell apart, and I was with a man
who lowered his palms, coughed again, and bled.

2
With the staples gone, the scar gleams like an inverted,
upper-case letter C through the most radical haircut

my father's ever had. The cortisone has reduced
the swelling in his brain, giving him a freedom of speech

and body he's never known. He is openly flirtatious,
asking the entire nursing station to join him

for dinner when he's better. They all said yes.
It's an invitation none will have to honour.

3
My father was assisted by a driver to his death –
a measured, battery-powered pack beside the bed

that eased a clear cocktail into his blood.
Euthanasia is illegal in Australia only on paper.

Hours before he died, emerging from his coma,
he sat up and clawed the air, saying *I am a mear cat.*

Then he went under. Holding his hand, his body
shutting down visibly, I remembered stories of light-

bulbs dimming, of wind bending glass when people died.
The light held on. The window glass moved

with a copy of my face when I looked at it.
His last breath was long, the exhalation silent.

When they came for him, he might have been someone
still expecting company – his open hands and mouth,

the comb-lines in his hair. He left the room on a false shelf
under a trolley laid out with towels, the woman steering him

pretending that this was nothing more
than laundry being taken down in the lift.

The Deep Scattering Layer

Up from the deep scattering layer, where spinner dolphins feed
 on globes and spirals

fleshed with the hunting luminosity of their kind – up through
the black from which
we crave understanding and poetry, the krill are blowing
attracted by halogen
lights rigged overhead as snares for squid with oil spills
around their eyes
and pliable arrowheads on the tapering sleeves of their bodies.
The krill could be milt
or wake water like aerated protein below the gunwales.
All night, long lines
set with lures fall and rise, spooling from drums to release
saltwatersparks
and the severed tentacles of squid that cough and suck
at tables of blacked-out mesh,
The machinery drones on. A deckhand smokes and stares.
Behind him, like a stripe
of shadow, strapped and loaded, a .303 Lee Enfield leans
into the wall. When asked,
he swears that rifle sound is enough to put the frighteners
on seals that follow
the living lines, though smiles when telling of how
the blue shark glides
and rolls its eyes as if amused to find itself in a bloodcloud,
Having said enough
he turns back under the fierce bulbs that burn and light
the krill, which are now
being culled at the edges by a school of cowanyoung –
bait fish with serrated flanks
and anal spurs, splintering the swell with a sound like gravel
cast over water.
They divide and reform, divide again as tuna work
at the speeding silver
plates of their undersides. Ink sheets into the windows.
Satellite tracking glows
on liquid crystal in the wheelhouse, showing the boat's
position and depth
of water being harvested. On the floor, in a tray, a frozen roast
cools the beer slab.
As a floodlit food chain circles stained timber, breaking
and mending itself,
white shapes surface to flip out onto the deck, where men
in rubber boots and overalls,

sleep-deprived or drunk, stand at the rails and smoke,
    staring, trying to avoid saying
too much, to themselves or others, in a squall of hard black rain.

Hammering at Clouds

Hammering at clouds is what it's like,
coming down from the sierra
some call mania, others
a heightening of the senses or the blue
touch paper of desire.
Medication is one option,
but so is a punch to the right hemisphere
of your dream-acquired brain injury.
Best to set fire to the scene
than have someone describe it for you.
One time I was gone for days.
Detectives were friends – they spoke
with their hands and took my keys.
I'd been out on the town, on my own,
and you know how that can go
prickly pear shaped. I woke up hammering
at a thunderhead, then changed my story.
Officer. I've been. Forgive me.
It's still unclear as to what happened next
and I've got the scars to prove it.
It's not always serious.
You might come to in the shower
at the home of a stranger
a state away, and it does not go like this:
Who's been abluting in *my* bathroom?
It's more like: next thing you've woken up
in bed, black-eyed and hammering
at mare's tails or a bit of circus nimbus,
and a nurse knows your name
mnemonically. You kiss him through
the refined skin of a tablet, then withdraw.
Surfacing, while clinical, is never deliberate.
And calling out in public is not my style,
though I do love oratorical grace and stamina,
the kind that gathers people in
and just as quickly disperses them.
Here's a list I made

from a ground-floor window in lucidity:
Being ill is always political.
A leather jacket is not straight.
A full moon is nothing but astrological.
Clouds are the hiss and steam from a water forge.
You get the picture.
Swimming and walking are restorative
and so is therapy, for a limited time only.
Too much for too long, and you emerge
full of talk, and that's the problem –
it's what brings you to grief
in the first and last place. Without it
you're reclusive as a dugong, whereas
being a blabbermouth attracts
bad company, and only pigeons will attend
to your needs and applaud your eloquence.
Have I mentioned love?
Who knows what it is and from where
it springs yet, when it's over
you know everything.
I have loved, and not metaphorically.
We held hands in sickness
and recovery. He understood why,
on re-entry, I had to work clouds into shape
and give a commentary.
His gift was silence and a scent
I could detect from a ward away.
In the end put himself to sleep.
In the only photo I have of him, he is wordless
and calm, and already making plans.
I visit him when I can.
Today I spoke to his name on the stone
saying how it's been a month
without episode or incident,
how no oxygen's been needed
for high altitude, no clouds aligned
for hammering a safe passage back to earth.
I know my way, and can tell a chemical
swing from a mood.
It's what professionals call
being stable. I call it time to make up
for lost time, to dream without coercion.

Tonight the sky is tethered
from hill to hill with mackerel cloud.
I'll walk, and consider
how blessed I am, and then keep walking.
It's only weather.

The Linesman

The telegraph wires have been set to open tuning.
In his harness up a pole on a country road,
a linesman is singing. He's so loud and off key
you'd be forgiven for thinking the glaze
on the porcelain pots at the top of the pole
might acquire more hair-line crazing.
As he sings, Apostle birds stop quizzing about
in the grass, and the wind gets up
out of a blazing canola crop to silence him.
His singing is louder now and completely atonal
and the words, if that's what they are,
enter a paddock where cattle, startled
from doing nothing, move off to do nothing again.
The wind gives up and dies down,
the Apostle birds seek each other's counsel.
When the linesman descends, the cattle
approach and circle him.
He sits on his heels and smokes in silence.
He only sings when he's alone, and high.

SARAH DAY 1958–

Sarah Day was born in Lancashire, England, and emigrated as a child with her family to Tasmania. She lives in Hobart with her partner and has two daughters. She was poetry editor of *Island* (1996–2003) and has been a member of the Literature Board of the Australia Council. She teaches Creative Writing at pretertiary level. Day has published five collections of poetry. Her poems are accomplished and lucid, but what elevates them is her empathy and her ability to surprise the reader.

A Hunger to Be Less Serious

When the bell rings at the canal bridge
it's as if the signal for release has sounded,
as if the people in motor cars unconsciously hoped for this all along,
as if they find themselves dismissed.

Doors open along the line.
The clay bank is suddenly colourful.

Upon the ringing of the bell, zebra gates, black and orange, swing to meet;
as they do, the whole silver body of the bridge veers in slow motion.
A Lego fantasy, a perfect mechanism.

The bridge marks its full arc then pauses,
describing a route for the reckless, the thrill-seeking, the desperate.
They picture it through windscreens: the brief ascent, the plummeting.

The water-surface puckers with the quick current,
underneath, the grey deepens steeply;
its effect is sobering, satisfying.

When she comes into view, the tub meets all expectations:
an old canoe-stern, trailing her fledgling nose-up in the wake,
sailing sublimely past the crowd and the procession of deserted vehicles,

away, away into the horizon,
carrying on board a gleaming catch
of strayed dreams and wish-fulfilments.

Stern Woman

Pleasure should be rationed, she says
beating along the garden path
with a good stiff brush of straw
that licks permanently to one side
from years of demonstrativeness,
a permanent cringer, brow-beaten,
voiceless complier to brusqueness.
If not the broom, it's a poker,
swatch or stick she has at hand,
an emphasizer, an adage.
Swearer of rods, she never spared them;
she was born stern, plain-spoken,
with a propensity for black.
She suffered neither childhood
nor levity nor temerity.
Hecate's image, she spurns sorcery
and remedy as shirking and illusion;
a firm believer in lots cast and just deserts,
she is perpetually bent – a lugger of burdens,
and bony, for the flesh is weak.
She dismisses dilemma,
countering uncertainty with her vocabulary,

the balance tips every time
with words like *should, ought, must.*
Pitting need against want and always wary
of disguises, she's from a line of puritans,
rigid, obdurate, dour.
She's scrupulous, this stern woman
and incorrigible.
She lives in my house and she won't go away.

Hens

I think I've been waiting for you all my life.
To glimpse you through the kitchen window
scratching between iris and daffodil,
disrupting roots, sprawling moll-like
in a patch of sun, wings spread flush
with the ground, a coquettish leg
in the air and rolling lascivious eye.
You're disruptive of course –
annuals, seedlings go by the wayside,
Christmas lilies cordoned off,
brassicas like khaki interns on parade –
but what small price
for that vigorous rustling
as mulch scatters from under hedges,
to have you beady at my side
grabbing worms as I pull up buttercups;
or whetting your beaks on the path, this side
that side, like good chefs sharpening knives.
I love the way you pose like weathervanes
on the axe handle,
to watch as I wash dishes
how today's menu, or tonic
is borage or bindweed or dock
that you will strip back
to a handful of cellulose spikes.
The way you share a laying box
when there is one for each of you
and midwife one another
through your confinements.
The way you lay eggs –
those warm white ellipses
on the straw.

Somehow for all the wreckage
the garden was never more alive.
You offer a remote conviviality
that I don't presume upon
as I would, say, a dog or cat,
I'm afraid it's species that I'm celebrating here,
not personality,
that atavistic sense of well-being you provoke
you unremarkably remarkable hens.
I'm grateful, watching you just now
splashing about in dust
for that reassurance you give,
of simple notions, like goodness.

CAROL JENKINS 1958–

Carol Jenkins grew up on the New South Wales central coast at Woy Woy and "left as soon as possible". She studied science at university and then obtained a graduate diploma in Labor Law and a Masters in Public Health. She worked in chemical regulation and assessment and in 2003 began a writing career. In 2007 she founded River Road Press, which produces audio CDs of Australian poetry. She lives in the Sydney harbourside suburb of Mosman, is married and has two children. Jenkins has published one collection of her poetry *Fishing in the Devonian* (2008). The American poet, Billy Collins described her work as "full of terrific conceits". Jenkins' poetry has a freshness and enthusiasm which sit intriguingly with the underlying hard intelligence, scientific exactness of observation, and sometimes bleak conclusions.

Fishing in the Devonian

Try Ellesmere Island when it's green and still attached
to Greenland. One fish, *Tiktaalik roseae*, is having second
thoughts about the water, it's perfectly clean
but there is the attractive ooze of mudflats
with morsels of scorpions and millipedes,
though you can't say millipedes in the Devonian
as there are no fingers to count on or Greek
prefixes for one thousand. The fish are inclined
to muddiness, mud being not much of a flavour
even for Devonians. How they throng
up and over the shore on their lobed fins so maybe
you don't have to throw a line in, in the classic sense
because the *Tiktaalika* is trying its best to get out,
get the morning papers and have a neck to look around.

Devonian fish come in metres so consider
scrupulously the best kind of hook and bait,
what kind of gloves you need to get that hook out.

Perhaps don't go out in a boat built
of spongy Devonian wood – not much
by way of secondary thickening
though a stout source of carbon. There is a lot
to think about in fishing in the Devonian. So,
pack thoughtfully.

Cloud Me

(Written on the 30th anniversary of *The Selfish Gene*)

With the clouding factor of being here,
in this brilliant light, and not being with you,
the blue bouncing like love gone crazy around the room,

I stand on the scales, at sea level,
with all the gravity I can muster, divide by ten
and multiply by seven to approximate my liquidity

that was once, and will be, pure cloud.
I read as thirty-eight litres of cloud potential,
thirty-eight litres of ebullient cumulus rising,

lapping through the water cycle I will be nimbus,
stratus, cirrus, altos, storm and ice.
We'll mix, rise, condense together, travel and rain apart,

separate from the DNA that codes for bones and muscles
to tilt a head that might revert to thinking about clouds,
and needs a body to bear it.

While those little squirls of code, the selfish species subsets,
swim to extinction, my enduring water,
returning cloud shaped, will outlast all organic parts of me.

When Years Take the Stars Away

If you're reading this in one-hundred-million,
two-thousand and seven AD, that is, after all the stars
have inched away, taking their tails of light with them,
far off to where the universe strikes a light against
what, at the time of writing, has no dimension, the timeless
place that time is coming to, I want to tell you
that here – right now – the sky is prinked

with nebulae in clusters and symposia,
the light is mostly white, so you get the true idea of blackness
and the abundance is such that it presses infinities
into the foreheads of children lying safe in their beds at night,
and those who can get out from the cities
and take the time to sit outside, make up elaborate
stories, concerning these embroideries of starlight, and if
a meteorite rushes, burning, into the earth's air,
wonderment bubbles up, into this strange satisfaction
which might be happiness. I want you to know, as you sit
reading this on your black and starless planet
that you should not find that blank
blanket of night a reason to believe that stars do not exist,
the galaxies, the Milky Ways and the jewel of Magellan's Clouds,
still shine and burn abundant in distant orbits.

Two Times Tables

A thunderstorm circles the house, blue-greenish –
and the schoolyard paddock across the road
is an amphitheatre lit by branding light,
and the sky's tearing itself to bits.
In the open doorway
– where she has said we would be electrocuted,
she sits, legs out straight, head turned skyward,
fat rain drops steam summer heat
from the concrete porch, and I watch her, watching
and I can't bear it and say come away from the door,
the lightning could get you,
"I don't care, it can," she says.
She might be thirty or thirty one, and I'm
pleading with her but she doesn't move, she is getting
wet and any moment could be hit by lightning.

Six years later she shuts herself into the walk-in wardrobe
with a large knife, muttering that she's not
going to cut her wrists,
but on account of how sharp
the knife is and the way her voice tapers off
to this frantic pitch, I know at twelve,
holding my two months
baby sister, that it would be a good idea to
get her, or the knife,

out of the wardrobe.
My elder brother and I coax and beg,
plead, argue and cajole, and she cries
and goes on and on,
the baby cries, and we talk about stuff
and say she can stay in there
but can she please give us the knife.

Clays Bookshop – Kings Cross

It's 1984 and one hundred dollars is in excess
of generous for a voucher. It seems certain,
even before I place it quietly on the counter,
that Miss Chapman, who has deduced the complexity
of what I like and want and should read, will find out.

She casts an eye from it to Judith Menzies, who steps over,
and they both look at the voucher. A blush is moving
from my throat to my face – "Oh," Miss Chapman says,
and I can hear her eyebrows rising but on her face
they are obedient to her person, "we wondered," and here
Judith M. concurs – "we wondered who that Young Man
belonged to" – her hand describes a vivid arc, "oh he bounced
and sprang around the shop – in a way we talked about for days,
so exuberant and charming," and both she and her hand stop short,
and we get down to business, "but we did not think it could be you
– we thought … that young man who's always with you …"

For a moment I study the Reference Section, and then I say,
"Oh, I work with James, and I live with Mark"
and like mirrors with a time delay, one eyebrow
of Judith Menzies' reflects that of Miss Chapman,
who stretches out the words, "Well, you are lucky,"
smiles at me, and at that moment, maybe I am.

MARK O'FLYNN 1958–

Mark O'Flynn was born in Melbourne and graduated in Arts from Swinburne Institute in 1979. He later completed a script-writing course at the Victorian College of the Arts and began writing for the theatre. He has had seven plays professionally produced and has published three collections of poetry and two novels as well as essays and short fictions. He now lives in the Blue Mountains of New South Wales. O'Flynn's poetry is consistently intelligent, and he is able to isolate oddities and strangeness with vivid economy.

The Stillness of Cows

Thirteen early morning cows
standing in the sugary ice of their shadows,
still as cairns. All about them the paddock thaws
but for cow-shaped maps to the west
white as mould on the dawning green.
One side of them slowly steaming in the light
while the dark flanks tic and shudder
a collective dream of the herd.
Something in me envies their stillness
waiting for the simultaneous moment
when they will lower their heads
in the frost's silence and kiss the ground.

Peasoup

("Fog is cloud that has lost the will to fly" – Bill Bryson)

After the downpour – a peasouper.
Fog so thick it is like glaucoma. The spirits
are said to be let loose in fog such as this.

I wanted to go to the centre of the oval
where even the dark silhouette
of the treeline disappears and you
can imagine the world evaporated.

Out there I found a bunch
of cricketers camouflaged in the mist
waiting for their blindness to lift
and the contest to resume. It felt distinctly odd
meeting them like steamed ghosts,
part cloud, part will-o'-the wisp standing
with the drowned worms in the grass.

PHILIP HODGINS 1959–1995

Philip Hodgins grew up on a dairy farm at Katandra West, a flat, mainly wheat-growing area of inland Victoria. An only child, he helped on the property from an early age, and farming life, viewed pragmatically, has been an important subject in his poetry. For his high school education he went to a private school in Geelong, from which he was expelled in his final year. He then worked for seven years with a publishing company in Melbourne as a sales representative. In 1983, at 24, Hodgins was diagnosed as having leukemia, and was given three years to live. His first book appeared in 1986, while he was a full-time student at the University of Melbourne. He later travelled in Europe and the United States. In 1990 he married the writer Janet Shaw (whose first collection of short stories was published that year). They moved to the country at Maryborough, central Victoria, and restored a derelict mud-brick farmhouse. Hodgins leukemia recurred and he died in Maryborough at the age of 36, survived by his wife and two daughters.

Hodgins published a novella in blank verse, *Dispossessed* (1994), about a family being evicted from a farm told in the laconic and brutally unillusioned style of a rural anecdote, but treated with an extraordinary artistic tact and discrimination. He published five other collections of poetry during his lifetime and a sixth, *Things Happen* (1995), was published posthumously. Hodgins is one of the exceptional Australian poets born after World War II, lucid, powerful and understated, and was struck down at the moment his poetry was demonstrating its greatest strengths.

The Birds

The time is nearly five a.m.
and all the birds are on the go.
They sound just like the frequencies
of many twiddled radios.

It's really bad the way it's gone –
I always used to sleep okay
and dream and miss the rural life
and never see the break of day.

But since I got the only part
in cancer's scripted dialogue
I've heard those birds a million times
and seen the sun come up a lot.

I've been rehearsing death each night,
and still I haven't got it right.

Walking through the Crop

It doesn't matter any more
the way the wheat is shivering
on such a beautiful hot day
late in the afternoon, in Spring.

I couldn't care about the sound
of insects frying in the heat
or how a flock of cockatoos
has gone up in a brilliant sheet.

I had a list I tried to keep.
Sometimes I even wrote it down.

It had all sorts of private things
like images, sensations, sounds …

There's nothing in these dying days.
I've given everything away.

Chopped Prose with Pigs

There was one old barrel-size boar
who just couldn't hold off
until the gate had been dragged open.
On that evening, after milking,
when we reversed down the lane
with a load of reject peaches from the cannery
this pig charged the electric fence
like some quixotic warrior whose time
had come. Knowing what the wires held
he started screaming with metallic vigour
way back before he got to the pain.
We stood on the trailer in filthy stasis
like two ham actors
upstaged by a member of the audience.
When it arrived the moment
was wonderful. The scream
went up to an ecstasy and the pig,
soaking with mud, hurled and dragged
itself frighteningly under the wires
while at the arch of contact
blue sparks burned into the twilight
and into my memory.
I had never seen so much intensity
for so many small peaches.

But pigs will eat other things as well,
including their offspring, and you.
There was a farmer up at Yabba North
who came unstuck in a pen
full of pigshit and duplicitous saddlebacks
one ordinary morning in January.
When they hosed out the place
they found about half the things
he had been wearing
plus all the bigger bones.
I saw his widow doing some shopping in town

not long after the funeral.
She was loaded down with supermarket bags
and grief.

Another time we found a bloated cow
tipped over in a far paddock.
The dead-cow truck wasn't coming round
so my father tied her to the tractor
and lurched her down the lane
like a small ship in a gentle swell.
We stopped in the smell of pigs
and while I rolled a cigarette
he broke her into half a dozen pieces
with an axe
and threw them over to the pigs.
When I went back early the next day
I stood rolling another cigarette
and looked at all the bigger bones
and the pigs lying round in the innocent mud.

It was one of those same pigs, a sow,
who got out of the churned-up paddock
and went down to the dairy one afternoon.
In the passageway there was a cattledog tied up
to keep cats out of the milkroom,
but he didn't worry about the pig.
She got in there
and tipped over an eight-gallon cream can
and then licked it all up.
We found her three days later
lying very still in an empty drain
with a relentless cream hangover.
Her eyes were so bloodshot
that whenever she opened them
it looked like she would bleed to death.

She recovered
but later on she did go out that way.
It happened early in the spring.
I coaxed her into a single pen mechanically
and smashed her between the eyes
with a hammer.
After pushing a knife through the jugular
I rolled her to one side

until most of the blood had pumped out.
It spread across the concrete
like an accident
and made me think how the cream
must have spread the same way.
I scalded and scoured her thoroughly
and when I hung her up
and drew the knife down her front
some of the guts pushed out
like odds and sods from an overloaded cupboard.
Reaching in for the rest
had me disgorging handfuls of animal warmth.

When the job was done
I hoisted her out of catreach
in muslin as clean as a bridal veil
and threw the chopped shinbones
to the cattledog.
I can still hear him
outside his tipped-over forty-four
chewing them with a sloppy broken rhythm.

Shooting the Dogs

There wasn't much else we could do
that final day on the farm.
We couldn't take them with us into town,
no-one round the district needed them
and the new people had their own.
It was one of those things.

You sometimes hear of dogs
who know they're about to be put down
and who look up along the barrel of the rifle
into responsible eyes that never forget
that look and so on,
but our dogs didn't seem to have a clue.

They only stopped for a short while
to look at the Bedford stacked with furniture
not hay
and then cleared off towards the swamp,
plunging through the thick paspalum
noses up, like speedboats.

They weren't without their faults.
The young one liked to terrorize the chooks
and eat the eggs.
Whenever he started doing this
we'd let him have an egg full of chilli paste
and then the chooks would get some peace.

The old one's weakness was rolling in dead sheep.
Sometimes after this he'd sit outside
the kitchen window at dinner time.
The stink would hit us all at once
and we'd grimace like the young dog
discovering what was in the egg.

But basically they were pretty good.
They worked well and added life to the place.
I called them back enthusiastically
and got the old one as he bounded up
and then the young one as he shot off
for his life.

I buried them behind the tool shed.
It was one of the last things I did before
we left.
Each time the gravel slid off the shovel
it sounded like something
trying to hang on by its nails.

So-and-so's Famous Poem

He probably just started with a single line,
some loose thread he hardly remembered picking up
on the edge of an uneventful afternoon.
It wouldn't have meant much to him on its own,
lying there without a context among his thoughts,
but even so there'd be no doubting its quirkiness.
On any wander through his big Collected Poems
that line still clings to you with its unexpectedness,
its atypical repose, saying at last the poet has relaxed.
The next few lines may well have been the same:
off-cuts, false starts and other by-products of his work
just thrown together to see how they looked.
It must have been luck, as much as anything else,
which made that opening part turn out the way it did:
four separate statements, each one quite bold

but not as disconnected as they first appear to be.
And perhaps it was here, with chance on his side,
he first arrived at the poem's exquisite form,
an enfolding of the old with the naturally new.
He would then have concentrated more on craft,
removing the slackness from each of the lines
and tying tight knots of rhyme at each second end.
By now he would have seen enough of the poem's shape
to know what sort of tension he was looking for
and teasing out new lines would be a bit easier.
The feeling of making something from almost nothing
should have been behind him and the poem's length
helping him along, one tied line suggesting another.
At this sweet point, with the fabric coming evenly together,
he might have wondered what the poem really was.
A love letter, an epitaph, or maybe a suicide note?
And if so, for whom was all the effort intended?
The obvious answer was that none of this mattered
and he would have got straight on with the job,
arranging his material with as much slow care
as a weaver working all day in front of a loom.
The further he went the more the poem would have
written itself, the pattern unfurling before him
until he would hardly have thought the poem his own.
He may even have felt the thing was commissioned
but he couldn't have said why or by whom.
It was like worship: these weren't the right questions.
The final lines, when they came, would have held
no surprise, as though they were already there
just waiting to be picked up by someone at hand.
And afterwards he would have been left with
a beautiful object, perfectly useless of course
but something to take to the grave, to anyone's grave.

The Meaning

Last night a pair of eyes
shone back at me
when I poked the torch out
the side door to see

what had made the dog
go off like a crude alarm,

echoing his urgency
across the still farm;

a pair of eyes
over near the chook shed,
low down, close together
and like Mars, faintly red.

Probably a neighbour's cat,
or a feral one,
its guts full of all
the damage it had done.

I told the dog to shut up
like you would a child
and went back to bed
where the doona was piled

roughly at the bottom
with the sheet,
a big sack of feathers
losing my body heat.

This morning at first light,
with a heavy frost
sheeting on the ground,
I counted the cost

of my mistake –
our six chooks dead
and scattered in bits
in their corrugated shed.

It looked as if there'd been
a pillow fight
that got out of hand:
blood on the white

feathers, dead eyes open
and astonished, legs
bitten off, and the remains
of broken eggs.

I happened to look up
and saw a fox
running away through
the white far paddocks.

It ferreted across
the grass's frozen quilt
with enough speed
to resemble guilt,

a wriggling blip
on the monochrome
of a large computer screen.
Heading back home

it stopped once,
and turned and scanned
this farm, as if blood
were the meaning of the land.

The Drinkers

All around the dam, sentry spaced,
are clumps of bitten-down and dried-out rushes:
bristling, defensively braced
echidnas in colour, size and shape.

They flourished outrageous spiky hairdos
that would pierce your skin,
which worked until
three hungry white goats were let in.

Now dozens of bees are drinking at the edge
of this relative ocean.
They hover up and down
like particles of energy bouncing in slow motion

and then all at once are dispersed
when Hattie wanders through them
unaware and contented
on her way to have a swim.

She forges out in a straight line, stops
and continues round and round
like a rudder-jammed boat,
drinking as she goes with a slurpy clopping sound.

Emerging on the farther shore
with her black pelt sleek with wet weight
she gives herself a staggering shake
that manages momentarily to imitate

the size of a peacock's raised display –
a water-drop composite fan
is thrown up, tinted by the sun
and drops away.

The curious goats come down for a drink as well,
chewing their cud.
They sink down closer to themselves
as their front legs make pole holes in the mud.

One goat lifts her stumpy tail to eliminate
a jackpot of black pellets,
which Hattie comes to investigate,
nodding while sniffing, as if making a count.

Across the other side, in the shallows,
each time breasting an instant ring of water,
two curvy swallows
are swooping down to scoop up tiny beakfuls.

Later, when the sunlight fails
kangaroos will have their turn,
sliding at the final muddy stage on temporary skis
and anchoring themselves with muscly tails.

Midday Horizon

The summer's worn-out paddocks
aligned as neatly as quatrains on a page,
one of those highly buffed duco skies,
and in between, a fine graph line
as nervy as a lot of black snakes in the heat.
Great sheets of mirage are lying there
as bright as new galvo.
You squint into the glare until your eyes
are nothing more than two short twitching lines
and see on the horizon
the standing shadow of a eucalyptus tree.
A big mob of sheep is moving to the left,
breaking up and catching up
in slow eddies like a lava flow.
Seen through the hot distorting air
clear flames seem to be tearing off the mob.
A man is walking sheep-slow behind them.
From where you are

his shape is continually being modified
as if he were walking through different dimensions.
Sometimes he seems to slip into separate pieces,
then pull back together, temporarily.
The same thing is happening to the tree.
The man stops
and a low piece of him draws right away this time.
It must be a dog.
You notice the silence, how near it is.
There's no threat that you can see
and yet the thin exposed horizon trembles.

Woman with an Axe

She sits on the splitting-block
in the middle of the afternoon,
leaning over her upturned axe

with one hand round the handle's neck,
the way someone else
might sit on a kitchen chair

at the end of a summer day
and strum a few slow chords
on a relaxed guitar.

An axestone fits into her other hand
coldly and firmly,
like a small coarse discus.

It makes a fine grinding sound
monotonous as flies,
in little insistent circles

like a killer killing time,
as it focuses the shiny edge
into an evil smile.

Up and down the nearby trunk
of a lemon-scented gum
a grey fantail moves from one

minute meal to another,
jabbing and then accelerating on
with shuttlecock speed.

The woman watches as if
listening to a faraway sound,
then tests the sharpened edge

gently, with her thumb,
the way you'd tease
a soft note from a guitar.

She looks at the green wood
laid out in front of her,
three new logs of red gum,

one still slowly shedding the hard tears
of its translucent colour
from a miraculous site,

and thinks how she'll chop
a length or two
for the primal pleasure it gives:

the knock of the swung head
impacting through the packed fibre,
the shock of it

rocketing back up the handle,
and the chips spinning off
to land in the grass.

Already she can smell
the resinous freshness
of the dry chiselled vee.

Close behind her,
up against the paling fence,
the sawn blocks of grey box

are stacked on their sides
with cellar neatness
in an insecure pyramid.

Each block on its end,
when struck with the axe,
will split in its own way.

Some will burst into halves
almost too easily,
as if spring-loaded.

Others will tear unwillingly
down the grain, and hang
together in a splintery embrace.

And one, there is always one,
will bounce the axe
like metal meeting metal.

She puts down her tools
and looks to their weatherboard house
where a slight rupture of smoke

is drilling straight up
from the pitted orange-brick chimney
of their wood-fire stove

that has burned continuously
since the First War,
if her mother is to be believed.

Two Dogs

The smell of fox is as strong as burnt hair.
Even my nose knows there's something there.

For Hattie's twitching snout it must be overload.
She eyes the thick coffee bushes beside the road

then crashes in and disappears from sight
though not from sound. I wait for the fight

to begin but all that happens is first one bush,
then others lurch as if given a sudden push.

Eventually a gingered fox steps out near me
and lopes away across the paddock casually

with Hattie following in a natural contrast,
running much more energetically but not as fast.

The further they go, these dogs, one wild, one tame,
the more obvious it is which has won the game.

The student keeps on losing ground to the master.
And gives up. Wild things are always faster.

The Last Few Days and Nights

So weakened by life he could just pass
through the world this hospital bed,
he lies as still as someone already dead.

Hi-tech machines surround him now like family.

Three floors below him lies the mortuary.
People there have been cleaned of their identity.
Impossible to tell who wore the business suits,
the pilot's uniform or the comfortable shorts.

A nurse comes in to tend to the machines.
Reaching across him to one of them her breast,
the left one, is momentarily pressed
into his face with pillow-pressure softness.

He opens his eyes as if to some memory.
She gives him a look as intimate as surgery.

Wordy Wordy Numb Numb

Death.
Now there's a word.
He wrote it down.

It didn't take up much space.
You could say it was discreet,
and patient.

He couldn't remember
the first time he'd heard it.
It seemed to have been always there,

like something he owned
as a kind of right or inheritance.
But he wasn't sure if this was true.

He liked the way it rhymed
with breath,
its natural opposite.

He liked it for many reasons,
and because of that
he wrote it down many times

in many different contexts
finding that it had
all sorts of meanings.

Later on, when words had passed,
he backed it up
by dying.

One thing
he had always remembered
was the arrogance of health,

those dumb days
when nothing can touch you,
when death is just one

of the familiar short words:
sun, moon, tree, bread, wine, house, love …
you know them,

each one worn smooth
as a river stone
with the flow of language

and death the odd one out,
not so much worn smooth
as numb.

Better not to think about it then
and come back to it later
when it comes back to you

like an unpaid debt
gathering interest
infinitely greater than what was lent.

MIKE LADD 1959–

Mike Ladd was born in California, of Australian parents, came to Australia aged one and grew up in the Adelaide hills. He studied philosophy and English at the University of Adelaide and became a singer/lyricist with the new wave punk band *The Lounge*. After travelling and working overseas, he returned and worked for the Australian Broadcasting Corporation as a sound engineer and then a producer. He presents a poetry program *Poetica* for ABC radio from Adelaide. Ladd has published five collections of his poetry. "Last Thoughts of a Famous Dog" is about Laika, the first living creature sent into space, launched in Sputnik II in 1957. She was a stray dog taken from the streets of Moscow. Her 'coffin' circled the Earth 2,570 times and burned up in the Earth's atmosphere in 1958.

Last Thoughts of a Famous Dog

In his grey coat, he seemed a friendly man,
leaning towards me with a piece of meat.
I followed, jumped into his van –
the last I saw of my Moscow street.

We drove through suburbs I didn't know,
I snuffled and scratched at the bars.
Those first flakes of Autumn snow
hit the windscreen and drifted off like stars.

A uniformed man lifted the boom,
we passed through the gates of an institute.
Washed and fed, kept in a sterile room,
I was named and numbered – a new recruit.

I remember a dark journey in another van
down roads that never seemed to end.
I sniffed the frozen air of Kazakhstan,
and scented something burnt in the wind.

From my porthole I see the sky's arc expand,
below me, the vanishing cosmodrome.
Noise and killing heat. Now I understand –
this famous dog is never coming home.

JORDIE ALBISTON 1961–

Jordie Albiston was born in Melbourne, where she grew up and lives. She studied flute at the Victoria College of the Arts, before turning to writing. She is the author of six poetry collections, and works as an editor, manuscript assessor, proofreader and mentor. She has two children. Albiston's poetry is cerebral, passionate, and sparing in its use of imagery. She often writes suites of poems – two of them are book-length – that examine a subject from various angles. Some shorter, more lyrical poems may have a logical development like a fugue. In a 2001 interview she said: "My poems are fairly structural, and I know I'm a bit formalistic for many people's tastes, but I do believe in things like unity, balance, symmetry … a poem doesn't necessarily have to *look* visually symmetrical to please me as a reader, but there has to be a very particular sense of organic order and cohesion: a beginning and an end, and a relationship between every part."

The Fall

People will gasp. They'll point at you in disbelief, but before they can absorb the reality of what they're witnessing, the miracle will be over. – Paul Auster

She takes a tall building as hers is to be a very long fall.
She was always going to fall, whether she got to the top
Or not. Depression is holy. You have to be called.
She hears the children cheering inside: there is no hope.

She was always going to fall, whether she got to the top
And jumped, or was pushed. It says so in the contract.

She remembers the small print: *There will be no hope:*
However, cleanse your heart with prayer before combat.

She will jump. Or she will be pushed. See contract.
From this height, West 33rd Street has a silent mystique.
Her heart is clean out of prayer: nothing will extract
The dread, the black-dog knowledge it is all a mistake.

From the eighty-sixth floor, West 33rd Street is silent.
There is no consolation for those who cling to the railing
Only dread. She believes this is what the prophet meant.
With her body in her throat, she lets go, and is falling.

There is no consolation for those who cling to the rails.
I don't think I'm lost, but I don't know where I am.
She has let go, hesitated in the air. She has yet to exhale.
Her body hangs over a matrix of chaos and desolation.

She is not lost, but falling like Eve into the Big Apple.
Each year takes a minute, each week a singing second:
Her body hangs over a matrix of chaos, as she topples
Downwards, too fast for those below to comprehend.

In the air, a moment can take on the time centuries span.
She falls through former selves above a thousand heads.
No one looks up. No one looks towards the bright sedan:
Within a handful of time, it will be her crumpled bed.

She falls, self by self, over a crowd of a thousand heads.
Failing always at physics, this falling is her punishment:
In seconds, her crumpled body will lie in its metal bed
Where she shall sleep, no matter what the prophet meant.

Physics having failed her, she falls at the speed of night.
She is spinning through childhood on a taut yo-yo string
Aching for God, and some sleep. She is alone alright:
The playground, the pool. She is the one with no wings.

She spins through a childhood and the cool New York
Night, clutching an orchid in her white-gloved hand.
Wingless, she is tumbling through twenty-three years
Of astonishing despair. She is the Angel of Manhattan.

Clutching an orchid, she flies through the rhyme We All
Fall Down and cannot get up (the pool, the playground).
She is often astonished at the depth of despair in her soul:
Still she tries to find God, endeavours to never look down.

She is falling down, cannot get up, and so goes the rhyme.
Her descent through adolescence with its paintbox of blood
Is final: she leaves her life and her longing for God behind.
If not this flight, then what in heaven can make her good?

She descends through adolescence, obsessed with its paints
And its blood. It feels always like falling (she never flew).
Nothing on earth can make her good, for she is tainted.
See, a stocking is down, she has already lost both her shoes.

Moments are made to be flown through: you climb, and
If you have the courage, leap. She knows this much is true.
Shoes gone, stocking down, orchid clutched in left hand
She hisses by on a seam of light only darkness could pursue.

If you have the courage, leap, the prophet may have said.
Clinging to life like a leaf in the suburbs, she never took
The plunge. But now, how she sings on that hissing thread!
How bright and thin the sound of her whistling rebuke!

She clings like a leaf to the life she never took to, falls
Towards womanhood where things start to look black.
The whistle of her descent becomes a God-awful squall:
In these final few feet, she knows there is no going back.

It is during womanhood that blacknesses start to appear.
Lay your hands upon me: cat! you feel my broken heart?
There is no going anywhere in these final falling years
No rehearsal, no second chance. This is the lonely part.

A broken heart can make a woman climb, and catapult.
(She flashes on being caught in her father's open arms.)
There is no rehearsal, no second chance, no way to halt
This lunge. She was always going to come to harm.

She falls into her father's arms from various heights:
This was the light that held her darknesses from her.
Now, as she plunges, she invites the harm of night.
Into the smog and the New York noise she is hurled.

Out of the darkness, she blurs into light for a moment.
No one has time to point or scream at the miraculous
Sight. The streetlights and smog receive an angel sent
From the Empire Deck. Those above are still oblivious.

And then the car. No one has time to point or scream:
The word Forgive is already forming on thickening lips

As she curls into metal, perfectly. The Empire is a dream
She always had. She was contracted to climb to the tip.

Her lipsticked mouth is locked around a word, Forgive.
Yes, depression is holy. (Another soul has just been called.)
The orchid is a contract she clutches in one hand: To live
You must climb to the very top, for it is a very long fall.

Playground Without Children

Ectopic event: five hundred thousand is a lot to lose
in one heroic tube. There are no kids on your swings.

There is not one toddler in various colours playing on
your slide. And no child wanders down by the water

and very nearly falls in. The see-saw see-saws with
ghost girls and boys balancing each other while mother

looks on. Each and every month you know you have
failed. The seasons continue with little interruption

to this lack of life. Christmases, you search the empty
stocking. You dream at night of knitting booties and

try your best to not recite the feast of tiny feet leaving.
(And still the snow lies round about – deep, crisp, even.)

ALISON CROGGON 1962–

Alison Croggon was born in Carltonville, South Africa, and came to Australia via Cornwall in the UK at age seven. She went to school in Ballarat and was a cadet journalist on the Melbourne *Herald*. She has published seven collections of poetry and a quartet of highly popular young adult fantasy novels, *Pellinor*. She has had nine works of theatre produced and is a theatre critic. Her husband is a playwright. Croggon's poetry asks for a passionate, almost theatrical declamation. In a 2003 email interview with Rebecca Seiferle, Croggon said: "Over the past couple of years I've become aware of and interested in the very long history of utopian writing by women ... the formal qualities of the work are as much part of the expression and imagining as any other part." In her most successful poems she is able to resolve the risk inherent in ecstatic/Utopian writing, by formal rigor and keeping the imagery specific.

The Elwood Organic Fruit and Vegetable Shop

I will go walking in Elwood with my mind as smooth as a marrow
winking at the unruffled sky throwing its light down for free
letting the gardens exude their well-groomed scents and thinking everything
good

to the Elwood Organic Fruit and Vegetable Shop:
for the counter is democratically in the centre and everyone smiles
for people go on with the civil business of buying and selling under the
handwritten notices
for bawling children are solaced with grapes and handled to leave no bruises
for the mangoes are soft yellow thighs and the strawberries are klaxons of
sweetness
for the mignonette purses its frilly lips and snowpeas pout their discreet
bellies and the melons hug their quirky shapes under their marvellous
rinds
for onions ringing their coppery globes and o the silver shallots and the
hairy trumpets of leeks
for the cabbages folding crisp linens and the broccolis blooming in purple
tulles and the dense green skirts of lettuces,
for peaches like breasts of angels and passionfruits hard and dark and
bursting with seed in your palm
for the dull gold flesh of pontiacs and knotty umbers of yams and new
potatoes like the heels of babies
for the tubs of sweet william and heart-lifting freesias and orchids damp
and beautiful as clitoral kisses
for poignant basil and maiden-haired fennel and prim bluelipped rosemary
and o! irrepressible mint!
how they nestle up the vegetables, promising them the fragrance of their
ardour!
the marriages which await them! the lips that moisten to meet them!
glorious speech of the earth!

Ode

We were woken too early, before the moths had died in the streets,
when buds had barely hardened in the frost, when stars are hurtful
and famished. They took us through gardens and past the halls
where once we had lingered, past the houses and doused markets.
Our footsteps echoed back like iron. Of course we were frightened,
that was a given, of course we remembered photographs we had studied
that then had nothing to do with us. The empty light of morning
made anything seem possible, even freedom, even God. We stumbled
on familiar roads, and everything turned away from us,
lamp-posts, windows, signs. They weren't ours any longer. Even the air
greeted us differently, pinching our skin to wake us from its dreams.

*

Words of course were beyond us. They were what killed us
to begin with. They were taken away from the mouths that loved them

and given to men who worked their sorceries in distant cities,
who said that difficult things were simple now and that simple things
no longer existed. It was hard to find our way, we understood
the tender magic of hands, we knew the magic of things not spoken,
but this was a trick we couldn't grasp. It lifted the world in a clump of glass
and when everything came back down the streets had vanished.
In their places were shoes and clotting puddles and sparking wires
and holes and bricks and other things that words have no words for
and that silence swelling the noise until you can't hear anything at all.

*

It's said that the dead don't dream, but I dream of flowers.
I could dream so many flowers – lilies like golden snow on water,
hyacinths the colours of summer evenings or those amaranths they call
love-lies-bleeding. I dream of none of those. I dream instead
of wind-blown roses that grew in our shabby yard, of daisies
glimpsed through the kitchen window, of marigolds that glowed
through nets of weed. But most of all, I dream of red anemones
that never grew in my garden. They rise on slender stalks,
their seven-petalled heads bobbing and weaving in the wind.
Wind-flowers, Pliny called them, because they open only in the wind,
and the wind scatters their petals over every waste in the world.

EMMA LEW 1962–

Emma Lew was born in Melbourne, studied Arts at the University of Melbourne and has worked as a deckhand, shop assistant, proofreader, receptionist and clerical assistant. She began writing poetry in 1993 and has published two collections. She likes forms that ring the changes on lines and phrases. Her usual poetic method is bricolage: the assembling and polishing of disparate phrases, that verge on meaning, usually not realised. She has an ability to suggest a whole historical era (such as the Russia of her ancestry) with an incisive lightness of touch. She published the following letter in *Quadrant* in November 2002:

> SIR: ... I ... wish to correct Patrick McCauley's misrepresentation of my work. He says: "Emma Lew's methodology involves writing down lines and phrases which take her eye from everywhere and anywhere ... She then arranges the lines, changes a word here and there, and bingo, a poem."
>
> This implication that what I do amounts to throwing together random fragments, and then passing it off as poetry, is false. Yes, I often use lines and phrases from a range of sources, but only as a starting point. Everything I use I work and rework, usually taking weeks to create what, for me, is a coherent poem with the sense and mood I'm seeking to convey. There's no "bingo" about it. The final draft would rarely contain even one line or phrase from the original material.

Detail for a Lily Scheme

When a woman gets married it is because she is hungry, thirsty or naked.
Take her straight from the fields and threshing floors.
Give her anything, so long as it's gold,
and a little bunch of those white flowers they sell on street corners.

Straight out of the fields and threshing floors,
she comes carrying the bloom of youth, and the threat,
and a little bunch of those white flowers they sell on street corners.
Her silence means consent.

Carrying with her the bloom of youth, and the threat,
she simmers like a bone in soup,
so that all you can hold against her is her silence.
It's autumn already. Can the forest burn?

She simmers like a bone in soup,
growing strong on the very pity she feels for herself.
It's autumn already. Can the forest burn?
But not even that would soften her hatred.

She grows strong on the very pity she feels for herself.
Give her anything, so long as it's gold,
though none of it will soften her hatred.
When a woman gets married it is because she is hungry, thirsty or naked.

Ghetto Poem

The spectacle is not so chilling after all.
By degrees the people become accustomed to the gate,
to the work, to the little injustice.
Still others find relief in poetry.
Anyone may stumble all of a sudden.
Trust is a laudable virtue only in ordinary times.
With awe and reverence, I am hiding
the pages that can tell about the quiet groans.
I have trifled with the fear of death,
the shameful recoiling and desire to strike.
But can one wear the clothes of someone who has perished?
Can one eat in the presence of a corpse?

They Flew Me in on the Concorde from Paris

They flew me in on the Concorde from Paris.
We were fortunate not to burn.
Over Shanghai I observed to my flautist husband,

"Such a metropolis needs a decent opera house."
He rejected me in late May.
I resolved in future to express my feelings through my garden,
With an archway of zucchinis and cucumbers,
A bed of apothecary roses and high-yield grass seeds.

In the carpark at the Institute of Space Research
Women workers were performing their role of holding up half the sky,
While shipping companies complained about reserves of grain
Silting up the anchorage and all the sputnik could do was bleep.

I lodged with a senior government official in four elegant pavilions
Named after four seasons and bedecked with imitation sheep carcasses.
It was almost unthinkable not to give,
But I had no hard currency and could not afford contraceptives.
Thus I took a tonic in winter to be able to hunt tiger in spring.

I delivered my acceptance speech in the Great Hall of the People.
Citing the Scripture of Mountains and Seas,
I began by calling on steel makers to take up the way of Lamaism.
"Let's start calming down!" I cried.
"Let's get off painting and onto banking.
Differences are secondary to common interests,
They should not affect bilateral ties in a larger sense."

I was applauded by reformists and conservatives alike.
Tell that to the lady in the morgue.
And tell her,
"When you get to heaven,
Maybe you'll get some answers."

Caught in the Act of Admiring Myself

I love it when my doctor laughs in spite of himself,
like we're equals.
The fact that he suggested I start
making medium-term plans
must mean he thinks I'm doing well,
because generally it's the better adjusted
who're up to making plans.
Consider,
he said,
working out
some aims professional/personal
and ways to achieve them –

a two-year/five-year plan.
But doctor,
I'm busy with the big nectarine in the fruit bowl
while the world plans around *me!*
Yes, and I sketched
a little gesture of doubt in the air
without moving my chin from my hand.

Berchtesgaden

She tells a strange story of Hitler's love of astrology
She saw Goebbels with a red weal on his face
She says Hess is an addict of heroin
And says of Himmler *He still suffers from the effects of*
venereal disease contracted when he was only
a lad of twenty
Coarse Goering is always cracking jokes
Contrary to popular belief, the Führer is a late riser
Lunch is his favourite meal and begins with vegetable soup
He has a passion for trout served with butter sauce
Sweet potatoes usually accompany the fish
Sometimes an eagle is seen circling in the blue air
Guests assemble on the balcony before the dinner hour
Munich radio brings them *Die Lustige Wittwe*
Rounded forms of crockery gleam in the great hall
The Führer's pockets are always filled with chocolates

Snow and Gold

So, on the heels of the army, our troupe moved.
I gave birth in the street and night nailed the great city to the earth.
I saw the plague stalking like a stranger whose language I could not understand.
My sores were dressed, my handkerchiefs hemmed.

It is one thing to listen to the heart and its murmurs.
A strange woman came to see me, saying that she was my lover's wife.
It was the twilight hour that is called the "grey hour", when mourners become lost and follow the wrong coffin.
We walked a little way together; and the talk burned like agate.

I know they say that one should speak well of the dead or not speak at all.
The winter came in one jump like the wolf.
An eye grew sightless because there were frightening scenes I did not wish to see.

I had talent for the noble virtues of blind faith even then.

An agile acrobat threw his plank across the ditch.
The wine now travelled from mouth to mouth.
The sentry's face clouded over, and he wept at the prompting of my fingers on the strings.
So the young men paid their precious francs.

The wagons pulled out to the east like a sunburst.
Of course I sang, like a log covered with ice.
We lived unbuttoned through the black country,
taking such great mouthfuls of bread, as though we were seagulls.

What was I besides the strength of my shadow?
I climbed up on the trains and tossed down coal.
The wind blew and merged with me, my childhood and my life, my passions and transgressions.
Even if they weren't gold, the trinkets glittered.

I often wonder how unpenitent people could live under a sky.
It was that kind of Tatyana I had come to be.
Let my father say as many harsh and stupid things as he likes,
but the skin of my hands was like fine snow.

Light Tasks

I arrived in bits,
furious at Copenhagen.
The swans were stretching their necks and biting.
The donkeys stumbled badly on the descent.

How nice your compliments sounded –
it was as if the lights in the priory hall
had been turned on all at once.
The cabbage was marvellous.
Oh! If only I were dressed better!

You seemed a little wanton.
Thistledown, someone said.
And all were weeping, men with white beards.
The dog had perhaps been noble and faithful.

Thousands of pineapples came
by steamer.
The policemen on the streets gave directions
in the most attentive fashion.
The church arches were splendid,

the pillars slender,
and when we were walking on the road
you wrote the word *changelessness* in the sand with your foot.

My mind was like an angel sinking.
Among the ruins of four walls you showed me the sea –
how it and the starry sky were constructed.
It was ebbtide. I undressed.
How many hearses in the coming year?

The children herding cows were so beautiful.
One questioned me about the darkness.
Ships with all their sails, I said.
All the melodies of pain at every shift,
and then the endless moon, growing and growing.

Nous

All things are formed from water
Our world is one of many
The sun at night does not go beneath
The earth is a flat disk resting on air

Each thing contains portions of all things
Each atom is solid, unchanging, uncreated
The soul is moved by a touch
The sun shines only because it is day

Thought is located in the blood
Sound is material, a bundle of atoms
The sun is formed of little sparks
From ether to earth and back is slow

Fire is the ultimate matter
The atoms swerve without a cause
The sun shines and forgets
Each world will be dissolved again

Darkness mixed with fire causes night and its stars
Love is an agreement between unlike things
Only the changeless sphere can exist
All things flow but everything returns

CRAIG SHERBORNE 1962–

Craig Sherborne was born in Sydney and went to live in country Victoria in 1987. He has written plays which have been performed for stage and radio, a verse play and two volumes of memoir: *Hoi Polloi* (2005) and *Muck* (2007). He has has been a senior writer for the Melbourne *Herald Sun* and has published two collections of poetry. "The Poem" is from Sherborne's first collection *Bullion* (1995). Many of the poems in this volume have a rural setting with finely observed details. The voice is sympathetic, but distanced. All of the other poems selected here are from his second book, *Necessary Evil* (2006). In this book Sherborne's poetry became startlingly autobiographical. There is an immediacy and nakedness. Sherborne was asked in an interview if there was anything he would not write about, and his answer was no. In "Suburban Confidential", "Randwick" refers to Randwick race course. In "Brett's Mum", "the Coolabah's dripping nose" is the nozzle of a cardboard cask of Coolabah wine, and "Alpines" are a mentholated cigarette.

The Poem

This is the poem that the town passes through.
A curved hedge of hill-scrub passes through it,
And a lookout road below the sun-dial of one tree –

That tree points a blunt shadow-finger this way
And leans in the wind that passes through the poem,
And the chaff blown from harvest lorries passes through it,

And the lorries themselves – at the join of dipping
Paddocks they swell from a pinpoint on frayed tar-seal
That lengthens like a river and passes through the poem,

And the roundabout it spools on passes through it,
And the plaiting rail-tracks and the soot-black carriage tubs,
And the barley dust lifting from platform cellars

With an odour of sacking damp and malt.
The elevator loading belts rattle through the poem,
And silence sometimes follows them,

And footsteps sometimes follow that,
And the poem is the centre where windscreens glimmer
Then vanish in a tunnel of park elms.

Crows hang like mobiles and pass through the poem,
They creak "OhOh" like a practised complaint,
And ducks in pond-weed pass through and back, feeding

Or mating like two waters fighting.
And the minutes ticking in the ground-clock of petunia
And seconds ticking in the sprinklers pass through it,

And the steam from strawed soil and water-darkened grass
And water-darkened courthouse paving.
Two men on the steps there laugh through the poem,

They smoke and confide and wait in their suitcoats.
A boy walks the wheels of his bike towards them
Then rides off the footpath and passes through the poem.

And the scratched breeze of a radio continually passes,
And the faint bark-coughs of the pound dogs,
And drifts of perfume and burning onions

And petrol spilt from the garage pumps.
The flaking gold names of the war-memorial pass
When butcher-birds take a piece of them for home.

Carrier bags cartwheel through the poem,
And a broom in the main street sweeps through it four times,
And shop-front awnings dim the poem

Behind their flapping green canvas windows.
The brick-yard storm drains trickle through it
Foamed and slimed with kitchen peelings,

And carpenters building the trotting-track stable
Build it on the poem, on ladders.
Houses fenced with roof iron sprawl through the poem,

And their bleached lawns sprawl, windrowed with rotting cuttings.
And vacant blocks grow saplings through it,
And sheep gaze through it, mouthing their food.

And the cemetery's stone beds crumble through the poem,
And the tip smoulders through it in shallow pits
Where magpies walk through the poem through mud

Along a whitewashed wall of sky and smoke.
The stray finds scattered there, are scattered
Through the poem – the fanged palings and tyre-licorice,

The shoe-heels and shattered glass.
They heat in the sun's light that passes through the poem
And has no message other than itself.

A Racing Life

My uncles and I weren't related.
They had something they did in Chinatown.
They poked a washboard of maths

on their betting stands, and wore
a white side-drummer's bag.

They flashed the badge of their stomachs
at my father, fist on hips, parting
the curtain of their suit-coats.
He flashed his stomach back,
took off his porkpie hat to lick
his thumb across its feather.
My mother chose what colour rose
he popped in his lapel.

You were in the know or you weren't.
You said "zilch" not "nothing".
You plunged on Comet Boy
at 33 to I because you got the wink
Presidium was nobbled.

That night my father trampolined on the bed,
flinging dollars from his mackintosh pockets.
My mother grabbed and shrieked,
heaping a pommel of them in her lap,
her temples wet from heat and drink
as if there was water in money-rain.

Trophy Hair

My mother slept in toilet paper.
She tore it from a roll in bandage lengths
and wrapped it round her hairdo.
"A military operation" my father called it,
staring into a Western as she bound
her steepled armour against
the pillow's dishevelling influence.

He'd push their separate beds together
and she'd spray and pat a spot like a headwound,
clipping the brittle turban into place with brush and comb hands.
From the television of her heart-shaped mirror
she rated each sculpture fresh from the salon –
"8 out of 10 on the social scene" –
then removed the performance of her face with Ponds,
the black fan-dance of her eyes.

Her real teeth were pulled because false ones don't yellow.
A string-of-pearls choker for her goiter's stitched smile,

a flaw she covered with her fingers in the time
it took to kill the lampshade light.

He'd help her lay it down to sleep with,
that rustling paper cap he cupped from behind,
its candy floss swirl peach-tinted and hollow,
face powder dandruffing her hairline.
"Peach is what they're wearing," she promised.
"If you touch it I'll just die."

Race Day

I help my mother into her bosom,
zip her spine till
the freckled cleft is in position
and the dress is a drum between her shoulder blades.
"Thank you, Half Man," she says, meaning *boy*.
"All that meat and no potatoes," my father jokes at her,
parting his hair to the skin.

Next comes a monocle of eyebrow and lashes.
Now the other.
The elastic sheen of her coloured-in mouth
and red glove of nails she blows on as if for luck.
Nylon legs, dark brown for varicose veins.
A list she ticks through with a finger
and ends with a prayer: "OK God. Let us play."

He usually does. Her pillow's tangs
are hairspray and whisky when
I kiss her good afternoon the next morning.
She murmurs without waking,
so I check for any coins on the floor
that she calls chicken feed.

Suburban Confidential

The pickpockets at Randwick called their business Skims.
They had Fly, Gloves and Legman instead of Christian names.
They said wads were Crops and talk was Mail.
Watches and bracelets were Tin.

Jockeys whip with a little oar. But *they*
called Whipping the fingering for black wallets
tucked like the skin of the heart.
How do you do it? I asked. "Practice. Practice."

I was crouched in walk-socks, underfoot of the people,
scouring for winnings among discarded slips.
There they stood in tracksuits, Love-Hate on their knuckles,
"We call you Periscope," they said. "The way you're updown in the Herd."

From the um-pah-pah rotunda I watched
their pincer-move below: Fly sauntered
anti-clockwise to the crowd and threaded
his arm in-out of the Joe.

Gloves took the pass in a newspaper mitt
and snuck it to Legman who squeezed into the sun
where a bugle called for Horsemen of the Optimists
to canter to the barrier please.

Practice. Practice – I tried it at home.
In my father's wardrobe there were seven empty suits.
I play-picked their pockets till the hangers
didn't swing fanning his smell's creamy lotions.

At my mother's end there were purses with crossed fingers:
I pried in their bladders with a soft unspring.
She had hair plaits and earrings like clip-on oysters,
pearl handfuls and chainy tangles.

I wore them with lipstick at her sit-down mirror,
and fell in love with my boy-woman skin.
When bored with wrapping her scarves into turbans
I kissed the glass in puckered mists

and searched the drawers for something confidential,
a secret compartment I could spy in.
Of course there was no such thing,
no glamorous code-books,

no false walls with diamonds.
Handkerchiefs and socks covered what was private:
a book of sex acts called *Danish Passions*,
an open pack of condoms.

Brett's Mum

She'd peck me on the lips like an extra son.
I'd lick away the crayon tang. Purse the red
on to my finger. My father called her
a glamour-puss. My mother called her 40.

She wore jeans and buckles with plastic flowers.
The day Van der Hum won the Melbourne Cup
she had a calf-skin top on, with lace-up buttons.
Brett was away, staying at his father's.

I passed club sandwiches around the lounge
to the Cup-muzak on the tele.
My mum conducted smoke with her cigarette.
Dad pinched the Coolabah's dripping nose.

In the kitchen she touched my arm a lot,
tucked my hand in her fist and went "Mmm",
offered me sips from her icy glass – I winced
at medical stings of gin. Who did what first?

There was a sliding door into her laundry,
a drier's Coke-bottle eye. The crack
of her bust rode up as the door rolled shut behind.
In close-up, lipstick stuck to her teeth like food.

She breathed herself up to my face – the Alpines
going bad, the drinks of the day –
lifted her goggle-bra to let me when
I reached through wire and nylon to her skin.

For the first time I saw pain-bliss on a face.
If something was said it was along the lines of:
"Brett mustn't know," whispered to my throat;
"I won't blab at school," muttered to her hair.

But then her forehead slumped to my shoulder.
She held my wrists so they couldn't move,
sobbed with no tears, just little sniffs and shrugs,
backing out the door to unskew clothing.

I touched the heat where her groin had used my knee.
The air of her smells cooled to lint, mouldy water.
She cut cheese on a platter.
The unsaid thing it said was: "That never happened."

Plastic Flowers

My tribe is roses that never peel back their foreskins,
taffeta leaves growless in the TV sun.
"You can't tell the difference," my mother warns
in case you try to look down your nose.
Here she comes now, the old girl, dressing gown gaping,

its faded leopard spots, her ankles swelled from too much sitting.
She straightens that photo of my ex-wife on the table,
The *ex* part of which she's never got used to.

Here's the old boy trying to change the subject,
hitching his walk-socks to stand for speeching.
"I'm in for more tests," he complains, excited,
unbuttoning his shirtfront to his scar.
"It's the doctor keeps *me* evergreen."

Ham sandwiches again for their dinner;
two fizzing Saccharine in each cuppa sweetens the air bitter.
What time is it? Time's no longer for watches.
It's *The Bold and The Beautiful* hour, *The Young and The Restless.*
Time of the week to dust with old undies
Nylon Frangipani, wire Queen Anne's Lace:
soothing them by their Christian names *That's Better; That's Nice.*

Ash Saturday

There is no God, I was made in *this* man's image:
those slate-dark eyes of his are mine,
the dented bridge of our his-my nose.
I laugh with his rasping cackle in me.
I walk with his stooping, trudging gait,
swearing his "Jesus bloody Christ"
in a sudden fist-curl of temper.
My right ear points like a flesh-antenna as his does,
and being my father I bear his name.
Haphazardries of kin passed on from birth
that to see him wizened on his cancer bed,
his insides turned to water,
is to view my own death, my own Dorian Gray
smiling, weeping in the drug-bliss of sleeping
or counting out life on his fingers:
"I've got more money than I thought," he says.
"And I can't even wipe my arse."
I soak a flannel and do it for him,
the first time I've touched his privates.
The doctor says he could go on for hours,
but no he won't, the nurse assures me.
She gives him a last injection.
"If there's something unsaid, best say it now.
He won't wake up from this one."

Now I scatter him in the surf.
This is what a man burns down to:
bone's grey grit like broken pebbles.
Not ash but grit and blood-brown dust
from the coffin they called "Mahogany".
The same salt 'n' pepper as his shaven stubble
that whiskered the sink-white from his razor,
the Brylcreemed hair he palmed skin-smooth
after combing with his tongue poked forward.
Some of him sticks to my swimming hands –
I shudder and dunk to wash him from me,
splash myself like an accidental ritual,
but it's too late, the symbol remains:
He always stood between me and death,
but now I'm next in line, I inherit his future,
a law bequeathed that's impossible to alter,
a murder-chain sanctioned as natural.

I've already moved into his death:
I've tried on his clothes for a decent fit
and sorted the rest for the Salvos.
I used his screwdriver to jemmy the plug
from this beige plastic tube he came in.
It exhaled a false puff of breath.
In a minute I'll escort my mother from the beach,
her taking my arm like a younger he,
casting his funeral flowers to the shallows.
"Looks cold that water," she'll worry with a shiver.
"You don't think we should have buried him?"
She'll complain how the pins-and-needles sand
is stinging her legs like mosquitoes.

She'll hope out loud there's nothing funny with his will
and expects her sister to be over for a hand-out.
Then we'll turn for one more chance to watch
where his slick dissolved in the buckled swell,
stretched into invisibility.
I'll blink and utter "Goodness" with her
as if death really was a mystery after all
and dwells out there in all that sea and twilight.
But death's no mystery, not to me, not now.
I am its DNA.

TRICIA DEARBORN 1963–

Tricia Dearborn was born in Glenn Innes, New South Wales. She has degrees in Biochemistry and Arts and has worked as a senior editor in an educational publishing house. She has published one collection of poetry *Frankenstein's Bathtub* (2001). Judith Rodriguez has described Dearborn's poetry as "a voice that's fresh, a mind in enquiry mode." In a note to "Come In, Lie Down" Dearborn said: "I'm a fan of clarity. I want the writing to get through, to get *in*, to hit me with its full force … not to lodge as a puzzle in my brain. For the latter, there are cryptic crosswords … the only autobiographical note I'd add is that there was an amusing moment beforehand where I said, 'There *is* something we need to talk about …', and X – the 'you' of the poem – said matter-of-factly, 'You're a lesbian'. He explained he'd seen the stickers on my car …"

The Pouch of Douglas

Although eponyms should be avoided, they are in frequent use and a guide to their meaning is useful – O'Rahilly, *Anatomy*

a friend who went for a pelvic ultrasound was relieved to hear she had no unusual fluids in her pouch of Douglas

what she didn't know was that the pouch of Douglas is a small pocket in the female body in which reside all the eponyms that physicians have tacked onto this extraordinary anatomy

filed alphabetically, and if you care to look you'll see Bartholin's glands right next to Frankenhauser's ganglion, which rubs up against the Graafian follicle

the canal of Nuck, on the other hand, will be found nestled between Mackinrodt's ligament and the tubules of Skene

so where exactly *is* this pouch of Douglas? it is in fact the little space between the back of the uterus and the front of the rectum

two good solid names that at least a woman can call her own

Schlieren Lines

imagine you pour a stream of
sugar solution into a beaker
of water, or pee into a bathtub
you see the twining translucent trails
as each solution curls around the
other, prior to their coalescence?

these are schlieren lines
my biochem hons supervisor –
the one who gave me to work with

radioactive compounds so old
they had no hope of giving me
cancer, let alone decent results –

taught me this much. I don't quite
forgive him the dodgy materials,
or for telling me in detail of his wife's
travails with cystitis, over a cup of tea
and a plain biscuit at 11, the old
laboratory ritual, with the autoclave

busily hissing steam and the smell
of dilute ethanol drifting from ranked test
tubes in gradated hues of pink. But I grant
that he gave me that unique pleasure
of having at last a word for
the thing I could never name.

At the Laundromat on Rue St Florent

My tired reflected face is framed
by the curving leap

of my jeans –
always the last to relinquish

the final skerricks of damp, not dry
till the rivets will brand your skin.

I watch as the jeans submit
with seeming grace, or joy,

tumbling to rest, then
leaning back legs spread

as they're lifted and tossed across
in streaming freefall.

Like the fearless girl lining up again
for the wildest ride;

or a child turned upside down
and swung and begging for

one more go.
Though later when the denim

flattens momentarily to the glass,
falls back, and is pressed again,

it's more like someone
get me out of here.

Come In, Lie Down

I'm new to you and your let's-get-to-it.
Flat on my back that first time
not five minutes after the front door

snicked behind you. New to this
excoriating tenderness passion
that leaves me stubble-scraped and scabbed

The shock of those miniscule nipples!
The lean hairy thigh that met my palm
and made me laugh out loud. Later you asked

was it OK, for sex with an alien?
Women are sea-creatures, you said,
one hand curved at the soft swell of my thigh.

Like seals. And men are goats. I like you
inside me when I want it. I like how you held my hair back
that first time we stood there kissing. You come

so close to sating me with touch, stroke into me
relaxation I rarely know.
Round up and banish ancient threats

whose names I'm beginning not to recognise. Still –
I miss that brine-lapped cleft, the way that sealskin
glides on sealskin. One day I must

go down to the seas again.

The Changes

Kissing Louise was a bell. Unlike
the chimes of the genteel drawing-room clock
it gave no warning before it struck.

It was more like the shock of the extra-early
morning alarm
on the day of the journey.

Or the sudden shrilling of a schoolroom bell,
calling me in
to a strange new lesson.

It rang sweet as a tardy dinner gong
summoning me to a meal
of scent and heat.

Resonated like a great church bell
calling the villagers over fields
to christenings, to benedictions.

My throat sang my body
swung my skin shone
and my old life shivered and fell from me

and lay like the sweat of the ringers in the tower.

JOHN KINSELLA 1963–

John Kinsella, born in Western Australia, has published over twenty collections of poetry, including *Peripheral Light, Selected and New Poems* (2003), which was chosen and introduced by the distinguished American critic, Harold Bloom. Kinsella has also published two books of fiction and a memoir. He has held positions at British, American and Australian universities, was the founder of the publisher *Salt*, edited the *Penguin Anthology of Australian Poetry* (2009) and shares a blog with his wife, Tracy Ryan: "Mutually Said: Poets Vegan Anarchist Pacifist". Kinsella's poetry reflects his growing up in rural Western Australia, or at other times the theories of L=A=N=G=U=A=G=E poetry in America, which he refers to as "the separation of self from text".

The Silo

Visitors, as if they knew, never remarked
on the old silo with its rammed earth walls
and high thatched roof, incongruous amongst
the new machinery and silver field bins.
Nor the workers brought in at harvest time,
trucks rolling past the ghostly whimperings,
snarls and sharp howls cutting the thick silo's
baffling. Nor when a bumper harvest filled
every bin and the farmer was hungry
for space – no one ever mentioned bringing
the old silo back into service. This
had been the way for as far back as could
be remembered. Thin sprays of baby's breath
grew around its foundations, while wedding
bouquet sprouted bizarrely from the grey
mat of thatching. The sun had bleached the walls

bone-white while the path to the heavily
bolted door was of red earth, a long thin
stream of unhealthy blood. Before those storms
which brew thickly on summer evenings
red-tailed black cockatoos settled in waves,
sparking the straw like a volcano, dark
fire erupting from the heart of the white
silo, trembling with energy deeper
than any anchorage earth could offer.
And lightning dragging a moon's bleak halo
to dampen the eruption, with thunder
echoing out over the bare paddocks
towards the farmhouse where an old farmer
consoled his bitter wife on the fly-proof
verandah, cursing the cockatoos, hands
describing a prison from which neither
could hope for parole, petition, release.

Drowning in Wheat

They'd been warned
on every farm
that playing
in the silos
would lead to death.
You sink in wheat.
Slowly. And the more
you struggle the worse it gets.
"You'll see a rat sail past
your face, nimble on its turf,
and then you'll disappear."
In there, hard work
has no reward.
So it became a kind of test
to see how far they could sink
without needing a rope
to help them out.
But in the midst of play
rituals miss a beat – like both
leaping in to resolve
an argument
as to who'd go first
and forgetting

to attach the rope.
Up to the waist
and afraid to move.
That even a call for help
would see the wheat
trickle down.
The painful consolidation
of time. The grains
in the hourglass
grotesquely swollen.
And that acrid
chemical smell
of treated wheat
coaxing them into
a near-dead sleep.

Goat

Goat gone feral comes in where the fence is open
comes in and makes hay and nips the tree seedlings
and climbs the granite and bleats, through its line-
through-the-bubble-of-a-spirit-level eyes it tracks
our progress and bleats again. Its Boer heritage
is scripted in its brown head, floppy basset-hound ears,
and wind-tunnelled horns, curved back for swiftness.
Boer goats merged prosaically into the feral population
to increase carcass quality. To make wild meat. Purity
cult of culling made vastly more profitable. It's a narrative.
Goat has one hoof missing – just a stump where it kicks
and scratches its chin, back left leg hobbling, counter-
balanced on rocks. Clots of hair hang like extra legs
off its flanks. It is beast to those who'd make devil
out of it, conjure it as Pan in the frolicking growth
of the rural, an easer of their psyches when drink
and blood flow in their mouths. To us, it is *Goat*
who deserves to live and its "wanton destruction"
the ranger cites as reason for shooting on sight
looks laughable as new houses go up, as dozers
push through the bush, as goats in their pens
bred for fibre and milk and meat nibble forage
down to the roots. Goat can live and we *don't know*
its whereabouts. It can live outside nationalist tropes.
Its hobble is powerful as it mounts the outcrop

and peers down the hill. Pathetic not to know
that it thinks as hard as we do, that it can loathe
and empathize. Goat tells me so. I am being literal.
It speaks to me and I am learning to hear it speak.
It knows where to find water when there's no water
to be found – it has learned to read the land
in its own lifetime and will breed and pass its learning
on and on if it can. Goat comes down and watches
us over its shoulder, shits on the wall of the rainwater
tank – our lifeline – and hobbles off
to where it prays, where it makes art.

TRACY RYAN 1964–

Tracy Ryan was born in Western Australia, where she now lives. She grew up in a large family, and after reading English at Curtin University, studied European languages at the University of Western Australia. She has translated French writers, including Helene Cixous, Maryline Desboilles and Francoise Han. She spent some years living in Britain and the USA where she worked in libraries, bookselling, editing and community journalism, and taught at universities. She has two children and is married to John Kinsella with whom she shares a blog: "Mutually Said: Poets Vegan Anarchist Pacifist".

First Burn

All day she has pitched dry grass, Hardyesque,
perched on the stack, helping to raze the block
in a race against shire deadlines: fire risk.

Only her colours are wrong – curls a stark
hedge in English autumn, young fragile skin
dead-of-winter white. But she will work

to feel she's useful, wanting to fit in,
all my cautions thrown to the easterly,
hot from the desert. I've done all I can –

this is the point, the moment beyond me
for which we've struggled, locked like Gabriel
and Jacob, though the outcome may not be

a blessing. She is tall and capable,
strong on the outside – surely that's enough.
To look at her now no one else could tell

what tinder, what touchwood she was made of.
By evening there appears a subtle glow
upon her shoulders, imprinted as if

someone had held her fast; by morning so
reddened and furious she is aflame
with reproaches, and cries: *You made me go*

to England and then you made me come home.
Non-sequitur, she knows, but all the same
I am the mother, I must wear the blame.

LUCY DOUGAN 1966–

Lucy Dougan was born and grew up in Perth where she now lives. She was poetry editor for HEAT magazine and has completed a Ph.D. She has published two books of her poetry. A note for "The Quilt" says that it "owes a debt to Gerald Brenan's *Personal Record 1920–1972* (Jonathan Cape, 1974) and to Mary Ann Caws's *Women of Bloomsbury* (Routledge, 1990)."

The Quilt

You are the only person. who notices what I wear – this green dress, who will see how lovely it is?

Carrington to Gerald Brenan

She had cut up all her old dresses
and sent a quilt for their wedding bed, so
that each square might yield his spent caresses.

He sleeps with his bride beneath an old embrace,
her scent, her clothes – all the moments he had held
and his dreams are peopled by an awkward grace –

her white legs, green dress, brown hands
trailed in the stream at Watendlath.
At her death he'll write: nobody understands.

Restless as always, he tosses off the gift, her cover,
and remembers (her words) the big and devastating love
that she held, with and without hope, for another,

When this big love dies she wears his jackets.
If I could sit here: alone just holding his clothes ...
she sends the residue to friends in packets

they don't want. Everyone gets a love that's patched.
Just before sleep he recalls the warmth of her letters
and how in their separate lives, at least, they had matched.

Kindergarten Story

There are windows stuck with stars
and hybrid things.
If you lie on the ground and look up
the sky strains in through
cut-out clouds, uncertain zodiacs.

Children with blunt scissors,
small originators of these skies,
tear out pieces of the world
and stick them back again,
refiguring whole constellations.

I slip back into a kind of making.
Someone has lain gauze over the afternoon
and lulled us quiet a little without our consent.
There is a hum, a room-sound
only, nothing that could count as words.

I stretch out on the trail of broken stars
and feel where my bones meet the floor,
how they tell a kind of story
through my clothes. This could be
a lesson about striving not to know.

I'm pleased with each breath that comes and goes,
a certain smell their working makes.
I rise up on my knees, the carpet bites.
When I falter, their cutting composes me.
We stick up more and shut out the day's last light.

Woman Bird Woman

Driving, you see a woman
make her way
between the mail and her front door.
Upright and white-haired,
one hand rests on the svelte tweed
of her hip, the other
casually thrust behind,
fans out five letters like the tail
of some unnamed bird.

Think of this place before
the suburbs for a moment,
but keep the mail-bird woman there,

in your need for her to be
hybrid, original:
how she struts and looks up into the pink evening,
and how it doesn't matter
what is in the letters.
They become pure decoration.

She inhabits Lautréamont's principle
with ease – in this intersection
of a woman's hand and white paper.
With the heat in your face
you wonder how it is that
we can only explain a thing exactly
by making it another,
by coercion, by a kind of learned
violent look.

At this point
(even though you cannot see them)
you know her eyes,
on either side of her wily head,
are cocked to the sky.
To enter the shining dark of her pupils
and see the world differently
would be enough.

GREG McLAREN 1967–

Greg McLaren was raised in the Hunter Valley coalfields and studied at the University of Sydney which awarded him a Ph.D. for a thesis on Buddhist influences in the poetry of Harold Stewart, Robert Gray and Judith Beveridge. He has published three poetry collections. Writing in the online magazine *Jacket*, Nick Riemer says: "McLaren's poems are loaded with the past and animated by the attempt to understand and recover it. Not simply a past characterized by loss, though that is the predominant tone: among the many other details of an earlier life that McLaren relates, he excels at capturing the iconic moments of childhood in a small town ... In less deft hands this could be hackneyed and inauthentic, but McLaren succeeds in making it his own, and his recreation of a childhood around the Hunter Valley town of Kurri Kurri or somewhere like it is, to my urban sensibility at least, utterly convincing."

Greyhounds at dusk

Women in thin head-scarves and their husbands
walk greyhounds at dusk, down lanes

lined with paspalum, backed with grey fences,
rickety gates, loose sheds. The clack of the railway

and its small amounts of coal. The yellow light
of kitchen windows falls into the dark
cast by the near hills. The moon is behind
thick clouds, grey-lined, massing over the east.

The dogs' heads strain at their muzzles,
choking, tight-leashed. Cigarettes are lit.
They bob and loop, gesticulating past
the reach of streetlights, damped flares.

Voices come from them, far off.
As they come near there's talk
of running the bitch through her paces,
claiming the insurance on the car:

I've got a cousin call help you with that.
Thin dogs, chasing stuffed rabbit smell,
arf and wheeze. In daylight the Hanleys
buy groceries, and grow pumpkins

and chokoes on the vine. One winter
they win money on the dogs. The Abermain
cops nod and wink, pockets full of hands. Kids
walk the train line with chaff bags,

picking spilt coal for the fire, and milk bottles
for change. They throw stones at each other,
and threaten with the size of fathers,
the speed of dogs. Hands bruise quietly,

quiet as if it were your father home from the pub.
You wait for your mother's shift at the shop
to finish; there is the strange green light,
religious, of the coke bottles.

The dogs tied outside are glowing with dew.
Their breath hangs, framed in the doorway.
Cars pass by, trailing taillights. The three hubcaps
we find at the bus stop next morning don't match.

We roll them across the road between cars,
and get to school late. On the cold mornings
the fog cuts us off from the railway
the other side of the road. You can see maybe

as far as the fence, or the fat green frog

flopping across the lawn.
The dog trainers' voices echo, too,
phlegmy and cranky in the cold blank air.

EMILY BALLOU 1968–

Emily Ballou was born in Milwaukee in the United States and moved to Australia in 1991, going to live in the Blue Mountains. She has published two novels and is a screenwriter. She currently lives in Scotland. *The Darwin Poems* (2009), her only published book of poetry, is a verse-portrait of Charles Darwin, and was written during an Australia Council for the Arts residency in County Monaghan, Ireland.

Plunge *(from* The Darwin Poems*)*

You thrust your head through a lid of water
open-eyed to the sting of salt
that takes some time to adjust to
then look around.
Your curls swim. Fish scatter.

Pink velvet starfish cling to the green
slopes of sub-aqueous rock pools, the diorama spill
of strange flowers, opening, shutting mouths
draw you deeper
past grey-eyed cuttlefish
the circular gills barely perceptible
feathered edges of constant motion among the waving
fronds of seaweed hair & the rise & pop of silver
domes of air.

Here a corrosive, rusted land
beneath land, a forgotten twin place
on Earth where Man
does not belong, where sea
divides head from body
so thoroughly it is exiled;
the floating flesh
so much whiter, more defenceless;
this total, plunging, breathless despair.

Terror makes you leap up
suddenly from the depths
& laugh to find you were dunked
head down in two feet of water.

Go now. Deeper. Into the blue swallow.
If you're lucky enough you'll catch
a fever of sting rays
soaring past the ship in sinuous series
the great, slate, rugose weights;
little bodies embedded in wings.

When you capture one
& flip over its flat white belly, on the sand,
a small false face appears:
the side-gazing eyes
the nose-holes of its snout, the slit
of mouth gills dimpled on either side
like a smile –
wide, distended, intelligent
underwater humanity
you slice with a knife.

Nights when the sea
& everything you touch
lights up green, pours over you
mass & massive
you will remember
Volta's batteries
which he called his electric fish
& which were puzzled out
from the anatomy
of stingrays.

Coralline *(from* The Darwin Poems*)*

1.

Charles would never forget the limb of vital life
Professor Sedgwick
first planted in his mind;
a spring of water that flowed
from a chalk hill
and left an elegant tracery of lime
in brushwork lines on twigs.
This bubbling cave of transmutation
Stendhal then turned to a staff of salt jewels
before his eyes
into which longing itself had crystallised.

Darwin, The Eager, had searched the source
and not satisfied with mere twig
had uprooted and flung an entire bush into the brook
hoping to come back
as love-caked as that
branching bone
he pulled from the water's spell.

2.
When love finally came
it accreted slowly,
gathering particle by particle
yet within a week it seemed
like the sheltered cave
of a shallow atoll
glittering with sand and sun
enclosing him
and he called her, his one,
coralline.

3.
They built their home
on the chalk downs
a silt bed of shell and bone
calcium carbonate
and filled the powdery rooms with stone
marble, wood, velvet, silk, calico.
They filled the pillows with down
feathers and papered the walls
with delicate mosaics
of petal and leaf, violet and rose.

Still the house soon grew
coralline too
spawning new babies and bodies
crystallising into a solid shape
regular, geometric as a frozen snowflake
a grain of salt
this colourless, time-telling, gem-encrusted form that love filled.

4.
A father and his four children, coral-handed, bandits all, take turns
strapping the magnifying glass across their eyes,

shuffling along the dining room wall
in search of Earth's most infinitesimal meanings
and the flicker of minutes
caught within the paper
enlarging to 300 times the power of the eye
the pale petrified postures
and skeletons of tiny sea creatures fossilised
beneath the flowers, preserved in chalk.

The children will ever afterwards
believe their house to be a giant barnacle
clinging to a buoy that sinks and rises again
with the weight of accretion,
some kind of sea-seeking
crystal palace. They lick
the north window panes on windy days
for the taste of salt.
Indeed, on winter nights the house windows glow
like Thompson's phosphorescence,
imperfectly known luminous points
on a raft of black sky;
yet when he sees them from the outside
the yellow lamps in his wife Emma's,
in his children's bedroom windows
he thinks
yes,
there is light
of the softest and most destructible tenderness.

5.
Love, love, our architectonic
is neither plant nor mineral
but both
neither animal nor island
but both
neither male nor female
but both
neither hard nor soft
but both
neither solitary nor colony
but both
neither fragile nor robust
but both

neither this nor that
and so both. And so all.
Microscopic, telescopic, generative,
we are home, architect and inhabitant;
love how we propagate
brain and branching
how we grow
from broken stems.

6.
And though she secretly hopes
you two will be for each other forever
you know
love will last as long as you last;
that you will return
to fossil, to salt, to chalk-
bones, your new home geology's strata
and your veins, your life force
will turn to quartz
your fingers to fossils, your brain
will become rock.
Soon, we too will be
wallpaper, my coralline.

Marriage *(from* The Darwin Poems*)*

"Detective Darwin," his wife would muse
as he sloshed in heavy-headed, mind-leaded from his room
"have you any extraordinary news, any vexing but enchanting clues
for me? A new barnacle perhaps, a perplexing addition
to your family tree we marine-wives at tea
teasingly call your Monster & Co? Though we don't mind
the slime of innuendo, or the wild surmising
when you & your heretical friends
(although I do like the chutney that Mr Hooker sends)
preach undersea reproduction
the stalks & sacks & budding of creatures;
we do not mind Mr *Arthrobalanus*, your deviant little barnacle,
nor the fact that you seem to be
increasingly cirripede-like (I have noticed your whiskers
waving at me), or even that you light your room
with luminous zoophytes at night
but I have been bothered by these strange constant leaks

of saltwater under doors
& do not speak of hermaphrodites
& double penes &c &c over the soup please,
at the very least when the children are present."

"Don't be cross at me dear wife & cousin Em, life is a contest
of forces, a Hegelian joust. Let the strongest forms
by their strength survive, & the weakest forms, well you see ...
& you, my sweet, are the perfect example
of the emergence of beauty
(though not order) from the struggle to be.
But I know you will wish me & my barnacles *al Diabolo*
when you hear of the half-inch female species, Mrs *Ibla*,
I found today, whose body, like a jacket, has two pockets
each manned by a tiny husband, & would you believe
what I do, that *'embedded in the flesh of their wives
they pass their whole lives ... as testis, mere bags of spermatozoa
& can never move again?'* But I shan't say
a word more about it, will upset you, except that I sense
my truth is a virtue & these minute males are truly
wonderful. Evidence that my species theory
(like confessing a murder I know) is *gospel*."

"It takes no quick work to know
that the wonder & riddle is one such as she,"
Emma said, "(the stronger sex indeed!)
who will put up with two useless, purple, sack-like chaps
affixed to her skirts & her bed for eternity without rest?
Asexual sprouting, or whatnot, no matter,
this cannot make for feminine happiness
with or without Heaven
but only proves as *gospel* what I, Emma,
dutiful and true, already knew:
that man & wife being constantly together for life
should have its limits.
Don't try to unseat me with your lance, dear Charley,
I have already budded seven for you."

BRONWYN LEA 1969–

Bronwyn Lea was born in Tasmania and grew up in Queensland and Papua New Guinea, with frequent moves as her father was in the construction industry. At seventeen she went to the United States, intending to stay for a year and stayed for twelve. She studied at California State University in San Diego. Returning to Australia, she completed a Ph.D. at the University of Queensland, where she now teaches in the School of English, Media Studies and Art History. She has a daughter who is a sculptor. Lea has published two collections of her poetry and a chap book. She said in an interview that she sees no dichotomy between the craft of a poem and its feeling: "A poem that is all feeling and no craft becomes kitsch, like a Hallmark card." She related to Dylan Thomas's approach: "to treat words as a craftsman does wood or stone – to hew, carve, mold, coil, polish, and plane words into patterns, sculptures, fugues of sound expressing some lyrical impulse, some dimly-seen truth that he must try to reach and realise." Lea has a note to "Standing in Bette Davis's Shoes" stating each sentence in the poem is spoken by a character played in a film by Bette Davis.

Original Sin

for RMD 1931–1997

Right before she died Rita said, *if*
I could live my life over again, I would
have more sex and fewer children.
and I believed her in Laguna Niguel,
sitting crosslegged at that French bistro,
ordering chocolate cake called *Original*
Sin, the pink rising in her English
cheeks like rice paper taking up the ink,
as she stared down the seven layers
of bittersweet wafer melded together
with cream and strawberries and floating
in a pool of hot maple syrup.
Fuck my diabetes, she whispered
after the handsome waiter left, *I'm eating.*
I can see her a teenage girl again,
lying among the backyard strawberries
this time to take her childhood sweetheart
now that she knows how: her heels and
shoulders, his elbows and knees pressing
into the loam, her back arched and falling
like a bridge. I can see her a young wife
standing in her kitchen, sipping scotch
and lifting her skirt for her husband

after work, her small hands gripping
the porcelain taps while he takes her
from behind. And the next morning,
arranging silk chrysanthemums in a vase,
then pushing aside the coffee table
with her foot, to straddle her husband's
best friend on the floor; while her only
child studies at school. And years later,
after all the suffering, after all his cheating
and her own, I am not surprised
to see Rita returning to her marriage bed,
her hands brushing the dry length
of her husband's limbs as if with flour,
kneading his soft muscle, their tongues
mingling with embarrassment, the shy
awkwardness of a man and woman
who have slept beside each other for forty-
five years making their hate known
and not remembering why.

Girls' Night on Long Island

We drink vodka martinis
with tiny onions and green olives,
eat popcorn and salty pork and talk
about circumcision. That's their problem,
we decide, their insecurity, the root
of their castration anxiety. Teresa laughs,
she's not complaining,
she thinks it's worth the sacrifice.
I shrug, fixing another drink, either way.
"What does she care?" Ruth asks,
"She's Australian!" and everybody laughs.
But Meg is happy at least one
woman's not fussy
because when her premature son
was born they stuck dozens of tubes
into his little red body,
and when he came out of ICU,
she just decided forget it. Ruth says
it was the same with her son,
though longer ago,
his lung burst in the delivery room –

from a resuscitator set at adult pressure –
and they took him to another hospital
to have the lung re-inflated.
For a week she cried,
without her child or any visitors,
and when she finally got him back,
she wouldn't let another doctor
touch him. And besides,
she laughs chewing on an olive,
all of her grandparents
and all of her uncles and all of her aunts
died at Auschwitz,
and she thought about this,
as she suckled her newborn son,
that if another Hitler came to power
at least he wouldn't get
this little Jew. And her words fall heavy
on the living room, just like the rain
falling outside. Meg is asleep.
Her second martini too much
after half a Xanex. Some of us turn
to the fire. Some of us turn
to the rain.

Bronwyn Lea

As Maureen O'Hara did, my mother named
her daughter after Anna Lee's Bronwyn Morgan
from *How Green Was My Valley*. I like to think

she did not know the burden she was inflicting
with a name meaning *white breast* – from the Welsh
braun meaning *fleshy & gwen* meaning *blessed* –

the metaphor was lost on schoolboys who came
up with more vulgar translations. Australian boys
hadn't heard of Branwen, daughter of King Llyr,

sent to Ireland to marry Matholwch, then banished
to the kitchen as a slave, her ears boxed daily
by the butcher – though if they had, I like to think

the boys might have been more gallant. Branwen
taught a starling to speak & sent it to Wales
to tell her brother Bran of her plight. His army

sailed to Ireland to rescue her, where a bloody battle
broke out: two kingdoms destroyed on her account,
Branwen fled to Aber Alaw & died of grief. Lea

means *meadow* – perhaps the one where Branwen was
buried – else a set of warp threads carried by a loop
of the heddle. Swapping vowels, *lee* is a place

sheltered from the wind, & back in Wales *lli*
becomes a stream. Always in the plural, *lees* is dregs –
as employed by Macbeth to himself on the state

of his soul: *Renown & grace is dead,*
The wine of life is drawn, & the mere lees
Is left this vault to brag of.

Said quickly, my name is an adverb: attached
to action so as to qualify it – as in, to travel *bronwynly*
which might be to travel within an ace of salvation

or to survive exile & die the first night home.
But it is my first not last name that leaps from the page –
I like to think it is my true family's name: Branwen

my foremother – ears bruised, pale breast exposed
to the pale Welsh sun – she walks upstream, leaving
no footprints, her vowels mutating through the years

her consonants & grief her only constants. She stares
at me – as a hunter stares down a deer – & smiles.
My name fits me perfectly as the arrow fits its wound.

Women of a Certain Age

Women of a certain age are waking up
in the middle of things – birth & death feel
blessedly far away – the raw edge of real
departure & arrival a distant memory –
days fleeting in restful harmony like leaves
seen through a window, drifting with all
the others until they are reimagined
again by light, time & rain. Women
of a certain age are waking to the sound
of their breathing which through the long dark
hours has frightened them. In their worry
to light up a few inches of the universe,
a fraction of the infinite, however minute,

they are waking before dawn to witness
a victory of light, the capture of every single
trench of shadow. The dawn will be theirs
to hold a little while – its lightness –
they will forget some of what they have
experienced & remember what they were
born with, including that which is too early
to remember. Women of a certain age – loving
this lightness – are rolling onto their sides,
rising out of their beds & out of their bodies,
imagining themselves free of the earth
& its drive to replace them, they are speeding
like comets over the edge of the universe,
falling & flying out of the familiar,
plummeting into the unknown to arrive
at a new hospitable household, having slipped
away without goodbyes only smoke as they burn –
bluer & bluer – on the last drop of fuel
found only in the bodies of women of a certain age.

Born Again

After the divorce he sold his house
by the beach & drove his Volkswagen
into the desert to die. He was gone
a year. I was living one vertical mile
above the desert floor – where he slept
in his car – in a house that overlooked
a great sweep of rocks & woodlands.
Instead of dying, god spoke to him.
God forgave all his trespasses. But I
didn't forgive his trespasses against me.
My heart was a long ledger. One day
he returned to collect our daughter.
My house was snowbound. I left him
to stand in the weather while I gathered
her things. It took a little while. When
I returned he was gone. Typical.
I looked around. Sparrows scratched
at the snow looking for seeds. I saw
a figure kneeling by a large granite
boulder. The ponderosa above him
was weighted with snow. The knees

of his jeans were wet. Snow drifts
on his shoulders & backs of his shoes.
Snow collected on his upturned palms.
I felt its coldness. Such intimacy
we had never shared. Sometimes grace
comes like that, it falls like snow.

Cheap Red Wine

Some nights I drink cheap red wine.
I drink it alone.
I drink from a Baccarat crystal wine glass
of which I have only one & that is why I must drink alone.
Popular wisdom tells me it is not good
to drink alone.
Especially cheap red wine.
The dank and cloying aroma is such that a feeling of sorrow
can too easily twist into despair.
That is why I sometimes think up an imaginary companion
to drink with. To ward off the despair. Last night,
for instance, I drank with Charles Baudelaire.
He drank from the bottle
owing to the single Baccarat wine glass.
Charles (he begged me to be familiar) said he was grateful
for the invitation. He hadn't been getting out
as much as he used to. I apologised for not thinking
to invite him sooner and asked after Jeanne Duval,
if he had seen much of her lately. He sighed.
Dans l'amour il y a toujours un qui soufre
pendant que l'autre s'ennui. In love,
there is always one who suffers while the other gets bored.
I nodded and refilled my glass.
Charles read to me from *Fleurs du Mal*,
as the evening breeze blew through the open window,
and I confessed to him my anthophobia,
how sometimes the scent of flowers can fill me
with unshakable dread. He nodded gravely.
Such a feeling, he said, inspired him to write
the lines: *arrangements of flowers encoffined in glass*
exhale their ultimate breath; & I prefer
the autumnal fruits over the banal blooms of Spring.
He shuddered and finished off the bottle. Deep into the night
Charles read to me, & as I fell asleep in his arms

I had the idea that communing with the dead
needn't be a mystical activity. It may require no more
than a glass or two of cheap red wine
& listening, intently, to the bodily meanings
of ghostly words.

Standing in Bette Davis's Shoes

Grauman's Chinese Theatre, Hollywood

You cad!
You dirty swine! No one
has any rights about me except me.
From head to foot, I'm one quivering mass
of loathing. If you could read
my mind you'd shrivel
where you stand. My passions are all
gathered together like fingers that make a fist.
You've the most amazing lack
of humour of anyone I've ever known!
You sound like a book & a very cheap one.
If I wanted to end up in the river
I'd have taken a jump off the Brooklyn Bridge.
If I weren't in such a hurry I'd break right down
& cry. I got things wrong with me
that all the doctors in the world can't fix.
If this is what you call living
I don't want any part of it. I'm humiliated
to the point I must thank you. Some will wind up
in the short end but not me
baby. If I don't get out of here I hope I die
& burn. There's only one person
in this town that does anybody a real favour.
That's the undertaker – carries them out.
I don't say things nicely. I don't want people
to like me. Nothing pleases me
more than when they don't like me –
means I don't belong. I know all the angles
& I think I'm smart enough to keep one step ahead
of them till I get enough to pack it all in
& live on Easy Street. I don't ask
for things I don't think I can get. I'll get you –
even if I have to crawl back from my grave to do it.

Good! Let's have blood & destruction.
I think I'll have a large order
of prognosis negative. Fasten your seat belts.
It's going to be a bumpy night.

Why I Write

Because up the coal road way the bees came out so nicely.
Because I have got my rifle cleaned out and she is bright as a whistle.
Because the geese are in and one of them lays.
Because it rained very heavily and some of the road washed away.
Because every jack one of our cows have got calves.
Because the baby is crying. Tiara is sewing. Ellee is propping her face up.
Because Dad and Mr Jackson got the maul and struck Jerry just above the nose.
Because when I am older I want to drive a twenty ton articulated tip truck.
Because do you know who it was? Well, it was Ben Price!
Because I get wild in a second.
Because Uncle and Dad and Uncle Charlie went out egging in the Mary.
Because Alfred Douglas has had 50 cuts with the cane.
Because I have had the cane once and stood on the form twice.
Because Fairy is a bit lame on her nearside foreleg. She had a stone in it.
Because they had the inquest in the new dinner room.
Because Lall said she won't be good friends with Carrie.
Because I am learning music.
Because Don says the orange trees will bear fruit in seven years.
Because I wish you many happy returns.
Because the bees came out so nicely and began to clean out their home.

JEMAL SHARAH 1969–

Jemal Sharah was born and brought up in Canberra until the death of her father in 1975, in a car crash of which she was the only survivor. This is the subject of "Kristallnacht" written when she was nineteen. After her father and brother's death she travelled overseas with her mother before settling in Sydney where she attended Sydney Girls High School and the University of Sydney. She works for the Department of Foreign Affairs and Trade in Canberra and has two children. She has published one collection of poems, *Path of Ghosts* (1994), poems that combined strong emotion with classical restraint. Recently Mike Ladd commented: "I've also been re-reading a first book, *Path of Ghosts* by Jemal Sharah. It's one of those first books that seems to have come out fully-formed, polished, and with a maturity that makes its author seem like a veteran ... *Path of Ghosts* remains her only slim volume ... but that doesn't matter; this book still stands up as a wonderful achievement."

Kristallnacht

Alone in the bush.
Before, they had been singing,
when the car was given a great push
off the road; rain tinkling.

And then she got a fright –
the only one awake;
the others' eyes stayed shut tight
no matter how she'd shake

and shove their arms.
She didn't think of death –
sleep wasn't any harm –
and there was her father's breath,

though harsh, asthmatic, sore.
Locked in a foggy sleep
it might have been a snore.
Except it seemed so deep.

And she – she was awash
with cubes of window-glass,
with one leg safely squashed
in a metal cast;

with such neatly shattered crystal.
Her father loved to buy
goblets, clear as the distilled
water from an eye.

Its rhinestones chained her wrists.
She waited as time passed:
one car sped by – missed
seeing them, it went so fast.

And no-one came to help
in spite of all her cries;
she was stuck there herself,
and adult blandishments were lies –

that to cry help was the proof
against perverts, loss, distress,
that the boy who had cried wolf
was gobbled through excess.

Vague rain, sickness in tides;
neither offered any answers.

Nor, later, did the pride
of howling ambulances.

A Small Song

There is a sparrow frozen on the lawn,
in the snow that lasted through the night
and the cold dawn
that killed it. Now sunlight
drops about the corpse a pall of white.

So ends an unimportant life, and brief.
It spent some seasons lightly on the earth,
then doubtless with relief
found one lungful of breath
was all that stood between itself and death.

Old Legend

Under a sky blue as the heart of flame
gleams a small city, like a string of pearls
broken and scattered loosely on the plain
in high country, among the violet hills.

There, in childhood's realm, thick stars rise
like minnows in the lake, when in duet
the nesting magpies cry to darkening skies
"Do not forget, do not, do not forget."

In that white capital I and my brother
played beneath flowering boughs of lemon trees
in the long sunlit hours before another
age delivered, cell by cell, lasting unease.

Poor child, poor child, what have they done to you?
The town is changed, the garden chopped away.
A chill voice at my shoulder breathes, "I too,
yes even I, have been in Arcady."

JANE GIBIAN 1972–

Jane Gibian was born in Sydney and works as a librarian and teacher of English as a second language. She has published three collections of poetry and has been awarded a residency in Hanoi. Her poetry is brilliantly coloured, the voice elusive and able to create logical coherence from the sparsest materials, then cut.

Vessels for the Lapse of Time

1. Nested squares

What could be held in a month
of your calendar, in the pleached grid
of those windows, that spills out of mine
like water overflowing the rectangular

depressions of an icecube tray? A day
melts and stretches lazily into evening
in the sudden summer, and we place
our palms flat against the sun's captured

heat, coursing from brick walls along
each street: from here each day's
a window, lined up in a crooked row
like teeth inside a laughing mouth.

Flattened grass in the shape of our bodies
was still there the day after: we tried
to hold those days in cupped hands
but they trickled slyly through your fingers.

Walking past a window uncovered
to the night, that flash of someone's life
added to the inventory of sights
I collected to make you smile, an answer

to the compressed biography of postcards,
bound to the span of time in its nested
squares. Daylong we crossed disputed
territories, daylong I looked into

the battered rectangle of a pocket mirror
with its cracked corner and saw myself
divided. In the calendar's endless fretwork
you give each part of the day equal

thought; weight them evenly in your grasp,
until it's time to pull at a thread in the day
and watch it unravel behind us.

2. Helicoid

From the cracked bowl of the morning
rises a roaring sea in your left ear, the helical
pulse unfurling into time passages made

convoluted by fingers tracing a slow
orbit around a breast. Taking an old stethoscope
from the table you heard the loud whispery

edges of your heartbeat; listened for
the murmurous parts of that country
absorbed awkwardly inside, down

to the intricate whorls of your knuckles,
like distorted incense spirals. In this vessel
rests a memory of eating rice picked

three days earlier, smoothed grains
in the coarse capsule of a sack, so recently
bound in curved terraces of wet rice

stretching in tiers towards the horizon;
the taste of earthiness and pith sparking
tender florescence in the reverent

chamber of the mouth. With a word balanced
on the tongue comes simultaneously
its echo in another language, coiled

beneath, entwined with an older image;
the round edges of a biscuit tin decorated
with english birds: pheasants, demure

water fowl, a robin; and the helix of the present
winds more tightly; three inseparable baskets.

LISA GORTON 1972–

Lisa Gorton, who grew up in Melbourne, was awarded a Rhodes Scholarship to Oxford University. After teaching at university in South Africa and a stint as a consultant in Sydney at the management consultants, McKinsey & Company, she returned to Melbourne where she now lives. She has published one poetry collection, *Press Release* (2007). She has writen essays and reviews for newspapers and journals, and a children's novel, *Cloudland* (2008). Like Geoff Page, she is a grandchild of an Australian prime minister, whose wife she writes about in "Solitaire". She has two sons. In a 2008 interview Gorton said: "I wrote my doctoral thesis on John Donne. I like the way his compressed and very complicated images bring a kind of electric charge to the poems. Reading, you all at once understand them and that sudden understanding feels like illumination." Gorton is herself a poet of compression and implication. "Beauty" is set in Potts Point's fashionable Challis Avenue which has views of Sydney's CBD. The unindented lines of the poem can be read sequentially, with the indented stanzas perhaps being an extended commentary.

Graffiti

I wonder this wall can bear the weight of such words
   – Graffiti on a wall in Pompeii

The city is smaller than you expected.
Its houses turn their backs on streets –

   And given half a chance
   who wouldn't bunker down behind a stack of silence?
   An arm's length of wall permits any depth of
   meditative calm or your money back –

Its walls are made of potsherds, broken bricks and stone
cut from the hill's mouth, chain-lugged to the city –

   It happened just as you picture it:
   slaves bent double against the weight, whip cracks and flies,
   that crowd in the marketplace breaking off mid-sentence
   to see peace dragged in as a pile of stones –

The stucco of the city walls is everywhere
scratched with these piss-riddled importunities –

   – Cruel Lalagus, why don't you love me?
A wall can bear the weight
   – All the girls love Celadus the Gladiator
The weight is nothing to the wall
   – Caesius faithfully loves M[… name lost]
A wall can bear the weight
   – For a good time, turn right at the end of the street.

Out of the dark, ashes fall softly.
We have to stand up again and again to shake them off.
What a weight of light!
The dark is smaller than you expected.

Beauty

Challis Avenue, 5 a.m.

The art dealer promises a flower market

      It rained in the night. The street
      lights envy themselves in asphalt
      the way Elizabeth Taylor might
      watch "A Place in the Sun"

and the names: iris, star magnolia

I came from sleep to the still dark.
It is always day in dreams but the night
has secret hours when cars drive
into their lights like the idea of success

blazon the air, all neon expectation where he comes:

balding, rapacious, his eyes like
hands, his aficionado smile,
Whiteleys in his suitcase, Bromleys in his suite
and all the city's flowers in his palm.

Solitaire

i.m. Bettina Gorton

i

After lunch on sunstruck
afternoons I look for you in
the shaking out of light
from petrol haze –

I look for you on the combed
lawns of commuter suburbs
between the hedge and standard roses
with your back to the street –

When I come home from winter
holidays I can tell you have been there,
drinking window after window of light
till it is emptied and grey –

I think once I saw you
walking the curve of a disused rail line
where the track shrugged off its sleepers
and climbed into the heat –

ii

However early we woke, you were already waiting,
slippered in dawn's sedated light,
a first glassful of distance in hand and the cards set out
with the sound of somebody closing in: step step step turn,
step step turn, step turn, turn, only you had already gone
along paths of smoke into the smoke-coloured ways
where in place of footsteps, only ash falls followed you.

Because mallee scrub is the colour of thirst
with an infrastructure of patience,

you'd been divining a path across it ever since you sat down
on the screened-in verandah in that drought at war's end
and found even burning days would upholster you in stillness,
and nights antimacassar your hair till you could rest without stain
upon the fine print of promises.

iii

Out of smoke you came walking. Your face
made a cloud in that cloud-haunted absence
over the courtyard parterre where our noon
shadows snagged on our heels, planning to lengthen.
Then somebody saw the time and we left for the wake.

PETRA WHITE 1975–

Petra White was born and grew up in Adelaide and moved to Melbourne. She is a graduate in German and English literature from the University of Melbourne. She has held jobs in publishing, college tutoring, and as a government policy officer. She has published two poetry collections. White can write with great precision. In "Ricketts Point", for example, the reference to "soaked and pre-soaked shore" would seem to be to sand that is still wet from breaking waves, and sand above the waterline that is damp and drying out. Dedalus, mentioned in her poem "Voyage", was the architect in Greek myth who made a set of wings for his son, Icarus. As Icarus flew closer to the sun, the wax melted and he fell into the sea. The back cover of her second volume of poetry, *The Simplified World* (2010), states that some of her work "shows the shadow of depression: not so much expressing moods as touching on how depression dwells, finding its register so it can speak."

Ricketts Point

A slim girl playing by herself in the shallows,
like someone who's never been to the beach before,
and suddenly marvels at how the world
tips open to broad deep space, not fearsome.
Seawater cool as milk intimately swirling her.
Sand hospitably absorbing and releasing her feet,
her mounting dance of being, luminously alone
on the sea's hearth, its hissing welcome mat.
Two bearded men, perhaps her father and uncle,
identical as Kafka's lodgers, further out in the waves.
A third man out there with them hurls a ball;
they miss and laugh repeatedly, rolling like seals
under the waves and up again, under and over
their joy that won't stay under, and mirrors and magnifies

the separate joy of the girl, her not-to-be-tested trust.
Smiling at strangers perched on their towels
who can't help watching her, and smile back as if her world,
scribbled and wiped from soaked and pre-soaked shore
and flung from her hands in effortless wave-sprays,
was large or real enough to include them.

Voyage

for Clifford and Catherine Overton

The man who suddenly saw his five-year-old daughter
ascending the ski-lift alone and unbuckled
was not Dedalus, nor she Icarus.

She passed him as she passed the sun.
He could not tear his eyes away, and prayed
she wouldn't see him; one glimpse of his fear

might bring her tumbling sixty feet.
So he stood, a scarecrow of distraction on the snow
and dream-like she sailed up through the blind-white cloud.

Woman and Dog

A woman and a dog walked all day
beside the non-moving canal.
People who walk dogs displace themselves:

the dog sniffs and leads, harnesses
a human soul, spirit and flesh
willing or not. Its human-dog eyes

cradle the walkable world – a happy place –
a brimming here-and-yet. The canal
neither followed nor lagged behind.

There was the simplified world, on either side, green
fields and red houses. There was the little pub
they always got to.

So long they trudged, two bodies and one
soul, so many miles,
the paws began to bleed.

Little flecks of ruby blood glittered the black
rubbery pads, as if the dog was inking out
all the sadness of the woman.

And the woman, being just strong enough,
gathered up the dog (not a small one)
and carried it all the way home, wherever that was.

Older Sister

Deputy-mother of her maybe rivals,
love swings on and off.
Mary Poppins, Miss Hannigan,
spit-spot and slap-slap.

When parents say, she is shot like a comet
into adultness, to govern babies or keep
the ship of housework sailing.
Larger than adult, smaller than child,

chore-hungry and chore-fed,
a machine-child sweating at the iron.
Her fingers fly, her eyes are stone;
a ghost to herself, she body-and-soul becomes

the order that sorts the washing,
shyly perfecting the nappy's origami,
pressing the fatherly hankies
into high-piled civil squares.

On the floor, four toddlers sprawl
like dropped grenades: stilled by *Babar*,
that delicate French family of bourgeois-
monarch elephants and mint-

green apple-studded trees that float
through the screen and fill the timber house
that noses at the sky like Noah's Ark,
its cargo more than all the world.

It is like an order she has made:
four sisters, their hair still gleaming
in the braids she yanked into shape that morning.
Their future tantrums wait inside her throat,

she swallows them and keeps the peace.
The house teeters, creaks.
She slips out, climbs the voiceless apple tree,
squats quiet as a dove that ate the olive branch.

The babies drift by like clouds, their smiles
strung with cosmic spittle: she crouches,

a monster, hardened and un-hardened,
forming and re-forming,

eyes red with metamorphosis,
deep in the smell of feathers, wing-wax,
whirring breath,
she leaps from the apple tree,

lands in the kitchen, an angel,
and like four little kittens, the children
curl around her silk-slippered feet:
she pours them "baby tea" – six sugars, all milk.

Notes for the Time Being

How many sonnets must we write
before the great gong sounds in Heaven? Peter Porter

Relieved like a criminal
at last apprehended
and tricked out of daylight.
Will I be you again?

Too much freedom
is not enough.
How large or small the world
where time fits.

Terrible thing a head
from which no thought escapes.
As the world said
good-bye to you

it grew small and glazy,
a thing seen beneath tears
as when a child says good-bye
to a too-much-trouble pet.

~

Soul frees itself
(from something),
or tries to imagine
it gone, the heavy –

still carrying
what's precious
– the gold, the old –
and the fuse hope.

Thrown into light, thrown into dark,
etc. Where does illness live,
what does it want?
And sits before the Sybil,

begging for speech.
Describe your fear.
How do you feel out of 10?
Out of 9?

~

Soul is confused, sad for no reason,
can't remember;
sits in her chair and stares
like someone much older
who'll never again remember.

Weeps, as if out of the corner
of humanity's loose mouth;
her tears are lost coins, spilling down
the loud spiral of that machine,
somewhere in eternity, that codes them:

Grief 1, Grief 2, and
how unusual: Griefs 11 and 19.
And sometimes, of course, there is joy,
also for no reason – here you ask
what has reason got to do with it? –

AIDAN COLEMAN 1976–

Aidan Coleman was born in Aberystwyth, Wales, and lived in Nottingham as a child. His family migrated to Australia in the mid-1980s living at first in Wollongong and then settling in the Barossa Valley of South Australia. He studied Arts at the University of Adelaide and lives in the Adelaide suburb of Gawler, with his wife, where he teaches English and History. He has published one full-length collection of poetry, *Avenues and Runways* (2005). Coleman is a dedicated adherent of the Imagist approach in many of his poems, achieving a delicate understatement.

I Like Airports

for the big screen TV
of weather,
the city's hazy histogram
and the unsteady horizon.

But also nights:
a missing suburb
in sugary dark,
its capital
a small-scale city
of radar and eyes.

I like the way planes dwindle
to tail-lights, shed
their angry skins.

And every avenue ends in take-off:
every poem begins
on the ground
then is shot heavenward.

Estates

Here, on empty blocks,
the grass fists and flames,
sizzles by day
or hums with the dull voltage of insects.

The houses built are set out neat
as breakfast on a tray:
the water tank,
the shed, the velcro-lawn.

Now it's evening, lights come on.
You hear the echo
of a bouncing ball,
bikes rewinding the streets home.

A train brews to boil
then simmers;
the crossing bangs
its pots and pans.

Allnighter

Stepping out at three, for something
with more bite than coffee,
the uni hums like a program
left running: a mind turning over in sleep.

A sprinkler is chopping the night
into cool slices and, through trees,

are the red gels and molten-blues of the city,
where perhaps no one's awake;

paths and roads chilled in a soft-drink glow,
the river stilled to a lake.

STEPHEN McINERNEY 1976–

Born in Kiama, on the New South Wales south coast, Stephen McInerney attended boarding school in Sydney, and completed an Arts degree at the Australian National University in Canberra. He is a lecturer in English literature at a Catholic liberal arts college in Sydney's west. He was a postulant in a monastery, and is now married. He has published one collection of poetry, *In Your Absence* (2002). McInerney is a traditionalist in form, sentiment and belief. But this traditionalism is mitigated by a freshness and attractive hesitance. He is not afraid to choose uplifting subjects, using a carefully nuanced diction.

A Summer Morning, Sydney

Opening the bathroom window,
I can see
across the alleyway,
secretly,

this young woman
on the edge of her bed.
Like a stretch of sand
damply bared

by flourishing foam,
when the towel withdraws
beauty breathes
through her million pores.

Shoulders and neck, buttocks and back
are defined:
Le Violon d'Ingres
in outline,

lightly finished
by the brush of the sun,
and dusted with freckles
like cinnamon.

I know to turn away,
and yet I stare
on a scene as ordinary
as it is rare.

It might be an art-class
where eyes
trace with a brush
those breasts and thighs;

where charcoal, poised,
sets her waist
with delicate detachment
into place;

and where, discerning
her left shoulder
touched a moment by sun,
minds hold her

as they are held
in rapt attention:
all passion, all yearning distilled
to calm convention.

Unaware of me,
inwardly still,
she moves in and out
of the grasp of my will,

present and elusive
as the sun,
who takes her in his arms
and yet looks on.

Ideas for a Way of Life

A man will devote his life
to the art of handwriting; from day to night
he will work at perfecting letters;
the words will appear
in the mind, to be pondered and weighed, then shaped
into loops and curves – an f like a mayfly
in ink, balanced by invisible colour and light,
will become his favourite character;
just think
what delight will flood him, getting it right
the first time, then again in all sorts of patterns;
and the shapes will begin to make sense
as words;
perfection will lead to inquiry,

inquiry to a sentence
delicately formed and phrased
with balance and poise
like the mayfly, over
which he'll be taught to pause
by the letters themselves,
whose pause
will become his voice.
Often the words tumble over themselves unrestrained
by the curve of his letters, weighing
them down with urgency, bursting
their beautiful patterns –
but one word carefully chosen and soon
the noblest of thoughts will seek translation
in characters fine as themselves,
and the noblest of acts
will respond, and correspond
to those forms like bells
flourishing over the city, pulled on
with ropes
by boys, who drag and rise with their weight
like water
drawn from a well,
lifted and clear
and holding the sky, in search of dimensions,
brilliant and cold in its rocking reflection
each Sunday morning at nine;
slaking the thirst
of children, and widows of the church
and the cool, fluted minds of the Schoolmen,
with the formal perfection of a syllogism,
the blank rectitude of a rule and line,
the urgent restraint of a radical tract,
the transparency of a geographical statement –
Broadloaf is a town along the pacific, held in by rainforest –
and the world will begin to arrange itself
in a meaningful order again, a peaceable pact
of reason and faith; an order discerned not achieved,
an arrival acknowledged, received.

EMMA JONES 1977–

Emma Jones was born and raised in Sydney. She holds a Bachelor of Arts from the University of Sydney, and a Ph.D. in English from the University of Cambridge. She started writing poetry at the age of eight and became a compulsive writer. Jones has published one poetry collection, *The Striped World* (Faber & Faber, 2009). These are poems of much accomplishment: their imagery and syntax are adventurous and subtle. Jones writes with understatement and only sometimes in a personal vein. "Conversation" is one of these exceptions, a personal poem, written after her mother's death (she revealed in an interview). But even in this poem, a characteristic distance and understatement are maintained (combined with an intense, fragile, existential angst). In the conversation of the poem's title she shrugs off a question as to why she is reluctant "to go back". In the long urgent parenthesis which explains her feelings, the personal circumstances underlying this are undisclosed. In a 2009 interview she commented: "It is much more common now to be able to do a masters in creative writing but I never did anything like that. I have never written to learn the craft, I write because it is something I need to do and if I don't do it I'm unhappy." Jones went to Cambridge thinking she would become an academic, to support her vocation as a poet. But by the time she was finishing her Ph.D., she realised that "being an academic would not be good for my poetry". It would use up a lot of energy and concentration and she did not want to be "spending all day thinking and talking about poetry in an academic way".

Waking

Here it is again, light hoisting its terrible bells.
As though a world might wake up with it –

The moon shuts its eye. Down in the street
the same trolley is playing the pavestones.

For twenty-five years I've been waking
this way. There was one morning

when my mother woke and felt a twitch
inside, like the shifting of curtains.

She woke and so did I. I was like a bird
beating. She had no time for anaesthetic.

We just rolled from each other like indecent genies.
Even the nurses were startled.

Now she says the world and I were eager
from the start. But I was only waking.

Farming

The pearls were empire animals.
They'd been shucked from the heart of their grey mothers
which is why, so often, you'll find them

nestled at the neck and breast.
It stood to reason.
The sea was one long necklace,
and they often thought of that country.

Its customs waylaid them,
and it occupied their minds.
Nobody missed them.
The oysters felt nothing,
neither here nor there,
down on the farm and miles out to sea,
those swaying crops.

Rolled to create circumference.
Opened to accommodate
the small strange foreign irritant
that hones itself to a moon.
The oysters say
"it is a lulling stone, that outside heart
turned in, and beating."

They knit their fields of nacre, and are quiet.
The clouds converge.
It's a sad constabulary,
the clouds and the sea, and the boats.
Because piracy is common
the farmers carry guns. Does the sea
object, marshalling its edges?

Do the fish know
their glint, those inward birds,
in the fields of the Pacific?
It's a singing bone,
the indivisible pearl.
It's a bright barred thing. And pearls
are empire animals. And poems are pearls.

Conversation

"Oh this and that. But for various reasons" –
(the season, and the change in season, the season of grief

and retrospection, the rooftop pulled from the childhood
house, and the internal doll in its stuck seat,

that is, the fictive soul in its brute cathedral, and because of memory,
maybe, and organs in niches, and the beat to things,

and the knowledge that the body is the soul and vice versa,
but that false distinctions are sometimes meaningful,

and that difference, all difference, is just distance, not a state,
not a nation, and because nothing *matters*, not really,

or everything does, I don't mind being an animal, at all,
because a sentient thing is nothing else, and because toward matter

I feel neither love nor hate but the kind of shuttered Swiss
neutrality a watch might feel for time

if it had an animal's sentiments, knowing itself a symbol
and function, knowing itself a tool, and because I feel

the dull culmination of various phenomena informing me
and am that culmination, I feel ill in some small way,

though not ill really, just idle, and I prefer, you see,
to keep an impassive inviolable pact with things that tick,

with solitary, shifted things, and because my life's approximate act
is the sister to some other life, with different tints, I carry

and nurse, my diffident twin, I'm often morose, and think
of those statues that lean above themselves in water,

those fountains, stone, with commemorative light,
with disfiguring winds, and because reflection is an end in itself

and because there's an end even to reflection, and an end to the eye,
that heated room, I prefer to keep my artifice and my arsenal

suspended, close; like an angled man; like the stationed sun;
and because matter ends, or I should say, matter turns to matter,

and my small inalienable witness to this is real, I can't pretend
to wish to be a rooted thing, full-grown, concerned

with practical matters, in a rooted world, and careful of borders,
when an ineradicable small portion glints, my mind, that alma mater,

and says, make your work your vicarage) – "I put off going back".

ELIZABETH CAMPBELL 1980–

Elizabeth Campbell was born in Melbourne, where she lives. She spent much of her youth with horses in the Yarra Ranges and still keeps a horse. She is a graduate in English and History and since 2006 has taught English at Eltham High School. She has also worked as a florist, actor, singer, shopgirl, horse-riding instructor and waiter. Campbell is an uncompromising poet, who writes powerful, tough poems.

Martin Duwell reviewed her first (and so far only) poetry collection *Letters to the Tremulous Hand* (2007) as: "a pretty exhilarating first collection by someone who is more than a 'minor poet' … The poems are very difficult, especially for an innocent reader who has nothing but the text to work with, but it's the kind of difficulty that is not gratuitous. You feel that the poet has our interests at heart but also has a very complex view of life to share."

Proverb

"In the room
where onions are frying
even the cat weeps."

No more allegories – let's agree
proverbs help nobody.
No parables, I beg of you.

But then, who could love detail for its own sake?
Surely a gentle mind turns straight
away to symbol?

"Fact is the Kingdom of God.
Precision polishes the narrow heart.
Stories set us free."

The enemies of complexity prefer such
companionable summaries.
But Mother Doubt, you early laid on me

your threefold cradle-gifts:
sadness, restlessness,
and foremost of these, a hopeless

passion of reality. And so
my beloved cat, weep.
No more parables – let's just disagree.

Illuminations

Someone in a blue cloak belts someone else on the head
with a shovel in the frame ruled
for the sin of Rage. A French lady
adjusts the robes of a unicorn held
by a monkey whose rich commissioner kneels
before his saviour on the first page. A dog
contorts to lick his testes with a lizard's tongue.
Below, a bird-footed dragon bites the head
of a fourlegged man in an indigo tube

while a snake with a corkscrew neck eats his toes.
Pink turrets cower under currant-like projectiles
from a giant mangonel:Jerusalem!
Heretics swing jaunty from a mini gallow, weightless
necks cocked like holiday hats round the pole: May
in the Hours. In the initial the author
sits under arch penhanded, familiar at feet
like the pictured saint and lion or the open loggia
of annunciation in some floppy headgear, a babewyn beneath
aping his posture. Another monkey with a giant fork
feeds turds to a nun from a shit-pyramid.
The lion and his ministers rejoice and celebrate, eat and drink.
I promise you: an astronomer
in a red robe googles through an astrolabe.
Rabbits conduct a funeral.

Equus

what use is grief to a horse? – Peter Shaffer

My friend, mistaking the horse for a symbol, says
it wasn't meant. Born sick
the foal died through weeks of bitter tests

till xray showed her bones eaten away.
I held her motionless: her eyes
hit the straw open: dead before.

The mother touched the body with her face
apologise
then dragged it round and kicked it to be sure.

My friend, mistaking the earth for a gesture:
it just rejects some things. The mother
gouging lines of hide off with her toe.

My friend the playwright thinks
through blood's metaphor: *a kind of curse;*
she traces the shape of curse. The horse

learning faster than a woman that her child is dead
hangs her head, not confusing, *for everything*
a reason and a use: unseen

bacilli for the unread laws
of vaguely teeming gods. It's murder to believe
death meaningful. My friend mistakes

my grieving horse for *Horses,*
Horse, The Horse and with her pen
she puts out all our eyes.

Structure of the Horse's Eye

Under the sun, the horse's eye
is a glass dome over a petal, the pupil a raised bud
of pollinated velvet, bisected;

the horizon in it. Almost 360 –
a narrow corridor behind
and one spot in front of her nose, are blind.

Curious about the wolf? Find a fat horse
grazing at dozey noon her home paddock;
try to creep up.

In the waking night her eyes are flat opals
bouncing your torch as you pan the black
like a river for green-gold flakes,

or better; go sightless to hear
the known rhythm coming out the dark.
Within, the *tapetum*, mirrorlike, reflects all

available light back through her retina –
Homo sapiens, one of few mammals
lacking this useful aid, to nocturne,

mostly sleeps. *Equus* watches on her feet.
Sometimes a night visit sets them off –
swilling around you like surf in a tide pool

pushing the long bones
of their heads at you. The honest creature
investigates with her face, magnolia

nostrils cupping the scent
of palms up empty at arms length. Your image
shone back on the convex surface of the eye-pool

is macrocephalic, duck-billed, your skull
a helpless baby too heavy for itself.
If you want to better love the world,

ask counsel of those who never come inside;
her order, *perissodactyla*
(large mammals with odd numbered toes)

have largely failed. Taxonomy
progresses, dividing its names. Sometimes a life,
pressing on, proves its point

but Life does not. Let her advance –
she is herself, through flowering heads; eyes careful,
thinking nothing of advancement,

above lips tough enough to strip
the exquisite thistle-crown from its armoured stem.
How excellent is her tail! She draws all grass

through the bone-set strata of her teeth,
grazing 12 hours in her open-lidded present –
deep time made one dimension

by limited depth perception, wide world
made pasture and shelter. Let her head's long neck
lift to her clear-edged ear

whose hearing threads in darkness the Earth
to its sky. Let her steady herbivorous day
blink open and consume and close it all.

L. K. HOLT 1982–

Lucy Holt lives in Melbourne where she was born. Her childhood was mainly spent in Adelaide. She is a graduate in History from the University of Melbourne and at the time of writing is a master's student in English at that university. She has published a chapbook and two collections of poetry. Holt began as a visual artist, and says she switched to poetry (in her early twenties) because "of the control freak in me ... you're working with words which are easier to control than paint and clay and pencils." There is a strong visual sense in Holt's poems, and a controlled but mysterious development as the poem emerges from the structure she has chosen, which may be narrative or a conceit. The poem "5" is the fifth of a sequence of five "sonnets" from her second collection *Patience, Mutiny* (2010).

Grandmoth

On the wall the moth has fashioned itself
two-dimensionally, self as self-portrait.

Its eye-forgeries see everything in the room:
where I see memories it sees a great feast.

They are always fleeing, like thieves, like bits of dusk
left behind, at the opening of drawer or door, their stomachs

freshly full of coat or jewel-box lining; tweed and velvet

are left a demented lace of their hungry design.

From the box where I keep her necklace
(in non-existent photos I see her neck laced

with it, I see how it hangs consolingly beside
her one lonely breast) out stole a moth

and I thought it was her: my grandmother
returning as something hungry for time not lived.

A Problem of Filing

I could not find the saint or sentiment
for the time when I put on my shoes
then put on my father's over the top
and I just stood there, my tiny ankles
just holding me up, my love enclosed
in formality, my heart lost in a heart.

Poem for Nina

an axe age, a sword age (things shall be split)
a wind age, a wolf age (before the world sinks) *The Poetic Edda*

Time takes too much time! you sang as we took
to the wind, pulling our hair from our mouths

and breathing out air still spindrift.
In the two remaining greys of last light

the storm came in on the king tide's back;
by morning the jetty would be broken to bits.

That night we stood at the jetty's clinging root-end
and ran. The waves broke over both sides

to make us an arbour of threat and glisten;
we jumped the loosed planks that clacked

in retarded joy *sea! sea!* as we reached the sprig-end.
You clutched your crotch in happy fear

and lost your hat. The railings were all gone:
we were standing on a platter, offered up.

Dear Little Bastard Antoshevu,

(*from* Natalia Golden to Anton Chekhov)

You're having, I know, a merry free-for-all
in Moscow. I'm glad.

I cannot belong to you any more, now
        I've found for myself
a boy-tiger more suitable. I advise
        you not to marry:
you're still too young and write such rubbish to me.
        As for the main thing
that interests me more than anything else:
        your health – you don't talk
about that. You have two certain diseases,
        my Antoshevu,
amorousness of the blood and the spitting
        thereof – the first may
not prove lethal, but of the second, I ask
        please give me some words
if I give you the stamps. Perhaps you haven't
        yet forgotten your
Little Skeleton . . . . But if you have, she can
        imagine farewell

5.

The cliff is a wave of rock
that waits. Settled on top

is an albatross nestling, facing
the way its mother left at first light.

It will not move but to blink, *adagio,*
till she comes on the front of dusk.

You set me likewise on this rock
and ordered me to stay.

My heart a vessel
misemployed above the watermark,

the sea's black pelt gleaming
in the light underneath.

Steady is the pulse of the promisee's heart:
one beat mutinous; patient the other.

JOSEPHINE ROWE 1984–

Josephine Rowe was born in Melbourne. She published a collection of short fiction, *East of Here, Close to Water* in 2007, and in the same year a collection of poems and prose *Asynchrony*. She is a regular performer at Melbourne's spoken word venues. Poets she admires include Leonard Cohen, Ian McBryde and Jordie Albiston. Annie Clarkson has written that "Josephine Rowe has an ability to capture the core emotional truth in a given moment". Her poetry is able to do this by employing sudden and unexpected reversals of expectation, typical of some of the best performance poets.

In the Boot of Someone's Car

There is a woman
locked in the boot
of someone's car.
The darkness is pressing down on her
so hard she can't breathe
and she can't be sure
whether she's choking on fear
or petrol fumes
or the darkness.
The driver takes the corners too fast.
It hurts less if she just goes limp.
She can't remember how she got there
but she will be there forever
her voice hoarse from screaming
because I can't think of a way to get her out.
I know that somewhere
there's a cable release
or a toolbox with a crowbar
or a wrench.
She could jemmy the lock.
All she has to do is feel around in the dark
but her hands are tied behind her back
and I don't know what to do with her
once she's out.
I don't even know who the driver is.
So I leave her there
in the boot of someone's car.
I've run out of endings.
I leave women crying on doorsteps.
I leave lonely men
in empty carriages
on last trains to nowhere.
I leave families sleeping
as their houses burn to the ground.
I leave gamblers,

cocaine addicts, failed musicians,
prostitutes, lawyers, fathers,
at the top of buildings,
under bridges,
on freeways, train tracks, rooftops,
on the cracked linoleum floors of
restrooms in fast food restaurants
somewhere in the outer western suburbs,
or chain smoking at kitchen tables
watching the smoke curl up to
twenty five watt Homebrand lightbulbs
that flickflickflicker
as they wait for unfaithful lovers
to return home from work.
And I leave a man
with smoke in his eyes
both hands on the wheel
driving as far away as he can
on ten bucks of fuel
before he breaks down.
He calls me
to ask where we're going from here.
And I tell him that I don't know
because I've run out of endings.
I tell him that I'm sorry,
but there's a woman
locked in the boot
of his car.

ACKNOWLEDGMENTS

For permission to reprint work used in this anthology, grateful acknowledgment is made to authors, estates and literary agents, many of whom did not specifically request written acknowledgment, and to the following who did: University of Queensland Press for the poems of John Blight, which are from his *Selected Poems 1939–1990*; University of Queensland Press for the poems of John Manifold, which are from his *Collected Verse* (1978); University of Queensland Press for the poem of Dimitris Tsaloumas from *The Observatory* (1983); University of Queensland Press for poems of Bruce Beaver, which are from his *New and Selected Poems 1960–1990*; University of Queensland Press for the following poems of John Tranter, "After Hölderlin" and "Under Tuscan Skies" from *Urban Myths: 210 Poems: New and Selected* (2006) and "Columbo's Kangaroo" and "Little Dog" from *Starlight* (2009); University of Queensland Press for the following poems of Laurie Duggan "Dirty Weekend", "Five Poems", "from The Paperweight", "What I Came Onto", "South Coast Haiku", and "Blue Hills 23" from *New and Selected Poems 1971–1993*, "Blue Hills 44", "Boredom" and "Rainbow" from *Mangroves* (2003), "Blue Hills 52", "Blue Hills 53", "Blue Hills 55", and "Blue Hills 61" from *The Passenger* (2006); University of Queensland Press for the poems of David Malouf, which are from *Revolving Days* (2008); University of Queensland Press for the poems of Elizabeth Hodgson which are from *Skin Painting* (2008); University of Queensland Press for the following poems of Bronwyn Lea, "Original Sin" and "Girls' Night on Long Island" which are from *Flight Animals* (2001); Elaine van Kempen as Trustee for Estate of Late Eric Rolls for the poems of Eric Rolls; Tricia Dearborn for "Come in, lie down" published in *Southerly* and *The Best Australian Poetry 2008* (edited David Brooks, published UQP) and for "Schlieren Lines" and "The Pouch of Douglas" from *Frankenstein's Bathtub* (Interactive Press, 2001) and for "At the Laundromat on Rue St Florent" *Perverse Verse 2007: Queer Poets Read* (gay-ebooks.com.au); Sandy Fitts for her poem from her *View from the Lucky Hotel* (Five Islands Press, 2008); Martin Harrison for his poems from his *Wild Bees: New and Selected Poems* (UWA Press 2008); Golvan Arts Management Pty Ltd on behalf of Robert Adamson for his "from Sonnets to be Written from Prison (5)" from his *Mulberry Leaves: New and Selected Poems 1970–2001* (Paperbark Press 2001) and for all other poems of his being from his *The Golden Bird: New and Selected Poems* (Black Inc., 2008); Sheil Land Associates Ltd for poems of Randolph Stow, with "The Language of Flowers", "For One Dying", "The Ghost at Anlaby", "Ruins of the City of Hay", "The Land's Meaning", "Endymion" and "The Singing Bones" being from his *Selected Poems: A Counterfeit Silence* (Angus & Robertson, 1969) and "Frost-parrots" from *Visitants, Episodes from Other Novels, Poems, Stories, Interviews, and Essays*, edited by Anthony J. Hassall (UQP, 1990); Pearson Australia for poems of Bruce Dawe all from *Sometimes Gladness: Collected Poems 1954–2005* (Pearson Australia 2006); Pan Macmillan London for all poems of Clive James (except "Whitman and the Moth") which are from *Opal Sunset, Selected Poems, 1958–2008,* all Clive James poems being copyright © Clive James; HarperCollins for all Francis Webb poems, being from *Collected Poems* (1969), for J. R. Rowland's "Canberra in April" from *The Feast of Ancestors,* for all Nan McDonald poems which are from *Selected Poems* (1969), for James Devaney for "Song of the Captured Woman" from *Poems* (1950) and for "Dirrawan, the Song-Maker" from *The Vanished Tribes,* for Kenneth Slessor's "The Night Ride", "Dutch Seacoast", "Captain Dobbin", "Five Visions of Captain Cook", "The Country Ride", "North Country", "Last Trams", "Out of Time", "Five Bells" and "Beach Burial", all Slessor poems being reproduced from his *Collected Poems* (Angus & Robertson, 1994, edited by Dennis Haskell and Geoffrey Dutton), for Judith Wright's "For One Dying", "Halfway", "Finale" and "Small Town Dance", all Wright poems being reproduced from her *Collected Poems 1942–1985* (Angus & Robertson, 1994); Pan MacMillan Australia for all Dorothy Porter poems which are from *El Dorado* (Picador, 2007); the Strehlow Research Centre for all translations by T. G. H. Strehlow being from his *Songs of Central Australia*; Carcanet Press Limited for all poems of Vicki Raymond which are from *Small Arm Practice* (William Heinemann Australia, 1989); ∏ O for all his poems which are copyright © ∏ O and are from *Big Numbers: New and Selected Poems* (collective effort press, 2008).

All reasonable efforts were taken to obtain permission to use copyright material reproduced in this book, but in some cases copyright holders could not be traced. The editors welcome information in this regard.

INDEX OF POETS